INTERPRETING ALASKA'S HISTORY:

An Anthology

INTERPRETING ALASKA'S HISTORY:

AN ANTHOLOGY

Edited by

Mary Childers Mangusso
Fairbanks, Alaska

and

Stephen W. Haycox, History Department
University of Alaska Anchorage

ISBN 0-935094-14-8
Alaskana Series No. 43

Cover Photo from Clarence Andrews Collection,
University of Alaska Anchorage Archives and Manuscript Department

Published by

Alaska Pacific University Press
4101 University Drive
Anchorage, Alaska 99508

First Edition
First Printing, June 1989
Second Printing, September 1990
Third Printing, April 1993

TABLE OF CONTENTS

ACKNOWLEDGMENTS

This anthology is a tribute to all those who pursue a scholarly interest in Alaska history. We have tried to explain its purpose and context in the *Introduction.* The editors wish to express here their appreciation to all those who helped to make the work possible, and without whose generous assistance it could not have been completed. Most particularly, we thank Professors Morgan Sherwood, Richard Pierce, Lydia Black, Ted C. Hinckley, and Barbara Smith, whose support was essential. We also want to thank all those authors who graciously agreed to permit their work to be reprinted here, and the publishers and editors who also gave their permission, especially Lewis Saum of the *Pacific Northwest Quarterly*, Margaret Parker of the *Canadian Historical Review*, and Jim Ducker of *Alaska History*. Renee Blahuta and Marvin Falk generously offered suggestions about photographs and maps, respectively. We owe Sheri Layral of the University of Alaska Fairbanks history department special acknowledgement for her work in preparing the manuscript.

We particularly express our gratitude to Jan Ingram and the advisory board of Alaska Pacific University Press. Without their continuing faith in this project, it could not have been undertaken.

FOREWORD

Alaska's history, with its Indian, Eskimo, and Aleut heritage, its century of Russian colonization, its peoples' formidable struggles to wrest a living (or a fortune) from the North's isolated and harsh environment, and its relatively recent achievement of statehood, has been interesting, even exotic. Yet Alaska has far fewer serious book-length studies of its past than other states. Some of the best historical writing has been scattered in journals not readily accessible to the public. *Interpreting Alaska's History* gathers much of this literature together.

The articles included in this book record Alaska's history. Just as importantly, they interpret it. The editors point out that the views of the past presented by the authors of these articles have challenged earlier conceptions. Moreover, a number of the articles treat subjects--Native history and the environment--which were not in the mainstream of historical inquiry until the last couple decades.

The newer views may be correct, but they probably will not prove adequate. Just as the political pendulum has swung from the Great Society to the Reagan Revolution and the symbol of a progressive community has changed from a smokestack skyline to a greenbelt with a ribbon of bike trail, so the perception of what is reasonable, worthy, and far-sighted in our past changes. As these perceptions evolve, writers will address new topics and revisit older ones from fresh perspectives. They will retrieve from archives, libraries, and the oral tradition more of our past and make it speak to our world. They will do so just as the authors of the articles between these covers have; and they will do it better for the work of their forerunners.

James H. Ducker
Alaska History

November 22, 1988

INTRODUCTION

This anthology is a collection of articles and interpretations of Alaska history. It is intended to provide a deeper, more current understanding of significant events and developments in Alaska history than can be offered in general histories or in casual literature. It is designed to complement and extend the narrative histories of the region by providing critical analysis of salient aspects of the Alaskan past by specialists in the subject. It treats the more significant themes in Alaska history to which scholars of the subject have brought their training and attention. Every effort has been made to include as many contemporary writers in the field as possible, and most of the articles are written by practicing historians and researchers now active in the field. In addition, the editors have chosen to include a few older items which are regarded as classics, such as A.H. Brooks' physical description of Alaska and S.R. Tompkins' description of the negotiations which led to determination of the 1825 Alaska/Canada boundary.

Most of the selections were originally published in professional journals or in books. Together they represent the "state of the art" of historical study of Alaska at the present time.

I.

History is at once a scientific attempt to reconstruct the events of the past and an individual human attempt to understand their meaning. Historians, professional and amateur, constantly pursue both enterprises, sometimes simultaneously, sometimes separately. But the second aspect of writing history, interpretation, is not well understood. The image comes readily to mind of a researcher assembling old diaries, letters, reports and memos, and poring over their details so as to present an orderly progression of the sequence of events. But it is not well appreciated that the interpretation of such data, once assembled and ordered, is an act of individual judgment. It is often assumed either that the facts will tell their own meaning, and thus do not need interpretation, or else that the way they have been understood traditionally is the only way they can be understood.

History differs from science in that every writer, and every reader, understands the facts differently. Partly this is so because every act of reconstructing the past represents a different selection of the facts themselves. There are too many facts to be included in any one reconstruction of the past; some have to be left out. Which ones should be included and which not? The reader's first impulse is to answer that only the important ones should be included. But who is to be the judge of which are the most important ones? No two readers, or historians, will ever agree on which are the most important facts, and should be included, and which are the ones which should be left out.

In their reading of the very same letters and memoranda of officials in Alaska at the turn of the century, for example, Jeannette Nichols (who is not included in this collection directly) and William Wilson (who is included) came to different conclusions as to which were the most important facts, and what they meant. Nichols thought they meant that the federal government had been miserly in providing Alaska with support for development, given Alaska's special needs. But Wilson thought those facts meant that the federal government had been generous, given the level of its support to other developing territories.

As in any matter of judgment, either Nichols or Wilson could be right, though they themselves might not think so. It depends upon one's point of view. If one assumes that the federal government had a responsibility to provide more for Alaska, and one knows how critical transportation was to successful development, one is likely to agree with Nichols. On the other hand, if one assumes there were limitations on how much the government could do and knows something of the political and financial resources available, one is more likely to agree with Wilson. Their differing judgments demonstrate that the root of historical interpretation is not limited just to the question of which facts are the most important. It involves as well matters of the deepest personal judgment as to what the facts actually mean.

Every student of history, casual or professional, will come to an individual conclusion as to what the significance of a particular historical episode really is. And as in any intellectual enterprise, reasonable people will disagree. The credibility of any particular writer must be determined by the character of that writer's intellectual judgment and common sense, and how he or she has handled the factual evidence, i.e., whether the facts are accurate, and how they have been weighted in reaching conclusions and forming judgments. In this regard, history resembles any intellectual judgment or analysis in the present; it differs only in that its subject is mankind's past activity, and the analysts have the benefit of the passage of time.

Not all readers of history are aware of these subtleties. Some are impatient with differing interpretations, and particularly with new interpretations which challenge widely held, time-honored versions of the past. Reflection, though, suggests that truth is not easily obtained in any intellectual endeavor, and that it is not the product of popularity contests.

II.

Alaska history has been the beneficiary of much interpretation over the past several decades. As more scholars and students have joined those already practicing the historian's craft, subjects long neglected have been studied in greater detail, and the understanding of topics thought beyond change has been presented in new, sometimes dramatically different light. The purchase of Alaska, for example, usually axiomatically assumed to have been hugely unpopular in the United States, has been shown to have been heartily endorsed by most major newspaper editors, as well as by the two-thirds of the U.S. Senate necessary to pass the purchase treaty. The Alaska Highway, usually presented as a military supply road made necessary by war, has been shown to have been built for very different reasons and accepted only grudgingly by the U.S. Army. There are many other examples of familiar nostrums which have been challenged by closer, more recent study.

Most, though by no means all, of the work of reinterpretation has taken place in the professional historical journals which publish articles on Alaska history. These include, first and foremost, the *Pacific Northwest Quarterly*, which has been a steadfast friend to Alaska history for over half a century, but also such publications as *Pacific Historical Review*, *Western Historical Quarterly*, *Journal of the West*, *Pacific Historian*, *Arctic Anthropology*, and *Canadian Historical Review*, among others, and most recently, a newcomer to the field, *Alaska History*, sponsored by the Alaska Historical Society. Manuscripts submitted to all these journals are published only after approval by a panel of practicing historians or teachers of history and verification of the supporting documentation, thus insuring that they meet contemporary standards of historical accuracy, judgment, and writing style. Most of the articles in this anthology were originally printed in such journals.

The selections in this volume were chosen principally for their contribution to a more complete understanding of Alaska history, providing greater depth than is available in the more widely used narrative histories, and presenting, in the judgment of the editors, the best interpretations of those pivotal events and more significant themes in the Alaskan past to which writers have given their attention. The articles complement the region's history as presented in such texts as Ernest Gruening's *State of Alaska*, William R. Hunt's *Alaska: A Bicentennial History*, and Claus-M. Naske and Herman Slotnick's popular *Alaska: A History of the 49th State.* A similar anthology, edited by Professor Morgan Sherwood, a dean of Alaska history, was published in 1967. It is now out of print. There has been an explosion of Alaska historical research and writing in the last twenty years, and the need for a new anthology has been clearly expressed and keenly felt by many.

The collection includes anthropology and oral history as well as traditional documentary history. The new discipline of ethnohistory, a combination of the methods of anthropology and history, is represented by Lydia Black's work on Aleut culture. John Whitehead used the techniques of oral history in his work in comparing the Alaska and Hawaii statehood movements. Four of the articles deal directly with Alaska Natives and Native conditions, those by Black, Schneider, Haycox and Philp. Other articles also deal with Native affairs, though less directly. In addition to political history, the pieces treat economic development, social conditions, environmental concerns, and myth and ideology. Limited space has prevented treatment of many themes and topics and the inclusion of many articles which the editors would like to have reprinted. The editors have exercised their best judgment concerning the topics represented and the authors chosen.

III.

The theme of the Alaskan past most central to this collection is Alaska's relationship to broader contexts--geographical, political, environmental, economic, social and ideological. It has been common in much Alaskan historical writing to present the state's history either as if what happened here were independent of events, forces and ideas elsewhere, or, if not, should have been. Such a view is encouraged by the notion that Alaska is unique, and that its uniqueness pervades every aspect of its life and history. Certainly Alaska is unique in some ways. The largest state in the union, it is vast in size and diverse in resources. In many parts of the state population is sparse, and the number of persons per total acres of land is much lower than elsewhere in the U.S. Not only does Alaska have a significant Native population, but it has as well the only non-Indian aboriginal Native people in the United States, the Eskimos and Aleuts. Alaska is one of only two states not contiguous with the continental United States and was the first non-contiguous U.S. territorial acquisition.

But writers who have described Alaska have usually focused on the assumption that the people and the culture of Alaska are unique as well. Many have taken it as axiomatic that Alaskans are more independent, more self-reliant, and more individualistic than people in the rest of the U.S., and that they are less patient with the constraints which circumscribe thought and action in other parts of the country. People come to Alaska, it has been written, to live more freely and to be more fully themselves than is possible in the more settled, more heavily bureaucratic continental states. By extension, it has often been assumed that there is an Alaskan culture which is unique and which inspires a characteristically Alaskan self-reliance.

When this thesis of uniqueness has been applied to Alaska history, it has produced an interpretation particularly celebratory of individual heroes, such as sourdoughs, for example, and of individualistic enterprises, such as placer mining and fur trapping. At the same time, it has been critical of federal bureaucracy and the federal government's role in Alaska's development.

Like any interpretation, the thesis of Alaskan uniqueness is a way of understanding the facts, and like other interpretations, it explains some of them better than others. Today, with easy and nearly universal access to air travel and instant world-wide communication, people move into and out of Alaska with an ease not possible in earlier times and are as much a part of American culture as any other American residents with access to television, telephones, public schools and supermarkets. Essentially, non-Native Alaskans are virtually indistinguishable from people in the rest of the country in their experiences and attitudes.

Moreover, when historically considered, the thesis of Alaskan uniqueness contradicts Alaska's high degree of dependence on Outside investment and on the federal government for Alaskans' livelihood and development. Private investment in the Pacific salmon industry, in the industrial mining of gold and copper, and more recently, in oil, have comprised basic ingredients of the Alaskan economy. So have such public projects as construction of the Alaska Railroad, the Richardson Highway, and the numerous military facilities. Moreover, Alaska shares with the rest of the western states of the U.S. the transforming effect of World War II on its economic and social history. Its post-war development was categorically different from its pre-war period, being characterized by even greater federal investment and involvement.

Most of the interpretations in this collection, then, complement the notion of Alaskan uniqueness; some of them challenge it. They set Alaska history into broader contexts and show the relationships between Alaska and the Outside, between Alaskan experiences, ideas and circumstances and those of the rest of the U.S. and the world. Many recent writers have found that those relationships were much more complex than once supposed and that Alaskan dependence was much greater than has sometimes been understood.

The editors of this anthology will regard their work as successful in the task they set for themselves if readers take from it a deeper understanding of the true circumstances of the Alaskan past, a deeper understanding than that provided in the general treatments and casual representations which characterize popular literature. These have their necessary place. But this volume has been prepared to aid those who wish to go beyond popular history, to learn what the corps of dedicated researchers has found to be the meaning behind the facts, and how that meaning has changed as more is learned. The meaning of Alaska history will continue to change, as still more is learned through additional documentation, study, and reflection, and as the needs and circumstances of the present stimulate yet newer ways of understanding the past. As that work continues, this anthology will become outdated and will need to be replaced with yet another. We look forward to that day, for such is the true nature of history.

ALASKAN HISTORY: A PERSPECTIVE

The student of Alaskan history has to cope with a shorter time span than do history students in many parts of the world. Of course, Alaska has long been inhabited. Alaska's preliterate history extends back at least 10,000 years, and some scholars believe that humans migrated from Asia to the Americas across the Bering Sea Land Bridge 27,000 or 28,000 years ago. Whenever they came, these travelers included the ancestors of today's Haida and Tlingit of southeastern Alaska and of the Athabascan people of the interior. Eskimos and Aleuts, however, may have come later by boat, either across Bering Strait or via the Aleutians. In any case, they have been in western and northern Alaska and in the Aleutians for at least 8,000 years. Historians depend upon archeologists and anthropologists for information about the pre-contact lives of these Native Alaskans.

Alaskan history in the traditional sense (that is, as dependent upon written documentation or eyewitness account) began only in 1741. Despite its comparative brevity, Alaskan history is complex. For example, it encompasses a series of international rivalries, the collision of several cultures, and economic difficulties characteristic of any resource-rich but remote area.

In a political sense, Alaskan history may be divided into five eras: (1) the Russian period, 1741-1867; (2) the early American era, 1867-1897; (3) the gold rush years, 1897 to about 1912; (4) the territorial period, 1912-1959; and (5) the period since statehood, 1959 to the present. Some of these eras, such as the Russian period, may easily be subdivided. And naturally none of the periods is completely separate and distinct from that which preceded or followed it. But, for purposes of convenience, always remembering that this scheme of categorization is political and therefore somewhat artificial, such periodization may assist the reader to gain an understanding of general trends as well as of the significance of specific events.

The Russian Period, 1741-1867

In 1741 Vitus Bering led the first successful Russian expedition to Alaska. Although his crew landed on Kayak Island southeast of Cordova and charted part of the southcentral coast, the human toll was high; almost half of Bering's men perished. Those who survived, however, returned to Siberia in 1742 with many valuable furs, including fox, seal, and sea otter pelts.

The knowledge that pelts of high quality could be obtained readily in the islands east of Kamchatka led increasing numbers of *promyshlenniki* (fur hunters/traders) to the Commander Islands and the Aleutians. Whenever the *promyshlenniki* could not obtain pelts easily themselves, they forced the Aleuts to hunt for them. Within twenty years, the *promyshlenniki* reached Kodiak Island; within forty, Russian fur merchant Gregory Shelikhov had established a permanent settlement there.

Furs attracted other westerners, as well. Spain attempted to maintain its claim to all of the west coast of North America by sending at least seven expeditions into Alaskan waters between 1770 and the early 1790s. Great Britain sent Captain James Cook into the area in 1778. Private British and American traders followed. The Russian government, meanwhile, tried without success first to tax the Aleuts, then to protect them from the worst excesses perpetrated by the *promyshlenniki*.

Free-booting Russian exploitation of Alaska ended in 1799 with creation of the Russian American Company, a privately owned, government chartered monopoly modeled on Western European trading companies. Aleksandr Baranov, formerly resident manager of the Golikov-Shelikhov Company, became the Chief Manager, or "Governor," of Russian America. Baranov expanded the company's operations. He established a post at Sitka which, despite the open hostility of local Tlingits, became the company's Alaskan headquarters. Because of continual difficulty in procuring supplies, Baranov built a post in northern California (Ft. Ross) and twice attempted to set up trading posts in Hawaii. He also traded freely with British and American ship captains, upon whom he became increasingly dependent.

Russia's Imperial Navy objected to Baranov's dealings with foreigners and criticized his treatment of Natives, whom Baranov expected to work whenever and wherever required. He loaned Natives to foreign captains to poach otter on the California coast, and he also dispatched them to Ft. Ross and Hawaii. The Navy's opposition led to Baranov's removal in 1817, and Russian America subsequently fell under naval control.

Under the company's second and third charters, issued in 1821 and 1844 respectively, the colony's governor and his top assistants were to be naval officers, although the company remained nominally under the control of its stockholders, who continued to vote themselves handsome dividends. When he granted the second charter in 1821, Czar Alexander I also attempted to eliminate foreign trading in Alaska. He extended Russian America's boundary southward from 55° to 51°, and he decreed that no foreign ships were to be permitted within 100 miles of the coast. These directives brought immediate protests from Britain and the United States, also causing considerable hardship in Russian America by cutting off the colony's major sources of supply. Treaties between Russia and the United States (1824) and Russia and Great Britain (1825) reopened trade. The Anglo-Russian treaty of 1825 also delineated the Canadian-Russian American boundary. Russian America's supply problems remained unresolved until 1839, when company officials negotiated an agreement by which the Hudson's Bay Company leased what is now the mainland of southeastern Alaska in return for providing specified supplies annually to the Russians.

Under the second and third charters a distinctively Russian American culture began to emerge in the Aleutians, southcentral, and southeastern Alaska. Partly this resulted from the work of Russian Orthodox priests, especially Father Ioann Veniaminov. Veniaminov arrived at Unalaska in the 1820s, learned the Fox Aleut dialect, helped to devise a Fox alphabet, and through example converted many Natives to Christianity. Veniaminov soon moved to Sitka, where he established a seminary to train Native Alaskan priests. Despite his efforts, few of the local Tlingits converted to Russian Orthodoxy. The Russians, in fact, never subdued the Tlingits at all. But, among other Native employees of the company Veniaminov's influence was great.

Russian authorities took steps to improve the lives of Native workers as well as Christianizing them. Under the second charter, the "half-village rule" went into effect: only half of the men in any village could be conscripted for labor by the company at once, and the village headman had the right to determine who would go and who would stay. The Russians also tried several times to immunize people against smallpox. Their efforts proved partly successful during the continent-wide epidemic of the late 1830s.

As furs became depleted, the Russian American Company tried to diversify. Distance, transportation costs, and lack of skilled labor all operated to the company's disadvantage, however. Of potentially valuable exports, only ice proved profitable, but by 1860 the ice trade produced only about two percent of the company's revenues. Declining company income necessitated increased subsidies from the

Russian government, already beset with domestic financial difficulties. In addition, Russian officials in Alaska had watched the California gold rush of 1849 with alarm. California's population had increased from about 8,000 in 1848 to roughly 100,000 in 1850. Since the total number of Russians in Alaska probably never exceeded 800, obviously a stampede of that magnitude would have rendered Alaska ungovernable. And the Crimean War (1853-56) had further demonstrated Alaska's vulnerability; only the fact that Great Britain honored a mutual neutrality agreement negotiated by the Hudson's Bay and Russian American companies had saved Russian America from possible British attack and conquest. Russia's acquisition of the left bank of the Amur River from China in the 1850s brought Russia a new region far more accessible and potentially much more profitable than Alaska. For those reasons and others Czar Alexander II approved Alaska's sale to the United States in 1867 for $7,200,000.

The United States, traditionally expansionist, proved eager to buy Alaska, partly due to a desire to keep it out of British hands. But knowledge about Alaska's potential resources also contributed to Americans' willingness to purchase the area. Yankee whalers had exploited Alaskan waters for years, obtaining quantities of whale and walrus oil, baleen, and ivory. Scientists from the Smithsonian Institution had accompanied the Alaskan branch of the unsuccessful Western Union Telegraph Expedition (1865-66), and their glowing reports about potential wealth confirmed others' accounts. The formal transfer of Alaska from Russian to American hands occurred in October, 1867, some months prior to appropriation of the necessary purchase funds by the Congress. The speed with which the transfer was completed indicates the desire of both governments to consummate the deal quickly.

The Early American Era, 1867-1897

Following American acquisition of Alaska, the United States Congress designated it as a "customs and military district" and extended U.S. mining law to Alaska. In 1873, Congress categorized Alaska as "Indian territory" in order to prohibit the sale of distilled alcohol to Natives. No other governmental arrangements were made. No way existed to obtain title to land other than a mining claim. No civil government could be established legally. The United States Army was placed in control, but without formal declaration of martial law. The Army "governed" Alaska until 1877, when troops were withdrawn to suppress the Nez Perce rebellion in Washington and

Idaho. For two years the highest federal official in Alaska was the Customs Collector at Sitka. In 1879, following trouble between Tlingits and non-Natives at Sitka, U.S. authorities dispatched the Navy to govern Alaska, again without declaration of martial law. Naval personnel at least possessed the advantage of mobility, although they had little more success at governance than had army officers.

A number of land speculators and other optimists had moved to Alaska in 1867, confidently expecting the area to boom immediately under American rule. Alaska, however, did not develop quickly, a fact related to its geographic location, its size, and to the state of technology in the 1860s. New residents, in the way of frontiersmen throughout the American West, blamed the federal government for Alaska's problems. The government, they noted, had not provided adequate mail service, did not allow Alaska to be represented in Congress, had not passed a homestead law, and gave Alaska no right to self-government.

With hindsight it is apparent that Alaska in the late 1860s and early 1870s lacked any western-style economic base. Given the prevailing laissez-faire philosophy, the federal government could have done little to correct this condition. But slowly, without federal assistance, a western-based economy began to develop. Commercial salmon processing began in the late 1870s and grew rapidly. A major gold strike at Juneau in 1880 brought attention and outside investors to the area, and the Juneau-Douglas mines soon became the largest employers in Alaska.

Economics aside, the need for civil government became increasingly apparent. Alaska especially needed a judicial system. In both Sitka and Angoon, Tlingits with claims for compensation clearly legal under western law were denied redress by military authorities. In Angoon, the naval commander went so far as to punish the Tlingits, who had requested compensation for the death of a villager in a job-related accident, by shelling the village.

The Juneau gold strike; the census of 1880, which, although incomplete, found there to be more than 33,000 people in Alaska; the restiveness of the several hundred non-Natives drawn north by Alaska's apparent promise; pressure exerted in Washington, D.C., by Presbyterian leader Sheldon Jackson; and the obvious need for a fair and effective judicial system finally induced Congress to establish a rudimentary form of civil government in Alaska with the Organic Act of 1884. The act provided for a governor, a federal district judge, and various other court officials, each of whom would be appointed by the President and confirmed by the Senate. The laws of Oregon were to apply insofar as they did not conflict with federal law. The act reserved the Natives' rights to their land, pending final disposition of land claims by the United States Congress. And it created the post of General Agent of Education, a position occupied by Sheldon Jackson from 1885 until 1906, to oversee the schooling of Alaska's children "without regard to race."

Native Alaskans faced rapid social change during this period. Perhaps the greatest outside influence was that of missionaries. Sheldon Jackson encouraged Protestant missionaries to go north; at Jackson's suggestion, Protestants divided Alaska into exclusive districts to avoid competition and insure an Alaska-wide missionary effort. Roman Catholic missionaries soon followed their Protestant counterparts. Most missionaries combined the cultural assumptions of middle class Americans with a belief in saving souls. Thus, missionary activity in the early American era stressed education as well as Christianization, the goals being to avoid mistakes made earlier in the contiguous United States and to prepare Alaska's Natives for assimilation into America's mainstream. The missionaries exercised mixed influences, of course. They suppressed Native languages and cultural traditions. They also operated orphanages, supervised a reindeer-herding program instituted in northwestern Alaska by Jackson, and spread the Gospel. Perhaps they cushioned the worst of the cultural collisions. Certainly they helped many Natives prepare for the changes that the turn-of-the-century gold rushes brought.

The Gold Rush, 1897-1912

Alaska's gold rush era began, of course, with the Klondike strike in Canada's Yukon Territory. This strike affected Alaska in two ways. First, major routes to the gold fields crossed Alaska, resulting in a demand for goods and services by stampeders on their way north. By the time the stampeders of 1898 reached Dawson City, the best ground had already been staked. Many simply returned home, but others drifted into Alaska to seek gold. Knowledge of the Klondike also stimulated prospecting by Alaskan residents. Consequently major strikes occurred in Nome in 1898 and near Fairbanks in 1902. Each of these triggered a rush, as did several dozen other strikes throughout Alaska.

The gold rushes spurred other economic activity. The Alaska Syndicate, a consortium formed by J. P. Morgan, the Guggenheim brothers, and others, bought the Kennicott copper mine, built the Copper River and Northwestern Railroad, and operated gold mines, canneries, and a steamship line. Southcentral Alaska particularly benefited from the Syndicate's investments.

During the gold rush era, Alaska's population doubled in ten years. For the first time, a substantial non-Native population existed north of the Yukon River. Native Alaskans not previously affected by outside contact now experienced its effects. Miners brought influenza, measles, and smallpox. They depleted game in areas near gold fields. They disregarded traditional Native land use patterns. At the same time, jobs, education, and medical care became more widely available. Again, prolonged contact between cultures brought mixed results.

In political terms, the gold rushes brought the beginnings of self-government and increased federal attention. The government hurried to formalize settlement of a boundary dispute with Canada which stemmed from ambiguities in the 1825 Anglo-Russian treaty. Congress provided new civil and criminal codes expressly for Alaska and expanded the judicial system, permitted towns of more than three hundred people to incorporate and set up municipal services, granted non-Natives the right to homestead and Natives the right to acquire land allotments. Finally, in 1906 Congress allowed Alaskans to elect a non-voting delegate to the United States House of Representatives.

Despite these changes, many Alaskans remained dissatisfied. Natives worried about losing their land. At the same time, they sought the benefits of education and Western technology. Non-Natives became more frustrated than ever with federal control of Alaska's resources. Theodore Roosevelt's creation of the Tongass and Chugach National Forests and his withdrawal of Alaska's coal lands from public entry provoked spirited protests and sparked a debate about the proper federal role in Alaska which continues today.

The Territorial Period, 1912-1959

Alaska formally became a territory when Congress passed the Organic Act of 1912 establishing a legislature. The powers of the legislature were severely limited. For example, acts passed by the legislature could be vetoed by the governor (subject to override) or disallowed by the United States Congress. The Alaska legislature could pass no land laws. Neither the territory nor its incorporated municipalities could incur bonded indebtedness. These types of restrictions historically had applied to most U.S. territories. However, the Alaskan legislature operated under two unique restrictions: it could neither establish a territorial judicial system nor regulate fish, game, and fur-bearing animals. These restrictions resulted from pressure exerted by the salmon packers, who feared that a larger government would necessitate increased revenues, leading to higher taxes. The packers also benefited throughout this period from relatively lax federal fisheries regulation and thus preferred federal to territorial control.

In areas where the legislature could act, members generally favored Progressive measures. For instance, the first act passed by the first session of the first legislature gave women the right to vote.

Despite the promise of the gold rush years and federal funding of the Alaska Railroad in 1914, World War I brought depression to Alaska. Men left the territory to join the service, and many failed to return. Nature played a part, too; the Treadwell gold mines on Douglas Island closed following collapse and flooding. And after the war the prices of copper and salmon, Alaska's major products, fell sharply. Alaska's economy remained depressed throughout the 1920s in spite of efforts to promote tourism and encourage agriculture, the completion of the Alaska Railroad, and the introduction of air travel, a means by which to solve the territory's remaining transportation problems. Policymakers in Washington, D.C., could only contrast Alaska with the booming contiguous United States and conclude that something must be wrong with Alaska. Once again, expectations had been foiled by impersonal factors, particularly a geographic location which rendered large-scale industrial and agricultural development economically infeasible as yet.

The interwar years marked the entry into politics of the Tlingit and Haida, the first Native Alaskans to participate actively in the western-imposed political process. Tlingit lawyer William L. Paul, Sr., led the way, becoming in 1925 the first Native Alaska to serve in the territorial legislature. Paul also played a role in insuring that Alaskan Natives could establish village councils and qualify for the grants and loans provided by terms of the Indian Reorganization Act of 1934. Concern about land lost with the creation of Tongass National Forest led to a request for, and passage of, the Tlingit-Haida Jurisdictional Act of 1935, which permitted the Tlingit and Haida people to sue the United States government in the Court of Claims for compensation.

Other Alaskans continued to fret about federal-territorial relations, particularly the control which the federal government exercised over Alaska's land and resources. Federal fisheries policy remained a major issue as the size of the annual salmon pack began to decline beginning in 1937. The federal Bureau of Fisheries blamed the decline on Japanese fishing in Alaskan waters. Alaskans more correctly blamed it on overfishing as a result of ineffective regulation by the federal government.

Although Alaskans criticized some federal policies, residents also benefited from federal expenditures during the 1930s. The Civilian Conservation Corps, a New Deal relief program, employed both Natives and non-Natives on a variety of projects. The Public Works Administration furnished grants and loans to municipalities for proposals as diverse as a new schoolhouse in Skagway, a federal building in Fairbanks, and a bridge crossing Gastineau Channel to connect Douglas with Juneau. As the 1930s wore on, the Works Progress Administration began to finance defense-related projects, such as emergency landing strips. A major defense buildup began in 1939, leading to construction of military installations at Fairbanks, Anchorage, Kodiak, and Unalaska.

World War II changed Alaska even more drastically than had the gold rushes. People flooded into the territory--soldiers, contractors, construction workers, support personnel. The Japanese Navy came, too, bombing Dutch Harbor near Unalaska in early June, 1942, and occupying Kiska and Attu, the outermost Aleutian Islands, a few days later. A counteroffensive followed, driving the Japanese from Alaska by mid-1943. Eventually some of the airfields and harbors built for defense purposes would serve the burgeoning civilian population, as would the Alaska Highway, which for the first time provided an overland link to the "lower 48."

To all Alaskans the war brought confusion and inconvenience--travel restrictions, censorship of mail, shortages of specific commodities. To a few, it brought suffering. The Japanese interned the Aleuts captured on Attu in Hokkaido. More than forty percent died there. The United States government evacuated all other Aleuts from Unalaska west through the Pribilofs. Taken to southeastern Alaska, housed in deplorable and insanitary conditions, many returned home to find their houses demolished, their personal belongings vandalized and their communities surrounded by unsightly, often dangerous, military debris.

For other Alaskans, World War II meant promise for the future. Alaska's governor, Ernest Gruening, and Delegate to Congress Anthony J. (Tony) Dimond both believed that the attention drawn to Alaska by the war might insure statehood for the territory in the foreseeable future. Both worked to prepare. Gruening presented a tax reform proposal which the territorial legislature initially rejected but finally passed in 1949, insuring that Alaska could support a state government financially. And Dimond sponsored legislation enlarging the Alaskan legislature and apportioning its lower house according to population, thereby giving statehood advocates in the more populous districts a greater voice in legislation.

Defense spending had become increasingly important to Alaska's economy, and it continued to grow during the Cold War of the early 1950s. Alaska's population grew, as well. Many who had come to Alaska during the war remained. Others who had been in the territory in military service returned. More professionals came--teachers, doctors, lawyers--all necessary to provide the infrastructure required by a developing community. These people came from areas which possessed all the rights and privileges of United States citizens. They expected the government to provide many services, and they did not begrudge paying the taxes necessary to support such services. These newcomers, along with a cadre of reform-minded long-time residents, formed the core of the statehood movement.

Statehood proponents faced a long battle. Serious questions persisted as to Alaska's ability to support a state government financially. Opponents of statehood included the salmon packers; some Republicans in the U.S. Congress, who opposed admission of then-Democratic Alaska solely on partisan grounds; and many southern Democrats in the Congress who feared [correctly] that two more senators from a state with a sizeable minority population would equal two more votes for civil rights bills. A formula for conveyance of federal land to state ownership had to be worked out. Active opposition combined with indifference to delay statehood long enough to frustrate many initial supporters.

During the winter of 1955-56 the Alaska Constitutional Convention met on the University of Alaska campus at Fairbanks.

There, statehood advocates sought to demonstrate Alaskans' political maturity by adopting a model state constitution. No one knew whether or not that constitution would actually go into effect. The convention, however, galvanized the statehood movement. In 1956 Alaskan voters adopted the Tennessee Plan, so-named for the first area to use the device to speed the attainment of statehood. Under the Tennessee Plan, Alaskans selected an unofficial congressional delegation, one U.S. Representative and two Senators. Members of the Tennessee Plan delegation (Ernest Gruening, William Egan, and Ralph Rivers) joined Alaska's delegate to Congress (E. L. "Bob" Bartlett) in lobbying for statehood in Washington, D.C., and otherwise publicizing the cause.

Alaska became a state in 1959. The constitution drawn up three years earlier went into effect and remains, according to political scientists, one of the best in the nation.

Alaska Since Statehood

Statehood did not solve all of Alaska's problems, of course. The most immediate problems faced by the state proved to be financial ones. In 1959 the state had only $18.5 million in unrestricted revenues, much of that derived from personal and corporate income taxes. The state had anticipated revenue from sale of land, but conveyance to the state of the 103.5 million acres to which Alaska was entitled under terms of the statehood act proceeded very slowly. Essentially, the state depended upon periodic oil and gas lease sales for the revenue which enabled it to keep operating. The Prudhoe Bay oil strike, the Prudhoe Bay lease sale of 1969, and eventual completion of the pipeline in 1977 changed that. For the first time the state had more than adequate revenue, and Alaskans benefited from increased expenditures for education, from establishment of a state telecommunication network, and, in rural areas, from the improved health care that telecommunications made possible. Oil has replaced salmon as the mainstay of the economy, and at present the economy remains tied to a resource controlled by outside investors and world prices. The geographic imperative continues to operate.

Federal-state relations remain thorny. Passage of the Alaska Native Claims Settlement Act in 1971 and the Alaska National Interest Lands Conservation Act in 1980 have raised more questions regarding land management than they have solved. Environmentalists, development-minded Alaskans, and rural subsistence resource users remain pitted against each other, and often against the federal government, over land use and management practices. Solutions to many of today's problems will require care, thought, and time.

Statehood has undeniably brought many benefits to Alaska and its people. Alaskans now possess the same political rights and privileges as other United States citizens. Education, health care, and communications have improved. The salmon industry has recovered under state regulation. And while political structure can not alter geography, Alaskans now have a political framework in which to work together to solve common problems and to achieve common goals.

ALASKAN AND NORTH AMERICAN GEOGRAPHY*

Alfred Hulse Brooks

Just as the history of any region is shaped by its physical environment, Alaska is what it is partly because of where it is located in relation to the rest of the nation and to the world and its population centers. Impersonal forces, such as climate, topography, and natural resources, determine where and how Alaska's people live. Few people have understood the relationship between environment and historical development better than Alfred Hulse Brooks.

Brooks, a geologist, historian, and explorer, learned surveying as a youth. He earned a B.S. from Harvard in 1894 and began work for the United States Geological Survey the same year, leaving the agency briefly in 1897 to travel in Europe and study at the Sorbonne. In 1898 he returned to the USGS to work in Alaska. His duties included helping to survey the White and Tanana Rivers, reconnoitering a route from Pyramid Harbor in southeastern Alaska (now deserted) to Eagle, and investigating the Nome and Ketchikan areas and southcentral Alaska from Cook Inlet to the Alaska Range. After 1903 he headed the USGS's Alaska branch, turning down an offer to become the Survey's Chief Geologist in order to stay in Alaska. As a proponent of development, Brooks encouraged mining in numerous reports on Alaska's mineral deposits. He also served as vice-chairman of the Alaska Railroad Commission.

During World War I Brooks went to France as Chief Geologist with the Army Expeditionary Force, and in 1919 he became a consultant to the Paris Peace Commission. Following the war he travelled widely, returning to Alaska several times prior to his death in 1924.

This collection of articles opens with Brooks' discussion of Alaska's terrain, reprinted from *Blazing Alaska's Trails*. Brooks found four distinct geographic zones in Alaska: the Pacific mountain system, the central plateau, the Arctic mountains (now named the "Brooks Range" in his honor), and the Arctic slope. While modern geographers might quibble with his division of Alaska into only four regions, his classic description remains a good introduction to the subject. In it he explained the relationship of Alaska to North America and of Alaska's geographic regions to each other. He also emphasized the importance of Alaska's rivers to patterns of settlement. His essay not only connects Alaska geographically to the rest of the world but provides a necessary context within which to study Alaskan history.

---

*Alfred Hulse Brooks, *Blazing Alaska's Trails*, ed. Burton L. Fryxell (Caldwell, Idaho: Caxton Printers, Ltd., for University of Alaska and Arctic Institute of North America, 1953), pp. 1-27.

* * *

Alaska's Pacific shore line is bounded throughout much of its length by rugged mountains in which lie great snow fields giving rise to many glaciers. This coastal barrier is especially prominent from Portland Canal on the southeast to Kenai Peninsula on the southwest. West of Cook Inlet there is another range which, with its southwestern extension in the Alaska Peninsula, also forms a coastal barrier. Inland of these mountains and adjacent to them are other parallel ranges of high altitude. The whole constitutes a rugged system forming, indeed, one of the larger features of relief in North America. These high ranges include some of the loftiest peaks on the continent; and as many of them rise close to sea level, they present scenes of grandeur elsewhere unsurpassed. The steep slopes covered with snow and ice present a forbidding landscape; and where the dense coniferous forests clothe the lower reaches, they add to the sombreness of the scene.

It is this aspect of Alaska's relief which has been most strongly emphasized in descriptive writing, and the fact that beyond these ranges there is a region of broad fertile valleys and rolling uplands draining to Bering Sea through the Yukon and Kuskokwim rivers is often lost sight of. This great inland region is in strong contrast, both as to topography and climate, as well as vegetation and soil, with the coastal barrier. It is, in turn, separated from the Arctic by another mountain system which stretches across northern Alaska, and falls off on the north to the barren grounds that skirt the polar sea.

Alaska thus falls into four large physiographic provinces--two mountain systems, one bordering the Pacific and one paralleling the Arctic, an intermontane region of lesser relief, and a lowland area separating the northern system from the Arctic Ocean. Of these, the two mountain systems, together with the intermontane region, are a northwesterly extension of the Cordillera of North America that forms the grand feature of relief in western United States and Canada. The fourth province of Alaska corresponds in a general way to the Great Plains region, which stretches eastward from the base of the Rocky Mountains both in Canada and the United States.

These four provinces have been named, from south to north, the Pacific Mountain System, the Central Plateau Region, the Arctic Mountain System, and the Arctic Slope Region. Each has a certain topographic unity that distinguishes it from the adjacent province; each is also divisible into a number of lesser provinces differing from each other. Thus, the mountain systems are made up of numerous distinct ranges, and the Central Plateau Region includes uplands, broad lowlands, and some minor ranges.

These larger features of Alaska's topography have in large measure controlled the climate, the soil, and the distribution of vegetation and animal life and, because of this and of the barriers to communication, have had an important effect on man's occupation of the land. Therefore, Alaska's natural and political history can only be understood by a clear grasp of its physiographic features. These will therefore be described in some detail.

The rivers and streams have been a dominating influence in determining man's occupation of Alaska. These were important to the natives because they furnished a large part of the food supply and because the rivers marked the main routes of travel both in winter and in summer. The approach of the white man was also largely dominated by the watercourses. On the Pacific seaboard he was long held in check by the turbulent glacier-fed watercourses which drain this part of the Territory. On the other hand, easy access was had to the vast interior beyond the coastal barrier by the rivers emptying into Bering Sea. Along the rivers the pioneer could transport necessary supplies in crude rafts or boats built of the timber which grows on the banks; subsequently the steamboat succeeded craft propelled by hand. Later overland routes were determined by the river valleys, first followed by trails, then by wagon roads and railroads.

Not only has the drainage system determined the avenues of approach, but the valleys have yielded most of the placer gold and have provided the water power needed for industrial developments. Moreover, the best timber and most of the arable land are found on the river banks and along the valley floors and slopes. In short, the watercourses are and have been the most important physical features of inland Alaska. Therefore, the larger drainage features of the Territory first merit a brief description. A more detailed account of the principal rivers will be included in the description of the different physiographic provinces.

Alaska's drainage is tributary to three oceans--southward to the Pacific, westward to Bering Sea, and northward and northwestward to the Arctic. The waters of about one-fifth of its area, including the major part of the Pacific Mountain System, are carried to the Pacific. Nearly one-half, including the great interior region, finds its way to

Bering Sea, chiefly through the Yukon and Kuskokwim rivers; and the rest goes into the Arctic, whose watershed includes the northern part of the Territory.

In general it is true that the rivers emptying into the Pacific are turbulent and silt-laden, difficult to navigate in small boats, and impossible for steamers except in their lower courses. They drain a region of strong relief, and many spring directly from glaciers. In contrast to these, most of the rivers emptying into Bering Sea and the Arctic Ocean have sluggish currents for a long distance up from their mouths, making them navigable not only for small boats and canoes but also for steamers. These streams flow through regions of comparatively low relief, though some of their headwaters are in mountains and a few have their sources in glaciers. The Arctic drainage is in part of the turbulent type, in part rivers having sluggish meandering courses. A few small glaciers drain into the Arctic Ocean.

In looking at a map of Alaska one notices the great crescentic sweep of the southern coast line which partly envelops the Gulf of Alaska. This great bend of the shore is paralleled by all the larger features of the relief. The Pacific Mountain System trends northwesterly to about the meridian of Mount St. Elias, then bends westerly, and finally, in the longitude of Mount McKinley, trends to the southwest to be continued by the Alaska Peninsula and the Aleutian Islands. The Central Plateau Region makes a similar crescentic sweep, while the Arctic Mountain System, that trends east and west across Alaska, is continued to the southeast by a range that knits it to the northwesterly trend of the Canadian Rockies.

This crescentic surface plan of Alaska's relief is, then, the dominating feature of its topography and differentiates it from the rest of the North American cordillera, which preserves its northwesterly trend throughout the States and Western Canada. Just as the great peninsula of Alaska stretches out to the west and southwest to meet the northeastern extension of Asia, so its mountain ranges change their northwesterly trend to the west and south toward the northeasterly trend of the mountains of Siberia. Alaska is, therefore, the meeting place between the mountain trends of the Old World and the New. This great hinge line of the mountain systems of the two continents is a deep-seated structural feature of rock terranes which make up the mountains.

What has been described is the surface expression of the larger structures that dominate the bedrock formations. This change of trend line is especially striking in the Pacific Mountain System, which will first be considered.

Pacific Mountain System

The Pacific Mountain System is made up of a number of distinct ranges forming a mountainous belt paralleling the seaboard, together with some areas of lesser relief. In Southeastern Alaska it averages about 50 miles in width but broadens to the northwest so that at Prince William Sound it measures 200 miles across; it then narrows down again in the Alaska Peninsula. Its mean altitude varies from 5,000 to 10,000 feet, with many lofty peaks whose summits are from 10,000 to over 15,000 feet high and one, Mount McKinley, towering more than 20,000 feet above sea level. Some broad valleys, lowlands, and plateaus are included in the system, and the coastal barrier is traversed by a number of large rivers whose valleys lie athwart its course. It is these valleys and several passes which give access to the interior through the coastal barrier. The principal ranges of the system are the Coast, the St. Elias, the Chugach, and the Aleutian ranges, which lie close to the sea, and the Alaska Range, that forms the inland member of the system.

The mountains designated as the Coast Range stretch north from the boundary at Portland Canal for some 300 miles across the head of Lynn Canal and, again crossing the boundary, pass inland behind the St. Elias Range. They have no culminating crest line, but are made up of an irregular aggregate of peaks with connecting ridges, forming an elevated tract from 40 to 80 miles in width. Their general summit altitude has a marked uniformity, for only here and there a peak rises above the general level. At Portland Canal the relief is between 5,000 and 6,000 feet, but the altitude increases to the north, heights of 8,000 and 9,000 feet being reached at the head of Lynn Canal. Within the higher parts of the range there are some large ice and snow fields, and these give rise to numerous glaciers that discharge on both sides of the range, but the largest are on the seaward side. The boundaries of the Coast Range are ill-defined: on the south it is continued as the Coast Range of British Columbia; on the north and east it merges with the higher parts of the British Columbia plateau; on the west no sharp line can be drawn between it and the mountains of the Alexander Archipelago. Numerous fiords break the western face of the range, some of which penetrate far inland. Indeed, Portland Canal on the south cuts through almost the entire range.

Viewed from the sea these mountains present for the most part steep scarps rising from the water's edge or from narrow rocky beaches. The lower slopes are clothed in a dense growth of evergreens, giving the scene a sombre tone. Here and there a cataract leaps from a high basin to the sea, and most of the watercourses draining the west front of the range occupy narrow and steep valleys.

The boundary between Alaska and British Columbia lies within the Coast Range, so that only a small part of this mountain mass lies within Alaska. The boundary is an irregular line connecting some of the more prominent peaks that lie not far from the sea front of the range. Only at White and Chilkoot passes does the boundary follow the watersheds.

In the higher parts of the Coast Range most of the precipitation is in the form of snow, and much of the drainage is that of glaciers. On the lower slopes mountain torrents carry the heavy precipitation to the sea. Here and there a large stream emerges from the mountains through a steep-walled valley, but in general the drainage is through many smaller watercourses.

Several large rivers find their sources far beyond the Coast Range and reach the sea through valleys that traverse this barrier. The largest of these is the Stikine River, which drains a large area in northern British Columbia. It traverses the Coast Range through a steep-walled valley and here receives the discharge of several glaciers. The Stikine River has long been one of the routes into the interior, being used by the Hudson Bay Company as early as 1835. This route came into prominence during the Caribou gold excitement in 1865 and again during the Klondike rush in 1898. It is the only river traversing the Pacific Mountain System that is navigable for steamers.

South of the Stikine lies the Unuk River, whose source is in British Columbia beyond the Coast Range, while the same is true of the Taku River, which flows into Taku Inlet north of the Stikine. Both of these rivers afford routes into the interior that have been but little used, as they are not navigable.

There are but few passes through the Coast Range below the line of perpetual snow. The best known of these are the Chilkoot and

White passes, made famous by their use during the Klondike rush. Chilkoot Pass is about 20 miles from tidewater at Dyea Inlet, forming the lead of Lynn Canal. It is approached through a rather steep valley which reaches the foot of the final ascent 2,900 feet above the sea. From here a steep slope leads to the pass, 3,100 feet above the sea, which is but a narrow notch among high mountains that rise on either hand. It was this final ascent that taxed the strength of the gold seekers, for here no draft animals or sleds could be used, and all supplies had to be transported on men's backs. On the inland side a steep slope led down from the pass for about 500 feet to Crater Lake, and from here on the route was by water grade.

The White Pass, less than 25 miles south of the Chilkoot, is 2,800 feet high and also about 20 miles from tidewater at the mouth of Skagway River. The approach is by way of the Skagway valley, steep-walled and narrowing to almost canyon-like form. The steep ascent begins about ten miles from the coast, at an altitude of about 2,000 feet. The pass is wider than the Chilkoot, and to the north a gradual slope leads off to Lake Bennett. This pass was also extensively used by the Klondikers and is now crossed by the White Pass & Yukon Railroad, which runs from Skagway on the coast to navigable waters on the Yukon at Whitehorse, 110 miles from tidewater.

Northwest of Lynn Canal the Coast Range passes inland and beyond the boundary it merges with the British Columbia plateau. This part of the range is bounded on the south by the Chilkat valley, which separates it from the St. Elias Range to the southwest. At the head of the Chilkat River there are low passes leading into the Alsek basin, and these have long been used by the coast natives as a trading route into the interior.

West of Lynn Canal the St. Elias Range forms the coastal barrier. This lofty range stretches from Cross Sound and Icy Strait for over 250 miles to the northwest, with an average width of over 80 miles and a mean altitude of probably 8,000 to 10,000 feet. It probably has greater mass than any other range on the continent; and, rising, as it does, to great altitudes, almost direct from sea level, it presents a scene of grandeur unexcelled in the world.

A southerly extension of the St. Elias Range is to be found in the mountains which traverse the western part of Chichagof and Baranof islands. To the northwest it merges with the Chugach and

Wrangell mountains. The inland front of St. Elias Range is well defined, for it here presents a bold scarp toward the Central Plateau Region, which is of far lesser relief. The seaward face of the range rises boldly, in part almost direct from the sea, in part separated from tidewater by a coastal plain. Unlike the Coast Range, the St. Elias Range is but little broken by fiords. The exceptions are Lituya Bay--a T-shaped indentation with a narrow rocky entrance--and Disenchantment Bay, well known for its magnificent tributary glaciers. Except at these two embayments the shore line is but little broken.

The boundary between Canada and Alaska lies within the St. Elias Range, marked by a series of high peaks located near the seaward front of the range. This boundary has now been surveyed and marked. It is these surveys that have given us most of the available information about this mountain mass. The inland front of the range has also been traced, and the valley of the Alsek River has been traversed and the river ascended, but beyond this the range is almost unexplored.

The Alsek River valley cuts across the St. Elias Range, dividing it into two parts. Of these the eastern, stretching parallel to the coast to Glacier Bay, is called the Fairweather Mountains, and the western constitutes the St. Elias Mountains. The Fairweather Mountains rise from close to the sea up to altitudes of 8,000 to 15,000 feet and include an enormous ice cap that discharges into Glacier and Lituya bays, the Alsek River, and also directly into the sea. Among the highest peaks in this part of the range are Mount Fairweather (15,292 ft.), Mount Crillon (15,900 ft.), and Mount La Perouse (10,740 ft.). The St. Elias Mountains constitute the highest part of the range, averaging probably over 10,000 feet in height. Within the area marked out by lofty summits there is no stream flow, all precipitation being in the form of snow. Here the inequalities of topography are marked by great fields of ice and snow thousands of feet in thickness. These are drained to lower levels by huge glaciers, the largest of which discharge on the seaward flank of the range. Here the great piedmont ice sheets--the Malaspina and Bering glaciers--spread out over the coastal plain with a front of upwards of 150 miles.

The aspect of the range itself is essentially that of a sea of ice and snow, above which rise sharp pinnacles and spurs. While the lofty peak of Mount St. Elias (18,024 ft.) dominates the Alaskan part of the range, Mount Logan, on the Canadian side of the boundary, is still higher (19,500 ft.), and there are many other high summits, such as Mount Hubbard (16,000 ft.) and Mount Seattle (10,000 ft.). In places, foothill ranges intervene between Mount St. Elias and the sea. The most well-defined of these are the Robinson Mountains, which intervene between the Malaspina and Bering glaciers. They have a length of about 20 miles and are between 4,000 and 5,000 feet in altitude.

As has already been stated, most of the drainage from the St. Elias Range is through glaciers, and watercourses are as a rule limited to short streams springing from the front of ice masses. An exception is found in the Alsek River, which drains a great basin lying inland of the mountains and traverses the entire range through a steep-walled valley. Through this valley it takes a precipitous course to the sea and receives in its mountainous stretch the discharge of several huge glaciers. Most of the Alsek basin lies on the Canadian side of the boundary. So far as is known, there is no definite line of demarcation between the St. Elias Range and the Chugach Mountains, but the junction of the two occurs in an unexplored region. West of the boundary, however, which runs due north from Mount St. Elias, the range loses its unity by splitting up into a number of mountain masses. Of these, the southernmost is the Chugach Mountains, the northernmost the Nutzotin Mountains. The latter knits the northwest part of the St. Elias with the eastern part of the Alaska Range. Between the Chugach Mountains on the south and the Nutzotin Mountains on the north is an irregular group of volcanoes called the Wrangell Mountains. These three ranges constitute a broad mountainous belt upwards of 150 miles in width but broken into different units by broad valleys such as the Chitina and Copper.

The Chugach Mountains constitute the coastal barrier from about Mount St. Elias to the western part of Prince William Sound, a distance of about 200 miles, where they are extended to the southwest by the Kenai Mountains. These are well defined on the north by valleys of the Chitina and other tributaries of the Copper River and by the Matanuska valley, and at Prince William Sound their southern margin is close to the sea and here broken by numerous fiords. The Chugach Mountains have a rather uniform crest line varying from 6,000 to 8,000 feet, with a few peaks of over 10,000 feet. They constitute a belt probably averaging 7,000 feet high and from 60 to 75 miles in width. Their snow and ice fields are second only to those of the St. Elias Range and give rise to many glaciers. The largest of these flow directly toward the sea, but some find outlet in the Copper and Matanuska river basins. Most of the passes through the Chugach are at about the snow line, but Thompson Pass, crossed by the military road from Valdez to Fairbanks, is only 2,700 feet high. The Chugach Mountains are traversed by the Copper River through a steep-walled valley. This river is not navigable from the sea, but its valley has afforded a route for the Copper River & Northwestern Railroad.

North of the Chugach Mountains and separated from them by the broad trench occupied by the Chitina Valley lie the Wrangell Mountains. These comprise an irregular group of volcanoes, of which Mount Blackburn (16,200 ft.) is the highest and Mount Wrangell (14,100 ft.) is still active. This mountain group occupies a roughly circular area and on the east merges with the St. Elias Range, while its southern, western, and northern flanks are deeply buried in glacial silts and clays, and the watercourses have cut steep-walled canyons. The central part of the Wrangell mountains is buried in an ice cap, and from this many glaciers radiate and discharge at lower altitudes into streams which are chiefly tributary to the Copper River. A small part of the northern flank is drained by the Tanana River, this forming a part of the Yukon basin.

The Copper River rises in a glacier on the north flank of the Wrangell Mountains and thence by a great crescentic sweep encircles the western flank of the mountains, while its principal tributary, the Chitina River, drains the southern flank. Its basin is a broad area of relatively low relief separated from the Yukon basin on the north by the Alaska Range and on the south bounded by the Chugach Mountains through which it finds its way to the sea by the usual steep-walled valley. Much of this basin has been deeply buried in glacial silts and clays into which the Copper and its tributaries have entrenched their steep-walled valleys. The silt-filled part of its basin stands at 1,000 to 1,500 feet above sea level and has been called the Copper River plateau. Much of its surface is an ill-drained swampy area dotted with lakes and supporting only a scant vegetation of stunted spruce and moss. The valley bottom and slopes, however, have a more luxuriant growth of spruce and herbaceous plants.

The Copper River plateau stretches to the westward, where its margin is drained by streams flowing into the Susitna River. There is thus no well-defined watershed between the Copper drainage on the east and the Susitna on the west. Here the streams of the two watersheds interlock irregularly.

Beyond Prince William Sound the Chugach Mountains swing to the south and are continued by the Kenai Mountains, which form the backbone of the peninsula of the same name. This range rises steeply from the fiorded eastern shore of the Kenai Peninsula to altitudes of from 4,000 to 6,800 feet and is continued to its southernmost extremity. This mountain mass is from 30 to 60 miles in width with numerous sharp crest lines, in part broken by broad valleys. One of these furnishes the route of the government railroad extending inland from the town of Seward. Its higher southern portion is marked by a great ice cap above which only the higher peaks are exposed. On the west the Kenai Mountains fall off to a relatively flat upland that slopes down to the shores of Cook Inlet. Near the western margin of these mountains there are a number of large picturesque mountain lakes, the largest of which is called Kenai Lake. The shore of this lake is skirted by the government railroad.

The valley of the Matanuska River marks a broad depression separating the Chugach Mountains on the south from the Talkeetna Mountains on the north. This range comprises a roughly circular area in which peaks from 6,000 to 8,000 feet in altitude, with connecting sharp ridges, are rather irregularly distributed. The mass is broken by the valleys of several large rivers that flow westward to join the Susitna. To the north the range is connected by some irregular highlands with the Alaska Range; on the east they fall off through a series of foothills to the Copper River plateau.

The great depressed area, of which the lower part lies under the sea and forms Cook Inlet, stretches northward from tidewater for upwards of 100 miles. It here forms the Susitna lowland, traversed by the Susitna River and bounded on the east by the Talkeetna Mountains and on the west by the foothills of the Alaska Range. At the mouth of the Talkeetna River, the largest eastern tributary of the Susitna, the valley walls are contracted, and above this point the Susitna lowland is represented by only the flood plain of the river.

The Susitna River, which receives the drainage from much of the Talkeetna Mountains, springs from a glacier at the southern margin of the eastern part of the Alaska Range. It traverses a belt of foothills through a broad gravel-filled valley, then, bending westward for some 20 miles, cuts through its steep-walled rockbound canyon. Emerging from this canyon, it takes a southerly course through an open valley whose walls gradually recede to encompass the broad lowland of the lower Susitna.

West of the Susitna lowland is a series of foothills and beyond the snow-covered crest of the great Alaska Range. This is a rugged mountain mass which sweeps as a great crescent around the Susitna and Copper basins, constituting for the most part the watershed between the Pacific Ocean and Bering Sea. Trending northeastward from an unexplored region near Lake Clark, the range continues to the east as far as the Delta River. Here the axis takes a southeasterly direction and is continued, in the so-called Nutzotin Mountains, eastward to the international boundary on the White River.

The axis of this range, which has a parabolic form, is between 500 and 600 miles in length, and the range is from 50 to 80 miles wide. In the southern part of the range the peaks are from 5,000 to 8,000 feet in altitude. When traced northward and eastward, the crest line is found to maintain an altitude of 7,000 to 10,000 feet to the vicinity of Mentasta Pass, beyond which it is continued by the Nutzotin Mountains at a lower altitude. Its longitudinal extent, breadth, and mass make the Alaska Range one of the most prominent mountain chains of the continent. It is both higher and broader than the Sierra Nevada and of greater relief and extent than the Alps of Europe.

The region lying between Cook Inlet and Lake Clark, about 80 miles wide, has been little explored but is known to be of high relief. These mountains stretch northward for 100 miles and probably include a number of high ridges trending north and south, separated by rather broad valleys, and with peaks 8,000 to 9,000 feet high. From the Susitna lowland the eastern face of these mountains can be seen as a rather abrupt scarp which rises to a summit level covered with snow and is broken by a number of glaciers discharging into streams flowing into the Susitna River. In the headwater region of the Yentna there is a break in the Alaska Range, and several gaps from 2,900 to 3,000 feet high afford easy routes of travel between Cook Inlet and the Kuskokwim.

The Alaska Range maintains the same general character 100 miles northeast of the Skwentna basin. Here the inland slope rises abruptly from the gravel-floored plateau to the crest of the range, not more than five to ten miles distant from the mountain front. The crest line, a high serrated ridge 7,000 to 10,000 feet high, joins a series of dominating peaks, including Mount Dall (9,000 ft.), Mount Russell (11,350 ft.), and the two giant peaks, Mount Foraker (17,000 ft.) and Mount McKinley (20,300 ft.). East of the crest line are other high peaks which probably attain altitudes of 10,000 to 15,000 feet. Here valleys of the southeastward-flowing streams reach far back into the mountains and are, as a rule, filled with glacial ice well out toward the Susitna lowland. These glaciers form the most extensive ice sheets of inland Alaska. The valleys of the westward-flowing streams are short and are only in part filled with glacial ice.

That part of the range which lies between the head of the Chulitna, west fork of the Susitna, and the Tanana valley includes a mountainous area in which at least three subordinate ranges can be recognized, with an aggregate width of nearly 100 miles. The broad valley of the Nenana, traversing two of these ranges, is connected by a broad, low gap called Broad Pass (2,400 ft.) with the valley of the Chulitna, a stream that flows south.

The range is continued in a southeasterly direction by a broad mountain mass. Here the peaks are from 8,000 to 10,000 feet high, but the snow-capped summit of Mount Hayes stands over 13,000 feet above sea level. From the Delta River, which traverses the entire range, to Mentasta Pass the mountains are unbroken, the snow-covered crest line averaging probably 7,000 to 9,000 feet in altitude. Mentasta Pass is a broad, flat depression, 3,000 feet high. From Mentasta Pass the range finds its continuation to the southeast as far as White River in the Nutzotin Mountains, which embrace a rugged area 100 miles in length and 40 miles in width. These mountains stand at elevations between 7,000 and 8,000 feet, but above this level rise several peaks that are 9,000 to 10,000 feet high.

The southwestern part of the Alaska Range is separated from Cook Inlet by the Chigmit Mountains whose axis parallels Cook Inlet. Mount Spurr (10,500 ft.) and a number of peaks form the northeastern end of this range, which stretches to the southwest with decreasing altitude and at Iliamna Bay constitutes only a low, narrow ridge broken by numerous passes. Within the Chigmit Mountains are the two active volcanoes, Mount Iliamna (12,066 ft.) and Mount Redoubt (11,270 ft.).

Close to Cape Douglas, marking the entrance to Cook Inlet on the south, is a group of high snow-clad peaks which constitute the northeast end of the Aleutian Range. This range parallels the southern coast of the Alaska Peninsula. Near Cape Douglas the peaks reach altitudes of 5,000 feet and more, and here several glaciers of considerable size originate in the mountain mass whose crest line is here well defined. To the southwest the range decreases in altitude, though its crest is marked by many peaks, the highest of which are active or extinct volcanoes. If the range be traced to the southwest, its average summit level will be found to decrease in altitude, at Herendeen Bay the highest peaks being only about 4,000 feet in height. Here many broad, flat gaps break the continuity of the range. A further southwest extension is found in the mountainous Aleutian Islands, which carry the axis of the range for some 800 miles to the westward. Here the peaks reach altitudes of 4,000 to 8,000 feet. The peaks are all of volcanic origin, and the highest are found on Unimak Island where are the active volcanoes of Shishaldin (9,387 ft.), Pogromni (6,500 ft.), and Isanotski peaks (8,032 and 8,088 ft.).

The axes of the southern end of the Alaska Range and of the Aleutian Range are parallel. These highlands form the southwestern extension of the Pacific Mountain System. West of Cook Inlet the system has a width of some 40 or 50 miles, which gradually decreases to five to ten miles in the southwestern part of the Alaska Peninsula. North of Bristol Bay is a minor northeasterly-trending range called the Ahklun Mountains. Its relation to larger physiographic provinces has not been determined, for it lies in an unmapped region.

Central Plateau Region

Beyond the inland front of the Pacific Mountain System the aspect of the country changes abruptly. Rugged snow-clad ranges and narrow steep-walled valleys give way to a broad, rolling upland, diversified by extensive plains and broad, flat valleys. There are no glaciers in this part of Alaska, and the grasslands and timber, with the gentle slopes, give a pleasing aspect to the landscape. Here the interstream areas are in many instances flat-topped with a mesa-like form. Hence the name for this province, Central Plateau Region. A few minor ranges and many rounded domes rise above the general summit level. This region, a northwesterly extension of the central plateau of British Columbia, crosses the international boundary with a summit level of 3,000 to 4,000 feet and then sweeps westward with decreased altitude as it approaches Bering Sea. It has its minimum width near the meridian of Mount McKinley, where it measures some 150 miles between the front ranges of the Pacific Mountain System on the south and the Rocky Mountains on the north. To the westward it broadens out as the southerly system of ranges recedes.

This central province drains to Bering Sea, chiefly through the great Yukon and Kuskokwim rivers. While its general outline is fairly well defined, there are many places where it is not possible to make a sharp distinction between the Central Plateau Region and the bounding mountain system. It has a fairly definite southern boundary westward from the 141st meridian beyond Mount McKinley. Here the plateau province abuts abruptly against the inland front of the southern ranges, and here the flat, moss-covered interstream area abuts directly against the scarp marking the abrupt inland slope of the high ranges. Southwest of McKinley, so far as the region has been explored, there appears to be less of a contrast between the two provinces.

The northern boundary of this central province has only in part been explored, but it appears that here too the differentiation between plateau and mountains is not everywhere well defined. In places, however, as in the upper Koyukuk basin, the northern ranges fall off rather abruptly to the plateau level.

There is another element which complicates the topography of this region. Between the Yukon and Porcupine rivers the northwestern extension of the Rocky Mountain system penetrates the plateau province. In British Columbia and in the southern part of the Yukon Territory the eastern boundary of the plateau is fairly well defined by the front ranges of the Rocky Mountain system of Canada. The axis of these mountains on approaching Alaska swings gradually to the west, crossing the international boundary north of the Yukon, and is traversed by the valley of that river south of the town of Circle. Here the mountains are not well defined as a distinct topographic unit, but the extension of this uplift is found in the Crazy and White mountains west of Circle. These two minor ranges stand conspicuously above the general plateau level. It seems probable also that the same axis is to be recognized in the mountains which form the divide between the Yukon and Kuskokwim rivers in the Innoko-Iditarod region and to the southwest. West of the Yukon the Rocky Mountain element of the topography is by no means well marked, for the ranges described above do not form very conspicuous features of the relief as compared with the plateau features. This account of the northwesterly extension of the Rockies must be regarded as provisional until the region lying east of the upper Yukon and north of the lower Porcupine has been better explored.

The plateau region is also diversified by other minor ranges, such as the Glacier Mountains in the Fortymile basin, the Ahklun

Mountains north of Bristol Bay, and Kigluaik and Darby mountains of Seward Peninsula. A much more striking feature of the Central Plateau Region is the lowland areas. These include the broad coastal plain which marks the deltas of the Yukon and Kuskokwim rivers and extends northward to include much of the eastern shore of Norton Sound. They also include the broad basin lowlands which form a part of the valley system of the Yukon and Kuskokwim rivers and their tributaries. The best known of these is the Yukon Flats, lying adjacent to the Arctic Circle, but almost equally extensive are the basin lowlands of the lower Tanana, the upper Kuskokwim, and the middle Koyukuk rivers. These are of the same general type--flat areas across which the watercourses take meandering courses, bounded by the scarps of the upland. The main watercourses, traversing these lowlands in broad meanders, often enter and leave the basins through narrow steep-walled valleys.

Viewed in detail, the topography has certain striking characteristics. All except the smallest watercourses have rather broad flood plains; steep-walled valleys are the exception rather than the rule. Rounded forms and smooth slopes are the rule; scarps of bedrock and finely dissected slopes, the exception. The flood plains merge with the valley slopes at least on one side of the valley, and these slopes are continued to summit levels at low angles. The flat-topped interstream areas are broken here and there by rocky knobs which end abruptly on the smooth or moss-covered slopes.

Bering Sea receives the drainage of nearly all the vast Central Plateau Region and much of the inland slopes of its bordering ranges--an area comprising not only over half of Alaska but also a considerable part of Yukon Territory and northern British Columbia. Most of this large drainage finds its way to the sea through the Yukon and Kuskokwim rivers.

The Yukon is the largest stream of Alaska, the main artery of an extensive drainage system which gives easy access to much of the vast intermontane region. To the natives the river is and has been all important, for through countless generations its waters have furnished them fish for food and easy routes of travel by canoe and raft in summer, by sled and dog team in winter. The white men, too, found access to the interior by this river. The Russians, coming from the west in search of furs, dragged their clumsy boats for a thousand miles against its current; while the English traders, who reached its headwaters from the east, descended in their bark canoes for hundreds of miles. One of the headwater tributaries, rising in the Chilkoot Pass not two score miles from tidewater on the Pacific furnished an inland route to the coast natives and later to the prospectors who discovered the Yukon gold fields. Now the railway through the Coast Range makes the upper Yukon basin still more accessible. Scores of steamers navigate the Yukon during the summer months, and its frozen surface affords a highway for winter travel. In short, the settlement by natives and whites and the development of all the mining interest of the great interior region of Alaska and Northwest Canada were only made possible by the Yukon waterways.

The Yukon, with its longest tributary, the Lewes-Teslin, has a length of about 2,300 miles, of which about 2,000 miles are navigable, and a catchment area of about 330,000 square miles, over half of which is in Canada. The following table shows it to be fifth in rank among the rivers of North America:

Length and Drainage Area of Five Chief Rivers of North America

Rivers	Approximate Length (Miles)	Approximate area of drainage (Square Miles)
Mississippi, with Missouri	6,000	1,244,000
Winnipeg and Nelson	3,840	486,500
Mackenzie	2,868	677,400
St. Lawrence	2,600	565,000
Yukon, with Lewes and Teslin	2,300	330,000

The volume of the Yukon River, draining as it does a semiarid region, is far inferior to that of other streams draining equal areas. The measurements made by Porter and Davenport[1] at Eagle, near the international boundary showed the Yukon to have a volume of 100,100 cubic feet per second at a low-water stage in April and a volume of 249,000 cubic feet per second at a high-water stage in May. In 1900, G.R. Putnam computed the volume of the Yukon at the head of its delta (73 miles from the mouth), some 1,200 miles below the boundary, as 436,000 cubic feet per second in September, probably a medium low-water stage. Making allowance for high-water stage, it is estimated that the average discharge of the Yukon at its mouth is about 500,000 cubic feet per second. This may be compared with a discharge of 6,750,000 cubic feet per second for the Mississippi or even the 900,000 cubic feet per second of the St. Lawrence. The drainage basin of the latter is about two-fifths larger than that of the Yukon, and it also receives an average precipitation of about 35 inches, compared with about 12 inches for the Yukon.

The sources of the Yukon lie in British Columbia. All of its upper drainage channels trend north and northwest until it reaches the Arctic Circle, where it makes a right-angled bend to the southwest, and continues in this general course until it empties into Bering Sea. From latitude 60° to about latitude 65°, where it enters Alaska, it flows through the Yukon Territory, and less than half of its basin lies in Alaska.

The Yukon basin, comprising an irregular area in Alaska and adjacent portions of Yukon Territory and British Columbia, is roughly outlined on the north, east, and northeast by the Rocky Mountain system, and on the south by the Pacific Mountain system. There are no considerable highlands on the southeast, for there the tributaries of the Yukon, Liard, and Stikine interlock irregularly within the plateau region. The main tributaries of the Yukon are the Koyukuk, Tanana, Porcupine, White, Pelly, and Lewes, the main stream beginning with the junction of the Pelly and Lewes, which are entirely within Canadian territory.

The Yukon proper--that is, that part of the river below the junction of the Pelly and Lewes--has a length of about 1,500 miles. Its course is northwesterly, and for some 500 miles it flows through a steep-walled valley with only a narrow flood-plain as far as the town of Circle. The Yukon below Circle enters the great lowland called the Yukon Flats through which it takes a meandering course for some 200 miles. Within the flats and at the Arctic Circle the river makes its great bend from northwest to southwest. The Yukon Flats comprise a great lowland, swampy area bounded by a rim of highlands with a length of some 200 miles and a width of 40 to 100 miles. No surveys have been made of this part of the river, but in places the various channels probably include a width of 10 to 20 miles. It is here made up of an intricate network of shallow channels and sloughs. Many oxbow lakes have been formed by the shifting channels. From the steamer deck the Yukon Flats present a monotonous expanse of sand bars and low, densely forested spruce islands through which the boat follows a tortuous channel among a bewildering maze of tributary and distributary watercourses, with an occasional glimpse of the distant rim of the plateau which surrounds the lowland. The presence of man in this dreary tract is made manifest only in the clearings, from which the timber has been cut for fuel, or the occasional small trading post or Indian settlement. At low water 10 or 15 feet of silt are exposed in the banks, but during floods the river is almost even with the surface of the islands. The ever-shifting channels make navigation a constantly changing problem to pilots.

Within the flats the Yukon receives one of its largest tributaries, the Porcupine, whose mouth lies at the great bend of the main river and just within the Arctic Circle. The source of the Porcupine is within 60 miles of the Yukon, in latitude 65° 30', whence it flows northwesterly and, impinging on the mountain barrier which separates the Yukon and Mackenzie basins, bends sharply to the north and thence southwest, forming a great loop.

Within the flats the Yukon receives only two important tributaries, the Porcupine and Chandalar. Near the 66th parallel of latitude the flats end abruptly at a scarp which forms the northern boundary of a part of the plateau. This stands between 1,800 and 2,000 feet above sea level, and is often called the Lower Ramparts of the Yukon. The Yukon traverses this upland by a narrow, somewhat winding valley, whose walls often rise rampart-like, either directly from the water or from a narrow terrace. The stretch of the valley, about 120 miles long (measuring around the bends) and one-half to three miles wide, continues unbroken from the Yukon Flats to the mouth of the Tanana.

The Rampart region with the broad, sweeping curves of the river and the steep valley walls, clothed with spruce, cottonwood, and birch, varied by bare cliffs, is the most picturesque part of the Yukon. The Russian explorer, Lieut. L.A. Zagoskin, in 1843, reported the Yukon as unnavigable above the lower end of the ramparts, though its ascent and descent by steamers are attended by much less difficulty than in any other part of the river, for the current probably does not exceed five or six miles per hour, and there are few shifting sand bars to contend with.

The Ramparts end at the mouth of the Tanana, where there is an abrupt change in the contour of the valley. The gorge suddenly opens to a broad lowland, which along the Yukon is 15 to 20 miles in width, but which stretches up the tributary Tanana valley for a distance of 200 miles with a width of 20 to 100 miles. The northwestern boundary of the valley is a series of low mountains whose base the

Yukon hugs. The southern wall is 15 to 20 miles distant near the Tanana, but gradually approaches, thus reducing the width of the valley. Then for some ten miles the valley is well defined by both walls; but, ten miles below, the eastern wall recedes and is seldom visible from the river. Throughout its course to the head of the delta the Yukon continues to shirt the north bank, and the river itself flows through many channels and is broken by numerous islands and sand bars.

The delta begins near the 63rd parallel of latitude where the river divides into a number of divergent channels which find their way to the sea with generally northerly and northwesterly courses. Apoon Pass, the northernmost, and Kwikluak Pass, the most southerly of these waterways, reach the open sea at points about 75 miles apart in an air line and 40 or 50 miles from the head of the delta. An intricate maze of waterways lies between the two channels, some of which flow chiefly to the Bering Sea; others connect with such channels, but many are blind sloughs affected only by the ebb and flow of the tide. The interstream areas, not more than ten feet above low tide, are swampy and dotted with innumerable small lakes. Here, as in the flats, the Yukon is constantly shifting its channel. The changes are brought about largely by the current and tides, but aid is given by the scouring of the ice which accumulates in the delta after the break-up in the spring and forms dams that cause new channels to be cut and old ones to be silted up.

Though the Yukon delta properly includes only that part of the coastal plain included between the distributaries of the river, the broad lowland which embraces the deltas of the Yukon and the Kuskokwim has an extreme breadth of upward of 200 miles and might well be grouped with the delta flats. There can be no doubt that at some time a part of the Yukon water found its way across these lowlands and deposited the sediments by which they were made to encroach upon the sea. This region embraces a flat which is but a few feet above tidewater and is drained by sluggish, meandering rivers and dotted by many lakes. Its smooth surface is interrupted here and there by low, isolated hills, and the shore line is broken by inlets and tidal lagoons. At low tide this low coastal plain is extended a long distance seaward by mud flats.

The scenery of the lower Yukon offers but little of interest to the traveler. The mighty river, with its dark-yellow waters, is not without its grandeur, and the rounded valley slopes, dotted with spruce and deciduous trees, are not without picturesqueness; but for hundreds of miles there is almost no change in the aspect of the landscape. The upper reaches of the lower Yukon are heavily forested, but as the sea is approached the trees become more scattered and finally, a few miles above the delta, give way entirely to the tundra with its dreary, monotonous view. Inland the moss- and grass-covered lowlands stretch almost unbroken to the horizon except for distant, rounded highland masses, while seaward there is no break in the lowland, and its smooth surface merges with the plain of the sea. The delta supports a large, though migratory, Eskimo population which finds its way among the intricate waterways in large skin boats (umiaks) and kayaks, and is almost entirely dependent on the sea for food.

The Tanana River, the longest tributary of the Yukon whose basin lies entirely in Alaska, empties into the latter just where it emerges from the Ramparts and is about 400 miles long. The valley trends northwesterly, parallel to the main stream above the big bend, and drains an area of probably 25,000 square miles. The Alaska Range bounds the basin on the south and is the breeding ground of the glaciers from which most of the southern tributaries of the Tanana spring. The headwaters of the many tributaries from the north interlock with streams which flow directly into the Yukon above the Ramparts.

The Koyukuk joins the Yukon from the northwest about 450 miles from Bering Sea. Its drainage basin has an area of approximately 25,000 square miles and includes the southern ranges of the Arctic Mountain System which here form the Yukon-Arctic watershed. The valley of the Koyukuk, including that of its longest fork, is upward of 300 miles in length, while the river measured around the bends must be 600 or 700 miles long.

The area roughly blocked out by the Alaska and Aleutian ranges, the Tanana and Yukon rivers, and Bering Sea has been explored only in part. Its topography, as far as is known, consists of rounded hills and low mountains, seldom exceeding 2,000 feet in altitude, interpenetrated by broad river valleys and many lowlands; and the greater part of the drainage is carried to Bering Sea by the Kuskokwim River, the second in size in Alaska, possessing a catchment basin of probably more than 50,000 square miles.

Many headwater streams of the Kuskokwim rise in glaciers on the inland slope of the Alaska Range and flow northwesterly, their channels gradually uniting into four or five rivers which are tributary to the two trunk streams, whose junction in latitude 63° can be regarded as the beginning of the Kuskokwim proper. Geographic usage has applied the name Kuskokwim to the southern fork, while the other, whose valley trends northeast and southwest, is called the North Fork of the Kuskokwim. The Kuskokwim River proper rises in the unexplored mountain mass at the southern extension of the Alaska Range, and its headwaters probably interlock with streams tributary to Lake Clark.

The valley of the Kuskokwim below the forks is broad, and on the south the river is in most places bounded by wide lowlands that have been but little explored. One hundred miles above its delta the valley walls disappear, the uplands being represented only by occasional rounded hills or low ridges. The delta of the Kuskokwim on the north coalesces with that of the Yukon and is of the same general type. Unlike the Yukon delta, a relatively deep channel winds through the Kuskokwim delta, making it possible to bring small ocean vessels into the mouth of the river. Above, the river is navigable for river steamers for some 800 miles.

The Seward Peninsula, though it belongs to the Central Plateau Region, is isolated from the rest of the province. It is essentially a region of flat-topped uplands bounded near the sea by coastal plains. In places these give way to abrupt bluffs whose bases are washed by the waves of the ocean. This upland is diversified by some minor ranges, of which the Kigluaik, with peaks up to 4,000 and 5,000 feet in altitude, is the highest. The upland is broken by broad, flat valleys having gentle slopes. The drainage of the peninsula is both to the Arctic Ocean and Bering Sea.

Arctic Mountain System

The Central Plateau Region is bounded on the north by the Arctic Mountain System which stretches across northern Alaska as a broad highland belt forming the watershed between the Arctic Ocean and the Yukon basin.

The Arctic Mountain System enters Alaska as a broad belt north of the Porcupine River, here trending nearly east and west. It then bends somewhat to the southwest, terminating near Kotzebue Sound. These mountains are but imperfectly known.[2] At the boundary the system is made up of several parallel but ill-defined ranges, varying from 4,000 to 8,000 feet in altitude. Along the valley of the Colville River, whose course is at right angles to the system, two mountain axes are distinguishable, the southern-most of which has been termed the Endicott mountains. As it approaches the Arctic Ocean to the west, it loses its definiteness and is split up into several minor ranges by the valleys of the Selawik, Kobuk, and Noatak rivers, whose courses lie parallel to the general trend of the system. The northernmost of this group of ranges lying north of the Noatak valley has been called the DeLong Mountains. The Baird Mountains lie between the Kobuk and the Noatak; they are from 4,000 to 6,000 feet in height. The southern face of the Arctic mountain System is not everywhere sharply differentiated from the plateau region, for the two provinces merge through a series of foothills. The north face, on the other hand, falls off abruptly to a piedmont plateau to be described below.

The Arctic Mountain System is drained in three directions--southerly to Bering Sea and chiefly through the Yukon; westerly to the Arctic Ocean at Kotzebue Sound through the three large rivers, the Selawik, the Kobuk, and the Noatak; and northerly to the polar sea through many watercourses of which the Colville is the largest. This river rises in Chandler Lake, flows westerly, then, making a great bend, takes a northerly course to the sea. The aspect of the Arctic Mountain System is one of a rugged topography but broken by many broad gaps. Timber is found in only sheltered valleys, and much of the mountain mass is barren of vegetation except for moss. Few of the peaks rise to the line of perpetual snow, and there are only a few small glaciers in the entire mountain mass.

The Arctic Mountain System east of the boundary is knit to the northwestern extension of the Rocky Mountains by a minor range which forms the watershed between the Mackenzie and the Porcupine rivers. In Canada the plateau province is bounded on the east by the Rocky mountain system whose ranges, as has been shown, bend to the westward and, after crossing the boundary, are lost in the uplands of the plateau region.

Arctic Slope Region

At the international boundary the northern face of the Arctic Mountains rises almost directly from the sea, with only a few miles of low coastal plain between it and the Arctic Ocean. To the west the coast line bends northward and the mountain front retreats southward, thus widening out the coastal belt to more than 150 miles near the 156th meridian. This province, which embraces both a plateau and a coastal plain, is call the Arctic Slope Region.

Along the valley of the Colville River, the Anaktuvuk Plateau and the coastal plain go to make up the Arctic Slope Region. The former lies immediately adjacent to the mountain front, where it has a height of about 2,500 feet; thence it stretches northward, retaining its character as a rolling upland and sloping gently toward the Arctic for about 80 miles from the mountains, where the coastal plain begins. It is inferred that there is a gradual transition between the two topographic forms, their differences lying in the fact that the plateau has a gently rolling surface, while the plain is absolutely flat. In genesis, however, the two types differ, for the plateau is an uplifted, eroded surface, and the coastal plain is a constructional form, largely built up of horizontal stratified sediments.

It seems likely that the whole region lying north of the Arctic Mountains has essentially this type of topography, but it is almost unexplored. At Cape Lisburne there are remnants of a former plateau surface at an altitude of about 1,500 to 2,000 feet, which is probably a westward extension of the Anaktuvuk Plateau.

A number of rivers and streams traverse the Arctic slopes through broad valleys. These rise in the mountains, where they have steep gradients and swift currents. Emerging from the highlands, they take tortuous courses to the sea. The Colville, the largest of these watercourses and the only one surveyed, has already been described. The Arctic Slope Region is devoid of all timber except for a thin fringe of willow which hugs the watercourses. Grass, too, is scant, and most of the land is covered with moss and some herbaceous plants.[3]

ENDNOTES

[1]Porter, E.A. and Davenport, R.W., "The Discharge of the Yukon at Eagle, Alaska," *United States Geological Survey, Water Supply Paper, No. 345*, Washington, D.C., 1914.

[2]They are, of course, much better known now than they were when this manuscript was written. They are now called the Brooks Range in honor of the author of this book.--Burton L. Fryxell.

[3]A great deal of exploring and of more accurate mapping and surveying than is indicated in this chapter has been done in recent years. Of all this, Dr.

Brooks, of course, could have no knowledge when he wrote his manuscript. Consequently, a few of his references to nomenclature and some of his figures on mountain heights are subject to correction. For example, the Yukon River by official decree of the Canadian government is no longer considered to begin at the junction of the Pelly and Lewes, but now includes as part of its over-all length what was formerly known as the Lewes. Or again, the altitude of various mountains as given by Dr. Brooks is occasionally at variance with later, more precise measurements; nevertheless the figures quoted in his manuscript are the ones that have been used. In a number of instances, however, he had left blank spaces, apparently to be filled in later, for the heights of different peaks: these have been supplied by reference to *A Dictionary of Altitudes in the United States*, fourth edition, published by the United States Geological Survey as Bulletin No. 274, 1906.--Burton L. Fryxell.

RUSSIA MOVES TO THE EAST*

George V. Lantzeff and Richard A. Pierce

Few scholars have done as much during the last two decades to advance the study of Russian America as Professor Richard A. Pierce. Pierce, who taught at Queen's University, Kingston, Ontario, until his retirement, calls the period "the missing half of Alaska history." Now a member of the history department at the University of Alaska Fairbanks, Pierce earned his doctoral degree at the University of California (Berkeley) in 1956. He studied there under the Russian emigre scholar, Professor George V. Lantzeff, who also earned his doctorate at California. Lantzeff's dissertation on Russian colonial administration in Siberia, published in 1943, remains a fundamental work. He began working on *Eastward to Empire: Exploration and Conquest on the Russian Open Frontier, to 1750,* a survey, about 1950. Professor Pierce completed the work after Lantzeff's death in 1955.

In addition to numerous articles on Russian America, Pierce has published *Russia's Hawaiian Adventure, 1815-1817* (Berkeley: University of California Press, 1965) and *Builders of Alaska: The Russian Governors, 1818-1867* (Kingston: The Limestone Press, 1986). But he is most noted for a series of books on Russian America, published by The Limestone Press, which he founded. The series includes both primary and secondary works, some translated from Russian and others originally written in English. Examples include Kirill Khlebnikov's biography of Aleksandr Andreevich Baranov and Gavril Davydov's log of his travels in Russian America in 1805-06, as well as the work of such contemporary Soviet scholars as Svetlana Fedorova and Raisa Makarova. Now through thirty separate volumes, the contribution of this series has been monumental, opening an important but long neglected field to the scrutiny of students of Alaska history.

In the selection printed here from *Eastward to Empire,* Lantzeff and Pierce discuss Russian motivation for expansion into the Pacific. There had been a good deal of Russian activity in the North Pacific region before Bering's 1741 voyage of discovery, and the authors point out that while the principal motivation may have been scientific, the discovery opened North America to Russian fur trapping enterprises. Students also should note the work of Professor Raymond Fisher of the University of California, who has revolutionized understanding of the earliest phase of Russian American history in two indispensable books, *The Voyage of*

---

*This selection is excerpted from *Eastward to Empire, Exploration and Conquest on the Russian Open Frontier, to 1750* (Montreal: McGill-Queen's University Press, 1973), pp. 221-230, 252.

Semen Dezhnev in 1648: Bering's Precursor (London: The Hakluyt Society, 1981), in which he domonstrates the validity of Dezhnev's navigation of Bering Strait in 1648, and *Bering's Voyages: Whither and Why* (Seattle: University of Washington Press, 1977), in which he explains the state of geographic knowledge in the 18th century and the economic as well as scientific context of the Kamchatka expeditions.

* * *

The expansion of Russia poses problems in the reconstruction of events, the selection of significant agents, and generalization and analysis. The term "expansion" is itself an oversimplification, for behind it lie movements of various kinds. Relations in the east and south, usually sparsely populated by more primitive populations, differed from those in the west, which involved contact with settled states.

Diversity of Russian Eastward Expansion

The early Kievan state produced three currents of expansion eventually leading to Asia. One of these was directed toward the southern steppes to ward off the attacks of the Pechenegs and Polovtsy, who raided the Russian settlements and drove the people into captivity. "Defense lines" were developed, and various diplomatic means were employed to deal with the steppe peoples. The Russian princes tried to attract some of the nomads as allies, using one tribe against another, settling them to protect the frontier, or cementing ties by intermarriage.

A second current of expansion accompanied the decline of Kiev, in which, due in large part to the pressure of nomads and internal strife, some of the population moved away from Kiev into the less populated forest area along the Volga and Oka to the northeast. This movement was in fact a retreat in search of security, but it resulted in a great gain of territory. The movement was gradual and led to Russian infiltration among the scattered Finnish tribes, many of whom accepted Christianity and became assimilated. Together with the newcomers they formed what is known as the Great Russian branch of the Eastern Slavs. The princes followed the colonists; the strong Volga principalities came into existence; and more energetic and enterprising rulers encouraged further colonization in order to gain new subjects, soldiers, and taxpayers.

The rather peaceful expansion in the Volga-Oka area changed its character when the Russians came in contact with the numerous Finnic people of the Mordva, south of the River Oka, and with the Turkic people, the Bulgars, on the east bank of the Volga. In the first armed encounters, the advantage sometimes lay with the Bulgars and Mordva, but by the second half of the twelfth century the Volga princes led several successful expeditions into the lands of the Bulgars and Mordva, destroying their towns and villages and carrying away many prisoners. In 1221 the Russians founded a fortified town, Nizhnii Novgorod, at the confluence of the Oka and Volga, which for three centuries remained the Russian southern frontier terminal on the Volga.

A third current of expansion during the Kievan period started from the wealthy commercial city of Novgorod and went northeastward toward the Arctic Ocean and the Ural Mountains. The Novgorodians were interested in fish, salt, walrus ivory, and particularly in pelts of sables, ermine, foxes, and other animals, which were important items of their internal and external markets. Sailing along the northern rivers and their tributaries, they braved the hardships of difficult travel and obtained valuable furs and other articles from the natives by violence or by trade. Already, in the twelfth century, the Novgorodians reached the Urals and before long they became active in the northwestern corner of Siberia.

The early activities of the Novgorodians in the northeast of European Russia were in the nature of raids, but gradually permanent colonies appeared there, and, at least in the valley of the Northern Dvina, a sort of colonial administration was developed. East of the Dvina there were a very few Russian settlements, mostly temporary, serving as stations for the collection of furs brought by the aborigines for trade and as tribute. For a long time the Novgorodians were not disturbed in their "fur empire," but after the twelfth century they acquired competitors. The colonization of the Volga-Oka region began to overflow across the Volga and spread along its northern tributaries, which are separated by easily passable portages from the rivers descending into the Arctic Ocean--the Novgorodian northern trade routes. The Volga princes began to look enviously at the Novgorodian profits from the fur trade. With the aid of their own colonists north of the Volga and of rebellious Novgorodian colonists, they made a series of armed attempts to obtain a hold in the Novgorodian colonial possessions.

Novgorod was saved from these dangerous rivals by the Mongol invasion and for a time was able to exploit its northeastern territories without interference. Gradually, however, Mongol power declined, and the principality of Moscow rose not only to take the place of the earlier Volga principalities but to unify and liberate all of Russia. Novgorod resisted this renewed aggression from the Volga area until 1478, when she and her colonies were absorbed by Moscow.

Two of the currents of expansion noted earlier were thus joined. The third, toward the south, proceeded more slowly in the face of the Tatar overlords. Profiting from strife within the Golden Horde and the secession of Kazan and the Crimea, Moscow itself gained liberation in 1480. Striving to prevent the fragments of the Horde from recombining, employing adroit diplomacy, encouraging defectors, and building defense lines in the steppe, the Moscow rulers gradually extended their sway, although it would not be until the eighteenth century, with the annexation of the Crimean khanate, that the struggle in that sector would finally be won.

In the northeast, Moscow remained largely within the limits of Novgorod's erstwhile possessions until 1552, when Ivan the Terrible conquered Kazan, removing the road block on the easiest route to Siberia. A few years later the merchant family of the Stroganovs established a private chartered colony west of the Ural Range and financed the raid of Ermak and his cossacks east of the Urals. The successful outcome of this raid showed the government that Siberia was accessible and vulnerable and that possibilities existed for an enormous increase of state revenues from the exploitation of the Siberian fur resources.

The ensuing advance was at first systematic, controlled by the government, but during the "Time of Troubles" the initiative passed to local commanders, and thereafter the government usually lagged somewhat behind the forces of local commanders and private traders before finally establishing control. This lag was particularly noticeable in the Amur region and in Kamchatka. Even when they arrived on the scene, the government men were usually accompanied by frontier traders who augmented the fighting force of the expeditions and in turn benefited from the protection afforded by government troops. The valley of the Amur was conquered through the efforts of a frontier trader, Khabarov. He organized and financed the expedition himself, although assisted by the local administration. By the early eighteenth century, the Russians had explored Siberia and to a large degree exhausted its fabulous fur wealth. The Bering expedition gave a new impetus to the search for furs, causing merchants, fur traders, and cossacks to turn to the sea and eventually bring Russian dominion to the shores of North America.

Causes

Numerous attempts have been made to provide some comprehensive explanation of these movements and those of the eighteenth and nineteenth centuries which brought Russia to the Black Sea littoral, into the Caucasus, into Central Asia, and back to the Amur valley.

The interpretation put forward most persistently is that Russia expanded merely to satisfy an obsession for the acquisition of territory and a lust for power over other peoples. Such views have arisen whenever Russia has made new territorial gains or has aroused concern in other countries over her further intentions. But ideas of this sort are not borne out by the facts. With the exception of individual rulers, particularly Peter the Great and Catherine the Great, who had far-reaching ambitions, the several currents of expansion from Kievan times, the varied aims of trade and defense, the frequent exercise of private initiative, and pure chance create a record of diversity which refutes any theory based on mere megalomania on the part of those in power.

Others have claimed special qualities for the participants in the advance Thus, Johann Fischer, concluding his *History of Siberia*, published in 1744 under the auspices of the Russian Imperial Academy of Sciences, exclaims that "Greece, Rome, and the Old and New Worlds can take pride in their heroes and praise them as much as they please; I do not know if they would have dared to do what the Siberian heroes Buza, Perfil'ev, Nagiba, Khabarov, Stepanov, and many others did."[1]

Frank A. Golder, on the other hand, denying such singularity, states that

> entirely too much emphasis may be laid on the actors in the play at the expense of the play itself. The Siberians of the seventeenth and eighteenth centuries were part of a movement in which they were caught and carried along without leaving

> any impress of their personalities. They were men of more or less average ability, yet from the time of Muller to the present it has not been possible to speak of them with calmness. As soon as the banner bearing the magic word "promyshlennik" is waved we are expected to fall on our knees and bow to heroes. As a matter of fact they were, at best, very ordinary men and some of them were vicious and depraved...In every seaport town and in every frontier community one will find men who risk their lives and suffer hardships for the sake of pleasure and gain just like the Siberians did. There is nothing heroic about all this and if we stop to think it will be seen that it is very commonplace.[2]

Golder provides a needed antidote for the praise sometimes lavished on the promyshlenniks and cossacks, but he goes too far. The participants in the advance had many shortcomings, but it took more than "average ability" to achieve what they did. From the "very ordinary men" to be found in every seaport and frontier settlement might have come the rank-and-file--the followers--but the leaders, however reprehensible, were few and outstanding. They were brutal and ruthless, but they explored and took possession of a continent. Excluding any idea of hereditary traits shared by all the members of their group, one can still credit them with exceptional individual abilities, which were called to use by the challenge of their environment, and the good sense to make use of the fund of experience left by those who had gone before.

There is equally some foundation for explaining the Russian expansion in these sectors by factors of geographic determinism. That terrain, resources, and climate would help to set the direction of the various parts of this movement is inescapable. Thus, the flatness of the Russian plain has invited a search for defensible frontiers. The river system provided natural highways and had a centrifugal effect. Rough though they were, the participants in the advance can also be credited with some feeling for the great lands which they traversed. The lands ahead must have called them on, always to another river, another mountain range, in a supreme adventure which transcended mere hopes of personal gain.

Going beyond the undoubted effects of physical geography, however, many writers have attributed certain "instincts" for expansion to the Russians. Thus, in the United States the view was put forth repeatedly by Robert J. Kerner, a leading figure in Slavic studies, of a Russian "urge to the sea, a centuries-old national longing," which dominated Russian history.[3] Other writers have made similar assertions, but though recurrent, this line of reasoning is inadequate as a comprehensive explanation of Russian expansion. It is obvious, for example, that an enormous landlocked country like Russia would at various times seek an outlet to the sea, but such an explanation can hardly be applied to all areas of expansion. As John A. Morrison has pointed out in a penetrating critique of this concept, the greatest amount of Russian territory was gained for other reasons.[4]

As we have seen, the early acquisitions of Novgorod and Moscow in northeastern European Russia, and the later expansion of Moscow across Siberia involved a quest for furs. The expansion in the southern part of Russia was for centuries a form of defense against the attacks of nomadic peoples. Ivan the Terrible's aspiration to maritime trade by way of the Baltic and White Seas and Peter the Great's drive for "a window on Europe" bear out the hypothesis, but the Russian movement into central Asia grew out of the intention to establish a Russian land trade route to India and from the quest for secure frontiers. The reacquisition of the Amur valley in the nineteenth century was motivated in part by need of a good base for eastern Siberia and the Russian American colonies, and partly by fear that other powers might occupy the region. Georgia, in the Caucasus region, was acquired when the Russian government accepted that Christian country under a protectorate to defend it from Moslem Persia and Turkey. The conquest of the turbulent Caucasian tribes separating Georgia from Russia was undertaken in order to secure safe communications. The acquisition of the Black Sea coast did not become a goal until the eighteenth century, when the government for the first time became conscious of the possibility and desirability of reaching the Mediterranean trade. The effort to obtain a warm-water port in the Far East, from the 1890s,was a conscious aspiration of Russian leaders which foreigners chose to interpret as a late manifestation of an "age-old longing." It would seem, therefore, that although physical geography must be considered of great importance in Russian expansion, the variety of conditions at various periods makes it impossible to explain all the related movements by this single factor.

Another alleged cause of Russian eastward expansion, frequently suggested, has been the tendency of the Russian people toward migration and colonization. This tendency has been evident from early times, in the outward migration of peasants and in the formation of the various cossack groups. To the great Russian historian, S. M. Solov'ev, colonization was "one of the dominant phenomena of early Russian life",[5] while, in the oft-quoted words of the illustrious V. O. Kliuchevskii, "the history of Russia is the history of a country in the process of colonization,...migration and colonization have been the basic factor in our history."[6]

The importance of this factor can be demonstrated readily enough, although here, too, earlier foreign writers frequently took the matter to an absurd degree, attributing the movements to instincts peculiar to the Russian people. But did this colonization in any case play any particular role in the phases of Russian eastward expansion considered here? It would seem that it did apply to the steppe, with the growth of cossack communities and the gradual movement of peasants into lands secured by the defense lines. It does not appear, however, to have played any particular role in the initial advance into Siberia, nor in the subsequent exploration and conquest. The conquest of Siberia did not in itself mark a renewal of the colonization process, it merely prepared the way for that renewal. Consequently, colonization must be rejected as an important factor in connection with the advance into the region.

An economic motive suggested for the Russian advance into Siberia is more easily demonstrated. The desire of the state for revenue and of individuals for personal enrichment centered on furs. Although stressing that the economic life of Russia took many other channels as well, Raymond H. Fisher, in his detailed study of the role of this commodity, shows furs to have been pre-eminent among the raw products traded by the Russians from early Kievan times. The exhaustion of fur resources of the forest regions of the Dnepr River basin was a cause of the decline of the Kievan state. The fur wealth of northeastern Russia led to the rise of Novgorod and its commercial empire and in time caused inroads by the rising state of Moscow which resulted in the loss of Novgorodian independence and the appropriation of its territories. The quest for furs then became an important motive behind Ermak's crossing of the Urals and a primary cause of much of the subsequent advance.

Finally, in this quest for causes of Russian eastward expansion, one may single out the psychology of superiority characteristic of all expansionist peoples, convinced of their right to dispossess inferior and barbaric foes, to establish the true faith, and to reap the economic benefits of dominion.

In the Russian consciousness, this feeling dates back certainly to the acceptance of Christianity in 988, with all of the implied and expressed superiority of the believer over the unenlightened and the right to conquer and proselytize. The feeling intensified with the development of the "Third Rome" concept in the fifteenth century. It appears in the cloak of piety which was laid upon the conquest of Kazan in 1552 and upon every Muscovite conquest that followed. Contemporary accounts picture Ermak and his followers as chosen by God to vanquish the unbelievers. It appears in the contests with the Turk, the Tatar, and the Pole. It comes out strongly in the openly expansionistic elements in Russia in the nineteenth and early twentieth centuries.

These sentiments, almost as old as Russia, unite the seventeenth-century promyshlennik with the twentieth-century empire builder, and both with the Roman legionary, the Spanish conquistador, or the North American "Indian fighter."

Summing up, one may ascribe the Russian eastward advance to four main factors: (1) the physical features, particularly rivers and plains, which facilitated movement; (2) the qualities of the participants who, without recourse to innate "urge" or "instinct," responded ably, if not always nobly, to the challenge of their environment; (3) the drive for furs; and (4) the national psychology which permitted the participants to disregard the rights of the primitive peoples in their path and to take the land for Russia.

Effects

From consideration of the causes of Russian eastward expansion, one may turn to its effects. What influence did the advancing frontier exert upon Russia, upon those who pushed it forward, and upon the regions occupied?

The most comprehensive statement of any experience possibly analogous to that of Russia is F. J. Turner's famous hypothesis concerning the influence of the frontier upon the development of the United States.

Turner, it will be recalled, asserted in 1893 that "the existence of an area of free land, its continuous recession and the advance of American settlement westward, explain American development."[7] This development, he claimed, had been constantly conditioned by a succession of frontier zones. A social laboratory, the frontier had given rise to the doctrine of democracy and attitudes toward government, and from the common experience had emerged a distinctly American people.

This hypothesis, the most influential single contribution ever made to American history, has been discussed ever since, and although subjected to much criticism, still commands many adherents. Efforts also have been made to apply the hypothesis to other parts of the world with an advancing frontier. Thus, B. H. Sumner states that "throughout Russian history one dominating theme has been the frontier; the theme of the struggle for the mastering of the natural resources of an untamed country, expanded into a continent by the ever-shifting movement of the Russian people and their conquest of and intermingling with other peoples."[8]

Inasmuch as Russia's frontiers on the southern steppe and in Siberia, especially the latter, would seem in part analogous to the American frontier, some aspects of the Turner hypothesis might therefore seem applicable. Here, however, one must first make the distinction that Turner was talking mainly about the influence of the frontier upon the American colonies, or the societies into which they were transformed, rather than upon the motherland, England. Second, the limitation of the present study to the line of advance itself, rather than to the settlement and subsequent administrative, social, and economic development which occurred in its wake, excludes a number of possible similarities with the American West from discussion here. Only part of the hypothesis, that concerning the frontier as "the outer edge of the wave, the meeting point between savagery and civilization," can be applied. In this light, one may consider some of the remaining similarities, real or apparent. Thus, Turner sees "the American national character" developing as the frontier moved westward: "To study this advance, the men who grew up under these conditions, and the political, economic, and social results of it, is to study the really American part of our history." Assuming the existence in some degree of sets of qualities which distinguish one people from another, it would seem that the "national character" of Russia may well have been affected by centuries of contact and conflict with steppe peoples, but could hardly have been shaped by the rapid and relatively late movement of a few men across Siberia, any more than England or France were shaped by their American colonists. One cannot start with the Russian crossing of the Urals as if it were the equivalent of the landing of the Pilgrims at Massachusetts

Bay. If the origin of the majority of Russian characteristics is sought, one would have to examine as far as possible the earlier, largely prehistoric phase of Russian history, when the population lived for centuries under frontier conditions and worked out the considerable fund of culture already present by the ninth century, when Russian recorded history began. Involving a vastly greater period of time, the impact of that earlier frontier would have been more general and deeper than that of the later, shorter period of advance with which this study has been concerned.

Turner's assertion, with regard to the American people, that "the frontier promoted the formation of a composite nationality," can certainly be applied to Russia, but again one must also turn to very early times, even antedating the movements from Kiev into the frontier in the Volga region that resulted in a mixture with Finnic tribesmen to form the Great Russian branch of the Eastern Slavs. Again, just as the "isolation of the [American frontier] region increased its peculiarly American tendencies," so probably did the cultural isolation of early Russia help to shape the Russian character and to determine the nature of the later advance. On the other hand, it may have been the isolation of the frontier, rather than any "unifying tendencies," which furthered the differentiation of the Eastern Slavs into Great Russians, Ukrainians, and Belorussians.

Turner stated further that American development exhibits "not merely an advance along a single line, but a return to primitive conditions on a continually advancing frontier...Social development has been continually beginning over again on the frontier." This seems also applicable to Russia's successive Siberian frontiers. There, as in America, the experience gained on one frontier could be applied to the next.

This "constant readjustment" on successive American frontiers, which adherents of the hypothesis believe formed a pattern of attitudes and methods which became standard as the advance continued, probably resembles the experience which was gained in early Russia and passed on through successive advances eastward or southward. Thus, from need developed frontier self-help and initiative, while poor communications, the nature of the men involved, and the lag in establishment of central control fostered the frontier lawlessness so characteristic of both countries.

One may conclude from these points, then, that certain of the more general aspects of the Turner thesis do seem applicable to Russia. However, other analogies must be sought for European Russia, in periods antedating those considered in this study or in the course of the settlement which followed the line of advance. Nevertheless, with due allowance for its shortcomings and dissimilar features, this thesis would seem of some use as an approach to the study of the Russian frontier.

Achievements and Aims

Russian eastward expansion (and to that may be linked the earlier phases of southward expansion) thus followed many channels and stemmed from a variety of causes and motives. Is it possible to make any overall characterization of this enormous process, which resulted in the acquisition by Russia of the entire northern part of Asia?

In general, Russian historians have lauded this acquisition. After 1917 Pokrovskii, Bakhrushin, Ogorodnikov, and other Soviet historians for a time pointed out the misdeeds of the participants in the eastward advance, but in the 1930s official desires to lessen the resentment of minority peoples toward Russian dominance became expressed in a selective extolling of the men concerned as explorers and contributors to knowledge, with very little said about their clashes with the natives. Thus, the recent (1968-69) five-volume *Istoriia Sibiri* devotes barely twenty-five pages to the Russian takeover of Siberia and substitutes for the term "conquest" (*zavoevanie*) the milder "annexation" (*prisoedinenie*). It states that although there were cases of compulsion (for example, the conquest of the Siberian Khanate), there were other instances of passive or voluntary attitudes of the natives toward annexation. This variance in attitudes and circumstances existed, but using the rare instance of passivity to characterize the Russian takeover as something other than the generally forcible measure that it was would be like referring to Rome's "annexation" of Gaul, or Spain's "annexation" of Mexico and Peru on similar grounds.

Soviet historians now label this process, be it conquest or annexation, as "progressive," in that it brought Siberia out of age-old isolation into contact with the rest of the world and prepared the way for civilization. However, neither "progress" nor "civilization" are as clear-cut as they once were. In human and economic terms, the advance into Siberia was enormously destructive. The societies of the natives were shattered, their leaders were removed or bought, their economies were wrecked, and their numbers diminished by the conqueror's diseases and alcohol. The wealth of furs was plundered by uncontrolled hunting methods, almost exterminating the most valuable animals over vast areas, forcing the hunters to go ever farther afield.

Certainly, given the time and circumstances, these results were to be expected. Being but few in number, inhabiting a large area with valuable natural resources, the natives in the path of the advancing Russians, like the inhabitants of frontiers in other parts of the world, were certain to suffer this fate, paying the penalty of backwardness. If the Russians had not penetrated and appropriated the region, other peoples would have done so, as the stronger and more advanced have done in every corner of the globe. Similarly, it must be noted that the plundering of natural resources by the seventeenth- and eighteenth-century Russians was nothing unique, but merely an expression of attitudes which prevailed everywhere until now, when ideas of conservation are beginning to gain acceptance.

Nevertheless, although we cannot now act as a court of posterity on these Russian pioneers, we may gain a better understanding of our own times, motives, and deeds by achieving a better knowledge of theirs. In spite of its detrimental aspects, the Russian advance preceded a great economic achievement which still unfolds. If the problems accompanying this growth can be solved, the lands which once made up Russia's open frontier, along with other Arctic territories, will become increasingly important in world history.

ENDNOTES

[1]Raymond H. Fischer, *The Russian Fur Trade, 1550-1700* (Berkeley, 1943), pp. 630-31.

[2]Frank A. Golder, *Russian Expansion on the Pacific, 1641-1850...* (Cleveland, 1914), pp. 14-15.

[3]Robert J. Kerner, *The Urge to the Sea: The Course of Russian History. The Role of Rivers, Portages, Monasteries and Furs* (Berkeley, 1946), p. 103.

[4]John A. Morrison, "Russia and Warm Water: A Fallacious Generalization and its Consequences," U.S. Naval Institute, *Proceedings* (November, 1952) LXXVIII, 1169-79.

[5]S. M. Solov'ev, *Istoriia Rossii s drevneishikh vremen*, 29 vols. in 15 (Moscow, 1959-66) III, 314.

[6]V. O. Kliuchevskii, *Kurs russkoi istorii*, 8 vols. (in *Sochineniia*, Moscow, 1956-59), I, 31-32.

[7]Frederick J. Turner, *The Frontier in American History* (New York, 1920).

[8]B. H. Sumner, *A Short History of Russia* (New York, 1943), p. 1. Later reprints bear title *Survey of Russian History*.

ALASKA'S BOUNDARIES*[1]

Stuart R. Tompkins

Alaska's growing fur trade naturally attracted the attention of the other maritime powers during the late eighteenth and early nineteenth centuries. Spain ineffectually sought to maintain her claim to the entire west coast of North America, sending at least seven expeditions into Alaskan waters between 1770 and 1791. Captain James Cook visited Alaska in 1778, and his crewmen returned to Britain with tales of the fabulous prices paid for Alaskan furs by the Chinese at Canton. Private British and American traders began to frequent Alaskan waters.

Aleksandr Baranov, resident manager for the Golikov-Shelikhov Company from 1791 until 1799 and Chief Manager (or "Governor") of Russian America from 1799 through 1817, welcomed the foreign traders. While he deplored the foreigners' willingness to sell liquor and firearms to Alaska's Natives, Baranov never received adequate supplies from either the Golikov-Shelikhov Company or the Russian American Company. Consequently, he grew increasingly dependent upon foodstuffs and other trade goods brought from the United States and Great Britain. The Russian government, particularly the Imperial Navy, frowned upon Baranov's reliance upon foreigners, and in 1821 Czar Alexander I formally forbade any foreign vessel to enter Alaskan waters and unilaterally extended Alaska's boundary four degrees to the south. These actions, of course, sharply conflicted with British and American commercial and political goals and provoked immediate protests from both nations.

Historian Stuart Ramsay Tompkins examined international rivalry in the North Pacific in depth. Canadian-born, Tompkins received a doctorate from the University of Chicago in 1931 and taught for many years thereafter at the University of Oklahoma, retiring as Professor Emeritus. His general history, *Alaska: Promyshlennik and Sourdough* (Norman: University of Oklahoma Press, 1945) drew extensively upon primary sources and remains valuable today.

In the following article, reprinted from the *Canadian Historical Review*, Tompkins described the international rivalry along the Pacific Northwest coast. He explained the conflicting territorial claims, commercial interests, and political goals of the various nations involved. He explained how the United States and Great Britain arrived at trade agreements with Russia. His discussion of the Anglo-

---

*This article originally appeared in the *Canadian Historical Review* 26 (March 1945): 1-24.

Russian Canada-Alaska boundary settlement of 1825 is of particular interest. Little known outside scholarly circles, the 1825 treaty laid the basis for eventual determination of Alaska's present boundary.

* * *

Alaska's boundary seems to defy geography and common sense. The clean slash that marks the 141st meridian moves unerring from north to south across the ridges but stops just short of the Pacific. From St. Elias it straggles to the southeast across the mountains, enclosing a long appendage that reaches as far south as Dixon Entrance and bars access to the interior. This anomalous pattern was conceived a little over a century ago by diplomats of three powers called to reconcile competing national claims.

But in 1824 and 1825 the agreements grew in part only out of conflicting territorial claims in these regions. They reflected also the growing rift between Great Britain and Russia in their relation to the concert of Europe and the diplomatic crisis involving Spain's colonies that accompanied French intervention in Spain in 1823. One must therefore set the conflict in northwestern America against the general international background. Purely commercial interests, however, precipitated the diplomatic struggle.

The northwest coast of America had originally been regarded as Spain's under the claims she had established by the Papal Bull of 1493 and the Treaty of 1494 with Portugal. This claim for long was not seriously challenged. But beginning in 1741, Russian explorers had moved from Okhotsk in Siberia across the Pacific Ocean. The chance discovery of the sea-otter, for whose pelts keen demand arose in China, inspired a feverish search for this wealth by companies operating from Okhotsk. Posts were founded on the islands, and even the mainland came under Russian sway. Spain met this challenge by advancing her posts from Mexico northward into upper California and by dispatching maritime expeditions to the North Pacific. She showed only a languid interest in the fur trade, her principal aim being to exclude rivals.[2] But she began shortly to encounter more dangerous competitors, the English. Captain Cook's third voyage in 1778 and the wealth in furs disclosed stimulated English interest and enterprise in that region. After 1788 Spain had to face equally formidable rivals--the Yankee traders from Boston. In 1790 she engaged in a test of strength with England for possession of the coast, a struggle in which she came off second best. Thereafter she was gradually eased out of the North Pacific.[3]

The encroachment of English and American traders threatened Russian interest too, already weakened by feuds between rival companies and in 1799 the Russian government moved to put an end to this chaotic state of affairs by granting a monopoly in the fur trade on the northwest coast of America, the islands, and the coasts of Siberia to the Russian American Company. The charter granted this company the exclusive right to the fur trade on all parts of the American coast north of latitude 55° north. They (the company) were authorized to prosecute their explorations not only within these limits but also, "further to the south, and to occupy the new lands so discovered as Russian possessions, if they have not been previously occupied by, or been dependent on any other nation."[4] The charter was never notified to foreign governments but failure to challenge it later prejudiced the British case. Moreover, the Napoleonic Wars more and more hampered British commerce and by the end of the century the British flag had all but disappeared from the seas. Britain's interests were, however, being advanced from the landward side. Alexander McKenzie of the North West Company, the first explorer to cross the continent in latitudes north of Mexico, had pushed over the mountains to the mouth of the Bella Coola River in 1793. The North West Company had posts to the west of these mountains by 1806 and were in a fair way to reach the sea first had they not been forestalled by John Jacob Astor who planted a trading post at the mouth of the Columbia River in 1810.

American trade with the northwest coast had expanded phenomenally after 1800. This continued encroachment on the Russian monopoly led that government to lodge protests in Washington, particularly against the trade of the Yankee ship-owners in liquor and firearms, a deadly combination which imperiled Russia's tenuous control over the natives. These protests were disregarded, but Astor shrewdly sought to play on Russia's fears by a proposal to Baranov to divide the coast between them. While Baranov temporized, the War of 1812 and the loss of Astoria to the English North West Company extinguished Astor's interests. The restoration of Astoria to nominal American sovereignty in 1818 under the terms of the Treaty of Ghent was not intended to affect the claims of either side, though astute use was made of this by Adams to prejudice the claims of Great Britain.[5]

Meanwhile in 1811 the Russian American Company itself had thrown down the gauntlet not only to Spain but to their other rivals, the United States and Great Britain, by moving southward to latitude 38° (approximately) where they established Fort Ross near Bodega Bay, allegedly to supply the northern posts with grain and meat. This foothold was maintained against the protests of Spain in the hope that a favorable turn of events would render it permanent. It was not surrendered until 1841.[6]

The efforts to settle a number of outstanding differences between Great Britain and the United States led to these controversial issues being submitted to the Tsar Alexander for arbitration. The territorial question was, however, dealt with by a special commission consisting of Frederick J. Robinson and Henry Goulburn for Great Britain and Richard Rush and Albert Gallatin for the United States. It was found impossible to agree on a boundary and in lieu of this the Commissioners decided that all the country lying to the west of the Rocky Mountains should be open to the citizens of both countries on equal terms. While claims of both countries were specifically reserved, the United States rights were recognized for the first time in the territory north of the 49th parallel--a factor which was to play a considerable role in later negotiations.[7]

The following year the United States advanced her claim still further by signing with Spain the Adams-Onis Treaty of 1819 according to the terms of which the northern boundary of Spain's possessions was fixed at the 42nd parallel of latitude.[8] The whole situation, therefore, in the North Pacific was in a state of tension with three powers remaining in the contest--Russia, Great Britain, and the United States--all with claims that had to be recognized.

The first charter of the Russian American Company lapsed on July 8, 1819. On July 31 its privileges were provisionally extended to allow the Ministry of the Interior time (one year specifically) to gather information on the company's operations and to submit to the Emperor recommendations for his action.[9] A committee named for this purpose conducted hearings during the course of the following months and in due time submitted its report which dealt primarily with injury caused to its trade by American and English interlopers. On the basis of this an ukase proclaimed September 4/16, 1821, recited in the preamble how, "the trade of our subjects on the Aleutian Islands and on the northwest coast of America, appertaining to Russia, is subject, because of secret and illicit traffic, to oppression and impediments."[10] It specifically reserved to Russian subjects the pursuit of commerce, whaling, fishery, and all other industry within an area extending from Bering Strait to the 51st° of latitude on the American coast and on the Asiatic side, from the Strait to 45° 50' (the southern tip of Urup island in the Kuriles). Foreign vessels were not to approach within one hundred Italian miles of the coasts. On September 13/25 the new charter was finally issued. In somewhat more precise language the company was granted "the privilege of carrying on to the exclusion of other Russians and of the subjects of foreign states, all industries connected with the capture of wild animals and all fishing industries on the shores of northwestern America which have from time immemorial belonged to Russia, commencing from the northern point of the Island of Vancouver, under 51° north latitude to Bering Straits and beyond them, and on the islands which belong to that coast, as well as on the other situated between it and the eastern shore of Siberia, and also on the Kurile Islands where the Company has carried on industries, as far as the outer tip of the Island of Urup under 45° 50'."[11]

The purpose of this was effectively to exclude American and English ships from carrying on trade in furs in the coastal waters of the North Pacific. Instructions went forth at once to the ambassadors abroad to bring this pronouncement to the attention of the respective governments to which they were accredited.

The language of Castlereagh on hearing of this, "that His Britannic Majesty must be understood as hereby reserving all his rights" was the warning growl of the British lion. In Washington the action was less abrupt. "The President...has seen with surprise" were the words used by John Quincy Adams. The wheels of diplomacy began to revolve and three world powers prepared for a trial of strength for the possession of the areas bounding the South Seas.[12]

The preliminary negotiations opened at Washington in the early months of 1822. The ill health of Poletika, the Russian ambassador, led to their being interrupted. Meanwhile the Russian government appointed Baron Tuyll as the former's successor. Tuyll delayed his departure, and in the interval the Russian government, finding their position challenged by both Great Britain and the United States, saw the advantages of having negotiations with both powers conducted by the same plenipotentiaries. Since this could be done only at the Russian capital, they were transferred to St. Petersburg. Meanwhile, other more pressing matters tended to crowd the issue in the North Pacific into the background. As a result of the revolt in Greece, and the revolution in Spain, a call went out to the members of the Quadruple Alliance to send representatives to Vienna to consider the threat to Europe's peace.[13] Here, England standing aside, her allies gave France authority to invade Spain and to restore the power of King Ferdinand as absolute monarch. The dispute in the North Pacific was, it is true, broached by the Duke of Wellington,[14] but his somewhat perfunctory protest was met with the suggestion that these matters could better be discussed in St. Petersburg.

The ukase of September 4, 1821, contained two features that were objectionable alike from the British and American point of view; first, the exclusion of all foreign shipping from waters extending one hundred Italian miles from shore; secondly, the extension of Russia's territorial claims as far south as the 51st parallel of latitude.

The powers of a plenipotentiary were issued to Sir Charles Bagot on February 20, 1823, but these made no mention of the territorial dispute and provided solely for discussion with Russia. Before Bagot had been able to launch the negotiations they were, owing to a series of unforeseen complications, practically suspended for six months.

Meanwhile in Washington the recall of Pierre Poletika, the Russian ambassador, who had initiated the discussions, and the arrival of the new ambassador, Baron Tuyll, with a request from the Emperor that Henry Middleton, United States ambassador at St. Petersburg, receive powers as a plenipotentiary, suggested to the Secretary of State, John Quincy Adams, the advantages of acting jointly with England. The upshot was a suggestion to this effect, made to the British ambassador, and by him conveyed to the Foreign Secretary Canning.[15] The invitation which was cordial in tone contained this extraordinary statement, "He [Adams] added that the United States had no territorial claims of their own as high as the 51st degree of latitude..." This was relayed by George Canning to Bagot with this caution: "The part of the question in which the American government is peculiarly desirous of establishing a concert with this country is that which concerns the extravagant assumption of maritime jurisdiction...the other part of the question which relates to territorial claims and boundary is perhaps susceptible of separate adjustment."[16] Canning had not been officially approached by Rush in this matter. Hence the cautious wording of his despatch. Despite this Bagot interpreted this communication as a directive and he informed Nesselrode that he and Middleton would probably act together.

"Count Nesselrode being upon the eve of setting out to join the Emperor...I have thought it advisable even in the absence of those further instructions which you lead me to expect in your despatch No. 12, of the 12th of last month, to apprise him of the probability of Mr. Middleton and myself being soon instructed to act jointly in negotiating with him some proposition for the definitive settlement of that part at least of the question growing out of the Imperial Ukase of 4th (16th) September, 1821."[17]

Bagot expected further instructions but in the absence of these he adhered to the view that joint action with the United States was to be restricted to the question of "the extravagant assumption of maritime jurisdiction" marking time meanwhile on the territorial question.

The official documents give us an incomplete version of these preliminary discussions.[18] Turning to Bagot's private letters to Canning we find they reflect intense concern over the factors that had delayed negotiations and on which he was imperfectly informed. Moreover, the issues to be settled had not been clearly defined. Hence he asks in a letter of March 1, 1823: is he to negotiate for a line of demarcation, or (2) is he to negotiate for common occupancy; (3) is the virtual declaration of the North Pacific a *mare clausum* to be the subject of negotiation? A letter of June 2, 1823, indicates his impatience at the delay caused by the Russian government. By August 31 he had opened the battle by sounding out Nesselrode (in accordance with Canning's instructions of July 12), in the hope of forestalling his rival Middleton:

> I hope you will not think that I have run too fast in the American question. I have feared that Middleton might any day receive his instructions directly from Washington which might lead him to talk to Nesselrode before I had done so. This would have been inconvenient. As it is I have got hold of Nesselrode first and have put the matter to him in a way for which he is grateful. He hates Middleton and Jonathan *comme de raison*, and he has fairly acknowledged to me that he is delighted to have us to protect him against them and to keep them in order.[19]

Nevertheless he continued (as did Middleton) to assume that in the matter of maritime jurisdiction the two countries would treat jointly with Russia. In the course of these discussions Middleton revealed the negotiations undertaken the previous year (1822) when the first United States protests had been lodged against the ukase.

> Middleton now tells me what I was not before aware of, that he had last year by direction of the President several interviews with Count Nesselrode and Count Capodistrias upon the subject of this ukase and that it was at length agreed that he should inquire officially what were the intentions of the Imperial government in regard to the execution of it, an assurance being previously given that the answer he should receive would be satisfactory. Mr. Middleton has been good enough to furnish me with a copy of this answer, which I now enclose. As however, he considered the communication of the paper as personally confidential, I take the liberty of requesting that no public use be made of it.[20]

With regard to the territorial dispute, he writes: "I have explained to Count Nesselrode that the United States making no pretensions to territory so high as the 51st degree of north latitude, the question rests between His Majesty and the Emperor of Russia alone, and becomes therefore a matter for separate settlement by their respective governments..."[21] On these assumptions Bagot had begun his preliminary discussions directly with the Russian ministers on the question of boundary, leaving the maritime problem to be the subject of joint negotiations later, a course that was to be fruitful in misunderstandings.

The instructions to him had put the territorial question in the vaguest terms. Bagot himself on his own responsibility challenged Russia's claims south of 59° north latitude.[22] But Canning had suggested 57°.[23] Two considerations made a parallel of latitude an awkward boundary line. One was the general northwest to southeast trend of the coast south of Yakutat Bay; the other was the uncertainty as to how far east such cession should reach. Too great an extent would threaten the trading rights of the Hudson's Bay Company in the Mackenzie River valley as well as in the area between the Rocky Mountains and the sea. During the course of Bagot's discussions with Poletika this became obvious. As he turned the matter over in his mind, it occurred to Bagot that he could meet these difficulties by a novel solution. Still continuing to mark time while waiting for definite word from London, he wrote to Canning:

> I have half a mind to exceed my instructions and try if I cannot get a degree of longitude instead of latitude for our line of

> demarcation. It appears to me that if we take a degree of latitude we leave Russia with undefined pretensions to the eastward and in the interior of the continent, whereas a degree of longitude would describe both the boundary on the coast and within the continent at the same time. I do not know whether Russia would listen to such a proposition but it would, I think, be a great point if we could get somewhere about the 139th degree of west longitude as the line. This would cut the coast about Bering's Bay (Yakutat) to the south of which Russia has in fact no pretensions whatever, to discovery or anything else. This would make the latitude of our boundary about 59.5° instead of 57° with which you say you would be contented. If I am to secure 57° it may at all events be as well to begin by claiming something more, and I have some notion of bringing forward this idea...You may depend upon it that the Americans will try to interfere somehow or other in our boundary negotiations as distinguished from the maritime jurisdiction question. Mr. Middleton has already told me clearly that he thinks the United States have an interest in the business and upon what grounds? Because Spain had, by treaty, the right to trade with our coasts in that quarter and that the United States by their last treaty have acquired all the rights in that respect and stand in her shoes. Is not this preposterous?[24]

Still the word so impatiently awaited did not come.

Some days later Bagot's composure was rudely disturbed when he discovered that both he and George Canning had been in the dark as to the real intentions of the United States. This was owing to the facile assurance given by Stratford Canning that the United States had no "territorial pretensions as high as the fifty-first degree of north latitude."[25] Canning had been misled and far from being entirely disinterested in the territorial issue, the United States was prepared to assert equal claims with Great Britain to the whole of the northwest coast.[26] Even Bagot had allowed his better judgment to be overborne. His disillusionment but strengthened him in his original resolution to pursue the territorial discussions separately. Signs of growing Russian confidence impelled him to endeavor to come to terms with Russia at once before broaching the subject with the United States. But to his great disquiet the home government was showing signs of weakening, as is seen from the following note received from the Foreign Office: "It is probable that since the settlement of Sitka, the Russians may have extended their possessions to the great adjacent island (Baranof). I should think therefore that if latitude 56° which takes in the whole of that island and longitude 225° (or what is the same thing 135° west) were assigned as the Russian limits, Chatham Strait, Lynn Canal, and a line running from the head of the latter in the direction of northwest, would form an unobjectionable boundary. Perhaps a sketch of this part of the chart might accompany Sir Charles Bagot's instructions."[27] But by the time of its receipt Canning's instructions directing him to conduct his entire negotiations apart from his American colleague were on the way.

So far we have followed events in Washington and St. Petersburg, a method which gives an incomplete picture. It was in London that we can see the impact of the various forces that were shaping events. Here the struggle for a few miles of rugged and inhospitable coast was overshadowed by the rise of the new republics in South America and the feverish partisanship that this evoked in the Old World. Great Britain had in international affairs been veering from her allies in the Quadruple Alliance in their policy of constituting themselves custodians of Europe's peace and the implacable foes of revolution. In general, England's strong commercial ties, as well as her own revolutionary tradition, evoked sympathy with the constitutional government of Spain and the new states in South America and brought her interests into harmony with those of the United States where public feeling was on the side of Spain's revolting colonies. But it was more or less by chance that this opportunity, fleeting as it was, arose for England and her own emancipated colonies to find a common interest in the cause of freedom.

Shortly after George Canning had become Secretary of State for Foreign Affairs in succession to Castlereagh, John Quincy Adams with his tireless energy had once more addressed himself to clearing up a number of matters that had remained unsettled since the signing of the Treaty of Ghent. He accordingly sent a series of despatches to Richard Rush with instructions that he approach Mr. Canning and initiate negotiations on these problems. The documents reached Rush on July 29, 1823, and he was told that a seventh to follow would deal with the northwest coast.[28] Rush had his first interview with Canning on August 16 on the subjects covered in the first six despatches, omitting to deal with the northwest coast, instructions on which had not then arrived. At the conclusion of this interview Rush referred to still another matter on which he appears to have had some lead from Adams. "The proper object of it [the interview] over, I transiently asked him whether notwithstanding the late news from Spain, we might not still hope that the Spaniards would get the better of their difficulties."

He further suggested that: "...Should France ultimately effect her purpose of overthrowing the constitutional government in Spain, there was at least the consolation left, that Great Britain would not allow her to go further and stop the progress of emancipation in the colonies."[29] The words struck a responsive chord in Canning, but for the moment he contented himself with innocuous platitudes and the conference was at an end. Canning, however, carefully weighed Rush's remarks and at his next interview on August 22 returned to the subject of South America. On this occasion he proposed that Great Britain and the United States should issue a joint declaration on the subject of the Spanish-American colonies. Thus negotiations between Rush and Canning took an entirely new direction.

In a subsequent interview (August 27) Rush pressed Canning for recognition by Great Britain "of the independence of the new communities" as a necessary condition of such joint action.[30] But Canning balked at this as he considered recognition by England premature. The matter continued, however, to be discussed in later interviews until November 26 when, an agreement having proved impossible, it was dropped. At this point Canning began to pick up once more the threads of the controversy of the northwest coast not yet included in the agenda of matters to be discussed at London.

On December 12, as he was about to give Bagot final instructions for his guidance in this matter at St. Petersburg, he suggested that Rush communicate to him the views of the United States government on this matter. Canning in the meantime being taken down with gout, the scene is shifted to the sick room in Gloucester Lodge which, on the occasion of their next discussion, became the audience chamber of the Minister of State. There, propped up on pillows, and with his maps spread out before him, Canning listened to Rush explain the demands of the United States to be a party to any territorial settlement between Great Britain and Russia. Whatever his feelings he restrained them and merely murmured, as Rush took his leave, that "our claim seemed much beyond anything England had anticipated."[31]

For two weeks the American ambassador heard nothing. Whether it was the gout, or whether it was the shock of the disclosures that had overtaxed the patient, Canning remained in the seclusion of his home. Then at the end of a fortnight he had sufficiently recovered from both to pen this message to Rush: "What can this intend? Our northern question is with Russia as our southern is with the United States. But do the United States mean to travel north to get between us and Russia?" Rush's laconic reply that "it was even so" did not spare the sick man. The shock caused by this revelation had scarcely worn off when the text of President Monroe's message to Congress came to hand. The words--"that the American continents...are henceforth not to be considered as subjects for future colonization by any European power,"[32] directed in the first instance against Russia, were now ostensibly turned against England. Canning, at length recovered, braced himself for the struggle and drew up the final instructions to Bagot which would take account of this new complication.

The long delay of London in coming to some decision on the matter of joint negotiations is only partly to be explained by preoccupation with other matters. Misunderstanding also played its part. It appears that Adams had intended to reach an agreement with England on the northwest coast before proceeding to joint negotiations in St. Petersburg. The northwest coast was only one among seven different matters which it was proposed to refer to a special commission. Indeed, Adams, in his letter of instructions to Rush, distinctly says, "Among the subjects of negotiation with Great Britain which are pressing upon the attention of this Government is the present condition of the northwest coast of this continent."[33] There was, therefore, no reason why Rush should hurry Canning on this matter since it would be dealt with in due course. But apparently both Canning and Rush were at cross purposes, the former waiting for a fuller communication from Washington while Rush rather leisurely proceeded to gather up the threads of negotiations in London, unconcerned over those proceeding at St. Petersburg. It was only when word had been received back in London from the Russian capital that Canning had approached Rush:

> Upon receipt of Your Excellency's dispatch No. 48 reporting the arrival of Mr. Hughes at St. Petersburg with the instructions of the Government of the United States to Mr. Middleton, I applied to Mr. Rush for information as to the tenor of these instructions. I then found what I had not before been led to expect, that Mr. Rush had himself authority to enter into negotiations with us as to the respective claims of Great

> Britain and the United States on the northwest coast of America, although he does not appear to have been instructed to invite such negotiation here if we should prefer leaving it to be conducted at St. Petersburg.[34]

Canning had from the beginning been reluctant to reopen England's dispute with the United States since the agreement of 1818 had still five years to run.[35] But in failing to do so he allowed the United States to become, under the terms of the Convention of 1818, a party to settling the boundary between Britain and Russia.[36]

When Adams invited Great Britain to take part in joint negotiations he had casually disclaimed (at least Stratford Canning had so asserted) any interest for the United States beyond the 51st parallel of latitude. In his instructions to his ministers in London and St. Petersburg he gives signs of no such disinterestedness. In a document called "Observations on the Claim of Russia to Territorial Possessions on the Continent of North America," communicated with Mr. Adams's letter of July 22, 1823, to Mr. Middleton we read: "With the exception of the British establishments north of the United States, the remainder of both the American continents must henceforth be left to the management of American hands...the United States can in no wise admit the right of Russia to exclusive territorial possession on any part of the continent of North America south of the 60th degree of north latitude."[37] He instructed Middleton--"With regard to territorial claims...we are willing to agree to the boundary line within which the Emperor Paul granted exclusive privileges to the Russian American Company, that is to say, latitude 55°." A passing reference to Great Britain's claim and a hint at the possibility of joint negotiations dismisses Britain's case. It is suggested that--"as the British Ambassador at St. Petersburg is authorized and instructed to negotiate likewise upon this subject, it may be proper to adjust the interests and claims of the three powers by a joint convention."[38] He enclosed a project for a treaty between the United States and Russia setting the 55th parallel of latitude as their boundary.

Adams's intentions are set forth with greater fullness in his letter of instructions of the same day to Rush in London. In these, 55° and 51° assume a slightly different aspect, the one the British boundary as against Russia in the north, the other as against the United States to the south. Bagot was partly prepared for the revelation that the United States had extensive claims north of 51°, but the announcement of President Monroe's message to Congress on December 2 and the decision of Canning to proceed alone, marked the end of the truce and brought the two ambassadors at the Russian capital face to face. "What do you think those original instructions [from Adams to Middleton] were? Nothing less than to proceed to divide the whole coast between Her and the United States to our entire exclusion...Now there does appear to me to be a baseness in this business on the part of Adams which nobody but Adams was capable of. But this trick has failed...I shall conclude certainly speedily, and I think satisfactorily, our separate arrangements and Adams may bellow as much as he pleases."[39] Evidently the period of waiting had resulted in a certain exacerbation of feelings (of which Russia was not slow to avail herself). Finally on February 12, 1824, the Russian plenipotentiaries received their powers. Bagot was now in receipt of his final instructions from Canning and official conferences were opened.

Nor had Middleton been inactive during the interlude. He had submitted his first confidential memorial to the Emperor in December, 1823, and apparently had conversations with Bagot regarding the respective claims of their countries. Of the discussion between them, Bagot had this to say in a private letter to Canning: "This project is, I have no doubt, the modification of that which Mr. Middleton was originally furnished to negotiate about territorial demarcation and everything else, without us and to our exclusion...The duplicity of the American government as it regards us, has, you may depend upon it been extreme and I heartily hope that Squinty Adams may lose his election of it."[40]

The negotiations were thus begun by each country separately and carried on independently with little communication between the British and the American representatives. Middleton, however, at the start served notice on both the Russian government and Sir Charles Bagot "that if any attempt was made to negotiate upon territorial questions without our participation, it would become my duty to protest in the strongest terms." He also asserted the claim of the United States, till then officially unknown to Bagot, that "the said [United] States have concurrent rights, claims and pretensions with Great Britain to whatever point here may be considered to extend."[41] On the first point Bagot had already been instructed by Canning to make reservation of the claims of the United States as had been done in the convention of 1818, that "the agreement between the contracting powers should not be taken to affect the claims of any other power or state in any part of the said country."

The conferences of Middleton proceeded without further incident. At the outset, after some preliminary sparring, he offered the Russians in return for abrogation of the offending maritime clause in the ukase of 1821, and for trading privileges along the coast, recognition of the territorial boundary of 55°, thus at the beginning, proposing to buy concessions by a horse trade.[42] With this bait dangled before them the Russian plenipotentiaries made little difficulty and by the first of April they had succeeded in hammering out a convention that was mutually satisfactory. It was agreed that the parallel of 54° 40' north latitude was to be the southern limit of Russian occupation or settlement, and the northern limit of such by citizens of the United States.[43] All parts of the North Pacific Ocean were to be open to the subjects of both powers without discrimination for purposes of trade or fishing, with the stipulation that they were not to resort to a part of the coast occupied by the other power without permission. For ten years the ships of both powers were to be free to frequent coastal waters. Traffic in firearms and liquor was forbidden.

The conferences between Bagot and the Russian plenipotentiaries opened on February 28 and ran concurrently with those with the United States ambassador. From the beginning there was a stiffness and lack of cordiality that boded no good. At the outset Bagot submitted a proposal originally suggested by Count Lieven in London on January 21 that, "The question of strict right should be provisionally waived on both sides and that the adjustment of our mutual pretensions should be made upon the sole principle of the respective convenience of both countries." This was accepted.

Two things hampered the British representative from the beginning. First the retention of the 55th° of latitude as an approximate southern boundary was made by the Russians a face-saving issue.[44] The other was that the United States' representative had, despite his assertion of claim of United States rights concurrent with the British as far north as the extreme limit of their claims, already indicated that they were prepared to forget this if they secured the trading concessions which they wished. Moreover Bagot, following Canning's instructions of January 15, had modified his original proposal to take Cross Sound as the line separating Russian from British territory. But the selection of a north and south line dividing Prince of Wales Island from the mainland, would give United States ships access to the coastal waters (in British possession) and so render their exclusion from Russian waters difficult.[45] Bagot therefore was forced by the invincible opposition of the Russian plenipotentiaries to agree to an east and west line --"the fifty-fifth degree of latitude as her boundary on the islands"--in order to preserve also an uninterrupted British access to the Pacific Ocean.[46] This necessarily involved imposing some eastward limit. To secure all the coastal waters the frontier must be some distance from the coast, which would give Russia a littoral.[47] This point was reluctantly conceded by Sir Charles but he sought to fix the southern limit of such a coastal strip at the 56th parallel. From the point where this parallel cut the coast the new line was to pass out through Sumner Strait to the ocean so as to assign Sitka and Baranof Island to Russia but Prince of Wales Island to Great Britain. This proposal was rejected by the Russians, however, who returned to their original terms, a frontier that would secure Russia possession of the whole of Prince of Wales Island, then traverse Portland Canal to the summit of the mountains (which were assumed to border the coast), and then pass along the summit of these mountains to the 139th° of longitude. Along this meridian it would proceed to the Arctic Ocean.[48]

This concession Bagot refused as going beyond his original instructions. Negotiations were thereupon broken off and Bagot decided to toss the problem of territorial delimitation back to the Home government. He assumed that the question of maritime jurisdiction could be dealt with. But Nesselrode refused to negotiate on one point till the other was settled and asserted that the offending article in the ukase of September 4, 1821, would stand until Russia's terms were met. Bagot's disappointment and chagrin at his discomfiture came out in his personal letter to Canning:

> They [the Russian government] must be dealt with as you would deal with a horse dealer. Their whole conduct in the late negotiations has been of the most huckstering and peddlarlike character and in my opinion they will not be brought to reason unless they are told roundly that if they will not arrange the matter equitably and according to our mutual present convenience, they shall not be allowed to settle anywhere upon these islands south of their present lowest establishment, viz, Sitca. They [Poletica and Nesselrode] are both under the dominion of the Russian American Company at the head of which is an old Admiral Mordvinoff, an honest man but mighty obstinate who mistakes obstinacy for patriotism.[49]

With matters reaching this complete deadlock Bagot referred the dispute back to Canning.

The secret of the unyielding attitude of Russia which Bagot characterized as that of "a horsetrader" is abundantly clear from the letter which Nesselrode penned to Lieven to guide him in the discussions he was instructed to open with Canning. He had chosen the convention of 1818 with the United States as the weak joint in Britain's armor.[50] By admitting the Americans to an equal share in the exploitation of the region beyond the mountains she had conceded the weakness of her claims to exclusive sovereignty. Russia having further strengthened her case by coming to terms with Britain's partner and rival, there was nothing left for Britain but to acquiesce and to accept the same or a similar boundary. Having now attained her main purpose, a settlement of the long-standing difficulties with the United States, Russia could afford to sit back and wait for England to come to her terms. To make it more palatable to Englishmen Lieven was to represent Russia's retreat from her extreme pretensions as proof of her moderation.[51] Nesselrode ironically suggested that Britain should compensate herself by an extension of her claims southward into Oregon.

Canning, already struggling in a maze of unsolved problems, was forced to take up this task anew. Caught as he was in a difficult international situation he had no choice but to compromise and on July 12 he forwarded to Bagot a draft convention seasoned to Muscovite taste by the master chef, Lieven himself. All he now hoped to achieve, aside from saving some fragment of self-esteem, was to secure trading privileges at Novo-Arkhangel'sk and along the coast; to restrict within the narrowest limits the Russian American Company's hold on the mainland. But compromise was of little use. Full capitulation was to be the price paid for the treaty. The offer of the right to trade at Novo-Arkhangel'sk without time limit was withdrawn.[52] Liberty to navigate and trade *forever* along the coast of the *lisiere* was also refused, as well as the right to frequent other parts of the northwest coast (this refers to the parts of Alaska beyond the area in dispute) though it is only fair to Russia to add that these had not been contained in Russia's original offer. Bagot, therefore, threw up his hands, refused to sign and returned the "project" with a "counter project" of the Russians to London for final decision. He rightly saw that the traditional British methods of conciliation and compromise had broken down.

The publication of the convention with the United States had raised a clamor of protests against the supposed sacrifice of Russian interests, Bagot pointed out. "Nesselrode and Poletika are now afraid of signing anything upon the subject in which there are not great and signal advantages secured to Russia....I should like to have been the person to sign a treaty of such magnitude and importance and 1 should have ended my days here handsomely by doing so. But *Dis aliter visum est...*"[53]

Bagot left St. Petersburg in the summer of 1824 without reaching an understanding with Russia. By early winter the British Cabinet had decided to yield on the major issues and Stratford Canning was sent over to bring negotiations to a conclusion. His instructions were "if the present project is agreeable to Russia we are ready to conclude and sign a treaty."[54] The only point now at issue was the width of the *lisiere* to be conceded to Russia along the coast and the methods by which its boundaries should be fixed. Canning was determined to restrict it within the narrowest limits and, with this in mind, preferred to have the frontier run along the base of the mountains, a proposal that was rejected by the Russians for a suggestion that the crest of the range be followed. Canning yielded on this but insisted that it should at no point exceed ten marine leagues in width. This was grudgingly accepted by the Russians and on this sour note the negotiations came to an end.[55] One important concession came to the British more or less as an afterthought. This was the shifting of the line that ran north from Mount St. Elias 2° westward.[56]

A further incident troubled the diplomatic waters. Adams records in his diary that one day in December, 1824, before the treaty could come before the Senate, he received a mysterious call from Baron Tuyll, the Russian ambassador. With evident embarrassment the latter informed him that the Russian government wished, in view of an outcry that had arisen against the clauses admitting United States ships to Russian coasts everywhere in the Pacific, to amend the treaty. Tuyll brought the suggestion that on the occasion of the exchange of ratifications an explanatory note be issued modifying the treaty to the extent of restricting commercial intercourse of Americans in the North Pacific to that part of the American coast south of latitude 57°. Adams at once warned the Russian envoy that such tampering with the treaty would certainly mean its failure to secure ratification in the Senate, but agreed once this was assured to do something to meet Russia's wishes. Hence the curious instructions issued by the Russian American Company to the Governor at Sitka and apparently acquiesced in by the United States, limiting commercial intercourse of Americans to that part of the American coast south of Yakutat (Bering) Bay.[57] In the British treaty this was provided for by Article VII which says, "During the period of ten years, to date from the signing of this convention the vessels of the high powers or those belonging to their respective subjects, shall have equally the right to frequent, without any let or hindrance whatever, all the interior seas, the gulfs, havens and creeks in those parts of the coast mentioned in Article III, in order to carry on fishing and to trade with the natives."[58]

Shortly after Middleton had finished negotiating the treaty he wrote to Adams bewailing the fact that Congress had apparently taken no action toward the occupation of the Pacific coast. Middleton (like Adams) was one with many of his countrymen in regarding the convention of 1818 as but a momentary check in the progress of American expansion. Proposals of this kind made in 1821 had been the subject of a heated protest by Stratford Canning and an equally heated rejoinder by Adams.[59] The proposal in 1821 never got past the committee stage though it did become the subject of diplomatic discussions. But a similar motion made in 1823 by Congressman Floyd "to inquire into the expediency of occupying the Columbia or the Oregon River," emerged in January, 1824, as a bill for the despatch of troops to the west coast, a course supported by the Quartermaster-General Jesup. Fortunately the Senate rejected the bill and thus spared the administration the embarrassment of a move that was inspired by anti-British feelings.[60]

The settlement of the dispute over the northwest coast was based neither on any abstract title nor on "mutual convenience." Spain had had the most clear-cut claim but a Papal Bull had no standing with heretics outside the Roman Catholic fold. It was of little use to invoke "mutual convenience" since the governments were ill-informed on actual conditions in these remote regions. None of those participating in the discussions had ever been to the northwest coast. The maps used were imperfect and antiquated. The British placed their reliance on those of Vancouver, who, gazing from the deck of his ship had fancied the serrated peaks forming the eastward horizon were a continuous and well-defined ridge. A group of diplomats sitting around tables on the other side of the globe, working under such handicaps with defective, out-of-date maps could hardly produce satisfactory boundaries. Canning's quip of "bobbing for whale *ipsis in faucibus Beringi*" was mildly satirical of the air of academic unreality that hung over the negotiations. The convention was but one incident of a diplomatic game in which the participants were playing for stakes not always visible on the board.

Considered by itself the issue was less one between the Anglo-Saxon powers and Russia as it seemed to be, than a phase of the struggle between Great Britain and the United States for the possession of the continent. It is questionable whether Russia could ever have made a serious bid for power in the North Pacific against either of her rivals. She had an insecure foothold on the continent. The original Shelekhov-Golikov Company had never penetrated further east and south than Lituya Bay (approximately latitude 59° 30' north).[61] Baranov had been subsequently instructed to extend his operations to the south and east but when he did so, such extension was made from commercial motives and not out of deference to Russia's political aspirations.[62] Russia's tenure was constantly threatened by native risings. Russian occupation, Baranov continued to regard as provisional.[63] At the very time when negotiations were under way in the capital, the Board of Directors had already authorized abandonment of Sitka, a fact carefully suppressed during the discussions.[64] Moreover, up to 1825, Russia had one by one relinquished most of the mainland posts. The methods by which the Russian American Company obtained their furs tended to exhaust rather than preserve its resources and thus to render their rule transitory.

The "non-colonization" doctrine already foreshadowed by Adams and proclaimed by Monroe played relatively little role in the actual discussions. It was, however, implicit in the attitude of Adams and others, and it did not need to be insisted on to exert an influence on events. Bagot's anger against Adams was perhaps due to the latter's skill in cloaking a policy of exclusion with the mantle of a righteous crusade against tyranny. Yet Rush believed that this novel "pretension on the part of his Government was intended as a set-off against the maritime pretension of the Russian ukase."[65] The principle had not been adhered to in the settlement with Russia and Adams was probably ready for a deal with Canning. It is apparently this combination of extravagant claims with a show of moderation that explains the inconsistency which Bagot called "duplicity." In the midst of Adams' campaign for the presidency there could be no weakening in the emphasis on "manifest destiny."

ENDNOTES

[1]The original Monroe Doctrine emphasized two guiding principles in Europe's relation to the American continent; (1) non-intervention as regards the Latin American states then struggling for independence; (2) non-colonization of unoccupied parts of the continent. Studies of the Monroe Doctrine give scant attention to the second, and general works on the diplomacy of this period are of

little help in discussing it.

2Regarding Spain's interest in the fur trade see Adele Ogden, *The California Sea Otter Trade, 1784-1848* (University of California Publications in History, XXVI, Berkeley and Los Angeles, 1941).

3The convention of the Escurial in 1790 ostensibly settled only the rights of Britain at Nootka Sound and agreed that her ships were free to navigate the waters of the northwest coast. But whatever the wording of the treaty, contemporaries regarded it as ringing down the curtain on Spain's monopoly and the recognition of England's claims on the coast. See the admission of the Spanish king in 1790 as reported in Floridablanca's letter to Iriarte, November 21, 1790. "English trade and settlements were limited to that part of the coast north of Nootka," William Ray Manning, "The Nootka Sound Controversy" (*Annual Report of the American Historical Association 1904*, 458).

4*Proceedings of the Alaska Boundary Tribunal Convened at London... under the Treaty concluded at Washington, January 24, 1903*...(Washington, Government Printing Office, 1904, 7 vols., 56-2, Sen. Doc. 162, Ser. 4000), II, App. 23-5; hereinafter cited as *Alaska Boundary Tribunal*. Also *Polnoe Sobranie Zakonov Rossiiskoi Imperii* (Complete Collection of Laws of the Russian Empire) (44 vols., St. Petersburg, 1830), XXV, Text 19, 233. Russia's occupation of Fort Ross near Bodega Bay on the California coast would come under this head.

5See memorandum of H. U. Addington, May 10, 1826, in Edward John Stapleton (ed.), *Some Official Correspondence of George Canning, 1821-1827* (2 vols., London, 1887), II, 113-15. According to Addington, in spite of the admonition of Castlereagh that in restoring Astoria, special reservation was to be made of English rights, such reservation was not made in writing; and "by an equal fatality, the reservation of the territorial claims enjoined by Earl Bathurst on those appointed to deliver Fort Astoria...to the Americans in 1818, was omitted in the Publick Act passed on that occasion between the parties."

The only account taken of this by Adams appears in his instructions to Rush, July 22, 1822, "about the time of the conclusion of the Convention of 1818, some vague intimation was given by Mr. Bagot of British claims on the northwest coast. The restoration of the place and the convention of 1818 [on the joint use of the subjects of both countries of the land lying west of the Rocky Mountains] was considered as a final disposition of Mr. Bagot's objections" (*Alaska Boundary Tribunal*, II, App. 55).

6The occupation of Fort Ross was the work of the company and could, as a last resort, be disavowed. The persistence with which the post was retained, is a pretty good indication that the government countenanced such retention and would ultimately turn it to account. Muraviev is authority for the statement that in 1823 the government had refused the company's request to take over California (Ivan Barsukov, *Graf Nikolai Nikolaevich Muraviev-Amurskii*, Moscow, 1891, I, 321).

7The instructions to this commission, the negotiations, and the convention finally agreed on are to be found in *American State Papers, Foreign Relations*, IV, 370-406.

8Ibid., 623-4. The Treaty with Spain provides in Article 3: "The United States hereby cedes to His Catholic Majesty, and renounces forever all the rights, claims, and pretensions to the territories lying west and south of the said line; and in like manner, His Catholic Majesty cedes to the United States all his rights, claims and pretensions to any territories east and north of the said line, and, for himself, his heirs, and successors, renounces all claim to the said territories forever." This somewhat indefinite provision would not seem to be of much value as a title deed to any special tract of land. It was, however, later invoked by Adams in his despatch to Rush, July 22, 1823 (ibid., V, 446), but was never regarded as other than the lawyer's formula "or in the alternative."

[9]*Polnoe Sobranie*, XXXVI, Text 27,906, decree of July 31, 1819.

[10]Ibid., XXXVII, Text 28,747. An English translation containing the essential parts is to be found in *Alaska Boundary Tribunal*, II, App. 25, 26.

[11]*Polnoe Sobranie*, XXXVII, Text 28,756, and *Alaska Boundary Tribunal*, II, App. 27. The word industry (in the sense of craft) is a direct translation of the Russian word "promysl"--a general term applied to hunting, trapping, and fishing. The word "promyshlenniki"--literally craftsmen--are those who carry on such crafts or "industries."

[12]The Russian government, pending a peaceful settlement wisely decided not to enforce the rules. See footnote 20.

[13]Later moved to Verona.

[14]Named plenipotentiary to take the place of Castlereagh who had just died.

[15]*Alaska Boundary Tribunal*, II, App. 120-1, Despatch of Mr. Stratford Canning to Mr. George Canning, dated Washington, May 3, 1823 (received June 12).

[16]Ibid., App. 123-4, Despatch of Mr. George Canning to Sir Charles Bagot, July 12, 1823.

[17]*Fur Seal Arbitration, Proceedings of Tribunal of Arbitration convened at Paris* (Washington, Government Printing Office, 1895, 53-2, Sen. Doc. 177, Ser. 3166), part 4, IV, 407-81, Despatch of Sir Charles Bagot to Mr. George Canning, August 19/31, 1823 (received September 23).

[18]Preliminary because neither the American nor the Russian plenipotentiaries had received their powers. Middleton's did not arrive till October, 1823; those of Nesselrode and Poletika were not issued till 1824.

[19]Bagot Papers, II, part 3, Letters from Sir Charles Bagot to Mr. George Canning, March 22, June 2, and August 31, 1823. The direct quotation is from the letter of August 31.

The Public Archives of Canada have copies of the private correspondence of Sir Charles Bagot with Canning, carried on while Ambassador at Washington and St. Petersburg.

[20]*Alaska Boundary Tribunal*, II, App. 126, Despatch Sir Charles Bagot to Mr. George Canning, August 19/31, 1823 (received September 23). These negotiations touched not so much on the offending provisions of the ukase with regard to the exclusions of foreign (i.e., non-Russian) shipping, as on their enforcement. To render the atmosphere more favorable for negotiations on this delicate matter, the Russian government agreed for the time being not to attempt to enforce the offending clauses without, however, withdrawing the ukase. Much the same information had been conveyed indirectly to the English. See despatch of Middleton to Adams, August 8, 1822, giving account of the former's interview with Capodistrias and the enclosures, letter addressed to Nesselrode (July 27) and the reply (August 1). In his letter to Nesselrode Middleton calls himself "envoy extraordinary and minister plenipotentiary" although his powers were not received

till a year later (ibid., App. 42-6).

The same assurance was conveyed to the United States government on his arrival in Washington. See Despatch of Nesselrode to Tuyll, July 13 (o.s.), 1822, "Correspondence of the Russian Ministers in Washington, 1818-1825," *American Historical Review* 18 (Jan. 1913): 335-44.

[21]*Alaska Boundary Tribunal*, II, App. 126, Despatch of Sir Charles Bagot to Mr. George Canning, August 19/31, 1823 (received September 23).

[22]Ibid.

[23]Ibid., App. 124.

[24]Bagot Papers, II, part 3, Letter from Sir Charles Bagot to Mr. George Canning, October 5, 1823.

[25]Conveyed in his despatch of May 3, 1823. See footnote 15.

[26]*Alaska Boundary Tribunal*, II, App. 129-30. Confidential despatch from Sir Charles Bagot to Mr. George Canning, October 17/29, 1823.

[27]Bagot Papers, Correspondence Foreign Office, Document dated January 13, (1824--in pencil). Probably a minute drawn up by a clerk to serve as a basis for instructions to Sir Charles Bagot.

[28]Richard Rush, *Memoranda of a Residence at the Court of London* (Philadelphia, 1845), p. 390.

[29]Ibid., p. 399.

[30]The United States had already agreed to recognize the new governments.

[31]The circumstances of the famous interview and of the subsequent correspondence is recounted in Rush, *Memoranda*, 467-9.

[32]*American State Papers, Foreign Relations*, V, 246, Message of the President of the United States at the commencement of the 1st Session of the Eighteenth Congress, December 2, 1823.

[33]*Alaska Boundary Tribunal*, II, App. 52, Despatch of Mr. Adams to Mr. Rush, July 22, 1823.

[34]Ibid., App. 144-9, Despatch of Mr. George Canning to Sir Charles Bagot, January 15, 1824.

[35]Ibid.

[36]Stratford Canning had on Christmas Eve, 1823, warned the Foreign Secretary that of the two matters at issue with Russia the maritime could not be adjusted without settling the territorial. To achieve the latter, a prior understanding must be reached with the United States.

He opposed the tri-partite agreement which Canning was considering and strongly recommended coming to terms with the United States essential to a satisfactory settlement with Russia, emphasizing the paramountcy of England's interest in the region of the Columbia River over those to the north. "Is it not primarily by contracting our claws to the north we may hope to obtain a permanent share in the possession of the great wealth of the Columbia"? Canning failed to take this good advice and by attempting to settle with Russia without coming to a prior understanding with the United States, suffered a diplomatic defeat. See Bagot Papers, Correspondence regarding the Russian ukase of 1821, 48, Letter of Mr. Stratford Canning to Mr. George Canning, December 24, 1823, Berkeley Square.

[37]*American State Papers, Foreign Relations*, V, 445-6.

[38]*Alaska Boundary Tribunal*, II, App. 47-51, Letter of Adams to Middleton, July 22, 1823.

[39]Bagot Papers, II, Part 3, Letter of Sir Charles Bagot to Mr. George Canning, February 17, 1824.

[40]Ibid., Letter of Sir Charles Bagot to Mr. George Canning, February 28, 1824.

[41]*Alaska Boundary Tribunal*, II App. 70-1, Despatch from Middleton to Adams, April 7/19, 1824. It is questionable whether Middleton's statement is true. For specific terms of the convention see *American State Papers, Foreign Relations*, IV, 406, footnote 8.

[42]This does not seem to have been lost on Canning, for he wrote: "It does not seem very uncharitable to suppose that the object of the United States in making a selection, otherwise wholly arbitrary, of these two points of limitation for British dominion, was to avoid collision with Russia themselves, and to gratify Russia at the expense of Great Britain" (*Alaska Boundary Tribunal*, II, App. 146, Despatch of Mr. George Canning to Sir Charles Bagot, January 15, 1824).

[43]The boundary was set at 54° 40' instead of 55° since the latter would have cut Prince of Wales Island. It seemed preferable to assign to Russia the whole of the island to do which it was necessary to fix the boundary so that it would pass south of the southern extremity (*American State Papers, Foreign Relations*, V, 459, 465; *Alaska Boundary Tribunal*, II, App. 161).

[44]The Russian stand was in flat contradiction of the principle of "mutual convenience" which they had accepted. Logic perhaps was against them but the facts were with them. The United States having conceded this boundary, there was no alternative for Britain but to follow suit. The arguments are to be found in the letter of M. Poletika to Count Nesselrode, November 3, 1823 (o.s.) (*Alaska Boundary Tribunal*, II, App. 141) and in the letter from Count Nesselrode to Count Lieven, April 5/17 (ibid., App. 173-5).

[45]This first proposal of Bagot had been made during his preliminary discussions with Poletika at a conference apparently on October 2, 1823. The line would run through Cross Sound and up Lynn Canal and then north along the 135th meridian of longitude, the head of Lynn Canal being slightly west of this meridian. It, of course, had no official validity and was presumably disavowed by Canning to permit Novo-Arkhangel'sk (Sitka) to be given to Russia (ibid., App. 129-31, Letter (confidential) from Sir Charles Bagot to Mr. George Canning, October 17/29, 1823; Letter from M. Poletika to Count Nesselrode, with English translation, November 3 (o.s.), 1823 (received November 7/19, 1823), 132-42; also ibid., U. S. Atlas, Map 3.

[46]The various stages in the negotiations of Bagot with the Russian plenipotentiaries are set forth in a despatch of March 17/29 from St. Petersburg and received in London, April 13 (ibid., II, App. 153-7). See also ibid, U.S. Atlas, Map 3, for various British proposals.

[47]This argument that such a strip was necessary to bar the progress of the Hudson's Bay Company was advanced by Count de Lambert appointed to represent the Russian American Company in a conference with Poletika (ibid., II, 137-8, Letter of M. Poletika to Count Nesselrode, November 3, 1823).

[48]Counter draft by the Russian plenipotentiaries (date as shown in the Russian archives, 12/24 February, 1824) enclosed in a letter from Sir Charles Bagot to Mr. George Canning, March 17/29, 1824 (Ibid., II, App. 158).

The width of this "lisiere" as conceived by the Russian American

Company was somewhat vague. Admiral Mordvinov claimed for Russia everything up to the Rocky Mountains. Letter of Admiral Mordvinov to Count Nesselrode, 20 February, 3 March, 1824 (ibid., App. 152).

[49]Bagot Papers, II, part 3, Letter from Sir Charles Bagot to Mr. George Canning, March 29, 1824.

[50]This was not an afterthought on Nesselrode's part. He had written to Tuyll from Verona, December 2/14, 1822, that "by the convention of 1818 the territories adjacent to ours are to belong to both England and the United States for ten years" "Letter of Nesselrode to Tuyll" *American Historical Review* 18 (Jan., 1913): 335-44.

[51]*Alaska Boundary Tribunal*, II, App. 172-5, Despatch from Count Nesselrode to Count Lieven, April 5/17, 1824. The fallacy of advancing an extravagant claim and later to cite readiness to yield as proof of a conciliatory spirit was not lost on Bagot. See above private letter from Bagot to Canning. The subtle suggestion with regard to Oregon shows how cleverly Nesselrode played the two rivals off against one another.

[52]It is probable that this change was due to an unguarded statement of Canning's. The offer had originally been conveyed in the counter draft by the Russian plenipotentiaries, February 12/24, 1824 (ibid., App. 158). That Nesselrode had been quite prepared to yield this point is evident from his letter to Lieven on April 5/17, 1824, cited above. But in writing to Count Lieven on May 29, 1824, Canning had said, "It can hardly be expected that we should not also put in our claim for like privileges of trade as are or may be stipulated with Russia by any other nation" (ibid., App. 180). As the rights of the United States in this regard had been restricted to ten years it seems reasonable to suppose that Nesselrode had taken advantage of Canning's slip.

[53]Bagot Papers, II, part 3, Personal letter from Sir Charles Bagot to Mr. George Canning, August 24, 1824.

[54]*Alaska Boundary Tribunal*, II, App., 212, Letter from Mr. George Canning to Mr. Stratford Canning, December 8, 1824.

[55]It seems strange that so trifling a matter should have called forth a peevish protest from Lieven. "Even before the receipt of that document, I had made it my duty to remark to the Secretary of State how ungracious the refusal of the English Government" (ibid., App. 230, Letter of Count Lieven to Count Nesselrode, May 8/20, 1825).

[56]This very substantial set-off which ultimately gave Canada what was to be the Klondike goldfields was secured by Canning's tenacity, but was apparently due originally to the prompting of Sir Charles Bagot. As early as March, 1824, Bagot had written: "If by the cession of Prince of Wales Island...some equivalent concession can be obtained in respect of the longitudinal demarcation to the westwards (sic), in the higher latitudes, I may find it advisable to exceed...the letter of your instructions..." (Bagot Papers, II, part 3, Letter of Sir Charles Bagot to Mr. George Canning, March 10, 1824). The suggestion was not lost sight of for we find Lieven noticing "with pleasure that the English Government entirely renounced the demand which it had recently made with regard to fixing upon a degree of longitude farther to the west than the boundary assigned by our court...and that the boundary shall be formed by...the 139th degree of longitude" (*Alaska Boundary Tribunal*, II, App. 186, Despatch from Count Lieven to Count

Nesselrode, July 13/25, 1824, received August 7/19). The omission was made good and, on December 8, Stratford Canning was instructed to require that north of latitude 59° the boundary should be altered from the 139th meridian to the 141st (ibid. App. 211, Letter of Instructions from Mr. George Canning to Mr. Stratford Canning, December 8, 1824).

57John Quincy Adams, *Memoirs*, edited by Charles Francis Adams (Philadelphia, 1874-7), VI, 435 ff. Further light is thrown on this incident by *Bering Sea Tribunal, Fur Seal Arbitration, Proceedings*, VII, 156 and S. B. Okun, *Rossiisko-Amerikanskaya Kompaniya* (The Russian American Company) (Lennigrad, 1939), 108. Two alternative points were suggested as marking the furthest limits of commercial intercourse for U. S. ships--Cross Sound in latitude 57° north or Yakutat Bay, nearly 2° farther north (the latter only if the United States resisted the former). Yakutat Bay was finally decided on (*Alaska Boundary Tribunal*, II, App. 93, Letter of the Minister of Finance to the Board of Directors of the Russian American Company, September 4 (o.s.), 1824, signed by Lieutenant-General Kankrin, Minister of Finance and Yu. Druzhinin, Director [of the company]).

58Ibid., II, App. 222.

59Ibid., II, App. 92, Letter from Middleton to Adams, August 18/30, 1824.

60Floyd, the mover, made no secret of his feelings. The preamble stated that "the Columbia was the only point on the globe where a naval power can reach the East India possessions of our eternal enemy, Great Britain" (H. H. Bancroft, *The History of the Northwest Coast*, 2 vols., San Francisco, 1886, I, 353-4; Annals of Congress, 18th Cong., 2nd Sess., 14-27, 36-61). In his message to Congress in 1824 President Monroe actually suggested "the propriety of establishing a military post at the mouth of the Columbia or at some other point in that quarter within our acknowledged limits" (*American State Papers, Foreign Relations*, V, 358).

61This was the extreme limit of the concession granted in 1798 when the government sanctioned the merger of the rival companies in the North American trade. The charter of 1799, however, carried the boundary forward 3 1/2°. The so-called Act of Union, August 5, 1798, is given in Polnoe Sobranie, 1799, Text 19,030; an English translation of the first chapter is in *Alaska Boundary Tribunal*, II, App. 23. The claim to the American coast as far south as 55° north latitude appeared first in the time of Catherine and was advanced by Muller by virtue of Chirikov's discovery. See *Doklad Komiteta ob Ustroistvye Russkikh Amerikanskikh Kolonii* (2 vols., St. Petersburg, 1863), I, App. 279.

62Records of the Russian American Company, Instructions from the Board of Directors, St. Petersburg to the Governor of the Colonies (Baranov), April 18, 1802. These records of the Russian American Company's Sitka office consist for the most part of correspondence exchanged between the Directors at St. Petersburg and the Governor of the colonies at Sitka (or Novo-Arkhangel'sk). They were handed over to the United States by the terms of the Treaty of Cession of March 30, 1867. They remained for years in the custody of the State Department but are now in the National Archives. Files for the years 1802 (except for one or two communications) to 1817 are missing.

63Baranov's views are given in a letter on Kodiak to Larionov at

Unalaska, March 3, 1798, given in P. Tikhmenev, *Istoricheskoe obozrenie obrazovaniya Ross. Am. Kompanii i dyeistvii eya do nastoyasnago vremeni* (Historical Survey of the Formation of the Russian American Company and its Activity down to the present) (2 vols., St. Petersburg, 1861-3).

[64]Records of the Russian American Company, Letter from the Board of Directors to the Chief Factor of the American Colonies, Muraviev, February 22, 1822.

[65]*Alaska Boundary Tribunal*, II, App. 147, Despatch Mr. George Canning to Sir Charles Bagot, January 15, 1824.

ALEUTS AND RUSSIANS*

Lydia T. Black

Professor Lydia Black of the anthropology department at the University of Alaska Fairbanks has devoted her academic career over the last decade to questions relating to contact between Russians and the Aleut and Eskimo people of Alaska, and to the Russian Orthodox mission in Russian America. A prolific writer and thorough researcher, her studies have opened this particularly rich aspect of Alaska history to students and other scholars and have dispelled many false and damaging myths.

Earning her doctorate at the University of Massachusetts in 1973, Professor Black taught at Providence College, where she headed the anthropology division. She was a visiting professor at the University of Alaska Fairbanks before moving there permanently in 1985. She has published numerous articles on Aleut and Eskimo history and pre-history, and on art and artifacts. Her work on the Orthodox missionary Hiermonk Gideon was published by The Limestone Press in 1987. She edited the Yukon journals of the Aleut Orthodox priest Iakov Netsvetov, published by Limestone in 1984, and helped prepare the Limestone edition of Ioann Veniaminov's *Notes on the Islands of Unalaska District,* also in 1984.

In the article printed here, Professor Black discusses the work of the Orthodox priest Ioann Veniaminov among the Fox Island Aleut, the people of Unalaska and vicinity, in the 1820s. Father Veniaminov is usually credited with developing a Fox Aleut alphabet in which Orthodox liturgical works could be written, a monumental achievement equal to the development of a Cherokee alphabet by the warrior-scholar Sequoyah in 1821. Creation of an alphabet in one's mother-tongue would seem to have profound implications for the preservation of cultural integrity. Black finds that an Aleut headman, Ivan Pan'kov, played a central role in helping Veniaminov in his work of bringing literacy to the islands, a role which Veniaminov did not want forgotten.

---

*This paper was originally presented at the Spring Meeting of the American Ethnological Society, March 31 to April 3, 1976, in Atlanta, Georgia. It was presented at a session entitled "Native American Leaders and Their Relationship to Native Culture." [It first appeared in print in *Arctic Anthropology* 14, no. 1, (1977): 94-107.]

* * *

This paper is about an Aleut chief who lived over 150 years ago, at a time when his people faced one of the most difficult periods in their history: adjustment to a new social, economic and ideological order imposed by invading Russians. Soon after Russian entry into the Aleut area, the Aleuts became converted to Orthodox Christianity. The Orthodox Church became a vehicle for maintenance of group identity and group solidarity, replacing the aboriginal religion. Less well known is the fact that literacy was a concomitant introduction: Aleuts became literate in their own language. I shall attempt to demonstrate that at least in the Fox Islands this change was facilitated by the activity of Ivan Pan'kov, the Aleut chief of Tigal'da Island, and that he was an active participant in the events that made the Orthodox Church in a very deep sense the Aleut Church and Aleut literacy a heritage of the Aleut people.

I am deeply grateful to His Grace, Gregory, Bishop of Sitka and Alaska, for permission to use the original manuscript of Veniaminov's papers and to Father Paul Merculief and his wife Elizabeth, originally from the island of St. George, in whose hospitable home in Kodiak I worked on these manuscripts.

Thanks are also due to Phyllis Nottingham, Librarian, and the entire staff of the State Historical Library at Juneau, Alaska, and to the staff of the Manuscript Division, Library of Congress, Washington, D.C. for unfailing help in locating archival materials which enabled me to piece together the story presented in this article.

I am also indebted to the following persons with whom I have discussed some of the points mentioned in this paper: Dr. William S. Laughlin, Department of Biobehavioral Sciences, University of Connecticut; Rev. Innokentii (Gordon H. Marsh); Dr. Dorothy M. Jones, University of Alaska, Anchorage; Dr. Michael Krauss, Director, Native Languages Program, University of Alaska, Fairbanks; Mrs. Beverly Holmes, Department of Biobehavioral Sciences, University of Connecticut. All generously shared their knowledge, which I have put to use in marshalling my arguments. The interpretations presented here, however, are my own and no one shares any blame for any shortcomings or errors of fact and/or opinion.

The Aleuts, a Native American group inhabiting the Aleutian Islands since prehistoric times, are known in ethnological and anthropological literature primarily as representatives of an ancient population of the Bering land bridge. Very little has been written about the modern Aleuts, and nothing about their recent history. Yet, as of February 1976, there were 3060 registered shareholders in The Aleut Corporation[1] and during the last U.S. Census (1972), 6352 Alaska citizens identified themselves as Aleut.[2]

Reams of paper have been devoted to bemoaning the demise the Aleuts, postulated to have occurred with the Russian invasion of the 18th century:

> Aleuts now might raise potatoes (as many of them did) and cattle (occasionally), but there evidently was not much pride in the new life...The burning of tobacco was no substitute for the inner fire that had gone out of them.[3]

> Today there are fewer than 800 Aleuts left! Furthermore, the decline is continuing despite U.S. Government reports to the contrary. This demise of a race and its culture is a sorry testimonial to our own inability to cope with complex factors that are responsible for such a tragedy...Today only a few older Aleuts remember any details concerning the former customs and beliefs of their people. Young Aleuts seldom even express an interest in the past. In another thirty or fifty years, it will be too late to look for Aleut informants, or to help them.[4]

It is true that in the course of the last two centuries Aleut culture has changed. Aleuts are predominantly members of the Orthodox branch of the Christian Church, are participants in the modern economic and political order, and have been *literate in their own language for over 150 years.* The Aleuts are concerned with their heritage; they take great pride in their literary legacy.[5] As far as the alleged lack of interest in history is concerned, the problem may lie not among the "young Aleuts" but among the investigators who look for the wrong kind of history--a history that is no longer pertinent to the Aleuts.[6] Aleuts want to know about themselves as people--about their ancestors and about their political and spiritual leaders. They want to know about persons and the events in which these persons acted. Most Aleut tradition which relates the events of the recent past remains to be published. I have recently begun to focus on information about the conversion of the Aleuts to Christianity and the creation of Aleut literacy, although this was originally tangential to my research interests.[7] Gradually, I formed a mental picture of several Aleut leaders who were active at various times in the last two centuries. One man stands out, and it is clear that his role in the conversion process and in creation of Aleut literacy was very important. He was a close associate of the great missionary priest Ioann Veniaminov (Innokentii),[8] and because of this association, his life can be reconstructed from the records in considerable detail.

The name of this Aleut leader was Ivan Pan'kov. Specialists know him as Veniaminov's collaborator in the translation of various Church publications into the Aleut language. I assert that he was much more than that: that it was through his efforts that the literacy "took hold" and spread fast, and that the new faith grew to be identified as the "Aleut faith" or "Aleut Church" by Aleuts and non-Aleuts alike.[9] I believe that the rapid change in the realm of ideology and spiritual culture, which occurred in less than half a century, was the direct result of support by influential Aleut leaders of the time.[10]

Veniaminov came to the Aleutians from Irkutsk. He accepted the Bishop's call for missionary duty after a meeting with Ivan Kriukov--a Russian settler in the Fox Islands. Ivan Kriukov, an "Old Voyager"--that is, someone who participated in the early Russian exploration and exploitation of the Aleutians prior to the establishment of Russian-American Company in 1799--spent over 40 years in the islands, and was married to an Aleutian woman, presumably of Umnak Island. He was probably the founder of the first chapel in the Fox Islands (St. Nicholas at the Village of Nikol'ski) in 1806. His son, Stefan Kriukov, built the new chapel in 1826-28 and was the manager of the Russian American Company at Umnak. He was also in charge of sealing operations in the Pribilofs. Both father and son presumably were the leaders in the local "Church."[11] Later, in his old age, the son, Stefan Kriukov, is styled in various records as the Chief of Nikol'ski. To this day, direct descendants hold both the offices of lay readers and chiefs. Ivan Kriukov passionately pleaded with Veniaminov to come to the Aleutians. Veniaminov responded.[12] He came, accompanied by his wife Katherine, three small children (the then youngest was born *en route* at Sitka; four more were born to the Veniaminovs at Unalaska), his brother Stefan, aged 18, who was later to marry an Unalaska girl, and his aged mother Fekla. At the time of his arrival, Veniaminov was 27 years old. Though he began the study of the Aleut language while on the way to the Aleutians (at Sitka), he did not speak it. However, he planned to establish a school for the Aleuts to be conducted both in Aleut and Russian. This he accomplished, and the school continued to exist in accordance with the lines he laid down until the middle 1920s.

At the time of Veniaminov's arrival in the Aleutians, Ivan Pan'kov was 46 years old, so that a birth date of 1778 may be postulated.[13] He was married[14] and had children, among them at least one adult son, Semen,[15] and possibly others.[16]

Ivan Pan'kov was at that time the chief *(toion)*[17] of the Island of Tigal'da, one of the most populous Fox Islands at the time, which together with the island of Akun accounted for a large proportion of Aleut population in the District.[18] He apparently was influential as far as the Alaska Peninsula and the Shumagin Islands. Only a generation earlier, in the 1760s, the Krenitzyn Islands, notably Akutan, Akun and Tigal'da, provided the leadership and organizational talent for Aleut "war" against the Russian intruders.[19] Aleut tradition records that the Akun and Tigal'da chiefs, famed throughout the archipelago, ruled with an iron hand.[20]

There is no question that Pan'kov was an important leader of the Aleut community. Moreover, he also acted as the representative of the Russian American Company in the area where there were no Russian settlers.[21] He was well known to the General Management of the Russian American Company in St. Petersburg.[22] His rank in the community, however, may be judged on the basis of more direct evidence. On August 1, 1824,[23] immediately upon arrival, Veniaminov was presented, by his parishioners-to-be, a written address and a sum of money, designed to ease his adjustment in the unfamiliar situation and to help him establish his household.[24] Two hundred three persons donated.[25] The list is headed by Rodion Petrovsky, the General Manager of the Russian American Company of the District, who gave the largest donation of 30.00 rubles, and Semen Petelin, company clerk, who gave the second largest donation of 15.00 rubles.[26] Stefan Kriukov (see previous discussion regarding his status in the Aleut community of the time) also gave 15.00 rubles. Five Aleut *toions* are listed as contributors. The minimum contribution was 1.00 ruble; the average was 4.36 rubles; very few contributions, by Russians or Aleuts, exceeded 5.00 rubles. Of the five Aleut *toions* who contributed, only one, Vassilii Davydov of Umnak, contributed 10.00 rubles. Other *toions* donated in the range from 2.00 to 3.00 rubles. Ivan Pan'kov gave 11.00 rubles and his son Semen 10.00 rubles, well in excess of other *toions* and Russian settlers. Four other Pan'kovs contributed 11.00 rubles total and a Cherepanov, for whom a link to the Pan'kovs may be postulated (see below), gave a donation of 7.00 rubles--well above the average.

Ivan Pan'kov was bilingual and literate. He knew and understood Orthodox theology. There is evidence that he preached Orthodox tenets to the Aleuts on his own.[27] The entry in Veniaminov's journal for April 24, 1828 reads: "Though there is no need to reiterate the story of the reception of myself and of my teachings by the Aleuts, as it would only constitute useless repetition, I cannot omit to mention the inhabitants of the islands I just visited [The Krenitzyn islands are meant here. L.B.]. They are very diligent and attentive to the word of God and appreciative of instruction. I must witness, though, to the work of Ivan Pan'kov. He instructs the most respected men in Christian Law on many feast days. This they told me themselves."

Toward the end of his life, Pan'kov was instrumental in the establishment of two chapels, one built in 1842 on the island of Akun and consecrated to the Assumption of the Holy Mother of God in 1843, and one on Tigal'da, built and consecrated in 1844 in the name of St. Ioann (John) Lestvinnik.[28] According to the Annual Reports on the Status of the Church,[29] these chapels were "created by the care, effort and diligence" of Toion Ivan Pan'kov. The same documents note that these chapels were constructed by Aleut workmen, that the services were conducted by laymen, and that the iconostasies (the altar screens) were of "fine Aleut workmanship." There is some indication that these chapels might have been located at or near places sacred to the Aleuts in pre-contact times.

Ivan Pan'kov died presumably near the end of the decade or possibly in the beginning of the next, certainly prior to 1855.[30] Until the 1880s his descendants seemed to be important in Aleut affairs.[31] Today, to my knowledge, the name Pan'kov does not appear on the rolls of the shareholders in the Aleut Corporation, though several descendants linked to the Pan'kov family through women still are resident in the islands.[32]

It is not known when Veniaminov and Ivan Pan'kov met for the first time or under what circumstances the meeting occurred. Nothing indicates the impression the meeting must have left on both men. It is apparent, however, that their association began not too long after Veniaminov's arrival in the islands, continued until his departure ten years later and probably was not forgotten when Veniaminov became Bishop of the Aleutians. The character of this association may be deduced on the basis of frequent references in the documents; it is clear that in Veniaminov's communication with the Aleuts, be it propagation of the Word of God, discussions with the "knowledgeable men," visits to remote areas of his parish, or simply a "celebration," Pan'kov was Veniaminov's constant companion, mentor, guide, interpreter and sponsor. Often they traveled together. There are mentions of trips in *baidarka* (the kayak) or on foot, of treks across mountains, overnights on deserted islands; sometimes danger and privation, and sometimes pleasure. One can only surmise the conversations carried on and the relationship that must have grown between the older Aleut and much younger Russian.[33]

It is pertinent, at this point, to reiterate the fact that Pan'kov was literate and knowledgeable in the tenets of the Orthodox faith. The question then arises: when and how did he gain this knowledge? The official record is silent, but inferences are possible. Of the several possible explanations, I think the most likely relates to Pan'kov's father, Gavriil Pan'kov, who, judging by his name of record, was already baptized a Christian. We must look at the events that took place in the lifetime of the previous generation, in the early Russian-Aleut contact situation, and at the identity and character of the individual Russian *promyshlenniki*.[34] Some of them--Glotov, Druzhinin, Soloviev--are well known to historians and to the Aleuts; they are associated with the brutal breaking of the Aleut resistance to the Russian invasion. Such men are detested by the Aleuts. The role of some (e.g., Glotov, Korovin) is ambivalent. The names of others either have passed out of history, or are known only to specialists, but many survive as the surnames of modern Aleuts. Careful attention to historical detail, Aleut traditions, and localization of surnames in the islands permit us to postulate certain activities of the individual *promyshlenniki* in the islands. There is no doubt that some of the *promyshlenniki* established and maintained cordial relations with the Aleuts; still others settled among them. (It is even possible that in the conflicts that raged in the 1760s some of the *promyshlenniki* might have aided the Aleuts.)[35]

I suggest that two of the *promyshlenniki*, Merchant Stefan Cherepanov and Navigator Dimitrii Pan'kov might have belonged to the latter class; that the two were familiar with, and at various times called to, the Krenitzyn Islands; and that both men formed personal links with some Aleuts in that area. It is notable that the names Pan'kov and Cherepanov have been localized in the Krenitzyn Islands. Members of the Cherepanov family still reside on the island of Akutan and are very influential members of that community.

There is a record of two voyages by Stefan Cherepanov (1759 to 1762 and 1768 to 1773) and of three by Dimitrii Pan'kov (1758 to 1763; 1770 to 1774; 1780 to 1786). However, this record does not indicate the total time spent by the men in the islands. Many a man who outfitted a ship or became skipper, so that his name appears in the historical record, first sailed as a member of the crew. If financial success may be taken as an indication of diplomatic skill, Cherepanov and Pan'kov were, indeed, first rate diplomats: in the years when their fellow hunters were attacked by the Aleuts, their ships burned and the crews killed throughout all the Fox Islands, from Unimak to the Four Mountains, Cherepanov and Pan'kov, operating in the same area, brought home the richest cargoes, and there are no published reports of encountered violence.[36] Cherepanov's report (giving his location as Andreanof Islands) indicates that his relations with the Aleuts were good, that he was sympathetic to Aleut religious expressions and that through spontaneous sharing of food at meals with Aleuts who happened to come by at such times, he and his crew came to be considered "kinsmen by affinity."[37] Similar conduct could be postulated for Cherepanov when he hunted in other areas. Pan'kov, of course, reached Unimak on his first voyage, and is credited with the discovery of that island by Russian historians.[38] He operated in the Fox Islands and in the Krenitzyns in the years 1761 to 1763--the years when Druzhinin, Medvedev, Korovin and others suffered gravely. It is known that at least once D. Pan'kov and S. Cherepanov became partners: they joined forces on Pan'kov's second voyage (1770 to 1774).

It is well known, too, that some *promyshlenniki* acted as missionaries, and many administered baptism (in Orthodox religion laymen may baptize). As a rule, the newly baptized Aleut was given a Christian name (quite often the name of the saint whose feast fell on that day) and the surname of the Russian who stood as his sponsor--as godfather. Further, apparently on the basis of such ritual link, economic partnerships were created. It is well within the realm of probability that Navigator Dimitrii Pan'kov formed such a relationship with either Ivan Pan'kov's father Gavriil or one of his senior kinsmen. If Pan'kov, like his friend and partner Cherepanov, was a religious man, he would have taken his role as godfather very seriously indeed.

In Russian ideology, godparents are responsible for spiritual and educational needs of their godchildren. This obligation would extend to the children of an Aleut with whom such a ritual connection was formed. It is possible to postulate that Pan'kov urged education of Gavriil's son and that he (or another skipper whom Gavriil trusted) was charged with the supervision of Ivan's schooling. Ivan, who at the time of the conclusion of Pan'kov's last voyage of record in 1786 would have been about eight years old, probably was taken to Russia.[39]

I see, then, a very small Aleut boy, possibly a hostage, perhaps a godson, taken on a Russian ship to one of the ports on the Pacific and possibly traveling to a Russian town. I see him sent to school, surely at his sponsor's expense, perhaps living in his sponsor's household, a literate and religious household.[40] I see a young man returning to the islands to assume his position in the Aleut social order as chief or chief-to-be, trying to make sense out of his experience in two different and conflicting worlds. And I see a mature man seizing the opportunity, provided by his meeting with Veniaminov, to reconcile these worlds. Did Pan'kov discern the parallels in the Aleut and Russian world view?[41] Did he discuss them with Veniaminov? This we shall never know, but we do know that Pan'kov engineered a meeting between Veniaminov and an Aleut shaman and that at the end of that meeting, with Pan'kov translating the dialogue, the priest proclaimed the shaman a Man of God. I shall let the words of Veniaminov speak for themselves.[42]

> By nature and upbringing I am very far from believing various superstitions and still less inclined to invent false miracles. Yet, I have no wish to hide from your Grace anything, including my weaknesses, and therefore I want to appraise Your Grace of the following occurrence, which is not impossible, as the ways of the Lord are unfathomable and the strength of His mercy does not diminish, but nevertheless an event most rare and unheard of in these our times.
>
> During my stay in April of 1828 on the island of Akun and the other three islands belonging to the former, I learned through the interpreter Ivan Pan'kov that the resident of the village Recheshnoye on the island of Akun, on its SE side, about 10 *versts* [a *verst* is equal to 1.0668 km. or 0.6629 miles. 500 sazhen' make up one *verst*. (*Sovetskaia Entsiklopediia*, 3rd ed.) L.B.] from the main settlement on the island, Ivan

Smirennikov, an old man of about 60 years of age, is regarded by the local inhabitants and by many others as well, as a shaman, not an ordinary person, at least.

1) The wife of the Toion of the village Artelnovskoye, one Fedor Zhirov, on October of 1825 was caught in a fox trap, and her leg was badly hurt. There were no means to help her, and she was expected to die momentarily. The trap hit her at the kneecap by all three iron teeth, about two *vershok* [a *vershok* is equal to 44.45 mm. or approximately 1.75 inches (*loc. cit.*) L.B.] in length. Her kinsmen secretly asked the said old man Smirennikov to cure her. After thinking the matter over, he said that the patient will be well by morning. And, indeed, the woman rose in the morning from her deathbed, and is even now entirely well, not suffering any pain;

2) In the winter of the same year, 1825, the inhabitants of Akun suffered great lack of food, and some of them asked Smirennikov to pray for a whale to be washed ashore. After a short time the old man instructed the people to go to a certain place, where they indeed found a fresh whale carcass--precisely in the spot designated;

3) Last fall I planned to visit Akun, but because of the arrival of state ships from Russia, I had to postpone the trip. Yet, the Akun people sent an escort and all expected my arrival. Only Smirennikov boldly asserted that I would not come that fall, but should be expected next spring. And so it happened, contrary winds did not permit my departure, then the cold weather set in, and I was forced to delay my visit until spring.

There are many additional instances which prove his gift of clairvoyance, but I shall omit them here.

Such tales, confirmed by trustworthy informants, convinced me that I should meet Smirennikov in person and personally inquire how is it that he knows the future and what means does he employ to learn it? He thanked me for my interest and told me the following:

Soon after being baptized by Hieromonk Makarii[43] there appeared to him first one, later two spirits, not to be seen by any other man. The spirits had the appearance of humans, light of face, dressed in white robes and, according to his description, these robes resembled church vestments and were trimmed with rose bands. 1) They told him they were sent to him by God to instruct, teach, and preserve him, and they continued to appear to him for thirty years almost daily. The spirits instructed him in Christian teaching. 2) They granted his requests, and through him requests of others (though pretty seldom); they repeated to him my own teachings and told him not to confess his sins to anyone, listen to my teachings and not to listen to *promyshlenniki*, that is the Russians. Even this very day, as he was *en route*, they appeared and told him that I am calling him and for what reason, and instructed him to tell me all, not to be afraid, that no evil shall befall him.

I asked him, what did he feel when the spirits appeared--sorrow or joy? He said that only if he was conscious of having done something bad did he feel a twinge of conscience, but otherwise he did not experience any fear. Moreover, as the people regard him as shaman, and he does not want to be a shaman, he asked the spirits to leave him alone; the spirits replied that they are not demons and cannot leave him. To his question, why they do not appear to others, the spirits replied that they were so ordered.

It is possible to suppose that this man has heard from me or from somebody else the teaching of our faith he recounted and only for effect or out of vanity invented the appearance of the spirits. Yet, I must state that Aleuts do not fall prey to pride, vanity and empty bragging. Moreover 1) I, when preaching, for the sake of brevity and in order to avoid complications, omitted the story of creation, the fall of angels, of the tree of knowledge of good and evil, of the first murderer, of Noah, Abraham and John the Baptist and usually also the story of the Annunciation of the Birth of Christ. But he, Smirennikov, told me these stories in detail. When I preached, he was the first to confirm the truth of my words in the tone of a person conversant with the Holy Writ; 2) Aleuts who live here, all except the interpreter Pan'kov and very few others, even though they had Faith and prayed prior to my arrival, had little knowledge to whom they pray. Hieromonk Makarii, my predecessor here in 1794 and 1795 did not instruct the people here for lack of any kind of interpreter. It is only very recently that interpreters are on hand and among them Pan'kov is the best and most intelligent. But he, Pan'kov, afraid to fall into error, and having firm faith in the One God, never entered into any conversations with the old man and he also protested and tried to restrain others when they called on the help of Smirennikov. This fact was attested by many Aleuts, and therefore there was no one from whom Smirennikov could have learned in the matters of Church teaching; 3) He himself is illiterate and does not know any Russian; therefore, he could not have read about it and finally, 4) I asked him if I could meet with his protectors--the spirits. He replied that he does not know, but that he will ask. Shortly thereafter, in about an hour, he came and told me their answer: What does he want? Does he consider us demons? If he insists, he can see and converse with us. And then they said something very flattering to me, which I omit here. But I refused the meeting with the spirits. One could ask why did I do so? My answer is that there was no need for me to meet them. Why should I want to see them personally when their teaching is Christian teaching? Out of curiosity, to learn who they are? For this I should ask the blessing of my Archbishop, to avoid the pitfall of error, should I meet those spirits.

All of the above is attested to by Smirennikov under oath, and transmitted by me not word for word but true to the meaning, without additions or omissions. Moreover, the freedom, fearlessness and even pleasure of his discourse, and above all his clean manner of life, convinced me and confirmed me in the conviction that the spirits which appear to this old man (if they appear) are not demons. Demons may sometimes assume the image of Angels of Light, but never for the purpose of instruction, teaching and salvation of human beings, but always for their perdition. As the tree of evil cannot bear the fruit of good, these spirits must be the servants sent to those who seek salvation. Therefore, in order not to weaken (among the people) the faith and hope in the One Omniscient God, I, until I receive instruction from Your Grace, determined to render the following decision: "I see that the spirits which appear to thee are not demons and therefore I instruct thee to listen to their teachings and instructions, as long as these do not contradict the teachings I deliver in the assembly; just tell those who ask your advice about the future and request your help, to address themselves directly to God, as He is common Father to all. I do not forbid thee to cure the sick, but ask thee to tell those thou curest that thou doest so not by thy own powers, but by the power of God and to instruct them to pray diligently and thank the Sole God. I do not forbid thee to teach either, but only instruct thee to confine this teaching to the minors." I told the other Aleuts who were present not to call him a Shaman, not to ask him for favors, but to ask God.

In reporting to you, Your Grace, I deemed it necessary to ask Ivan Pan'kov who translated my words and those of the Old Man Smirennikov, to sign this statement, in witness of the truth of my story and the correctness of his translation. I also requested him to keep this matter secret for the time being. I beg your Grace to let me know if my decision was right and if there is any need for me to meet with the spirits which appear to the old man, and if so, what precautions I should take. If I erred, forgive me.

Signed: Your Grace's Priest Ioann Veniaminov, of the Church of Ascension in Unalashka, June 1828;

Signed: below by interpreter Pan'kov as follows:

To the truth of the words of Priest Ioann Veniaminov and the accuracy of translation of the words of the old man Ivan Smirennikov attests Tigal'da Toion Ivan Pan'kov.

True copy of the original, Tobol'sk, 5 November, 1829.

Strange, indeed, this acceptance of the Aleut shaman on the part of the priest, but not so strange if one considers the implications of his relationship with Ivan Pan'kov: the age differential mentioned previously, the obvious ability to converse on an equal level, the role of Pan'kov as his companion and sponsor in the strange, new Aleut world. When one reads the terse scattered remarks in Veniaminov's official papers one cannot escape the impression that there was trust, friendship, respect. A glimpse is afforded by Veniaminov's letter to Archbishop Michael requesting a reward in recognition of Ivan Pankov's aid. Noteworthy is the suggestion that the most suitable gift for Pan'kov, in his opinion, would be a book:

> I should like to draw your Grace's attention to the diligence of the Toion Ivan Pan'kov in the matters of the propagation of the faith. As you know, he helped me consistently with the catechism. He responded with pleasure to my invitation, and continued to work with me, sometimes at cost and inconvenience to himself. Prior to my visits to the Aleuts under his jurisdiction, he--often, as I was told--on every conceivable occasion taught the Faith to the leading men. Such constant effort deserves recognition, and therefore I ask Your Grace to send at the most pleasing and suitable gift, a book possibly inscribed in your own hand...[44]

By 1828, when Veniaminov went on his first extended visit to the Krenitzyn Islands, the two men were close friends indeed. An escort was sent for Veniaminov from Akun; they traveled in five *baidarkas*--one three-hatch *baidarka* and four two-hatch ones. Throughout the trip Ivan Pan'kov was at his side. It is through Pan'kov that Veniaminov addressed the leading men on Akun,[45] then on Tigal'da (where, as Veniaminov notes, were also assembled the residents of the Island of Ugamak), and on Avatanok, then returning to Akun to celebrate the feast of St. Alexander Nevsky.[46] On April 23, 1828, Veniaminov did not go to the bedside of a dying woman because Pan'kov was not able to come along, having developed trouble in one of his legs. Instead, the ailing person was brought to their camp.[47] It is on this day that Pan'kov arranged the meeting between Veniaminov and the shaman Smirennikov "locally known as a sorcerer,"[48] cited above, and on Akun he was introduced to the old woman who told him the story of Aleut defeat and destruction by Soloviev. Pan'kov must have been very sure of his man to have risked these meetings. Indeed, by that time the two men had shared two years of collaboration on the first book in Aleut--the Catechism--and on the design of Aleut alphabet. By March 1826 the following entry is made in Veniaminov's journal:

> In the beginning of this month arrived the Tigal'da Toion Ivan Pan'kov at my invitation and respectful plea.[49] Together *we* checked my translation of the catechism up to the Creed and began work on further chapters.[50]

And further:

> By Easter *we* finished the work on the catechism, and during Easter checked it over.[51]

That Pan'kov helped Veniaminov with Aleut phonology is clear from Veniaminov's note that in the course of the work on the catechism he corrected the diacritical marks over letters designed to represent sounds of the Aleut language. Thus, Pan'kov participated in the design of the alphabet itself.

By May of 1826 Veniaminov made a clean copy of the catechism and sent it to Archbishop Michael of Irkutsk for submission to the Synod and permission to print. The copy of the catechism was accompanied by a petition signed by several Aleut leading men who understood Russian. The list was headed by the name of Ivan Pan'kov and in the covering letter Veniaminov wrote:

> ...not trusting to my own knowledge I called upon the aid of Toion Ivan Gavriil Pan'kov, the best interpreter in the entire Chain. He is a native born Aleut, but knows Russian language well, speaking it without any accent and he is literate. He is forty nine years of age, lives in a settlement where reside only Aleuts, so that there can be no doubt about his perfect knowledge of his own language. The catechism was translated with his help, but I, not deeming the work yet finished, did the following: I read from this work in Aleut assemblies throughout my voyage through the Eastern part of my parish [Krenitzyn Islands. L.B.]; I discussed the text with the wisest among the Aleuts and solicited their opinions on the merit of the work; they approved the text and expressed the wish to have it...[52]

The letter, the petition and the manuscript were forwarded to St. Petersburg, where on the 19 November 1829, the Synod rejected it. The reason for rejection was the fact that in the meantime a new, abridged catechism was approved in Russia as a text for religious instruction, that is, the Russian text used by Veniaminov as the basis for the first Aleut catechism was superseded. The Synod instructed Veniaminov to proceed immediately with translation of the new text and a copy was sent to him for this purpose. Once again, Veniaminov called on Ivan Pan'kov and by July 1830 the new translation of the catechism, still in use today, was well underway.[53] But this task receives bare mention in Veniaminov's journal of the time, because in the meantime the two men were busy on a matter they considered of much greater significance: they were engaged in the translation of the Gospels into Aleut. This time they worked on Akun, where Veniaminov traveled to join Pan'kov, traveling to that island at least two times, and continued to work into the fall of 1829. Into that period falls the time of most intensive effort, when the Gospel of St. Matthew was translated into the Aleut language. The work did not go on when Pan'kov was absent. Once Veniaminov missed him, and the work had to be postponed until Pan'kov's return. Interruptions, when one of the men was called to attend to his other duties, as for example, when Veniaminov had to visit the sick, were kept to a minimum:

> In response to a call from a sick Aleut who lived at about fifteen *versts*' distance, Pan'kov and I went to him, first traveling in *baidarka*, then on foot, and having administered the rites, we returned immediately to our task.[54]

They began this, what they considered their most important task, on September 10th:

> Having called on the aid of God-the-Word...and this day translated the first two chapters.[55]

It was literally, as Veniaminov tells us in his Journal, the product of "sleepless labor."

> We worked in the following manner: from early morning till nightfall we worked on the translation; evenings, in the assembly of the most intelligent of the Aleut, and in the presence of all those who wished to come, we read aloud what has been translated during that day.[56]

Veniaminov notes that news of their enterprise traveled through the villages and that many Aleuts were coming from outlying settlements to listen and to watch.[57] Toward the end of the task, they worked around the clock:

> We finished at nine o-clock in the morning with the Lord's help, through the prayers of the Holy Apostles and Evangelist Matthew, the translation of this Gospel, to the very end, except two verses: to wit, VII-17 and IX-17. The first we omitted because in the local language there are no names for any items mentioned therein, the second, because the essence of its meaning appears obscure to many. We supplemented instead with verses from other Gospels on the subject of suffering of Our Lord.[58]

On Sunday, October 6th, in Unalaska, a service of thanksgiving was held to mark the completion of the task.[59] A clean copy was made, distributed to several bilingual and literate persons, and then sent to St. Petersburg. After some delays, the first Gospel printed in Aleut was published in 1840. In the Church of the Holy Ascension of Christ in Unalaska is presented a first edition of this work. It is beautifully bound in a silver cover, decorated with miniature icons on enamel insets, and annotated in the hand of Veniaminov marking chapters to be read in the course of the annual ritual cycle. It is today an Aleut treasure. On its title page, as on the title page of the first 1826 catechism, next to the name of Ioann Veniaminov appears the name of "Toion Ivan Pan'kov," an Aleut Chief.

Veniaminov never intended Pan'kov's name to be forgotten. In his "Introduction"' to the Gospels (see edition of 1898 page III), and in the "Introduction" to the *Catechism*, he gives Pan'kov full credit. Without his aid, Veniaminov's message hardly would have been made intelligible to the Aleut so effectively and so soon.

I believe it is no exaggeration to say that Ivan Pan'kov, Chief of Tigal'da, was instrumental in creating Aleut literacy and making Orthodoxy the "Aleut Church."[60]

ENDNOTES

[1]*The Aleutian Current* (Aleut Corporation newsletter), February 1976, 4: 2.

[2]The discrepancy between the enrollment in The Aleut Corporation (established under Alaska Native Claims Settlement Act of 1971) and the U.S. Census Bureau data must be understood in the light of the fact that many Alaskans other than the descendants of the aboriginal occupants of the Aleutian Archipelago *per se*, and some who are technically not eligible for enrollment under the Act, identify themselves as "Aleuts" to outsiders. This problem merits special attention by social anthropologists.

[3]Margaret Lantis, ed., *Ethnohistory in Southwestern Alaska and the Southern Yukon, Method and Content* (Lexington: University of Kentucky Press, 1970), p. 291.

[4]Ted Bank II and R. Williams, "Urgently Needed Research on Aleut Culture," *Bulletin of the International Committee on Urgent Anthropological and Ethnological Research*, No. 17 (Vienna, Austria), p. 7.

[5]The only published work on the importance of Aleut literacy is that by J. E. Ransom. [See Jay Ellis Ransom, "Writing as a Medium of Acculturation among the Aleut," *Southwestern Journal of Anthropology* 1, no. 3 (1945): 333-

344.] Gerald D. Berreman, "Inquiry into Community Integration in an Aleutian Village," *American Anthropologist* 57 (1955): 49-59, noted the importance of Aleut literacy and identified the Orthodox Church as the mechanism of social solidarity in modern times, but treats the subject only in passing. William S. Laughlin and G. H. Marsh, "A New View of the History of the Aleutians," *Arctic* 4, no. 2 (1951): 87, identified the importance of written Aleut for language maintenance and published a sample of printed Aleut. However, their discussion on this point is very brief.

[6]Cf., Joan Chandler, "Anthropologists' Perceptions of U.S. Indians in the Southwest, 1928-1966," paper presented at the 73rd annual meeting of the American Anthropological Association, November 19-24, 1974, Mexico City, for the discussion of the effect on the structure of research design pertaining to the Native Americans of the prevailing ideology held by investigators as to what is and what is not "Indian." Chandler convincingly demonstrates for her area (American Southwest) that groups which early adapted to the Western impact received little or no attention in American anthropology of the late 19th and, until recently, 20th centuries. The Aleut case is most blatant; their very existence is frequently denied.

[7]Several Aleuts asked me to provide precise data on the establishment of the Church of the Holy Ascension of Christ in Unalaska, founded by Veniaminov and considered the "Mother Church" of the Aleutians. Its 150th anniversary is being celebrated in 1975-1976, and recently the Church has been declared a National Historic Landmark (Site).

[8]Ioann Veniaminov (later Innokentii, Bishop, then Archbishop, of Kamchatka, the Kuriles, and the Aleutian Islands, and finally Metropolitan of Moscow and Kolomna, the head of the Russian Orthodox Church) is known world-wide as a scholar and churchman. His authoritative ethnography of the Aleutian peoples, *Zapiski ob ostrovakh Unalashkinskogo otdela* [*Notes from Unalaska District*] (1840, St. Petersburg) has never been superseded. His analysis and command of the Aleut language stands up today as the best extant (Dr. Michael Krauss, Director, Native Language Program, University of Alaska, personal communication). His *Indication of the Way to the Kingdom of Heaven*, originally composed in the Aleut language in 1833 and first published in Aleut in 1840, was translated later into Russian (and in 1952 into English) and is used as an instructional text in Orthodox communities throughout the world.

Veniaminov's parish comprised the Fox Islands, the Krenitzyn Islands (the largest of this group being Akun, Akutan and Tigal'da), the Shumagin Islands, the Alaska Peninsula, and the Pribilof Islands in the Bering Sea. The Andreanof Islands, the Rat and Near Islands (Atkha, Amlia, Adak, Attu etc.), together with the Kommandor Islands (now within the jurisdiction of the USSR) and the Northern Kuriles comprised the Atkha District of the Russian American Company administration and constituted a separate parish. In 1828 Yakov Netzvetov, son of a Russian settler and Atkha Aleut woman, became the first priest of the Atkha district. Netzvetov adapted the texts Veniaminov worked out as well as the alphabet to the Atkha dialect.

[9]Such identification is apparent through perusal of the official reports, travel and memoir literature for the American period (post-1867), and persists to this day (field data 1975 obtained from various residents in Unalaska, and personal communication by Beverly Holmes, formerly a long time resident of the Aleutians).

[10]A role analogous to that of Pan'kov seems to have been played in the Andreanof Islands by Amlia Chief Vassilii Dediukhin (Yakov Netzvetov journals, Alaska Church Collection, Manuscript Division, Library of Congress, Washington, D.C.).

[11]Aleut tradition, Gordon H. Marsh, personal communication.

[12]Ivan P. Barsukov, *Innokentii, Mitropolit Moskovskii i Kolomenskii, po ego sochineniiam, pis'mam i rasskazam sovremennikov* [*Innokentii, Metropolitan of Moscow and Kolomna, as Reflected in His Works, Letters and the Recollections of His Contemporaries*] (Moskva: Synod, 1883).

[13]In various documents Pan'kov's age is given as 46 (in 1824); 48 (for 1828); and 49 (for 1827).

[14]In the index to correspondence in Veniaminov's archive Pan'kov's "marriage case" is listed separately in the register for July 1825, relatively soon after Veniaminov's arrival. See Innokentii (Ioann Veniaminov), *Bumagi* [Papers] (including journals), Ms. holdings, St. Herman Pastoral School, Kodiak, Alaska, Folio 263. [This collection is hereafter cited as *Bumagi*.] It is possible to postulate that Pan'kov was anxious to solemnize and "regularize" his marriage. While baptisms and burial services could be conducted by laymen, marriages could not be, and the rite had to await the presence of a regular consecrated priest. Marriages in those times were solemnized *post factum* and often *en masse*: Veniaminov records up to twenty per day.

[15]Semen's age is given as 39 for 1833, making his year of birth 1794. He became Veniaminov's official interpreter in 1832 (toward the end of the latter's stay in the islands when he had no functional need for an interpreter). This birthdate would account for 16 years' age differential between Ivan Pan'kov and Semen. However, Aleut men married early (between the ages of 16 and 18, when they achieved the status of hunters; William S. Laughlin, personal communication) and a potential chief would have been expected to marry earlier than his peers. That a father/son relationship existed between Ivan and Semen Pan'kov is stated in correspondence between the Priest of Unalaska Sizov (or Sizoy) with the then Bishop Innokentii. Sizoy rejected the aid of the Pan'kovs in the work on Gospel translations. Soon thereafter, this priest was replaced (presumably on further orders of the Bishop Veniaminov) by Innokentii Shaiashnikoff, who was a Fox Island "creole." The gospels Sizoy translated were not published. (Manuscript in Alaska Church Collection.)

[16]In 1824 at least six male adult Pan'kovs were present in the District. In addition to Ivan and Semen, Mitrofan, Luka, Prokopii and Yakov Pan'kov are listed. Their relationship to each other is not known at this time (Innokentii *Bumagi*, Folios 134-135).

[17]*Toion*--a term of Siberian origin, possibly Yakut, applied by the Russians to designate native leadership positions (frequently anglicized as "toyon").

[18]In 1824, of the total Aleut population of 1509 (Innokentii *Bumagi*, Folio 171), the Krenitzyn Islands accounted for 451--a number equaling Unalaska population and far exceeding that of Umnak. It should be kept in mind that Unalaska, by that time, as center of the Russian American Company activities in the Fox Islands and Pribilofs experienced some growth through immigration and resettlement from other areas in the Archipelago.

[19]A. Sokolov, "Expedition to the Aleutian Islands by the Captains Krenitsyn and Levashev, 1764-1769," *Notes on the Hydrographic Department* (St. Petersburg) 10 (1852): 88; A. I. Andreyev, ed., *Russkiie otkrytiia v Tikhom okeane i Severnoi Amerike v XVIII v. Sbornik materialov* [*Russian Discoveries in the Pacific Ocean and North America in the 18th Century. Collection of Materials*] (Moscow-Leningrad: Akademiia Nauk, 1948).

[20]William S. Laughlin, personal communication.

[21]*Bumagi* Folio 359.

[22]*Bumagi*, Folio 276 and 359 verso.

[23]All dates are in Julianic calendar. To translate 19th century dates into Gregorian calendar, 13 days should be added to the date as given.

[24]Russian priests normally received minimal salaries from the Church and were supported mainly through parishioners' contributions. The missionary priests in Alaska constituted an exception in that their salaries, very substantial for the times, were paid by the Russian American Company. Veniaminov was to reject any contribution by his parishioners and to refuse payment for life crisis rites. At the time of his arrival, however, his parishioners' gesture reflected their recognition of the normal situation as well as of the difficulty a person faced in adjusting to life in the Aleutians.

[25]The donors represented fewer than one fifth of the District' s population, including Aleuts, Russians and Creoles (persons who traced their descent to Russian ancestry). Extensive population data are available in Veniaminov's "Papers" (Innokentii *Bumagi*) and in Alaska Church Collection.

[26]Veniaminov's eldest daughter, Katherine, later married Semen Petelin's son (by an Aleut woman), Ivan Petelin. Ivan Petelin, one of the first students in Veniaminov's school in Unalaska, became a priest and served as missionary in the Eskimo area of Alaska.

[27]Innokentii *Bumagi*, Folios 190; 276v.; 359; 360; Ivan P. Barsukov, *Pis'ma Innokentiia, Metropolita Moskovskogo i Kolomenskogo, 1828-1878* [*Letters of Innokentii, Metropolitan of Moscow and Kolomna, 1828-1878*] (St. Petersburg: Synod, 1897-1901), p. 5.

[28]The date of construction of these chapels is interesting. It is the time when Ioann Veniaminov had returned to Alaska as Bishop. Previous to that time, the only chapel in the Eastern Aleutians, aside from the authorized church in Unalaska, was one at Umnak built originally in 1806; a new building was erected in 1826-28 by Stefan Kriukov (see above) according to Veniaminov's design. The

Church administration at that time discouraged what was considered unnecessary proliferation of churches and chapels which could not be staffed by clergy. It was possible to rebuild the chapel at Umnak in 1826 only because Archbishop Michael of Irkutsk, in ruling on Veniaminov's request to permit such construction, while ostensibly prohibiting it, left a carefully constructed loophole for independent local action (Innokentii *Bumagi*, Folio 158). In the 1840s, as Bishop, Veniaminov had the authority to permit chapel and church construction. The name of the saint to whom the Chapel on Tigal'da has been dedicated, is, of course, Veniaminov's (and Pan'kov's) given name.

[29]*Vedomost' o Tserkvi*, Alaska Church Collection, Box 249, 1st set.

[30]Annual Report on the Status of the Church for 1855 lists Tigal'da and Akun chapels as having been built by "the *late* Toion Ivan Pan'kov" (Alaska Church Collection, Box 249, 1st set).

[31]If monetary contributions toward the maintenance of the symbolic system may be taken to indicate relative status. In the 1880s the Aleut community was building the new Church in Unalaska (the present building). The actual construction was carried out under the auspices of the Alaska Commercial Company, but the funds for construction, in very large measure, were donated by the parishioners. Donations, as preferred by the Alaska Commercial Company, were mostly in sea otter skins. The Pan'kovs of Tigal'da contributed several choice pelts. This information is contained in a handwritten ledger, property of Mr. L. Shaishnikoff of Unalaska. The ledger was kept by Mr. Shaishnikoff's kinsman, Vassilii, who at that time was the harbor chief at Unalaska. I am indebted to Mr. Shaishnikoff for showing me the ledger in the summer of 1975.

[32]There are persons bearing the surname Pan'kov living in the Kommandor Islands. They must have moved there sometime in the last decade of the 19th century or at the beginning of the 20th.

[33]Very little of Veniaminov's private correspondence has been published. I doubt that it has survived. Barsukov (1897-1901) apparently selected from Veniaminov's private letters only those addressed to or dealing with affairs of his two children who entered the ecclesiastical life (the younger son became a missionary priest in the Amur region; one daughter entered a convent). Veniaminov's "Journals" in *Bumagi* are not a private diary, but an official record kept for presentation to ecclesiastical superiors. Only occasionally does a personal note creep in.

[34]*Promyshlennik* (plural *promyshlenniki*) is a term which entered American historical literature to designate the Russian commercial fur hunters of the period. The term is largely untranslatable, connotes a hunter, a provider, and a commercial entrepreneur simultaneously.

[35]In this conflict Aleuts used firearms. It is generally assumed that those were captured weapons. I have very tenuous evidence that some might have been acquired by other means. That some *promyshlenniki* aided Aleuts in their own conflicts is mentioned by Veniaminov in his *Notes of Unalaska District*. He states that according to Aleut tradition Glotov wiped out the Four Mountains and adjacent

islands' population on behest of Umnak Aleuts, who were in a conflict of long standing with the former.

[36]R. V. Makarova, *Russkiie na Tikhom okeane vo vtoroi polovine XVIII v.* [*Russians on the Pacific, 1743-1799*] (Moscow: Nauka, 1968), pp. 56-59, 70-71, 79; Vassilii Berkh, *A Chronological History of the Discovery of the Aleutian Islands or the Exploits of Russian Merchants*, trans. Dimitri Krenov, ed. Richard A. Pierce (Kingston, Ont.: The Limestone Press, 1974), p. 21.

[37]Andreyev, *Russkiie otkrytiia.*

[38]Makarova, *Russkiie na Tikhom okeane.*

[39]Since the earliest contact, *promyshlenniki* brought young Aleuts to home ports, and some were educated in Russian schools. Initially, many of these were hostages--*amanats*. As a rule, *amanats* were sons or close kinsmen (male) of the Aleut chiefs and leading men, and the preferred age was from 8 to 14 years. Too young children were difficult to care for; the older teenagers, too dangerous to keep, demanding constant watch. By the 1780s relatively many young Aleuts, sons of leading citizens, were sent by their fathers to Russia for schooling, along with the *amanats*. Moreover, *promyshlenniki* who spent many years on a single voyage, sometimes became personally attached to their small hostages. There is some evidence that occasionally some of these men instructed the Aleut hostages in language and religion. I reject the possibility that Ivan Pan'kov was a Russian hostage in the islands because he, evidently, was relatively well educated and spoke Russian without any trace of an accent--residence in Russia seems much more likely. For the same reason, I reject the possibility that he traveled to Russia as an adult. Hostage status is possible but seems unlikely because of Pan'kov's obvious sympathy for the Russian culture and his loyalty to Orthodoxy. For these reasons I postulate a sponsorship and young age as well as residence in Russia.

[40]Both Cherepanov and Pan'kov were literate men. Cherepanov's report (in Andreyev) was signed in his own hand; Pan'kov's literacy is inferred from the fact that he was a navigator (*shturman* not a *morekhod*), that is, he must have been a graduate of Navigators' School. Cherepanov's piety was referred to earlier and is based on close reading of his report cited above; Pan'kov's attitudes may be only guessed.

[41]The existence of such parallels has been discussed informally by W. S. Laughlin, Gordon Marsh and myself in recent conversations and correspondence. In the summer of 1975, an Aleut informant brought up the subject in conversation.

[42]The letter was published by Barsukov (1897-1901) with the additional commentary indicating that Veniaminov was so impressed by the meeting that he recounted the incident to the then Governor-General Muraviev. In the summer of 1975 I identified a handwritten copy of the original letter in the "Miscellaneous Papers," Russian Church, in the archival holdings of the Alaska Historical Library. This copy was used for the translation offered here.

[43]Hieromonk Makarii, member of the first Orthodox mission (the Kadiak Mission) to Alaska, arrived in the Aleutian Islands in 1795. He traveled widely through the islands, from Unga to the Four Mountains Islands, he baptized many,

without instruction, as he did not speak Aleut, left the island in 1796 accompanied by several important Aleut men, for Irkutsk and hence for St. Petersburg, to present a case against *promyshlenniki's* treatment of the native inhabitants. He perished in the wreck of *Phoenix*, presumably off the coast of Unalaska, in 1799, on his return voyage. See Michael George Kovach, "The Russian Orthodox Church in America" (Ph.D. thesis, University of Pittsburg, 1957), p. 80.

[44] *Bumagi*, Folio 208-209 verso.

[45] Ibid., Folio 359.

[46] It is interesting to note that the chapel on the island of Akutan, the most recent of all Aleut chapels, is dedicated to St. Alexander Nevsky. Akutan was resettled by Aleuts from Akun and other Krenitzyn Islands. One wonders if there is any connection between the first service held in Akun by Veniaminov in 1828 and eventual dedication of the chapel to this saint.

[47] *Bumagi*, Folio 360.

[48] Ibid.

[49] Russian expression used by Veniaminov reads "po moiemu priglasheniiu i moiemu prosheniiu"--the element of supplication is emphasized. The entire tone of the passage is one of respect.

[50] *Bumagi*, Folio 338v; emphasis mine.

[51] Ibid., Folio 340; emphasis mine.

[52] Ibid., June 21, 1827.

[53] The new Aleut version was approved by Synod by 1832. This indicates the speed with which the two friends worked by now, especially if one takes into account the enormous time it took to communicate with St. Petersburg. Four hundred copies were printed by 1837, and sent to Alaska, but printing errors were so numerous that Veniaminov did not deem it fit for distribution. He determined to supervise a new printing himself. The situation was enough to try the patience of the Man of God--and his correspondence indicates the fact. The new corrected edition done under Veniaminov's personal supervision appeared in 1840 and is known under the title *Nachatki Christianskogo Ucheniia ili Kratkaia Sviashchennaya Istoriia i Kratkii Christianskii Katechisis/Beginnings of Christian Teaching or the Short Sacred History and Short Christian Catechism.* No copies of the faulty edition have been located. The original 1826 manuscript survives and is located at the St. Herman Pastoral School, Kodiak, forming part of Veniaminov's *Bumagi*.

[54] *Bumagi*, Folio 378, entry for Monday, September 16, 1829.

[55] Ibid., 377 verso.

[56] Ibid., Folio 378, entry for September 24, 1829.

[57] Ibid., footnote, Folio 378.

[58] Ibid., Folio 378.

[59] Ibid., Folio 379.

[60] That the Church served as the vehicle for maintenance of group identity and group solidarity among the Aleuts has been noticed by several investigators, notably Berreman, "Inquiry into Community Integration" and "A Contemporary

Study of Nikolski, an Aleutian Village" (Master's thesis, University of Oregon, 1953) and Dorothy Jones (personal communication). BIA teachers were aware of the fact, and were, as a rule, hostile to the Church. A notable exception is Phoebe West, "An Educational Program for an Aleut Village" (M.S. thesis, University of Washington, 1938). The best evidence, however, is the negative one originating from persons who economically exploited the region. I cite but from one example of many: Knut B. Birkeland, *The Whalers of Akutan. An Account of Modern Whaling in the Aleutian Islands* (New Haven: Yale University Press, 1926), pp. 79-85:

> It was natural for me to think that the natives would come around looking for jobs, but they did not do so. Evidently they expected us to go to them. I did not know at the time that the Russian system of village administration was so methodically carried out in any part of America as I later found it to be at Akutan.
>
> If anyone is in need of workers from one of the small villages in the Aleutian Islands, he will first have to consult with the village chief, who will call his men together and discuss the matter with them. It is for the members of his council to decide which ones shall go to work and at what wages. Once when we were in need of men I went to the little village of Bjorka, on the island south of Unalaska. I stayed on board the *Kodiak* while the captain went ashore with the interpreter to find out from the chief if any men were to be had. I could see the villagers assembling in consultation, and pretty soon the meeting broke up and everybody went into the church. After a brief service all the able bodied men of the village came on board, ready to start work...
>
> ...At the time the United States bought Alaska, together with the Aleutian Islands, from Russia, the latter reserved a right the scope of which the purchaser probably did not understand at that time. Russia obtained a guarantee from the United States that it would not in any way interfere with the religion or the religious customs and practices of the natives...
>
> After Alaska was deeded to the United States, the priests, as officials of the Russian government, continued to govern the natives in accordance with the orders of Russian government, and pictures of the czar remained over the altars in native churches. The Russian system of village administration could not be interfered with by the United States, because it was part of the religious customs...
>
> ...Until the recent revolution, Russia consistently made use of the privilege which it had reserved at the time of transferring Alaska to the

United States. This made it impossible to do efficient missionary work among the natives, and the same may be said of the attempt to make them learn the English language. These natives call themselves Christians, but it is my opinion that their religion is nothing but plain paganism. They have a number of holy days which are rigorously observed.

[A passage to the effect that drinking accompanies celebration of feast days is omitted. L. B.]

The natives were never able to work much on the day following a celebration, which, of course, interfered considerably with our work at the station. It was especially annoying that they should be celebrating one of their holy days on the other side of the bay when the weather was fine and the whales were coming in regularly; for such a practice greatly hampered the progress of our work. I wondered for some time if we could not eliminate a few of their holy days during the whaling season, making up for lost pleasures during the wintertime....

COLONIAL RUSSIAN AMERICA*

James R. Gibson

In the 1800s control of southern and southwestern Alaska fell to the Russian American Company, a privately owned trading company modeled upon British and French regional monopolies. Created in 1799, the Russian American Company received a twenty-year government charter, and the Russian government renewed this charter twice, one in 1821 and again in 1844. With the second (1821) charter, the government strengthened its ability to oversee the company by requiring that all upper administrative posts in Alaska be filled only by Russian naval officers on detached duty. In theory, therefore, Alaska became a tightly controlled colony, administered by men who answered to the government as well as to the company's board of directors. On paper, the government should have exercised at least as much authority in Alaska as in Siberia, also still a Russian frontier. But geography inevitably played a role, for distance diminished the effectiveness of formal authority.

Siberia had been a fur frontier, as was Alaska. Yet, no single trading company had gained control over Siberia. And Siberia differed from Alaska in many other important ways. James R. Gibson, Professor of Geography at York University, Toronto, Canada, examined many of these differences in a paper originally delivered at a conference in Sitka, Alaska, sponsored by the Kennan Institute for Advanced Russian Studies of the Woodrow Wilson International Center for Scholars and by the American Historical Association.

Gibson received his Ph.D. from the University of Wisconsin-Madison. He is noted for his studies of eastern Siberia and the North Pacific. His major works include *Feeding the Russian Fur Trade: Provisionment of the Okhotsk Seaboard and the Kamchatka Peninsula, 1639-1856* (1969), *Imperial Russia in Frontier America: The Changing Geography of Supply of Russian America, 1784-1867* (1976), and *Farming the Frontier: The Agricultural Opening of the Oregon Country, 1786-1846* (1985). His most recent book is a history of the maritime fur trade along the Pacific Northwest coast. He also serves as an associate editor of *Soviet Geography.*

In the following article, which appeared in *Russia's American Colony,* a compilation of the papers presented at the Sitka conference, Gibson examines numerous differences between Siberia and Alaska. He concludes that these differences explain why Alaska became increasingly untenable for the Russians and why Russia ultimately chose to sell the colony.

---

*This article originally appeared in, *Russia's American Colony*, S. Frederick Starr, ed. (Durham: Duke University Press, 1987), pp. 32-40, 371-374.

* * *

In 1812, as Emperor Napoleon Bonaparte's Grande Armee was nearing Moscow, Collegiate Councillor Ivan Kuskov's motley band was founding Fort Ross on the North American coast in New Albion. This outpost represented the farthest reach of a process of relentless eastward expansion that had been unleashed in 1582, when the renegade cossack Ermak had captured Isker, the capital of the Western Siberian Khanate and the last obstacle in the path of Muscovy's advance to the Pacific.[1] The next formidable obstacle was not encountered until two centuries later on the Northwest Coast of America, where the Russians finally came up against their westward-moving fellow imperialists from Great Britain, Spain, and the United States. Russia's open eastern frontier finally began to close, and with the rise of the United States and Japan as Pacific powers, Russia became as vulnerable to encircling alliances as the leading European states.

Meanwhile, the bulk of the Russian Empire had been won, thanks to the enterprise of a surprisingly small number of cossacks, *promyshlenniki* (trappers), *muzhiki* (peasants), and *meshchane* (townsmen). Largely on their own initiative--because their government was preoccupied with European affairs, and rightly so--these frontiersmen moved rapidly eastward in search of "soft gold."[2] Some sought adventure or solitude, many craved free farmland, others fled conscription or serfdom, and still others were exiled;[3] but initially, at least, the fur trade was the raison d'etre of the Russian occupation of Siberia and Alaska. In the process, the intruders altered the numbers and the mores of the aborigines by introducing their European diseases and spirits, Russian language, Orthodox faith, capitalistic exploitation, authoritarian bureaucracy, and inegalitarian society. And although the native cultures were changed less drastically and less bloodily than in New Spain, New France, or New England, they and their lands were nevertheless unmistakably Russified.

Thus, Russian expansion across Siberia and into America had certain features in common. But in a number of ways the two movements were significantly different. First of all, although both phases of expansion were spawned by the fur trade, in Siberia the sable was king, whereas in Alaska the sea otter reigned supreme.[4] Both were among the most valuable of furbearers. But the sable, a rather solitary and largely nocturnal creature, bears up to five young annually, whereas the "sea beaver," a daytime animal that congregates in large groups, drops only one offspring yearly, and the pelt of the female, moreover, was more valuable than that of her mate. So sea otters were depleted more rapidly than sables, and accordingly Russian occupancy in Alaska was less stable and less lengthy than in Siberia. Also, the sable is a land animal confined to the Siberian taiga. The sea otter, by contrast, is native to the coastal waters of the northern Pacific between Hokkaido and California. This contrast between continental and maritime fur trades--or between what Meinig has termed riverine and coastal empires[5]--was important. While the Russians were accustomed to, and competent in, the acquisition of pelts through tribute, barter, and hunting on land, they were ill-prepared for the maritime milieu of the far North Pacific. Partly for this reason, it took them only sixty-eight years after crossing the Urals to move across Asia and found a permanent port on the Pacific at Okhotsk in 1649, but up to 137 years--twice as long--after reaching the Pacific to move across the Bering Sea and establish a permanent post in America at Captain's Harbor on Unalaska Island in the middle 1770s and at Three Saints Harbor on Kodiak Island in 1784, despite the fact that the latter distance was far less than the former. The uncharted and stormy waters between Siberia and Alaska required ships and sailors and entailed far more risk and expense than land travel.

It was fortunate for the Russians that sea otter fur was even more prized than sable. In 1817, for example, a sea otter skin was worth ten times as much to the Russian American Company as a beaver pelt and forty times as much as a sable pelt.[6] In addition, sables were usually hunted in winter, when their tracks are more evident and their fur is thicker and longer, whereas sea otters were normally hunted in spring and summer, when the North Pacific weather is less inclement. Consequently, farming suffered more from temporal conflict with hunting in Alaska than in Siberia (where, however, there was some spatial clash). Also, the lack of winter hunting in America meant the absence therein of Siberia's *zimov'ia* or winter camps. These were replaced by Aleut hunting parties, which spent several weeks at sea during the warm season under a Russian foreman. *Ostrogi* (forts) were found in both regions but not *reduty* (redoubts, or ungarrisoned stockades) and *odinochki* (one-man posts); these were peculiar to Alaska, undoubtedly because of its shortage of manpower. Furthermore, the Russians had the sea otter trade all to themselves for half a century, and they controlled the habitats of the most valuable varieties of the animal. Great Britain and the United

States did not enter the trade until the late 1780s, long after Bering's second voyage of the early 1740s had launched the Russian enterprise, and they concentrated their hunting on the Californian and Northwest Coast otters, which were less valuable than their better-furred but sorely depleted Aleutian, Kamchatkan, and Kurilian cousins.[7]

Fortunately, too, for the Russians, they controlled the Aleuts, whose skill in the use of kayak and harpoon made them unrivaled as hunters of sea otters.[8] "They are extremely expert in managing their canoes, and...are excellent marksmen with the rifle and spear," noted a Scottish seaman in 1807.[9] These "marine cossacks" managed even to learn European seamanship faster than their Russian conquerors. As a result, the Russians never mastered the chase, and indeed did not themselves do the hunting in America as they had in Siberia. Hence, the Aleuts were more ruthlessly exploited than any aboriginal group had been in Siberia, where the Russians equaled or surpassed the natives as trappers. The Aleuts were virtually enslaved; beginning in 1799 all males between eighteen and fifty years of age had to labor for the Russian American Company. The resultant toll in lives was appalling but not surprising. At least 80 percent of the Aleut population perished during the first and second generations of Russian contact.[10]

The markets for sable and sea otter also differed. Sable pelts were sold mostly in Europe, especially at Moscow and Leipzig as well as in Holland and England, where they were exchanged for a variety of hardware, metals, textiles, beverages, and foodstuffs. By contrast sea otter fur, not as warm as sable and therefore more suitable for trim, was marketed primarily in North China where it commanded higher prices than in European Russia. It became the royal fur of the Middle Kingdom, whose Manchu upper class exerted a strong demand. Although some sable was transacted, it was mainly the lustrous sea otter that enabled Russia to obtain such exotic Oriental commodities as tea, silk, and porcelain. In much the same way, the Americans' shortage of specie towards the end of the eighteenth century made it desirable for them to acquire the same goods by trade in furs.[11] In a very real sense the sea otter trade supported the Russians' tea habit. More important, it facilitated Russian-Chinese contact, commercial and otherwise. The China trade blossomed at a time when Canadian furs were taking the European market away from Siberian furs. The sea otter provided the Russians with a timely response to the Canadian beaver.

The fur trade dominated the economy of Russian America much more than that of Siberia. In 1719, for example, 60 percent of Siberia's Russian male population were peasants,[12] whereas at a roughly comparable stage of development in 1833 probably 90 percent of Alaska's Russian males were fur traders. Already by the eighteenth century agriculture was Siberia's principal economic activity.[13] Mining for gold, silver, copper, lead, and salt, plus smelting, were also important; and some brewing, milling, tanning, glass making, and cloth making were carried on, as were considerable fishing and hunting. But in America the fur trade remained the preeminent occupation. The local market was too small, and foreign markets too distant, to warrant much diversification; it was cheaper to import from European or Asiatic Russia or, better yet, from California or the Oregon Country.[14] Some farming and shipbuilding were attempted, but merely to serve the needs of the fur trade. And they did not prosper.

Little wonder that when the fur trade ended, so did Russian America. Its monolithic economy was simply too vulnerable. And because its maritime economy was less diversified and hence less autonomous than Siberia's, Alaska had to engage in more external commerce, so traffic with New England, the Californias, the Oregon Country, the Sandwich Islands, and occasionally even Chile and the Philippines loomed large. Alaska's trade was even responsible for some of Siberia's commerce, for Russian American sea otters dominated the traffic at Kiakhta.

The more specialized economy of Alaska also meant that it was dominated by one major town. This pattern was commonly exhibited by colonial territories. Novo-Arkhangel'sk (New Archangel), with half of the colony's Russian population and capital assets, was the primary center. The more varied economy of Siberia, however, gave rise to several towns of prominent rank--Tobol'sk, Tiumen', Eniseisk, Irkutsk, and Iakutsk.[15] Thus, in an economic sense Alaska was more "colonial" than Siberia, since its economy was more mercantile, that is, more directed to serving the needs of the mother country than its own.

The American entry into the maritime fur trade of the North Pacific reveals another contrast with the continental business of Siberia. In Siberia, following the defeat of Kuchum Khan, the Russians encountered no serious opposition from the mostly paleolithic natives, who were neither numerous nor united, particularly in the face of Russian firearms. And no foreign power challenged the Muscovite conquest. The two states that could have done so--China and Japan--became isolationistic with the advent of, respectively, the Manchu (Ching) Dynasty (1644-1912) and the Tokugawa Shogunate (1603-1867), just as Russia was advancing across Siberia. But America presented no such power vacuum. At first Russia was unopposed on the Northwest Coast, but soon Spain and then Great Britain and the United States became alarmed, especially when Cook's last voyage revealed that there was something worth competing for in the form of *Enhydra lutris*.[16] By 1800 American and British shipmasters had halted the Russian advance down the coast, undermining its basis by outtrading the tsar's men. Furthermore, the Yankees in particular were not above bartering firearms (including cannons) to the coastal Indians and inciting them against the Russians.[17] The Tlingits even managed to capture the Russian American Company's colonial capital of Novo-Arkhangel'sk in 1802. Indeed, thanks to their bountiful economy and cohesive society as well as to American military aid, the Tlingits resisted Russian encroachment more successfully than any other indigenous group in the course of tsarist eastward expansion, the sole possible exception being the Chukchi. By the middle of the nineteenth century Russia realized that she was overextended in America. In the climate of reform following the disastrous Crimean War she withdrew from the American Northwest and consolidated her position in Asia in the face of burgeoning American power. Alaska thus became the only part of the Russian Empire ever to be relinquished by the tsarist regime.

Nevertheless, expansion into America did--for a while, at least--make Russia more of a maritime power in the Pacific, whereas expansion across Siberia, an Asian land base, gave Russia about one-third of the Asian continent and thereby a vested interest in its affairs. It also brought Russia into contact with China much earlier than other European states. The Treaty of Nerchinsk of 1689, which delineated the Amurian frontier, was the first accord to be signed by the Celestial Empire with a European country. Siberia also brought Russia to the Pacific, albeit precariously, for until the acquisition of Amuria the Russian Far East was a tenuous oceanic foothold.[18] It was not until Russia crossed the Bering Sea to Alaska that she became a full-fledged Pacific power with designs on borderlands like California and archipelagos like Hawaii.[19]

Russia's fledgling navy was bolstered by round-the-world voyages to her American colonies, but it was no match either for the power of Great Britain's naval force or for the acumen of the United States merchant marine. Additional ships were bought and built and more sailors were trained in order to show the flag in the North Pacific arena, make voyages of exploration, trade with maritime nations, and supply the Russian Far East and Russian America.[20] Russian maritime strength in the North Pacific was restricted, however, by the closure of Chinese ports to the tsar's vessels until 1858. Consequently, Russian America marketed its sea otters by land at Kiakhta via the protracted Okhotsk-Iakutsk-Irkutsk route rather than by sea via the more expeditious route from Novo-Arkhangel'sk to Canton.

Russian America also made the Russian Empire more "colonial" to the extent that "colonialism" implies overseas or noncontiguous expansion. This situation did not, of course, apply to Siberia. With the acquisition of Alaska Russia joined the ranks of Great Britain, France, Spain, Holland, and other European colonial powers. But there was a difference. Alaska, unlike Canada, Mexico, or South Africa, was never the object of settlement by numerous colonists from the motherland. Many Russians, particularly serfs, migrated to land-rich and seigneur-free Siberia but few were willing to go as far as America.

Once in America, colonists found a situation that differed militarily from what prevailed in Siberia. In Siberia furs had for a long time been obtained not only by trapping and trading but also by tribute. As a result, cossacks and soldiers had to be stationed there to enforce collection, as well as to suppress the Western Siberian Tatars, repel the Kirgiz in the southern steppe, and guard the Amur frontier against China. In Alaska after 1768 the exaction of tribute was officially banned. Notwithstanding the unruly Tlingits, no nomadic hordes or standing armies threatened the colony's borders, so the military was less prominent than in Siberia.

There were other important differences between Alaska and Siberia stemming from Alaska's more "colonial" nature. The Russian male population of Alaska was 563 in 1833; at a roughly comparable state of development in 1719 Siberia, with nine times as much territory, had 169,000, or 300 times as many.[21]

Females were scarce in Alaska, constituting only 10 percent of its Russian population in 1833.[22] This sexual imbalance prompted many Russian men to take native wives; their offspring, who were called creoles, came to form up to one-fifth of the colonial population, even outnumbering the Russians themselves. An important body of semi-skilled labor, this mixed-blood element was comparable to the metis of Canada and the mestizos of Latin America.[23] Far less intermarriage took place in Siberia than in Alaska. This greater degree of contact in Alaska likely meant a higher native toll from introduced diseases like syphilis, smallpox, and influenza. During the smallpox epidemic of the last half of the 1830s, for example, Alaska's natives suffered a fatality rate of 25 percent.[24]

Few, if any, exiles were sent to America. So many were banished to Siberia, by contrast, that they colored the very name of the region. The general dearth of Russian settlers was one of Russian America's basic weaknesses, for colonization was the surest way to substantiate territorial claims. With the sale of Alaska, Russia was able, in a sense, to escape charges of colonialism, although in fact her colonialism differed from that of other European countries mainly in that it was directed against contiguous territories, namely Transcaucasia and Central Asia, rather than overseas. And no doubt partly because Alaska was not contiguous to the rest of Russia it was considered more expendable than Siberia.

The few Russians who did venture to America distributed themselves in a settlement pattern that differed markedly from Siberia's. The Siberian pattern was linear, with settlements being strung first along rivers, then along tracks, and finally along railway lines; the main sites for settlement were commonly native villages, arterial portages, and transportation junctions. In Alaska the pattern was likewise linear, but strictly coastal. The usual sites of posts were promontories (*kekury*) at the mouths of rivers or at the heads of bays. Such were the locational requirements of the sea otter and fur seal business and of marine transport. Few settlements were found inland, which was neglected by the Russians (with the exceptions of the lower reaches of the Yukon and Kuskokwim Rivers). This neglect further weakened their tenure, which remained marginal, literally and figuratively.

Missionary activity may have been greater in America than in Siberia. The church's missionary activity increased in post-Petrine Russia,[25] just as expansion to America occurred. The success of Catholic missionaries in the New World also provided a stimulus. The relative vigor of Orthodox mission work in Alaska was due particularly to the extraordinary work of one man, Ivan Veniaminov

(1797-1879), whose untiring and versatile efforts earned him the unofficial title of "apostle of Alaska" and the official title of Metropolitan of Moscow and Kolomna, the Russian Orthodox church's second highest office. Veniaminov's American mission still exists.

A further contrast is significant. In Siberia furs, tusks, gems, and other natural products were obtained by a host of individuals and companies competing against each other. Not so in Russian America, where no individual entrepreneur could afford the expense of acquiring, outfitting, and manning a ship for a voyage of several years. As the sea otters receded farther eastward and southward, voyages became longer and riskier, costs rose, and returns fell. Competition became viciously keen, occasionally erupting into warfare, which occurred mainly at the expense of the hapless Aleuts.[26] The government was eventually obliged to intervene in order to keep the peace and save the trade, particularly in the face of increasing international contact on the Northwest Coast. The result was the formation in 1799 of the Russian American Company, which the Russian government empowered to administer and exploit Alaska.[27] Despite a number of able governors, the joint-stock monopoly soon became stodgy and cautious, disabilities that weakened its capacity to compete with American and British traders. Another monopoly, the Hudson's Bay Company, fared much better against the Americans, so perhaps Russian entrepreneurial backwardness was more at fault than monopolistic privilege per se. In any event, these were shortcomings that the Russians in America could ill afford in view of their other difficulties.

Perhaps the most crucial of these additional problems was supply. Provisioning was relatively simple in Siberia for several reasons. First, more of the land was arable, especially in the steppe of western Siberia, with its virgin *chernozem*. Second, the warmer and drier climate of Siberia was better for crops and livestock. Third, some of the native groups (such as the Tatars, Buriats, and Iakuts) were at a relatively advanced technological level, high enough, at least, to practice farming and therefore enabling the Russians to use them as sources of provisions. Fourth, Siberia was, of course, much closer to European Russia and its pool of personnel and materiel. The situation was much worse in Alaska, with its rocky and hilly terrain, cool and damp climate year round, nonagricultural indigenes, and extreme remoteness from the Russian heartland. That the environment was rich in fish and, to a lesser extent, timber merely alleviated rather than resolved the supply problem. The Russians perforce turned to American skippers, Californian missionaries, and Hudson's Bay Company factors. These were able to meet the Russian demand, but they were also rivals of the Muscovites for control of the territory and resources of the Northwest Coast. In this way the search for provisions critically undermined Russia's presence in America.[28]

Indeed, most of the contrasts between Russian expansion in Siberia and Alaska underscore the flaws of the latter.[29] Ruthless exploitation of hunters and fur-bearing animals alike, stiff international opposition, monopolistic complacency, precarious logistics--these are some of the compelling factors that persuaded Russia to retreat to a more tenable position in Siberian Asia, with its promising imperial opportunities to the southeast in Amuria[30] and to the southwest in Turkestan.[31] These opportunities more than compensated for the loss of Russian America, where the tsarist imperial system, so successful in Siberia,[32] failed to withstand the extreme strain. To extend a Siberian proverb, Russian expansion in Alaska failed because God was too high above and the tsar was too far away.

ENDNOTES

This paper appeared in somewhat different form in *The Geographical Review* 70 (1980): 127-36, and appears here with the permission of Douglas McManis, the editor.

[1]See George V. Lantzeff and Richard A. Pierce, *Eastward to Empire: Exploration and Conquest on the Russian Open Frontier, to 1750* (Montreal and London, 1973). Also see John A. Harrison, *The Founding of the Russian Empire in Asia and America* (Coral Gables, 1971), and George Alexander Lensen, ed., *Russia's Eastward Expansion* (Englewood Cliffs, 1964).

[2]See Raymond H. Fisher, *The Russian Fur Trade, 1550-1700* (Berkeley and Los Angeles, 1943); P. N. Pavlov, *Pushnoi promysel v Sibiri XVII v.* (Kras[n]oiarsk, 1972); and P. N. Pavlov, *Promyslovaia kolonizatsiia Sibiri v XVII v.* (Krasnoiarsk, 1974).

[3]See Donald W. Treadgold, *The Great Siberian Migration: Government and Peasant in Resettlement from Emancipation to the First World War* (Princeton, 1957); M. M. Gromyko, *Zapadnaia Sibir' v XVIII v.: Russkoe naselenie i zemledel'cheskoe osvoenie* (Novosibirsk, 1965); Francois-Xavier Coquin, *La Siberie.: Peuplement et immigration paysanne au XIXe siecle* (Paris, 1969); George Kennan, *Siberia and the Exile System*, 2 vols. (New York, 1891); and L. M. Goriushkin, ed., *Ssylka i katorga v Sibiri* (XVIII-nachalo XX v.) (Novosibirsk, 1975).

[4]See James R. Gibson, "Sables to Sea Otters: Russia Enters the Pacific," *Alaska Review* 3 (1968-69): 203-17.

[5]D. W. Meinig, "A Macrogeography of Western Imperialism: Some Morphologies of Moving Frontiers of Political Control," in *Settlement & Encounter: Geographical Studies Presented to Sir Grenfell Price*, ed. Fay Gale and G. H. Lawton (Melbourne, 1969), 213-40.

[6]Richard A. Pierce, ed., *Documents on the History of the Russian-American Company*, trans. Marina Ramsay (Kingston, 1976), 38.

[7]See James R. Gibson,"The Russian Fur Trade," in *Old Trails and New Directions: Papers of the Third North American Fur Trade Conference*, ed. Carol M. Judd and Arthur J. Ray (Toronto, 1980), 217-30.

[8]See R. G. Liapunova, *Ocherki po etnografii Aleutov (konets XVIII-pervaia polovina XIX v.)* (Leningrad, 1975).

[9]Archibald Campbell, *A Voyage Round the World...* (Honolulu, 1967), 46.

[10]Margaret Lantis,"The Aleut Social System, 1750 to 1810, From Early Historical Sources," in *Ethnohistory in Southwestern Alaska and the Southern Yukon*, ed. Margaret Lantis (Lexington, 1970), 179.

[11]See Clifford M. Foust, *Muscovite and Mandarin: Russia's Trade with China and Its Setting, 1727-1805* (Chapel Hill, 1969).

[12]A. P. Okladnikov and V. I. Shunkov, eds., *Istoriia Sibiri* (Leningrad, 1968), 2: 183.

[13]See V. I. Shunkov, *Ocherki po istorii zemledeliia Sibiri (XVII vek)* (Moscow, 1956).

[14]James R. Gibson, *Imperial Russia in Frontier America: The Changing Geography of Supply of Russian America, 1784-1867* (New York, 1976), 20.

[15]See R. M. Kabo, *Goroda Zapadnoi Sibiri: Ocherki istoriko-ekonomicheskoi geografii (XVII-pervaia polovina XIX vv.)* (Moscow, 1949); O. N. Vilkov, ed., *Goroda Sibiri (ekonomika, upravlenie i kul'tura gorodov Sibiri v dosovetskii period)* (Novosibirsk, 1974); O. N. Vilkov, ed., *Istoriia gorodov Sibiri dosovetskogo perioda (XVII-nachalo XX v.)* (Novosibirsk, 1977); 0. N. Vilkov, ed., *Goroda Sibiri (epokha feodalizma i kapitalizma)* (Novosibirsk, 1978); and O. N. Vilkov, ed., *Sibirskie goroda XVII-nachala XX veka* (Novosibirsk, 1981).

[16]See James R. Gibson, "The Significance of Cook's Third Voyage to Russian Tenure in the North Pacific," *Pacific Studies* 1 (1978): 119-46.

[17]See Mary E. Wheeler, "Empires in Conflict and Cooperation: The 'Bostonians' and the Russian-American Company," *Pacific Historical Review* 40 (1971): 419-41. Also see Howard I. Kushner, *Conflict on the Northwest Coast: American-Russian Rivalry in the Pacific Northwest, 1790-1867* (Westport, 1975); and James R. Gibson, "Bostonians and Muscovites on the Northwest Coast, 1788-1841," in *The Western Shore: Oregon Country Essays Honoring the American Revolution,* ed. Thomas Vaughan (Portland, 1975), 81-119.

[18]See James R. Gibson, *Feeding the Russian Fur Trade: Provisionment of the Okhotsk Seaboard and the Kamchatka Peninsula, 1639-1856* (Madison, 1969).

[19]See Richard A. Pierce, *Russia's Hawaiian Adventure, 1815-1817* (Berkeley and Los Angeles, 1965).

[20]See N. Nozikov, *Russian Voyages Round the World,* trans. Ernst and Mira Lesser (London, n.d.); and E. F. McCartan, "The Long Voyages--Early Russian Circumnavigation," *Russian Review* 22 (1963): 30-37.

[21]Gibson, *Imperial Russia*, 18; Okladnikov and Shunkov, *Istoriia Sibiri*, 2: 183.

[22]Gibson, *Imperial Russia*, 18.

[23]See Svetlana G. Fedorova, *The Russian Population in Alaska and California Late 18th Century-1867*, trans. Richard A. Pierce and Alton S. Donnelly (Kingston, 1973).

[24]Gibson, *Imperial Russia*, 47. Also see James R. Gibson, "Smallpox on the Northwest Coast, 1835-1838," *BC Studies* 56 (1982-83): 61-81.

[25]R. M. French, *The Eastern Orthodox Church* (London, 1961), 108. Also see Ernst Benz, *The Eastern Orthodox Church* (Garden City, 1963), chap. 7, especially 121-125.

[26]See R. V. Makarova, *Russians on the Pacific 1743-1799*, trans. Richard A. Pierce and Alton S. Donnelly (Kingston, 1975). Also see Mary E. Wheeler, "The Origins of the Russian-American Company," *Jahrbucher fur Geschichte Osteuropas* 14 (1966): 485-94.

[27]See P. A. Tikhmenev, *History of the Russian-American Company*, trans. and ed. Richard A. Pierce and Alton S. Donnelly (Seattle, 1978). Also see S. B. Okun, *The Russian-American Company*, trans. Carl Ginsburg (Cambridge, 1951).

[28]See Gibson, *Imperial Russia*.

[29]See James R. Gibson, "Old Russia in the New World: Adversaries and Adversities in Russian America," in *European Settlement and Development in North America: Essays on Geographical Change in Honour and Memory of Andrew Hill Clark*, ed. James R. Gibson (Toronto, 1978), 46-65.

[30]See James R. Gibson, "Russia on the Pacific: The Role of the Amur," *The Canadian Geographer* 12 (1968): 15-27. Also see Mark Bassin, "The Russian Geographical Society, the 'Amur Epoch,' and the Great Siberian Expedition, 1855-1863," *Annals of the Association of American Geographers* 73 (1983): 240-56; P. I. Kavanov, *Amurskii vopros* (Blagoveshchensk, 1959); R. K. I. Quested, *The Expansion of Russia in East Asia, 1857-1860* (Kuala Lumpur and Singapore, 1968); John J. Stephan, *Sakhalin: A History* (Oxford, 1971); and John J. Stephan, *The Kuril Islands: Russo-Japanese Frontier in the Pacific* (Oxford, 1974).

[31]See Geoffrey Wheeler, "Russian Conquest and Colonization of Central Asia," in *Russian Imperialism from Ivan the Great to the Revolution*, ed Taras Hunczak (New Brunswick, 1974), 264-98. Also see Richard A. Pierce, *Russian Central Asia, 1867-1971: A Study in Colonial Rule* (Berkeley and Los Angeles, 1960).

[32]See James R. Gibson, "The Significance of Siberia to Tsarist Russia," *Canadian Slavonic Papers* 14 (1972): 442-53.

RUSSIA SELLS ALASKA*

Ronald J. Jensen

Russia's sale of Alaska to the United States has long been a popular topic. Hector Chevigny concluded in his *Russian America--The Great Alaskan Venture* (Portland, OR: Binford & Mort, 1979 reprint) that Russia did not want to sell Alaska and that the United States did not want to buy it. Each nation, diplomatically isolated, acted against its better judgment in order to please the other, a potentially valuable ally. Varieties of this interpretation prevailed widely, and many casual acquaintances of Alaskan history apparently still believe that Russia relinquished Alaska reluctantly.

Chevigny's conclusion, however, contradicted much of the evidence he offered in advance. He noted that the Crimean War had demonstrated Russian America's vulnerability. Russia's Minister in the United States, Edouard de Stoeckl, had long regarded Americans as aggressive, even violent, and feared that the concept of "manifest destiny" might soon be directed northward. Constantine, the czar's brother, believed in laissez-faire and objected to the existence of an officially sanctioned monopoly per se. And Russia had acquired the north bank of the Amur River; the Amur region afforded economic opportunities in an area both more accessible and more defensible than Alaska.

Other scholars note that Russia had additional reasons to sell, as well. In 1861 Alexander II freed the serfs, compensating their former owners for the loss of their services. The serfs were to repay the government over a 49-year period. Compensation to former owners of serfs and other domestic and foreign obligations drained Russia's treasury. Meanwhile, the Russian American Company became increasingly unprofitable and required larger government subsidies to remain in operation.

Ronald Jensen's *The Alaska Purchase and Russian America Relations* (Seattle: University of Washington Press, 1975) is an example of a more recent scholarly study of the sale of Alaska and its purchase by the United States. Jensen's first chapter, reprinted here, described the abortive low-level sale/purchase negotiations between Russians and Americans during the 1850s. His findings confirm the view that Russia had valid reasons for wanting to sell Alaska to the United States many years before being able to do so.

---

*This selection originally appeared as Chapter 1 in *The Alaska Purchase and Russian-American Relations* (Seattle: University of Washington Press, 1975), pp. 3-22, 143-146.

* * *

The long series of rumors, recommendations, and negotiations that produced the sale of Russian-America actually began in 1854. Stories of earlier efforts, running all the way back to the time of President Martin Van Buren, appeared in the congressional debates of 1867 and 1868, but these reports lack foundation. Charles Sumner thought that the idea of purchasing Alaska had first taken shape under President James K. Polk, while Congressman Nathaniel P. Banks reported that Van Buren's administration had made a formal offer for the territory. But these were hearsay reports, made by purchase advocates anxious to add the weight of time to their arguments. No one offered proof for these assertions, nor could they.[1]

The preliminary negotiations in fact had grown out of conditions quite unforeseen by Van Buren or Polk, and unrelated to American considerations. The Crimean War and an attempted fraud set events moving toward the Alaska purchase. In the autumn of 1853 Russia and Turkey had gone to war, and Britain and France prepared to enter on the Ottoman side. Starting as a local Balkan clash, the war threatened to become worldwide, and possibly might involve Russia's distant colony in North America. That isolated outpost maintained only a handful of soldiers, behind wooden stockades, as a defense against Indians. It could never have stood against an assault from the sea. Nor could the colony have expected help from the Russian fleet, for in 1853 British warships outnumbered Russian by over two to one; in quality and experience the margin of British naval superiority was even greater. Russian-America would have been helpless in 1853 had a British expedition seized it.[2]

To prevent such a catastrophe the agent for the Russian-American Company and Russia's vice consul at San Francisco, Peter S. Kostromitinov, hatched a scheme to sell the territory to an American firm. According to the Charter of 1799, the Russian-American Company had sole authority to administer the colony as its domain. Conceivably, the company could sell out to a foreign firm and prevent its property's capture by Great Britain. Of course Kostromitinov planned only to feign a sale. When the threat of attack subsided, the company would reclaim its territory from the fictitious buyer.

The Russian agent had no problem finding an accomplice for his scheme. Indeed, the presence of a ready conspirator may have helped suggest the plan. For over a year the Russian-American Company had maintained close business relations with a group of San Francisco merchants who had incorporated under the confusing name, the American-Russian Commercial Company. The company included San Francisco's mayor, Charles J. Brenham; Abel Guy, a wealthy attorney; and, as president, Beverly C. Sanders, who was related by marriage to Daniel Webster. Sanders' group had contracted with the Russians to supply ice to the booming California coast. In return for an exclusive contract to distribute Alaskan ice, the San Francisco company paid thirty-five dollars per ton for ice it would then wholesale for seventy-five dollars. It was an especially profitable contract for the Americans because the Russian company did all the work and absorbed most of the expenses. It cut the ice, carried it to San Francisco, and even paid for the ice house in that city. The California firm merely sold the product. Between 1852 and 1859, over 20,000 tons of Alaskan lake ice reached the west coast.[3] Neither party wished to interrupt such a lucrative arrangement.

On 30 January 1854 Lucien Herman, vice president of the American-Russian Commercial Company, and Peter Kostromitinov drew up a contract to transfer the "property and franchises" of the Russian-American Company to the American firm for a period of three years. Leaving blanks for the date and price, they forwarded it to the Russian legation in Washington for approval. The San Francisco agent acted entirely without instructions, and until the contract reached the legation neither Russia's foreign ministry nor the Russian-American Company knew of the plan.[4]

Russia's representative in America, Edouard de Stoeckl, became the recipient of this strange contract. The "Baron," as he was erroneously called, had just assumed, by accident, the duties of charge d'affaire. Although he had served in the Washington legation before, Stoeckl had arrived in the United States during the winter of 1854 en route to Hawaii to become consul general. Upon arrival in New York he learned that Minister Alexander Bodisco was dead and that he was expected to take charge of the legation. He remained for fifteen years.[5] Stoeckl's continental manners and fluent English made him immediately popular in Washington society, while his country's liberal attitude on neutral rights--long an American goal in foreign policy--insured a welcome in the office of Secretary of State William L. Marcy. The Russian charge could expect friendly advice at the State Department, even on so delicate a matter as a fictitious transfer of

Russian-America, because of the hostility of both Russians and Americans to Great Britain.

Anglo-Russian enmity dated from the 1830s and arose primarily out of the ambitious policies both pursued in the Near East. When Nicholas I's government concluded a mutual security treaty with the Ottoman sultan at Unkiar Skelessi in 1833, British statesmen, especially Lord Palmerston, became convinced that Russia aimed to dominate Turkey. And Turkey was becoming a lively marketplace for English goods. Subsequent Russian intrigues in Persia and Central Asia appeared to threaten India and served to intensify British hostility prior to the Crimean War. It was only natural, then, that Russian policymakers cultivate the friendship of any power with a history of conflict with Great Britain. Once Russia found itself at war, and without allies in Europe, the government played on those issues calculated to ensure American support. It instructed Alexander Bodisco to tempt Americans with Britain's share of Russian trade, in return for allowing Russia to hire and outfit privateers in American ports. Bodisco's temporary successor, Constantine Catacazy, even entertained a plot to exploit the American position on neutral rights to Russia's advantage. He proposed to hire an American merchant vessel to challenge the British blockade. When the royal navy captured the ship, the United States government would insist that the cargo in a neutral ship could not be seized (the flag covers the goods); Britain would deny this interpretation and inflame American opinion. Stoeckl took over the office before the plan could be implemented and canceled it as too risky. He valued the cooperation of Marcy and the Pierce administration too much to compromise it with such a scheme, although Stoeckl did continue to search for a way to hire American privateers.

The United States government responded to Russia's calculated friendship by adopting a position of sympathetic neutrality. The Pierce administration allowed the sale of Russian merchant vessels interned in American ports after the declaration of war and forced Great Britain to accept the right of neutral vessels to trade with belligerents--a victory for blockaded Russia as well as American trade. In addition, Marcy offered Stoeckl his government's services as mediator, but that plan dragged on unfulfilled until the war ended. Some members of the American government even encouraged Stoeckl to hope for privateers, regardless of international law. California's Senator William M. Gwin told him that the prospects for fitting out such vessels in San Francisco were good, while Gwin's friend,

Beverly Sanders, offered his steamships and services. Marcy refused to commit himself or the government that far, but his letters to his minister in St. Petersburg do demonstrate consistent support for Russia. On 1 October 1855 he wrote: "Between no two Nations on the Globe are the relations of peace and amity so likely to be enduring. It is scarcely possible that the political policy of the one would interfere with that of the other."[6] Such cordiality was not at all one-sided. When Marcy asked Stoeckl that same year how St. Petersburg might view American annexation of the Sandwich Islands, he found the Russian minister very cooperative. Marcy's attitude did not extend to risking neutrality for Russia, but it did guarantee that Stoeckl could discuss sensitive political issues freely with him and others in the American government.

Stoeckl naturally asked Marcy and Gwin for advice on the Russian-America "sale"; both thought the plan too transparent to fool anyone. It would be "impossible," they advised, "to prove that the contract is not fictitious and that, in particular, it was drawn up before the war." Such an obvious deception could not save Russian-America and might embroil the United States, so the two Americans suggested that Stoeckl forget the scheme.[7]

Before the charge could relay these events to his home office, Alaska was saved through official channels. Although its representatives in the United States were unaware of it, the Russian-American Company directors in St. Petersburg had appealed to the Hudson's Bay Company for a mutual guarantee of lands in northwestern America. It is difficult to understand why the British government should have accepted such a proposal, since the Russians could not defend their own colony let alone threaten the Hudson's Bay Company holdings. Apparently the British cabinet decided against attacking Russian-America because it did not think the rewards of such an operation were worth the cost. So Britain, on 31 March, agreed to exclude Russian-America from the war. In St. Petersburg this surprising gesture did not appear as an expression of magnanimity. According to Prince Gorchakov, the British government feared that the Russians would cede the land to the United States if it were not neutral. The British legation in Washington kept on the lookout for just such a possibility throughout the war.[8]

Publication of the neutrality agreement saved Stoeckl from considering the transfer, and he forgot the plan. That would have stopped talk of an Alaska transaction, if the newspapers had not picked up word of a deal. Four months after the scheme was buried, the *New York Herald*, quoting the *Dublin University Magazine*, reported Russia anxious to cede its holdings in North America to the United States. An editorial from the *Herald* for 25 July 1854 asserted that Russia had made an offer. Papers from Baltimore and San Francisco picked up the story, and embellished it. None of the editors seemed aware that the transaction they were so eagerly reporting had died months earlier.[9]

Rumors of a sale were so persistent that even those persons privy to the San Francisco plan began to ask questions. It was just possible that Russia did want to sell and had proposed the fictitious deal to gauge American interest. Accordingly, Marcy and Gwin sought out Stoeckl for a second informal conversation concerning Russian-America. Gossip or not, the Pierce administration would not ignore a possibility for expansion.[10]

Both Marcy and Gwin had more than a passing curiosity in Pacific territories. In 1854 Marcy was busily negotiating a treaty of annexation with the Hawaiian Kingdom, while Gwin, always entranced by schemes, looked beyond the islands to a commercial empire in the Pacific. By employing islands as bases to bridge the Pacific, and by obtaining Russia's cooperation, he believed that the United States might oust Britain so as to become the primary power in Pacific commerce. The state of California naturally would be the center of such an American empire. In 1852 Gwin had secured federal funds to survey the Bering Strait and the northern Pacific "for naval and commercial purposes," and he followed this with plans for steamship and telegraph lines. The senator surely saw Alaska as a stepping stone to something or somewhere in the Pacific.[11]

The two Americans approached Stoeckl with the rumors of cession and in the course of conversation inquired about the availability of Russia's American lands. According to Stoeckl, Gwin and Marcy mentioned purchase only as a "vague project," and the Russian assured them that the territory was not for sale and the rumors were false.[12] That conversation ended the matter for the time, but the stories of sale had done their work. They had raised American interest in Alaska, and had reminded the Russians that a buyer was available if ever the emperor's government wanted one.

The purchase project lay dormant for several years, awaiting Russia's pleasure. Sale also required a willing seller, and Russia had never been anxious to divest itself of territory. The treaty ending the Crimean War gave Russian statesmen far more serious worries than the future of a few trading posts on another continent. The 1856 Treaty of Paris rolled back Russian influence in the Balkans, reduced the emperor's prestige in the councils of Europe, and opened the Black Sea to Russia's enemies. The recent war exposed grave social and financial weaknesses inside the empire. Alexander II, who succeeded his father in February 1855, was not anxious for reform, but, urged on by his younger brother Constantine, he recognized that recovery required change. In addition to advising his brother and serving on reform committees, Grand Duke Constantine commanded the Russian navy, the department that supervised the administration of Russian-America.

It was in this office that the grand duke connected Russian-America with the question of postwar recovery. Thanks to the sums swallowed up in war and the chaotic budgetary system, the Russian government faced a huge deficit. Economy was essential in every department. But any saving that Constantine might make in his naval budget would be minute, and also might weaken defense. Constantine sought other solutions, and on 3 April 1857 he suggested one of them to Gorchakov. He advised that in view of the financial dilemma in Russia "we would do well to take advantage of the excess of money at the present time in the treasury of the United States of America and sell them our North American colonies."[13]

A more personal motive also drew the grand duke's attention to matters of economy in the spring of 1857. In spite of its debts, the government had just invested 2,001,000 rubles in the Russian Steam Navigation Company--a commercial shipping firm founded by Constantine to trade in the Levant. The company began operating one month after Constantine's letter to Gorchakov.[14]

If Constantine was aware of the overture made by Americans in 1854, he did not mention it. Yet he had no doubt that the United States would buy the colony considering that country's desire to "dominate undivided the whole of North America." Impressed by the force of manifest destiny, he warned that if Russian-America were not offered for sale, the United States would "take the afore mentioned colonies from us and we [should] not be able to regain them." Constantine not only outlined his preliminary argument for the sale but ordered the step necessary to get the plan moving in St. Petersburg. Since the Russian-American Company would require compensation,

Constantine suggested asking the ex-governors of the colony for an assessment of Alaska's worth, "keeping in mind however that they may have somewhat prejudiced points of view."[15] As quickly as it took the mail to pass from the grand duke's retreat in Nice to the foreign ministry in St. Petersburg, Russian officials began to think of sale.

When he had written to Gorchakov, Constantine was aware that opposition to the sale of Russian-America probably would come from the directors of the Russian-American Company, and he soon appeared to guess accurately the nature of Gorchakov's opposition. The foreign minister, of course, canvassed the opinions of the company's major stockholders and directors. The governor of the Russian-American Company in the 1830s and later chairman of the board, Baron Ferdinand Wrangell, answered first. Wrangell politely registered opposition to the grand duke's proposal, arguing that the company and its territory showed great promise and that selling would deprive Russia of an "enlivening stimulus to maritime trade."[16] In reality, the company had discouraged trade more than stimulated it, for its government subsidies and monopoly privileges kept stock prices high and sustained the company in spite of its inefficiency and declining markets.[17] Wrangell especially opposed liquidating in favor of the Americans. During his days as governor this quick-tempered Baltic German had canceled part of the 1824 agreement with the United States. The 1824 treaty had allowed American vessels access to waters near Alaska's shore. According to Wrangell, American sailors abused the privilege, at this time, by coming ashore and cheating natives out of oil and pelts.[18] As a precaution against sale, the red-bearded baron made a generous estimate of the colony's worth. Actually he made two estimates. Figuring from the inflated value of shares outstanding, Wrangell gauged capital investment at 3,721,400 silver rubles, or about 500 rubles for each share. Granting the government an equal measure, Wrangell placed the total price of the territory at 7,442,800 rubles ($5,600,000). That, he thought, was its minimum value in 1857, but if one were to include prospective worth he suggested that Russia should demand 20,000,000 rubles.[19] If the company had to liquidate, Wrangell wanted a decent profit.

Three weeks after receiving the estimate, Gorchakov's office sent Constantine a long memorandum detailing conditions under which cession might take place. The memorandum accepted Wrangell's first estimate, 7,442,800 rubles. The study even noted the possibility of reckoning the asking price according to the twenty-million-ruble estimate, but left that to be decided later. Constantine might get his sale, but only if the United States would meet the company's price. Other stipulations included a four-year postponement to allow the company's charter to expire. Thus Gorchakov seemed to accept the principle of cession, while managing to delay it. Without actually opposing the emperor's brother, the cautious foreign minister had done what he could to stall the matter.[20] It was six months before a petty claim in San Francisco and an outrageous rumor from Washington gave Constantine an opportunity to press for cession again.

The petty claim in San Francisco was a complex matter. For some time the American-Russian Commercial Company had claimed trading concessions in Russian-America, dating from a contract which the Russian company had concluded during the Crimean War. At that time Russia's colony depended on San Francisco for supplies. To secure them it accepted a contract offered by Sanders, obliging the Russians to sell ice, timber, coal, and fish at cost, in return for half of the profits realized by the San Francisco firm. Backed by the war crisis and credentials obtained from the American president and Russia's representative in Washington, Sanders managed to persuade the governors of the Russian company to sign a twenty-year agreement on that basis. After the war the Russians ignored the contract. Stoeckl, however, accepted the American claim as just and warned St. Petersburg of future embarrassment and injury to Russian-American relations unless the company lifted its monopoly on Alaska trade.[21]

A month later, 3 December 1857, Stoeckl again warned the chancellery of trouble with the United States over Alaska. He had received reports that Brigham Young's Mormons might try to emigrate to Canada or, possibly, Russian-America. In a recent conversation, President Buchanan had "alluded to that eventuality." "It is for you to settle that question," Buchanan told Stoeckl, "as for us we shall be very happy to be rid of them." Stoeckl advised that the rumor seemed premature, yet the possibility was important enough to draw the attention of the emperor. "This supports the idea of settling henceforth the question of our American possessions," Alexander noted in the margin of the dispatch.[22]

Conflict between Americans and Russians over Alaska was by no means confined to rumors, or to peaceful contract disputes. The Russian-American Company's refusal to sanction foreign trade in

Alaskan ports or foreign fishermen in Alaskan waters, coupled with its inability to enforce its ban, seemed to encourage illicit whalers and traders. In the mid-1850s, according to an official Russian report, over four hundred unauthorized whalers penetrated colonial waters each year; and most of these represented American fisheries. Other intrusions by smugglers anxious to exchange guns and rum for otter pelts, or merely to steal the Indian's catch, multiplied. This not only deprived the company of furs and cheated the Indians, but also endangered Alaskan colonists. Smugglers occasionally supplied hostile natives with powder and arms. The company, of course, had protested these invasions through the minister in Washington, but to no avail.[23] Without sufficient force to prevent or even capture violators, the company would continue to suffer losses. At the same time legitimate American businessmen would continue to protest their exclusion from Alaska, since Russian ships were welcome in American ports. Minister Stoeckl could only relay the complaints from both sides to the proper authorities and urge his government to seek a permanent solution before these petty conflicts endangered the countries' relationship.

Stoeckl's report provided Constantine with the ammunition that he needed to renew the cession proposal. In a letter to Gorchakov the grand duke called attention to Stoeckl's warning that the Russian-American Company had jeopardized relations with the United States. At the very least, the company's exclusive policy would upset Russian commerce with the country. Constantine reminded the foreign minister that his proposal for sale would prevent these clashes and, at the same time, would add American gold to Russian coffers. The grand duke assumed, as he had in April 1857, that America was bound, "following the natural order of things, to possess the whole of North America," and that the Russian government could not prevent it. Surely it would be better to recognize this at once and sell the territory, "solving in a friendly and, at the same time, in a profitable manner, the question which may otherwise be decided against us by conquest."[24] Constantine also attacked the Russian company, denouncing the practice of trading companies acting both as merchants and administrators. Such a system, he argued, whether in India or North America, subjected people to second-rate administrators whose directors in London or St. Petersburg could not properly supervise. Whether Russian-America were sold to the United States or not, Constantine wanted the system reviewed, and he asked Gorchakov to send a committee of civil servants and naval officers to investigate administration in the territory.[25]

Constantine's opposition to the Russian-American Company and his stand on the question of sale involved more than financial and government considerations or fear of American aggression. He acted in accord with the feeling that Russian energy and resources should find employment at home to strengthen the country and remedy the ills revealed by the Crimean War. For Constantine a colony on the continent of North America was a luxury that Russia could not afford. He advised Gorchakov that "Russia must endeavor as far as possible to become stronger in her center, in those fundamentally Russian regions which constitute her main power in population and in faith, and Russia must develop the strength of this center in order to be able to hold those extremities which bring her real benefit."[26]

The grand duke's advice echoed that given four years earlier by the governor general of Siberia, Nicholai M. Muraviev. The latter had expanded Russian power in the Far East since his appointment in 1847. He sought for Russia the important Amur basin and, eventually, hoped to see his country displace Britain as the major influence in China. At a meeting with Emperor Nicholas in 1853, attended by Constantine and Alexander, Muraviev had advocated ceding Russian-America to the United States and concentrating Russia's resources along the Amur. Such a strategy, he thought, would increase Russia's weight in the Far East while establishing the United States as a counter to Great Britain. Like Constantine, Muraviev had believed that the United States was destined to dominate all North America anyway. Constantine's letter to Gorchakov was not that explicit, but contained more than a hint of Muraviev's influence.[27]

Gorchakov met the grand duke's attack with his usual strategy of delay. The courtly, gray-haired foreign minister favored no radical strategy. The old bureaucrat looked to Europe for Russia's foreign relations, and he was slow to adopt change. His popularity with the emperor was in large measure a reward for his reassuring conservatism. Besides, forty years of experience in the foreign service did not condition Gorchakov to liquidate his country's possessions, however rational the argument. He suggested that Constantine put off any investigation until the company's authorization expired in 1862, in order to maintain public confidence. A government inquiry at present might undermine the firm's credit, whereas in two years such an investigation would appear as a routine preparation for revising its charter. The demands of business weighed heavily even in an autocracy.

As an effort to give some visible result to the grand duke's wishes, Gorchakov authorized Stoeckl to see if he could "carefully advance to the Washington cabinet the idea of inducing Russia to cede the colonies on favorable terms." The envoy must somehow put the thought of purchase into American heads without compromising himself or the imperial government, or openly suggesting that Alaska was for sale.[28] Six months earlier the foreign minister had informed Stoeckl that cession was being considered; now Stoeckl might discreetly discuss the matter.

Stoeckl proved a more aggressive salesman than Gorchakov may have wished. Already his dispatches had augmented the cessionist argument; after 1857 they would grow increasingly outspoken on the subject. By then the bearded envoy had gained the experience and stature to become an effective diplomat. Stoeckl was a familiar figure in Washington and a successful one. He could claim partial responsibility for the steady support Americans had shown for Russia during the Crimean War and for the cordial relationship that followed. In 1854 and 1855 Stoeckl had helped negotiate a mutually desirable naval convention between the two nations, and had encouraged the exchange of commerce. As a reward for his services and in recognition of the new value placed on Russian-American relations, Alexander promoted Stoeckl to the position of minister in August 1857, and then on Christmas awarded him the rank of actual counselor of state. In the meantime Stoeckl had enhanced his popularity in Washington by marrying a Massachusetts lady, Elizabeth Howard--"American, Protestant, without property" as his dispatch described her.[29]

In spite of Stoeckl's position and inclination, Gorchakov's awkward instructions precluded rapid progress on the cession question. Gorchakov refused to allow Stoeckl to take the initiative. When the minister visited St. Petersburg on leave at the end of 1858, he could report no hint of any movement by the Americans. He returned to Washington to await an overture.[30] In January 1860 Stoeckl finally transmitted to the foreign ministry a new proposal for the purchase of Russian-America by the government of the United States, and it came, as before, from Senator William Gwin. The overture by the ebullient senator from California was an interesting affair--as were all propositions from that expansive gentleman. The senator's hope of capturing the North Pacific for American commerce had not diminished in the years since 1854. Gwin's interest in Alaska and in the Atlantic cable project, which his vote in the Senate saved in

1857, led him to notice Russian colonization of the Amur region and link it with the China market. In August 1860 he told a crowd in Stockton: "We must look to the hundreds of millions of people who inhabit China and Japan, and to the hosts Russia will soon have planted in her possessions on the Amoor River, for a market of our surplus products...Upon our intercourse with these regions of the earth hinges our greatness as a people." To achieve this goal Gwin had advocated a steamship line between San Francisco and northern Asia, and a telegraph cable from the United States up the west coast to Alaska, across the Bering Strait to the Amur. The line would eventually stretch across Russia to Europe, where it would connect with the Atlantic cable.[31] Acquisition of Russian-America, with its island chain stretching across the Pacific, would complement Gwin's efforts neatly. Besides narrowing the gap between the United States and Asia, its purchase would solve the problem of trading rights in Alaska, to the satisfaction of Californians. The senator met repeatedly during the 1850s with Minister Stoeckl to resolve disputes over contracts arising from policies of the Russian-American Company. Stoeckl sympathized with Gwin, deplored the conflict, but could not alter the situation.[32] Sometime in December 1859, while the two men sat discussing the claims of Gwin's constituents, the senator asked Russia's minister if the imperial government would be willing to cede the disputed territory to the United States. This was no casual inquiry for, Gwin added, "I have communicated my idea to the President, whom I have found quite disposed to adopt it." According to Stoeckl's description of the meeting, the senator listed the resources of the territory and reminded him that Russia was "too far away to exploit them. We are nearby and can get more profit from them." This was the standard argument for manifest destiny, and, as his dispatch demonstrated, proved most persuasive for Stoeckl.[33]

Stoeckl had responded cautiously, as instructed, pretending to know nothing about his government's view of such a proposition, as if he had never discussed cession in St. Petersburg. Nor would he venture an opinion. If the United States would submit a formal proposal he would bring it to Gorchakov's attention, but Stoeckl would not open delicate negotiations with St. Petersburg without a more definite request from the administration, and Gwin represented the government only indirectly. A few days later, after consulting Buchanan, Gwin again called on Stoeckl, this time to present Buchanan's instructions. The president wanted the cession proposal conveyed to St. Petersburg as a "mere idea," without official character. "To avoid even the shadow of formality," Gwin told him, "the President will abstain from talking with you on this subject either directly or through the Secretary of State."[34] The caution was understandable. In 1860, secrecy in such a matter was imperative, for a hint of extending American territory, even in the far northwest, would have redoubled the free-slave quarrel in Congress. The acquisition of Alaska would have been interpreted by pro-slavery elements as an effort to extend free soil, as many had viewed the Kansas-Nebraska Act in the Pierce administration. Clearly sectional politics forced expansionist advocates to tread warily. Perhaps only Gwin's credentials as a southerner (he was born and raised in Mississippi) encouraged the administration to sanction these tentative negotiations at all.

Stoeckl respected the senator's instructions and talked neither to Buchanan nor to Secretary of State Lewis Cass, but he still had no idea of how serious the United States government was about Russian-America, and he realized that the foreign ministry in St. Petersburg was not in the habit of committing itself to mere ideas. Stoeckl finally received confirmation of the President's interest in Alaska from Assistant Secretary of State John Appleton, a confidant of the president and the real locus of power in the State Department.[35] Appleton repeated Gwin's statement, and assured the minister that Buchanan was ready to follow up the project if the Russians decided to cede the colony. Until that was known, the affair had to remain unofficial, kept secret even from Secretary Cass.

Appleton's talk convinced Stoeckl that the proposition was genuine and the minister immediately sent a message by courier to St. Petersburg. Along with a description of the meetings with Gwin and Appleton, Stoeckl appended his own recommendation in favor of ceding Alaska to the United States. His argument adopted Gwin's view that Russia was in no position to exploit its North American territory, and he seemed as convinced as Constantine that the Russian-American Company had no future, observing that the company had grown little in the past twenty years. Stoeckl doubted if the territory was worth more than five million dollars, a figure that Gwin had suggested in one of their talks. Since the Russian minister had for some time regarded the company as a threat to American relations, five million looked even more like a fair price.[36]

Like Muraviev, Stoeckl had great hopes for his country's future in Asia, in the Amur basin, and he advised his superior that Russia should develop its possessions there rather than in North

America: "It is on our Asiatic possessions that our interests lie and it is there that we must concentrate our energy." Four years earlier Stoeckl had tried to promote development in the Amur area by sponsoring an American commercial agent in the region.[37]

Gorchakov had heard most of these arguments before, though not so forcefully expressed, by a subordinate. Indeed, Constantine's views were so similar as to suggest correspondence with Stoeckl or, perhaps, a conversation during the minister's previous visit to St. Petersburg. Stoeckl did add one important reason for ceding Alaska that Constantine had not suggested. By selling the territory to the United States, Russia would not only drop a millstone, but would strike a blow against its principal rival Great Britain. "If the United States becomes master of our possessions British Oregon will be closed in by the Americans on the north and on the south and will with difficulty avoid their aggressions."

Stoeckl's dispatch reopened the question of cession in the Russian capital. It even reached the attention of the emperor, although the latter decided only that "this must be considered further."[38] And there was further support. Within a few days another advocate of cession, Rear Admiral Andrei Alexandrovich Popov, laid a detailed memorandum before the Ministry of Foreign Affairs. Popov commanded Russia's Pacific fleet, and was familiar with both Russian-America and the United States. He also held sufficient rank to speak freely. The admiral roundly condemned the Russian-American Company, charging its officials with greed, maladministration, and mistreatment of the natives. He flatly denied that the company had brought any advantage whatever to Russian commerce, and supported his contentions. Apparently the company regularly overcharged its customers in St. Petersburg several hundred percent for furs it purchased from Alaskan natives. According to Popov, the company was not even useful for the training of Russian seamen, as its defenders claimed; the company preferred to use experienced foreign crews on its oceangoing vessels. Regardless of Alaska's value, Popov, like Constantine and Stoeckl, believed that the colony was destined to fall to the Americans. The "doctrine of manifest destiny," he claimed, "is entering more and more into the veins of the people, and new generations are sucking it in with their mother's milk and inhaling it with every breath of air." To Popov it seemed only a matter of time before the United States would occupy the entire continent. Since Russian-America could not be defended from the Americans, it should be ceded to them "in good time and voluntarily," and its Russian population settled on the Amur.[39]

Faced with such mounting criticism of the company, and the new advocates of cession, Gorchakov now began to seriously consider the American proposal. The arguments of Stoeckl and Popov had followed Constantine's advice too closely to be ignored, yet the foreign minister still doubted that cession would be in Russia's interest. Once more he decided to stall. He informed his minister in Washington that he opposed cession, but told Stoeckl not to end negotiations, since financial considerations might persuade him to reconsider. The United States would have to offer more than Gwin's proposed $5,000,000. In spite of the fact that Gorchakov had accepted an assessment of $5,600,000 in the foreign ministry memorandum of 1857, the foreign minister claimed that the American offer was "entirely inadequate and much below the real value of the colonies." He instructed Stoeckl to seek a higher price, and commit himself to nothing until the company charter expired.[40]

By the time Gorchakov's order reached Washington in April 1860, the United States government was not longer in a position to negotiate. The sectional crisis had deepened; Buchanan's popularity had fallen. According to Gwin, "the hostility of Congress toward the administration is such that it would suffice for the President to present a project to have it rejected." But for these circumstances Gwin was ready to deal and willing to raise the bid for Alaska. His Pacific-coast colleagues would go along, Gwin told the Russian minister, but consent of the other states would be more difficult to obtain: "The only motive which might induce them to acquire your colonies would be the prospect of augmenting in the quarters of the Pacific the power and influence of the United States to the detriment of England. That political consideration...will without any doubt have a favorable influence on Congress."

For the moment, congressional animosity toward Buchanan, and the intense sectional rivalry, prevented any purchase. Gwin advised Stoeckl to wait for the next administration, and for the congress that would meet in December 1861, when presumably both sides, Russia and the United States, would be ready to talk.[41] But with the Lincoln administration came civil war, and six years of waiting for Minister Stoeckl.

ENDNOTES

[1]Charles Sumner, *Charles Sumner, His Complete Works* (Boston: Lee and Shepard, 1900) 15: 185; U.S. Congress, House, *Congressional Globe*, 40th Cong., 2d sess., 1868, 3662; David Hunter Miller discusses these reports at length in his manuscript "The Alaska Treaty," National Archives, pp. 56-64. He finds that Robert J. Walker, lobbyist for the sale and treasury secretary under Polk, mentioned prior negotiations, but without evidence that they actually took place.

[2]S. B. Okun, *The Russian-American Company*, trans. by Carl Ginsburg (Cambridge: Harvard University Press, 1951), p. 234.

[3]Howard Kushner, "American-Russian Rivalry in the Pacific Northwest, 1790-1867" (Ph.D. diss., Cornell University, 1970), pp. 174-76; Pavel N. Golovin, *Obzor Russkikh kolonii v Severnoi Amerike* [Review of the Russian colonies in North America], pt. 2 of *Materialy dlia istorii Russkikh zaselenii po beregam vostochnago okeano* [Materials for the history of Russian settlement on the shores of the eastern ocean], trans. Ivan Petroff, p. 183 (hereafter cited as Golovin, *Review*); see also H. H. Bancroft, *History of Alaska 1730-1885* (San Francisco: A.L. Bancroft and Co., 1886), pp. 587-88, and E. L. Keithahn, "Alaska Ice, Inc.," *Pacific Northwest Quarterly* 36 (1945): 121-22.

[4]Okun, *Russian-American Company*, pp. 237-38; F. A. Golder, "The Purchase of Alaska," *American Historical Review* 25 (1920): 411-12.

[5]F. A. Golder outlines Stoeckl's career in "The American Civil War through the Eyes of a Russian Diplomat," *American Historical Review* 26 (1921): 454-55.

[6]Marcy to Seymour, 14 April and 9 May 1854, 1 October 1855, William L. Marcy Papers, Library of Congress, Washington, D.C.; see also F. A. Golder, "Russian-American Relations During the Crimean War," *American Historical Review* 31 (1926): 462-65.

[7]Stoeckl to Gorchakov, August 1854, quoted in Okun, *Russian-American Company*, p. 240.

[8]Gorchakov Memorandum, quoting Stoeckl, December 1855, Annex 12, Papers Relating to the Cession of Alaska, National Archives; J. S. Galbraith's *The Hudson's Bay Company as an Imperial Factor, 1821-1869* (Berkeley: University of California Press, 1957), pp. 264-67, discusses the British decision on Alaska.

[9]*New York Herald*, 20 and 25 July 1854; *Times* (London), 8 August 1854; *Daily Alta California*, 11 September 1854, quoting *Baltimore American*, 28 July 1854.

[10]Stoeckl to Gorchakov, August 1854, quoted in Okun, *Russian-American Company*, p. 242.

[11]U.S. Congress, Senate, *Congressional Globe*, 33d Cong., 1st sess., 1852, 876-83; *Congressional Globe*, 32nd Cong., 1st sess., 1850, 2452: Gwin to Marcy, 20 April 1855, Marcy Papers; see also Hallie M. McPherson, "The Interest of William McKendree Gwin in the Purchase of Alaska," *Pacific Historical Review* 3 (1934): 28-38.

[12]Stoeckl to Gorchakov, 4 January 1860, Annex 8, Alaska Cession, N. A.; Golder, "Purchase of Alaska," p. 412.

[13]Constantine to Gorchakov, 3 April 1857, Documents Relating to the

Cession of Alaska, Archives of the Russian Ministry of Foreign Affairs 1857-1868: Asiatic Department, Manuscripts Division, Library of Congress.

[14]W. E. Mosse, "Russia and the Levant, 1856-1862; Grand Duke Constantine Nicolaevich and the Russian Steam Navigation Company," *Journal of Modern History* 26 (1954): 40-41.

[15]Constantine to Gorchakov, 3 April 1857, Alaska, Min. For. Affairs, L. C.

[16]Wrangell Memorandum, 10 April 1857, Alaska, Min. For. Affairs, L. C. Wrangell served as governor of Russian-American Company from 1830 to 1835 and then returned to St. Petersburg as a member and, eventually, as chairman of its board of directors.

[17]Okun, *Russian-American Company*, pp. 225-31, examines company finances.

[18]Hector Chevigny, *Russian America, 1741-1867* (New York: Viking Press, 1965), pp. 180-90.

[19]Wrangell Memorandum; Hunter Miller, "Alaska Treaty," pp. 94-102.

[20]Gorchakov to Constantine, 29 April 1957, Alaska, Min. For. Affairs, L. C.

[21]The contract was finally broken by mutual agreement in 1859, and a new contract, only for ice, established to run through 1862. The new contract bound Americans to pay $7/ton for at least 3000 tons and pay $8/ton in freight charges. Golovin, *Review*, pp. 183-255, Stoeckl to Gorchakov, 13 November 1857, Annex 4, Alaska Cession, N. A.

[22]Stoeckl to Gorchakov, 13 December 1857, Annex 5, Alaska Cession, N. A.

[23]*Diklad komiteta ob ustroistve Russkikh Amerikanskikh kolonii* [Report of the committee on organization of the Russian American colonies], trans. Ivan Petroff, pt. 1, p. 162, 230; for an able discussion of American interest in the northwest coast, see chapters five and six of Kushner's dissertation cited above.

[24]Constantine to Gorchakov, 7 December 1857, Alaska, Min. For. Affairs, L. C.

[25]Ibid.

[26]Ibid.

[27]Muraviev's report of March 1853 is quoted in B. V. Struve, *Vospominaniia o Sibiri, 1848-1854* [Memoirs of Siberia] (St. Petersburg: Obshchestvennaia pol'za tip., 1889), pp. 155-56. The foreign ministry feared repercussions from Muraviev's aggressive tactics and consistently opposed him, but Alexander, like his father, usually overrode their objections. Muraviev continued to implement his ambitious policy until his retirement in 1861.

[28]Gorchakov to Constantine, December 1857, Alaska, Min. For. Affairs, L. C.

[29]Ministry of Foreign Affairs to Stoeckl, 26 August, 25 December 1857, (O. S.), in F. A. Golder, *Guide to Materials for American History in Russian Archives* (Washington, D.C.: Carnegie Institution of Washington, 1917-1937), 2: 15-17; see also Golder's "Russian-American Relations During the Crimean War," pp. 474-75.

[30]Stoeckl to Gorchakov, 4 January 1860, Annex 6, Alaska Cession, N. A., recalls conversation in St. Petersburg.

[31]*San Francisco Herald*, 31 August 1860, see also Lately Thomas, [pseud. of Robert V. Steele], *Between Two Empires; The Life Story of California's First William McKendree Gwin* (Boston: Houghton Mifflin, 1969), pp. 155-56.

[32]Gwin's efforts to pierce the Alaska monopoly are described in Admiral Popov's Memorandum, 7 February 1860, Alaska, Min. For. Affairs, L. C.

[33]Stoeckl to Gorchakov, 4 January 1860, Annex 6, Alaska Cession, N. A., Lately Thomas [pseud.], *Between Two Empires*, pp. 155-56.

[34]Ibid.

[35]Philip S. Klein, *President James Buchanan: A Biography* (University Park, PA: Pennsylvania State University Press, 1962), p. 275.

[36]Stoeckl to Gorchakov, 4 January 1860, Annex 6, Alaska Cession, N. A. As early as March 1854, Stoeckl had argued that if Russia insisted on restricting American vessels in Russian-America the U.S. would retaliate, Golder, *Guide*, 1: 72.

[37]Perry McDonough Collins to President Pierce, 29 February 1856, Consular Despatches, Amoor River, N. A., reports Stoeckl's cooperation.

[38]Alexander wrote in the margin of Stoeckl's dispatch of 4 January 1860.

[39]Popov Memorandum, 7 February 1860, Alaska, Min. For. Affairs, L. C.

[40]Golder, "Purchase of Alaska," pp. 416-17; Stoeckl to Gorchakov, 16 July 1860, Annex 10, Alaska Cession, N. A., repeats Gorchakov's instructions; T. M. Batueva, "Prokhozhdenie dogovora o pokupke Aliaski v congresse SShA v 1867-1868 gg." [Passing the treaty on the purchase of Alaska in the U.S.A. congress in 1867-1868] *Novaia i novieshchaia istoriia* [New and contemporary history] 4 (1971):118, 26 May 1860.

[41]Stoeckl to Gorchakov, 16 July 1860, Annex 10, Alaska Cession, N. A.

BUYING ALASKA: THE MYTH OF "ICEBERGIA"*

Richard E. Welch, Jr.

It has been accepted as axiomatic by writers of American history that the purchase of Alaska was unpopular. Terms such as "Icebergia," "Walrussia," and "Seward's Folly" have been repeated from newspapers of the time to suggest that Americans thought the territory was a land of perpetual ice and snow, and that it was worthless. Several often reprinted editorial cartoons of the era have contributed to the familiar interpretation.

There is significant evidence that the purchase was not as unpopular as the traditional interpretation holds. There was in fact a considerable body of accurate information on Alaska available in 1867, collected by observers and scientists from several nations over the years, including the U.S. Moreover, Alaska was purchased by treaty. A treaty does not become law under the U.S. constitution unless ratified by a two-thirds majority of the Senate. Supporters of the Alaska treaty, most particularly the chairman of the Senate Foreign Relations Committee, Massachusetts Senator Charles Sumner, obtained the necessary vote on the first try, when the count was 27 to 12. The final official tally was 37 to 2. Sumner's speech to the Senate on the day of the vote shows that he was quite familiar with real Alaska conditions. America was in an expansionist mood at the time, and William Seward was a generally popular Secretary of State. It should not be surprising, therefore, that despite the fact that Alaska was the first non-contiguous acquisition of the U.S., the two-thirds majority was fairly handily obtained.

Why, then, has the myth of unpopularity been so persistent? This is partly because it is consistent with a general ignorance about Alaska on the part of most Americans, including the writers of general textbooks. But also, there was considerably less enthusiasm in the Congress for the notion of purchasing Alaska than there was for spending the money necessary to administer it, to which there was significant opposition. Also, at the very time of the purchase, the Congress was involved in two of the most significant constitutional crises in American history, southern Reconstruction and the impeachment of Andrew Johnson, leading to much acrimonious criticism of the executive branch.

Three decades ago Professor Richard Welch of the history department at Lafayette College in Pennsylvania surveyed the major newspapers in the U.S. at the time of the purchase. He found that nearly all of them either supported the purchase editorially, or at least did not oppose it. We reprint Welch's article here,

---

*This article originally appeared in *American Slavic and East European Review* 17 (1958): 481-94.

as Morgan Sherwood did in 1967, in the hope that it will raise awareness concerning the complex nature of the reaction to the Alaska purchase and lay to rest "once and for all" the traditional myth.

Students should note also a new analysis of the charges of bribery associated with Alaska purchase, Paul Holbo's *Tarnished Expansion: The Alaska Scandal, the Press, and Congress, 1867-1871* (Knoxville: University of Tennessee Press, 1983).

* * *

The American purchase of Alaska from Russia in 1867 is often cited today as an example of providential intervention in behalf of America's national security. Commentators shudder at the thought of Soviet air bases in what was once Russian America and praise the near miraculous foresight of Secretary of State William Seward.

Comprising as it does the only real estate transaction ever completed by Russia and America, Seward's annexation of Alaska properly holds a rather unique place in the diplomatic annals of both countries. The tendency of textbook writers to over-dramatize the role of Providence and to imply that Seward alone saw the value of Russian America is, however, both mistaken and unfortunate.[1] It tends to make the Alaskan Treaty of 1867 the mysterious property of a single individual, a thing foisted on the American people and accepted by them, reluctantly, only from a sense of obligation to Russia for her supposed aid to the Union government during the Civil War. It is possibly congenial to our current self-esteem to believe that only in our generation have Americans appreciated the value of American ownership of Alaska. Such a view, if gratifying, is incorrect. Contemporary public opinion--as reflected in the newspapers of the day--was far from universally opposed to our purchase of Alaska.[2]

The initial response of certain newspapers, upon hearing of the unexpected transaction, was one of some bewilderment. But the editorial mind of many was soon affected by the March 30th dispatch of the Associated Press, by the quantities of information eagerly supplied by the State Department, or by a reasoned weighing of the increasingly available evidence. Each of these influences requires perhaps a brief explanation.

The March 30th dispatch of the Associate Press was a lengthy account, relating the existence of the treaty, its chief provisions, and its supposed origin.[3] It was not dictated by Secretary Seward, but he was certainly its anonymous, responsible source. The dispatch implied that the Johnson Administration, inspired by a concern for the economic welfare of our citizens in the Washington Territory, was solely responsible for initiating the treaty. The implication was clear. If this treaty was rejected, the innocent and obliging Russian Emperor would consider himself insulted and betrayed, and let all remember that Alexander II was the one European monarch who had "befriended" the United States during the Civil War.

The influence of the State Department on the American Press, in general, though apparent, was not conclusive. Surely Secretary Seward "planted" some information, and made available to the press certain letters he had received,[4] various official scientific reports, and copies of Charles Sumner's eloquent speech in the Senate; surely all the information so distributed was favorable to the purchase. This need neither surprise the historian, however, nor give rise to the assumption that the press was bribed or controlled by Secretary Seward. Charges current at the time, and later, that vast sums of government money were expended by Seward to subsidize large portions of the press, seem definitely unfounded. What Seward termed his "education campaign" was neither extravagant nor illegal; indeed, it has perhaps been rather over-emphasized by certain writers. Indirectly, this educational campaign influenced both congressional approval and the acquiescence of a large part of the articulate public. It did not alone create this approval and acquiescence. Any belief in Seward's omnipotence is perhaps disproved by the fate of the Secretary's West Indian project.

For the purpose of this paper the *extent* of Seward's influence on the press is somewhat irrelevant. It is with the opinions and given reasons of American journalists that we are concerned; whether they obtained these opinions and reasons from prepared releases or original research is relatively unimportant.

The press was not dependent for information on Alaska solely from Secretary Seward, in any case. It is quite erroneous to believe that Alaska was *terra incognita* for all Americans in March, 1867. Not only had New England whalers brought back news of seal furs and walrus ivory, as well as sperm oil and ambergris, but the mishaps of the Perry Collins-Western Union Telegraph project, and the exploits of the "Rebel pirate," *Shenandoah* had acquainted various Americans with Alaska's existence. Moreover, after March, 1867, information on Alaska increased considerably, thanks to the reports of the combined coast survey-scientific expedition sent out by the Government in 1867; the research efforts of Professors Baird, Bannister, and Henry of the Smithsonian Institute; the literary labors of Fredrick Whymper, artist of the ill-fated "Telegraph Expedition"; and the "Alaskan lectures" of the indefatigable William H. Dall.

Editors would also, of course, consult local leaders whose views would reflect local economic interests. New England papers, for example, mentioned the whalers of New Bedford; West Coast papers, the needs and desires of Louis Goldstone and the California fur traders.[5]

As the initial bewilderment of many papers was overcome by second thoughts and growing information, one must not accept the first editorial comment as the considered judgment of a paper; neither must one confuse a touch of good-natured raillery with confirmed antagonism. The walrus and the polar bear lent themselves to jest and remarks of supposed wit, and even many pro-Alaska editors could not resist a facetious comment or two. James Gordon Bennett of the New York *Herald* favored the treaty, but could not forbear to print certain editor-manufactured advertisements to the effect that any impoverished European monarch who wanted to sell worthless territory "should apply to W.H. Seward, State Department, Washington, D.C."[6]

The forty-eight newspapers consulted (for the months of April, 1867, and July, 1868) constitute, it is believed, a reasonably representative sample, geographically and politically. Most of the quotations will be found to carry an April, 1867, dateline. Very few editors seem to have taken the trouble to express any real interest in the House proceedings of July, 1868, when the appropriation bill was debated. This can perhaps be accounted for on the grounds that the physical transfer of the territory was then an accomplished fact, and the presidential campaign of 1868 well under way.

The papers consulted will be divided geographically. Chief concentration will be placed on the Eastern newspaper capitals of Boston, New York, and Philadelphia, and for all sections only those papers will be mentioned which offered opinionated editorial comment concerning the Alaskan Purchase.

The Boston press was almost uniformly favorable to the purchase, evincing no trace of fear that the Alaskan fishing grounds would affect adversely New England interests in the North Atlantic fisheries.

The Boston *Herald* (moderate Republican) of April 11, 1867, declared, regarding Alaska, that:

> ...those who know most about it, estimate it most highly. The climate on the Pacific side [at that latitude] is not to be compared to that on the Atlantic side of the continent...The country is reported to abound in furs, forest, and minerals, while its rivers and bays on its coast swarm with as fine fish as ever were caught. [Alaskan timber] will be particularly valuable in the development of our domain on the Pacific coast and the commerce of the Pacific which has just been entered upon. As to the price, there can be but one opinion--it is dog cheap.

The Boston *Daily Evening Transcript* (April 3, 1867) emphasized "the great value and growing importance of our fisheries, both for whale and cod, in the waters of the North Pacific..." Though by no means ardent in its favor of the purchase, the *Transcript* seemed to think Alaska a reasonably good buy at $7,200,000. It had not changed its mind fifteen months later, though it expressed shock at the rumors that only four of the seven millions would reach Russian soil.[7]

The Boston *Advertiser* (Democratic) warned that the "treaty is not a matter to be dismissed lightly in ignorance." There was involved "the great whale fishery of the Northern Pacific and of Behring Straits, in which Massachusetts is so deeply interested." The western tip of Alaska, moreover, would provide a commanding naval station. (April 6).

A letter to the editor (April 9) declared that the Aleutian Islands would make fine coaling stations between our country and China, and that the products of India would soon be flowing across the Pacific to America, in ever-mounting quantities.

The Republican *Daily Evening Traveller* gloated over the supposed excitement the purchase had caused among the British, and editorialized to the effect that Alaska's "chief value is now its fur trade and its fisheries; but...of vastly more importance than all other things, will be the command it will give us of the western and the northwestern territory of this continent."

This paper could not resist mocking (April 12) the "great change [that] has come over the American mind with respect to Russian America. Everybody is looking at Russian America, and it is discovered that that country, which *once* was scarcely supposed fit for the presence of civilized men, is one of the finest parts of the globe." The *Traveller*, however, by no means condemned the turn the public mind had taken. "It deserves praise rather than censure." Whether the bargain would be a good or bad one would depend in the final analysis on the use that should be made by America of the acquisition. "...the change in Russian America, there is reason to hope and expect, will prove as great as that which within living memory has taken place in the country purchased from Napoleon..."

The Boston *Journal* (Republican) made little editorial comment on the purchase, but its Washington correspondent proclaimed that Sitka would follow the example of San Francisco, and in ten years would be a city of 50,000 persons.

The leading northern New England papers of the period were the Bangor (Maine) *Daily Times* and the Manchester (New Hampshire) *Daily Union*. Though for a time rather neutral, both finally concluded that the purchase was a good thing. In the opinion of the editor of the *Daily Union* (Democratic), it was well worth seven millions "to get good boundaries like the Pacific and Arctic Oceans." (April 10).

Of the seven New England papers consulted not one may be classified as an opponent of Alaskan annexation.

Among New York papers was the great journalistic opponent of the treaty, Horace Greeley's New York *Tribune* (then radical Republican). It opened fire on April 1 with a charge that the Administration was trying to divert attention from its domestic difficulties by plunging the country into foreign complications. We had no use for this territory and were putting "ourselves in the attitude of seeking ostentatiously the friendship of a power not friendly to England, and of contracting what is tantamount to an alliance for the sake of an affront."

By April 8 the *Tribune* was complaining that "national good will does not usually extend so far that one nation will sacrifice its interest merely to oblige another," and warning that Alaska was "territory on which Great Britain holds a virtual mortgage, and in which her fishermen and hunters will have equal rights with ours." On the following day the *Tribune* printed a story to the effect that Admiral Fox had once been told by Prince Gortchakoff that Russia would gladly *give* Alaska to the United States, just to be rid of it. The lobbying activities of Seward and his "Esquimaux ring" were steadily criticized by Greeley, and the Senate, when it ratified the treaty, was accused of land mania--"if it is at the North Pole, no matter." (April 10).

The *Tribune* initially expressed the hope that the House would refuse to appropriate the money to effect this hideously expensive and tax-burdensome folly, this acquisition of impossible "deserts of snow" (April 11); but by July 16, 1868, was grandly conceding: "We have not felt justified in urging the House to refuse the acquisition appropriation. We believe it was advisable to pay the money. Having received it, we wish Russia would consent to receive back the territory as a free gift from the Republic."

Of the other New York papers only the *Independent* (April 18, 1867) and the *Sun* (July 1, 20, 1868) joined the *Tribune* in real opposition to the acquisition of Alaska. The *World, Commercial Advertiser, Times,* and *Herald* were all on the other side of the fence.

The New York *World* (Democratic) was increasingly favorable to the acquisition as the first week of April, 1867, wore on. In its first editorial (April 1), it asked: "But have we done wisely in buying it? If estimated by what it is now, certainly no; if by what the purchase may hereafter lead to, perhaps yes." As an advocate of expansion the *World* was inclined to favor the treaty because, "It is an advancing step in that manifest destiny which is yet to give us British North America."

Twenty-four hours were sufficient to evoke other arguments in the treaty's favor. "The whaling merchants of New England and settlers in Oregon and California will no doubt find some way of profiting by the annexation...Our commerce...ought pretty certainly to be benefited by the opening of ports along this extreme verge of the continent, and by the attendant expansion of the fur trade and the fisheries."[8]

The New York *Commercial Advertiser* (Democratic) was both pro-Seward and pro-treaty, and in the New York *Times* the purchase had one of its most influential advocates.

> While narrow minded political bigots have been exhausting all their resources in branding him [Seward] as a traitor to his party, he has been quietly pursuing great objects of permanent and paramount interest for his country. The main importance of this acquisition grows out of its bearing upon our future trade with Japan, China, and the other countries of Eastern Asia...Reluctant as that body [the Senate] may be to accept even so great a boon as this from the hands of the President and Mr. Seward, its sense of public duty will constrain its ratification. (*Times*, April 1).

With its next issue the *Times* was ready boldly to declare that the purchase was "a natural though perhaps unexpected consummation of negotiations dating back to the time of Monroe, and its tendency is to lessen the likelihood of 'further entanglements' by removing Russia from the diplomatic area so far as the future policy of this continent is concerned."[9]

In later editorials it mentioned the undeveloped coal seams of the new territory, spoke of the possibilities of the Aleutian Islands as a naval station, and declared that seven millions "was a mere bagatelle compared with the magnitude and importance of the acquisition." (April 8, 10).[10]

The New York *Herald* (Republican) favored the treaty mainly on grounds of international policy:

> Politically considered, however, this cession of Russian Alaska becomes a matter of great importance. It indicates the extent to which Russia is ready to carry out her "entente cordiale" with the United States...it places British possessions on the Pacific coast in the uncomfortable position of a hostile cockney with a watchful Yankee on each side of him...[It is a] flank movement for this greater object [Canada]...we are satisfied that the proposed purchase from its political bearings will be at once approved by the public sentiment of the country and will, perhaps, be considered a bargain at seven million, simply as a speculation in fish oil and the fur business. (April 1).

The *Herald* was a sharp critic of the "pushing" tactics of Mr. Seward, however, and with reference to Seward's "promotional" dinner parties declared: "But with his Pennsylvania roast beef, his

Virginia oysters, his smoked walrus from Bering Strait, his Esquimaux stews and ice, his California wines and Kentucky Bourbon, his seven million and the lobby, the undaunted Seward, perhaps, will best them yet." (April 9).

Despite such exercises in literary irony, the *Herald* was a treaty advocate. The leading paper in extracting names and quotes from the executive sessions of the Senate, and the first paper to publish the treaty text, the *Herald* was sure that this new empire, "in area more than twice the size of France" would prove valuable as a factor in the international scene and valuable, too, for its fisheries, whales, fur trade, and coal. (April 12).

The New York Evening *Post* demonstrated an inexplicable example of editorial indecision. In its first edition of April 1, it declared that the territory was a "frozen, sterile, desert region...of no value present or prospective..." In its second edition of the same date, it asserted: "The purchase of the Russian Territory is a step towards the retrieval of this blunder [the Oregon 'Compromise' of 1846] not only by giving us the undisputed prominence on the American coast of the Pacific, but by pushing it out of the power of England to extend her territory in that quarter." The forests there were immensely valuable, its agricultural capabilities had never been developed, and, as for its fisheries, "the advantage of our whaling and fishing interest in these northern seas, in having always ports of their own country to run into, will develop its value with the advance of our population in the Pacific."

On April 8, however, the *Post* declared, "We hope the Senate will reject the proposed purchase." The next day it spoke in resigned tones of the acquisition, and on April 19, went so far as to make plans for the future of the various areas of Alaska when "the increase of population and of trade requires a division of the territory."

The only thing that seems certain about the attitude of the *Post* is that it was neither decisively for or against the treaty. Of the seven New York papers which took a definite stand, four were, on balance, favorable to Alaskan annexation.

In Philadelphia the editor of the *Inquirer* (Republican) was a most ardent advocate of the purchase:

> [Alaska] might become very useful to any power having naval interests in the Pacific...A time may come, when the possession of this territory will give us the command over the Pacific, which our extensive possessions there require. (April 1).
>
> ...If there is any value in the timber, furs, and fisheries of that region, and it must be great, the consideration of the cost of the territorial government is not worthy of a moment's thought. (April 8).

The *Inquirer's* Washington correspondent was equally enthusiastic over the territory's possibilities and spoke of the Pacific Coast's desire for Alaska, and of the treaty's value in preserving the Union Party in the Far West. Numerous letters to the editor were published, all of them favorable to the purchase.

The Philadelphia *Ledger* (Democratic) was less decided in its support of the treaty, but despite some merriment over the possibilities of political elections among the polar bears (April 11), offered no real objection to the treaty. The expansionist-minded *North American Gazette* (Republican) also favored the results of Seward's latest project. Philadelphia, indeed, produced little or no journalistic opposition to Seward's treaty.

Moving South, the press of Washington, D.C. was generally favorable. The Washington *Evening Star* scouted the opposition to the treaty, jibing that it paralleled the foolish reluctance of some in 1803 to accept the Louisiana Purchase. It viewed the treaty as a proper piece of expansionism and dogmatically pronounced: "There are few full-blooded Americans who do not devoutly believe in the doctrine that this country is to absorb not only Russian America, but all the British possessions in North America." (December 21).

The *National Intelligencer* was equally convinced:

> The Russian possessions will secure us furs, fish and lumber in the greatest abundance to say nothing of the undisputed route of an overland telegraph. The fisheries, in the hands of our hardy seamen, would be of priceless value, and, as we are soon to have the Pacific railway, which will give an extraordinary impetus, we wonder that American statesmen should hesitate. (April 5).

The *National Republican* voiced its support in turn. In an editorial entitled, "Now is the Day and Hour for the Confirmation of the Treaty with Russia" (April 6), it lectured to the following effect: "American civilization has pushed itself through to the Pacific sea, where a commerce is growing up...which demands that the United States have absolute sovereignty over the entire coast from California to Bhering [*sic*] Straits." In listing various reasons for desiring the territory, the *National Republican* mentioned the protection it would afford our fisheries and fishermen there, the splendid nature of the rivers and harbors of Russian America, the territory's use as a broad base of trade with Japan and China, and the chance it gave us to fill out and protect our Continental Republic. The friendship of Russia was noted by way of further justification, and the warning given that "if we shall ever need the aid of any foreign power...it will be the immense and almost immaculate power of Russia." (April 8).

Whatever might have been the case when the purchase was before the House, it is most likely that John Forney's *Daily Morning Chronicle* was a free and unbribed agent in April, 1867, quite uninfluenced by the labors of former Senator Robert Walker or the purse of Minister Stoeckl. In this early and "amateur" phase, the *Chronicle* heartily applauded the treaty, if not with the violence it was to exhibit later: "Our people have faith in the manifest destiny of the nation. They look to the eventual absorption of the whole North American continent, and the Senate has undoubtedly gratified a national instinct in ratifying the treaty..." (April 11).

The favor with which the *Chronicle* received this treaty is indicated by its quoting in full--and with marked approval--an editorial in the Rochester (New York) *Democrat*, which virtually eulogized the possibilities of the Alaskan territory.

The Wilmington (Delaware) *Daily Commercial* favored the acquisition of the territory, but opposed its purchase: "It seems to us the worst of policies, for it...is certainly to become ultimately the property of our Yankee nation, and we consider it fair to presume at a price next to nothing at all. If this were our last chance, and the lowest offer likely to be made, we might urge its acceptance..." (April 4).

The Baltimore *Sun* (Democratic) and *American and Commercial Advertiser* (Republican) were not so economy-minded. The latter printed the highly favorable and nationally quoted Associated Press dispatch of March 31 as its first news of the treaty, and followed this up with a pair of editorials in which the value of the area's fisheries and fur trade was discussed at great length.

The *Daily Journal* of Wilmington, North Carolina approved the purchase only "in view of ulterior events." The expansion of the fur trade and whale fisheries on the Pacific Coast and the increased likelihood of garnering the British possessions in North America furnished such "events." (April 4).

The Louisville (Kentucky) *Daily Journal* favored the treaty, observing: "The great commercial advantages secured by it are universally admitted." (April 3).

The Memphis *Daily Post* (moderate Republican) urged the purchase in these terms:

> In view of our growing commerce in the Pacific, the establishment of lines of steamers to run regularly between China, Japan, and Australia, the increase of the coastwise trade, the completion of the Pacific Railroad and the Russo-American telegraph...the acquisition of this vast possession is desirable, and seven millions of dollars is a small consideration to pay for it. (April 5).

The Memphis paper, however, reviled the manner in which Seward had "unscrupulously urged" the treaty, and insisted that the actions of the Secretary and the President in this connection would further damn them in the eyes of the public. (April 15).

The Washington dispatches of both the Savannah *Daily Republican* and the Augusta *Daily Press* included press releases, telegrams and Seward-inspired "reports from Washington" highly favorable to the purchase.

Of the New Orleans papers the *Commercial Bulletin* seems to have been the most enthusiastic, virtually urging an alliance between the now-enlarged Northwest and the South:

> The demands for cotton goods in the new region of the Northwest will be enormous, and there is no reason why these goods should not be manufactured in the South, thereby employing our poor and industrious population, and adding greatly to our resources...it will be seen that the South will be

greatly advanced by the acquisition and settlement of the Russian American possessions. (April 15).

The New Orleans *Times* and the newborn New Orleans *Republican* contained a large number of dispatches and letters favorable to the purchase, but *La Tribune de la Nouvelle-Orleans* had mild doubts about the value of the territory. It suspected that if the Russians were willing to shed the territory it must be of little value. ("...evidemment inutile aux Russes, elle ne peut pas etre d'un bien grand profit pour les Americains.") (April 3).

The Galveston *Republican*, though making no editorial comment, printed at considerable length the panegyric on Alaska delivered by Representative Banks during the debate in the House. (July 13).

Of the sixteen Southern newspapers consulted, only two may be labeled outright opponents of the Alaskan Purchase.

In the Middle West, the city of Chicago saw its two leading papers somewhat divided on the desirability of Alaska. The *Evening Journal* cheered the purchase without qualification of any kind, but the reaction of the *Republican* was less clear. The Washington correspondent of that paper was vehemently anti-treaty; its editor, tepidly favorable. The same issue of the *Republican* that found the correspondent calling the treaty a "huge farce," found the editor pontificating that it was "very natural that Russia and the United States should form an alliance...Russia has demonstrated her good faith in this matter by ceding to our Government all her possessions on the American continent." (April 1). Even though the editor jocosely declared some four days later that the real reason for the purchase was to give the Fenians a base of operations, and even later (April 13) spoke of the danger of soon seeing in the House a representative from Sitka "dressed in a grizzly bear-skin overcoat and seal-skin unmentionables," the attitude of the paper seems to have been, on the whole, one of hesitant favor. "As evidence of the good will of the Russian Government toward the United States, this treaty has its chief significance. Future explorations may prove it to be rich in mines, while it will undoubtedly prove of increasing value to the Pacific states for its fisheries." (April 10).

The Cincinnati *Daily Gazette* rather opposed the purchase, but its sister paper, the *Commercial*, favored it. Other affirmative voices were those of the Detroit *Free Press* and the St. Louis *Times* and *Daily Missouri Democrat.* The latter stressed the wonderful effect of the Japanese current on the climate of Alaska, and asserted that the acquisition "affords another perspective of Uncle Samuel's 'manifest destiny' to absorb the continent." (April 11).

The Alaskan Treaty does not seem to have interested Mid-Western editors to the extent it did those on the East and West coasts, but even the few examples given show that the press of this section was in no sense solidly opposed to the purchase.

What then can be said of the reaction of the press as a whole?[11] First, that all statements to the effect that the newspapers were uniformly unfavorable to the treaty are erroneous. Secondly, that though the sample of newspapers consulted is perhaps too small to support any sweeping generalizations, it can be suggested that a majority of the American press seems either to have favored the treaty or at least not to have been opposed to it.[12] Thirdly, that neither the political allegiance nor the geographic location of a newspaper was usually decisive in determining its stand. Finally, that the main arguments advanced by the press in support of the purchase, listed perhaps in order of increasing importance, were: the propriety of maintaining the friendship of Russia; the possibility that the purhase would facilitate the acquisition of British Columbia and generally promote our predestined expansion and power; and the probability that we should derive great economic benefits from the purchase.[13]

"Russian friendship" and the "assistance" Russia gave the Federal Government during the Civil War was often mentioned by the American press, though usually as an auxiliary argument.[14]

Contemporary press opinion indicates that there was a good deal of latent expansionism in the United States in 1867. The Civil War had caused certain Americans to think for the first time of the desirability of such objects as naval and commercial bases, and that quasi-mystical doctrine, "Manifest Destiny," had still its supporters. Belief in the inevitable and benevolent assimilation of North America by the politically and morally superior United States was nutured in many an editorial heart and column. In so far as Manifest Destiny was basically an agrarian movement, the desire of certain Americans for Alaska was not an offshoot of Manifest Destiny. But Manifest Destiny also had its "commercial" side, and in this sense, the Purchase was the vestigial remain of that nation-shaping doctrine. Certain papers emphasized the importance of Alaska's harbors for our Oriental trade, and more spoke of the necessity of checking British expansion and securing a favorable balance of power for the United States in the Pacific West. Various editors on the Pacific Coast went to far as to express hope that the purchase of Alaska, by putting British Columbia in "an American vice," would mean the ultimate acquisition of that choice and strategic area by the United States.[15]

The chief argument of those members of the press who supported the purchase, however, was that, in economic terms, Alaska was worth the purchase price. Because of its supposed resources in fish, whales, furs, timber, and minerals, because of its very real commercial value, Alaska was thought a good bargain.

Those were arguments and motives that could have clear appeal for the average educated American. Surely they were such as to deter press or public from howling in united chorus, "Seward's Folly!"

ENDNOTES

[1]One receives from many secondary accounts the impression that virtually the only American who did not think the acquisition a complete folly was Mr. Seward. That gentleman by lobbying and legerdemain somehow forced the United States to accept his treaty despite a solid hoot of derision from the American public. See, for example: Hubert Howe Bancroft, *History of Alaska* (San Francisco, 1890), vi; Henry Wadsworth Clark, *History of Alaska* (New York, 1930), pp. 78-81; Asa E. Martin, *History of the United States* (Boston, 1931), II, 334; Foster Rhea Dulles, *America in the Pacific: A Century of Expansion*, 2d ed. (Boston, 1938), pp. 83-88; R.E. Riegel; D.F. Long, *The American Story* (New York, 1955), I, 423; Oscar Handlin, *Chance or Destiny* (Boston, 1955), p. 119; H.U. Faulkner, *American Political and Social History*, 7th ed. (New York, 1957), p. 626.

The last four works cited testify to the persistence of this view despite the provocative article by Professor Thomas A. Bailey, "Why the United States Purchased Alaska," in the *Pacific Historical Review* 3 (1934): 39-49. Bailey sampled contemporary editorial opinion in six Pacific Coast newspapers and reached the conclusion that these newspapers were definitely favorable to the Alaskan Treaty. He admits, however, that geographic proximity and special commercial interests could have made opinion in the Far West a rather special case.

[2]The measure to which newspaper opinion reflects public opinion must always be a point of dispute. It is surely a component part of the public opinion of a period, and, to a degree, usually both influences and mirrors general contemporary opinion.

[3]See in this connection Victor J. Farrar's excellent monograph, *The*

Annexation of Russian America (Washington, 1937), pp. 56-57.

[4]*House Exec. Doc.* #117, 6-109.

[5]A group of California fur traders headed by Louis Goldstone had for some years envied the favored position which the Hudson's Bay Company enjoyed under charter in Russian America. Using Senator-elect Cornelius Cole of California as intermediary, they began in 1866 to negotiate with Russian Minister Stoeckl for the expiring rights of the British company. Baron Stoeckl led them on, and, after they had made a formal request, made his refusal the opening wedge in his March, 1867, talks with Seward.

[6]New York *Herald*, April 12, 1867.

[7]This is a reference to the old "mass bribery charge" that was well disposed of by Professor William A. Dunning in 1912, but which still crops up on occasion. For the origins of this charge see the New York *Sun* of November 30, 1868, the Worcester *Spy* of December 4, 1868 (Worcester, Massachusetts), and Reports of the Committee on Public Expenditures, *House Reports* (40th Cong., 3d Sess.), #35; #1388.

Professor Dunning's article, "Paying for Alaska" is to be found in the *Political Science Quarterly* 27 (1912): 385-98. See, also, Ellis P. Oberholtzer, *A History of the United States Since the Civil War* (New York, 1917), I, 556; Reinhard L. Luthin, "The ale of Alaska," *The Slavonic and East European Review* 16 (1937): 168-182.

[8]Though the *World* favored this extension of our boundaries, it was sufficiently anti-Seward to mock the arguments and methods used by the Secretary to help effect the purchase, and to mock the self-conflicting extravagances of the treaty advocates. "Tropical Disadvantages Offset by the Value of the Ice Trade--Secretary Seward's New Ice-othermal Line--A Great Opening for Soda-Water Fountains and Skating Ponds" ran the headline of April 9.

[9]Like many Eastern papers, the *Times* printed large sections from Charles Sumner's famous and scholarly address in the Senate. Sumner's speech, incidentally, was most influential in producing the large pro-ratification majority in the Senate, and had probable influence as well on American press opinion.

[10]The *Times* still strongly favored the purchase fifteen months later, but on abstract constitutional grounds agreed with the pretensions of the "House Constitutionalists." (July 15).

A group of "House Constitutionalists" or "House Rights Men" succeeded initially in attaching to the Alaskan Appropriation Bill the Loughridge Amendment. By this amendment the House of Representatives asserted its right to be "previously consulted" respecting any future purchase of territory. It was but an exhibition of jealousy by the House over senatorial prerogative in treaty-making, similar to that demonstrated in connection with the Jay Treaty. In both cases, the House had finally to give way.

For the views of the "House Constitutionalists" see *Congressional Globe*, 40th Cong., 2d Sess., IV, 3621-25; 4052-55; V, 4392-94.

[11]The writer has not made a sufficient study of contemporary periodical literature to warrant any over-all conclusions in that area. Of the fifteen "national" periodicals consulted, however, only three expressed an editorial opinion adverse to the Alaskan Purchase: *Leslie's Weekly*; the New York *Nation*; and *Harper's Weekly*.

[12]Though there was much initial hesitation on the part of many editors to

express a definite opinion, the statement of Theodore Clark Smith that "the bewildered comments of the newspaper press during the week when the treaty was pending indicate clearly the absence of any popular feeling for or against annexation" is a statement of doubtful validity. T. C. Smith, "Expansion After the Civil War, 1865-1871," *Political Science Quarterly* 16 (1901): 415.

[13]These arguments were interestingly enough almost identical to those made in Congress during the ratification and appropriation debates. All can be found in Senator Sumner's speech (*House Exec. Doc.* #177, 124-188). In the House of Representatives see the speeches of Representatives Schenck and Banks on "Russian Friendship"; Representatives Orth, Donnelly, Maynard, Myers, Spalding, and Munger on "Expansion and British Columbia"; and Representatives Munger, Higby, Johnson, and Banks on "Economic Value." *Congressional Globe*, 40th Cong., 2d Sess., IV, 3625-27; 3659-60; 4054 and V, Appendix, 386-432.

These arguments and motives also appear prominently in the private letters received by Senator Sumner in 1867 from such correspondents as Professor Spencer Baird, G. V. Fox, Commander John Rodgers, Major General Meigs, W. Beach Lawrence, John M. Forbes, and Louis Agassiz. Sumner Correspondence for the year 1867, *Sumner Papers*, Widener Library, Harvard University.

[14]It was an argument and "motive," however. The statement of John G. Latane to the effect that the research of Professor Frank A. Golder in the Moscow archives "leaves one with the impression that Russian friendship can no longer be considered an important factor in the purchase of Alaska" is erroneous. Golder's concern was the motives of Seward and the Johnson Administration, not public opinion and its inspiration. Myths have as much influence on public opinion as facts. Latane, *A History of American Foreign Policy* (New York, 1927), pp. 424-25. Golder, "The Purchase of Alaska," *American Historical Review* 25 (1920): 411 ff, "The Russian Fleet and the Civil War," 20 (1915): 801 ff.

[15]Bailey, "Why the United States Purchased Alaska," *loc. cit.* See, especially, Sacramento *Daily Union*, April 1, 1867; Seattle *Puget Sound Gazette*, April-May, 1867. See, too, Chicago *Evening Journal*, April 1, 1867.

MISSIONARIES, INDIANS AND POLITICS*

Ted C. Hinckley

American missionaries first arrived in Alaska ten years after its purchase by the United States. It is apparent today that the missionaries' own cultural and intellectual heritage led many of them (although not all) to view all cultures in "superior"/"inferior" terms. They simply had no concept of the value of cultural diversity. Their own culture, they believed, was undeniably superior; "inferior" societies, including those of Alaska's Native inhabitants, had merely not yet evolved from hunter-gatherer through herding and then agriculture to reach the most fully "civilized" form, that of industrial democracy. One of their tasks, they felt, was to assist this evolutionary process so that Alaska's Native people (but not necessarily their cultures) might survive into the twentieth century. Thus, they were assimilationists as well as Christianizers.

One is most likely to think of Presbyterian leader Sheldon Jackson when one hears the word "missionary." But Jackson never engaged in parish work in Alaska at all. Instead, he organized missionary activity, directed the acculturation of Alaska's Natives, and raised public and private funds for both purposes from the contiguous United States. From 1885 until 1906 Jackson also served as General Agent of Education in Alaska, a position established by the Organic Act of 1884. To accomplish his goals, Jackson maintained residency in Washington, D.C., and travelled extensively throughout the rest of the country, visiting Alaska each summer.

Historian Ted C. Hinckley of San Jose State University has written a number of articles about Jackson and his contemporaries. Hinckley's research extends to other aspects of Alaskans' experiences during the early American period as well. His publications include accounts of William Seward's only visit to Alaska, of the U.S. Navy's shelling of the village of Angoon in 1882, and of the Tlingits' concerns about non-Native encroachment onto their lands and traditional fishing sites. Hinckley's major publications include *The Americanization of Alaska, 1867-1897* (Palo Alto, CA: Pacific Books, Publ., 1972) and a biography of gold rush era governor *Alaskan John G. Brady: Missionary, Businessman, Judge, and Governor, 1878-1918* (Published for Miami University by Ohio State University Press, 1982). Hinckley presently is preparing a history of the Tlingit people following United States acquisition of Alaska.

---

*This article originally appeared in *Journal of Presbyterian History* 46 (September 1968): 175-196.

In the following selection, Hinckley discusses Samuel Hall Young, the resident Presbyterian leader in Alaska for many years. The article suggests that the missionary experience in Alaska was more varied than those familiar only with Jackson might suppose. It also demonstrates that Jackson had both rivals and critics.

* * *

The survival and durability of the Puritan tradition into nineteenth and even twentieth century America is a remarkable phenomenon. A splendid example of this legacy in action is the career of Samuel Hall Young. An evaluation of his early Christian labor in and for Alaska is particularly valuable as the forty-ninth state celebrated its 1867-1967 centennial.

Samuel Hall Young was born in Butler, Pennsylvania, on September 2, 1847. Young's parentage was of solid Calvinist persuasion. His mother, Mrs. Margaret (Johnston) Young was particularly proud of one extension of the family tree--none other than Oliver Cromwell's eldest daughter. Typically independent-minded, her American forebearers had come to represent every type of Presbyterianism: Seceders, Oldside Covenanters, Newside Covenanters, United Presbyterians, *ad infinitum*. Sectarian divisiveness was no less evident on S. Hall Young's father's side.

The Young and Johnston families, like their Puritan ancestors, seem to have respected the power of a formal education. At the dawn of the nineteenth century, after New England grandfather Robert Young had moved his family into Western Virginia, Robert served as a part-time teacher. One of his sons, S. Hall's father Loyal Young, completed his education at Allegheny's Western Theological Seminary. His graduation occurred in 1832. That same year America's western champion was triumphantly reelected, and Andrew Jackson's "Democracy" revealed a nation burgeoning with unpredictable confidence. Many years later Loyal's son reflected how well the young Republic's amazing social mix had diluted Puritan predestination. "I would not emphasize heredity too strongly," S. Hall Young wrote. "We are what we are. Our blood may have power to sway us this way or that, and environment is still more potent; but every strong man is 'captain of his soul...'"[1]

Samuel Hall Young grew up in the penury familiar to a rural manse. Whether it was Scotch-Irish testiness, or simply boyish embarrassment over initials that spelled SHY, the youth chose Hall as his name, and it stuck. The deprivations of a rural ministry in Western Pennsylvania do not seem to have injured seriously the happiness of Hall Young and his seven brothers and sisters. But there is no mistaking the sacrifice and spartan simplicity which guided their home life. Hall's grammar school education was spotty, partially because his affection for outdoor romps would not surrender to the confinement of a one-room school house. Severe discipline was meted out to him. Unfortunately this liberal application of the rod plus his rather poor health resulted in much of his boyhood education being of the "Lincoln home study" type: the *Bible* and *Pilgrim's Progress*. The recently published historical poems of Longfellow, such as "Hiawatha" and "The Courtship of Miles Standish," provided entertaining dinner recitations.

In later years Young expressed his relief that the hell-fire ideology to which his youth had exposed him was balanced by the ever-present sweetness of his parents' love. Once during his teens he had momentarily experienced that love was not simply happiness. The sight of his parents literally risking their lives as conductors on the underground railroad shook him. Very likely the fear written on the faces of the runaway slaves frightened the youth more than the very real hazards confronting his parents.

Adolescence and poor health kept Hall from joining his brothers in the ranks of the Union Army. Nonetheless, the monumental humanitarian issues which exploded in the Civil War were ever present in the sensitive lad's mind. After the war Young joined two of his brothers in Michigan. He had planned to study law. Like many a minister's son, Young had carried his religion rather automatically. Now, suddenly, unexpectedly, the twenty-year-old, whose constitution had been toughened by demanding physical labor, was converted. "I joined the Church...and the whole tide of my life flowed towards the Christian ministry and evangelization of those who 'sat in darkness'; I was a missionary from the moment of my conversion."[2]

Further education was therefore mandatory, and in 1871 Young entered Wooster College. Founded only five years before, Wooster faced considerable collegiate competition and was not reluctant to promote its virtues. One blurb ran: "It is better to give a son a complete education than to give him a farm. He will then be able to earn far more in a year than a farm could produce, and he may besides wield a great influence for good."[3] It was the latter wish that Young sought to fulfill, but due to "constant poverty," he finished at Wooster one year late. Eager to sit at the feet of Princeton Theological Seminary's esteemed Dr. Charles Hodge, Young traveled to New Jersey. One year was enough. Hodge was far more interested in his Greek Testament than his students, and, Young later declared, he got "more good" from New York City's Madison Square meetings of Moody and Sankey than he got from his whole seminary year.[4] He finished seminary at Western Seminary, Allegheny, Ohio. Sandwiched between his studies were valuable preaching and teaching experiences.

No different from hundreds of other ministerial novices, Young had frequently dreamed of foreign service. The achievements of nineteenth century missionaries in Africa, Asia and America's Far West were immensely challenging. Men like David Livingstone, Adoniram Judson, and Marcus Whitman enjoyed a fame and public acclaim that went far beyond sectarian or even Christian circles.[5] But Young's poor health record seemed to disqualify him for harsh missionary rigors. His reservations vanished, however, when he encountered another minister who years before had also been told to seek a comfortable eastern parish because of weak physique, and who had then subsequently become the Presbyterian Church's Far Western "Rocky Mountain Superintendent."

It was just before Christmas in 1877 when this popular home missionary organizer, Dr. Sheldon Jackson, spoke at Western Seminary. The pint-sized Jackson declaimed on the needs of America's most recent territorial acquisition--giant-sized Alaska.[6] In his inimitable way ramrod Jackson quickened a mandate for Christian service. As Young later recalled, "Alaska became a land of enchantment...Its heathen multitudes were a reproach to Christendom." Forthwith Young volunteered himself to the Board of Home Missions.[7]

Alaska in 1878 was badly in need of dedicated Americans who would assume responsible civilizing roles. During the preceding year the United States Army had withdrawn its forces from the northern territory, and only the thinnest veneer of either government or American society existed there. Here was a country one-fifth that of the contiguous United States, inhabited by some thirty thousand natives, many of whom had never heard of the Christian faith--for a tyro minister it posed a tremendous challenge.

Sparked by the "Rocky Mountain Superintendent," who would himself in a few years devote his entire attention to the Far Northern frontier, Young sought the facts.[8] From Aaron L. Lindsley, pastor of the First Presbyterian Church of Portland, Oregon, and from Mrs. Amanda R. McFarland, the pioneer Presbyterian missionary to Alaska, he obtained additional information of what would be required. Mrs. McFarland's replies were strong medicine. The harsh picture which she painted of indigenous social disintegration in Wrangell, Alaska, left no doubt that evangelization there must be coupled with, if not preceded by, social action.[9] Despite Mrs. McFarland's sobering accounts, Hall Young was impatient for his last year of seminary to end. Young's impatience with a student's life only grew when soon after the New Year of 1878 he heard that John Green Brady, a graduate of Union Theological Seminary, and Miss Fannie E. Kellogg, Lindsley's niece, had already reinforced Mrs. McFarland in Alaska. In the spring of 1878, the Board of Home Missions commissioned him for Alaska. Sheldon Jackson editorialized: "The action of the Board is none too soon, as the Jesuits are also entering the field."[10]

Before Young left for his new assignment in late spring of 1878, Dr. Henry Kendall, Secretary to the Board of Home Missions, told the ministerial recruit half jestingly, half seriously, "If those Indians scalp you, we will canonize you as a martyr, but don't let them do it if you can help it." Young docked at Fort Wrangell on July 10, 1878.[11] To welcome him was a crowd of two: an ex-soldier who had fallen in love with the misty, mountainous Alexander Archipelago, and an Indian covered with lampblack. Prior to his departure, Kendall had urged Young to "find a wife." Upon disembarking at Wrangell, a Hudson's Bay agent counselled him, "Don't become an Indian." Within a few days Young had found his wife, and a distinguished fifty-year career would testify that he never "went native." Yet, like almost every other educated man or woman who dared the Alaskan frontier, Young found intervals of state-side service indispensable. Alaska was beautiful but it was also brutal and barbarous.

Before commencing his work as Mrs. McFarland's co-worker, the apprentice's curiosity about his Presbyterian peers at Sitka had to be satisfied. Continuing aboard the steamer, he journeyed up the Inside Passage to the District capital. Sitka, Young discovered, had changed little since Russian days. He soon met John G. Brady and Miss Fannie Kellogg; the former proved to be quite as industrious as Young while the latter proved to be most charming. Certainly Miss

Kellogg wasted no time. She took the missionary novice on a tour of historic "Lovers' Lane" to Indian River, and, as Young later confessed, "the stately trees of hemlock and spruce impressed me much less than the lively young lady at my side."[12] Miss Kellogg had already built a mission school with over fifty students, although their attendance was about as predictable as a Sitka sunbeam. In age they ranged from six to sixty. Her enthusiasm and capabilities, not to mention her feminine attractiveness, were what Young had hoped to find--but never in Alaska. On December 15 Fannie became his wife and joined him at the Wrangell mission.[13]

A worthy career had begun, but as fate would have it, it had been flawed even before it began. The controversial place of Aaron L. Lindsley, Fannie's uncle and pastor of Portland's First Presbyterian Church, still needs to be evaluated. Regrettably both he and Sheldon Jackson, for all their abilities, unabashedly scrambled after the historic distinction of having pioneered the Presbyterian Church in Alaska. When their respective partisans got into the unseemly quarrel, their contest became more than a case of two egos in collision. In the author's opinion, and in the view of Dr. Charles A. Anderson, one-time Secretary of the Presbyterian Historical Society, Lindsley bungled much of what he attempted in Alaska.[14] To call him the "Father of Alaska Missions," as Young later did, is historically incorrect.[15] And to describe Lindsley as the "loving and bountiful parent of all the early missionaries" is laughable. Alaska's first Presbyterian missionary, Mrs. Amanda McFarland, thoroughly distrusted Portland's eminent divine. Young's superior, Dr. Henry Kendall, surely had no doubt about Lindsley's troublesome role.[16] The only substantial aid which his church seems to have rendered Alaska missions during the 1880's was to the Wrangell mission, and it was minimal compared with the support forwarded by the New York Board. Whatever the verdict of history, Young unsuccessfully tried to remain neutral in the Jackson-Lindsley feud.

Presbyterians are everything but neutral. By 1884 Lindsley was of no real significance to Alaska missions, while Jackson's territorial role, both in and out of the Church, had skyrocketed. Because of the success of his spreading mission school system, Jackson in 1885 was appointed, under the United States Bureau of Education, General Agent for Education for all of Alaska. Unlike Young, John G. Brady had been an unqualified pro-Jackson man from the outset. Blessed by a warm personality, a quick mind, and legal training, Brady would ultimately become Alaska's governor. He would achieve the high office on his own merits, but Jackson's political leverage at the nation's capital certainly did not hurt him.

Jackson never broke with his younger fellow missionary, S. Hall Young. Yet they never achieved the mutual confidence and deep friendship which Jackson and Brady came to enjoy. Many years later Young made various invidious comparisons between himself and Jackson's protege--especially how he had remained a minister while Brady had abandoned the cloth.[17] Clearly it was a case of sour grapes, for Young also suffered from the political itch and if fate had afforded him a chance to substitute the gavel for the collar, he would probably have done so.

By the fall of 1878, Young was totally immersed in educational work with Mrs. McFarland and the Wrangell mission. His correspondence bubbled with the optimism of the tyro. "Six tribes look to us for light." The Indians "learn rapidly and are delighted with the school...I preach twice every Sabbath to the Indians and once to the whites. We have Sabbath School after the morning service. Our congregations are large and orderly...Wrangell's future is assured and its rapid growth is certain." Young was wrong about a Wrangell boom. Yet his approach to founding a church was completely practical. "We cannot think of organizing a church yet...I am about organizing a catechetical class of men. I wish to train material for elders, deacons, and private members."[18] In less than a year, on August 3, 1879, to be exact, Wrangell had its Presbyterian Church with "eighteen Native and five white communicants." Present to honor the occasion were Messrs. Kendall, Jackson and Lindsley, and their wives.[19] Despite the tension between Lindsley and Jackson, everyone could rejoice at the mission station structures: a church 35 by 55 feet and a two-story girls' industrial school 40 by 60 feet.[20]

During 1879 Young had done considerably more than teach, preach and pound nails. Drawn by the challenge of Archipelago "pagans" outside the mission's influence, he took to the water. Accompanying him was none other than the California naturalist John Muir. Muir recalled how "even those chiefs who were not at all inclined to anything like piety were yet anxious to procure schools and churches that their people should not miss the temporal advantages of knowledge which...they were not slow to recognize." At the meeting with the Chilkats an old chief patiently listened to the young minister and then replied:

> I might say that through all my long life I have never until now heard a white man speak. It has always seemed to me while trying to speak to traders and those seeking gold mines that it was like speaking to a person across a broad stream that was running fast over stones and making so loud a noise that scarce a single word could be heard. But now for the first time, the Indian and the white man are on the same side of the river, eye to eye, heart to heart.[21]

Young not only had many chances to explore the hearts of men, but in company with Muir he explored regions not previously investigated by white men.[22] Later, without Muir, Young made two "long voyages of discovery and missionary work": one a four-hundred-fifty-mile circuit of Prince of Wales Island and another southward to the Cape Fox and Tongass tribes.[23]

One thing Young had quickly discovered in Alaska was the latent immediacy of violence. Murderous altercations occasionally erupted among the white miners who crowded into Wrangell during the winter months. And if the usual forms of civil justice were lacking, prompt legal decisions were not. One time Young found himself officiating at a funeral which laid to rest both the victim and the murderer.[24] The local aborigines spared white men, at least near the settlements, but not each other. One of the worst blows which befell Young was the loss of two of his Christian Indians, Moses and Tow-a-att. The quarrel which claimed their lives had begun over the destruction of some native hoochinoo, or hooch.[25] From the very first the American military as well as the later Christian teachers had struggled to separate the indigenes from all forms of liquor. In Alaska as in other regions of the Pacific and Far West, "fire water" reduced to rubble certain native societies.

On his famous canoe voyage with John Muir, Young had encountered a whole village "afire with bad whiskey." As the naturalist later commented, "This was the first time in my life that I learned the meaning of the phrase "a howling drunk."[26] In conjunction with the United States Navy, Young did everything he could to beat back the flow of rot gut. Illustrated classroom lectures on the evils of drink, actual physical destruction of stills, and a whole battery of efforts were fired at the beverage nemesis. Around the zones of settlement, at least, the dry campaign accomplished some good.[27]

Another campaign in which Young involved himself was the Juneau meeting of Alaskans "for the purpose of taking some action toward procurement of recognition and representation of this Territory by the United States Government." Juneau, in July, 1881, was still not yet designated as Juneau, and its population was largely itinerant miners. In fact, the rush to this remote site was hardly a year old, but with typical Western impatience, a territorial convention had been called. S. Hall Young came as one of the Wrangell delegates and was elected secretary of the one-day convention. As the Juneau historian, Robert N. De Armond, has noted, the popular vote that seated Young and his fellow delegates was ridiculously small. Understandably Congress did not take their demands for increased civil government very seriously. But for Young, no doubt, the convention was a heady affair.[28]

That spring Young escorted twelve Archipelago boys and girls to the United States Indian Training School at Forest Grove, Oregon. This institution had copied some features of Captain Richard H. Pratt's Carlisle establishment and taught a similar polytechnical curriculum with a heavy emphasis on English language instruction. Inspection of the Forest Grove plant stimulated Young's hopes for a similar school at Wrangell.[29] Before returning home, he made some public addresses and met with the Presbytery of Oregon. A. L. Lindsley's duchy endorsed his work. Because he had earlier complicated the work of the Board of Home Missions, neither Jackson nor Kendall wanted any further involvement with the Portland pastor. Indeed, in the preceding year, Jackson had requested the General Assembly either to organize a Presbytery of Alaska or to place the missionaries under the Presbytery of Puget Sound.[30] Although an attempt by the Presbytery of Oregon to lay claim to Alaska was blocked, it was not until May of 1883 that the Presbytery of Alaska was constituted. By that time Young's territorial duties had undergone a marked change.[31]

Certainly the mission personnel perplexities which beset Young were not the product of his sloth or lack of imagination. A sample of his non-teaching non-preaching tasks were: substituting for the local Wrangell Customs Officer; writing copy for the *Evangelist*; trying to outbluff a native shaman "doctoring" a sick native; and "logging in the mission's winter supply of salmon." As if all this were not enough, he urged his seniors to forward a boat so that the mission's evangelizing radius might be expanded. "Such a boat as I contemplate would need only three men or at most four." Dollar-conscious Home Board secretaries could only shake their heads. What he "contemplated" would have doubled the Wrangell staff.[32]

Certain factors appear to have injured S. Hall Young's early ministry. Not only did Young's very enthusiasm intimidate those with less drive, but due to his exuberant loquacity, tact occasionally fled. Alaska, like all remote missionary fields, was an inviting preserve for gossip. Fannie Young's aggressive abilities, plus the Young link with her uncle's Portland church, did not help mend this affliction. During the early 1880's the Young team irritated virtually every missionary working at Sitka and Wrangell.[33] A letter from Captain Henry Glass, commanding officer of the *U.S.S. Wachusetts*, clearly reveals how difficult it was for Young to restrain both tongue and pen.[34] The truth was, notwithstanding his ambition to move large groups of men, Young had been cast as a vivacious Christian whose triumphs would lie in the small-scale, person-to-person realm. In the full vigor of early manhood he could not know this.

On February 9, 1883, the Home for Wrangell's Indian girls which Mrs. McFarland had labored so hard to build burned to the ground. One year earlier, the mission structure at Sitka had met a similar fate. The result was that in 1884 the McFarland Home was moved to Alaska's capital. Well before the Wrangell conflagration Young had pressed upon the Home Board the desirability of an agricultural school for boys. With typical ebullience, and confidence that it could be made self-supporting, he inquired of Jackson, "Can't you do something for our boys? This farm scheme is not visionary for it is simply business. The chance seems providential. It would be a saving to our outlay. We could keep fifty head of cattle there without more work than the labor of one or two more."[35] No less than her husband, Fannie wanted a speed-up in social amelioration. During October of 1881 she had commenced to agitate for a hospital. Wrangell's medical needs were publicized in the *Presbyterian Home Missions*, and by November Hall boasted, "Mrs. Young's hospital gets along well and the Lord keeps ahead of her all the time in money and Indian Food...The place looks very tidy and neat."[36]

Shortly after the destruction of the McFarland Home, Young steamed southward for aid. Actually by this time the Wrangell mission's day school and the coeducational boarding facilities had received additional personnel. The Sitka station, as well as other new mission Panhandle posts, was thriving. Almost all of this had been accomplished under the authority and with the support of the Church's

Board of Home Missions. Young must have made quite a plea to the Presbytery of Oregon. Food, money and nine cases of clothing were promptly dispatched as succor.[37]

In his pocket Young carried a petition from the five Alaska missionaries (Sheldon Jackson, J. Loomis Gould, J. W. McFarland, Eugene Willard, John G. Brady, and himself) urging the 1883 General Assembly to create a Presbytery of Alaska.[38] Recognizing the handwriting on the wall, the Presbytery of Oregon not only seconded the action of their northern colleagues but elected Young as Commissioner to General Assembly.[39] To help assure that the Youngs arrived at the Saratoga Springs, New York, General Assembly, Jackson secured them half-rate ministerial railway tickets.[40] Young described the Saratoga Springs gathering as "a momentous one for Alaska." An Alaska Presbytery was officially instituted at this General Assembly. The really momentous part for Young was the aftermath. He had a wonderful time showing off his attractive wife and talking Alaska before eastern church groups.

> A constant whirl of social and church activities kept us busy; a series of missionary conventions in New York, Pennsylvania and New Jersey, with trips as far east as Rhode Island and as far west as Chicago, and south to West Virginia and Kentucky, kept us speaking almost daily.

Young further commented that the "response of the churches was more than we anticipated. The Board had to put on the brakes."[41]

What in fact had happened was that he and his eager wife had gone considerably beyond what their Home Board employers had expected. It was not that Hall and Fannie had raised money to build an independent boarding home for Wrangell natives which was so disconcerting, but that the Portland church once again appeared to be competing with the Church's Home Board. The Church's governing bodies rightly wanted Sheldon Jackson to win any prospective, forthcoming federal appointment for administering Alaska mission schools. Lindsley, however, lobbied for the partially experienced S. Hall Young. The Portland pastor, no doubt, believed he could have some control over Young.[42] Predictably it was asked, "Why start another boarding school when the Sitka Industrial School and its unification with the late McFarland Home already left everything in such an embryonic state?" Members of the Wrangell day school staff were no less perplexed and a bit angry.[43]

Fannie Kellogg later claimed that she founded her Tlinkit Training Academy in 1882. If she meant that she and Hall informally adopted some youngsters into their home in 1882, this is correct.[44] Actually the academy seems to have been born in 1884 when the United States Government authorized a free lease of some old abandoned garrison buildings for sleeping quarters and classrooms, and even permitted service rifles to be issued for hunting purposes.[45] Aided by his brother, James W. Young, and his Indian students, Hall transformed the barracks into a carpenter-cabinet-shoe shop and dormitory for boys and girls. A farm nine miles from Fort Wrangell in the Stickeen River delta was purchased for five hundred dollars, in order that the Academy might meet its own food requirements.[46] Fannie told how, "Our aim from the first has been to make the institution as nearly self-supporting as practicable." By November of 1885 the Tlinkit Training Academy boasted nineteen boys and eight girls.[47] James Young worked as farm foreman and mechanic while Young's cousin from West Virginia, Miss Lydia McAvoy, assisted as teacher. It appears the Youngs eventually planned to have boy boarders only.

Fannie and Hall were in full earnest when they spoke of a "self-supporting" institution. In the spring and summer months the native lads applied themselves to farm chores during the morning, while the afternoon was spent in study. As Young described it for the *Presbyterian Journal*, there was plenty to do:

> They are putting in sixty bushels of potatoes, besides plenty of oats, buckwheat, peas, turnips and garden seeds. Foragers are sent out every day for a supply of game and fish. Ducks, geese, grouse, and bears are abundant and close at hand. Then the supply of salt salmon and trout, dried small fish and dried berries will be put up for the winter.

To further assist the school, each student would be given a "Christian name" by "some individual or society" which promised to donate sixty dollars a year for his support. What would the boys receive for their labor? Young summed it up, "We are protecting these promising boys from temptations which would else surely prove their destruction, keeping them busy, pushing forward their English, Christian education, and striving to 'thoroughly furnish' them for the future."[48]

Throughout 1885 and 1886 the Youngs really threw their hearts into the Tlinkit Academy effort. Principal Hall Young also sought to maintain his work as Home Board preacher-teacher at Wrangell; inevitably there were Sundays when the ranch chores kept him from his village pulpit.[49] Concerned over inadequate mission communication, Jackson encouraged him to initiate a needed United States mail link. For a period Young assisted as Wrangell's unofficial postmaster.[50] In 1885 Governor A. P. Swineford visited the Tlinkit school and reported that the "training academy...had effected a great deal in the civilization and Christianization of the Indians."[51] One tourist noted that the ranch had "fifteen hundred acres...raising potatoes, turnips, etc. Mr. Young informed us that one thousand acres could be cut with a mower. They intend to demonstrate that there is good soil in Alaska for farming purposes." Stock was brought in to supply both power and food; indeed, Fannie's team of horses may have been Wrangell's first.[52]

At approximately the same time that Sheldon Jackson received his appointment as General Agent for Education in Alaska, the United States Congress began to authorize funds for native education in Alaska. By 1885 Jackson had begun to coordinate (in a loose fashion) the Moravian, Episcopalian, Methodist and Congregational high commands in a common assault on Alaska. Each was to assume a special region in which to labor. Naturally General Agent Jackson would do all he could to abet church missions with federal aid.[53] This problematically constitutional design had been adumbrated by President U. S. Grant's earlier, well-publicized Peace Policy for the Far West Indian population.[54] Although Jackson's scheme was better organized, it was not without its deficiencies. Among the incipient common schools now funded by Uncle Sam (and in which the precursor missionaries understandably would have a major role) was the Home Board's Wrangell Day School now transformed into a Government Common School. Young's cousin, Lydia McAvoy, assumed this billet in mid-1885, and a year later Hall ejaculated, "We have had the best day-school this year ever held in Wrangell [sic]....the progress of the children has been remarkable."[55]

It was not all triumph. A building fire proved too much for one girl and she "jumped through a window and cut her hand dreadfully...three girls...took their chances to run off." Indian boy-girl relations frequently horrified the Victorian mission staff. Once Fannie had to expel some boys for "insubordination and impudence," and to keep them fed was a herculean labor. One year's larder required the killing of "one hundred and twenty-one deer, eleven seals, one bear, about one hundred fifty wild geese, over three hundred ducks, and numerous other grouse, porcupines, marmots...they caught all the salmon, halibut, codfish, trout, herrings, flounders, crabs, clams, etc. needed."[56] Costs always outran income. To expand their public relations, and hopefully enlarge donations, Fannie and Hall initiated a school newspaper, *The Glacier*. The monthly ran from December 1885 to May 1888. *The Glacier* was a one-page sheet; an annual subscription was fifty cents; and its copy was local chit-chat, mission happenings and the progress of Christianity among the natives. What was not reported were the sexual propensities of the young student body that kept the missionaries in "constant trouble both at Wrangell and Sitka."[57]

In order to balance their constant expenses, Young had early attempted to barrel and ship salmon.[58] With the initiation of federal support, he no doubt hoped that Jackson would exert himself in support of the Tlinkit Training Academy as he had for the Sitka Training School. Jackson did not do so. In fact he actually discouraged what money might have been forthcoming. In answer to an inquiry from the Commissioner of Indian Affairs, the newly appointed General Agent for Education replied, "there is already one [Training School in Alaska]...And instead of having two starved ones in the same region of the country it is better to have one well sustained and efficient."[59] Fannie took the bit in her mouth and protested directly to the Secretary of the Interior, Honorable L. Q. C. Lamar.

> Of the appropriation, voted by Congress of Fifteen Thousand Dollars for Industrial Schools in Alaska, for the fiscal year ending June 30th, 1885, Eleven Thousand was given to the Sitka Training School, and our application for the unexpended balance sent on in May with the endorsement of the Civil Officers...was stated by the Department to have been received too late, the balance having been already paid back into the Treasury.[60]

It seems highly doubtful that the parsimonious Jackson permitted a single penny of any appropriation to go unspent. Whatever the case, the Academy's costs continued to mount and reality demanded an economic answer. On October 15, 1885, Hall wrote to Oregon's Senator J. N. Dolph. He admitted the school was in serious financial trouble and that the farm "on which we based our principal hope of self-support failed to realize these hopes." His solution was to let "the Government take up this school, using the shops, farm, printing press and supplies on hand."[61] Unfortunately

Congress' ridiculously small allocation for Jackson's expanding school system precluded another training school 150 miles from Sitka. However, in 1887-1888, the Bureau of Indian Affairs' budget did supply some temporary relief: for her twenty-five students the government promised $167 per annum.[62] Alaska's capital newspaper rejoiced at the news. Declared *The Alaskan*: "Heretofore this school has been supported by voluntary contributions, and the donation to it of a large part of Mr. Young's salary as a missionary, and a person of less indomitable will and energy than good Mrs. Young is possessed of would have abandoned the work long ago."[63]

Certainly Fannie had given her best. On January 1886, her husband reluctantly reported to *Glacier* readers:

> Our institution is now motherless. Mrs. Young has been doing the work of three. Our funds were not sufficient to warrant the employment of the needed assistants. Mrs. Young was not very strong to begin with; and the constant strain upon bodily and mental powers told severely upon her health and developed a heart trouble that was growing to dangerous proportions. So we sent her down to Portland by this month's steamer, for the double purpose of obtaining medical advice and giving her a much needed rest.[64]

Fannie recovered, but a year later the Youngs suffered the tragic loss of their youngest daughter, Fannie Louise, because, as her sorrowing father wrote, "The delicate health of this little one could not be recruited amidst the rigors of the Alaskan climate." Both Reverends Lindsley and Jackson participated in the resultant funeral ceremonies.[65]

The 1887 government aid was just not enough to sustain the Academy's momentum. Despite Fannie's will and Hall's industry, the institution's end appeared in sight. In the fall of that year United States Commissioner James Sheakley visited the Wrangell School.

> In the conscientious discharge of my official duties I had to decide a case against Mrs. Young and her so called Training school; and the facts developed by the investigation proved that she had no training school at all and that she was keeping nothing but an Indian boarding house of rather inferior grade. I have the kindest of feelings toward the Young family and have put myself to some inconvenience to assist and

> accommodate them and will do so still but the facts and the law are against her and I could not decide otherwise.

The upshot was that the Commissioner (later to become Governor Sheakley) strongly urged the Youngs "to abandon their effort...and seek some employment better adapted to their capacity." He reported they had "decided to act upon [his advice] and will make ready to leave this place by early spring."[66] The following spring Sheakley was surprised to discover that Fannie "was making a determined effort to continue the so-called training school." "The farm," he insisted, "is of no value. It has never produced anything but debts and an annual loss of about a thousand dollars." One good training school in the Territory is all that is required and the one at Sitka now in successful operation is sufficient to accommodate all who need such educational advantages."[67]

Aware that the Young enterprise was about to collapse, Jackson sent Mr. and Mrs. H. F. Lake to salvage enough for a far simpler mission school operation. The transition was understandably not always pleasant for either Mrs. Clara Lake or Fannie Young. "It is indeed very fortunate," penned Mrs. Lake, "that Mr. Lake and I are not troubled with being sensitive--those that are she worries the life out of."[68] Clearly Fannie and Hall had exhausted themselves. No doubt they accepted the news that the Office of Indian Affairs had not renewed their contract less as a *coup de grace* than as a reprieve. Hall felt the lack of civilization was deteriorating him "mentally and spiritually." He had grown to loathe preaching in Chinook and Tlinget.[69] By July, Young was on his way to scout out a California parish assignment, and faithful Fannie labored to close down the late Tlinkit Academy. Writing to the Commissioner of Education, Sheakley commented "that the closing of Mrs. Young's 'so called training school' is a good thing for all concerned." To Jackson he wrote a laconic "All is well that ends well."[70]

Regrettably it was not that graceful. Before Fannie could disengage herself from Wrangell, she got into a legal battle with a petty representative, spiteful, it would appear, of the United States Government. To hasten her departure, the officer placed six locks on her home, commenting, "Won't that old hairpin be surprised when she comes home and finds her doors locked." The "old hairpin" was furious, and both the frontier press and the Sitka Judge, none other than her old co-worker John G. Brady, heard about "A LADY

MISSIONARY PERSECUTED." Flemming, the government official, beat a hasty retreat.[71]

Happily Fannie and Hall enjoyed their own well-earned retreat. His new ministry took him to the Southern California coastal community of Long Beach. With the old enthusiasm he informed Jackson, "I am well suited in my location here--am by the sea, in a delightful climate and a beautiful country. Am 22 miles from Los Angeles with Railroad connection. The town is rapidly growing and the church which was only organized in June has excellent prospects."[72] But the Golden State could not match Alaska. Neither could subsequent pastorates at Cedar Falls, Iowa, Cabery, Illinois, nor a college pastorate at Wooster, Ohio. The Great Land was in his blood, and in another ten years S. Hall Young would again be in the north, but serving a new role and in a completely different part of Alaska.[73]

It seems rather obvious why S. Hall Young's Wrangell efforts did not produce the result for which he and his loyal wife labored so assiduously. First of all, their sweat and vivacity could not outweigh lack of money, lack of Home Board support and a farming operation for which neither Wrangell's soil nor settlement was adapted. If Wrangell had been a thriving town everything would have been stimulated. As it was, the place by 1888 was a haunt of its former self. One visitor referred to it as a "ghost town," with its main street covered by knee high grass.[74] Furthermore, Jackson was right about an ill-advised training school duplication. There is no way to prove that Jackson's *bete noir*, Aaron L. Lindsley, kept encouraging the Tlinkit institution to spite the Church's Home Board leadership, but circumstantial evidence is tantalizing. Surely if he had wanted to promote the Presbyterian Church in Alaska he should have told the exuberant and naive Pennsylvania novice to play the team game, that is, keep his shoulder behind one of the regularly constituted Panhandle missions.

But maybe this does Lindsley a grave injustice. Possible he did attempt to restrain Young and his dynamic wife in their academic independence. To judge from Young's later career, in which he lunged from one assignment to another, the man's impetuosity was very unpredictable. Young was never one to soft-pedal his achievements. But then neither was he incapable of admitting his deficiencies. Gazing back on his Wrangell ministry from the perspective of the 1920's, the grey-haired Young declared, "My mistakes were many, and I regret them, both those mentioned, and more of which I cannot tell."[75]

Any fair-minded student who seeks to evaluate the early 1878-1888 career of S. Hall Young and/or his Alaska co-workers must admit that equipped with all the money in the world, the missionaries' goals were next to impossible to fulfill. An age which is a bit wiser in the enormous variables and complexity of acculturation can either scoff at their temerity or express respect for their steadfast sacrifices. Estimating a missionary's worth, like measuring the successful teacher, is largely impossible; one must weigh *future* achievement. In 1893 Rev. Clarence Thwing, Presbyterian minister in charge at Wrangell, wrote, "In spite of any irregularity about the latter enterprise, [the Tlinkit Academy] and its unfortunate (almost ignominious) termination, there are twenty or more fine young men, now just entering manhood, who were more or less educated or trained in the Academy. Mr. Young's works do follow him.'"[76] Add to these visible signs S. Hall Young's countless words and deeds for his native, as well as white, parishioners. Surely the verdict must be that he left Alaska a better place in which to live.

ENDNOTES

[1]The best source of information of S. Hall Young's family background is his autobiography, *Hall Young of Alaska: the Mushing Parson* (New York, 1927). Both the Presbyterian Historical Society in Philadelphia and the San Francisco Theological Seminary contain documents of his life's story.

[2]Ibid., p. 52.

[3]Frederick Rudolph, *The American College and University: A History* (New York 1962), p. 65.

[4]Young, *Hall Young*, p. 59.

[5]Clifton E. Olmstead, *History of Religion in the United States* (Englewood Cliffs, N.J., 1960), p. 496; William Warren Sweet, *The Story of Religion in America* (New York, 1930), p. 357.

[6]Still the only really complete biography of the remarkable Sheldon Jackson is the biography which he authorized Robert Laird Stewart to write, *Sheldon Jackson: Pathfinder and Prospector of the Missionary Vanguard in the Rocky Mountains and Alaska* (New York, 1908). For Jackson's Rocky Mountain achievements see also the pamphlet, *An Historical Sketch of the Presbyteries, Church and Mission Work of the Synod of Colorado*, and the articles by Andrew E. Murray in the *Journal of the Presbyterian Historical Society* 27 (March, June and September, 1950).

[7]Letter from S. Hall Young to Sheldon Jackson, Dec. 15, 1877. Jackson Correspondence Collection, Presbyterian Historical Society, Philadelphia,

Pennsylvania. Vol. 7, p. 199. Hereafter this collection referred to as J. Corr.

[8]Along with a study of medical books, the book on Alaska which S. Hall Young promptly turned to was the pioneer work by William H. Dall, *Alaska and Its Resources* (London, 1870).

[9]Jackson gave maximum publicity to her heart-rending descriptions in his own newspaper, *The Rocky Mountain Presbyterian*. Most of her letters are available in Charles A. Anderson's (ed.) "Letters of Amanda R. McFarland," *Journal of the Presbyterian Historical Society* 34 (June and Dec., 1956): 83-102; 226-244.

[10]*The Rocky Mountain Presbyterian*, April, 1878. A complete file of Sheldon Jackson's monthly is now available on microfilm from the Board of Microtext, Dr. Raymond P. Morris, Yale Divinity School Library, 409 Prospect St., New Haven, Conn. 06511.

[11]Young, *Hall Young*, p. 66. Young formally began his work at the Wrangell mission on August 8, 1878. Sheldon Jackson, *The Presbyterian Church in Alaska: An Official Sketch of Its Rise and Progress 1877-1884*...(Washington, D. C., 1886), p. 4.

[12]Young, *Hall Young*, p. 78.

[13]Ivan Petroff referred to her as a "highly intelligent lady." Ted and Caryl Hinckley (eds.), "Ivan Petroff's Journal of a Trip to Alaska in 1878," *Journal of the West* 5 (Jan. 1966): 23. Sheldon Jackson, *Alaska, and Missions on the North Pacific Coast* (New York, 1880), p. 215.

[14]Conversations with author, July 1959, Philadelphia, Pa. For details of Jackson-Lindsley feud see: Ted C. Hinckley, "The Alaska Labors of Sheldon Jackson, 1877-1890" (unpublished Ph.D. dissertation, Indiana University, 1960), pp. 23-39.

[15]Young, *Hall Young*, p. 69. See also: National Archives Microfilm Series No. 430, Interior Dept., Alaska. Roll 1, Letter of S. Hall Young to President Rutherford B. Hayes, Dec. 24, 1880.

[16]Thomas Stratton Goslin, "Henry Kendall and the Evangelization of a Continent" (unpublished Ph.D. dissertation, University of Pennsylvania, 1948), p. 337.

[17]S. Hall Young, *What Every Presbyterian Should Know about Alaska* (n.p., n.d.). Young, *Hall Young*, p. 79.

[18]*Rocky Mountain Presbyterian*, Feb., 1879; S. Hall Young to Sheldon Jackson, Nov. 11, 1878, J. Corr., Vol. 9, p. 3.

[19]Jackson, *The Presbyterian Church*, p. 4. It was the first and apparently the last time Lindsley visited Alaska. Jackson would make, with a few exceptions, an annual tour of the Far North frontier until after the turn of the century.

[20]*The Alaska Appeal*, Sept. 15, 1879.

[21]John Muir, *Travels in Alaska* (Boston, 1915), pp. 127 and 172.

[22]Morgan Sherwood, *Exploration of Alaska, 1865-1900* (New Haven, 1965), p. 74.

[23]S. Hall Young, *Alaska Days with John Muir* (New York, 1915), pp. 126-127.

[24]Young, *Hall Young*, pp. 163-164.

[25]Newspaper clipping by S. Hall Young in Sheldon Jackson Scrapbooks, Presbyterian Historical Society, Philadelphia, Pa., Vol. 8, pp. 29 and 59-61. Hereafter collection referred to as J. Scrap.

[26]Muir, *Travels*, pp. 131-133.

[27]On the Presbyterian battle to separate Alaska's native population from liquor see: Morgan B. Sherwood, "Ardent Spirits: Hooch and the Osprey Affair at

Sitka," *Journal of the West* 4 (July 1965): 301-344; Ted C. Hinckley, "Punitive Action at Angoon," *Alaska Sportsman* 24 (Jan. and Feb., 1963): 8ff and 14ff; and "Sheldon Jackson and Benjamin Harrison: Presbyterians and the Administration of Alaska," *Pacific Northwest Quarterly* 54 (April 1963): 66-74.

[28]Robert N. De Armond, *The Founding of Juneau* (Juneau, 1967), pp. 118-122.

[29]Young, *Hall Young*, pp. 255-257; S Hall Young to S. Jackson March 24, 1881; J. Corr., Vol 11, p. 105; S. Hall Young to S. Jackson, March 8, 1881, Ibid., p. 8D. *Annual Report of the Commissioner of Indian Affairs to the Secretary of the Interior-1881* (Wash., D. C., 1881), p. xxxvii.

[30]S. Hall Young to S. Jackson, May 16, 1881, J. Corr., Vol. 11, p. 164; *Minutes of the General Assembly, 1880* (New York, 1880), p. 44.

[31]Jackson, *The Presbyterian Church*, p. 8; *Minutes of the General Assembly*, p. 590.

[32]J. S. Oakford, Deputy Collector to William G. Morris, April 26, 1882, Alaska Custom House Records, Alaska State Historical Library, Juneau, Alaska, Vol. 22. Hereafter collection cited as Custom House. S. Hall Young to S. Jackson, Aug. 15, 1882, J. Corr., Vol. 12, p. 258; S. Hall Young to S. Jackson, Jan. 9, 1882, Ibid., p. 48.

[33]S. Hall Young to S. Jackson, June 4, 1881, J. Corr., Vol. 11, p. 186; H. Kendall to S. Jackson, June 10, 1881, Ibid., p. 195; Mrs. E. S. Willard to S. Jackson, June 29, 1881, Ibid., p. 241; Eugene S. Willard to S. Jackson, Oct. 29, 1881, Ibid., p. 282; S. Jackson to Mrs. Jackson, July 10, 1881, Ibid., p. 219; S. Hall Young to S. Jackson, Dec. 14, 1881, Ibid., p. 48; Maggie McFarland to Mrs. McFarland, Sept. 17, 1883, J. Corr., Vol. 13, p. 204; A. E. Austin to S. Jackson, Nov. 19, 1883, Ibid., p. 240; Maggie McFarland to Mrs. McFarland, April 15, 1884, Ibid., p. 336.

[34]Henry Glass to S. Jackson, Nov. 14, 1882, J. Corr., Vol. 12, p. 291; S. Hall Young to S. Jackson, Nov. 15, 1882, Ibid., p. 305.

[35]*Presbyterian Home Missions*, Nov. 15, 1880, p. 227; S. Hall Young to S. Jackson, Nov. 22, 1880, J. Corr., Vol. 10, p. 358.

[36]Jackson, *The Presbyterian Church*, p. 4; S. H. Young to S. Jackson, Nov. 15, 1881, J. Corr., Vol. 11, p. 305.

[37]S. Hall Young to S. Jackson, March 12, 1883, J. Corr., Vol. 13, p. 60.

[38]J. Loomis Gould arrived in Alaska in 1882; he was Young's second cousin and took over the Howkan Mission Station. J. W. McFarland arrived in Alaska in 1880; he was a nephew of Amanda McFarland's late husband. After marrying Miss Maggie Dunbar of the Wrangell staff, he joined the Wrangell team. Rev. Eugene S. Willard arrived in Alaska in July, 1881, and commenced work at Portage Bay. Jackson, *The Presbyterian Church*, pp. 4-6.

[39]Young, *Hall Young*, p. 267.

[40]S. Hall Young to S. Jackson, March 12, 1883, J. Corr., Vol. 13, p. 60.

[41]Young, *Hall Young*, p. 269.

[42]J. Corr., Vol. 13, p. 384, O. D. Eaton to H. Teller, June 24, 1884.

[43]Maggie McFarland to S. Jackson, Aug. 13, 1883, J. Corr., Vol. 13, p. 194, Maggie McFarland to S. Jackson, Feb. 25, 1884, Ibid., p. 309.

[44]Fannie E. Young to Hon. L. Q. C. Lamar, Secretary of the Interior, Nov. 7, 1885, Miscellaneous Correspondence, National Archives, Washington, D. C., Bureau of Education. Hereafter cited as National Archives.

45H. F. French to Collector of Customs, Dec. 8, 1883, Custom House Records, Vol. 26; C. J. Folger to Collector, June 12, 1884, Ibid.; Thomas A. Willson to Peter French, April 20, 1886, Ibid., Vol. 30; *Juneau City Mining Record*, October 4, 1888.

46Young, *Hall Young*, p. 271; *The Evangelist*, Aug. 9, 1884. A contemporary, missionary John W. McFarland, stated that the farm was acquired "for 400. also oxen and farming implements." John W. McFarland to S. Jackson, April 15, 1884, J. Corr., Vol. 13, p. 334.

47F. Young to L. Q. C. Lamar, Nov. 7, 1885, National Archives. This is the way the school's name was spelled in the Academy's newspaper, not the way S. Hall Young spelled it in his autobiography. There he identifies the institution as the Thlingit Training Academy for Boys. Young, *Hall Young*, p. 269.

48*The Presbyterian Journal*, June 12, 1884. While there were to be a number of fine products of the Presbyterian missionary institutions in Alaska, the most outstanding was Edward Marsden. For his life story see: William Gilbert Beattie, *Marsden of Alaska: A Modern Indian* (New York, 1955).

49Francis C. Sessions, *From Yellowstone Park to Alaska* (New York, 1890), pp. 58-59.

50Hinckley, "The Alaska Labors," pp. 188ff. The excellent compilation by Melvin Ricks, *Directory of Alaska Post Offices and Postmasters* (Ketchikan, 1965) does not list Hall; however, his wife Fannie is credited as Sitka's Postmistress July, 1878-November, 1878, p. 58.

51*The Alaskan* (Sitka), Jan. 16, 1886.

52Sessions, *Yellowstone*, pp. 58-59.

53For background details of this enterprise see: Hinckley, "Alaska Labors," Chapter 10, and the *Annual Reports of the Commissioner of Education* for the 1880's (Washington, D. C.).

54Two extremely useful books for understanding this phase of Indian history are: Loring Benson Priest, *Uncle Sam's Step-Children: The Reformation of the United States Indian Policy, 1865-1887*; and Henry E. Fritz, *The Movement for Indian Assimilation, 1860-1890* (Philadelphia, 1963).

55S. Hall Young to S. Jackson, May 13, 1886, J. Corr., Vol. 14, p. 210.

56Maggie D. McFarland to Mrs. Jackson, April 15, 1884, J. Corr., Vol. 13, p. 336; *The Alaskan* (Sitka), Feb. 20, 1886; John McFarland to S. Jackson, April 15, 1884, J. Corr., Vol. 13, p. 334.

57*The Alaskan* (Sitka), Jan. 30, 1886. The author possesses some *Tlinkit* fragments but knows of no full-run file of this useful publication. James Wickersham, *A Bibliography of Alaskan Literature: 1724-1924* (Cordova, 1927), p. 260; Young, *Hall Young*, p. 309.

58*The Presbyterian*, June 12, 1884.

59S. Jackson to D. C. Atkins, July 20, 1885, "Alaska Schools," Vol. I, p. 248, Sheldon Jackson Manuscripts Collection, Princeton Theological Seminary, Speer Library, Princeton, N. J. Hereafter this manuscript collection referred to as PTS.

60F. Young to L. Q. C. Lamar, Nov. 7, 1885, National Archives.

61S. Hall Young to Senator J. N. Dolph, Oct. 15, 1885, Miscellaneous Educational Materials in Sheldon Jackson Collection, Presbyterian Historical Society. A. B. Upshaw to N. H. R. Dawson, August 8, 1888, National Archives.

62S. Jackson to H. Kendall, July 31, 1886, "Alaska Schools," PTS, Vol. 4, p. 175.

[63]*The Alaskan* (Sitka), Dec. 18, 1886.

[64]*The Glacier*, Jan., 1886.

[65]*The Glacier*, June, 1887; *The Occident*, June 8, 1887; and Clipping, J. Scrap, Vol. 18, p. 20.

[66]James Sheakley to S. Jackson, Oct. 31, 1887, J. Corr., Vol. 14, p. 137.

[67]James Sheakley to S. Jackson, May 23, 1888, J. Corr., Vol. 15, p. 124C.

[68]J. F. Lake to S. Jackson, June 20, 1888, Ibid., p. 67; Mrs. (J. F.) Clara Lake to S. Jackson, April 7, 1888, Ibid., p. 15.

[69]D. C. Atkins to N. H. R. Dawson, May 11, 1888, National Archives; S. Jackson to Mrs. C. E. Walker, July 11, 1888, J. Corr., Vol. 26, pp. 238-241; Young, *Hall Young*, p. 312.

[70]James Sheakley to N. H. R. Dawson, June 16, 1888, National Archives; James Sheakley to S. Jackson, July 7, 1888, J. Corr., Vol. 15, p. 75.

[71]William Irwin to S. Jackson, Sept. 10, 1888, Ibid., p. 93; James Sheakley to S. Jackson, Sept. 29, 1888, Ibid., p. 97; *Juneau City Mining Record*, Oct. 4, 1888.

[72]S. Hall Young to S. Jackson, 1888, J. Corr., Vol. 15, p. 103.

[73]*New York Times*, Sept. 4, 1927; and Young, *Hall Young*, Chapter 31ff.

[74]Septima M. Collis, *A Woman's Trip to Alaska . . . 1890* (New York, 1890), pp. 78-79.

[75]Young, *Hall Young*, p. 313. The statement in the *Dictionary of American Biography*, Vol. 20, p. 20, that, "By 1888, when Young resigned his place at Fort Wrangell, Christian missionary work was proceeding in all the principal tribes of Southern Alaska largely because of his initiative" exaggerates his fine work.

[76]Dr. Clarence Thwing to Mr. Boyd, Feb. 24, 1893, Thwing Letter Book, San Francisco Theological Seminary, San Anselmo, California. An edited version of this letter book is: Ted C. Hinckley's (ed.) "Excerpts from the Letters of Dr. Clarence Thwing, Presbyterian Missionary to Wrangell, Alaska, during the Mid-1890's," *Journal of Presbyterian History* 41 (March 1963): 37-55.

"KLONDICITIS:" SEATTLE AND THE RUSH NORTH*

Pierre Berton

Pierre Berton was born in 1920 in Dawson, Yukon Territory, where his father had gone on the trek of 1898. He has achieved fame as a broadcaster and writer, and as editor of *Maclean's Magazine.* One of his chief interests has been the way the people of the United States understand and interpret Canada. His book, *Hollywood's Canada* is a classic on the subject.

Berton has written one of the best books on the Klondike gold rush, and on the gold rush era, *Klondike Fever: The Life and Death of the Last Great Gold Rush* (New York: Alfred A. Knopf, 1982). His principal thesis is that, although most of the 40,000 or so argonauts who trudged north in 1897 and 1898 did not find any gold, they found something far more valuable: themselves. The gold was secondary, Berton argues, for the adventure became a test of the men and women who engaged in it, a test of their motivation, and their perseverance, and their character. For most, he says, it was the experience of a lifetime, the encounter which taught them who they were and what they would be capable of later on.

In the selection printed here, Berton discusses the early phase of the gold rush when many an otherwise stable individual became infected with "Klondicitis," as he calls it, the itch to join in the trek north. "Klondicitis" was not an altogether accidental phenomenon, Berton argues, for there were those who made it their business to promote it. Be that as it may, there is no doubt that it took some truly bizarre forms.

* * *

In the fevered chorus chanting anthems to the Klondike, a few reedlike voices could be heard faintly counseling caution. On July 28 the white-bearded Louis Sloss, one of the founders of the Alaska Commercial Company, said flatly: "I regard it as a crime for any transportation company to encourage men to go to the Yukon this fall...The Seattle people who are booming the steamship lines may be sincere, but a heavy responsibility will rest on their shoulders should starvation and crime prevail in Dawson City next winter...It is a crime to encourage this rush, which can only lead to disaster for three quarters of the new arrivals." This statement, coming from the head of a pioneer company which stood to gain immeasurably from

*This selection is excerpted from *Klondike Fever* (New York: Alfred A. Knopf, 1959), pp. 120-136.

the stampede, could be counted as an honest and reliable appraisal of the situation. Few heeded it, perhaps preferring the advice of the colorful Joaquin Miller, published the same day. The gray-bearded "Poet of the Sierras," a veteran of earlier Rocky Mountain stampedes, was already en route to the Klondike as one of Mr. Hearst's quintet of journalists. He announced that there was "no possible chance of famine" and that "the dangers and hardships and cost of getting through have been greatly exaggerated." Miller, who was almost sixty years old, boasted that he was traveling light, with very little in the way of provisions or equipment--a fact that was to cause him great distress before the year was out.

There were further warnings. The Travellers' Insurance Company announced it would refuse insurance to any stampeder. An Ottawa paper published, in the form of a "Miner's Catechism," a series of questions that every would-be prospector should ask himself before setting out for the Klondike:

> Have I a capital of at least five hundred dollars? Am I subject to any organism or chronic disease, especially rheumatism? Am I physically sound in every way and able to walk thirty miles a day with a fifty pound pack on my back? Am I willing to put up with rough fare, sleep anywhere and anyhow, do my own cooking and washing, mend my own clothes? Can I leave home perfectly free, leaving no one dependent on me in any manner for support? Can I do entirely without spirituous liquors? Can I work like a galley slave for months, if need be, on poor fare and sometimes not enough of that, and still keep up a cheerful and brave spirit? Am I pretty handy with tools and not subject to lazy fits? Can I swim and handle boats and canoes; put up with extremes of heat and cold, and bear incessant tortures from countless swarms of mosquitoes, gnats and sand flies?

Only a fraction of the tens of thousands who streamed across the passes in the months that followed could say *yes* to these questions. Most of them were sedentary workers, clerks and salesmen and office help, but once they caught the fever they were not to be deterred by mere words, especially when many newspaper writers, egged on by local chambers of commerce, were painting the journey to the goldfields in the most vivid and enthusiastic terms.

Ambrose Bierce was a rare exception, one of the handful of journalists who took a jaundiced view of the stampede. "The California gold hunter did good by accident and crowed to find it fame," he wrote in the San Francisco *Examiner*. "But the blue-nosed mosquito-slapper of Greater Dawson, what is he for? Is he going to lay broad and deep the foundations of Empire [for Great Britain]? Will he bear the banner of progress into that paleocrystic waste? Will he clear the way for even a dog sled civilization and a reindeer religion? Nothing will come of him. He is a word in the wind, a brother to the fog. At the scene of his activity no memory of him will remain. The gravel that he thawed and sifted will freeze again. In the shanty that he builded, the she-wolf will rear her poddy litter, and from its eaves the moose will crop the esculent icicle unafraid. The snows will close over his trail and all be as before."

By August 10 the U.S. Secretary of the Interior, C. N. Bliss, felt it necessary to issue a state paper warning against anyone attempting to get to the Klondike that season. Clifford Sifton, the Canadian Minister of the Interior, had already published a similar plea, but both warnings fell on deaf ears. The *Excelsior* landed in San Francisco with a second cargo of gold, and this time the newspapers did not underestimate the quantity. There was only about half a million dollars on board, but the press reports made it two and a half millions, exciting such enthusiasm that the publicity-shy William Ogilvie, who was a passenger, had to disguise himself as a crew member to escape the reporters. There was further excitement when it was learned that a U.S. government revenue cutter was escorting the *Portland* down the coast on her second trip to protect her from Chinese pirates said to be lying in wait to capture the two million dollars reported aboard her.

Such tales lent impetus to the rush which was gathering speed, snowball-fashion. When the government warning was issued, three thousand people were already hived in the erupting tent towns of Dyea and Skagway, at the foot of the passes, together with two thousand tons of baggage. Thousands of horses were already struggling, dying, and rotting on the trails. Before the warning was a fortnight old, twenty-one more steamers as well as three sailing-vessels and two scows, all jammed with men and animals and freight, had put out from Pacific-coast ports, steaming toward the Lynn Canal. In one single week in mid-August, twenty-eight hundred people left Seattle for the Klondike. By September 1 nine thousand people and thirty-six thousand tons of freight had left the port.

Although few would believe it, there was by this time no chance of any traveler reaching the diggings before the following summer. This fact was conveniently glossed over by the merchants of the various coastal ports who were bidding for the Klondike outfitting trade. Every city was a madhouse. The streets of Victoria, British Columbia, bustled with strange men--Scots, Irish, French, German, Australian, American--garbed in outlandish costumes and dragging oxen and horses through roadways piled high with sacks of provisions, knockdown boats, fur robes, and Klondike knickknackery. In Seattle the streets were crowded all night long. Unable to get lodgings, the stampeders slept in stables and washed at fire hydrants. All the coastal ports--San Francisco, Tacoma, Portland, Seattle, and Victoria--were locked in an intense struggle for the lion's share of the booty, each city screaming that it was the only possible outfitting port for the Klondike. The Canadians cried that every would-be miner ought to buy his goods in Canada since the Klondike was on British soil and a stiff duty would be levied on American outfits crossing the line. Victoria merchants went so far as to dispatch agents to Seattle to spread this news among the stampeders who were pouring off the trains. The Americans shouted just as loudly that every miner would have to cross the isthmus of the Alaska Panhandle, where he must pay duty on Canadian goods or else pay U.S. guards a fee to accompany bonded supplies to the Canadian line.

Up and down the coast the arguments reverberated. Seattle papers published bitter editorials attacking the claims of Tacoma and San Francisco, and the rival cities retorted in kind. One San Francisco merchant displayed in his window a poster showing two stampeders. One was depicted tired and beaten at the foot of the Chilkoot, complaining: "I outfitted in Seattle." The other was shown fresh as a daisy atop the pass, crowing triumphantly: "I bought *my* goods in San Francisco."

But it was Seattle in the end that seized the bulk of the gold-rush trade with a campaign planned as carefully as any military exercise. Within a week of the *Portland's* arrival the Chamber of Commerce had organized a committee to boost Seattle as the only possible outfitting port. The city's subsequent paid advertising in the nation's press exceeded that of its competitors fivefold, but it was the superiority of Seattle's free advertising that won the day.

This was largely due to the secretary of the advertising committee, a veteran newspaperman of subtle ingenuity named Erastus

Brainerd, a Harvard graduate who had once been an art-gallery curator. The term "public-relations man" had yet to be coined, but Brainerd was a worthy forerunner of the PR breed. In publicizing Seattle he left nothing to chance. He inserted advertisements in small-town newspapers until he calculated he had a total circulation for them of almost ten million. He saw that the Klondike edition of the Seattle *P-I* was sent to seventy thousand U.S. postmasters, six thousand libraries, and four thousand mayors; then, for good measure, he distributed fifteen thousand to the Great Northern and Northern Pacific railroads for prospective stampeders heading for the west coast. Brainerd was a student of psychology, and one of his most successful schemes was to persuade Seattleites of recent origin to send letters back to their home towns, to friends and local editors, exhorting their former neighbors to go to the Klondike via Seattle. Brainerd made it easy to send such letters, for he wrote them himself, leaving blanks for names and signatures, supplied the postage, and even dropped them in the mailbox. Another scheme involved the sending of Klondike views, with Seattle's compliments, as Christmas gifts to the crowned heads of Europe. This worked out satisfactorily in all cases but one: the German Kaiser refused to open his package for fear that it might contain dynamite.

Brainerd had printed a series of circulars of various kinds which he sent to newspapers, diplomats, prospective migrants, governors and mayors, congressmen and Senators. These documents looked more like personally dictated letters than advertising throwaways, and received wide attention. In one such circular Brainerd quoted the correspondent of *Harper's Weekly* on the superiority of Seattle for Alaskan trade. He did not mention that the correspondent of *Harper's Weekly* was Erastus Brainerd.

Another circular tried to suggest that the Klondike trip was not much more arduous than a casual stroll after lunch--an idea that was fostered by all the Pacific-coast ports. Shooting the Whitehorse Rapids was made to appear mere child's play: "Of those who have gone in...not more than half a dozen have lost their lives and these from carelessness in fording." The last phrase was a masterpiece, for it seemed to imply that the crossing of the various Yukon torrents was not much more than a wading expedition. Brainerd persuaded the Secretary of State for Washington to sign this circular, which he sent to foreign diplomats. This gave it the status of an official communication, and it was immediately relayed to overseas capitals, where it was widely published and distributed.

In addition, Brainerd and the Chamber worked out an espionage system which (a) quietly gave Seattle merchants the names of potential customers and (b) informed the city of its rivals' plans so that steps could be taken to forestall them. All this energy paid big dividends for the city, which by the early spring of 1898 had garnered twenty-five million dollars in Klondike trade as compared with the five million that went through the other ports. As for Brainerd, he became so mesmerized by his own campaign that, when spring came, he started for the Klondike himself.

Gathering momentum swiftly in the late summer months, the great stampede was moving at express-train speed by midwinter, its course illuminated by the various quirks and eccentricities, personal tragedies, follies, fortunes, and excitements which mark any large exodus of people. The Klondike was certainly responsible for one of the strangest mass movements in history. All that winter and through most of the following summer, men and women by the tens of thousands crossed oceans and continents, moving by train, steamship, scow, horseback, oxcart, foot, and raft to reach the magic land. The movement was truly world-wide. A sloop with ninety Norwegians left Christiania in October, sailed around the Horn, and reached San Francisco in April en route to the Klondike. In February the *Cape Otway* left Sydney, Australia, for Alaska with two hundred and twelve passengers crammed aboard her. A Greek in Jerusalem wrote to the Central Pacific Railroad that he and a group of fellow countrymen were heading for Dawson with stores of goods to trade. An expedition of three hundred Scotsmen sailed for Montreal in January on their way to the goldfields. A steam yacht, complete with orchestra, personal valets, and Parisian chefs, left England in February loaded with young aristocrats. A company of young Italians moved through San Francisco in the spring, announcing that they were an advance guard for an expedition of several hundred. Belted earls and washerwomen, congressmen and card sharps, millionaires and paupers all rubbed shoulders on the trails that led north. Sir Charles Tupper, the ex-Prime Minister of Canada, wrote from England that one hundred thousand stampeders would sail from that country alone. This turned out to be an overestimate, but it has been reckoned that in the winter of 1897-8 one million people laid plans to leave home and family to seek their fortune in the Klondike and that, at the very least, one hundred thousand actually set out.

The transportation companies were as eager for the Klondike business as the coast cities. Every train traveling across the continent had its own "gold-rush car," the walls lined with glass jars full of nuggets and dust and papered with photographs of the mining areas, and the side cabinets and tables cluttered with books, maps, and pamphlets, picks, pans, shovels, hammers, quicksilver, fur, parkas, and heavy boots.

In the fall of '97 steamship tickets sold at fantastic prices. Before the *Excelsior* left on her return voyage from San Francisco to St. Michael, the agents had been forced to turn away ten times her passenger list. On July 29 one man who had bought a ticket aboard her was able to sell it for fifteen hundred dollars, which was ten times its value. By midwinter the fare settled down to a straight one thousand. Suddenly money had become very cheap. Stampeders were willing to gamble almost any sum to reach their goal. In March 1898 the *Review of Reviews* estimated that the argonauts had already spent sixty million dollars in purchasing rail and ocean transport and Klondike outfits. The Klondike had been oversold: its gold-production for the year 1898 did not exceed ten millions.

The stampeders snapped up almost anything that was offered them. They bought sleds powered by gasoline motors and others powered by steam. They bought "automatic" gold-pans set on a spindle and operated by clockwork on the gramophone principle. They bought scurvy cures, portable cabins, food tablets, earmuffs, frost cures, and a variety of useless bric-a-brac that even included "nugget-in-the-slot" machines for dispensing cigars, paper envelopes, scenes of great battles, and similar northern essentials. Bunko men rushed to the Pacific coast to take advantage of the suckers pouring through the various towns. Arthur Dietz, a God-fearing New Yorker who arrived in Seattle in February on his way to Alaska, described it as "more wicked than Sodom." Dietz wrote that "the Devil reigned supreme. It was a gigantic chaos of crime and the city government, as an institution, protected evil." The streets were infested with agents and beggars and confidence men hawking everything from bottled mercury to evaporated beans. Gambling-houses, saloons, and brothels ran wide open. Government stores got rid of army surplus blankets, tents, and knapsacks, many of them worn out and useless. Dietz and his party bought one hundred pounds of evaporated eggs from an agent who poured some of the yellow powder out of the sack and cooked it before their eyes to demonstrate his honesty. It tasted like scrambled eggs, but when the party reached the shores of Alaska and opened the sack they discovered that the salesman, by sleight of hand, had substituted yellow cornmeal. Dozens of other parties reported similar experiences.

The so-called "Klondike Bicycle" was a popular item with the stampeders, for the Klondike strike came at the height of the bicycle craze. The velocipede was to the 1890's what the television set came to be to the 1950's. Sunday newspapers actually found their circulation decreasing because everyone spent the Sabbath on wheels. When the New York *Journal* held a contest to name the ten most popular bicyclists and send them on a tour of Europe, it received six and one half million responses. Everybody from princes to policemen pedaled, and the *Herald* reported with approbation that one woman had tracked down her faithless husband on a bicycle and thus secured a divorce. It was freely predicted that the next war would be fought on bicycles, and the Sunday-supplement drawings of what the world would look like a hundred years hence invariably showed the entire populace pedaling determinedly down the streets. Such was the faith in the bicycle that thousands were prepared to believe that this was the ideal way of crossing the mountain passes. Two youths, cycling around the world for a Chicago paper, switched plans and began propelling themselves toward Alaska. On September 20 the Misses Olga McKenna and Nellie Ritchie, described as "two of the best wheel-women in Boston," started pedaling north, announcing that they expected to enlist one thousand women in their move to cycle to Dawson City. Two wheel-men from a Brooklyn club were a day ahead of them, pumping furiously across the continent wearing broad-brimmed slouch hats, blue shirts, knee trousers, heavy woolen stockings, and bicycle shoes, a costume they described as being halfway between a cyclist's and a miner's garb.

A New York syndicate meanwhile was busily marketing machines designed especially for the stampede to which were attached four-wheeled trailers with a freight capacity of five hundred pounds. There were also "ice bicycles" with a forward ski, and something else called "bicycle skates." Two New Yorkers in the fall of '97 left for the Klondike on a strange contraption consisting of two bicycles joined together with iron bars heavy enough to support a small rowboat containing their outfit. They declared they would reach the Klondike in ninety days by this method, but the ensuing winter found them still at the foot of the White Pass.

Another much-advertised contrivance was the Klondike "boat-sled," a sectional steel vessel which was purported to be amphibious.

Sails were provided to propel it across northern lakes; on land, a couple of panels at the side were supposed to be let down to form a flat surface under the keel, which was hollow, being fitted with air chambers to ensure buoyancy, and a burglar-proof compartment in which to store the gold dust that everybody expected to dig from the ground as easily as if it were so much sand.

Like so many others, the boat-sled scheme flopped miserably. There seemed to be no end to the ingenuity and impracticability of the inventions that sprang up during the stampede. A noted electrical expert of the times, Nikalo Tesla, a onetime associate of Thomas Edison, attempted to market an X-ray machine which he said was essential for prospectors because it could detect the presence of gold hidden in small beds of sand and gravel. Three Washington State men worked out a scheme to suck gold from the riverbeds, using compressed air. Another optimist headed north with diving-equipment, explaining that he planned to walk along the bed of the Yukon River picking up nuggets. The Secretary of the Treasury, Lyman Gage, actually gave his blessing to a snow train, propelled by a giant sprocketed wheel, that bore a remarkable resemblance to the modern snowmobile (but which never worked). An organization called the Trans-Alaskan Gopher Co. offered shares at a dollar apiece and promised returns of ten dollars a minute when it got into operation: it proposed to take contracts for digging tunnels in Klondike claims with trained gophers. A root-beer salesman announced he was leaving for the Chilkoot pass with a thousand packages of root beer; it was his intention to sell the beverage to thirsty argonauts at an eight-hundred-per-cent profit. A Dr. Armand Ravol, the city bacteriologist of St. Louis, planned to go to the Klondike armed with packages of deadly germs suitable for eliminating mosquitoes. And there was that abortive corporation with the jawbreaking name known as The Klondike and Cuba Ice Towing and Anti-Yellow Fever Company, which proposed, with a wild disregard for ocean geography, to tow icebergs from the Klondike to the South Seas, where, it was believed, they could be transformed into cold compresses to alleviate the suffering of fever victims.

Portus B. Weare, the balding and distinguished chairman of the board of the North American Trading and Transportation Company in Chicago, was the target of a small platoon of fortune-seekers who wanted financial backing for a variety of wild schemes. A lady clairvoyant cornered him in his office and asked for two thousand dollars. She claimed to be able to find the hiding-places of nuggets, no matter how far they were below the surface. A penny-dreadful writer asked Weare for a few thousands to go to the Klondike, which, he felt, must be swarming with notorious criminals in hiding. It was his plan to use his detective-novel knowledge to capture them and claim the rewards.

There were several projects afoot to invade the goldfields with lighter-than-air craft, for the balloon was the sensation of the age and just six days before the *Portland's* arrival in Seattle, Salomon Augustus Andree, the Swedish polar explorer, had set out to reach the North Pole by balloon. In Dublin an Irish gold-seeker announced the construction of an enormous balloon large enough to take fifty passengers to the Klondike. In New York one Leo Stevens, Jr., adopting the more romantic title of Don Carlos Stevens, raised one hundred and fifty thousand dollars and announced he was building the biggest balloon in the world, which would take off from a point near Juneau and soar over the coastal mountains into the Klondike carrying eight to ten passengers and six or seven tons of freight. In Kalamazoo another entrepreneur declared that he would establish a regular balloon route to the Klondike, each balloon to carry a ton of goods and make a return trip in a fortnight. People all over the country wrote to him offering ridiculous sums for passage or even "a berth in steerage," and one Illinois citizen even sent along a bank draft for five hundred dollars. But after Andree was swallowed by the polar mists, the enthusiasm over balloons began to fade.

One of the periodic features of the stampede was the emergence of the "syndicate of wealthy New Yorkers," a vague and shadowy group of titans who continually popped up, propounding various get-rich-quick schemes. One "syndicate of wealthy New Yorkers" was said to be establishing a reindeer postal service to the Klondike along the lines of the pony express, while another syndicate of wealthy New Yorkers was reported engaged in building a bicycle path to the Klondike to service a chain of trading posts.

A scheme devised by a Milwaukee man involved the use of carrier pigeons to establish communication between the Klondike and the rest of the world. A series of pigeon stations was envisaged, with the birds carrying letters that had been photographically reduced to the size of a needle point. These were to be enlarged at Victoria, British Columbia, and remailed from there. The trouble with this idea was that nobody could work out a fast way of getting the pigeons to the Klondike.

If these schemes were taken seriously, it was because of the peculiar blindness produced by the Klondike fever. One plan actually entertained by responsible businessmen in Canada and the United States called for the construction of a railway from Chesterfield Inlet on Hudson Bay across seven hundred miles of Arctic tundra to Great Slave Lake, a region almost totally unexplored, unmapped, and unknown. This was only part of a grandiose rail-and-water route which was pictured as stretching all the way from Sault Ste. Marie to Dawson City, a distance of more than four thousand miles--and thence on to the Bering Strait, where a ferry line would link North America with Russia. A writer in the Toronto *Globe* reckoned that by this route a traveler could reach Dawson in seven days. A group of Canadian businessmen actually secured a charter for it, and the *Financial Times* of London commented favorably on the scheme. Needless to say, no such railway has ever been built, but there is little doubt that the Klondike boom spurred the tremendous railway expansion that marked the development of Canada in the first decade of the twentieth century. By 1910 the Canadians had constructed two more transcontinental railways, in addition to the Canadian Pacific. Both eventually went bankrupt.

But in the fall of 1897 the wildest plans seemed practical, the most impossible ventures attainable. There was the Irishwoman who planned to take a group of children to the Klondike: she would teach them lessons by day, they would dig gold by night. There was the dancing-master who planned to practice his craft in Dawson City: he would teach the two-step to Indians and miners all winter and dig gold all summer. "Dig" was the operative word. To many, it was as simple as that: you stuck your spade into the golden soil and shoveled the results into the bank. There were those who actually took gunnysacks with them on the trip north to serve as containers for the nuggets.

All across the land, syndicates, co-operatives, investment and colonization companies were being formed to exploit some aspect of the Klondike. On August 1 the New York *World* carried a solid page of advertisements for Klondike organizations of one kind or another. By the end of August there were eighty-five syndicates in operation in twenty-two American cities, with a total capitalization of one hundred and sixty-five million dollars. Dozens more were forming almost hourly.

These syndicates and co-operatives operated with a board of directors or executive; each member paid a weekly sum to finance a few men to go to the Klondike and strike it rich for the whole. Some of the syndicates were fairly farfetched: a group of Chicago spiritualists formed a syndicate, gazed into crystal balls, drew maps with the aid of clairvoyance, and sent a representative to the Klondike; a group of barbers met and formed a syndicate to shave the beards off Klondike miners, an enterprise generally considered rewarding in view of the whiskers sported by prospectors debarking from the treasure ships. The Bowery Mission of New York formed a syndicate and sent an expedition of seven men to the Klondike, headed by a reformed gambler who proposed to convert his fellow stampeders en route and dig for gold at the same time. Dozens of Bowery habitues tried to go along, threatening to empty the mission.

In Philadelphia a promoter talked twelve technical-school students into persuading their fathers to buy a schooner and send them around Cape Horn to the Klondike. It was a measure of the madness that the fathers acquiesced. The promoter was supposed to be a navigator, but turned out to be a very poor one. After a series of fits and starts, delays and bunglings, storms and calms, the vessel finally stumbled into Juneau, Alaska, where it foundered. All of the boys went home except one, a particularly determined youth named Frank Neal who was not deterred by shipwrecks or bankruptcy. He continued to press on toward the Klondike and finally reached his goal in the summer of 1900. The gold was all gone, but, as others were to discover, it was not all in the ground. Neal made a small fortune hauling logs, used it to get a start in the construction business in Long Island, and did well enough to marry and make a wedding trip back to the Klondike.

Of the colonization schemes, the most intriguing was a plan, launched by members of the congregation of the Beecher Memorial Church of Brooklyn, to charter a boat and build a second Brooklyn City on the Yukon River, from which gamblers, drinkers, and other un-Christian citizens would be banned. The group announced that the city would be eventually the largest on the western side of the continent. None of the participants seemed very sure of where it was they were going, but their literature placed the site at the foot of "a mountain which is said to be the fountainhead of the gold field."

The single status of ninety-eight per cent of the Klondike miners was not lost on the entrepreneurs promoting various expeditions to the goldfields, or upon the hundreds of spinsters who put personal ads in the newspapers offering to accompany men to the Klondike "in any capacity." The movement for emancipation was well under way in the nineties, and the distaff side was beginning to insist with increasing vigor that anything men could do, women could do better. One of these was Charlotte Smith, a well-known sociologist of the era, who talked up a scheme to transport four thousand spinsters from the sweatshops and factories of New England to the Klondike. She received thousands of applications but no financing. There were other ideas along the same lines. A midwife announced that she would guarantee a yearly income of fifty thousand dollars to any partner who would invest five hundred in a hospital she planned to build in Dawson. There were no takers. A man from Pittsburgh laid plans to establish a matrimonial agency in the Klondike: he said he would secure employment in advance for groups of one hundred women, "poor but thoroughly respectable." Their future employers would advance funds for the trip north and "under their influence the camp would take on a homelike appearance and the miners would not feel a sense of isolation which sends so many to their graves."

Another promoter in South Dakota, described as "a strict Presbyterian," proposed to send a consignment of marriageable women north, plus a clergyman to marry them. Each maiden was asked to sign a pledge that she would not get off the steamboat until she and her would-be spouse had taken the vows and paid a commission.

Several women's Klondike expeditions were actually financed and organized. One ambitious group, promoted by a New York newspaperwoman, planned to travel in caravans which could be collapsed and taken on horseback over the passes and then floated down the river on rafts. There were to be five vans for every twenty people, three of them to be fitted with portable sleepers to accommodate seven women in each.

Few of these schemes got under way, but one party of women actually did set out for the Klondike under the aegis of Mrs. Hannah S. Gould, a nurse and businesswoman who booked passage for five hundred passengers, mostly widows, to the goldfields as part of the Women's Clondyke Expedition. The company chartered the steamship *City of Columbia*, painted a four-leaf clover on the smokestack, and announced that they would sail it on a twenty-thousand-mile voyage around the Horn to Alaska. J. J. Clements, one of the original stakers of Eldorado, broke a bottle of champagne over the ship's bow in New York harbor, while Mrs. Gould, in a natty yachting-cap and pea jacket, toasted the voyage in wine, talking all the while of establishing a library, church, recreation hall, restaurant, and hospital in Dawson. One hundred cases of champagne were stowed away below decks as a cure for seasickness, and the ship got under way. The champagne came in handy in the Strait of Magellan, where the entire expedition was shipwrecked and the luckless women marooned for twenty-four hours on a bleak rock off Tierra del Fuego. Here Mrs. Gould had a brief but unhappy encounter with a Patagonian cannibal who, as far as could be determined, was attempting a proposal of marriage. The doughy widow refused to be swerved from her Klondike objective, which, at this point, was quite literally at the other end of the earth. "Go away, you ugly brute!" she exclaimed and led her flock back aboard the patched-up vessel, which limped on into Valparaiso. By this time the company was on its last legs.

The unhappy women scraped up twenty-eight thousand dollars to repair the ship, and reached Seattle in April, all their savings dissipated. They had paid in advance for outfits which were supposed to be awaiting them in Seattle, and also for their steamer passage north, but there was nothing for them on arrival. The entire party disbanded, their dreams of rich husbands shattered. Only one ever reached the Klondike, a determined little woman with snapping black eyes named Nettie Hoven simply walked aboard the steamship *Hayden Brown* worked her way north as a stewardess.

The great majority of the Klondike syndicates met similar fates. Few paid off for the investors who stayed behind. In spring of 1898 Captain W. B. Richardson of the U.S. Army, who had been sent to Alaska the previous fall, reported from St. Michael that almost all the syndicates had labored under incapable management and with insufficient means, and that "in nearly all instances" had come to ultimate grief or abandonment.

SHAKING THE BIG STICK: TR AND THE ALASKA BOUNDARY*

Thomas A. Bailey

The Canada-Alaska boundary had been determined on paper by the 1825 Anglo-Russian agreement described earlier in this volume in Stuart Ramsay Tompkins' article. The on-site border had not been determined precisely, however, and the 1825 treaty terms regarding its location in southeastern Alaska proved unclear. The 1825 treaty specified that the Alaska/British Columbia boundary should run along the crest of the coastal mountain range but also that it should not lie more than ten marine leagues from the coast. The issue of the border's precise location lay dormant until the Klondike gold rush. Then, since no clear "crest" of the coastal mountain range existed, Canadians claimed that the heads of all major inlets lay in Canadian territory. Had this been true, it would have provided all-Canadian access to the interior. The United States, on the other hand, argued that the boundary should fall precisely ten leagues inside the mainland coast at all points. The inlets would then lie entirely within United States territory.

The ensuing diplomatic dispute and accompanying display of American bravado have been described by Thomas A. Bailey. Bailey, who earned a doctorate from Stanford University in 1927, subsequently taught at Johns Hopkins, Harvard, and Stanford. He became one of the best renowned and most prolific diplomatic historians in the nation. His *Diplomatic History of the American People* (Englewood Cliffs, NJ: Prentice-Hall, Inc., 1980) is now in its tenth edition.

In the excerpt from that work reprinted here, Bailey examines settlement of the dispute and attributes its resolution to Theodore Roosevelt's less than diplomatic maneuvers. Indeed, Roosevelt's handling of the boundary question seems consistent with his general approach to affairs in North and Central America and the Caribbean.

* * *

Of the half dozen or so substantial secondary accounts relating to the Alaska boundary settlement, only one, that by Mr. Henry Pringle, is the result of a systematic survey of the Roosevelt papers; and by limiting himself to three pages on this subject Mr. Pringle has either consciously omitted, or unintentionally overlooked, certain bits of information which, pieced together, throw a somewhat different

---

*This article originally appeared in the *Canadian Historical Review* 18 (June 1937): 123-30.

light on the affair. The object of this study is to review the entire episode as revealed in the Roosevelt papers, while avoiding, in so far as possible, the repetition of familiar details.

The background of the story is briefly this: the Alaska boundary, which had been ambiguously defined in the Anglo-Russian treaty of 1825, seems to have been the object of no particular concern until 1896, when gold was discovered in the Klondike. Desirous of securing a deep-water route through the Alaska panhandle to the gold-fields, the Canadians advanced the claim that the boundary did not follow the sinuosities of the coast but cut through the most important inlets in such a way as to leave their heads in the possession of Canada. The dispute was temporarily adjusted by a *modus vivendi* arranged by Secretary of State John Hay in 1899; and when both British and Canadian high officials evinced an increasing willingness to make a permanent settlement, a convention was signed in 1903 which provided for a tribunal of "six impartial jurists of repute," three to be appointed by the president of the United States and three by his Britannic majesty. Two prominent Canadians, one of whom had had judicial experience, and Lord Alverstone, lord chief justice of England, were chosen to represent Great Britain. Roosevelt appointed Secretary of War Root, Senator Henry Cabot Lodge of Massachusetts, and ex-Senator George Turner of Washington. None of these three men had acquired any considerable "repute" in a judicial capacity, and there were grave doubts as to the impartiality of each one on the Alaska question, particularly so in the case of Senator Lodge, who was not only one of the leading professional Anglophobes in America but had already publicly committed himself against the Canadian claim. The tribunal met in London late in 1903, and by a vote of four to two, Lord Alverstone siding with the Americans, sustained the main contention of the United States, that regarding the inlets. The equal division of four small islands in dispute, as well as the adjustment of the boundary from the 56th parallel to the 141st meridian, strongly suggests that the decision was a compromise rather than a purely judicial award.

Throughout the controversy Roosevelt was unshaken in his conviction that the Canadian allegations did not "have a leg to stand on" and that they were "dangerously near blackmail."[1] In support of his view he asserted in numerous letters that the official British maps, even those presented to the tribunal, upheld the American line. He believed that the Canadians had advanced an extravagant claim in order to extort some substantial concession from the United States by a compromise settlement; and that they were trading upon their loyalty during the recent Boer War to enlist the support of a somewhat unwilling mother country.[2] Roosevelt felt that by consenting to the treaty of 1903 he was giving the Canadians their last chance to emerge gracefully from the bad hole into which they had worked themselves by insistence upon an indefensible claim. He also believed that it would be wise to settle the dispute before the turbulent mining element got out of control and precipitated a crisis.[3]

The joint commission which met at London was not an arbitral tribunal in the generally accepted sense of the term, for the Americans could expect nothing worse than a deadlock and they had an excellent chance of winning. It is clear from Roosevelt's letters that he had no intention of submitting the dispute to arbitration, and that he did not regard the Alaska tribunal as an arbitral body at all.[4] He explained his attitude fully to F. W. Holls:

> An arbitration is where some outside body decides the question at issue between two parties. To call a meeting between representatives of two parties in the endeavor to come to an agreement an "arbitration" is in my idea a foolish misuse of words...There is no "proposition for an arbitration", with an uneven or an even number of judges, or under any name, or upon any condition, which ever has received or ever will receive my sanction; and to call the proposed tribunal an "arbitration" is as absurd as to speak of the correspondence that has gone on between the foreign office and the State Department for the last year and a half on the subject by the same name.[5]

But with regard to the four tiny islands in the Portland canal, Roosevelt was willing to admit that the Canadians had a case, and he was even prepared to submit this phase of the question to arbitration.[6]

Lest there be any mistake and the American commissioners regard themselves as judicially-minded arbiters, Roosevelt wrote all three, shortly after their appointment, positive but somewhat contradictory instructions. "You will," he said, "impartially judge the questions that come before you for decision," but "in the principle involved there will of course be no compromise." He declared that he was issuing such instructions because Sir Wilfrid Laurier, the Canadian premier, had recently made a speech in which he had virtually given the two Canadian commissioners a mandate to uphold the Canadian view.[7] It is interesting to observe, however, that nearly a year before, when the question of the joint commission was under discussion, Roosevelt had informed Hay: "I will appoint three commissioners to meet three of their commissioners, if they so desire, but I think I shall instruct our three commissioners when appointed that they are in no case to yield any of our claim."[8]

The British and the Canadians appear to have consented to the treaty of 1903 with the understanding that the three American jurists would be judicially-minded men taken directly from the supreme court or perhaps some lesser tribunal. In view of the fact that Roosevelt was accused of having hoodwinked the British and the Canadians in his appointments, it is only fair to say that he offered, or said that he offered, a place on the tribunal to two of the supreme court justices, presumably Holmes and White, both of whom declined.[9] But even granting that the supreme bench was closed to him, Roosevelt could certainly have found capable and unobjectionable men elsewhere among the federal courts had he intended in good faith to appoint "impartial jurists of repute." He explained his extraordinary choices by writing to Mr. Justice Holmes that "No man in public life in any position of prominence could have possibly avoided committing himself on the proposition"[10]--which was patently not true. The questions at issue were unusually complicated; and it would probably be fair to say that relatively few men in public life, judicial or political, had either formed any opinion on the question or had committed themselves on it. Even granting that Roosevelt finally decided to appoint commissioners with closed minds who would staunchly defend the American view, he certainly could have chosen men less offensive to the British and Canadians than Senator Lodge and ex-Senator Turner.

A number of years after the event, Senator Lodge wrote that when the Alaska convention came before the senate it encountered strong opposition from those, particularly from the northwest states, who feared that the president might appoint commissioners who would not stand fast on the American contention. Lodge then went to the president and secured from him in confidence the names of the men whom he would choose, whereupon the opposition collapsed and the convention was approved.[11] Assuming that Roosevelt approached the two supreme court justices before this arrangement with Lodge, the story hangs together remarkably well, and has the added merit of providing what is perhaps the only rational explanation of why Roosevelt could have made such incredibly improper choices. We do know that the convention encountered enough difficulty in the senate to cause Hay considerable worry; and that the opposition suddenly ceased and the agreement was approved almost unanimously.[12] We also know that Hay, in explaining the appointments to Henry White, wrote, "the President thought it was impossible to get the treaty through the Senate without the earnest and devoted assistance of Lodge and Turner and of the groups which they represented."[13] Probably this is what Hay had reference to when he wrote to Roosevelt, "The Alaska treaty went through beautifully--thanks to your engineering."[14]

As a matter of pure speculation, it is interesting to consider what would have happened had the two supreme court justices consented to serve. The day after the decision of the London tribunal, Mr. Justice Holmes wrote to Roosevelt: "[Mr. Justice] White, the only person with whom I have talked here except my wife, was saying yesterday that with our judicial scepticism neither of us could have taken so convinced an attitude [as the tribunal?] and we agreed that it was a personal triumph of yours."[15] This interesting statement suggests that if Holmes and White had represented the United States, the Canadians probably would have secured a good deal more. But Roosevelt appears to have thought differently, for six weeks later he wrote to Arthur Lee that if the two supreme court justices had served, Canada probably would have got nothing.

> You speak of your regret that the Commission was not composed exclusively of judges. I asked two judges of our Supreme Court, whom I thought most fit for the positions, to serve. They both declined; and as I now think, wisely. On this Commission we needed to have jurists who were statesmen. If the decision had been rendered purely judicially, *the Canadians would not have received the two islands which they did receive at the mouth of the Portland Canal*; and one of the judges to whom I offered the appointment has told me that on that account he would have been unable to sign the award. He would have felt that he was sitting purely as a judge, and that judicially the case did not admit of a compromise. Personally, while I think the American case even as regards these islands was the stronger, I yet attach so great importance to having the case settled that I am glad that our commissioners yielded to Lord Alverstone and thus rendered it possible for a decision to be made. But my belief is that if you had had two of our Supreme Court judges on the American Commission,

> they would have stood out steadily for a decision on every point in favor of the American view--a determination which I think would have been technically proper, but in its results most unfortunate.[16]

Assuming that the president was referring to the above-quoted letter of Mr. Justice Holmes, which seems probable, it would appear that his memory was not altogether reliable.

In certain respects the Alaska difficulty is an outstanding example of Roosevelt's big-stick technique. He was determined to secure a settlement in his own way or no settlement at all. In March, 1902, he dispatched orders to the secretary of war to have "additional troops sent as quietly and unostentatiously as possible to Southern Alaska."[17] He wrote numerous letters to Root, Lodge, Hay, and Henry White in which he expressed his determination, if the commission failed, to occupy the disputed area by force, if necessary. Roosevelt's repetition of this theme was so frequent[18] as to suggest that he wanted his views to percolate to British officialdom through these intermediaries. He used a somewhat cruder approach in a remarkable letter to Mr. Justice Holmes, who was then in England. At the outset Roosevelt informed him that he was "entirely at liberty" to tell Joseph Chamberlain, British colonial secretary, "what I say, although of course it must be privately and unofficially." This is the passage that Roosevelt undoubtedly had in mind:

> ...If there is a disagreement I wish it distinctly understood, not only that there will be no arbitration of the matter, but that in my message to Congress I shall take a position which will prevent any possibility of arbitration hereafter; a position I am inclined to believe, which will render it necessary for Congress to give me the authority to run the line as we claim it, by our own people, without any further regard to the attitude of England and Canada.[19]

Mr. Justice Holmes showed his letter in confidence to two prominent men whom he met in England, including the chairman of the Canadian Grand Trunk, and then he had an interview with Chamberlain in a purely unofficial capacity. Holmes's report to Roosevelt is both interesting and significant:

> He expressed regret at the attitude and said that so far as he had examined there seemed to him to be a reasonable case on the

> other side. I said that I knew nothing about the question although experience had led me to regard most things as open to argument. He thought it would have been a step forward for this world [?] if men with wholly open minds had been appointed. As to this particular controversy he did not care much but England had to back up Canada...He was amiable, but considered the implications of your letter as exceedingly grave and to be regretted.[20]

Other attempts to browbeat the British were more subtle. Late in September, 1903, Roosevelt wrote a letter to Henry White, secretary of the American embassy in London, in which he expressed his determination to use strong measures.[21] The president evidently expected White to convey this information to high British officials, which White later testified he did.[22] About the same time Secretary Hay, who had become somewhat alarmed by Roosevelt's bellicose talk, advised White to see that the president's views were conveyed to Prime Minister Balfour. White, presuming on his friendship, had an interview with the prime minister early in October, 1903, and reported that he had "left no doubt upon his [Balfour's] mind as to the importance of the settlement nor as to the result of a failure to agree."[23] Two days after his conversation with White, Balfour was closeted twice with Lord Alverstone, who undoubtedly was informed of the seriousness of the situation. About the same time, Lodge, who knew of Roosevelt's views, also discussed the matter at some length with Balfour.[24] A few days earlier, Ambassador Choate reported that he had had an interview with Lord Lansdowne, British foreign secretary, "in which I pressed upon him very urgently the views of the President as expressed by him in our interview in June..."[25]

Roosevelt evidently believed that his big-stick methods contributed materially to the final result. Shortly after receiving word of the decision he reminded Mr. Justice Holmes: "If you will turn back to the letter I wrote you in July last, and which you showed to Chamberlain, you will notice how exactly the Alaska boundary decision went along the lines I there indicated. I cannot help having a certain feeling that your showing that letter to Chamberlain and others was not without its indirect effect on the decision."[26] But Holmes was not so sure. He replied: "What you say strikes me as extremely probable, although the circumstance will remain among the arcana of history. The English are very touchy about any suggestion of a threat and I said to Mr. C.[hamberlain] that I did not for a moment suppose that it was intended in that sense--although he said and fully realized that the intimation was grave."[27]

Roosevelt undoubtedly over-estimated the effect of the Holmes letter; but his combined efforts, direct and indirect, to bring pressure on high British officials probably were not without effect. It is unthinkable that the colonial secretary, the foreign secretary, or the prime minister could have failed to convey this information to Lord Alverstone, who, faced with the Canadian clamor on the one hand and with the knowledge that an adverse decision might cause Roosevelt to take steps that might lead to war on the other, was in an unenviable position. It is also difficult to believe that Lord Alverstone, who had long known the seamy side of politics before ascending the bench, was entirely immune from such pressure, though he may not consciously have yielded to it.[28] This may in part explain why he signed the final compromise decision, which was unpalatable to a purely judicial mind, and gave way on the southern extremity, where even Roosevelt admitted that the Canadians had a case.

Dr. Tyler Dennett is of the opinion that Roosevelt's handling of the dispute suggests that he was looking for an issue in the campaign of 1904.[29] But Roosevelt's own professions, if they mean anything, indicate that he consented to the final arrangements somewhat reluctantly, and that he did not want this problem unnecessarily aroused on the eve of a presidential election.[30] Nevertheless he was pleased with the advantageous settlement, writing to White: "The Alaska and Panama settlements coming in one year make a very good showing, do they not? I shall get Cuban reciprocity through, too."[31]

As in the case of Panama, Roosevelt got what he wanted by questionable tactics--and at the cost of a neighbor's ill-will.[32] Had he been willing to make haste more slowly, he probably would have secured substantially what he desired in both cases without the accompanying heritage of distrust. And one of the most curious things about the whole Alaska episode is that Roosevelt seems never to have realized how deeply his clumsy tactics hurt the Canadians. As he wrote to Mr. Justice White shortly after the news of the decision, "Our case was ironclad, and the chief need was a mixture of unyielding firmness in essentials and a good-humored courtesy in *everything*!"[33] The result, Roosevelt asserted with perhaps unconscious irony, "furnished a signal proof of the fairness and good will with which two friendly nations can approach and determine issues."[34] Such is not the verdict of history.

ENDNOTES

[1]*Roosevelt Papers*: Roosevelt to Strachey, July 18, 1902; Roosevelt to Hay, July 10, 1902. Unless otherwise indicated, all correspondence hereafter cited may be found in the Roosevelt collection in the Library of Congress, Washington, D.C.

[2]Roosevelt to Strachey, July 18, 1902; Roosevelt to Root, Aug. 8, 1903.

[3]Roosevelt to Morley, Dec. 12, 1903.

[4]Roosevelt wrote to Hay, "I have not regarded the question as one open to reasonable doubt, and for that reason have refused to permit any arbitration upon it..." (Roosevelt to Hay, Jan. 14, 1903); see also Roosevelt to Ted (Theodore, Jr.), Oct. 20, 1903.

[5]Roosevelt to F. W. Holls, Feb. 3, 1903.

[6]Roosevelt to Hay, Sept. 15, 1903.

[7]Roosevelt to Lodge, Turner, and Root, March 25, 1903.

[8]Roosevelt to Hay, July 16, 1902; also Roosevelt to Hay, July 10, 1902.

[9]Roosevelt to Arthur Lee, Dec. 7, 1903. Although it cannot be definitely determined that Holmes and White were the two justices, the internal evidence indicates that they were, strongly so in the case of Holmes.

[10]Roosevelt to Holmes, July 25, 1903.

[11]C. G. Washburn, "Memoir of Henry Cabot Lodge," *Massachusetts Historical Society Proceedings* 58 (1924-5): 340.

[12]Tyler Dennett, *John Hay* (New York, 1934), p. 362; New York *Times*, Feb. 6, 1903, 8, col. 1.

[13]Allan Nevins, *Henry White* (New York, 1930), p. 195.

[14]Hay to Roosevelt, Feb. 11, 1903.

[15]Holmes to Roosevelt, Oct. 21 1903.

[16]Roosevelt to Lee, Dec. 7, 1903; italics Roosevelt's.

[17]Henry Pringle, *Theodore Roosevelt* (New York, 1931), p. 290.

[18]In February, 1903, Roosevelt told the German ambassador substantially the same thing (*Die Grosse Politik*, XVII, 292).

[19]Roosevelt to Holmes, July 25, 1903.

[20]Holmes to Roosevelt, Oct. 11, 1903.

[21]Roosevelt to White, Sept. 26, 1903.

[22]Nevins, *White*, p. 199.

[23]Ibid., p. 200. Probably White read Roosevelt's letter of September 26 to Balfour.

[24]Ibid., p. 200.

[25]A. L. P. Dennis, *Adventures in American Diplomacy* (New York, 1928), p. 154: Choate to Hay, Oct. 20, 1903; also Roosevelt to Hay, June 29, 1903.

[26]Roosevelt to Holmes, Oct. 20, 1903; also Roosevelt to Ted, Oct. 20, 1903.

[27]Holmes to Roosevelt, Oct. 21, 1903.

[28]The testimony of the two Canadian commissioners supports the presumption that Lord Alverstone yielded to a compromise settlement (James White, "Henry Cabot Lodge and the Alaska boundary award," *Canadian Historical Review* 6 (Dec., 1925): 345.

[29]Dennett, *Hay*, p. 359.

[30]Roosevelt to Lodge, July 8, 1903; Roosevelt to Hay, June 29, 1903; Roosevelt to Lodge, June 29, 1903.

[31]Roosevelt to White, Nov. 26, 1903.

[32]Perhaps the intemperance of Roosevelt's language regarding the Canadians is explainable in part by the fact that when the Alaska matter was coming to a head Roosevelt was in a fever over the unwillingness of the "blackmailers of Bogota" to ratify the Panama canal treaty. He even used some of the same vituperative expressions in referring both to the Canadians and to the Colombians. See particularly Roosevelt to Hay, Sept. 21, 1903.

[33]Roosevelt to White, Oct. 19, 1903; italics Roosevelt's.

[34]Annual message to Congress, Dec. 7, 1903 *Congressional Record*, 58 cong., 2 sess., p. 5.

WRITING ALASKAN*

William R. Hunt

Many people who never thought of leaving home to seek a fortune in the Klondike, Nome, or Fairbanks found the gold rushes vicariously thrilling. These people constituted a sizeable audience for northern adventure stories, be they factual or fictional. Accordingly, the market for northern literature boomed.

North American readers, of course, were already familiar with the Horatio Alger stories, moralistic tales about poor boys who gained fame, fortune, and happiness by virtue of hard work and dogged persistence in the face of adversity. And the dime novels popular in the late nineteenth century, especially those about rugged, quick shooting western heros, whetted readers' appetites for adventure. In fact, much gold rush literature consisted of typical western topics transposed to a northern setting. Rex Beach's *The Spoilers* is probably the classic example of this genre, even though it is based upon events which actually occurred in Nome (thereby proving that some western rascals did move north). Literary realism and naturalism in the late nineteenth and early twentieth centuries further prepared readers for gritty accounts of endurance and tenacity in grim circumstances. And the often sentimental poets popular at the turn of the century, particularly Henry Wadsworth Longfellow and Rudyard Kipling, paved the way for Robert Service's northern verse.

William R. Hunt, Professor Emeritus of History at the University of Alaska Fairbanks, has written a number of articles and books on Alaska and the north. His major works include *Arctic Passage* (New York: Charles Scribner's Sons, 1975), a history of the Bering Sea and its people; *To Stand at the Pole* (New York: Stein and Day, Publishers, 1981), an account of the controversy generated when Robert Peary and Frederick Cook each claimed to have reached the North Pole first; and *Stef* (Vancouver: University of British Columbia Press, 1986), a biography of Viljalmur Stefansson.

In the following selection from *North of 53°: The Wild Days of the Yukon-Alaska Mining Frontier, 1870-1914*, Hunt discusses Jack London, Robert Service, and Rex Beach, each of whom built his reputation writing about the north. Hunt analyzes why northern literature, like the gold rush era itself, proved short-lived. And he concludes that adventure and self-discovery were themes as important for writers as for the prospectors themselves.

---

*This selection originally appeared in *North of 53°--The Wild Days of the Alaska-Yukon Mining Frontier, 1870-1914* (New York: Macmillan Publishing Co., Inc., 1974), pp. 286-96, 308-309, (Chapter 34 and Epilogue).

* * *

The North was a brutal frontier, raw and desolate, demanding of all the stamina and courage men could muster against it. Mesmerized by their lust for gold, they endured excruciating harships on the trail, faced incredible obstacles of distance and a savage climate and struggled on to a triumphant achievement of their goal--or to failure and frustration. Their tenacious efforts in a harsh land were memorialized in contemporary journalism and autobiographical accounts, and in a popular literature that encapsulated all the drama and rugged romance of their collective experience. Countless millions shared vicariously in the travails of the gold seeker, welcoming avidly the birth of a new frontier hero in story and verse.

Towering over all those who enshrined the heroes and rogues of America's last frontier adventurers in popular fiction was Jack London. His rowdy youth as oyster pirate, hobo, and seal poacher was as colorful as that of any of his fictional characters, London stampeded to the Klondike in 1897. There he prospected, mined, suffered from scurvy--the miner's curse--and failed to strike a bonanza. All these were common enough vicissitudes but they provided the basis for a literary outpouring that was to springboard the young writer to worldwide fame. In eleven books London served up his highly seasoned conception of the northern scene, the violent world of the Malemute Kid, Sitka Charlie, Old Tarwater, and the indomitable Buck. He created characters of commanding strength--men, and women too, who strode over snowy mountains and frigid tundra in fulfillment of their unique destinies. They could not be intimidated; their courage, resourcefulness, and sagacity made their progress irresistible; they exemplified Thomas Huxley's theory that the fittest survive at the expense of inferiors. As one scholar put it, "the age of heroes was not dead, but they had emigrated to the frozen north."[1]

Among the strongest intellectual influences upon Jack London were Thomas Huxley, Charles Darwin, and Rudyard Kipling. From the first two, the writer gleaned a particular interpretation of the theories of evolution and the survival of the fittest, concepts that easily supported London's reading of Kipling. Clearly, the Anglo-Saxons demonstrated a racial superiority condoned by the laws of the universe. It was obvious among the jungle fauna, on the Indian subcontinent, and equally so, with the inhabitants of the high latitudes who peopled London's stories. In novels like *Burning Daylight* and

Call of the Wild, short stories like "Love of Life" and "Son of Wolf," London's characters loom huge to display their surmounting mettle.

London drew on his own Yukon and Alaskan travels and on the lore he gathered from others. Old Tarwater of "Like Argus of Ancient Times" was modeled on the aged rusher who joined London's party on their ascent of the Chilkoot; his would-be egg profiteer of "One Thousand Dozen" owed much to an actual incident related to the writer. These figures and others like them were transmuted by the novelist's alchemy into the dramatic personae of his literary world. Critics might dispute the verisimilitude of London's creatures, but his northern tales still exercise their fascination over readers. No other writer's depiction of events of the North has approached London's in popularity. Today, London's books are more widely read in some European countries than in America. In Russia he holds the place of best-known American writer. As one Russian put it, "This is the first cigar we smoke in our youth."[2]

In 1899 the *Overland Monthly* published nine of London's short stories, most of which later appeared in his first book. In 1900 eastern journals became aware of London's work and published ten more of his stories. For five years after his return from the Klondike, dead broke and scurvy-ridden, his output of novels and stories with northern settings was snapped up eagerly by editors anxious to assuage the appetite of magazine and book buyers. "I never realized a cent from any property I had interest in up there," London wrote a friend in 1900, "still, I have been managing to pan out a living since on the strength of the trip."[3] London discovered a literary mother lode and drew from it throughout his career.

Wilson Mizner, the wittiest of all the stampeders, once made fun of the "London school" of Klondike fiction, with "its supermen and superdogs, its abysmal brutes and exquisite ingenues."[4] Other critics have complained that London's craft consisted of turning men into brutes, and brutes into men. Yet a close examination of London's stories reveals their basic strength aside from any dependence on ideology. They are good stories that are well told.

What did pioneer northerners think of London's fiction? It is difficult to generalize about this beyond noting that they read London's work eagerly. Obviously they did not accept every facet of the writer's interpretations. Will Ballou, the Rampart miner, read *Call of the Wild* in the spring of 1901 and remarked that it was one man's version of Alaskan life. The only feature he criticized in particular was London's endowment of squaw men, whites living with Indians, with heroic qualities. Miners did not view such men so favorably because they corrupted natives by getting liquor for them and because of racist attitudes.

Robert Service

Another writer who established a reputation through his northern residence was the poet Robert Service. The going was not easy for this Scot who threw up his bank clerk's position in the Old World to emigrate to North America. He hoboed his way to California, lived on oranges and an occasional mission handout, and read about the gold rush in the stories of Jack London and others, little dreaming that, "while other men were seeking Eldorado, they were also making one for me."[5] In 1904 the young Scot took a job with a Canadian bank and was sent to Whitehorse, the interior head of the railroad built in 1899 from Skagway to Whitehorse. As he steamed north on the passage, Service marveled at the rugged grandeur of the coastal mountain ranges and mused on his future. He hoped to be a writer, knowing himself as a "poor wretch with dreams, but somehow different from the crowd." From the steamer deck he reveled in the sublime, moonlit scenery "inspired...to sordid schemes of self-enrichment, because in the end they mean escape to freedom."[6] His years as bum and minstrel, thumping out his own songs on a guitar to unresponsive listeners, had not reconciled him to a resumption of a bank clerk's life. Yet, by an accident of fate, he was voyaging towards the land that would be his artistic catalyst and where all his dreams would find fulfillment.

The Skagway at which Service disembarked was a sleepy little town, very different from the wild port known to the Dawson argonauts. Now there were no crowds, no excitement, no threats from lawless gangs. Travelers to the interior could ride the White Pass and Yukon Railway safely and comfortably over the coastal range to the interior. Far below his coach Service could see the distinct markings of the stampeders' trail. It looked tough enough, and the poet did not long for its drama. "I was glad I had not been one of those grim stalwarts of the Great Stampede."[7] Strange comment from the writer whose verses were to romanticize the gold era for generations of enraptured readers of "The Cremation of Sam McGee" and "The Shooting of Dan McGrew," but quite in keeping with his no-nonsense character. Once established in Whitehorse, Service plugged away at his commercial duties, avoided the drinking crowd, and saved his money. This austere regime was to bring him closer to the old Klondike mood than any amount of wassailing in saloons could have done.

In his spare time Service was in demand at social gatherings for his recitations of dramatic poems. "Casey at the Bat," "Gunga Din," and "The Face on the Barroom Floor" were universal favorites of the day and his own verse efforts were in the same vein. Though he recited other mens' poems he had the satisfaction of seeing some of his own early work in print. Little fame or fortune attended the occasional appearance of a poem in the *Whitehorse Star*, the town's newspaper; still, it was an encouragement to his lonely aspirations.

Service's ambitions got a nudge in the proper direction from Stroller White of the Star, one of the best-known newsmen of the North. White urged the young banker, who had been asked to recite at a church concert, to do something original: "Give us something about our own little bit of earth...there's a rich paystreak waiting for someone to work. Why don't you go on in and stake it?"[8]

Musing on White's suggestion, Service took a long walk, searching for a poetic theme. Nothing came. Back in the bank, where he could work in quiet after closing, he gnawed a pencil and stared at his blank notepaper. Faintly he heard sounds of merriment from a neighboring saloon--it was Saturday night and revelry time. "A bunch of the boys were whooping it up in the Malemute Saloon," he wrote. Suddenly, there was the roar of a pistol in his ear. The bank's nightwatchman had mistaken Service for a burglar and fired at him. After calming the watchman, the poet scribbled feverishly through the night. His theme--a shooting at the Malemute Saloon, and the lurid narrative of unrequited love and vengeance unfolded itself. By 5 A.M. the ballad "was in the bag." "The Shooting of Dan McGrew" had taken form.

A delighted audience heard Service's "Dan McGrew" at a church concert. Afterwards, one of them, a Dawson mining man, buttonholed the poet to tell "a story Jack London never got." One wonders what Jack London might have done with the miner's story of the prospector who cremated his partner, but it gave Service a masterpiece. After the concert Service walked for hours, brooding on the incident and searching for a theme. Then it came--"There are strange things done in the midnight sun." Verse after verse fell into place as emerged "The Cremation of Sam McGee," which was to be the keystone of the poet's success. Before Service stumbled into bed he had completed the last verse celebrating the miner who finally got in from the cold.

And there sat Sam, looking cool and calm, in the heart of
the furnace roar;
And he wore a smile you could see a mile, and he said:
"Please close that door.
It's fine in here, but I greatly fear you'll let in the cold
and storm --
Since I left Plumtree, down in Tennessee, it's the first
time I've been warm."[9]

The *Songs of a Sourdough*, Service's first book of poems, met with instantaneous acclaim. Immensely readable and, even more important, recitable, the ballads appeared in edition after edition--the twentieth by 1909, and never out of print since.

Rex Beach

Next to Jack London the most popular fictional portrayer of the northern gold scene was Rex Beach. Beach was a law student in Chicago when he heard the call of the Klondike. The burly youth had joined the school's football and water polo teams for the privilege of free dining and he was eager to escape the playing field. The hardship and privation on the trail did not worry him. "Freezing was far more pleasant than drowning...and as for hunger, I was starved most of the time, anyhow."[10] With a grubstake from his brothers, equipped with sleeping bag, rifle, doeskin suit, and mandolin, Beach set out.

Beach spent two years at Rampart working at mining, logging, and various odd jobs, including music-making. A writer's career did not cross his mind at the time; he was just one of many drudging away to make a living. The question of the literary possibilities of the northern frontier was discussed on occasion, but mining men did not find their own work glamorous. A journalist acquaintance at Rampart assured Beach that the North would never produce a Mark Twain or Bret Harte--the writers who immortalized the California gold era in fiction--"There's no drama up here, no comedy, no warmth. Life is as pale and cold as the snow." How could colorful stories be told of such a drab and dreary country?[11]

At the time Beach agreed with the journalist. Life did seem hard and unromantic on the Yukon compared to sunny California. Later he reflected on this conversation in amazement at what he had almost missed. "Color, comedy, drama indeed! There we were, some fifteen hundred souls, and twelve saloon keepers, all dumped out on the bank of the Yukon to shift for ourselves in a region unmapped and unexplored." The men had arrived in Rampart late in the fall; grub was short; stoves were scarce; and all were newcomers. "Not one in ten knew how to toss a flapjack or tear a footrag." None knew what gold looked like in its "native state." Neither roads nor well-marked trails existed. "Every valley was a no-man's land, every rushing river was a highway to adventure and every gulch [was] filled to the brim with a purple haze of mystery." Surely the stuff of romance was there![12]

He was only 24 when he left the North and had not yet thought of becoming a writer. In Chicago he joined a building materials firm as a salesman and moved up rapidly in the business world. One day he met a Yukon acquaintance who had just earned $10 from the sale of an article on Alaska. "Here was news more incredible than the Klondike discovery, viz., paydirt on Michigan Avenue running ten dollars to the pan!" Beach exclaims, recounting this episode humorously in his memoirs. As he described it, he was fearful that the news of such easy money would leak out and start a literary stampede: "I implored my friend to keep it under his hat at least until I could get some stakes down." Exaggeration aside, the incident did, for some reason, stimulate Beach to try his hand at writing.[13]

His first story was based on an anecdote told to him by a Rampart miner. This piece was submitted to the popular *McClure's Magazine* and promptly accepted. With some pride the fledgling author displayed a $50 McClure's check to his boss who pretended amazement at such a windfall. His business colleagues' taunts did not divert Beach from further writing. By this time he had been promoted to a vice-presidency in his firm, but he devoted evenings, Sundays and holidays to authorship: "I wrote on railroad trains, in waiting rooms or wherever I could hold a suit case on my knees."[14] Before long his income from writing equaled his salary and Beach gave up business to become a full-time author.

S. S. McClure, the magazine editor, suggested that Beach try a novel. A good plot came readily to mind--the brazen conspiracy of Alexander McKenzie and Judge Noyes to oust the Nome discoverers from their rich claims. "About all I had to do was add a little imagination, flavor with love interest, season to taste and serve."[15] After completing *The Spoilers*, a fictional account of the "boldest buccaneering raid directed at the North," Beach wrote a muckraking article, "The Looting of Alaska," based on the same incident.[16] McClure liked the article but made the mistake of letting another publisher get the novel. *The Spoilers* became a best-selling book and a Hollywood film. In fact moviemen have liked *The Spoilers* well enough to base films on the story three times over the years.

Roy Glenister is the hero of *The Spoilers*. He is depicted as one of the mine owners whom the conspirators tried to defraud. To some extent former reindeer herdsman Jafet Lindeberg served as a model. The young miner proves himself too dominant a figure to stand aside in the face of judicial chicanery, and triumphs over the legal minions and thugs set against him. For all Glenister's gentlemanly qualities he was essentially an untamed force, bottling up under the veneer of civilized conduct a fierce, half-savage spirit. Glenister has to struggle against his demon and the consequences of his love for a girl, who happens to be a loyal niece of the perfidious judge.

Among Beach's thirty-two books are other novels set in Alaska. *The Barrier* draws on Beach's experiences on the Yukon at Rampart, but is not based upon actual events--and does not hang together as well as *The Spoilers*. Beach turned to another chapter of Alaskan history in *The Iron Trail*. Here the rivalry of railroad builders driving to complete a route to the rich Kennecott Company copper mines forms the substance of the plot. In Beach's works the secondary characters are pale foils to the leading hero and villain. Regardless of their efforts at humor and their varying vernacular, they cannot balance the overpowering weight of the main figures, men almost too good or evil to believe in.

Beach's stories still have readers, particularly *The Spoilers* and *The Iron Trail*; *The Iron Trail* has been recently reprinted in paperback. But Beach's popularity over the years has not kept pace with that of Jack London--and for obvious reasons. London was a craftsman of much superior ability, his plots and characters were much better than Beach's. Nor could Beach's descriptive powers approach those of London. London's North may have been somewhat unreal at times, but it never lacked vividness. Despite Beach's extensive experience at Rampart and Nome, he fails to communicate the atmosphere of those lively towns. His highly charged scenes set in saloons and elsewhere are dramatic enough, yet often are not marked by any particular quality of their northern background.

London and Beach have not had a long line of successors. For all the popularity of northern stories in the early years of the century, when noted writers like Jules Verne tried their hand, the interest has not been maintained. Popular fiction depends upon ready points of reference among readers, and the decline of interest in the North since the gold rush days has diminished the opportunities for such work. While the appeal of the colorful history of the Old West's frontier never wanes, and is encouraged endlessly by films and television, the fictional field of the North lies fallow. It is conceivable that popular writers might rediscover the North and exploit the material that brought prominence to London and Beach. Alaska's current oil boom might help to prepare the ground for tales of hearty dog mushers and the quest of fortune in frozen regions, but a resurgence cannot be predicted with any confidence. The weary cycle of Deadwood shoot-outs, Apache battles, and hard-riding cattle-rustling grinds on relentlessly while the rich adventures of northern mining camps are forgotten.

Perhaps the pessimistic prophecy of Ambrose Bierce has been partially fulfilled as far as the North's literary heritage is concerned. Bierce made his name writing about the California gold rush but could see nothing of permanent value resulting from the Klondike stampede. He doubted that even a "dog sled civilization and a reindeer religion" would survive,

> Nothing will come of him [the stampeder]. He is a world in the wind, a brother to the fog. At the scene of his activity no memory of him will remain. The gravel that he thawed and sifted will freeze again...The snows will cover over his trail and all be as before.[17]

But, of course, the North was changed radically and permanently by the gold developments. Some of the trails became roads. Yet the literary gravel did freeze up after it was worked brilliantly by London, Service, and Beach.

Too bad--but such neglect is understandable. America's Alaskan frontier experience has not fixed itself in the national consciousness. Fleetingly, in the skilled efforts of Jack London and

Rex Beach, the North became part of the frontier legend, then was crowded from popular imagination by more familiar western exploits. Alaska was too strange, too distant and obscure to preserve its place. The handful of historians and creative writers of the North have not been able to reverse the trend. Soapy Smith, Wilson Mizner, Swiftwater Bill Gates, and other northern worthies toss restlessly in their graves, longing, one might suppose, for their just share of prime television time.

EPILOGUE

In distant Europe huge armies were fiercely engaged in the trench warfare of the Western Front as the little steamboat *Pelican* voyaged along the Yukon and its tributaries. The rivers themselves had not changed much over the 30-odd years since Lieutenant Schwatka's raft had floated down from the Yukon's headwaters to St. Michael. Waters yellow with silt poured into the Bering Sea as always, draining the great basin of the interior in an unending flow. Much that Lt. Frederick Schwatka had seen on his exploratory expedition in 1883 was observed also by Reverend Hudson Stuck from the deck of the *Pelican.* Of course there had been momentous changes as well. In the intervening years between these two voyages the North had boomed. Its ancient, gold encrusted stream beds had lured the adventurous, yielded up fortunes and created cities in the wilderness. The North known to Lieutenant Schwatka could never be again.

What evaluation can be made of this tumultuous chapter of the region's history? Stuck's reflections were gloomy indeed as the *Pelican* steamed downriver to Dawson and Forty Mile in the Yukon Territory, crossed the American border to Eagle, Circle, and Fort Yukon, then ascended the Tanana to Fairbanks. The Episcopal priest observed all the interior's principal gold camps, including Ruby on the lower Yukon, and Iditarod on the Innoku River, and reported on others: Wiseman, Coldfoot, Caro, and Nome. Few of the gold towns showed much bustle at the time of Stuck's visits, though many signs of former prosperity could be noted. A brief life was characteristic of a placer town: "However it may grow and flourish, however comfortable its homes and however attached to them people become, however...conditions of living become more and more pleasant, the whole thing is without substantial foundation, and inevitably temporary."[18] Unlike longer lasting quartz mines, placer deposits were soon worked out and when they failed after a few years, the communities dependent upon them also failed. Forty Mile, Eagle, Circle, and Rampart were dead, and elsewhere mining activity was declining. Dawson was still alive, but the dredges operating there were gathering the last remains of alluvial gold in the district and would soon have all there was. Dawson was a "doomed city" and so were virtually all the others that had not yet become ghost towns. Stuck thought that Fairbanks might survive with the aid of the government railroad to the coast, "its market-gardens and its launderies," but he was not overly optimistic.[19] With reason a Fairbanks newspaper had labeled the minister a Prophet of Despair for uttering such sentiments on other occasions.

Surely the great boom had come and gone and with it had departed Swiftwater Bill Gates, Wilson Mizner, Jack Hines, Tex Rickard, Rex Beach, Jack Kearns, and thousands of lesser known stampeders. But the collapse of the boom did not obviate community life in the interior. Alaska's population declined; yet a small mining industry sustained the pioneers of Nome, Fairbanks, and other towns. Tenacious men and women defied the predictions of those who argued that a region without agricultural potential could not survive. These northern settlers did not enjoy great prosperity. The remoteness of the North and the high costs of transporting most of the necessities from the Outside made their lives hard, yet they had discovered other values that reconciled them to Alaskan conditions. Neither a romantic nor an adventurous spirit sustained them; it was simply a preference for a life style that for a variety of reasons appealed to them. Against all the formidable odds of isolation, distance, and a harsh climate, they nurtured their frontier communities, ignoring the death toll sounded by Reverend Stuck and other pessimists. Many could echo the sentiments of George Pilcher whose adventures of 1898 ripened into a lifetime commitment to life in the North:

> I came to this Alaska a young man full of energy, industry and a will to win. I am now well into my 67th year and can feel the tug of time. I have failed to win wealth but have maintained my self-respect and am convinced that I hold the respect of all--or most all--others. This is worth more than gold.[20]

But there was also a meaning in the northern experience for the tens of thousands who did not settle permanently. Men like Fred Walker, an Englishman, who was lured to the North in quest of adventure and stopped only fleetingly in Alaska before moving on to other parts of the world, looked back on his journeys there as one of "the high spots" of a varied career.[21] Another favorable commentator, Johnny Walker, a veteran of the stampedes, had fond memories of his early experiences: "I'm an old man now, but in those days of my youth I lived, ate, and slept adventure. I made fortunes and spent them, lived like a prince, and like an Indian."[22]

Most of the argonauts seemed to have appreciated their individual gains as participants in the stirring events of the gold era. Very few of them expressed the disenchantment and bitterness of Arthur Dietz, whose sorry journey over the Malaspina Glacier was reported earlier in these pages. More typically, the rushers were like Charles Angel, who after suffering severe hardship on the trail and the climax of a near disaster at sea, watched from shipboard the land of so many golden dreams and shattered hopes recede.

> True, I had found no gold. But I was no poorer than when I arrived; I enjoyed the best of health, and surely no more soul-satisfying adventures could have befallen me. No, I had no regrets.[23]

For Angel and others, the Alaskan adventure was well summed up in the verse of an anonymous poet:

A million dollar gold bond
Could never, never buy,
My memories of the Northland --
I'll keep them 'till I die.
I'll treasure them like a miser,
His hoard of gleaming gold
My memories are my treasure,
And never may be sold.[24]

ENDNOTES

[1]Calder-Marshall, *Bodley Head Jack London* (London: The Bodley Head, 1966), Vol. IV, p. 10.

[2]Richard O'Connor, *Jack London* (Boston: Little, Brown, 1964), p. 6.

[3]Franklin Walker, *Jack London and the Klondike* (San Marino: Huntington Library, 1966), p. 213.

[4]O'Connor, *Jack London*, p. 84.

[5]Robert W. Service, *Ploughman of the Moon* (London: Benn, 1946), p. 257.

[6]Ibid., p. 262.

[7]Ibid.

[8]Ibid., p. 274.

[9]Robert W. Service, *Collected Poems* (New York: Dodd, Mead, 1968), p. 36.

[10]Beach, *Personal Exposures* (New York: Harper & Brothers, 1940), p. 20.

[11]Ibid., p. 28.

[12]Ibid., p. 32.

[13]Ibid., p. 27.

[14]Ibid., p. 24.

[15]Ibid., p. 22.

[16]Ibid., p. 28.

[17]O'Connor, *Jack London*, p. 81.

[18]Hudson Stuck, *Voyages on the Yukon and Its Tributaries* (New York: Scribner's Sons, 1917), p. 51.

[19]Ibid.

[20]George H. Pilcher Diary, University of Alaska Archives, Fairbanks, December 31, 1930.

[21]Fred Walker, *Destination Unknown--The Autobiography of a Wandering Boy* (London: Harrap, 1934), p. 106.

[22]Jonny Walker, as told to Louis Whittaker. "Bonanza Days," *Alaska Sportsman* November 1943, p. 12.

[23]Charles Wilkes Angel, "And Going Home We Lost the Rudder!" *Alaska Sportsman* September 1943, p. 29.

[24]James Wickersham, *Old Yukon* (Washington: Washington Law Book, 1938), p. 24.

CROSS-CULTURAL CONTACT IN THE WILDERNESS*

William Schneider

Morgan Sherwood asserted in *Exploration of Alaska, 1865-1900* (New Haven, CT: Yale University Press, 1965) that the United States government did not ignore Alaska during the early American period, contrary to the charges of the several hundred non-Native inhabitants who regularly sought some form or another of federal assistance. In fact, Sherwood found that the federal government rather generously funded research and exploration by such institutions as the United States Geological Survey, the Smithsonian Institution, and the United States Army. These activities were documented by those who did them, and the accounts understandably reflect the western culture's point of view.

William S. Schneider has examined exploration and initial Native/non-Native contact from the Native point of view. Schneider, who received a Ph.D. in Anthropology from Bryn Mawr in 1976, is Curator of the Oral History Collection in the Alaska and Polar Regions Department of the Elmer Rasmuson Library, University of Alaska Fairbanks. Schneider helped to create that collection and implemented the first systematic statewide oral history indexing system. His research projects have included an oral history of the Alaska Steamship Company and interviews for the Alaska Statehood Commission. The bulk of his work, however, has been with Native Alaskans. He initiated the Life History Series, which resulted in the publication of Moses Cruikshank's *The Life I've Been Living* (Fairbanks: University of Alaska Press, 1986), and he is presently working through that program on a biography of Waldo Bodfish, Inupiat whaling captain.

In the following article, which first appeared in the Alaska Historical Society's new journal, *Alaska History,* Schneider describes Lt. Joseph Herron's 1899 expedition to the Upper Kuskokwim and explains that Herron and his men probably would have perished had they not been rescued by Athabascan Chief Sesui and his people. Schneider concludes that the incident is an example of positive cultural adaptation among Chief Sesui's band and suggests that because of their location Upper Kuskokwim Athabascans were able to maintain an unusually high level of cultural integrity following contact with non-Natives.

* * *

In 1899 Joseph Herron, a first Lieutenant in the 8th Cavalry, United States Army, led a small detachment of soldiers through the Alaska Range into the Upper Kuskokwim drainage. Enroute to the

---

*This article original appear in *Alaska History* 1, no. 2 (Fall/Winter 1985): 1-18.

Yukon, this party became lost in the broad flat lands of the Upper Kuskokwim and was rescued by the Athabascan Chief Sesui (Shesoie or Shesuie) and his followers. The soldiers were cared for and then led to Tanana on the Yukon where a new military post had just been established.[1]

The story of that extraordinary rescue is dramatic, but the events leading up to the rescue and the conditions of the rescue provide fascinating clues to the successful cultural adaptation of the Natives in the upper Kuskokwim. Examples of positive cultural adaptation by Native peoples in times of rapid change are few. The usual pattern is marked by disruption of the seasonal cycle of hunting and fishing, strains on the social system and curtailment of culturally valued activities. That does not seem to have happened in the Upper Kuskokwim. Indeed, the Upper Kuskokwim Natives, living in an area remote from outside supply and maintaining a high level of flexibility and trading options for much of their history, were able to sustain a high level of cultural integrity and to take advantage of economic opportunities which finally developed in their region.

For years the Native population of the Upper Kuskokwim had engaged in limited contact with traders, missionaries, and perhaps the lone prospector. But they had not, until Herron's expedition in 1899, experienced prolonged interaction with a non-Native population in the heart of their homeland. As 1899 is a comparatively late date in the history of white-Native contact in Alaska,[2] the event therefore provides a good setting for evaluating the ways that Native people at the local level learned about outsiders before they actually arrived in their homeland and how they selectively incorporated the foreigners' goods and way of life. The expedition reports and Native oral accounts which persist even today provide rich detail on the response of the Upper Kuskokwim people to Herron and his men. And the circumstances surrounding the expedition help to explain the history of exploration in Interior Alaska.

These circumstances gain added significance because rather shortly after Herron's trip, the Upper Kuskokwim was traversed by the two major trail systems which brought prospectors and employment opportunities for the Native population. The Natives' success in exploiting these opportunities stands in marked contrast to many other parts of Alaska where development signaled dislocation and disruption, particularly of subsistence pursuits. A consideration of developments in this area can therefore provide insights on the effects of culture contact and change in general.

For many years, the U. S. government showed little interest in governing the territory of Alaska. The military, in name, was to provide the major federal presence but it was not until a large influx of gold seekers in the 1890s that the Army gained authority and resources to play an active role in the Territory. The gold seekers were headed for the Yukon River, to rich proven ground on the upper river, or down river to new prospects on the tributaries. The prospectors expected to find supplies plentiful enough to support their needs and they assumed there would be law and order. Often they were disappointed on both counts. They found that the transportation companies which ran the steamboats on the Yukon River could not be depended upon to meet their needs; shallow water and limited service meant few goods and exorbitant prices.

In addition, as gold mining developed, Americans became concerned that Canadians might seek to control access to the gold fields of the Upper Yukon in Alaska. In the 1890s access to the Upper Yukon was by three basic routes. Each had particular problems. One route led over the Chilkoot and other passes from tidewater at Skagway and Dyea into the Yukon territory of Canada and then down the Yukon River. Another way was by the Old Hudson's Bay Company route through northern Canada and down the porcupine River to Fort Yukon. The third way was by ship to St. Michael and then by steamboat up the Yukon. This route while avoiding the Canadian problem was blocked in winter by sea ice, and in summer, shallows on the river created special problems for supply.

These were the conditions that finally prompted the government to action. In 1897, Captain P. H. Ray of the U. S. Army was sent to Alaska under special assignment from the president of the United States to report on conditions in the Interior. Ray was a keen observer, an extremely competent leader under pressure, and he had influence back in Washington.[3] In the fall of 1897, Ray experienced problems of supply firsthand, and soon after his arrival he formulated recommendations for alternative routes in Interior Alaska, overland "All-American" routes from tidewater to the Yukon River.

Ray based his recommendations on hearing of Native trails from the mouth of the Tanana River to the Copper River, Cook Inlet, and the Upper Kuskokwim River. Ray reported on these trails and urged military exploration from Cook Inlet or Valdez Inlet to the mouth of the Tanana.[4] The War Department accepted his proposals and in the summers of 1898 and 1899, the Army mounted expeditions from Prince William Sound and Cook Inlet. While Ray's report provided the principal justification for Lieutenant Herron's expedition in 1899, additional support for the Upper Kuskokwim route to the Yukon was provided by a United States Geological Survey geologist, Josiah Edward Spurr. During the summer of 1898, Spurr led a geological expedition from Cook Inlet up the Susitna River and through the Alaska Range to the Upper Kuskokwim, down that river and thence across the Alaska Peninsula. This journey marked the first scientific investigation of the Upper Kuskokwim, but Spurr's trip is noteworthy because of his observations on the potential for a transportation route from Cook Inlet to the Upper Kuskokwim and thence to the Tanana drainage. This may very well have added fuel to Ray's plea for an "All-American" route and certainly influenced the plans for Herron's expedition the following year. Spurr wrote:

> From the shores of Cook Inlet to the Tordrillo Mountains the way lies over a comparatively level plateau with practically no irregularities and the Tordrillo Mountains themselves offer convenient passes near the place where they were crossed... On the Kuskokwim side of the mountains the same low, level plateau reaches down to the perfectly flat country through which such a large portion of the Upper Kuskokwim flows. Thus for a wagon road or a railroad there are few engineering difficulties to surmount. From the Upper Kuskokwim communication with neighboring districts is easy. The divide between the Upper Kuskokwim and the Lower Tanana consists of low mountains which offer few obstacles; indeed, a well-known native route to the Kuskokwim is by way of the Toclat River, which enters the Lower Tanana and which communicates with a tributary of the Kuskokwim. It is probable that a wagon road or railroad across the divide would also be a very simple matter.[5]

Spurr's enticing description had appeal but the "well-known native route" was to prove elusive for Herron.

In 1899, Herron led his expedition from Cook Inlet through the Alaska Range and into the Upper Kuskokwim in search of an "All-American" route from tidewater to the Yukon. Joseph Herron was a graduate of the U. S. Military Academy, graduating in the class of

1891. Eight years later, he found himself the leader of a major expedition which, by the standards of the military of his day, was a success. He traversed over five hundred miles of unknown territory, experienced tremendous hard-ships, and produced a detailed map and description of the country.[6] In October, 1901, two years after the trip, he was advanced to the rank of captain.[7]

Like many of the other expeditions of 1898 and 1899, Herron and his party of eight men were heavily loaded for extensive overland travel in dense forest cover. They began with, among other items, six hundred pounds of bacon and a thousand pounds of flour. Fifteen horses and eight men carried a total weight of 3,300 pounds.[8] The previous year there had been considerable trouble in acquiring trained horses for explorations because military horses were in demand for the Spanish-American War. Whether this was also true of Herron's expedition is not clear. What is evident is the unsuitability of horses for the traverse. The animals became bogged down in the heavy brush; there were difficulties in finding sufficient graze; and the animals were not suited for the swift streams that had to be crossed. The animals were finally abandoned. The expedition was forced to cache many of its foodstuffs, a decision that ironically aided their eventual rescue.

Herron's destination was Rampart on the Yukon River, the site of prospecting activities and near the location where John Mynook had discovered gold in 1893.[9] By this time, the Yukon was well known; Captain Charles Raymond's trip up the river by steamboat in 1869 had demonstrated its navigability by river steamer, and by the mid-1870s traders such as Arthur Harper, Jack McQuesten and Al Mayo had carried on a lively trade for furs. McQuesten was instrumental in broadcasting the gold mining potential of the streams. He grubstaked some of the early prospectors working in the Yukon Valley.[10]

Lt. Herron acquired two Native guides at Susitna station, an Alaska Commercial Company trading post on the Susitna River. The party did not get started until June 27th when the season was quite advanced.[11] They traveled up the Susitna to the Yentna, up the Yentna to the Kichatna, then through Simpson Pass to the Upper Kuskokwim where they eventually became bogged down. The Upper Kuskokwim is complicated and provides unusual challenges. The numerous tributaries and the broad expanse of the lowlands create a veritable maze to the uninitiated. The two guides, Slenkta and Stepan, abandoned the party before they reached Egypt Mountain, a landmark and traditional Native trading site. The expedition was in serious trouble. The reasons for the Natives' desertion are unclear. Perhaps they lacked knowledge of the country beyond that point or they may have feared reprisal from Upper Kuskokwim people who would recall unfavorable treatment they had received from Tanaina traders at an earlier time.[12] The expedition continued without Native guides. Floundering in an area near Telida, the men cached supplies and abandoned the remaining horses.

Both written and oral accounts tell of the rescue. Herron's report tells how a bear broke into their cache and consumed bacon they had put there. The bear was killed by the Telida Indians and, upon discovering the bacon in its stomach, the Indians backtracked its trail to Herron's cache and then were able to track the soldiers. Herron reported: "September 19 we found an Indian, who, 1 learned later, was the one who had killed the bear that had robbed our cache; or rather, the Indian found us."[13] Judge James Wickersham has also provided a written ac-count of the rescue which he undoubtedly gathered from oral accounts while in the Kantishna. He wrote:

> Shesoie, the chief of the Telida (Tena) village was out hunting one day and ran across and followed a bear's trail until he found the animal and killed it. He ascertained the bear had been eating bacon; and being interested in learning where it had obtained this white man's food he followed on its back track, which finally led him to one of Lieutenant Herron's caches at which the bear had obtained the bacon. Until that moment the Indian had not known there were white men, or bacon, in his country. He immediately set out to follow the white man's trail, and so found Lieutenant Herron and his soldiers afoot, lost and starving, in the maze of the Kuskokwim marshes. He took them safely to his village where he sheltered them and fed them for two months, and then guided them over his Cosna trail to the Tanana River and put them on that highway to Fort Gibbon.[14]

Oral accounts of the rescue tell how Carl Sesui, son of Chief Sesui, saw horse tracks and droppings. He asked his father what they were. Chief Sesui told him that was the white man's dog, his way of describing the horse. One version of the story tells how Carl Sesui and his father saw the tracks and droppings which Chief Sesui identified for his son. They went on and shot a bear. They discovered the bear had bacon in its stomach and then they went back to the horse tracks and followed them until they came to Herron's camp. They found Herron and his men there.[15] Charlene LeFebre, an anthropologist who met Carl Sesui while looking for archaeological sites in the Upper Kuskokwim was told by him:

> My father went down with a canoe and he took me down below my place. We see on other bank some kind of track there. He says "horse." That summer he been to Tanana and he see white man and horse. That what he know. And he talk me that is white man and I don't believe it because I don't see that kind of track...nails and funny thing stick out behind...heel. I don't believe it. I don't know that game. That is some kind of animal. Go down 4-5 mile and see horse and my father told me we see horse. Still alive. And few miles further father find men. Thought this was Tanana. Make raft. Find this neck and make fire and my father show them how the Kuskokwim and Tanana and Cochaket and Kantishna meet. Got down to old village and put him in cabin--don't know how long he stay there. An started to get cold and my father and mother make moccasins, mits, fur cap and father make snowshoes for those fellow. And he started to walk and went thru to Minchumina and Cochaket and don't cost nothing. Just help that guy that all.[16]

Herron's account also told how they were taken to Telida and housed, fed, and clothed for their trip to the Yukon:

> I proceeded to go into camp there for two months, until we could get winter clothes and socks made of our horse blankets, procure mits, fur caps, moccasins, and snowshoes for the party from the Indians, and to wait until conditions were favorable for snowshoe travel.[17]

On November 25th, they were guided by four Telida Natives to Tanana following the Native trail to Lake Minchumina, and the Cosna River trail to the Tanana, and down river to Fort Gibbon, the newly established army post at Tanana. They had expected to proceed to Rampart but Fort Gibbon had been built that summer (1899) and therefore became their immediate destination.[18] News of their pending arrival was passed through local groups but their appearance at the post created quite a stir. Robert Farnsworth, son of Captain Farnsworth, the post commander, reported:

> Arriving at our cabin they could hardly walk. We asked them in, but Lieutenant Herron refused to even shake hands, saying they were covered with lice. So they were taken to the post laundry, which was only partly finished. Their clothes were soaked in the much valued kerosene, then the men were shaved and had haircuts and baths...
>
> The Indians also got cleaned up and came to the cabin for a recommendation and money for supplies...A recommendation was written out for them on the typewriter and also an order for some food, but they refused to take either, saying they were no good. The documents had to be written in longhand before they would accept them.[19]

The Herron expedition marked a major achievement in the description and mapping of an uncharted portion of the Interior. Portions of their route would be retraced by gold seekers in the years that followed, on routes such as the Iditarod Trail. Besides describing unrecorded country, Herron's experience demonstrated that the western slope of the Alaska Range was not the best "All-American" route to the Yukon. The Valdez Trail to Eagle and the Fortymile proved to be a more appropriate route, because of the distances involved and because of the economic opportunities for miners which continued to be available in the Upper Yukon.

Herron's expedition marked the end of an era, the end of large overland military expeditions in Alaska. The attention of the Army shifted to the posts on the Yukon. The role of exploration and description of Alaskan territory was inherited by the United States Geological Survey. They employed quite different methods. They sent out small parties of professional geologists equipped with lighter outfits. They also were unhampered by the formal chain of command which typified the Army expeditions.[20]

Herron's rescue stands out in the record of Native-white relations because Chief Sesui and his followers demonstrated so much knowledge of white men and their ways. Native assistance to military expeditions in the Interior was not unique--Lieutenant Henry Allen was guided on the upper Copper River by Chief Nicolai and Lieutenant J. C. Castner depended upon Native assistance, particularly on the Volkmar.[21] However, the Herron rescue stands out because of the many details which Sesui noticed and used in finding and assisting Herron. The discovery of foreign food (bacon), the tracking process, knowledge of horses, and the preparations for the trip to the Yukon point to the very sophisticated knowledge that these people had of white men.

Considering that this was the first intrusion of white men in the heartland of their territory, it would seem that the Upper Kuskokwim people must have traveled extensively outside of the upper river, and relied upon a wealth of detail about white men gleaned from accounts from neighboring groups. Both of these assumptions are substantiated by the historical record going back to the period of Russian and British traders, before the Treaty of Cession in 1867.

In the early years of the nineteenth century, Russian traders extended their search for profitable furbearers, entering the Interior and finally establishing a post at Kolmakovsky (Kolmakov Redoubt) on the Kuskokwim River in 1841. From there the Russian-American Company maintained a seasonal trading site at Vinasale in the 1850s, some twenty river miles below present-day McGrath.[22] Vinasale became a trading focus for some Upper Kuskokwim people although they also met Tanaina Athabascans from Cook Inlet at trading sites close to the place Medfra called Itstynoo[23] and near Egypt Mountain on the north side of Rainy pass.[24]

Russian expansion on the Yukon River was from St. Michael up the Yukon to Nulato where a post was established in 1839. The Hudson's Bay Company, also in search of fur, gradually extended a network of posts across Canada, finally entering Alaska and establishing Fort Yukon in 1847. From this post, they sometimes made the trip down river after break-up to the confluence of the Tanana and the Yukon where they traded with the Native groups gathered there.[25] The Russians also made spring trips to trade, but they had to wait until the ice cleared Nulato and rarely went further up river than the mouth of the Tanana.[26]

Some of the trade goods from the Yukon-Tanana trade must certainly have made their way to the Upper Kuskokwim people, although we do not have much information on this critical question. However, by Herron's time, the Upper Kuskokwim people had an established route to the Tanana River and were familiar with the settlement of Tanana, having been there to trade.[27]

The importance of trade and travel to Tanana deserves some additional consideration. The newly established post at Tanana, Fort

Gibbon, was near the location of the traditional spring gathering where Athabascan groups came to trade,[28] a gathering enriched by the Hudson's Bay and Russian-American Company traders before the American purchase of Alaska. The location continued to be important after the purchase when the Church of England established St. James Mission at the mouth of the Tozitna, some eighteen miles from the confluence of the Yukon and the Tanana, near a trading post called Fort Adams. The mission was taken over by the Episcopal Church in 1891[29] and this is where the Indians of the Tanana, Koyukuk, and surrounding Yukon drainages went for religious and trading purposes. The church's influence extended as far as Lake Minchumina where the Natives held allegiance to the Episcopal Church, but the Upper Kuskokwim people were Russian Orthodox and maintained religious connections down river. However, in the last quarter of the nineteenth century, their trading allegiances may have been oriented toward Tanana. As noted, the Upper Kuskokwim people's trade with the Tanaina of Cook Inlet was interrupted sometime late in the century, largely as the result of a serious incident involving Diqelas Tukda, a Tanaina trader who allegedly deceived them.[30] After this incident, the Upper Kuskokwim people turned to other sources of trade,[31] and it is likely that the trading posts on the Yukon and specifically at Tanana, increased in importance. Genealogical work with the residents of Telida and Nikolai may indicate kinship and other social ties at this time with the Yukon people. On the Kuskokwim River, after the Treaty of Cession, the Russian-American Company was replaced by independent traders, and eventually by the Alaska Commercial Company. White traders did not pursue trade on the upper Kuskokwim River as vigorously as on the Yukon, where there was a larger population and concentration of activity, until the development of gold mining on the lower and middle Kuskokwim after the turn of the century.[32]

The Upper Kuskokwim people were ready to assist Herron on his way through and they were ready to assist the hundreds of others that came in the early years of the twentieth century on their way to gold strikes farther down river and at Nome. This readiness is rather unique for Indian groups which experienced gold rush activities and can be credited to a number of factors. A prolonged period of indirect contact facilitated cultural integrity. The Upper Kuskokwim is geographically distant from the major western supply lines; therefore, Native services were vital to travelers. The Upper Kuskokwim Natives had flexibility to develop culturally appropriate and economically remunerative roles in activities of the gold rush--

activities such as running roadhouses, supplying fish and game, and serving as dog team mail carriers.

In 1908 the Iditarod Trail was surveyed and became a winter route of travel for prospectors headed for Southwest and Northwest Alaska. In 1923, with the completion of the Alaska Railroad, the Kantishna/Upper Kuskokwim trail also became an important winter travel route. These two trails crossed the Upper Kuskokwim and were traveled by many people headed for the distant gold mining areas.[33]

Strikes in Fairbanks in 1902 and Kantishna in 1905 also brought gold seekers who spilled over into the Upper Kuskokwim. To support the newcomers, roadhouses were built along the trails, and Upper Kuskokwim Natives were employed to work at these sites, and to provide food for the travelers and their dog teams. Some Natives were employed to carry the mail. In some cases the roadhouses were run and owned by Natives.[34]

The introduction of fishwheels by 1918 on the upper river signaled a major technological advance that permitted Upper Kuskokwim people to catch large quantities of salmon on the main river. Fish were also caught in traps in the streams and sold to the roadhouses to feed travelers and their dog teams.[35] The dramatic picture that emerges is of a small Native population which very quickly and effectively provided basic services on the trails and at the roadhouses. The services involved some skills that they had used all of their lives: hunting, fishing, and dog team driving. The introduction of fishwheels was advantageous and, along with the traditional fish traps, provided a ready source of fish near the main travel routes. The ownership of roadhouses and the entrepreneurial skills that this demanded are of considerable interest.

The Upper Kuskokwim presented unique problems of supply. In summer, river steamers could operate dependably as far up river as McGrath,[36] but the roadhouses farther upriver had to depend on shallow-draft boats, and, of course, winter supply over the trails. One suspects that for these roadhouses, local--meaning Native--supply was very important, more important than elsewhere where white traders could depend upon steamboats for supply. The geographical remoteness from outside supply necessitated a dependence on local resources, and therefore permitted a relatively high degree of local control, paralleling in some respects the situation Herron found himself in during his stay at Telida.

Unfortunately, the period of employment and entrepreneurship was short-lived, lasting only until the 1930s when the airplane signaled an end to dog team mail delivery. Many of the roadhouses and even the trails ceased to be important.[37] The employment opportunities decreased dramatically. By then, the hordes of prospectors were gone. Those who had found paying quantities of gold were established in a few locales, most outside the Upper Kuskokwim. The traffic had decreased, the wage labor opportunities were few, and people returned to much of the trapping life that they had practiced before, only now the area was less isolated and white trappers shared in the rich fur resources.

Reflecting on the historical events surrounding Herron and the gold seekers, we are left with the strong feeling that the Upper Kuskokwim Natives not only culturally survived but thrived during the early phases of direct contact. In at least one important respect, the situation is reminiscent of descriptions of the "Dawson Boys," the Peel River Kutchin from Canada, who participated in the Klondike Gold Rush of 1897-99.[38] In both cases, the Natives were able to contribute culturally-valued skills in demand by the prospectors--most notably by hunting and by guiding travelers. Some Peel River Natives left their homeland temporarily in order to participate in the gold rush, whereas the Upper Kuskokwim Natives experienced large numbers of people traveling through their country. But, in both cases, the important point that emerges is that the Native group was able to control the type and amount of interaction. For the Peel River people, there was the chance to decide if they wanted to go to Dawson or to the mining camps. And for the Upper Kuskokwim people, control came from their unique position along a major route which was isolated from the centers of western supply.

The Herron expedition demonstrates that the Upper Kuskokwim people were also well prepared to meet these opportunities. Years of indirect contact from many different directions provided opportunities for these people to gain a very sophisticated knowledge of white civilization and to incorporate this information into their own lives. When the prospectors came, the Indians relied upon their knowledge of traditional skills to fulfill the needs of the travelers, and they expressed a willingness to do so. Therefore a very special situation was created for the traveler and for the Natives. The willingness and interest of the Upper Kuskokwim people to capitalize on the opportunities which came with the trails is of particular interest, and it is suggested here that the Natives' ability to provide locally available services on their own terms created a favorable situation for cultural contact between the two groups.

Unlike many other parts of Alaska where direct contact in a home territory followed rather quickly after indirect contact and necessitated immediate change, the Upper Kuskokwim people maintained insulation for a long time, absorbing what they wanted and declining what they did not want. For many years they dealt with strangers on their own terms, and that may have influenced their willingness to exploit the opportunities that finally developed in their home territory. The people who entered their territory had destinations elsewhere. They sought gold outside that territory and did not provide direct competition for the employment opportunities. A contact situation was thus created which permitted the resident population ample opportunity to maintain its integrity and to benefit from their geographically remote location.

ENDNOTES

[1]Joseph S. Herron, *Explorations in Alaska, 1899, for an All American Overland Route from Cook Inlet, Pacific Ocean to the Yukon* (Washington, D. C.: Government Printing Office, 1909).

[2]The lower reaches of their homeland were visited by Russian traders and explorers but the middle and upper reaches remained insulated from prolonged contact with outsiders until Herron's expedition in 1899. Josiah E. Spurr, a United States Geological Survey geologist, conducted a reconnaissance of the Kuskokwim in 1898, descending the river after portaging to the headwaters from the Susitna. That party made no prolonged stops once they reached the Kuskokwim. However, Spurr's report provides some specific information on prospectors and traders who had traveled through the Upper Kuskokwim country. See Josiah Edward Spurr, "A Reconnaissance in Southwestern Alaska in 1898" in *Explorations in Alaska in 1898*, pt. 7 of *Twentieth Annual report of the United States Geological Survey to the Secretary of the Interior, 1898-99* (Washington, D. C.: Government Printing Office, 1900), 95. For further discussion of the territory, see Edward H. Hosley, "Kolchan" in *Handbook of North American Indians*, Vol. 6 *Subarctic*, William Sturtevant, general editor, June Helm, volume editor, (Washington, D. C.: Smithsonian Institution, 1981), 618-22; and Wendell H. Oswalt, *Historic Settlements along the Kuskokwim river, Alaska* Alaska State Historical Monograph No. 7 (Juneau: Alaska Division of State Libraries and Museums, 1980), 81.

The present paper defines the Upper Kuskokwim Natives' territory differently from Hosley's more expansive definition of the territory before 1900. The restrictive use of the term here is not meant to contradict Hosley but to focus the discussion on the middle and upper reaches of the Upper Kuskokwim Natives' traditional territory.

[3]For a more detailed discussion of P. H. Ray and his assignment in Alaska, see William Schneider, "P. H. Ray on the Alaskan Frontier in the Fall of 1897" (1985). Manuscript available from the author.

[4]See Ray's letters of September 15 and November 15, 1897 to the Adjutant General in *Compilation of Narratives of Explorations in Alaska* (Washington, D. C.: Government Printing Office, 1900), 525-28, 544-45. Further reference can be found in a telegram from Brigadier General Merriam to Adjutant General, (summarizing Ray's letters), 1 February 1898, Record Group 107, National Archives and Records Service.

[5]Spurr, 96.

[6]Herron, 7-8.

[7]Francis B. Heitman, *Historical Register and Dictionary of the United States Army from its Organization, September 29, 1789 to March 2, 1903* (Washington, D. C.: Government Printing Office, 1903), 526. (Republished by University of Illinois Press, 1965).

[8]Herron, 24-27.

[9]Alfred Hulse Brooks, *Blazing Alaska's Trails* (Caldwell, Id.: Caxton Printers, for the University of Alaska and the Arctic Institute of North America, 1953), 332.

[10]Charles P. Raymond, "Reconnaissance of the Yukon River," in *Compilation of Narratives of Explorations in Alaska*, 23. Discussion of the pioneer traders Harper, McQuesten and Mayo can be found in Brooks, 316-20.

[11]Herron, 20-21, 27.

[12]For many years the Tanaina Athabascans enjoyed an advantageous trading position with the Upper Kuskokwim Natives. But when the Upper Kuskokwim people discovered that the Tanaina were becoming rich off their trade, they became angry. This point is made in the oral account of Diqelas Tukda, a Tanaina who was forced to flee from a trading session when it was discovered that he was charging exorbitant prices for trade goods. The Upper Kuskokwim people said, "He took too much from us...let's throw him in the river." This story is found in Shem Pete, *Diqelas Tukda, the Story of a Tanaina Chief* (Fairbanks: Alaska Native Language Center, 1977), 25-26.

[13]Herron, 38-42.

[14]James Wickersham, *Old Yukon: Tales, Trails and Trials* (Washington, D: C.: Washington Law Book Co., 1938), 259.

[15]Leonard and Hazel Menke, personal communication, 1980 and 1983. The account of this story was collected at Lake Minchumina from the Menkes who had heard the story from Carl Sesui. It was told again for the author in 1983 with elaboration on the tracking process. Hazel Menke recalled that Carl Sesui said he was about twelve years old when the rescue was made.

[16]Charlene LeFebre, Field Notes, 7 July 1949, 3.

[17]Herron, 42.

[18]Captain P. H. Ray suggested the site of the Tanana Post, Fort Gibbon,

in a letter to the Adjutant General dated 15 September 1897 in *Compilation of Narratives of Explorations in Alaska*, 525. Subsequent letters also mention the desirability of this location, so the establishment of the post probably came as no surprise to Herron and his men.

[19]Robert J. Farnsworth, "An Army Brat Goes to Alaska: Conclusion--Building Fort Gibbon," *Alaska Journal* 7 (Autumn 1977): 216.

[20]Morgan B. Sherwood, *Exploration of Alaska, 1865-1900* (New Haven: Yale University Press, 1965), 167-68, 181-82; Jonathan Nielson, "Soldiers on A Northern Frontier: The Military in Alaska's History, 1867-1983," (Anchorage: Report to the Alaska Historical Commission, 1980), 89.

[21]Henry T. Allen, "Military Reconnaissance in Alaska," in *Compilation of Narratives of Explorations in Alaska*, 432-37; J. C. Castner, "A Story of Hardship and Suffering in Alaska," Ibid., 691-92.

[22]Oswalt, 47, 86.

[23]C. M. Brown, "Navigable and Non-navigable Waters in the Upper Kuskokwim River Basin," Bureau of Land Management, Anchorage, 6 May 1980, photocopy, 7.

[24]Personal communication from Nikolai elder Bobby Esai, 1980.

[25]Brooks, 175.

[26]Ibid., 233; see George R. Adams, *Life on the Yukon, 1865-67* (Kingston, Ontario: Limestone Press, 1982), 73.

[27]Charlene LeFebre's field notes indicate that Chief Sesui had been to Tanana before Herron arrived. LeFebre, Field Notes, 7 July 1949, 3.

[28]The exact location of the post is described in "Copy of a Military Historical Sketch of Fort Gibbon, Alaska," Box 1, Folder 1, Major General C. S. Farnsworth Papers, University of Alaska Archives, Fairbanks.

[29]Hudson Stuck, *The Alaskan Missions of the Episcopal Church* (New York: Domestic and Foreign Missionary Society, 1920), 41-44.

[30]Pete, 25, 27, 30.

[31]James Fall references the story of Diqelas Tukda and also indicates the break in trading relations which undoubtedly occurred after 1877. James Arthur Fall, "Patterns of Upper Inlet Tanaina Leadership, 1741-1918," (Ph.D. Dissertation, University of Wisconsin, 1981), 207-9.

[32]L. D. Kitchener, *Flag over the North* (Seattle: Superior Publishing Co., 1954), 176; Oswalt, 11, 86.

[33]Oswalt, 14-15. See also William Schneider, Dianne Gudgel-Holmes and John Dalle-Molle, "Land Use in the North Additions of Denali National Park and Preserve: An Historical Perspective," 24-26, 1985 Draft Report available at Denali National Park.

[34]Schneider, et. al., 26.

[35]Jeff Stokes, "Subsistence Salmon Fishing in the Upper Kuskokwim River System, 1981-82," Juneau, Department of Fish and Game, Division of Subsistence, 1982, 1-29.

For reference to the introduction of fishwheels on the Kuskokwim, see Hosley, 550-51. As noted, fish fences and traps were used on the clear water, up river tributaries until the mid-1960s. Stokes claims that most salmon were taken with this method up to that date. I suspect that this was a localized take; the introduction of fishwheels along the main rivers must have greatly facilitated fishing while the roadhouses were in operation and had a large demand for fish.

[36]Oswalt, 55.

[37]Brown, 89; and Schneider, et. al., 27.

[38]Richard Slobodin, "The Dawson Boys--Peel River Indians and the Klondike Gold Rush," *Polar Notes* 5 (June, 1963): 24-36.

I am very appreciative of the assistance of many people who read earlier drafts of this paper. Particularly I would like to thank Dianne Gudgel-Holmes, Joan Antonson, Lyman Woodman, Jon Nielson, Barbara Smith, Marvin Falk, Paul McCarthy, Doug Best, Jeff Stokes, Charlene LeFebre, and Morgan Sherwood.

NATIONAL POLITICS AND ALASKA*

Herman Slotnick

There are several points at which Alaska briefly enters the general history texts in American history. The Ballinger-Pinchot controversy is one of those. Like the purchase of Alaska in 1867, or the Klondike gold rush in 1898, or the discovery of oil at Prudhoe Bay in 1968, the dispute between President William Howard Taft's Secretary of the Interior and his Chief Forester attracted the attention of the nation and held it long enough for Alaska to become, for awhile at least, a household word. When Theodore Roosevelt decided to form a third party to run against Taft and Woodrow Wilson in 1912, he chose the bull moose as his party's mascot, partly because it reminded voters of Alaska and Taft's supposed anti-conservationist policies there.

In his article from the *Journal of the West* printed here, Herman Slotnick analyzes the role of the Ballinger-Pinchot controversy in Alaska. Professor Slotnick earned his doctorate at the University of Washington and, until his retirement a few years ago, represented the second generation of historians at the University of Alaska in Fairbanks, following the tenure of Professor Cecil Robe who had preceded him. Slotnick published a number of articles in the *Western Political Quarterly* analyzing Alaska elections in the 1960s and in 1979 joined with University of Alaska historian Claus-M. Naske in writing *Alaska: A History of the 49th State.* That successful text has been republished in 1987 by the University of Oklahoma Press.

In his study of the effect of the Ballinger-Pinchot controversy in Alaska Slotnick found that Alaskans felt themselves somewhat victimized. Few people understood the real issues as they affected Alaska, Slotnick found, and the publicity had much more to do with national politics than with Alaska.

Readers should remember that Gifford Pinchot and Richard Ballinger both had served in Roosevelt's administration, in different cabinet-level departments, Ballinger as head of the General Land Office in the Department of Interior, and Pinchot as head of the U. S. Forest Service in the Department of Agriculture. Roosevelt's Secretary of the Interior had been James Garfield, who was supportive of Roosevelt's conservation policies. Pinchot was a close personal friend of Roosevelt's, and both men had expected that when Taft became president, he would retain Garfield at Interior. When Taft instead appointed the development-minded

---

*This article originally appeared in *Journal of the West* 10, no. 2 (April 1971): 337-347.

Ballinger as Secretary of the Interior, Pinchot, Roosevelt, and conservationists around the country felt betrayed. The Ballinger-Pinchot controversy had its origins partly in that sense of betrayal. As Slotnick points out, the affair was to some degree a rehearsal for today's environmentalist-development debate.

* * *

With the discovery of huge oil deposits in the Arctic North Slope, Alaska once again has become the scene of a great battle between conservationists and developers. In 1910, the conflict was called the Ballinger-Pinchot Affair, taking its name from two members of President William Howard Taft's official family, Richard Ballinger, the Secretary of the Interior, and Gifford Pinchot, the chief forester of the United States, each of whom had differing views concerning the utilization of the nation's natural resources. Their controversy did much to embitter relations between President Taft and his predecessor, Theodore Roosevelt, causing a split in the Republican party which helped elect Woodrow Wilson as Taft's successor in the White House. Testimony given by witnesses before a joint congressional committee which had been formed to investigate the dispute filled thousands of pages. Numerous books, magazine articles and newspaper stories have added to the accounts of the fray.

In 1940, Harold Ickes, then Secretary of the Interior, in Franklin D. Roosevelt's administration, re-opened the case when he wrote in a series of articles published in the *Saturday Evening Post* that Ballinger had been a much maligned man, which Pinchot promptly denied. Those who have written or been concerned about the Ballinger-Pinchot Affair have stressed its significance, quite properly, as a national issue important in the party politics of the period and in the struggle to establish a sound conservation policy for the United States. Little has been said of how the controversy was viewed in Alaska, although one of the leading issues involved the disposition of Alaska's coal lands, almost all of which was in the public domain.

At the time of the affair, less than one percent of the land in Alaska had come into private ownership. Congress, which was in effect the legislative body for Alaska--Alaska did not have a territorial legislature--had made a half-hearted effort to find a solution for the utilization of Alaska's natural resources. In 1900, the coal mining laws of the United States had been extended to Alaska, but no provisions had been made to survey the public lands. Four years later, an amendment to the act allowed private persons to make surveys, but at their own expense. Operators of coal mines complained that Congress, by limiting the size of the tracts to 160 acres, had virtually made coal mining uneconomical in Alaska. It was generally admitted that the situation encouraged fraud. Coal operators tended to combine their holdings contrary to law, in order to make mining profitable.

President Roosevelt, himself a leading conservationist, regarded the law as unworkable, and issued an executive order in 1906 withdrawing all lands thought to contain coal from public entry. He called upon the Congress to enact new legislation designed to benefit the coal men by removing these arbitrary restrictions as well as protecting the interests of the American people by preventing any individual or group from securing a monopoly. But Congress failed to act immediately, and it was not until 1915 that a law was passed making the mining of coal in Alaska once again legal.

Among those who had attempted to obtain coal lands in Alaska prior to the Roosevelt withdrawals were thirty-two persons who had given Clarence Cunningham the power-of-attorney to make selections for them. Acting on their behalf Cunningham had taken an option on 5,280 acres of land in the Bering River area, which subsequently was to be incorporated into the newly established Chugach National Forest by Roosevelt in 1908. His efforts to obtain patents for the land had been fraught with repeated delays. Rumors had begun to circulate almost immediately after Cunningham had filed the necessary forms that he and the group he represented had never intended to mine coal themselves as the law required, but that they had formed their association precisely for the purpose of transferring their claims to the Alaska Syndicate, a consortium of the Guggenheim Brothers and J. P. Morgan & Company, which had extensive business interests in Alaska. Several agents of the Department of the Interior were subsequently sent to Alaska to investigate the substance of the charge.

Among them was Louis Glavis, who became convinced, as a result of his investigations, that Richard Ballinger, the man named by President Taft as Secretary of the Interior in 1909, was preparing to validate the transfer of Cunningham claims to the syndicate. Glavis consulted Pinchot who advised him to submit his findings to the President, which he did. Taft, after reading Glavis' report, ordered Ballinger to dismiss him "for filing a disingenuous statement unjustly impeaching the integrity of his superior officers."

Glavis, following his retirement from government service, wrote and sent to *Collier's*, a leading magazine, his version of the controversy, which was published in the November 13, 1909, issue, and immediately created a furor. Glavis professed that he was not making charges against anyone, but the editors, without consulting him, chose as the title of the article, "The Whitewashing of Ballinger," while the cover of the magazine posed the question, "Are the Guggenheims in charge of the Department of the Interior?" with the question mark, printed in red, encircling a picture of Ballinger.[1]

A joint congressional committee was then formed to investigate the Department of the Interior as well as the Forest Service, pernicious activities of certain officers Ballinger complained, "had inspired the charges against his department."[2] Pinchot himself was subsequently fired on charges of insubordination for having written a letter to Senator Dolliver, which was read on the floor of the Senate. It was highly critical of Taft's handling of the affair and of his support of Ballinger.

Richard Ballinger was a Seattle attorney whose connection with Cunningham was of long standing, ante-dating his appointment as Secretary of the Interior in 1909. He had been the commissioner of the General Land Office in the Roosevelt administration when Cunningham had first applied for patents on behalf of his clients. Ballinger resigned in 1908. As a private attorney he had advised the Cunningham group on the procedures to be followed in processing their claims. As Secretary of the Interior he succeeded James Garfield, a leading conservationist and friend of Gifford Pinchot. Ballinger, while not the foe of conservation, as his enemies claimed, could hardly be called an enthusiast. He did believe that conservation as practiced by Pinchot and Garfield obstructed the "logical development of the country," and that some of the land withdrawals made during the Roosevelt administration for conservation purposes were of questionable legality.[3]

Pinchot, Ballinger's opponent, had been called the first professional forester in the United States. He had been trained abroad, and under his direction, the Bureau of Forestry became a highly professional agency. Pinchot had been particularly close to Theodore Roosevelt, but much less influential with Taft, a constitutional lawyer, who, like Ballinger, regarded Roosevelt's actions in setting aside laws of Congress as being of doubtful validity at best. Pinchot professed the view that the government had a responsibility to administer the resources of the country for the benefit of the people of the United States and had made many enemies by attacking the "vested interests" who were spoiling the nation's heritage.

Voting on almost strictly party lines the majority, composed of stalwart Republicans exonerated Ballinger of any wrong-doing, while the Democrats and one progressive Republican found him guilty of violating his trust. Ballinger resigned in the summer of 1911 and was succeeded as Secretary of the Interior by Walter Fisher, the vice-president of the National Conservation Association, an organization headed by Gifford Pinchot.

Inside Alaska the Ballinger-Pinchot Affair attracted much attention and excited a great deal of comment although the newspaper accounts were quite spotty. Alaskans seemed to be not so much interested in the merits of the controversy as in the issues and personalities relating to the affair. Ballinger, Pinchot, Cunningham, the Guggenheims all came in for their share of attention. Alaskans delighted in the publicity given to the territory by the affair and hoped that the problems of Alaska might soon receive a hearing in the Congress.

Alaskans were prone to sympathize with Clarence Cunningham, whose long struggle to obtain title to the coal lands for himself and the group he represented symbolized the wrongs done to Alaska by an absentee government. He was pictured as the prototype of all prospectors, a man who had endured incredible hardships in locating his claims. He and his associates were honest men who had attempted mainly to comply with laws patently absurd; their violations were mere technicalities, not the wrong-doing of deliberate lawbreakers. Encouraged, it was alleged, by laws passed by Congress for the "apparent purpose of inducing citizens to locate claims and develop them," they had spent thousands of dollars only to see their work completely destroyed when President Roosevelt, in violation of their constitutional rights, abrogated the laws and withdrew located lands and other land. Thus under "the American flag" wrote the editorial writer in the *Fairbanks Times* there are these "people who have worked, sweated, starved and spent their last cent in trying to develop the coal lands of Alaska," and then have everything swept away by one stroke of "as tyrannical a pen as any despot ever wielded."[4] Alaska's non-voting delegate to the Congress, Thomas Cale, gave official support to the Cunningham claims when he introduced a bill into the House of Representatives in 1908 backed by the then commissioner of the General Land Office, Richard Ballinger, to confer title to the lands they sought to acquire.

Ballinger was very popular in Alaska. His continuous support of the Cunningham claims was attributed to a selfless interest in the welfare of Alaska, and a realization that the government should help rather than hinder those who wanted to mine coal in the territory. As a Westerner his admirers asserted he was more cognizant of Alaska's needs than the Easterner Pinchot, and was very much aware that prosperity depended upon having cheap fuel.

Ballinger was frequently portrayed as a most honorable and wronged man, the victim of a conspiracy fostered by an ambitious subordinate, Glavis, who had sought to advance his own interest at the expense of his superior. Glavis, in turn, had been aided and abetted in his "sinister deeds" by Pinchot, who regarded the head of the Department of the Interior as the "chief obstacle" to the various theories he sought "to foist upon Alaska." Both men were accused of having offered "inferences and apprehensions instead of facts" in their attacks upon Ballinger.

The Secretary was praised as a man who had conducted his office "as the law directed" and not as he thought "it should have been" in marked contrast to his predecessor, Garfield, who had "set himself above the law" by withdrawing lands contrary to the intent of Congress.[5]

Major Strong, a newspaper editor, of Katalla, whom Woodrow Wilson appointed governor of Alaska in 1913, expressed his dismay with the "results of the alleged investigations of the coal situation by agents of the Department of the Interior" and found it deplorable that Glavis "should attempt to make Judge Ballinger a crook in the eyes of the people." Glavis evidently was "more eager to discover a mare's nest than to give a square deal to the men who have honestly complied with entry laws in taking up Alaska's coal land."[6] An editorial in the *Seward Gateway* warned that any "efforts to unearth something against Ballinger was futile, for among those who knew him he was respected" as a man among men.[7]

Gifford Pinchot, Ballinger's great antagonist, suffered by contrast. He was accused of having done more than any man to hinder the development of Alaska. When asked what was wrong with

Alaska, many Alaskans simply replied, "Pinchot." He was derided with such epithets as a "woolly headed theorist," an "impractical visionary," a "degenerate," the "lord high executioner of Alaska," and was accused of being consumed with a desire to "lock up the resources of Alaska for posterity."[8]

Within Alaska the term "Pinchotism" came to be synonymous, as it was in other parts of the United States, with an extreme form of conservation. The more charitable of Pinchot's critics were willing to concede that he was a man of upright character and an able administrator, but that his usefulness had been seriously impaired by the lack of a restraining hand to guide his many ill-conceived activities. He and Roosevelt were chided for their ignorance of Alaskan conditions, and were said to be interested in Alaska only as a testing ground for their experiments.

Falcon Joslin, the president of the Tanana Valley Railroad, even denied that he was a good forester, while a consulting engineer from Valdez found that people "throughout the West think more highly of Ballinger than of the great forest preserver, Pinchot, who somehow has failed, to date, to show even the smallest area of our national forests scientifically and practically cultivated, planted or improved in the way that French or German forests are maintained as a source of revenue...all his vociferous magazine articles not withstanding."[9] Pinchot was characterized as being power-mad and obsessed with the over-riding ambition to be President of the United States, and there were a few who suggested that he had deliberately planned the destruction of Alaska's coal industry in order to preserve the Pacific coal market for the Pocahontos Coal Company of Pennsylvania, which was erroneously attributed as belonging to his family.[10]

More than anyone else Gifford Pinchot was blamed for the federal government's policies, which the critics claimed were hampering the development of the territory. He was depicted as the evil genius behind Roosevelt, the real author of the executive order that had brought coal mining to a halt in Alaska and effectively ended railroad construction in the territory, for no investor would continue to put money into an industry such as railroads, which were so dependent upon cheap fuel. All of this, apparently part of a great design, for Pinchot and his cohorts did not rest content with tieing up and withdrawing from entry one of the chief resources of the territory--namely the coal lands--but had then thrown "a vast domain...into the Chugach Forest Reserve." Here in the Chugach, the *Valdez*

Prospector complained, "the indefatigable Pinchot discovered trees where everybody knew there were no trees, discovered water power in every hollow where there was heavy dew and the colonel (Roosevelt) reserved and reserved until they had nearly everything bottled up."[11]

The Seward Commercial Club ridiculed the establishment of a reserve in an area of 8,000 square miles where, it was alleged "less than 800 are covered with a scattering growth of hemlock, spruce and cottonwood timber, the few trees are mature and super mature, and the timber is strictly for local use; not a foot of it has been, or ever will be, shipped out of Alaska." In the opinion of the Club members, the "only business in the Forest Reserve Alaskans are interested in is mining and its subsidiary industries," and they duly protested that "the hardships the Forest Service works on miners and prospectors" is a "notorious scandal."[12]

Demonstrations in a number of Alaskan towns directed against Pinchot were staged as a means of protesting federal policies in Alaska which he presumably had instigated. At Cordova, the port used by the Alaska Syndicate to supply their copper mines in the interior, "a coal party," patterned after the famous Boston Tea party of 1773, was staged on May 3, 1911, a few months after the joint congressional committee concluded its hearing in the Ballinger-Pinchot Affair. Some three hundred residents of the town raided the docks where coal imported from Canada by the Copper River and Northwestern Railroad was stored, threw the coal into Controller Bay, and burned Pinchot in effigy. Signs were displayed at the wharves in Cordova, Valdez and Seward stating, "Let us mine our own coal." At Katalla, the village closest to the Cunningham claims, Pinchot again was burned in effigy, and fire was set to a copy of Roosevelt's proclamation withdrawing the coal lands from entry. Placards posted at several places along the streets bawled out:

> Pinchot: my policy: No patents to coal; All timber to forest reserves; Bottle up Alaska; Put Alaska in forest reserves; Save Alaska for all time to come.[13]

Pinchot himself visited Alaska a few months after the coal dumping incident. He had come, he said, to view the problems of Alaska at first hand. He met with a mixed reception even judging from his own testimony. He wrote from Seward that "Never in my life have I had more courteous treatment than since reaching Alaska," but also admitted that it had been necessary for Jack Dalton to "come down to the dock with two guns on to prevent certain citizens of Cordova from carrying out their doubtless laudable purpose of keeping me from landing from the steamer."[14]

Opposition against him was lead by the *Cordova Daily Alaskan*, described as the organ of the Guggenheims, which referred to him as "a deposed and discredited government official whose day of usefulness and obstruction had ended." Alaskans were counselled to treat him as they would any "tramp tourist." When Pinchot cancelled a trip to Katalla, because of bad weather, he was mocked as an "effete Easterner," fearful of a little snow and rain. According to the *Daily Alaskan*, the Cordova Chamber of Commerce, which had a "reputation" for graciously receiving visitors, deliberately snubbed Pinchot and refused to send a delegation to greet him upon his arrival. Arrangements were made, however, by a committee of Cordovan citizens to hire a hall so that they might hear him speak.[15]

Pinchot attempted to answer his Alaskan critics. He reminded them time and time again that it was "land frauds rather that conservation" that was responsible for the "bottling up of Alaska's resources," and that his activity in the Ballinger-Pinchot Affair was simply "an effort to prevent the men who were trying to plunder and monopolize Alaska from carrying out their plan." He insisted that he had been trying since 1906 to get Congress to pass laws opening up Alaska that would be "fair to the people and not favorable to monopoly."[16]

His protests were of little avail. To many he was the symbol of the conservation movement and it was as a conservationist that he was mostly condemned. To many of the "developers" it was really Pinchot and the conservation movement that were really on trial at the hearings of the joint congressional committee. Conservation was condemned as the fad of the moment, comparable to the "Yellow Peril," "free silver" and "vegetarianism"--a utopian scheme inapplicable to Alaskan conditions. Conservationists were thus opposed to progress, they were "not of the energetic class that do things," and "if all were conservationists, the process of evolution from the ape age would have been slow indeed" for "some of us would still be hanging by our prehensile tails in an ambitious endeavor to gather a few coconuts." It was alleged also that conservationists were engaged in a subtle plot to bring all the territory's resources under governmental ownership.[17]

Major Strong, a very vocal critic of Pinchot and Glavis during the affair, conceded that conservation served a useful function, but stressed the differences between those conservationists who were seeking to prevent waste and the radicals "who wanted to lock up" Alaskan resources. He and other "moderates" were in agreement that conservation had been most beneficial in checking rapicious exploitation and potential monopolies in the more highly settled areas of the United States, but that conservation in Alaska, where the resources had hardly been touched, was both harmful and wrong.

Alaskan development had already suffered much from the activities of the conservationists. Her citizens had been forbidden by law to mine coal, and forced to import coal at ruinous prices or else burn wood as a fuel. Unless conservation policies were altered Alaskan interests would continue to be sacrificed to those of the United States, her resources kept in a "deep freeze" until those of other parts of the country had been exhausted. Conservationists were chided that their policies toward Alaska were based on error: the resources of Alaska were not the property of the people of the United States to hold in perpetuity, but belonged to those who were willing to invest their capital and labor in making them usable.[18]

Among the developers, charges of wrong doing by the Guggenheims and their associates, which had formed so prominent a part in the Ballinger-Pinchot proceedings were treated with disdain. Falcon Joslin declared that Pinchot had invented the "Guggenheim dragon" that was "about to gobble up Alaska" so that he could pose as "the heroic defender of the rights of the whole people."[19] A number of newspapers censured the conservationists for causing distrust of the Guggenheims and impugning their motives.[20] Fred Heilig of the *Times* wrote that the "Guggenheims' bugaboo" had been overworked, and that there was "a need in Alaska for one thousand such monopolies" to help bring about the development of the territory.[21] The *Dispatch* charged that "Pinchot and his followers got the nation so wrought up over efforts of certain interests to possess the riches of Alaska that Congress evidently feared to act lest it violate the doctrines sacred to radical conservationists."[22]

The *Seward Gateway* noted that "while some condemn the syndicate as an octopus the fact remains that it is spending millions of dollars in Alaska's development."[23] In similar tones, the *Cordova Daily Alaskan* was certain that an "examination of the facts" would "demonstrate the falsity of the charges that the Guggenheims are trying to gobble up the whole of Alaska," and asked that if it were not true instead that the people of Alaska owed the Guggenheims a "debt of gratitude for opening up and making possible permanent growth, development and population" of the territory. Supporters of the Guggenheims frequently cited the testimony of Alfred Brooks, the noted geologist, to refute the arguments of conservationists that the syndicate planned to establish a monopoly in Alaska. Brooks, without mentioning the Guggenheims by name, had stated his opinion at the Ballinger-Pinchot hearings that the coal deposits of Alaska were virtually inexhaustable, and that it was practically impossible for any Corporation to secure a monopoly of mining rights.[24]

Whatever support there was for Pinchot and the conservationists came from the anti-Guggenheim forces. James Wickersham, the Alaskan delegate to Congress, who had run on an anti-Guggenheim platform, telegraphed Ballinger early in the controversy that he had the support of all Alaska. Later Wickersham denounced Ballinger as the tool of the Guggenheims and praised Pinchot and Glavis whose "bold actions" had prevented the syndicate from taking over even more of Alaska than it already owned. Wickersham said that he was most anxious to have the Coal mines of Alaska opened up, but that he was not willing to turn the territory over to one giant corporation just to have it developed.[25]

The *Cordova North Star* wrote that it was with the Guggenheims in their "efforts to build railroads, open coal mines and develop the resources of the country to the extent that this would benefit the whole people," but was unalterably opposed to their domination of Alaska.[26] The *Nome Nugget* denounced the Guggenheims as the "real bogey men of Alaska" who were "playing a close careful game" with the "stakes all of Alaska's deposits" and warned that unless something was done to "place an estoppage on their plans and schemes...Uncle Sam will realize that he is the vast owner of the territory in name only."[27]

In an editorial urging the defeat of the Beverage Bill, a measure providing for the establishment of a commission appointed by the President to govern Alaska, the *Skagway Daily Alaskan* lauded Glavis and Pinchot for having saved the Alaska coal lands from coming under the control of the syndicate. Residents of the territory were advised to seek home rule as the means of making the syndicate pay its fair share of taxes and preventing any special interest group from gaining possession of Alaska's resources.

The affair affected Alaskan politics only slightly. A half-hearted attempt was made by the Democrats to exploit the Ballinger-Pinchot dispute. Republicans were blamed, because a Republican administration had passed the mining laws, which were so inadequate; a Republican President had withdrawn the coal lands from entry, and the same administration had established the forest reserves, which had limited the activities of the miners even more. Ballinger, Pinchot, Taft, and Roosevelt, it was pointed out, were all Republicans, and only Ballinger was deemed to be a friend of Alaska. Wickersham, the Republican Alaskan delegate to Congress, was attacked in the campaign of 1912 for his hostility to the Guggenheims and his alleged opposition to the development of the territory.

While most Americans had thought of the Ballinger-Pinchot Affair as being primarily political, to Alaskans it had been something quite different. There were few in the territory who really cared as to how the affair had affected the fortunes of the major political parties or a few individuals. Alaskans had been interested because the setting of the affair had been in Alaska.

Ballinger and Pinchot merely symbolized two radically opposed approaches to the future of Alaska. Ballinger had received the support of the articulate newspaper owners and business men because he presumably stood for the economic development of the territory while Pinchot and the conservationists--who never really got a hearing as to their point of view--were accused of having tied up the resources of Alaska, of having brought coal mining to a standstill, and hence being responsible for Alaska's economic woes. In the minds of the developers there had to be some reason why Alaska was not growing. And the simplest explanation seemed to be that a sinister coalition of muckrakers and conservationists had been successful in leading a far away and absentee government to pursue policies that were holding Alaska down.

ENDNOTES

[1]M. Nelson McGreary, *Gifford Pinchot, Forester-Politician*, (Princeton, 1960), pp. 145-6. I am indebted to Professor McGreary for his excellent account of the background of the Affair.

[2]Ibid, pp. 151-2.

[3]Ibid, pp. 118-24, *passim.*

[4]Quote from *Fairbanks Daily Times*, July 6, 1910, p. 4. See also

editorial from *Valdez Prospector* reprinted in Cordova *Daily Alaskan*, March 15, 1910, p. 2; *Seward Gateway*, April 23, 1910, p. 3, S. C. Eby, "The Cunningham Story and Ethics of Coal Situation in Alaska", *Alaska-Yukon Magazine*, (May, 1910), 388-396, *passim*.

[5]*Fairbanks Daily Times*, May 31, 1911, p. 2. Testimonials favorable to Ballinger from a number of leading Alaskans and others appear in an article, "R. A. Ballinger," *Alaska-Yukon Magazine* (May, 1910), 371-3.

[6]*Seward Gateway*, February 18, 1911, p. 2.

[7]Ibid, April 23, 1910, p. 3.

[8]See *Cordova Alaskan*, issues of February 26, 1910, September 18, 1911, p. 1, September 11, 1911, p. 1. Falcon Joslin, "The Conservation Policy in Alaska", *Alaska Yukon Magazine*, Vol. IX, 347-8, F. J. Dyer, "Gifford Pinchot," Ibid, pp. 368-71.

[9]See Joslin, "The Conservation Policy in Alaska", pp. 347-8 and letter from Consulting Engineer of Valdez to *McClure's Magazine*, "Too Much Cry of Wolf Retards Alaska Development," published in *Alaska-Yukon Magazine*, (February 1910), 174-77.

[10]*Cordova Alaskan*, February 3, 1910, p. 2.

[11]Quote from *Valdez Prospector* editorial printed in *Fairbanks Daily Times*, June 12, 1910, p. 2. See also Dyer, "Gifford Pinchot," pp. 368-71.

[12]*Seward Gateway*, March 19, 1910, p. 4.

[13]Jeannette P. Nichols, *Alaska: A History of its Administration, Exploration and Industrial Development During Its First Half Century Under the Rule of the United States*, (Cleveland, 1924), pp. 369-70 and footnote, p. 370.

[14]McGreary, pp 208-9.

[15]Compare *Cordova Daily Alaskan*, September 15, 1911, p. 2 with (Juneau) *Daily Alaskan Dispatch*, October 6, 1911, p. 1.

[16]McGreary, p. 208.

[17]Quoted from *Seward Gateway*, April 16, 1910, p. 2; see also (Skagway) *Daily Alaskan*, March 17, 1911, p. 2.

[18]The May, 1910, issue of the *Alaskan-Yukon Magazine*, Volume IX, centers about the theme of conservation and contains a number of articles by prominent Alaskans. See J. F. A. Strong, "The Development of Alaska," pp. 350-53, Falcon Joslin, "The Conservation Policy in Alaska," pp. 341-50, S. C. Eby, "Home Rule in Conservation," pp. 354-7; Frederick Heilig, "Most Urgent Needs of Alaska," Lafe Spray, "Some of the Urgent Needs of Alaska," pp. 405-7, J. J. Finnegan, "Alaska's Greatest Needs," pp. 407-10, D. H. Sleem "The Urgent Needs of Alaska Today," pp. 410-14. Gifford Pinchot visited Alaska in September, 1911. Almost all of the issues of the newspaper *Cordova Daily Alaskan* for that month contain editorials highly critical of the conservationists.

[19]See Joslin, "The Conservation Policy in Alaska," p. 347.

[20]Quoted in (Juneau) *Alaska Daily Dispatch*, February 18, 1911, p. 3.

[21](Juneau) *Daily Alaskan Dispatch*, June 11, 1910, p. 2.

[22]*Seward Gateway*, March 31, 1910, p. 2.

[23]*Cordova Daily Alaskan*, September 18, 1910, p. 1.

[24]See testimony of Alfred Brooks in Senate Document 719, 61st Congress, 3rd Session, *Investigation of the Department of the Interior and the Bureau of Forestries*, Vol. IV, pp. 2887-2895. See also editorial from *Valdez Prospector* in *Cordova Daily Alaskan*, May 17, 1910, p. 2.

[25]See introduction to Nichols' *Alaska* by James Wickersham, pp 28-9. *Seward Gateway*, March 25, 1911, pp. 1, 2, *Juneau Daily Record*, February 21, 1910, p. 1, *Fairbanks Times*, June 30, 1910, p. 1; McGreary, p. 208.

[26]Editorial from *Cordova North Star* reprinted in (Juneau) *Daily Dispatch*, March 26, 1910, p. 2.

[27]Editorial from *Nome Gold Digger* reprinted in *Dispatch*, January 28, 1910, p. 2.

THE URBAN FRONTIER IN THE NORTH*

William H. Wilson

William H. Wilson is an historian of the Alaska Railroad. His *Railroad in the Clouds: The Alaska Railroad in the Age of Steam, 1914-1945* (Boulder, CO: Pruett Publishing Co., 1977) tells the story of the founding of the railroad and its role in Alaska's development in the 1920s and 1930s.

Having taught at the University of Alaska in Fairbanks for a number of years, Professor Wilson now teaches at North Texas State University. He has published a number of important articles in Alaska history, including "Ahead of the Times: The Alaska Railroad and Tourism, 1924-1941" in *Alaska Journal*, Spring 1977, and "Alaska's Past, Alaska's Future," in *Alaska Review*, 1970. In the latter, he forcefully presented the thesis which unites all his work on Alaska: that Alaska's history is much more similar to that of other western states than it is different, and that most historians, "traditionalists," as he calls them, have erred in seeing Alaska as unique. Most particularly, Wilson argues that the federal government should be viewed historically as a helpmate to Alaska's development rather than as an impediment. He also argues that while absentee-owned industries, such as the salmon canneries, dominated the Alaska economy, they may not have been as ruthless in their exploitation of Alaska's resources as commonly held in popular histories.

The article printed here deals with the first part of Wilson's useful critique of Alaska historiography, the role of the federal government. He points out that Alaska's major city, Anchorage, came into existence essentially as a government project. The federal Alaska Engineering Commission, which built the Alaska Railroad, planned the city, provided its basic necessities, including light, water and sewer, and drew up its first enabling rules and regulations. Moreover, it provided the city's economic base: railroad construction, and in later years railroad operations, and a subsidiary, coal production. The federal commission running the city was planned to expire after five years, Wilson writes, but Anchorageites had become so used to their federal support that many were reluctant to take on the responsibilities of self-government, a view of Alaskan self-reliance markedly different from that suggested in many histories of Alaska.

---

*This article originally appeared in *Pacific Northwest Quarterly* 58, no. 3 (July 1967): 130-141.

* * *

In a low basin flanked by prominent tablelands at the mouth of Ship Creek, Alaska, a homesteader with an insubstantial claim had planted a garden patch among fire-killed spruce and scrubby birch. A few other settlers had established themselves farther up the creek. But at best Ship Creek had been used only as an occasional lighterage and transfer point on Knik Arm of Cook Inlet, when President Wilson announced on April 10, 1915, that it was to be a major construction base for the government railroad in Alaska.

The announcement set off a rush to the creek flats reminiscent of the earlier mining stampedes. By June about 2,000 adventurers were on the ground, living in a collection of ragged, unsanitary tents and temporary wooden buildings, north across the creek from present downtown Anchorage. Each week at least a hundred more boomers debarked from steamers or hiked in from the end of steel on the Alaska Northern Railway, a physically and financially shaky line which the federal government had purchased to form the first 70 miles of the railroad out of Seward.[1]

In one important respect this boom was unlike the others, for the Interior Department intended to control the area in and around the railyards to make certain that no private interest would impede the project and that the town itself would develop in an orderly way, free from the usual "hell on wheels" construction-camp atmosphere. Thus began a unique experiment in federal operation of a frontier municipality 3,500 miles from the seat of national government. The experiment lasted for more than five years and embraced every aspect of local affairs. It was a commentary on the realism of the government's hopes for the townsite, on the behavior of pioneers whose activities were under close federal control, and on the attitudes and actions of federal officials who, although untrained in municipal government, were armed with broad powers and were required to balance local demands with political and economic necessities as Washington saw them.[2]

Frederick Mears, a member of the Alaskan Engineering Commission, directed operations at Ship Creek. He urged the General Land Office to act quickly in surveying the high, thickly timbered tableland south of the camp so that the sale of lots in the permanent settlement could begin. Mears was an experienced construction engineer and army officer who fretted, in lengthy and anguished letters to his superiors, over delays in railroad work. Efficiency was not his only concern however; the health of the settlers was at stake. In May the Commission surgeon warned that the water supply would probably become contaminated if the settlement on the flats continued much longer. Settlers in the temporary location freely criticized the government's delay. The Department of the Interior must cut red tape, Mears wrote, and allow the local authorities to proceed in this project which was so "important from a sanitary and construction standpoint as well as from a political standpoint." Mears also asked for regulations which would prohibit liquor traffic in the new townsite. His recommendations were seconded by Andrew Christensen, the Land Office chief of field division in charge of the surveys.[3]

As early as November, 1914, after the government had withdrawn several parcels of land as potential townsites, Christensen had pleaded with the Land Office to develop an administrative policy for the proposed new towns. But his superiors took no action until the local residents demanded to know why the Ship Creek site was not ready. Instructions from Washington finally reached the Land Office in Juneau on May 6. Christensen arrived at Anchorage with a survey party eighteen days later--good time considering the preparations required and the transportation problems involved. Because there were no direct cable communications between Anchorage and Washington, officials in both areas had agreed to forego time-consuming formalities. The survey of the 350-acre site was quickly completed, approval received, and a date fixed--July 10--for the lot auction. Mears and Christensen worked closely together, made on-the-spot decisions, and kept their superiors informed.

To control lot sales and establish a basis for future government, President Wilson, on June 19, issued the "Alaska Railroad Townsite Regulations." These detailed rules provided for the conditional sale of lots at public auction to be conducted by a superintendent of sales who was to appraise all lots and have full charge of the proceedings. No lot could be sold for less than $25. The purchaser was to pay in full or one-third down and the balance in five equal installments, depending upon the sale price. One clause reflected hopes for high standards of sobriety and behavior by rough construction crews. It required that the lots and the payments made for them would be forfeited if the property were "used for the purpose of manufacturing, selling, or otherwise disposing of intoxicating liquors as a beverage, or for gambling, prostitution, or any unlawful purpose..." If the purchaser paid his bid price and the assessments for improvements, and if he prohibited improper conduct on his lot, he was to receive patent to the land at the end of five years.[4]

Before the auction began, Christensen, who was also the superintendent of sales, spoke from a platform erected at the Ship Creek campsite. He promised permanent improvements and heavy expenditures at Anchorage. His expansive speech, as well as the high spirit of the occasion, spurred the stampeders into active competition for business and residential lots. Bidding became so brisk that some prospective owners who had conspired to hold down prices "lost their heads," Christensen reported, and when he closed the sale on July 18, he had sold 655 lots at just under $150,000. Despite earlier fears that the auction system would invite speculators and squeeze out legitimate interests, Christensen could claim that the sale had "injected confidence into the people of the town." The Land Office, and later the Commission, continued to open new additions, sell lots and tracts, and lease business sites in the terminal area. After two successful sales during November, when the short days were cold and heavy snows covered the frozen ground, Christensen exulted, "I could sell lots every day if I were in Anchorage; it seems that the demand for them never ceases."[5]

An uncompromising removal order issued to residents of the Ship Creek flats helped the confident little town to spread over the rigid rectangular pattern of the Land Office survey. But neither the survey nor the sale escaped criticism. A student of city planning described the uniform block townsite as "this T-square community of Anchorage," and, after comparing a 5-acre recreational reserve and a 17-acre cemetery tract, he concluded that "Anchorage has been figured to be a place to die in, but not much of a place to live in..." In truth, Commission officials had little knowledge of town planning. They did grade one winding drive overlooking Cook Inlet, but only because topographical conditions dictated it. They named east-west streets numerically and north-south streets alphabetically. According to Clay Tallman, Land Office commissioner, the only excuse for such a lack of imagination was that the town had been urgently needed and was hurriedly laid out by engineers whose primary purpose was to build a railroad.[6]

In a sense, government had begun before the auction--when Mears landed at Ship Creek and opened a post office. Acting together, Mears and Commission Chairman William C. Edes had appointed a physician to be sanitary officer, and they had selected J. A. Moore, a special agent of the Land Office, to be temporary townsite manager. The new appointees quickly drew up and issued sanitation and fire control regulations. Some essentials of an orderly, healthy community were thus provided for, but policies regarding other necessary services--lighting, telephone, sewer, water systems--were yet to be decided. Neither Edes nor Mears wished to become deeply involved in running the town. Civic government was outside their experience, and the energy they invested in administering Anchorage would be lost to railroad construction. Having assumed responsibility for sanitation and fire protection, however, they found it difficult to avoid operating a complete utilities system.

The problem was not one the Commission could decide at its leisure, for the new town was rapidly taking shape, and people were clamoring for the right to install telephones and electric lights. The Chamber of Commerce, on the other hand, had resolved that lighting and telephone systems be "conducted by the government and not by private corporations..." Although Edes declared that he was neither "advocating Government ownership" nor "hunting for additional responsibility," he wrote to the Secretary of the Interior, Franklin K. Lane, that providing water was an inescapable part of assuming control of fire protection and sanitation, and that lighting and telephone systems should also be constructed and operated by the Commission. If private parties owned and managed the lights and telephones, he maintained, they would insist on rates high enough to return substantial profits. Under private ownership, the Commission would license and supervise the companies and thus be closely identified with them. The public then would blame the Commission if they failed. Anchorage, Edes concluded, "is our child and we are responsible for its well being until it can care for itself."

On September 1, Lane authorized the installation of a water system, and the Commission began pumping water from a sand filter bed in Ship Creek to the townsite above. Electric light and power were extended in 1916, though gingerly. By 1917 the Commission had so many customers that there was fear of overloading the plant. Accordingly, new users were added only after the utilities superintendent called upon some of the commercial customers and persuaded them to reduce their wattage.[7]

The telephone problem was more difficult to solve. In May a stampeder shipped in telephone equipment which he had bought on credit. He was confident that he could install it because he possessed the qualifications which were most essential in an Alaska camp--he was first on the ground with the necessary supplies. Much to his dismay and to the displeasure of his suppliers and creditors, the Commission refused to grant him permission to string his wire and insisted on referring the matter to Washington. On October 4, Lane authorized the Commission to install telephones, and Mears relieved an embarrassing situation by purchasing all the equipment belonging to the would-be entrepreneur.[8]

In 1917 a sewer system, replacing inadequate cesspools, was installed to serve the business district. When the initial street work was completed, improvements proceeded at the request of residents after the townsite office had determined that the affected lot owners could afford to pay the assessments.[9]

These actions met the immediate needs, but the Commission's commitment to govern for five years demanded comprehensive townsite control. Every alternative to systematic federal administration was confronted by the facts that the town could not incorporate, govern itself, or tax itself unless the government surrendered land titles as well as its conception of Anchorage as a model construction camp. Furthermore, the townspeople preferred federal direction. Anchorage citizens assumed that the Commission, because it was not required to make a profit, could manage the utilities more cheaply. Besides, they believed that federal townsite administration would free them from "petty city politics."[10]

From the Commission's viewpoint, the first arrangements were inefficient and cumbersome. The Land Office was responsible for investigating and reporting all violations of townsite regulations, including failure to pay improvement assessments, while the Commission was supposed to make improvements, issue assessments, and have general authority over the townsite. Because of overlapping functions and divided responsibility, policy and administrative matters had to be decided in conferences of Land Office and townsite officials--Christensen, Mears, Moore, the temporary townsite manager, and J. G. Watts, the townsite engineer.[11]

During another series of conferences lasting through August, Christensen and the commissioners developed plans for a Land and Industrial Department of the Commission to supervise most matters outside the sphere of engineering and construction. Though Secretary Lane did not sign the order creating the department until April 12,

1916, it is evident from Christensen's role as unofficial townsite adviser that he was expecting to leave the Land Office to become the department's manager. The department was established at Seward and later moved with other Commission offices to Anchorage.[12]

Christensen was a forthright, diligent, and decisive public servant whose previous experience had been in land and railroad legal matters. He had no technical knowledge of local government, but more than that he needed a full measure of calm and self-confidence to cope with the breakdown of law enforcement involving liquor, gambling, and prostitution.

Bootleggers who catered to thirsty construction crews throve on the heavy shipments from the licensed saloon at Knik, 30 miles up Knik Arm from Anchorage. In a town of scarcely 3,000, gambling games ran wide open, and dealers worked in shifts in the jam-packed back rooms of the dozen or so false-fronted pool halls and cigar stores along the rim of tableland overlooking Ship Creek. Characters with nicknames such as "Dago Jim," "Creampuff Bill," and "The Pale Faced Kid" strolled Anchorage's dirt streets and disappeared behind swinging doors where, day and night, the click of billiards mingled with the clink of chips.

In tents and cabins southeast of the built-up section, "Little Annie," "Montana Bessie," and thirty or forty other members of the oldest profession followed their calling in Alaska's newest townsite. Theirs was a sordid exile. Forced into a "restricted district," forbidden by stern local custom from mingling on the main streets with the townspeople, and dependent on a "messenger" who carried their provisions, the girls on "the line" were at the mercy of the pimps who had organized them.

Prostitution was the nexus between the frontier underworld and the world of government and law. The Commission shared responsibility with the deputy marshal's office for restricting the prostitutes to one section rather than permitting them to settle anywhere in town or attempting to prohibit them entirely. In July, 1916, the Commission decided to sell lots and acre tracts in the district, and it ordered the prostitutes off the site by the first of October. On October 2 a delegation from the Chamber of Commerce event to the Commission with a stiffly worded complaint: prostitutes were overrunning the town and endangering its morals. The Land and Industrial Department must establish another district. Christensen,

Watts (now townsite manager), and the deputy marshal collaborated on selecting a new location.[13]

The men of the Commission shared much of the responsibility for the restricted district, but information gathered by Commission operatives showed that a few pimps and their allies in the marshal's office reaped the rewards. The leading maque had formed such an effective league with one of the deputies that prostitutes who refused to buy liquor from him were jailed, and, if they did not correct their errors, they were handed one-way tickets out of town. The same pimp reportedly exacted protection money from the gambling dens. The deputy in question owned the lot upon which one of the most notorious gambling establishments stood, and he was openly living with a lady bootlegger who was not his wife. Christensen and his co-workers were in an unenviable position; they believed that they had to permit prostitution, partly to protect the town's respectable women, and, at the same time, prevent the corruption of law enforcement and the graft and liquor traffic that were its consequences.

Gambling and the lax attitude of the marshal's office toward it disturbed the Commission even more, for the blatant gaming preyed upon the eager construction stiffs newly arrived from the wilderness isolation of "the front." One operative found a big card game in progress at a pool hall. The exceptional pot of between $1,200 and $1,500 had drawn such a large, excited crowd that he could not enter the back room and had to follow developments by word passed from the onlookers inside. But when he informed the chief deputy of the facts, the lawman regarded him calmly and remarked, "I guess I'll have to touch 'em up a little." To the operative's disgust, the chief deputy took his usual action in such cases--he did nothing. Although Commission men were exasperated with the chief deputy, they could never discover clear links between him and the underworld, nor could they decide whether he was stupidly indifferent, intimidated, or involved in illicit profits. Their evidence, however, suggests all three.[14]

Bootlegging flourished alongside gambling and prostitution. Commission informants and agents alleged that liquor and beer were dispensed from drugstores, general merchandise stores, and residences, as well as from "the line." The deputy marshal's office only sporadically enforced the law against the three offenses. When the deputies did move, they acted merely to assist a pimp in controlling his prostitutes, to appease the aggressive assistant district attorney who was periodically dispatched to Anchorage, to quiet the Commission whenever its agents brought in overwhelming evidence, or to increase official revenues through fines levied with the mutual understanding that they were business taxes upon the violators.

On the face of it, the Commission's remedy was simple. Townsite regulations provided for forfeiture of lots used for prohibited purposes. Hence the Commission could at any time have begun forfeiture proceedings by bringing charges against lot owners to the field division of the Land Office. Actually, the procedure was potentially so slow and cumbersome that federal officials hesitated to become involved in a series of forfeiture hearings. Besides, they wanted Anchorage to develop from a construction camp into a stable center for the railroad, light industry, and the agricultural and mineral hinterland. But the town could not mature with the threat of forfeiture hanging over every lot, and the territorial banking board had warned against real estate loans on land which was so liable to loss. Even in cases of clear violation, forfeiture could have been an injustice, for the regulations did not forbid leasing or assigning by quitclaim deed, and a lessee or assignee could invite forfeiture of another's lot by his illegal pursuits. Finally, if the townsite administrators moved against the owners of lots given over to gambling, for consistency's sake they should also prosecute for violations of sanitary or fire regulations. Yet forfeiture for such petty violations was a punishment scarcely fitting the crime. It was easier to do nothing than to determine the degree or kind of violation that warranted forfeiture.[15]

The alternative--enforcing federal laws on gambling and liquor--was more attractive, but it too was beset by practical difficulties. The Commission had no desire to limit prostitution beyond confining it to the restricted district. Yet it was unable to enlist the aid of prostitutes in its antiliquor campaign, not only because they made money by reselling whisky and beer, but also because they lived in fear of exportation and dared not inform on their liquor-selling pimps. "The girls," one of them told Christensen, "never squeal." It was nearly impossible to stop the flow of liquor through its other channels because the government had to prove at least one sale--a difficult business which required purchases by undercover agents. It was also difficult to prosecute gamblers successfully because the testimony of a participant in the game--provided that he could be persuaded to testify and thereby incriminate himself--was not sufficient evidence to convict a gambler. The testimony of a spectator was necessary in addition to that of a player or dealer, and no jury could be counted on to return an adverse verdict. Gamblers, after all, provided one of the town's principal forms of recreation.[16]

Despite these handicaps, Christensen decided to conduct his own raid on a gambling den with the help of the assistant district attorney and an out-of-town deputy marshal. He did not ask for aid from the local chief deputy whose raids the gamblers always seemed to be well informed about in advance. On November 17, 1916, after secret preparations, Christensen and his band descended upon a pool hall--named, with whimsey and accuracy, "The Bank"--and arrested fourteen dealers and players. Christensen soon discovered that arrest was easier than conviction. At the first trial before the local commissioner, the marshals, who were responsible for selecting the jury, waited until the prosecution had exhausted its challenges, then sent in a gambler to sit in judgment upon his peers. The jury failed to agree, and a second trial was held. Again the marshals managed to pack the jury. The exasperated Christensen wrote in despair to Edes:

> No stronger case of gambling could be made. People who played in the game, who paid the dealer the money and saw the dealer take his rake-off on every pot testified. In fact the scene in the pool hall was clearly enacted before the jury. There was no doubt whatever as to the facts and yet the jury let him off.

Christensen was further disconcerted when government witnesses were intimidated and spirited away, two undercover men were expelled from the local labor union and all of them were ostracized, and courtroom spectators demonstrated against the prosecution during the trials.[17]

Commission officials finally decided that the only solution to the law-enforcement problem was to change the law-enforcement officers. Consequently, they appealed to the Department of Justice for an overhaul of the marshal's office. At the end of November, the chief deputy found himself transferred to the insignificant Matanuska townsite, and the deputy who had enjoyed such a close relationship with underworld elements was removed from office. The change stuck despite a petition which was signed by some of the town's leading businessmen and directed to the district marshal at Valdez. The petition praised the chief deputy for his "honesty, integrity and moral uprightness" and requested his return.

Although Christensen criticized the temporary deputy marshal for his lack of "initiative" and "energy," the new man was, he believed, "one with whom you can work." Arrests mounted, but so did public feeling against the Commission. Convictions were as difficult as ever to obtain. Gamblers and bootleggers, however, realized that they faced constant harassment following the loss of their comfortable working arrangement with the marshal's office. After a mid-December conference with Commission officials, government attorneys, and the temporary deputy marshal, the gamblers tore out the partitions of their notorious back rooms, and bootlegging declined. The permanent deputy arrived in January, 1917, and thereafter illegal activity dwindled to manageable proportions.[18]

The perplexities of providing adequate schools for Anchorage children paralleled those of law enforcement and proved as difficult to resolve. With schools as with law enforcement, the Commission faced a situation compounded from administrative oversight and divided authority. Schools had inadvertently been omitted from the list of specific items for which the Commission could assess Anchorage lots. The problem of financing the schools was impossible of easy solution. The Commission was required by circumstances to assume responsibility, yet there was no way, under the townsite regulations, to compel residents to pay for their children's schooling.

There were, however, some sources of financial aid. Under the so-called Nelson law of 1905 residents of Alaska could organize school districts outside incorporated towns. Such a district would be eligible for aid from the "Alaska fund," which was comprised of 25 per cent of the receipts from federal licenses on businesses located in unincorporated areas and was to be used annually for school maintenance. In addition, the district could expect $1,000 in territorial aid for school construction and possibly more for certain operating expenses.[19]

The Commission and the newly formed school board quickly learned that territorial funds were inadequate for the needs of Anchorage. The legislature could be of no help, because it was forbidden by the Alaska Organic Act of 1912 from writing "local or special" school laws. The governor, in his capacity as ex-officio superintendent of public instruction, was reluctant to requisition the "Alaska fund" because the Nelson law and other similar laws were designed for hamlets or scattered settlements. They were not intended to cover the needs of a community which, during the summer of 1916, had a population of 3,332, including about 200 of school age. Anchorage was a metropolis by Alaska standards of the time. All the legislation assumed that it would incorporate and care for its own schools.

Anchorage, of course, could not incorporate. Its residents concluded that, because the federal government had failed to foresee the school situation, it should accept responsibility for finding a way to finance education. Alaskans outside Anchorage and the other townsites believed that they should not be required to support schools in "government towns." An unstated but surely significant reason for the governor's reluctance to spend "Alaska fund" revenues for Anchorage was the fact that the town contained no saloons which contributed license fees to the fund. Thus an appropriation for Anchorage would bestow upon this federal boomtown benefits out of all proportion to its contributions.[20]

Although these problems later became pressing, they were unimportant in the early days of the town's existence. Under the Comptroller-General's liberal interpretation of the broad grant of power in the Alaska railroad act, the Commission constructed a schoolhouse in the fall of 1915, and residents raised a subscription to supplement "Alaska fund" money which the governor had granted until, as everyone confidently believed, Congress would provide for carrying on the schools.

Though the first school year passed without incident, a crisis developed during 1916. In July the director of the Anchorage school board reported to the Commission on the shortcomings of the first, hastily constructed frame school. The building lacked a safe foundation, paint, inside toilets, running water, and a satisfactory heating system. Its unheated outside toilets did not conform to sanitary regulations. Townsite Manager Watts concluded from his own investigation that the school was "entirely inadequate," "insanitary," and was generally "of an order of the early Eighteenth Century." He agreed with the recommendation of a Commission engineer that the building should be abandoned and an adequate structure built. The Commission decided to construct a new and larger school, while the board undertook to rent the additional space needed until completion of the building. But other problems still were unresolved.[21]

Late in the summer of 1916, the board and the Commission appealed to Governor John F. Strong, but he was unwilling to advance any substantial sum for maintaining and operating the school. The Governor reminded Edes that the territory had allotted about $6,000 to the Anchorage school for the academic year 1915-16. He complained that the pupil population had fallen below expectations and charged that the board had been remiss in failing to send him regular reports as required by law. Later, the board informed Strong that more than $14,000 would be needed to operate the school for the second year, and the Commission reinforced the board's plea with the assertion that without adequate financing the school would soon be forced to close. But Strong refused to budge. "I cannot coax money from a fund that is exhausted," he once exclaimed, and though he exaggerated the lack of money, his allocation of what was available made it plain that he intended to care for other districts in unincorporated areas before attending to Anchorage.[22]

While the Commission was pressing Strong to act, it was urging Secretary Lane to authorize aid for the school. Lane's refusals were as uncompromising as Strong's, and the matter became a contest between the federal and the territorial governments to see which of them could force the other to assume the burden. When Mears reported on November 10 that the teachers were not being paid and were living on credit extended by the merchants, Lane relented and authorized the use of federal funds until about the time of the Christmas recess. The next month the harassed school board informed Christensen that, if the Commission did not immediately assume fiscal responsibility, the school would remain closed at the end of the vacation. On receipt of this news, Lane capitulated and agreed to advance funds until another source could be found.

Although federal officials could scarcely escape the obligation to support education, they were hardly happy with the new task. This was especially the case with Christensen, whom Edes appointed to assume operation of the school during the time Commission money was spent for its maintenance. Edes told Christensen that he hoped a permanent solution would be found, but "in the meantime you can be school director in addition to your other duties."[23]

Christensen wondered why the school board "appeared much relieved" when he announced that he was taking over. He soon discovered that he had inherited a personnel problem. The principal had transferred one of the teachers from the high school to the third and fourth grades, and the board had sustained the principal when the teacher complained. Christensen decided to reassign the demoted teacher to the high school, but he determined to give both principal and teacher "a good talking to." He told the teacher "to stop gossiping, complaining and criticizing, and to bring her work up to the standard." The principal was told that "he must quit going to the pool halls and must get down to business." Another problem that plagued the new director was overcrowded classrooms. One teacher, he wrote to Edes, had charge of seventy primary students and was instructing them in half-day shifts. "It is a troublesome question," Edes agreed, "and I wish we were rid of it."[24]

Establishing a permanent source of funds to finance the school was an equally troublesome question. Since the spring of 1916, the Commission had campaigned for congressional action to return half the lot-sale receipts to the townsite for public improvements. The school crisis and congressional critics of the Commission's expenditures for education quickened interest in finding a way to avoid spending railroad money for school financing. On April 17, 1917, an act allowing 50 per cent of the lot-sale money for schools and other permanent improvements was passed as part of a deficiency bill. The "fifty per cent fund," as it applied to the schools, was limited to construction expenses only and did nothing to ease the shortage of maintenance and operating funds.[25]

During the previous month, Congress had responded to another Interior Department request by repealing the restrictions on schools imposed upon the Alaska legislature by the 1912 Organic Act. When Christensen went to the legislature in April to explain the need for special legislation, he found the lawmakers willing to extend territorial aid to Anchorage equitably with other larger Alaska towns. For the rest, the legislators believed, the town or the Commission should be responsible. Working with Christensen, they quickly drew up and enacted a bill giving unincorporated towns having at least a hundred settlers and a school-age population of at least thirty the right to elect a school board with power to evaluate real and personal property in its district and to levy a tax of up to one per cent of the valuation. That summer Anchorage voted in a new board under the provisions of the act. In December the Commission completed the new school and, because construction costs had been reimbursed from the "fifty per cent fund," donated the $45,000 building to the district free of charge.[26]

Special problems aside, effective administration of Anchorage was a continuing responsibility that required the consent of at least some of the governed. Commission managers were employers, high salaried and socially important in the town. It was natural, then, for them to refer to "the Anchorage Chamber of Commerce and Commercial Club, representing the people," and to form close ties with the town's merchants through the Chamber and other commercial organizations. The merchants found the Commission a willing partner in plans for promotion and development of Anchorage and its tributary agricultural and mining region.[27]

Relationships were not always harmonious. Disagreements usually concerned such matters as the operation of the railroad's retail commissary, which the Chamber wanted closed, or commercial opportunities in construction areas, which the Commission wished to restrict. On matters of government, Commission leaders and merchants generally agreed. The Chamber repaid the Commission for its recognition by endorsing Commission appropriation requests and appeals to the territorial legislature and by printing and giving wide circulation to a pamphlet which praised the Commission's work.[28]

Although the relationship was mutually satisfactory, it failed to hide the fact that the Chamber was not popularly elected. Both the Commission and local citizens recommended the formation of a group similar to a city council, which could advise on townsite management. As a result, an Advisory Council was established. Its bylaws called for an at-large election of seven members by the adult lot-holders, a clause that cut off the large transient labor and boarding group from representation on the new body. The Council, chosen in September, 1917, was recommendatory only, dealt mostly with routine matters, and failed to supplant the commercial organization in the Commission's confidence. The initiative in affairs of importance continued to rest with the Chamber.[29]

No other area of administration affected the residents so palpably as the financial demands of the townsite office. That office levied three types of assessments.

First, it charged for townsite operation and maintenance under the terms of sale requiring lot purchasers to comply with regulations regarding streets, sanitation, and fire protection. Assessments comparable to property taxes were raised to meet ordinary municipal costs such as maintenance, garbage collection, office expenses, and engineering. Watts argued that they were not like property taxes, but rather were charges levied for the services each lot received, without reference to its property value. But this argument failed to convince people who saw Anchorage's business lots assessed at only three times the rate for unimproved parcels on the fringes of the townsite. Opposition to the crude one-to-three ratio of the first assessment was so strong that townsite officials later worked out monthly service charges for eight classes of lots, each carefully defined by location. Although they maintained the service charge fiction, they in fact levied operation and maintenance assessments in proportion to lot values.[30]

Second, sale regulations justified assessments for improvements including sewers, water main extensions, sidewalks, and grubbing, grading, and surfacing of streets. Improvement assessments were issued against benefited property on a front-foot basis, just like special tax bills in incorporated communities.

Third, the Commission compelled Anchorage residents to pay a portion of the costs of the first permanent water main. In 1915 the Commission had approached the Chamber of Commerce on the subject, and the commercial body had authorized the installation. Owners of affected lots were to repay in four equal installments.[31]

Watts tried to prove to townsite residents that Commission government was a bargain for them. For example, in 1918 he compared the average Anchorage operation and maintenance costs of about $32,000 per year with figures of $60,000 for Juneau and $35,000 for Fairbanks, towns of comparable size. Accepting the Anchorage school board's valuation of $2,000,000, Watts figured the total assessments at 1.93 per cent of valuation, slightly below the maximum legal rate of 2 per cent for incorporated towns. In any case, the Commission received few complaints about assessment rates. Further, the number of delinquencies does not seem abnormally high, doubtless because the Commission unhesitatingly reported delinquent lots to the Land Office for forfeiture.[32]

Anchorage received other benefits. By the end of 1917, the "fifty per cent fund" had paid for the first two schools, the firehouse, park improvements, and some street and utilities construction. Though the Commission repeatedly raised water rates in an attempt to erase its operating deficit, its charges compared favorably with those in other coastal towns, even though they were served by less expensive gravity systems.[33]

The townsite manager and his one or two assistants struggled with the minutiae of administration as well as with the large issues of townsite government. A stream of regulations, including a solemn warning to dog-team drivers to stay off the sidewalks, issued from the townsite office. The office encouraged lot assignees to register there, sent assessment notices to them rather than to owners of record, and published in the official *Alaska Railroad Record* installment information received from the Land Office at Juneau. Believing that they were obligated to control roaming dogs, townsite officials also operated a pound, though it was without much legal authority and was heavily criticized by "self-styled admirers of dogs," as Watts put it.[34]

During the Commission's administration, Anchorage evolved from a rough construction camp into an established railroad town, though it retained its frontier flavor. Near the end of 1917, it reached a population peak it would not exceed for several years: a reasonably accurate count showed 3,928 persons living in the townsite and terminal yards.

The Commission contributed to Anchorage's amenities in many ways. It constructed a hospital for its employees which was also open to others, built a dock, ran excursion trains, founded a YMCA, encouraged gardening, athletics, and beautification, established parks and recreational reserves, and assisted with controlling the spread of influenza during the 1918 epidemic. World War I drained men away from Anchorage, and by 1920 the population had recovered to only 1,856.[35]

"Personally," Christensen had written in December, 1915, "I should think it would be a good idea to always have in mind the withdrawal from the management of these towns, so that it can be done gracefully and with dignity." Almost five years later, the time had come for Anchorage.[36]

Did the citizens of the town desire independence from Commission government? Many did not. The Governor, members of the territorial legislature, and territorial delegates to Congress had sharply criticized the unrepresentative nature of Commission control, but they did not live in Anchorage. Local residents knew that they had a good thing in federal paternalism. Despite many personnel changes, townsite administration was relatively efficient, economical, scandal-free, and, for the residents, carefree. They were loath to assume responsibility, grew increasingly apprehensive as the end of the period of federal tutelage approached, and threatened to balk at organizing their own municipal affairs.[37]

Beginning in the spring of 1920, the Commission and a committee of the Chamber of Commerce worked closely together to establish plans for local control. The committee most wanted to know what property the government would give the town. The Commission told the townspeople that they would receive the schoolhouse and grounds, the "municipal block" reservation, the firehouse, the water mains, and the streets, sidewalks, and alleys. This was not enough for the Chamber. It threatened a negative vote on incorporation unless the Commission met what the Chamber said was a popular demand by deeding unsold and forfeited lots to the town and by selling Commission cottages to permit a tax levy against them. The Commission declined to be stampeded, though it did agree to discuss assumption of a proportionate share of town expenses, based on unsold lots and government property within the corporate limits.

The Commission's concessions were not tempting enough, for sentiment still seemed to run against incorporation. Officials were worried. Under territorial law, incorporation required a two-thirds majority, and if the vote failed, Anchorage would fall into an administrative limbo.

Obviously, some plain speaking was necessary. At a mass meeting held on the night of October 28, 1920, Burton H. Barndollar, the Commission's chief accountant, bluntly told the gathering that the government's control period, contracted for in the lot purchase agreements, had ended and that it would have "no more to do with the management of the town...than it would have to do with the management of the City of Seattle..." He flung back at the assemblage the Alaskan's continual cry of bureaucratic domination from Washington and warned that Anchorage must not repudiate its opportunity for self-government. Failure to seize it would suggest to Washington that Alaska was populated by political hypocrites. When asked whether Commission fire protection would continue if incorporation failed, Barndollar replied, "No." Interested residents in the town would have to find their own means of firefighting. That statement brought the meeting around. Anchorage would have to incorporate and tax for a fire department, or there would be no protection and fire insurance would be unobtainable. After Barndollar had finished, the meeting nominated a slate of candidates for the council election to be held on November 1, concurrently with the balloting for incorporation.[38]

One last legal hurdle remained. The vote showed a majority for incorporation, but whether it was a two-thirds majority depended upon how 85 blank ballots were to be counted. If the 85 were included in the grand total vote, the majority would fall short of two-thirds, but if they were excluded, the total vote would drop to 458, giving more than the required majority to the 328 favorable votes.

Consternation reigned in the Commission offices when the district judge counted the 85 blanks in the total and declared incorporation defeated. Mears fired off a telegram to the district attorney, urging him to prepare an opinion against inclusion of the blanks. The district attorney agreed that the blanks should not be counted as votes because they carried no expression of opinion. He convinced the judge, who reversed himself and on November 23, 1920, declared Anchorage to be incorporated.[39]

More than five years had passed since the day Frederick Mears landed at Ship Creek to build the government railroad in Alaska and found that townsite matters competed for his attention against problems of supply, labor, and construction. The men of the Commission had to assume responsibility for Anchorage, though they were reluctant to add the tasks of municipal government to those of railroad building. They failed to create a model construction camp, but they fashioned a modern community from the frontier wilderness. They contained the caterers to human frailty who threatened to overwhelm the town, they provided education for the children, and they kept a reasonable degree of order.

To accomplish all this, they had to work with ambiguous and inadequate laws and regulations and live with local criticisms, made in most cases without an understanding of the sometimes conflicting restrictions and responsibilities placed upon them. Frederick Mears, Burton Barndollar, and the others may be forgiven their irritation with the critics who so cautiously assumed the burdens which these men had borne beyond their allotted time.

ENDNOTES

[1]This article is based on the files of the Alaska Railroad, presently housed in the railroads headquarters building, Anchorage, Alaska. First citations are to file folders which contain the principal sources for the topic under discussion; subsequent notes are confined to material outside those sources. The following

folders contain the most important material pertaining to the founding of Anchorage and its first few months of existence: Headquarters Files 47.01, 48, 48.3, and 48.31 (hereafter cited as HF); Land and Industrial Department Files 25.202-203, Anch. Lots, 1915-20 (hereafter cited as LIDF, folder cited by number only), and LIDF 040.3, Report on situation with respect to townsites along RR, 1915-16 (folder hereafter cited by number only). See also New York *Times*, April 11, 1915, and "Annual Report of the Alaskan Engineering Commission, Calendar Year 1915," 16, typescript (hereafter cited as AEC 1915 Report). The official reasons given for selecting a wilderness area as a construction base, although the established town of Seward was available, were that the railroad could be built toward the Matanuska coal fields from Ship Creek, and that Anchorage would be a convenient coal port during the navigation season on Cook Inlet. Evangeline Atwood, however, advances another reason: the speculative greed of those having heavy investments in Seward property forced the Commission to seek a different location. See Atwood, *Anchorage: All-America City* (Portland, 1957), 4.

[2]The usual townsite procedure conferred no extraordinary powers on the official serving as townsite trustee, whose duties ended after the public lot sale which would establish the town. For a comparison of the usual procedure with the special arrangements for Anchorage and other railroad townsites, see *Circular Instructions Relating to the Acquisition of Title to Public Lands in the Territory of Alaska*, Dept. of the Interior, General Land Office, Circular No. 491 (Washington, D.C., 1916). Anchorage was the first and by far the largest and most important of the several railroad townsites.

[3]Mears to Lane, June 2, 1915, HF 48.3.

[4]The regulations appear in various circulars and in separate printed forms. Copies are in LIDF 040.3. The lot purchase installments, payable to the Land Office at Juneau, must not be confused with the lot assessments issued by the Commission and paid to the Anchorage townsite office. For the convenience of lot holders, lot payment information was carried in the weekly *Alaska Railroad Record* (hereafter cited as *ARRec*), though the Commission had no formal connection with lot payment matters. Lot payments due during and after August, 1918, were suspended one year by Executive Order No. 2982, Oct. 25, 1918, because of wartime stringencies in Alaska.

[5]Christensen to Clay Tallman, July 21, Dec. 9, 1915, LIDF 25.202-203; "Annual Report of the Chairman of the Alaskan Engineering Commission to the Secretary of the Interior, January 1 to December 31, 1916," 56, typescript (hereafter cited as AEC 1916 Report); "Report of the Chairman, Alaskan Engineering Commission, to the Secretary of the Interior, Calendar Year 1917," 63-64, 78, typescript (hereafter cited as AEC 1917 Report).

[6]"City Planing--Minus," by J. Horace McFarland, typescript, HF 48. For criticisms of Anchorage and the lot sale caused by the jealousy of other Alaska towns, see Christensen to Tallman, Dec. 13, 1915, and to William C. Edes, June 18, 1917, LIDF 040, Injury Suit Threat of John E. Ballaine (1916) 1917; Christensen to Edes, Feb. 11, 1918, LIDF G-12.71, Land and Ind.--Miscellaneous

(folder hereafter cited by letter and number only); Edes memorandum May 15, 1919, LIDF G-1.7, Constr.--General. "Anchorage" became the commonly used, and later the officially accepted, townsite name, though a vote on the question gave a plurality to "Alaska City." See "Resolution to Change the Name of Anchorage," Chamber of Commerce, undated copy; Edes to Christensen, and Christensen to Edes, Oct. 17, 1915, telegrams; Mears to Edes, Oct. 18, 1915, LIDF 172, Resolution--to change name of Anchorage to Alaska City, 1915. The civic myth that the name "Anchorage" won at the election was powerful enough to prompt a full-scale celebration on the 50th anniversary of the supposed naming, Anchorage *Daily News*, Aug. 9, 11, 1965; Anchorage *Daily Times*, Aug. 11, 1965.

[7]Memorandum of conference Aug. 6, 1915, "between Commissioner Mears... and Messrs. Moore Watts and Christensen...," HF 48.33; Resolution passed by the Chamber of Commerce, Anchorage, Aug. 20, 1915, and covering letter, Carl Almy to Mears, Aug. 21, 1915, HF 48.3; Edes to Franklin K. Lane, Aug. 30, 1915, LIDF 002, "Handling Townsite Matters at Seward, 1915-1918" (folder hereafter cited by number only); E. R. McFarland to Mears, March 7, 1917, and Mears to McFarland, March 8, 1917, HF 434.200.1. The Alaska railroad act allowed the government to do almost anything necessary to advance the project. See 38 Stat 305 (1914). General summaries of utilities and local government matters are in the AEC annual reports, 1915 through 1920.

[8]Lane to Edes, Oct. 4, 1915, LIDF 25.044, Public School, 1915-18 (folder hereafter cited by number and dates only); H. J. Emard to Kellogg Switchboard & Supply Co., Aug. 26, 1915, R. H. Coyne, Kellogg Switchboard & Supply Co. to Lane, Oct. 6, 1915, and Mears to Coyne, Nov. 6, 1915, HF 27.2.

[9]AEC 1916 Report, 42; AEC 1917 Report, 73, 74; Christensen and Edes to J A Moore, Townsite Manager, and J. C. [*sic*] Watts, Engineer, Aug. 29, 1915, and Christensen to Mears, Aug. 29, 1915, HF 48.37.

[10]Christensen to Tallman, Aug. 31, Dec. 10, 1915, LIDF 040.3.

[11]Christensen to Tallman, Aug. 31, 1915, LIDF 040.3.

[12]The order gave most of the townsite responsibilities previously held by the General Land Office to the Land and Industrial Department. See LIDF 002, and *ARRec*, Vol. 1, No. 1 (Nov. 14, 1916): 4.

[13]Law enforcement problems are the subject of material in LIDF 25.202, Sale of Anch. Lots, 1918-19; HF 47.02 and HF 48.301.

[14]Christensen to William A. Munly, assistant U.S. district attorney, Jan. 4, 1917, attachment No. 1, HF 48.301.

[15]There was so little confidence in the security of lots that, as soon as the law enforcement situation improved, Executive Order No. 2641, June 18 1917, revoked provisions of the townsite regulations for forfeiture in case of illegality or immorality. A few of the most notorious liquor violators had been punished with forfeiture prior to that time. For discussions of considerations and problems in relation to lot forfeiture, see U. S. Attorney at Valdez to the Attorney-General, April 25, 1917, copy, LIDF 25.129-501, Liquor Forfeiture Cases, 1916-17 (folder hereafter cited by number only); Christensen to Edes and Mears, Jan. 18, 1917, and

C. R. Arundell to Tallman, April 13, 1917, LIDF 129, Self-government of towns on Railroad, 1917-19 (folder hereafter cited by number only). After June 22, 1917, the Commission reported failure to pay lot assessments directly to the Commissioner of the General Land Office. See *Amending Procedure for Forfeiture of Lots Under Alaskan Railroad Townsite Regulations*, Dept. of the Interior, General Land Office, Circular No. 554.

[16]Christensen to Munly, Jan. 4, 1917, attachment No. 5, HF 48.301; Munly to Mears, Feb. 21, 1916, with copies of proposed federal legislation, and Mears to Edes, Feb. 28, 1916, HF 71.1.

[17]Christensen to Edes, Dec. 2, 1916. HF 48.301.

[18]Christensen to Mears, Dec. 6, 1916, enclosing undated petition to H. E. Brenneman, United States Marshal, Valdez, copy, Christensen to Edes and Mears, Dec. 15, 1916, Christensen to Edes, Jan. 20, 31, Feb. 17, 1917, LIDF 25.129-501.

[19]33 Stat. 616 (1905); Territory of Alaska, *Session Laws, Resolutions, and Memorials* (1915): 110-14.

[20]For correspondence on school problems, see LIDF 25.044 (1913-18); see also Ernest Gruening, *The State of Alaska* (New York, 1954), p. 152.

[21]Watts to Christensen, Aug. 16, 1916, LIDF 25.044 (1915-18).

[22]Strong to Edes, Oct. 11, 1916, telegram, LIDF 25.044 (1913-18); Christensen to Strong, Dec. 18, and Strong to Christensen, Dec. 20, 1916, LIDF 044, Schools, General (folder hereafter cited by number only).

[23]Edes to Christensen, Dec. 29, 1916, LIDF 25.044 (1915-18).

[24]Christensen to Edes and Mears, Jan. 6, 1917, LIDF A-12.5 Land and Ind.--Schools (folder hereafter cited by letter and number only); Edes to Christensen, Jan. 23, 1917, LIDF 25.129-501. Christensen had to worry over many details. See LIDF 25.044-1, Public Schools, 1917.

[25]LIDF 129.1, Fifty per cent of money received from sale of town lots to lbe used for self government, 1916-20; LIDF 25.044 (1915-18), *ARRec*, Vol. 1, No. 27 (May 15, 1917): 213.

[26]LIDF 044; LIDF A-12.5; *ARRec*, Vol. 1, No. 32 (June 9, 1917): 255-56, No. 33 (June 26, 1917): 263, No. 37 (July 24, 1917); [292], Vol. 2, No. 3 (Dec. 11, 1917): 32; *Senate Journal of the Third Legislature of the Territory of Alaska* (1917), 234; "Report of the Manager, Land and Industrial Department, for the Period October 1, 1916 to December 31, 1917," 97-98, typescript.

[27]Christensen to Edes, Jan. 5, 1916, HF 48.33.

[28]"Conference Between Anchorage Chamber of Commerce and Alaskan Engineering Commission in re Commissary," Jan. 26, 1916, LIDF 030.6, Anch. C of C--Abolishing Commissary 1916-18; William Gerig, memorandum for Colonel Mears, Feb. 25, 1920, HF 1.61; *ARRec*, Vol. 2, No. 36 (July 16, 1918): 281. For the commissary and related labor matters, see LIDF A-6.3, Wages; LIDF A-11.5, Comms'y--Misc; LIDF A-12.1, Land and Ind. Dept.--Townsites; LIDF 010, Labor-wages, 1915-17; HF 11.221.1; HF 13.20; *ARRec*, Vol. 3, No. 15 (Feb. 18, 1919): 117, and No. 24 (April 22, 1919): 186; Territory of Alaska,

Journal of the House of Representatives of the Third Legislature (1917), 64-63.

[29]HF 48; HF 48.3; LIDF 040.4, *ARRec*, Vol. 2, No. 43 (Sept 3, 1918): 340, No. 44 (Sept. 10, 1918): 348, No. 45 (Sept. 17, 1918): [353].

[30]*ARRec*, Vol. 1, No. 9 (Jan. 9, 1917): [65]-66, Vol. 2. No. 40 (Aug. 3, 1918): 314. Military men were exempt from assessment payments during World War I. See *ARRec*, Vol. 3, No. 28 (May 20, 1919): 219.

[31]HF 48.33, *ARRec*, Vol. 1, No. 13 (Feb. 6, 1917): [97], Vol. 2, No. 5 (Dec. 11, 1917): 38-39.

[32]*ARRec*, Vol. 2, No. 25 (April 30, 1918): 197; AEC 1917 Report, Appendix L.

[33]HF 48.33, AEC 1917 Report, Appendix L.

[34]Watts to Christensen, May 25, Oct. 29, 1917, with memorandum, LIDF 139, Laws & regulations regarding Fisheries in Alaska: Dogs in towns, 1916-19.

[35]HF 18.31; HF 47.01; HF 48; LIDF 25.202, Anch. Lots--Regulations 1920; LIDF 040.102. Requests for reports and general information, 1917-18; LIDF G-1.3, Constru.--Cost; *Census of Population: 1950* (Washington, D.C., 1953), Vol. 2, *Characteristics of the Population*, Part 51, p. 4, Table 2. The census figures are indications of the resident population, rather than the seasonal population which approximately doubled the town's size during each summer.

[36]Christensen to Tallman, Dec. 10, 1915, LIDF 040.3.

[37]References to criticism are in Arundell to Tallman, April 13, 1917, and Christensen to Edes, April 17, 1917, LIDF 129, and Atwood, *Anchorage*, 13. Personnel changes in the Land and Industrial Department and the townsite management are listed in *ARRec* and annual reports. In the only such instance uncovered in the Alaska Railroad archives, Watts was cleared of corrupt intent but censured for his poor judgment in granting permission to the townsite sewer foreman to contract for private connections as work progressed on the main. Independent plumbing contractors criticized Watt's action. John H. Robinson, special inspector, to Mears, Sept 27. 1917, and Christensen to Watts, Oct. 26, 1917, LIDF 029.0--029.2, Using and selling govt. property, Forwarding personal belongings, Reservations, 1916-20. There were complaints of petty employment grafting and theft from townsite supply stocks, but the management was not implicated in these activities nor did it condone them.

[38]Burton H. Barndollar to Mears, Oct. 29, 1920, and transcript of Barndollar's remarks, HF 48. The problem of certifying town lots paid and issuing patents on them was a separate matter under General Land Office supervision. It was not a major obstacle to incorporation, because Anchorage did not assume its own government until after the end of the five-year period for most lots. Under territorial law, a petition requesting incorporation, and giving information about the community, was filed with the district judge, who then announced a hearing on the subject. If the judge satisfied himself that the petition was legitimate, he fixed the date for an incorporation election in the community. Mears discussed fire insurance problems in a letter to H. T. Fowler, Nov. 11, 1919, HF 48.5, 1937.

[39]HF 48.

TOURING ALASKA*

Frank Norris

Regular tourism began in Alaska with steamship cruises up the "Inside Passage" to Glacier Bay in the early 1880s. John Muir despaired of Kodak-toting travelers cluttering up the front of the glacier. He called them "arm-chair tourists" because they never got off the boat except to buy curios in waterfront shops where they complained of the poor quality of the surroundings and the high prices.

But tourism grew steadily from its early beginnings and by World War I was an established if modest factor in the Alaska economy. Still, getting off the boat could be expensive. A tour from Skagway to Whitehorse on the railroad, then down the Yukon River to Dawson and on around via the Tanana River to Fairbanks, and along the Alaska Railroad to McKinley Park, Anchorage and Seward in 1932 cost about $600.00, if one included the $100 steamship ticket to and from Seattle or Portland. That was about the same as the cost of a six-week summer sojourn in Europe.

Those who could afford such trips came anyway, according to Frank Norris, whose article is printed here. One of the growing number of historians working for public agencies in Alaska and elsewhere, Norris worked for the National Park Service in Skagway before leaving to attend graduate school.

Norris concludes that while tourism was a small industry, the number of Alaskans who depended on it continued to grow after World War I, making tourist enterprises vital to the territory's economy.

* * *

Alaska's vast expanses of undisturbed wilderness and pristine scenery give its visitors a sense of discovering something new and untrampled. Yet, no matter how fresh the experience may be for the traveler, today's tourists had their predecessors over a century ago. Moreover, since the 1870s, people have garnered an income from showing off the north's attractions.

---

*This article originally appeared in *Alaska History* 2, no.2 (Fall 1987): 1-18.

For the tourist trade's first several decades, sight-seers left little wealth behind them and created very little employment in the territory. Prior to World War I, visitors spent most of their money and time on steamers which cruised through the Southeast, but were based Outside. They made a few contributions to the local economy by purchasing Alaskan curios, most of which were created by Natives. Otherwise, excursionists furnished almost no support for local hotels, restaurants, or transportation firms.

After World War I, the industry experienced dramatic changes. Spurred on by a nation-wide boom in leisure activity and a multiplication of Alaskan travel routes, people flocked northward in increasing numbers. The new routes brought many travelers inland, where they helped support hotels, eating establishments, and local touring companies. More tourists also prompted those businesses retailing Native handicrafts to expand their operations. Alaskans began to reap substantial financial benefits from tourism. By the eve of World War II, tourism was a significant industry, touching the lives of many residents of the territory.

Though some have suggested that an excursion by William Seward in 1869 was the first Alaskan tourist trip, others claim that an 1878 tour led by Captain George S. Wright to the Stikine River initiated the industry. Several pioneer tourist groups wandered through southeastern Alaska in the early 1880s, and by 1884 a regularly scheduled loop, the so-called "Inside Passage Tour," had been established. This excursion usually began in Portland or a Puget Sound port. Northbound ships wended their way up the coast of British Columbia, then steamed on to Wrangell. The gold camps of Juneau and Douglas were next on the tour; they were followed by a visit to Muir Glacier in Glacier Bay. Returning south, ships stopped at the Native village of Killisnoo, near Angoon; they then put in at Sitka before returning to the United States. The tour quickly gained popularity; 1,650 sight-seers took the cruise in 1884, but six years later that figure had more than tripled.[1]

The Inside Passage Tour remained the mainstay of the Alaskan tourist trade for decades. Specific stops changed--for instance, Skagway and Ketchikan were added and Taku Glacier replaced Muir Glacier on the tour about 1900--but the basic route stayed much the same. It was the only steamship tour advertised before 1900, and in later years travelers who chose to explore other areas of the territory usually passed through the ports of Southeast.[2]

In the fading years of the nineteenth century an embryonic rail and riverboat network developed that allowed greater route choices and took tourists into the Canadian Yukon. The White Pass and Yukon Route furnished the first inland service available to tourists. Sight-seers' eagerness to take to the rails was such that during the summer of 1898 several parties rode on open flatcars when scarcely four miles of track had been laid.[3]

The rails reached Whitehorse in 1900, and shortly afterwards the WP&YR began operating a system of riverboats and lake steamers. Though the company had built the line for the mining trade, it wasted little time in promoting its services to tourists. Beginning in 1907 the WP&YR published attractive booklets, and by 1910 it brought a steadily growing stream of visitors to Whitehorse, Dawson, Atlin, and the summit of White Pass. Most early tourists who took the WP&YR confined their travels to these spots, but an intrepid few continued down the Yukon to Fort Yukon, Fairbanks, St. Michael, and Nome.[4]

The north country had much to lure the tourist before World War I. Besides the Inside Passage's magnificent scenery, each port boasted points of interest within walking distance of its dock. In Ketchikan, visitors ambled over to Ketchikan Creek to observe the salmon migration, viewed the totem poles downtown, and climbed to the overlook near the town's high school. At Wrangell, Chief Shakes Island, numerous totem poles, and remnants of an old fort were major attractions. Travelers to Sitka stopped at the Russian Orthodox Cathedral and looked over the Presbyterian mission school and museum before continuing on to lush Indian River Park, with its impressive collection of Haida totem poles that had been erected about 1905. Juneau area tourists visited the Treadwell Mine complex, a Native village, or hiked up Gold Creek Canyon. Most of those landing at Skagway stayed on Broadway Street, but some proceeded to the Gold Rush Cemetery in search of con man "Soapy" Smith's grave.[5] Those who continued inland to Canada thrilled to the beauty of White Pass Canyon, Whitehorse Rapids, and Midnight Dome at Dawson. Some also took a train or stage up Bonanza Creek to witness gold mining in the heart of the Klondike country.[6]

An air of informality characterized northern tourism before World War I. Visitors normally found their way to each attraction on their own, and few amenities existed at the points of interest. The only places sponsoring organized tours were noisy Treadwell Mine (where guides communicated by shouting and dramatic waving), Chief Shakes' house, the Presbyterian mission school, Sitka's Russian Orthodox Cathedral, and the excursions up Bonanza Creek. Only the last two tours charged a fee.[7] Some steamship captains doubled as tour guides; they loved to tell visitors anecdotes of Alaskan life, and assisted in giving directions to attractions.[8] Local residents also volunteered their services. In Ketchikan and Sitka, townspeople sometimes met tourists at the dock and escorted them without charge to the sights. In many towns residents invited travelers into their homes. For example, in Ketchikan the widow of an early Hudson's Bay Company trader told visitors about local Indian lore. In Juneau retired prospector Dick Willoughby regaled guests perched on stools and cartons scattered about his home with spellbinding bear stories, prospecting tales, and other real or imagined anecdotes.[9]

Individual personalities dominated other stops as well. Sporting a gaudy military uniform, Chief Kitchnatti entertained visitors to Killisnoo. At Metlakatla, the arrival of a tourist boat gave the town's founder, Rev. William Duncan, an opportunity to publicize his "progressive Indian experiment." To impress his guests, the Anglican missionary often arranged for a Native marching band to play when ships docked, after which he escorted the visitors to the town's cannery and shops and gave them a speech in Metlakatla's church.[10]

The economic contributions of tourism before World War I were both small and localized. Although thousands ventured north each summer, few spent their money in Alaskan towns. The tourist steamers, which served as hotels, restaurants, and stores, were chartered, staffed, and supplied in the West Coast states. Visitors spent only a few hours at each town along the Inside Passage.[11] The frontier aspect of the ports, while a source of curiosity, was too primitive for the standards demanded by the tourist trade. Early visitors were warned that there were "no Palace Hotels in Alaska"; they seldom remained overnight off the ship. Until 1910, many traveled on steamers reserved primarily for "roundtrippers." Hostages to the steamer schedule, they were cautioned that "you will go when and where the steamer goes." Travelers going inland were similarly cloistered; passengers ticketed to Atlin and Dawson, for example, stayed overnight on the lake and river steamers. The only substantial items tourists purchased in Alaska were train tickets, inland boat tickets, and curios. The combined revenues from these sources were insufficient to awaken most Alaskans to the economic benefits of the industry.[12]

The curio trade was the oldest indigenous segment of the Alaskan tourist industry. When tourists began traveling up the Inside Passage, both Natives and non-Native shop owners reacted by selling the newcomers whatever artifacts were available, regardless of value. Merchants hawked antique Russian samovars, whalebone creations, eagle-skin robes, and practically anything else portable as pieces of genuine Alaskana. The Natives, who too often recognized only an assured profit, sold many of their own tools and ceremonial objects to tourists, and in their zeal pillaged abandoned villages for whatever curios might be obtained.[13]

By 1890, the regularity of tourist trips had created a small cottage industry among southeastern Indians. The occupation was seasonally defined; Natives created their goods in the winter and sold them in the summer.[14] To present their wares to the tourists, Natives lined the wharves and main streets of the principal steamer stops. At Sitka, Wrangell, and Douglas a "curio line" assembled at the wharf on steamer days. Natives also situated themselves along Sitka's Lincoln Street and Skagway's Broadway Street. Natives peddled their wares in various locations in downtown Juneau. When visitors stopped at Yakutat, many never left the ship, so Natives crowded near the railing to display their goods. Before 1900, curio sellers even stationed themselves near the face of Muir Glacier in Glacier Bay. An exasperated John Muir noted that many passengers "turned from the great thundering crystal world of ice to look curiously at the Indians that came alongside [the ship] to sell trinkets."[15]

Although each Native family typically produced only a few types of craft items, there was often little similarity in the goods produced by Natives in different families or different ports. As a result, a refreshing variety of curios was available to the early Alaskan tourist. For example, a 1900 visitor to Wrangell wrote that the Natives offered "baskets, diminutive totem poles, beads and shellworks." Several years later, stocks had diversified into "labrets, silver bracelets, carved horn and wooden spoons, reed-baskets, halibut-hooks, gaily painted canoe paddles, the carved rattles of the Shamans, and fine carvings in slate." Metlakatla Indians sold silver bracelets, wood carvings, and colored baskets. Indians near Glacier Bay offered toys, baskets, and slippers. In 1907 Sitka Natives marketed baskets, beadwork, deer antlers, blankets, moccasins, woven bark matting, and small totem poles; the last featured inlaid mother-of-pearl, shells, pebbles, and walrus ivory in flint.[16]

Most of the items for sale were a logical part of the Native life style. In Killisnoo, however, villagers retailed items from outside their area. They sold reindeer moccasins and so-called "Eskimo dolls," as well as locally made bracelets and miniature canoes. A few early curios reflected the desire among tourists for gifts symbolic of Alaska. Noting such goods in a Wrangell shop, Muir decried the "shabby stuff manufactured expressly for the tourist trade."[17]

The best known curios were Native baskets. Excursion passengers snapped them up as early as the 1880s, and by the first decade of the twentieth century basket collecting became a fad. Firms carrying tourists, such as the Alaska Steamship Company, quickly recognized and promoted the craze. Their brochures advised that "no home is complete now-a-days without a neat and artistically arranged basket corner." Some baskets could be obtained in towns along the main steamer routes. The advertisements noted, however, that only in the remote villages (reached, not surprisingly, by that company's ships) would there be Natives who would be "ready and eager to display their baskets, odd carved totems and fine bead work." Several guidebooks recommended stops at villages to acquire craft items. Some travelers who followed this counsel found excellent Native handiwork, but others ended up paying high prices for worn or discarded works.[18]

Though most tourists purchased craft goods directly from Natives, many general stores, drug stores, photo shops, and jewelry retailers developed a trade in curios well before the turn of the century. Prior to World War I, these merchants sold a limited variety of local items. Wrangell shops in 1900 marketed locally made baskets and miniature totem poles, as well as Stikine River garnets. Most curios sold at a St. Michael shop were made of walrus ivory, while Unalaska outlets specialized in Aleut products, such as Attu baskets and other woven items. Stores in Skagway and Juneau sold a greater variety of goods. One Juneau shop marketed "photographs, beads, totem poles, wooden dolls, attractive little gold nuggets for rings, chain mountings, etc.; also skins of the otter, seal, beaver, squirrel and other animals...[and] fish salmon plates, which are purchased by the visitors simply as mementoes of the place."[19]

The Alaskan tourist industry remained economically insignificant until approximately 1910. However, the next decade witnessed consistent growth. Successful advertising, particularly by the WP&YR, played a role, as did World War I, which interrupted the traditional Grand Tour vacation route to Europe. Alaskan transportation companies encouraged the tourist traffic by improving their services. Amenities such as fresh fruit and vegetables first appeared on Atlin steamers in 1909. Soon after, the WP&YR upgraded its steamboats by adding more crew members, redesigning dining areas, and building more cabins. In 1912 the company converted the first of many railroad coaches into parlor cars. Three years later the firm operated its first tourist-only Midnight Sun Excursion boat from Whitehorse to Fort Yukon, and in 1917 it conducted its inaugural tour from Carcross to the Ben-My-Chree homestead at the south end of Lake Tagish.[20]

The tourist business expanded rapidly in the decade after World War I. The WP&YR system, which was indicative of the industry as a whole, enjoyed remarkable growth. In 1915 fewer than 2,500 tourists purchased tickets on the system. Four years later over 3,750 bought fares, and by 1927 over 9,800 did so. Travel diminished significantly during the Great Depression. In 1933 only 5,200 tourists ventured over the WP&YR. Recovery, however, was dramatic. By 1938 the company proudly noted that over 16,200 tourists had ridden its parlor cars and steamboats that year.[21]

The tourist business proved a boon to the line. Nearly 40 percent of WP&YR's passenger revenue came from tourists in 1915, and by 1924 over 70 percent of such income came from tourists. The shift was so striking that in 1923, the superintendent of the WP&YR's River Division wrote that, "time after time this summer, I noticed the absence of one way passengers leaving here [Whitehorse], and we have been very lucky to have been able to work up a passenger business to replace the old time movement [of miners] in and out of the country."[22]

In the early 1920s, several new routes opened up to Alaskan visitors. Each involved steamship passage to ports in Southcentral Alaska, an area seen by few tourists before World War I.[23] Some sight-seers confined themselves to brief visits to the coastal towns of

Yakutat, Cordova, Valdez, and Seward. However, most ventured into the Interior. Many traveled over the Copper River & Northwestern Railway from Cordova to McCarthy. Others were guided along the Richardson Highway to Fairbanks, and still others rode the Alaska Railroad, opened to Fairbanks in 1923.[24]

Transportation companies, individually and in concert with each other, worked to capitalize on the tourist trade. The Alaska Railroad, for example, usually doubled the number of trains in the summer; many of its extra runs went to the Kenai Peninsula's Spencer Glacier, Anchorage, McKinley Park, and other points of interest. The CR&NW similarly augmented its passenger service, and along the Richardson Highway several touring companies competed for the tourists' dollars.[25]

Travelers had greater flexibility in making vacation plans when, in the mid-1920s, rail and steamship lines began to coordinate their schedules. The Great Circle Tour guided sightseers from Skagway to Whitehorse by rail, down the Yukon to Fairbanks on a WP&YR steamer, and south to Seward on the Alaska Railroad. The Golden Belt Tour took tourists from Cordova to Chitina on the CR&NW, from Chitina to Fairbanks via the Richardson Highway, and returned them to saltwater on the Alaska Railroad. A short alternative to the Golden Belt Tour had travelers turn south at Chitina on touring cars for Valdez. Tourists could take these trips in either direction.[26]

The development of new routes boosted the Alaskan tourist industry because it meant that tourists spent more time off the steamships. All the new routes headed inland; both the Great Circle and Golden Belt tours took the traveler away from the coast for at least five days. This spurred business for lodging and feeding establishments. The Atlin Inn, built by the WP&YR in 1916, was erected specifically for tourists, and many other businesses were expanded or upgraded.[27] The most successful tourist hotels were at the major transfer points of Skagway, Whitehorse, Fairbanks, and Seward; at the terminus of tourist routes, such as Dawson and Atlin; and in the larger towns of Anchorage, Juneau, Ketchikan, and Sitka.[28] Along the Alaska Railroad, tourists stayed at the Curry Hotel built in 1925, and most Richardson Highway tourists lodged at the Upper Tonsina and Paxson roadhouses.[29]

Restaurants catering to tourists were widely scattered. The Bennett station house, between Skagway and Carcross on the WP&YR, was a well-known eating house in the north country. It offered a unique "sourdough lunch" that reputedly featured moose meat stew. The five-course meal was served *table d'hote* style on the station's long wooden tables, allowing customers to eat their fill.[30]

Tourists discovered that the meals served in local restaurants and roadhouses were both tasty and hearty. They were pleasantly surprised to find that tipping was not a custom, and that restaurants often served locally caught game. Tourists encountered such menu delicacies as ptarmigan, grouse, mountain sheep, caribou, and mountain goat. Beef and pork, however, were either expensive or were not available. Alaskan eating places, moreover, did not provide a wide choice of food, and most made no menu modifications for the tourist trade. As one guidebook declared, "no allowance is made for delicate or jaded appetites." Those requiring special diets were generally advised to stay home.[31]

Nevertheless, some restaurants did go out of their way to lure the tourists. Harriet Pullen, proprietress of Skagway's Pullen House, served fresh milk and cream to her guests. Few Alaskans were able to have fresh dairy products, but a small dairy herd on Pullen's Dyea homestead kept her patrons well supplied. Dawson's Arcade Cafe was popular with tourists because of its tongue-in-cheek menu. Called the Cheechako Bill of Fare, it advertised such tempting delights as "combination salad, pick and shovel dressing," "leg of pork and bonanza apple sauce," "glacier apple pie," and "skookum jim coffee."[32]

In the larger towns, the entire retail sector benefited from tourism. In Ketchikan, for example, businesses ranging from drug stores to photographers advertised for the visitor. One Ketchikan company sold "Totem Stationery," and innumerable taverns created "iceworm cocktails" by including bits of spaghetti in their ice cubes. Sitka, Anchorage, and Juneau gained similar benefits from the tourist trade.[33]

Local merchants recognized the value of tourism. By the late 1920s many chambers of commerce and similar civic bodies advertised local attractions. In Ketchikan, even the salmon industry helped promote tourism. In the mid-1930s, one of the first things tourists saw in town was a great arch spanning Dock Street. The arch, constructed by the local packers' association, proclaimed "Welcome Visitors," and at the apex of the arch was painted a large Alaskan salmon can.[34]

Although postwar vacationers continued to walk to a few points of interest, most towns offered far more sights via expanded road systems. Alaskan entrepreneurs augmented and modernized their taxi fleets, and some purchased large touring cars to carry people to these attractions. Group tours were the rule; the rental car industry had not yet developed, and virtually no tourists brought their own vehicles.[35]

Most Southeast towns had some commercial tours during the 1920s and 1930s. Visitors to Ketchikan often rode out the Tongass Highway to see the fish canneries, or continued on to nearby Ward Lake. Those who stopped at Petersburg could take a twelve-mile ride out the road that paralleled Wrangell Narrows.[36] At Skagway, Martin Itjen drove tourists to local sights in his "Skagway Streetcar." Juneau offered several tours. Some visitors rode up Gold Creek Canyon, a few went south to the Alaska-Gastineau mill at Thane, and others hopped aboard scenic flights over the surrounding countryside. Most, however, headed north to Mendenhall Glacier and Auke Lake. Along the way they passed a dairy and hay ranch, which one guidebook suggested made tourists "forget that they are in Alaska."[37]

Motor and air tours seemed in vogue throughout the north country. For example, taxis from the Whitehorse railroad station supplanted the previous walking tour to Miles Canyon, while touring companies took Dawson visitors to Bonanza Creek and Midnight Dome.[38] At Fairbanks guides in the 1920s drove visitors to the territorial college, which featured a museum and an agricultural experiment station, and to the gold mines along the Chatanika River and Ester and Goldstream creeks. Anchorage visitors enjoyed an auto or train ride to Lake Spenard, or a jaunt out the Eagle River road. While some sight-seers at Seward took the train to Lawing on Kenai Lake, others boarded an auto excursion to the lake, where boats took them to the resort. By the late 1920s pilots offered scenic flights out of Anchorage and Fairbanks. Key attractions were Mount McKinley and the midnight sun.[39]

Southeastern Alaska developed several revenue-producing attractions in the 1920s and 1930s. In Juneau, the Alaska Historical Museum opened in 1921. Five years later a short-lived museum began in Skagway, and a local resident opened a Soapy Smith Museum in 1935. Skagway pioneered the north country musical pageant in 1926, when the "Days of '98 Show" had its premiere.[40]

The curio trade also underwent major changes between the two world wars. But unlike the shifts that took place in other sectors of the tourist industry, those in the curio market were not directly attributable to the expansion of travel routes. As routes to Fairbanks and along the Yukon River became popular, some Interior Indians began to sell handicraft items at roadhouses and steamer stops. These Natives produced furs, birch bark baskets, and beadwork. However, tourists bought relatively few of these items; craft work of Interior Natives was not considered as appealing as that of the coastal groups. Fairbanks and Anchorage, large as they were, had few curio shops before World War II.[41]

While some Natives continued to sell their wares directly to tourists, the postwar period witnessed the emergence of several large shops selling tourist goods. In Sitka the Native street market still dominated the trade, but most of the other southeastern ports sported several curio stores by the mid-1920s. The Nugget Shop and Winter & Pond's in Juneau; Pruell's and Billingsley's in Ketchikan; and Kirmse's, Keller's, and Richter's in Skagway all consistently advertised to tourists.[42] Each depended on tourists for much of their income.

Curio shops developed and prospered because they attracted customers too timid to haggle with Natives, and because they offered a retreat from the capricious Alaskan weather. Furthermore, they retailed Native crafts from various regions of Alaska, and not simply the locally manufactured handicrafts offered by Native curio sellers. E. H. Richter in Skagway, for example, sold such diverse items as silver and copper spoons, moccasins, beads, bracelets, wood totem poles, along with cribbage boards, paper knives, and paper weights made from mastodon ivory. Pruell's Gift Shop in Ketchikan went even farther afield for its goods. It stocked slate totems from British Columbia's Queen Charlotte Islands as well as Attu baskets, Alaskan carved ivory, Tlingit and Haida baskets, and Chilkat blankets.[43]

Curio shops were also successful because they sold items not made by Natives. Native vendors were limited to selling traditional handicrafts such as baskets, wood and bone carvings, beads, and fur clothing. The curio shops sold more diverse merchandise. In Juneau, the Nugget Shop advertised nugget jewelry, pictures, and postcards. Kirmse's curio store in Skagway sold polar bear rugs, Alaskan views, books, and postcards. Both shops also sold a variety of Native handicrafts.[44]

The growing trade in Native handicrafts fostered by the curio shops provided expanding opportunities for Natives, including those off the major tourist routes. By the 1920s artisans in several Eskimo communities, as well as in Tlingit villages away from the steamer lines, created curios. In the late 1930s a government study indicated that over a score of settlements, mostly Eskimo, supported themselves to some extent through the creation of these goods.[45]

Unfortunately for Alaska's Native cultures, the manufacture of items for the tourist trade required conformance to the demands of visitors. To satisfy their market, Natives created items that bore little relation to the traditional objects that were expressions of their life style. In the process they found themselves in a very uncomfortable position. It became emotionally difficult for Natives to "carve and paint for grumbling, patronizing white people," but many had little economic alternative.[46]

Instead of traditional Native goods, tourists wanted items which were either useful within the context of white society or symbolically Alaskan. In the first category were the salt shakers, ash trays, cribbage boards, gavels, paper weights, rings, and umbrella handles that King Island Eskimos fashioned from walrus tusks and fossil ivory, and the book ends, lamps, and candlesticks produced by Natives at Yakutat.[47]

More destructive may have been the move to symbolic art. This included the predecessors of those post-World War II creations which anthropologist Dorothy Jean Ray condemned as "a decoction of all the worst seals on an ice cake, howling and hard-working sled dogs, half-drowned walruses, and staring polar bears...in a word, 'Eskimoland'."[48] The demand for symbolic art considerably narrowed the range of traditional objects created by Native artists. Thus the tourists unwittingly helped dilute a culture they purported to admire.[49]

Tourists sometimes went to the extreme in their craving for symbolic art and popularized items supposedly related to Native culture that in reality were invented by whites. One example of this was the Anaktuvuk mask, which passed as a Native ceremonial object, but which was never used by the Native groups which produced them. Better known was the billiken. Although Alaska Natives often manufactured them, this good luck charm was designed outside of the territory and introduced to Alaska about 1910 by Florence Pretz, a Missouri school teacher.[50]

Another unfortunate, if inevitable, consequence of tourism was the emergence of cheap, mass-produced curios. These appeared in the 1920s and 1930s and often served in advertisements to entice customers into stores. For example, a Ketchikan store sold walrus teeth, medicine men charms, and "Native" baskets for a dollar or less apiece. A Cordova curio shop advertised "Indian" moccasins that sold for between fifty-eight cents and a dollar per pair, and another merchant gave away a free "souvenir Alaska husky sled dog" to lady travelers.[51]

These items, which were produced by non-Native companies, angered those involved in the legitimate curio trade. Owners of shops that sold genuine Native products scoffed at such goods, and tourist publications repeatedly warned against "Native" products made in Connecticut or Japan. In the late 1930s, merchants instituted reforms. Most shop owners agreed to segregate mass-produced curios from those made by Natives. Also, they adopted a legal trademark to distinguish Native-made articles, but it is uncertain how effective these reforms were.[52]

By the late 1930s the Alaskan tourist industry was clearly important to the territorial economy. Owners and employees of many hostelries, eating houses, transportation companies, and curio shops depended heavily on the patronage of visitors to the north. Many Alaska Natives supplemented their income by selling their handicrafts. One observer declared in 1939 that "the revenue derived from the [tourist] industry contributes immensely to the business and income of the people of the territory." The flow of visitors and their money remained at a high level through the 1941 season; then, because of the wartime emergency, casual travelers were prohibited from coming to Alaska. However, the war brought changes which caused territorial boosters to see a booming future for the industry once peace returned. In 1945 Governor Ernest Gruening spoke for many Alaskans when he predicted that tourism would some day be bigger than the fifty million dollar salmon business.[53]

His vision proved prophetic. After the war, tourism claimed three important advantages it lacked before hostilities began: commercial air travel to and from the territory, a highway link to the outside world, and governmental support through the Alaska Development Board. As a result, the industry grew quickly. It has been so successful that the number of annual visitors now exceeds the state's population and nets more than half a billion dollars and nine thousand jobs for Alaskans.[54] The industry, which was born soon after America took possession of Alaska, matured dramatically in the 1920s, and is today a healthy, consistently growing industry in a state marked by an inconsistent economy.

ENDNOTES

[1]Robert DeArmond, interview with author, Juneau, 13 March 1987; C. L. Andrews, *The Story of Alaska* (Caldwell, Idaho: Caxton Printers, 1940), 167; Ted C. Hinckley, "The Inside Passage: A Popular Gilded Age Tour," *Pacific Northwest Quarterly* 56 (April 1965): 69-71.

This article is based on research funded by the Alaska Historical Commission. Some of its findings earlier appeared in a report for the Commission entitled "Gawking at the Midnight Sun: The Tourist in Early Alaska" (1985).

[2]Dave Bohn, *Glacier Bay, The Land and the Silence* (Anchorage: Alaska National Parks and Monuments Association, 1967), 73-76.

[3]*Skaguay Alaskan*, 25 July 1898, 26 August 1898.

[4]Art Downs, *Paddlewheels on the Frontier* (Sidney, B.C.: Gray's Publishing Co., 1972), 148; "Route Earnings" 1916, 1921-1938, Folder IV-1, White Pass and Yukon Route Collection, Yukon Archives, Whitehorse; WP&YR Traffic Department, *What Travelers Say About the Trip to Alaska and the Klondike* [1907].

[5]Mrs. James Edwin Morris, *A Pacific Coast Vacation* (London: Abbey Press, 1901), 113; Charles M. Taylor, Jr., *Touring Alaska and the Yellowstone* (Philadelphia: George W. Jacobs and Co., 1901), 269; Karl Baedeker, *The Dominion of Canada, with Newfoundland and an Excursion to Alaska* (Leipzig: the author, 1907), 305; *Skagway Alaskan*, 20 July 1908.

[6]WP&YR, *What Travelers Say*.

[7]Morris, *A Pacific Coast Vacation*, 113; Taylor, *Touring Alaska*, 269; Baedeker, *The Dominion of Canada*, 305.

[8]Hinckley, "The Inside Passage," 70; "Soapy Smith's Skull: An Ironic Monument to the Two-Gun Tyrant," *Literary Digest*, 3 September 1927, 38.

[9]Caroline Sheldon, "The Puget Sound and Alaska," *Chautauquan* 51 (July 1908): 187; Myrth Benjamin Sarvela, "Blarney Stone at Sitka," in *The Alaska Book: The Story of Our Northern Treasureland* (Chicago: J. G. Ferguson, 1960), 103; Walter J. Stalder to Governor John W. Troy, 18 August 1937, Records of the Office of Territorial Governors, Record Group 101 (hereafter cited as Governors' Papers), Box 543, Folder 64-2, Alaska State Archives; Taylor, *Touring Alaska*, 174; Lloyd W. MacDowell, *The Totem Poles of Alaska and Indian Mythology*

(Seattle: Alaska Steamship Co., 1905); H. P. Corser, *Totem Lore and the Land of the Totem*, 8th ed. (Juneau: Nugget Shop, [1928]), 73.

[10]Taylor, *Touring Alaska*, 251, 257; R. W. W. Cryan, "Diary Jottings in Alaska," *Westminster Review* 153 (May 1900): 564; Morris, *A Pacific Coast Vacation*, 60-63.

[11]Hinckley, "The Inside Passage," 69-73; R. L. Polk, *Polk's Alaska-Yukon Directory and Gazetteer*, editions for 1902, 1905-1906, 1909-1910, and 1917-1918.

[12]Pacific Coast Steamship Co., *Alaska Via the Totem Pole Route, 1906 Excursions*; Pacific Coast Steamship Co., "Passenger List of the *Spokane*, July 7, 1903," Pacific Coast Steamship Collection, MS 68, Alaska Historical Library, Juneau; Alaska Club, *Alaska Club Almanac* (1907), 59; Merle Colby, *A Guide to Alaska* (New York: Macmillan, 1939), lv; Earl S. Pomeroy, *In Search of the Golden West: The Tourist in Western America* (New York: Knopf, 1957), 57-58; Baedeker, *The Dominion of Canada*, 295.

[13]Hinckley, "The Inside Passage," 71.

[14]C. L. Andrews, *The Story of Sitka* (Seattle: Lowman and Hanford, 1922), 93; Alaska Club, *Alaska Club Almanac* (Seattle: Harrison Publishing Co., 1909).

[15]Taylor, *Touring Alaska*, 180, 188, 268-69; Andrews, *The Story of Sitka*, 93; Si Dennis, Sr., interview with author, Skagway, 5 March 1985; Morris, *A Pacific Coast Vacation*, 91; John Muir, *Travels in Alaska* (Boston: Houghton Mifflin, 1915), 293; Florence E. Nowell, "The Alaska That Was," *Overland*, May 1920, 396.

[16]Taylor, *Touring Alaska*, 147, 157; Baedeker, *The Dominion of Canada*, 299; Morris, *A Pacific Coast Vacation*, 91-92; Sheldon, "The Puget Sound and Alaska," 190.

[17]Cryan, "Diary Jottings in Alaska," 564; Muir, *Travels in Alaska*, 276.

[18]Lloyd W. MacDowell, *Alaska Indian Basketry* (Seattle: Alaska Steamship Co., 1905), 3-4; William H. Goetzmann and Kay Sloan, *Looking Far North: The Harriman Expedition to Alaska, 1899* (New York: Viking Press, 1982), 87; *Alaska and the Midnight Sun* (Boston: Raymond-Whitcomb Tours, 1917), 12; Taylor, *Touring Alaska*, 247-48.

[19]Mrs. Maria L. Ferguson, *Dawson City, Yukon Territory and Alaska Directory and Gazetteer* (n.p., 1901); R. L. Polk, *Polk's Alaska-Yukon Business Directory* (Seattle: R. L. Polk Inc,, 1903); Alaska Club, *Alaska Club Almanac* (Seattle: Harrison Publishing Co., 1905); Cryan, "Diary Jottings in Alaska," 559; John Scudder McLain, *Alaska and the Klondike* (New York: McClure, Phillips and Co., 1905), 130; Edith Newman Plaut, "Arctic Cruise," *Alaska Sportsman*, February 1935, 16; Taylor, *Touring Alaska*, 172-73.

Business directories are poor indicators of the number of curio shops, particularly before the 1920s. Although diaries and other travel accounts suggest that a score or more curio shops may have existed in the 1900-1910 period, none of the above directories list more than three in Alaska. This discrepancy exists because most shops which sold tourist goods gained year-round revenues from sales of other commodities.

[20]WP&YR, "Superintendent's Annual Report on Operations," of 1909, 1915, 1917, and 1921, Folder II-1, WP&YR Collection; Leslie Cole, "Ben-My-Chree, A Garden in the Wilderness," *The Beaver* 315 (Spring 1984): 43-47. The Midnight Sun Express ran to 1920; the Ben-My-Chree trips proved a long-term

success, operating until 1955.

[21]WP&YR, "Route Earnings," 1915, 1921-1938, Folder IV-1, WP&YR Collection.

[22]WP&YR, "Route Earnings," 1921, 1927, Folder IV-1 and WP&YR, "Superintendent's Reports," Folder II-1, WP&YR Collection.

[23]Col. Claude Cane, *Summer and Fall in Western Alaska* (London: Horace Cox, 1903), 13; Ella Higginson, "Alaska, the Dream-Voyage" *Alaska-Yukon Magazine*, September 1906, 15; Copper River Railway, *Finding of an Empire* (1909): 1.

[24]Numerous contemporary listings and brochures detail the main tour routes. Examples are Alaska Railroad, *Alaska* (1927), 9-23; "Let's Pack Up and Go," *Literary Digest*, 2 June 1928, 68-70; and Alaska Steamship Co., "Alaska Excursion Bulletin," versions of 1910-1917.

[25]Alaska Railroad, "Annual Report" for fiscal years 1925, 1927, and 1928, Records of the Alaska Railroad, Record Group 322, Boxes 15-17, Federal Archives and Records Center, Seattle; Richardson Highway Transportation Co., *Summer Schedule* (1930); Alaska Railroad, *See Alaska Via the Alaska Railroad* (1930).

[26]Alaska Railroad, *See Alaska Via the Alaska Railroad*, 6; Alaska Steamship Co., *Alaska* (1926), 1-9. The development of these routes is described in Alaska Railroad, "Information for 1924 Fiscal Year Report," 5, Box 15, RG 322, Alaska Railroad Collection, and William H. Wilson, *Railroad in the Clouds: The Alaska Railroad in the Age of Steam, 1914-1945* (Boulder, Colorado: Pruett Publishing Company, 1977), 84.

[27]WP&YR, "Superintendent's Report," 1916 and 1937; "Cruising to Skagway," *House Beautiful*, March 1939, 130-31; Lucille Elsner, interview with author, Skagway, 15 June 1985.

[28]Alaska Club, *Alaska Club Almanac* (1905), 6; Harold Griffin, *Alaska and the Canadian Northwest, Our New Frontier* (New York: W. W. Norton, 1944), 132; Sunny Joyce, "Alaska is Different," *Alaska Sportsman*, August 1938, 9; Sherman Rogers, "Alaska the Misunderstood," *Outlook*, 6 December 1922, 609; Canadian National Railway, *Alaska* [1926]; W. M. Dynes, *Dynes' Tours of Alaska* (Juneau: Dynes' Alaska Directory Co., 1921), 119. Cordova, which was also a transfer point, did not have a tourist hotel; passengers transferred directly between steamship and train. Grace A. Hill, "Along the Alaska Coast," *Overland Monthly*, September 1917, 220-21.

[29]Richardson Highway Transportation Co., *Summer Schedule* (1930); Alaska Railroad, *Annual Report*, 1925, 11, Box 15, RG 322, Alaska Railroad Collection. Before World War II, the shortage of hotels was an intermittent problem. It became acute after 1945, and was solved only when large tour arrangers constructed hotels for package tour patrons. Herb and Miriam Hilscher, *Alaska, U.S.A.* (Boston: Little, Brown and Co., 1959), 155-66; Charles B. West, *Mr. Alaska: The Chuck West Story* (Seattle: Weslee Publishing Company, 1985), 54-59.

[30]Leta Sisley, "We Went to Alaska," *Sunset*, January 1930, 14-15; Anna True (former waitress at Bennett), interview with author, Skagway, 17 March 1985.

[31]Nellie Wright Allen, *Alaska! The Great Country* [1925]; Colby, *A Guide to Alaska*, xxii.

[32]Howard Clifford, *The Skagway Story* (Anchorage: Alaska Northwest, 1975), 60; Fred Ordway, "Up the Mighty Yukon," *Alaska Sportsman*, April 1938, 20.

[33]"Special Tourist Supplement," *Alaska Sportsman*, July 1936, 14-A;

Alaska Railroad, "Annual Report," 1927; Colby, *A Guide to Alaska*, 168, 199; Dynes, *Dynes' Tours of Alaska*, 135; Advertisement, *Alaska Sportsman*, April 1936, 25.

[34]Skagway Commercial Club, stationery, [1910], Trail of '98 Museum, Skagway; Juneau Commercial Association, *Juneau, Alaska: Capital of the Territory* [1921], in Box 666, Folder 17, Governors' Papers; Alaska Territorial Chamber of Commerce, *Glimpses of Alaska As It Was and As It Is*, editions of 1935 and 1937; *Alaska Sportsman*, November 1937, 15.

[35]Alaska Planning Council, *General Information Regarding Alaska* (Juneau, 1941), 72-73; *Alaska: The Richardson Road, Valdez to Fairbanks* (1922), 2; Dynes, *Dynes' Tours of Alaska*, 55.

[36]Dorothy Irving Mead, "Hang Your Hat on a Totem Pole," *Sunset*, April 1930, 22; Dynes, *Dynes' Tours of Alaska*, 15; *Alaska Sportsman*, July 1937, 42; Lois Allen, "He Takes 'Em For a Ride," *Alaska Sportsman*, September 1940, 14-15, 22-27.

[37]Dynes, *Dynes' Tours of Alaska*, 36; Rand McNally, *Guide to Alaska and Yukon for Tourists, Investors, Homeseekers and Sportsmen* (New York, 1922), 106.

[38]Griffin, *Alaska and the Canadian Northwest*, 132; Mrs. George Diack, diary, Klondike Gold Rush National Historical Park Collection, Skagway; Colby, *A Guide to Alaska*, 200.

[39]Criswell Travel Service, *Alaska* (1929), 50-51.

[40]Alaska Historical Library and Museum, *Biennial Report of Progress and Condition*, 1937-38; Interview, author with George Rapuzzi, Skagway, 13 March 1986; Catherine H. Blee, Robert L. Spude, and Paul C. Cloyd, *Historic Structure Reports for Ten Buildings* (Denver: National Park Service, 1984), 180, 370; James Warner Bellah, "Alaska," in *Holiday Magazine's American norama* (Garden City, N.Y.: Doubleday and Co., 1960), 12; Agnes Rush Burr, *Alaska, Our Beautiful Northland of Opportunity* (Boston: Page and Co., 1919), 223. Skagway's play, which has since been rewritten many times, recently celebrated its sixty-second season.

[41]*Alaska: The Richardson Road*, 2, 11; Alaska Club, *Alaska Club Almanac* (1909), 71; Colby, *A Guide to Alaska*, 205; "Special Tourist Supplement," *Alaska Sportsman*, July 1936, 14A-B; Alaska Dispatch, *Alaska, The Golden Empire*, Golden Spike Edition, 1922.

[42]Barrett Willoughby, "The Passing Alaskan," *Sunset*, May 1926, 27-28; R. L. Polk, *Polk's Alaska-Yukon Directory and Gazetteer*, editions of 1920-21 and 1923-24; Alaska Directory Co., *Alaska Directory and Gazetteer*, editions of 1932-33 and 1934-35.

[43]Dynes' Alaska Directory Co., *Southeastern Alaska Directory* (Juneau, 1921), 127; Pruell's Gift Shop, *Alaska the Wonderland, A Guide to Ketchikan* [1935].

[44]Ernest F. Hall, *Under the Northern Lights* (Denver, 1932), 19; Willoughby, "The Passing Alaskan," 27-28; Dynes' Alaska Directory Co., *Southeastern Alaska Directory*, 66, 126.

[45]Edward L. Keithahn, *Alaska for the Curious* (Seattle: Superior Publishing Co., 1966), 119; Morris, *A Pacific Coast Vacation*, 59; U.S. House of Representatives, Subcommittee on Indian Affairs of the Committee on Public Lands, *Compilation of Material Relating to the Indians of the United States and the Territory of Alaska, Including Certain Laws and Treaties Affecting Such Indians*

(Washington, D.C., GPO, 1950), 900-1032, *passim*; McLain, *Alaska and the Klondike*, 246; Colby, *A Guide to Alaska*, 343.

[46]Willoughby, "The Passing Alaskan," 27-29.

[47]Colby, *A Guide to Alaska*, 385; Northwestern Alaska Chamber of Commerce, *Information Concerning Nome*, 8; Lona E. Morlander, "Steamboat Round the Bend!" *Alaska Sportsman*, March 1938, 6.

[48]Saradell Ard Frederick, "Alaska Eskimo Art Today," *Alaska Journal* 2 (Autumn 1972): 31.

[49]Goetzmann and Sloan, *Looking Far North*, 86.

[50]Keithahn, *Alaska for the Curious*, 22; Frederick, "Alaska Eskimo Art Today," 30.

[51]*The Alaska Pioneer*, May 1912, 1; "Special Tourist Supplement," *Alaska Sportsman*, July 1936, 14-B; Advertisement, *Alaska Sportsman*, August 1937, 23.

[52]Baedeker, *The Dominion of Canada*, 296; Sheldon, "The Puget Sound and Alaska," 187; Colby, *A Guide to Alaska*, xxxiv-xxxv; V. R. Farrell, "Native Goods Now Go To Market," *Alaska Life*, May 1938, 9.

[53]Marguerite Shaw Pilgrim, *Alaska, Its History, Resources, Geography and Government* (Caldwell, Idaho: Caxton Printers, 1939), 247-50; B. W. Denison, *Alaska Today* (Caldwell, Idaho: Caxton Printers, 1950), 127.

[54]Alaska, Division of Tourism, *Alaska Traveler Survey and Visitor Industry Analysis 1983: Overview*, 1-4.

RACISM, INDIANS AND TERRITORIAL POLITICS*

Stephen W. Haycox

During the 1920s the Tlingits of southeastern Alaska became the first Alaskan Native group to participate actively in territorial politics. The Alaska Native Brotherhood (ANB) had been organized in 1912 and the Sisterhood in 1915 to promote equal rights for Natives, mutual aid, and assimilation. In 1920 the Tlingit attorney, William L. Paul, Sr., began to channel the ANB's energy into politics. He developed a large enough political base to win election to the territorial House of Representatives in 1924 and 1926, becoming the first Alaskan Native to serve in the territorial legislature.

Prejudice flourished throughout white, middle class America during the 1920s, a result of the "100% Americanism" campaign of World War I and of the postwar Red Scare, characterized by anti-labor, anti-radical, and anti-immigrant sentiments. Anyone outside the mainstream was suspect. Alaska proved no exception to this trend, and Paul's political power provoked an anti-Native backlash.

Professor Stephen Haycox, a member of the history faculty at the University of Alaska at Anchorage, has worked extensively with the records of Alaska Native history and contemporary Native issues. His article "Sheldon Jackson in Historical Perspective: Alaska Native Schools and Mission Contracts, 1885-1894," appeared in *Pacific Historian,* Spring 1984, and his "'Races of a Questionable Ethnical Type': Origins of the Jurisdiction of the U. S. Bureau of Education in Alaska, 1867-1885" in *Pacific Northwest Quarterly* in October 1984. In 1988 he published *A Warm Past: Travels in Alaska History*. He is currently writing a history of the Alaska Native Brotherhood and federal Indian policy in Alaska before statehood.

In the following article, Haycox examines William Paul's political activities in the early 1920s. He describes the efforts of Paul's opponents to pass a territorial law requiring a literacy test for voters, and he concludes that Paul's opponents, racially motivated, hoped to use the literacy test to eliminate his political base.

* * *

In April 1925 the seventh Alaska Territorial Legislature enacted into law a measure requiring that voters in territorial elections be able to read and write the English language. Amended to meet significant

---

*This article originally appeared in *Alaska History* 2, no. 1 (Winter 1986): 17-37.

objections raised during legislative debate, the bill passed the House by a vote of 14-2 and cleared the Senate unanimously.[1] Passed after World War I in a period when racism and segregation became increasingly regimented throughout the United States, Alaska's literacy law clearly was consistent with a growing willingness on the part of white Americans to enact into law restrictions on the movement and civil participation of non-whites, including Indians as well as blacks. Restrictive legislation in the continental states often was a direct response to the growing political power and social mobility of these minorities, and was based on assumptions of racial inferiority, as well as a desire to maintain a social stability which accepted a subordinate role for minorities. That the same assumptions which obtained nationally also had come to Alaska seems manifest in the debate among politicians and publicists in the territory over whether or not to adopt the Alaska literacy law.

Literacy laws were a common device used by states to limit the opportunity to vote, and in 1925 such statutes were in effect in twenty states. Most of these were in the South and functioned to discourage voting by blacks. The measures have been interpreted as racist in character since the single criteria which seems to have attended their use was skin color, not educational attainment. In addition to the South, several western states had literacy laws. Since some of these western states also had significant Indian populations, Arizona and Washington for example, it may reasonably be asked whether the presence of literacy qualifications in these states was aimed at disenfranchisement of the minority Native population. A search of relevant sources and secondary literature does not yield a conclusive answer to this question, and no scholar seems yet to have reviewed the enactment and implementation of such laws with this question in mind. Certainly there is much evidence to suggest that assumptions of the cultural or racial inferiority of Indians prevailed in western states in the early twentieth century, including the belief in the inability of Indians to understand the subtleties of electoral politics. But with advancing educational standards in the United States after the turn of the century, literacy increasingly became a consideration in voting. And without direct evidence, it is difficult to establish that the intent of literacy acts was specifically to disenfranchise Indians. As a western and northern territory, Alaska also had a significant minority Native population, and it is reasonable to inquire into the circumstances of its adoption of a literacy act in 1925. Alaska had a tradition of liberality in regard to voting and other civic affairs, so it might be inferred that the primary purpose of the Alaska law was to ensure understanding of the electoral process. But this inference is only partially true, for while there was a great deal of rhetoric concerning understanding and education associated with the debate and passage of the Alaska measure, it is clear also that the measure was directed at one man, and at the disenfranchisement of voters he represented. Further, it is clear from the debate and commentary attendent upon the proposals for such an act that in some measure it was racially motivated. The man at whom the Alaska literacy act was aimed was the Tlingit Indian leader William Lewis Paul, who emerged in the early 1920s as a major force in Alaskan politics. The people he represented were the Tlingit and Haida Indians of southeast Alaska.[2]

Born of part-Indian parents in the southeast Alaska Indian village of Tongass in 1885, William Paul had gained an education at the Sheldon Jackson Presbyterian mission school at Sitka and later at the Carlisle Indian School in Pennsylvania, as well as at Banks Business College in Philadelphia and Whitworth College in Spokane. By the time he returned to Alaska in 1920, he had also earned a law degree through the LaSalle University extension program. He was an able orator and an articulate spokesman for the causes which attracted his attention. These included Native rights, and territorial politics.[3]

From the beginning of his political career Paul allied himself with the colorful Progressive Republican James Wickersham, who had served as territorial delegate from 1908 to 1920, and who was the major force in Alaskan electoral politics. Wickersham, who was not allied with the national or territorial leadership and organization of either the Democrat or Republican party, was a political maverick who succeeded through the force of his personality, and his insistence that Alaskans maintain as much independence as possible from the traditional parties. His proteg[e] and successor was Alaska miner and fisherman Dan Sutherland who served in the same post from 1921 to 1930. Both Wickersham and Sutherland were sensitive to Indian rights. So influential was Wickersham in the territory that most politicians and newspaper editors aligned either for or against him, and throughout the 1920s Sutherland and Paul usually were identified in editorial comment as leaders of the "Wickite" faction.[4]

Paul first attracted territorial attention at the eighth annual convention of the Alaska Native Brotherhood, a fraternal Native self-help organization founded at Sitka under the auspices of the Presbyterian church in 1912. Its goal prior to 1920 had been civilization through assimilation. At the 1920 convention of the ANB, held at Wrangell, William Paul and his brother Louis began to politicize the organization, and from then on it became a major political force for Native rights in Alaska politics. The Pauls' leadership, particularly that of William, lasted over a decade and a half.[5]

The issue the Pauls chose to pursue was the admission of Indian children to white schools. Education in the territory had been segregated from its beginnings in the 1880s, and the refusal of white schools to admit even assimilated Indian children had been an Indian complaint since 1906. In language clearly reflecting William Paul's influence, the 1920 convention adopted a resolution instructing ANB officials to "carry the matter forward to the federal courts as a test case" if necessary to achieve satisfaction. Sometime afterward the Pauls met with Charles Hawkesworth, head of Indian schools in Alaska, to present their demands. Hawkesworth was favorably disposed toward the Indian position, and after the meeting he announced the closing of the Indian school at Wrangell, William Paul's home town, for the following school year, 1921-1922. The effect of the closing would be to force Indian children into the white school at Wrangell, if they were to be taught at all.[6] White leaders in southeast Alaska, where most of the territory's assimilated Indians resided, expressed adamant opposition to the plan, and Hawkesworth later announced that the Indian school would stay open. But William Paul had made his mark. His insistence on equal rights for the Indians of southeast Alaska would be a factor in the region's future affairs.[7]

It is likely that Paul next set about organizing the Indians of Southeast into an effective political force. Indians had voted in elections in Alaska from the beginning of electoral politics, although there was some question over the legality of their so doing. The question of Indian citizenship was somewhat unclear, but the federal district attorney at Juneau had ruled in 1918 that even those Indians who had not qualified under the terms of the territorial citizenship act were citizens nonetheless and could vote if "living in accordance with the customs of civilization." Analysis of election returns from 1918 to 1926 for the First Division, which encompassed southeast Alaska, shows a significant increase in the number of votes from Indian villages starting in 1922, a greater percentage increase in votes than that recorded in the white towns. Additionally, there was an increase in the number of Indian villages where votes were recorded. Election judges in Indian villages were often themselves Indians, and it is likely that as a general practice, those Indians who wanted to vote, or were encouraged to do so, did so at will.[8]

Paul likely took advantage of this situation to weld together a dependable political machine for the Wickites. In later years he would admit that he provided guidance for Indian voters. His position as an officer of ANB would have taken him to the various Indian villages of southeast Alaska, and it would have been natural to use that opportunity to advise Natives on their rights, and on which candidates were most likely to be helpful in pursuing them. As an Indian, Paul enjoyed high credibility. His ability to meet with white leaders on their own terms because of his education and acumen doubtless enhanced his stature among many Indians. And with Wickersham's blessing, he commanded a significant following among white Progressive Republicans.[9]

Most of the Indians in southeast Alaska, however, still were illiterate. Perhaps Paul's most controversial act was to organize illiterate voters as well as literate ones, a fact which probably helps to explain the increase in Indian voting statistics. To ensure that Southeast Natives would know how to vote, as well as whom to vote for, Paul prepared sample ballots and cardboard cutouts which would cover all but the appropriate boxes when placed on the actual ballot. By placing an "X" in the squares showing through the cutouts, illiterate Indians could be sure of voting for Paul's choices. Most Indian votes in the 1922 election went for Sutherland, though just how many Indian votes there were would be a matter of continuing dispute. Opponents would argue that Paul controlled at least one thousand illiterate Indian votes; his supporters would argue that the number was only a few hundred.[10]

Directed voting by illiterate voters at the hands of an able and ambitious politician was offensive to a culture schooled in the notions of self-determination and free choice. It would have been problematical under any circumstances. At the hands of an Indian leader in a period when Americans still relied upon legal segregation in many places, and when many Indians still were not assimilated, it was intolerable to many whites. Political opponents of William Paul came to fear him greatly, for he represented the potential to control the outcome of any election in which his influence might be used. Beginning in 1922 the Paul "ticket" in southeast Alaska occupied the attention of newspaper editors and commentators like no other factor in election campaigns. It is understandable that many voters, whether or not opponents of Paul and the Wickites, would have found Paul's willingness to instruct illiterate voters morally reprehensible in the context of American ideals of freedom and individualism.

William Paul may not have been the first to use the device of ballot cutouts. In 1916 and 1918 Wickersham had contested the results of the delegate election between himself and Charles Sulzer, and Congressional committees had resolved the disputes after investigation, both times in favor of Wickersham. Charges were made in both disputes that large numbers of illiterate Indian votes had been organized for one or another of the opponents. But in both elections Congress had decided the result on other grounds, determining that the Indian vote had not been a significant factor in the outcome. The record is not clear on the point of who first utilized "cutouts" in these elections. Wickersham at one point charged that Sulzer had used them, and later, anti-Wickites would imply they had been used against Wickersham. But whether or not Paul was the first to use the device, his use of it clearly was more visible and effective than ever before.[11]

In the face of Paul's audacity, political leaders in Alaska looked for a way to counteract Paul's organizing efforts. Who first proposed the idea of a literacy law to stop bloc voting by illiterate Indians does not seem to be a matter of record. The measure was first debated, however, in the 1923 legislature, where it became one of the primary issues of the session. It would remain a major, divisive issue in Alaska politics for the next three years. Rep. Frank H. Foster, an anti-Wickersham Republican lawyer from Cordova, introduced the literacy bill in the legislature. The bill may have come as something of a surprise to many of the sixteen representatives and eight senators from Alaska's four election districts (the First in Southeast, the Second around Nome, the Third in southcentral Alaska, and the Fourth including Fairbanks and the Interior). At the start of the sixty-day biennial session the major newspaper in Juneau, the anti-Wickersham *Alaska Daily Empire*, predicted that roads, old age pensions, and aid for the territorial college and for schools would be the biggest issues. There was a hint of what might lie ahead, however, in Governor Scott Bone's address to the legislators. Though a Republican, Bone was often the object of Wickite attacks on the principle of federal control of Alaska. Although Bone declared that the territorial school system "will be wisely safeguarded," probably a reference to Paul's attempt to force white schools to educate Indian children, Bone urged that there be no change in the territory's election laws.[12]

But before the 1923 session was a week old, Foster had introduced his bill in the House. It provided simply that "no person who is unable to read the Constitution of the U.S. and to write the

English language shall be eligible to vote." The bill received quick consideration in the committee on elections, perhaps in an attempt to forestall extended debate. The committee reported the bill adversely. However, Rep. H. Royal Shepard of Juneau filed a minority statement, urging upon his colleagues the seriousness of the bill and the situation which called it into being.[13]

Like Foster, Shepard was an anti-Wickersham Republican. Unlike Foster, he had stood for election in William Paul's own district and thus was directly threatened by Paul's political power. In his statement Shepard articulated most of the arguments which would be used to support a literacy law over the next three years in Alaska and in the federal Congress. It was clear from Shepard's remarks that he was more concerned with politics than with the failure of most Natives to be able to read the Constitution. Shepard said that as a class, the Indians of Alaska constituted "practically all the illiterate voting population of the Territory." They numbered about one thousand out of seven or eight thousand votes, and thus, he said, held "the balance of power" in territorial elections. Without mentioning Paul by name, Shepard said it was reprehensible that manipulators held such a balance of power in the electorate and could use the votes of trusting Indians not for the Indians' good, but to support the manipulators' own ambitions. "The Indians, having no vague knowledge of our institutions and government, lend themselves to the machinations of political charlatans." He also claimed erroneously that the "illegality of large numbers of Indian votes" had been the principal question in Wickersham's elections in 1916 and 1918.[14]

Editorial support for Shepard's minority report came quickly from the large circulation, anti-Wickersham, anti-Paul *Daily Empire*. In territorial elections, the editor wrote, some had voted who not only could not read English, but also could not speak it. Voters had "admitted on the witness stand that they knew nothing" of the matters for which they had voted. The best interests of the Indians would be served by their attaining full citizenship, the *Empire* argued, not by being "led to the polls by another person and voted in droves." Other papers followed suit, and it quickly became apparent that the literacy bill would be a major issue of the session.[15]

Full hearings were held on the measure in the House on March 15 and 16, in the second full week of the session, and were well attended. From the start of debate supporters of the literacy measure focused on the issue of race, and charged that William Paul and the

Alaska Native Brotherhood used the Indian vote as their pawn. Rep. Joseph Murray, a mining lawyer from Valdez, argued that the question of whether illiterates should vote "resolves itself into whether or not the Senate and House and the Territory shall remain white." Foster asserted that those who opposed the measure did so for political reasons. William Paul himself appeared in opposition to the bill. He charged that politics motivated the bill's supporters, not its opponents. He admitted that there had been mass voting by Indians. It had taken place, he said, under careful guidance, with "some intelligence." Indians had voted with full knowledge of what they were doing. Rev. David Waggoner, a minister from Juneau, supported that notion in asserting that many of the best Indian thinkers could not read or write, but had provided good leadership. The right to vote, he implied, was the right to vote, unqualified. He might have added that in the history of the republic to that time probably more illiterate people had voted than literate. But Herbert Faulkner, former marshal of Juneau, argued that the right to vote was only the right to vote intelligently, and he praised Rep. Ernest Polley from Juneau who favored the law even though the Indian vote had gone for him in the 1922 election.[16]

Other important considerations were raised during debate on the measure. Rep. Cash Cole questioned the right of the territorial legislature to pass such a bill, implying that only the federal Congress could establish voter qualifications in the territory. One member argued that such illiteracy as existed in the territory was the fault of the federal government anyway, because adequate provision had not been made for the Indians' education. Some members were concerned that regular election judges would determine who qualified under the act and who did not. Election judges were often village residents, but in towns with a mixed population they were usually white people. Rep. Richard Decker, a Methodist minister from Nome who subsequently voted against the bill, offered an amendment calling for school board members and one missionary to make the certification, apparently assuming their judgments would be less susceptible to political or personal prejudice. The amendment was defeated. Tensions likely were high when Foster suggested that those who did not favor the bill were politically motivated. Decker said he greatly resented the implication that opponents of the bill were for "rotten politics."[17]

When the full House voted on the measure on March 17, it passed by a margin of 10 to 6. Eight Republicans, and an Independent and a Democrat voted for it, while two Republicans, three Independents and one Democrat opposed it. Of Alaska's four election districts, representatives from three split their four votes, two and two, including Southeast, where the bill would likely have the greatest impact, and the only region where Paul had organized the Indian vote. On the other hand, the Third Division, Southcentral, which often voted against the Southeast, voted solidly for the measure. It is most likely that in all cases the votes reflected personal views rather than partisan considerations. Personality counted more heavily than party loyalty in Alaskan politics, as Wickersham's career had demonstrated.[18]

Now it was the Senate's turn. Charles W. Brown, Jr., an Independent who lived in Nome in the summers but whose permanent home was actually in Seattle, was chairman of the committee on elections, and opposed the measure. But the Senate held hearings on the bill, and its debate often was conducted on a higher plane than the debate in the House, though emotions occasionally intruded in the upper body as well. In the debate some opponents argued that a literacy bill would be unfair to those many Indians who understood politics, but could not read or write. Fred Ayer, a Nome mining engineer, articulated the prevailing sentiment for assimilation of Natives when he said he was sympathetic to the Indians, but it would be good for them to learn English, and the literacy measure might force them to do so. Besides, even if William Paul voted them intelligently, as he claimed, he would die some day, and someone unscrupulous could replace him.[19]

Frank Aldrich, a Progressive Republican from Juneau, argued that the "fish trust" of wealthy absentee investors sought to eliminate the Indian vote because most Indians were fishermen, and voted with white fishermen for higher taxes on the industry, removal of fish traps, and other measures aimed at the industry. This was a common theme in Alaska politics in the 1920s; Delegate Dan Sutherland often charged in Congress that the "fish trust" lay behind the anti-Wickersham forces in the territory. The literacy bill, Aldrich said, was just an attempt to deliver territorial politics "into the hands of men who do not represent the people of the territory."[20]

Aldrich said that he had received a telegram from the Skagway Women's Club in support of the measure, but that he would oppose it anyway, on principle. Ketchikan Republican Forest Hunt said he had received a petition in support of the bill signed by eighty women of his city. E. E. Chamberlin, a Seward Independent, asserted that only one newspaper in the territory opposed the bill, and that on that basis he would support it. Ayer certainly expressed the thrust of editorial opinion when he said in support of the bill, "We do not want to be ruled by an inferior race, nor dominated by an illiterate one." Former territorial senator W. E. Britt argued that the federal government never intended that illiterate Indians should take part in the government of the territory. Anthony Dimond, the Valdez lawyer who later became a territorial delegate, disputed the claim that those unable to read and write still could vote intelligently. He noted there were no words in the Indian languages for the terms "delegate," "representative," "attorney-general," or "senator." The *Daily Empire* had already weighed in with its opinion that should the "citizenship of the Republic fall down on account of ignorance, illiteracy, or failure to comprehend the meaning of the Constitution, the Republic itself would fall." The secret ballot, "self arrived at," the editor argued, is what constitutes self government.[21]

Chamberlin attempted to salvage the bill by providing an amendment that it be held back to see if the United States Congress would enact similar legislation. This would also answer the objection of some witnesses that the territory did not have the authority to set voter qualifications. The amendment failed, perhaps owing to Alaskan resentment at being too much governed by the Congress already. As the vote approached, Rep. Shepard came over from the House to testify, sounding a threatening note when he vowed that Alaska was "white man's country," and warning that the whites would see "that the man who curries favor with the Indian vote by opposing this bill is not again elected," a barb aimed particularly at his first division colleague Aldrich. But John Dunn, an Independent from Ruby, struck a high tone in arguing that the measure was contrary to law, morality, and principle.[22]

When the vote finally was taken the tally was a tie, 4-4. As such, it failed, for to pass in the Senate, a measure needed a majority. As in the House vote, the Third Division members were unanimously in favor of the bill. The First and Second divisions split their votes, and the Fourth was unanimous against the bill. As in the House, party affiliation did not play a major role. It is likely that most legislators who routinely supported the Wickites and their call for more independence for Alaska supported Paul in voting against a literacy bill. But Alaskan politics were intensely personal in the absence of strong party organizations in this period, and many solons prided themselves on the individuality and independence of their political activity. Four members of the 1923 House had been elected as

Independents, as had three of the eight senators. Several others had run as "Non-partisan" candidates.[23]

Failure in the sixth territorial legislature did not quiet supporters of a literacy law. The legislature had made a mistake which will be rectified, predicted the *Daily Empire*. The *Empire* was right. The debate had aroused passions, and the vote had been close enough, just one vote short of passage, that the bill was bound to be an issue in the 1924 election campaign. Two developments combined to ensure that it would. First, in the spring William Paul filed as a candidate for election to the legislature from the First Division. Then, in May, Congress passed the Indian Citizenship Act, making citizens of all aborigines not already so classified. This meant that unless there were state or territorial laws to prevent it, all Indians henceforth would be voters. But in Alaska, a territorial literacy act would prevent a majority of Alaska Natives from voting since most were not literate, an implication not lost on advocates of such a law.[24]

As campaign rhetoric and editorial commentary during the primary in April and the general election in November made clear, Paul's candidacy was itself a test of the issues which underlay the literacy test measure. Paul himself seems to have broadened his platform to include issues which Indians shared in common with whites, most particularly opposition to the creation of federal fish reserves and support for higher taxes on the fishing industry. These were issues which Sutherland also emphasized in his campaign. But the *Empire* and other papers made illiterate voting by Indians the principal debate, as did a number of anti-Wickite candidates.

"A plan is on foot," read a large political ad in the *Empire* in March, "to extend to the Indians of Alaska all the privileges of whites, including the right to sit on juries, to vote irrespective of mental qualifications, and to send their children to the white schools to mingle, regardless of physical condition, with white children." "We do not believe," the ad continued, "that the Indians are yet ready to assume all the duties imposed on whites." Referring to the Wickite faction, the ad stated that an organization existed which was dedicated to enacting into law Indian interests, and that unless those who were opposed "to having Indians in the Legislatures" were also to organize, "the Indians are certain to have the balance of power." Supporting the signatories, who declared themselves in favor of a "law to prevent the mass voting of illiterate Indians," provided voters "an opportunity to keep the Indian in his place." The ad was signed by four anti-

Sutherland Republicans from the First Division, including H. R. Shepard, who had supported the 1923 literacy bill.[25]

The same candidates signed another ad in the *Empire* three weeks later which stated that regulation of Alaska fisheries and "the prevention of corrupt mass voting of illiterate Indians" were the major issues of the campaign. The candidates did not seek office for personal reasons, they asserted, but only "to avert what we believe to be a real danger; for if illiterate Indians control nominations and election of candidates for the legislature, serious trouble is bound to result to all, both white and Indians." Such an overtly racist appeal may have been too stark for many voters, for none of the four survived the primary to run in the November general election.[26]

William Paul, on the other hand, easily survived to run in the November general election, outpolling all but one candidate in a Republican field of thirteen House candidates. Whether this was due primarily to "mass" voting, or his support of Wickersham and Sutherland, or to other factors, is not possible to determine. Certainly the victory was a blow to the *Empire* and a triumph for those who opposed its tendentious condemnation of Indian voting, a campaign whose racist overtones were all but inescapable. Indians, clearly, had not been intimidated.[27]

Paul's victory in the primary exacerbated the already high level of tension in the territory resulting from the literacy issue, a tension clearly manifested in commentary and editorials when the general election campaign began. "If racial feeling should develop between whites and Indians in Alaska," the *Empire* asserted in early October, "the responsibility for it will lie with those who are giving the Indians either vicious or foolish advice...If those who are trying to rush the Indians to the polls in masses, literate and illiterate, to vote in a bloc, as Indians, have their way they will create a chasm between the races in Alaska that will...make this either a white man's country or an Indian's country for many years to come." Apparently the editor of the paper could not imagine a climate in which whites and Indians functioned as equal partners, "literate or illiterate."[28]

In the election campaign Sutherland supported William Paul and opposed the literacy law. Speaking in Cordova, Sutherland suggested that an educational qualification for voting might be unconstitutional. The most he could accept, he said, was a provision that voters be able to read the names on the ballot. At Ketchikan he said it would be "outrageous" to require that anyone be able to read the Constitution, and he sounded a note that would become increasingly important in the debate. "No one who has ever exercised the right of suffrage," he said, "should be denied that right today." On the other hand, Sutherland's opponent for delegate, Frank A. Boyle, a Juneau Democrat, charged that Sutherland was responsible for the "menace" of mass voting of illiterate Indians because he failed either to introduce federal legislation that would have prevented it or to oppose the Indian Citizenship Act, which encouraged it.[29]

"Menace" was a word which fired the imagination. Under the title "The Menace of Mr. Paul," the *Empire* charged that with his massed illiterate voters Paul would be able to force the legislature to impose ruinous taxes on the fishing industry, thereby bringing unemployment and depopulation in the territory. On the eve of the November election the paper told its readers: "Literacy Test Is Main Issue Before Voters." And in his final campaign ad, Boyle urged voters to "Keep Alaska and Its Schools Free From Indian Control." "The establishment of a Literacy Test for voters," he said, was the big issue in the election. Without such a law, "the Government of the Territory of Alaska, its institutions, its schools, the government of some of its towns, their institutions and the public schools, will inevitably pass into the hands of those controlling the votes of thousands of illiterates."[30]

But again voters rejected the appeal of those who castigated William Paul and Dan Sutherland. In the delegate election, Sutherland handily carried the First Division, 2,798 votes to 1,905 for Frank Boyle of Juneau, his opponent. For the territorial House, Paul received the third highest total, 2,098, behind tallies of 2,384 and 2,173 for the biggest winners. Sutherland's total in the First Division was seven hundred votes more than Paul's, perhaps reflecting voters who, while loyal to the Wickites, could not accept voting for Indians. The certified tally showed that the combined votes of the scattered Indian villages of Southeast, most of which went to Paul, were enough to overcome the leads most white candidates received over Paul in the white towns. The number of ballots cast in most Indian villages in the 1924 election was higher than in 1922. That may have been due to the fact that William Paul was the first Native ever to run for the territorial legislature. It may also have been a result of the Indians' having anticipated Congressional passage of the Indian Citizenship Act, and thus feeling freer to vote. But it is very likely that William Paul, on the ballot for the first time, and on record as favorably disposed toward "mass" voting, continued his assistance to illiterate Indian voters with sample ballots and cardboard cutouts.[31]

Rep. Shepard's prediction that white men would see that those who voted against the literacy measure in 1923 would not be re-elected proved not to be true. Of the six House members who voted against the bill in 1923, only two stood for election in 1925, one for the House, W. Grant of Wrangell, and Cash Cole of Juneau, who ran on a provisional ticket for governor. It was Grant who received the highest vote in the election. Cole also won. In the Senate, only two who voted against the measure were at the end of their four-year terms. Charles Brown of Nome was re-elected, while M. D. Snodgrass moved from Fairbanks to the Matanuska Valley and did not seek re-election.[32]

With Paul's victory the die was cast; now the question of a literacy act would be fought out again in the legislature, and this time the forces favoring it had plenty of time and plenty of ammunition. As the *Empire* essayed as the final results came in, "The Fight Has Just Begun."[33]

As the seventh territorial legislature opened at the beginning of March in 1925 there was considerable speculation over how representatives would line up on the literacy issue. The *Empire* reminded legislators that nearly all newspapers in the territory favored the law, including the *Anchorage Daily Times*, the *Anchorage Alaskan*, and the *Cordova Times*. Governor Bone, who in 1923 had advised no change in territorial election laws, now bowed to public opinion, or to the federally protected "fish trust" if the "Wickites" could be believed, and in his legislative address urged passage of the literacy measure.[34]

The fight was joined on the first day of business. Wickite Republican W. D. Grant of Wrangell attempted to effect a compromise by introducing a bill which would have required voters to be able to read and write, but would have imposed no penalty for violation of the law, and further, would have exempted anyone who had previously voted, a major change from the 1923 bill. Grant's bill was withdrawn, and replaced by a bill introduced by Anchorage Republican Benjamin Grier, which would have prohibited any illiterate from voting. Grier's bill represented the hardliners' position. In a surprise move, however, the House elections committee accepted the idea of exempting from the literacy regulation any persons who had previously voted. Debate would focus on which kind of law to adopt, Grier's proposal exempting no one, or the more liberal, amended version.[35]

Endorsements for the more restrictive bill rolled into Juneau from civic groups throughout southeastern Alaska. The Skagway School Board favored the bill, as did the Ketchikan Commercial Club and the Douglas Women's Club. Virtually every Southeast parent-teachers' association was heard from, favoring the original bill, and every chamber of commerce, likewise.[36]

Although hearings were scheduled in the House, the compromise apparently appealed to the members, for the hearings were preemptorily canceled, and the measure was speedily brought to a vote. Perhaps the legislators sought to avoid the acrimony and dissension which had characterized debate on the issue in 1923. Certainly the matter of previous voters represented at one and the same time both a problem and a solution to the issue. Richard Sundquist, a Republican miner from the Seward Peninsula probably helped push his colleagues toward the compromise measure when he pointed out that any bill prohibiting previous voters from voting again most likely would be declared invalid. In any case, quick action on the bill precluded a repeat of much of the emotional commentary which had been heard during the 1923 debate and the 1924 campaign. Supporters of the bill had little choice but to go along with the substitute measure. It still established a literacy qualification, but it protected the franchise for all who might have voted previously, including whites as well as Indians. For opponents, the compromise was likely the miracle they had been hoping for. Only in southeastern Alaska was the issue a significant one, for only there had large numbers of Natives ever voted. Those whom William Paul had organized had voted both in 1922 and 1924. With them "grandfathered" into the bill, it represented no threat to Paul's power. Yet, at the same time, it satisfied those whose support of the bill was on ideological and moral grounds. The supporters of the bill were trapped.[37]

The amended bill quickly passed the House, 14-2, with only H. H. Ross, a Fairbanks Independent and former Democrat, and Andy Nylen of Nome, also an Independent, dissenting. A practical compromise having been found, the solons easily dispatched the matter. It is likely that Paul was committed to voting for the compromise measure which he would have participated in developing, and a version of which was introduced by his Wickite colleague, Grant. The House having acted, the final clash would again be fought out in the Senate.[38]

The *Empire* fairly fumed. The Senate had yet to act, and if the bill should become law in its amended form, the paper editorialized "it would leave Southeast Alaska little, if any, better off than it is at the present time." It would not bar a single one of the one thousand or more "illiterate Indians who have been led to the ballot boxes and voted as a bloc at the dictation of a master." American Legion posts and their women's auxiliaries immediately protested the amendment, and Lester Henderson, head of territorial schools, wrote that the issue was not a matter of politics, but of "territorial welfare" that the Grier bill be passed in its original, unamended form.[39]

Action in the Senate came quickly. The bill came to the full body within six days of its passage in the House. Apparently the senators were as happy with the resolution of the volatile issue as their House colleagues. On April 18 Senator Dimond introduced an amendment to the House bill which would have eliminated the "grandfather" rights. This was the climactic test, for if the amendment failed, the compromise measure was certain to pass easily. There was apparently little to be said, for the arguments were brief. When the vote was taken four senators went against Dimond's amendment, killing it: Brown, who had been re-elected even though he voted against the 1923 bill, Dunn and Aldrich, who were serving in the second legislature of their four year terms and also had voted against the 1923 bill, and Forrest Hunt of Ketchikan, who had been re-elected and who had voted for the 1923 bill. Ketchikan was a Paul stronghold and Hunt a Paul ally. Voting as Paul did, he too likely felt that the "grandfathered" measure was the best bill obtainable. On April 20 the Senate voted on the House bill. As predicted, it passed unanimously.[40]

Alaska had adopted a literacy law for voters. But for William Paul the result was a significant victory, because the amendment to exempt any previous voter from the law meant that his political base in the villages of southeast Alaska was protected. However many illiterate votes Paul actually had influenced in those villages, a few hundred or over a thousand, the potential to draw upon them again was protected by the amended law.

Many Alaskans, including the anti-Wickersham, anti-Paul press, were unwilling to give up the fight. In an editorial titled "A White Man's Party Is Necessary," published the day after the Senate vote, the *Empire* wrote that the race problem was the "paramount political issue" in southeastern Alaska. The editor linked the issues which had fueled the literacy law debate, arguing that "the large illiterate Indian vote" accounted for a fifth of the First Division electorate, and was "likely to be expanded much beyond that in spite of the literacy test measure." The *Empire* continued that this vote "in the hands of a single ambitious politician as dictator [was] a menace to the Territory," and that it "threatens local municipal and school government in sections of Southeastern Alaska." The *Anchorage Daily Times* wrote the next day that those who voted against the original bill "will find difficulty in convincing their white constituencies that they acted in the best interests of Alaska." Having failed in Alaska, supporters of the measure prepared to take their case to the United States Congress. The Congress could pass legislation for the territories whenever it chose, of course, and literacy supporters hoped to get at the national level the absolute prohibition of illiterate voting that had eluded them at the territorial level.[41]

As he always had, Delegate Sutherland opposed any literacy measure, and could not be prevailed upon to introduce one in Congress. So Alaskan supporters went to Republican Rep. Wallace White of Maine, whose own state had a mild literacy law. Sutherland had been outspoken in his criticism of the administration, particularly of Commerce secretary Herbert Hoover, and Alaskan supporters of a literacy bill doubtless sought to capitalize on growing anti-Progressive sentiment in the Congress. The bill was referred to the House Committee on Territories, chaired by Charles F. Curry of California, well acquainted with Alaskan conditions. Sutherland had worked with Curry on legislation for the territory, and hoped he could persuade Curry to block the bill. But when the committee received endorsements from a large number of Alaskans, including the mayors of Juneau and Anchorage, various chambers of commerce and commercial clubs, American Legion posts, and even the Wrangell City Council, pressure to release the bill was irresistible, particularly considering that a literacy law had passed in the Alaska legislature. After debate, the committee reported out a bill just like the one which had failed in Alaska, an unqualified prohibition of illiterate voting. Sutherland now had the test in the Congress he had sought to avoid.[42]

Rather than contesting the Alaskan supporters of the bill who had written the committee, when the bill came to the House floor, Sutherland mounted a strong attack against its failure to exempt previous voters, as the Alaska law did. On the floor he developed a careful and prolonged review of the laws of the twenty states which had literacy laws, pointing out that seven of them had provisions similar to the Alaska law to protect previous voters. The sponsor's state, Maine, was among these, he reminded the solons, thus making support for the more restrictive measure seem inconsistent. Curry emphasized the same point, saying categorically that he did not wish to see any present voter lose the privilege to vote. Most likely had had considered the constitutionality as well as the sentimental appeal of that argument. Interestingly, James G. Strong of Kansas argued that enforcement of an act protecting previous voters was problematical since voting records were destroyed in Alaska each year. Under such circumstances, it would be impossible to verify who had voted and who had not. In any case, the presentation by Sutherland and Curry was successful, for after direct questions on the point, the full House amended the bill to include the exemption, and in that form it passed easily.[43]

Alaskan supporters of a stronger literacy law did not give up. Once again they sought to ensure passage of an acceptable bill in the Alaska territorial legislature, focusing on the November territorial election. Both Sutherland and Paul stood for re-election in 1926, and again editorial comment concerning the literacy act was unrelenting. The Fairbanks *News-Miner* accused Sutherland of opposing a strong literacy act to further his political ambitions. The *Anchorage Daily Times* hoped to persuade readers that illiterate voting constituted "more of a problem than is generally realized." Appearing at a Juneau rally for Sutherland, Wickersham charged that the Democrats had voted Indians against him. Their protest now, therefore, sounded a little hollow. In Juneau the *Empire* made much of Paul's program for the next legislature, which included amending the widow's and orphan's pension funds to include Indians for the first time, and to permit Indians' admission to the territorial pioneers' home in Sitka. Paul was a self-appointed dictator, the *Ketchikan Chronicle* charged, and in his political campaign stood convicted by his own acts as being "a hypocrite, a purveyor of falsehood and misrepresentation and a positive menace to Alaskan progress or the means of recognizing the higher aims of American citizenship." He had taken the Alaska Native Brotherhood into politics, the *Empire* reminded its readers, much to the detriment of the Territory. In the meantime, Sutherland's opponent, former mayor of Fairbanks Thomas Marquam, traveled throughout southeast Alaska attempting to rally votes by promising to purge the legislature of the influence of Indians, a frankly racist appeal.[44]

But the negative campaign was to no avail. Most voters probably considered the literacy issue moot since the legislature had acted. And Wickersham likely helped deflate the anti-Sutherland, anti-Paul press by suggesting many who opposed the literacy law in the legislature had done so because they considered the act to be a ploy of the "fish trust" which, the Wickites charged, opposed Indian voting as a way of diminishing support for higher taxes on the fishing industry. As he had throughout his political career, Wickersham relied on Alaskan chauvinism to win Sutherland votes. The *Empire* countered that William Paul had likely extracted a commitment of support from Wickersham and Sutherland for Paul's own future candidacy for delegate as his price for delivering the Indian vote in this and previous elections. Little had changed in the political rhetoric inspired by the issue.[45]

The results were the same as in 1924. Both Paul and Sutherland swept to comfortable victories.[46] That meant that the literacy measure really was a dead issue, for without a clear repudiation of Paul, supporters could not count on constituent support for tackling the measure another time. Moreover, the result confirmed the failure of the *Empire* and its supporters to rally Southeast voters around opposition to Paul and Indian voting. Apparently, most were less threatened by the "menace" of William Paul than the *Empire's* editor.

There was one final possibility for supporters of a stronger law, however. The United States Senate was due to take up Curry's House bill in the coming second session of the sixty-ninth Congress, and once again, supporters besieged the appropriate committee with endorsements. But when the Senate Committee on Territories reported its bill, it did so with the exemption for previous voters intact. Floor debate on the bill was desultory, C. C. Dill of Washington merely commenting that the measure was identical to the literacy law in his own state. With that, the law passed without further interest.[47]

Although it duplicated the 1925 Alaska act, the federal law finally signed by the President in 1927 was significant. Like any other territory, the Alaska legislature was prohibited from passing laws contrary to a federal law. And while it was theoretically possible, as a practical matter getting the Congress to reverse itself on a matter of such limited national interest was unlikely. Conceivably, continuing interest in Alaska might have caused the bill to be brought up again in the territorial legislature. But with the federal law in place, there would have been little point in making the attempt, for even if the supporters of a literacy measure had been successful in Alaska, they would have had to change the mind of Congress, or wait out a fight in the courts over their right to pass a literacy act different from the federal one. The effect of the federal law, then, was to inhibit any further action on the matter in Alaska, and effectively to conclude the business.

The Alaska literacy act of 1925, with its companion United States statute of 1927, represents an important chapter in Alaskan political and legislative history. William Paul's organization of illiterate voters, his support of Wickersham and Sutherland, and his own successful candidacy for the territorial legislature elicited shrill consternation from some voters, politicians, and newspaper editors who found their traditional assumptions about politics and cultural superiority directly challenged. Many responded in a fashion lamentably common in American politics of the age, impugning the motives and the capability of their opposition and injecting the issue of race into territorial politics. In so doing, they manifested the transfer to America's newest frontier of some of the culture's oldest and most destructive prejudices. Some opposed the bill for quite noble reasons, arguing that Indians had as much right to participation in the political process as other people, and in that argument, implied the substantive equality of Indians with whites. Some opposed the act for the very practical reason of electoral support. Supporters also had noble and practical motives for their positions. But the racism implicit in much of the political rhetoric unleashed by the battle must be seen as a negative development, for it surely helped to confirm many in their conviction that Indians were not ready for, and might never be capable of, equal rights and dignity with whites.

Perhaps the most significant consequence of the struggle over the bill was to confirm William Paul's position as a Native leader, and with it, the necessity and the potential for utilizing traditional American political structures to win and eventually to guarantee equal political rights for Natives. The struggle over the literacy act likely helped Paul to become the first Native elected to political office in the history of the territory. Certainly it was inextricably bound up with his two electoral campaigns. Paul would continue his work on behalf of Native rights for the rest of his life, though he would be eclipsed in later years by other Native leaders. After his two terms in the House he pursued his objectives primarily in the courts and administrative agencies, and as an ANB officer. No other Native would be elected to the Alaska legislature until 1946, perhaps because of the controversy raised by the literacy act episode. The ANB continued to serve as Paul's primary political vehicle until both it and he were superseded by the Tlingit-Haida Central Council, created in the 1940s. But the ANB supported no one for political office.

The literacy laws remained theoretically in force until eclipsed by the Alaska state constitution and the Statehood Act. Enforcement, however, was likely problematical, since accurate records were not kept of voters in all villages, and the determination of who had once voted was not easy to make. Moreover, the will to enforce the act probably did not exist in most places. There were apparently no court cases which tested the measure.[48] Whether or not the Alaska literacy act and its companion federal legislation in fact prevented Natives from voting, therefore, or impeded the development of political participation among Alaska Natives, is difficult to determine conclusively. The enforcement of voting regulations was lax in Alaska in the period. At the same time, education of Alaska Natives for literacy was well supported by both the territorial and federal governments, and had led to considerable success by the post-World War II years. By then the 1925 Alaska literacy law episode had been largely forgotten.

ENDNOTES

[1]*Session Laws of Alaska, 1925*, Chapter 27; *Senate Journal*, April 20, 1925, 143; *Alaska Daily Empire*, April 14, 1925, 1.

[2]Liberality in Alaska legislation concerning civic affairs is shown in the enfrancisement of women and in a Native citizenship act. (See *Session Laws of Alaska, 1913*, Chapter 1, and *Session Laws of Alaska, 1915*, Chapter 24.) Voting rights of Indians in western states are discussed in Gary C. Stein, "The Indian Citizenship Act of 1924," *New Mexico Historical Review* 47 (July 1972) and Francis Paul Prucha, *The Great Father: The United States Government and the American Indian* (Lincoln: University of Nebraska Press, 1984), II: 794ff.

[3]William L. Paul, Sr., "The Real Story of the Lincoln Totem," *Alaska Journal*, Summer 1971, 4-5.

[4]Evangeline Atwood, *Frontier Politics: Alaska's James Wickersham* (Portland: Binford & Mort, 1979), 351, 353, 360, 362; *Alaska Daily Empire*, October 26, 1926, 4, November 1, 1926, 1.

[5]Philip Drucker, *The Native Brotherhoods: Modern Intertribal Organizations on the Northwest Coast*, Bulletin 168, Bureau of American Ethnology (Washington, D.C.: GPO, 1956), 16-19, 38-39; Andrew Hope, III, *Founders of the Alaska Native Brotherhood* (Sitka: Andrew Hope, 1975).

[6]Hawkesworth to Gov. Thomas Riggs, Jan. 10, 1921, Henry Wellcome Papers, file 8, Federal Archives and Records Center (FARC), Seattle; *Wrangell Sentinel*, Jan. 13, 1921, 1 (reprinted from *Alaska Daily Empire*), Feb. 17, 1921, 1; ANB Minutes, 1920, file 71, Records of the Bureau of Indian Affairs, Record Group 75, FARC.

[7]*Wrangell Sentinel*, Feb. 17, 1921, 1.

[8]*Alaska Daily Empire*, Nov. 5, 1918, 2. Voting statistics were reported by a territorial canvassing board, and some survive in the governors' records (cited below, n. 31). Voting statistics for the First Division also were printed in the *Alaska Daily Empire*. The analysis of elections is based on the statistics printed in the following issues: Nov. 12, 1918, 5; Nov. 17, 1920, 7; Nov. 25, 1922, 8; Nov. 11, 1924, 8; Nov. 15, 1926, 8. The number of Indian villages voting was 7 in 1920, 4 in 1922 (data suspect), 11 in 1924, and 8 in 1926. The vote at Hoonah was 35 in 1920, 103 in 1924; at Kake, 11 in 1920, 104 in 1924.

[9]Drucker, *Native Brotherhoods*, 38-39; Mary Childers Mangusso, "Anthony J. Dimond: A Political Biography," (Ph.D. dissertation., Texas Tech University, 1978), 85-88; *Alaska Daily Empire*, October 1, 1924, 8.

[10]*Literacy Tests for Voters in the Territory of Alaska*, House Committee on Territories, 69th Cong., 1st sess., H. Rept. 728, 2; *Alaska Daily Empire*, March 16, 1923, 8; *Congressional Record*, June 30, 1926, 12371.

[11]*Contested Election Case--Wickersham v. Sulzer*, House Committee on Elections, 65th Cong., 3rd sess., H. Report. 839, 1415; *Delegate from Alaska*, 66th Cong., 1st sess., H. Doc. 74, 11-14; *Contested Election Case, Wickersham v. Sulzer and Grigsby*, House Committee on Elections, 66th Cong., 3rd sess., H. Rept. 1319, 9 (also minority report under same title); *Alaska Daily Empire*, March 14, 1923, 8.

[12]*Alaska Daily Empire*, March 5, 1923, 8, March 7, 1923, 8.

[13]Ibid., March 10, 1923, 1, March 14, 1923, 1, 8, April 4, 1923, 1.

[14]Ibid., March 14, 1923, 8.

[15]Ibid., April 16, 1923, 4 (reprinted from *Seward Gateway*), March 29, 1923, 4 (reprinted from *Cordova Times*), March 28, 1923, 4 (reprinted from *Ketchikan Chronicle*).

[16]Ibid., March 16, 1923, 8; see also *Alaska Fisherman*, a monthly paper edited by Paul, May 1924, 15.

[17]*Alaska Daily Empire*, March 16, 1923, 8, March 17, 1923, 8.

[18]Ibid., March 17, 1923, 8; Mangusso, "Anthony J. Dimond," 75.

[19]*Alaska Daily Empire*, April 2, 1923, 8, April 3, 1923, 3.

[20]Ibid., April 2, 1923, 8. For Paul, Sutherland, and Wickersham on the "fish trust," see *Alaska Daily Empire*, October 22, 1924, 4, October 11, 1926, 1.

[21]Ibid., April 2, 1923, 8, April 3, 1923, 1, 3, March 29, 1923, 4.

[22]*Senate Journal*, April 3, 1923, 113; *Alaska Daily Empire*, April 3, 1923, 1, 3, April 4, 1923, 1.

[23]*Senate Journal*, April 4, 1923, 121; *Alaska Daily Empire*, April 4, 1923, 1; Mangusso, "Anthony J. Dimond," 75-77; *Session Laws of Alaska*, 1923 and 1925, names of representatives; Evangeline Atwood and Robert N. DeArmond,

Who's Who in Alaskan Politics (Portland: Binford & Mort, 1977), biographical data on 1923 and 1925 representatives; various issues of the *Alaska Daily Empire*, *Anchorage Daily Times* and *Fairbanks News-Miner* in April and October, 1922 and 1924 for campaign reports and campaign ads for various candidates for legislative office.

[24]*Alaska Daily Empire*, April 5, 1923, 4; 43 U.S. Statutes, 253 (1924); Stein, "The Indian Citizenship Act of 1924," 257.

[25]*Alaska Daily Empire*, March 17, 1924, 3.

[26]Ibid., April 7, 1924, 3, May 7, 1924, 8.

[27]Ibid., November 25, 1922, 7, May 7, 1924, 8, November 11, 1924, 8.

[28]Ibid., October 3, 1924, 4.

[29]Ibid., October 4, 1924, 4 (citing the *Cordova Times*), November 3, 1924, 2.

[30]Ibid., October 7, 1924, 4, October 23, 1924, 4, November 3, 1924, 1, 3.

[31]Canvassing board report, 1922, Records of the Office of the Governor of Alaska, Alaska Historical Library, microcopy roll 92, file 19 (hereafter cited as Canvassing board report); *Alaska Daily Empire*, Nov. 11, 1924, 8, Nov. 25, 1922, 8.

[32]*Session Laws of Alaska, 1923*, 8-9; *Session Laws of Alaska, 1925*, 8; Canvassing board report, roll 111, file 18, Governors' Records; *Alaska Daily Empire*, April 21, 1923, 1; Atwood and DeArmond, *Who's Who in Alaskan Politics*, 93.

[33]*Alaska Daily Empire*, November 11, 1924, 4.

[34]Ibid., March 4, 1925, 3, March 5, 1925, 8, March 6, 1925, 4.

[35]Ibid., April 11, 1925, 1, April 10, 1925, 1-2.

[36]Ibid., April 10, 1925, 2, April 13, 1925, 8, April 14, 1925, 1, 8.

[37]Ibid., April 11, 1925, 1, 8, April 13, 1925, 1, April 15, 1925, 8.

[38]Ibid., April 14, 1925, 1, 8.

[39]Ibid., April 15, 1925, 4, April 17, 1925, 1.

[40]*Senate Journal*, April 18, 1925, 135, April 20, 1925, 143; *Alaska Daily Empire*, April 20, 1925, 1.

[41]*Alaska Daily Empire*, April 21, 1925, 4; *Anchorage Daily Times*, April 21, 1925, 4.

[42]*Literacy Tests*, H. Rept. 728, 1-4.

[43]*Congressional Records*, 69th Cong., 1st sess., April 19, 1926, 7785, June 30, 1926, 12370-74.

[44]*Alaska Daily Empire*, September 21, 1926, 1, 2, October 1, 1926, 4 (reprinted from *Fairbanks News-Miner*); October 2, 1926, 4 (reprinted from *Anchorage Daily Times*); October 30, 1926, 4 (reprinted from *Ketchikan Chronicle*); October 26, 1926, 4; Wickersham to Sutherland, December 29, 1926, James Wickersham Papers, Rasmuson Library, University of Alaska Fairbanks; *Anchorage Daily Times*, October 27, 1926, 1, *Fairbanks News-Miner*, October 29, 1926, 4.

[45]*Alaska Daily Empire*, October 11, 1926, 1, November 2, 1926, 1.

[46]Ibid., November 15, 1926, 7; Canvassing board report, roll 132, file 19, Governors' Records.

[47]*Congressional Record*, 69th Cong., 2d sess., February 16, 1927, 3977, February 26, 1927, 4890, March 1, 1927, 5221; 44 U.S. Statutes II, 1393, Chap. 363.

[48]*Alaska Digest*, 1st ed., V. III, "Indians," and same heading in the "pocket supplement."

POLITICAL ISSUES OF THE 1920s*

Mary Childers Mangusso

Mary Childers Mangusso taught in various capacities at the University of Alaska at Fairbanks from 1966 to 1988. She earned her doctoral degree at Texas Tech University in 1978 with a dissertation on the career of Anthony J. Dimond, Alaska's delegate to the U. S. Congress from 1933 to 1945. Her professional articles include work on Dimond (*Alaska Journal*) and on the Nome gold rush (*Pacific Northwest Quarterly*, January 1982, with Andrea R. C. Helms), and many papers presented at professional conferences as well as numerous reviews.

In the article printed here, taken from a chapter of her work on Dimond, Mangusso discusses territorial political issues in the 1920s and Dimond's role as senator in the territorial legislature. Alaska politics depended much more on dynamic personalities and the loyalty they could command than it did on party organization and discipline. Dimond was a major figure in territorial politics and earned a reputation for ethical conduct and intelligent investigation of issues.

Salmon canning was the principal economic factor in Alaska in the 1920s, and the question of territorial regulation and taxation of the industry occupied much political attention. For the most part regulation stayed with the U.S. Commerce Department despite territorial protestations that the fisheries should be controlled by the territory.

Another issue was the organization of territorial government. Many Alaskans resented the power of the "federal brigade," which included the governor, a presidential appointee, as well as the heads of the district offices of federal agencies with jurisdiction over Alaska affairs, such as the Bureau of Fisheries, the U. S. Forest Service, the Bureau of Education, and the judges in the court system, among others. But attempts to invest with substantive power officials who were elected in the Territory did not succeed.

Dimond was involved in these battles as well as in the fight over the Literacy Act. Throughout, Mangusso found, he supported progressive social legislation and tried to set a high ethical standard in the practice of territorial politics.

---

*Adapted from "Anthony J. Dimond, A Political Biography" (Ph.D. dissertation, Texas Tech University, 1978), Chapter 2, pp. 44-110.

* * *

When the sixth session of the Alaska legislature convened in March 1923, a squabble concerning selection of a permanent secretary delayed organization of the Senate. Anthony J. ("Tony") Dimond and his fellow senator from the Third Judicial Division (southcentral Alaska), backed by one member from the Second Division (northwestern Alaska) and another from the Fourth (the Interior), supported Miss Selma N. Scott of the Third Division for the position, while the other four senators favored Will Steel of the First (the Southeast). Three of the four men who supported Steel described themselves as Republicans; one, as an independent. Scott had the support of Dimond (a Democrat), two Republicans and an independent. A deadlock ensued until Steel solved the problem by withdrawing from consideration.[1] Obviously, neither party affiliation nor geographic origin necessarily determined how a senator might vote on a question of patronage, and the same held true for many other issues.

When Congress established the Alaskan legislature in 1912, only the most rudimentary party organizations existed within the territory. Parties consisted of sets shifting coalitions with no specific programs and no Alaska-wide machinery. This condition resulted in part from the absence of firmly established political traditions, since territory-wide politics had come into existence only in 1906, when voters had been empowered to send a non-voting delegate to Congress. However, absence of strong party systems also may be attributed to the character and personality of Alaska's major political figure, James Wickersham.[2]

Wickersham had come to Alaska in 1900 as a federal district judge and had entered politics in 1908, when he ran for the delegateship as a self-designated "Independent Republican" and defeated four opponents (a Republican, a Democrat, an independent, and a laborite). Vigorous and flamboyant, he dominated Alaskan politics for the next quarter century. No one could ignore him; individuals either supported him enthusiastically or abhorred him. His followers praised his energy, his combative style, and his courage. He hurled imaginative oratorical insults at his adversaries, who in turn accused him of self-aggrandizement and opportunism, often referring to him gleefully as "Flickering Wick." That appellation was not unearned, for Wickersham placed little apparent value upon political consistency. He won reelection as delegate in 1910 as an insurgent

Republican and in 1912 as a Progressive. In 1914 he again ran successfully, describing himself throughout most of Alaska as an independent supporting Democratic President Woodrow Wilson's politics. However, in some parts of the territory he called himself a Progressive Democrat. After 1916 he always identified himself as a Republican, although other Republicans did not necessarily agree. Since he was the only politician whose influence and reputation extended throughout the whole territory, his party-hopping produced considerable turmoil. Political alliances formed and disintegrated according to their members' opinions of Wickersham's activities. Both major parties split into pro- and anti-Wickersham factions, and these factions attacked each other with an intensity rivaling that of their attacks upon members of the opposing party.[3]

Internal party divisiveness also resulted from differing economic interests and local and regional jealousies. Many voters, their loyalties shaped by place of residence and means of livelihood, distrusted any office-seeker from another area. Alaska's size and the lack of adequate transportation made it difficult for anyone to campaign in all regions, and voters' sources of information often proved unenlightening. Newspaper publishers, for example, frequently demonstrated greater creativity than objectivity. As a result, misunderstandings, misinformation, and sectional rivalries contributed to a tendency among Alaskans to support a person rather than a party or a platform.[4]

Substantive issues existed, and often opposing candidates held remarkably similar views about them. However, the territorial legislature had no power to deal with many of these issues. In the Organic Act of 1912, which created the Alaska legislature, Congress imposed restrictions upon its powers greater than those imposed upon any other territorial law-making body in the United States. The legislature possessed limited power to tax and could not alter the existing system of license fees on business and trade or the federal laws allocating revenue from such fees. Legislators could not amend or alter those acts of Congress which established Alaska's executive and judicial departments, could not allocate land, and could not change, amend, or repeal federal laws relating to fish, game, fur seals, or fur-bearing animals. Neither the territory nor its incorporated municipalities could incur bonded indebtedness. While many of these limitations applied to all territorial legislatures, the sections which prevented creation of a territorial judicial system and which retained federal control over fish, game, and fur-bearing animals were unique to Alaska.[5]

While election to the Alaskan legislature certainly represented more than the "empty and profitless honor" that Dimond once described it to be, the Organic Act severely limited legislators' abilities to address many of Alaska's problems. In areas where action could be taken, inadequate revenue often restricted their options.[6] The legislature's weakness contributed to petty quarreling and to perpetuation of the cult of personality in territorial politics.

The cult of personality probably contributed to Dimond's political successes during the 1920s. Perhaps the best evidence of this can be found in letters from friends who urged as early as 1912 that he run for one or another office. Such suggestions sometimes included offers of money but never mentioned party affiliation, possibly because friends knew him to be a Democrat but more likely because they regarded party identification as relatively unimportant.[7]

Dimond first entered territorial politics in 1922, running for a Third Division territorial Senate seat. He faced no opposition in the primary. Republican Thomas A. Wade of Anchorage ran against Dimond in the general election. A resident of Valdez, Dimond had earned a reputation as a formidable defense lawyer throughout southcentral Alaska. However, by 1922 Anchorage had grown into the largest town in the division, and Dimond expected Wade to receive a majority of the votes cast there. Because of limited funds and uncompleted legal business, Dimond did not campaign extensively. But Wade proved to be an unexpectedly weak opponent, and Dimond won easily, carrying even the Anchorage precincts and receiving 1,406 votes to Wade's 872.[8]

As a freshman senator in 1923, Dimond served on the Committee on Mining, Manufacturing and Labor and the Committee on Engrossment and Enrollment, Per Diem and Mileage. He chaired the Committee on Judiciary and Federal Relations. The judiciary committee assignment took most of his time, for Alaska's attorney general inundated the Senate with forty-seven proposed bills intended to bring territorial law into conformity with recommendations made by federal judges in Alaska and by the United States Commission of Uniform Laws. Dimond himself proposed additional bills intended to regularize and strengthen existing laws.[9]

The mining committee undertook a general revision of territorial mining law, but after much discussion members could not agree upon the extent of the legislature's authority under the terms of the Organic Act and gave up their attempt. Dimond did introduce a bill to clarify the time limit for filing the affidavits of annual labor required on mining claims; this measure passed and received the governor's signature.[10]

Dimond generally supported progressive or reform legislation. In the 1922 general election voters had approved, by slightly more than two to one, a referendum which proposed that women be allowed to serve on juries. Dimond supported that measure[11] and introduced his own bill designed to insure that jurors would be chosen fairly. Formerly marshals or deputies had selected jurors for commissioners' courts, marshals had selected jurors for special venires, and in district courts the names of jurors had been drawn from a box containing the names of 300 persons eligible to serve. Dimond felt that the existing procedure could be abused too easily, especially in the case of commissioners' courts where juries could be virtually handpicked. The "Dimond Jury Law" provided that in all courts jurors would be chosen by drawing from a box containing the names of three-fourths of the persons in the area who had voted in the previous general election.[12]

Dimond also supported an act which permitted a married woman to dispose of her property without authorization from her husband[13] and an act giving fishermen and cannery workers preferred liens on property owned by the company employing them in case of nonpayment of wages.[14] He drafted and voted for an act which increased workmen's compensation benefits by thirty percent and extended coverage to more workers.[15]

All of the acts described above passed the Senate unanimously. Senators also accepted without dissent a bill intended to help fur farmers by raising the existing territorial bounty on eagles from fifty cents to one dollar per bird.[16] Obviously members shared certain assumptions, for each backed some types of social and legal reform, and all proved eager to reduce predation which seemed to threaten an infant industry. However, the legislators did not concur on all proposals; measures relating to regulation of commercial fisheries, reorganization of the executive branch of the government, and a literacy test for voters provoked spirited debate and revealed profound differences of opinion.

By the 1920s the annual value of Alaska's salmon pack had begun to decline sharply, falling from about $50,000,000 in 1918 to roughly half that amount in 1921. The drop in part reflected a post-war decline in prices, but also it resulted from overfishing and consequent depletion of supply.[17]

Responsibility for regulating the Alaskan salmon industry rested with Secretary of Commerce Herbert Hoover, whose purview included the Bureau of Fisheries. At Hoover's suggestion the Warren G. Harding administration attempted to halt the decline by creating two fish reserves to be administered by the Bureau of Fisheries, one located in the Aleutians and the other encompassing Bristol Bay and the Kodiak area. About forty percent of Alaska's commercial salmon fisheries fell within the reserves.[18]

Major corporations based outside the territory dominated the salmon industry and consistently blocked efforts to secure strict and effective regulation of fisheries by either federal or territorial authorities. Alaskans strongly resented both continued federal control of Alaska's resources and the powerful economic and political influences which the salmon packers undeniably exercised. Accordingly, most of the territory's residents interpreted establishment of the fish reserves as an effort to protect the interests of the large corporations at the expense of resident fishermen.[19]

A memorial to Congress introduced in the Alaskan House by Representative William D. Grant of Wrangell expressed this common belief:

> Irrespective of the good intentions of present officials, the privileges upon a reserve must, in the very nature of things, go to those who maintain the strongest lobby. It cannot be presumed that before the Bureau of Fisheries, any more than before a tribunal primarily created to administer justice, a claimant who can neither appear in person nor by counsel can possibly have an even chance with one who is constantly represented by men specially skilled in presenting facts.[20]

The memorial reportedly had been written by Dan Sutherland, then Alaska's delegate, Wickersham's protege, and a vigorous foe of Hoover's policy. Dimond felt the memorial to be weak because it suggested no remedy for the existing situation, but he viewed it more favorably following House adoption of an amendment which requested abolition of the reserves and establishment of territorial control over Alaska fisheries. When the Senate considered the proposal, Dimond and E. E. Chamberlain, the Third Division's senior senator, framed a somewhat more tightly worded substitute, which the Senate rejected. Both men eventually joined in approving the memorial as it had come from the House.[21]

Rejection by the Senate of the substitute memorial prepared by Chamberlain and Dimond probably resulted from a natural preference among Wickersham/Sutherland supporters for a draft reportedly written by Sutherland instead of a similar measure drawn up by someone else. But all members of the Senate certainly agreed as to the undesirability of fish reserves and the desire to protest such a policy.

However, a controversy soon arose regarding the means and extent of an effective protest. Senator Forest J. Hunt of Ketchikan introduced a resolution at Sutherland's request authorizing Alaska's attorney general to test the validity of the fish reserves. One section of the resolution instructed that official

> to protect and defend any private citizen or corporation of the United States against any charge of the violation of any rules or regulations promulgated by the secretary of commerce or bureau of fisheries attempting to deny to any person or corporation any right which in the opinion of the attorney general is vouchsafed to such person or corporation by the constitution or the laws of the United States, and, to that end, to defray the necessary expenses connected with his or its defense, including the engaging of attorneys to assist whenever he shall deem the same necessary.[22]

In considering the resolution Dimond acknowledged the need for conservation of salmon but questioned both the intent and the potential effectiveness of the reserve system. He disagreed with those who believed creation of the reserves to be unconstitutional, but he expressed willingness to have their validity tested in court. He refused, however, to support the resolution as written, objecting vehemently to the portion which directed the attorney general to defend and pay the legal expenses of anyone accused of violating federal fishing regulations. He contended that passage of such a resolution would be futile at best and, at worst, might encourage and abet open, violent rebellion against the government of the United States.[23]

During the discussion of Hunt's resolution, no one mentioned either the possible expense to the territory or the potential benefit to any corporation which might take advantage of the provision for territorial financing of a legal defense. Apparently everyone expected the governor to veto the measure if it passed, and it seems to have been introduced merely to lay a foundation for its sponsors' future partisan appeals. Dimond must have recognized the resolution's political origin and purpose. Yet he could not question the propriety of using territorial funds in such a manner without implying that his opponents had sold themselves to the cannery lobbyists, a move his belief in political fair play would not allow him to make. Instead, he attacked indirectly, stressing the danger of insurrection,[24] a point not entirely improbable when one considers the acknowledged magnitude during the 1920s of fish piracy (theft of fish from traps owned by major packers by Alaska residents, who then sold the fish to the packers from whom they'd been stolen).

The Senate considered an alternate resolution containing less explicit language than the original, but Dimond believed that the meaning remained essentially unchanged and refused to vote for the substitute. The Senate passed the alternate proposal by a five to three vote, with Dimond, Chamberlain, and Fred M. Ayer of Nome in the opposition. The House also adopted the substitute, which the governor vetoed.[25]

In addition to pushing through the fish reserve resolution, the Sutherland faction in the Senate proved strong enough to defeat a bill which would have required all voters to be able to read and write the English language. Proponents of the literacy qualification intended it as a means by which to restrict voting by Indians, thereby breaking the political power of Native leader William L. Paul. Paul, a Tlingit who had studied and traveled extensively in the contiguous United States, had politicized the Alaska Native Brotherhood and by 1923 reportedly controlled a bloc of about one thousand Native votes in southeastern Alaska, which he used in Sutherland's behalf. Many of Paul's followers were believed to be illiterate; at election time he allegedly supplied them with stencils to be placed over the official ballot and instructed them to mark an "x" in each cutout. Although hoping to eliminate Paul's political base and undercut Sutherland, the literacy test's backers described it as a reform designed primarily to reduce corruption.[26]

Dimond supported the measure, stressing that voting should be regarded as a privilege, not a right automatically accorded to every citizen. A working democracy, he argued, depended upon the participation of an enlightened electorate; voting by persons presumably unable to inform themselves adequately about public affairs perverted democratic ideals. He admitted that the proposal would affect Indians almost exclusively. The responsibility for educating Indians lay with the federal government, and properly qualified Alaskan voters should neither accept blame nor suffer inequities because the federal government had failed to fulfill its obligations. He noted that Paul openly admitted that the bill could deprive Sutherland of one thousand potential votes and characterized that admission as "an abject confession" of political impropriety.[27]

Had the literacy measure passed, it would have reduced somewhat the influence of the First Division in territorial affairs as well as undermining Republican support there. The boundaries of Alaska's four judicial divisions had been determined for the geographical convenience of the territory's four federal district judges. In the Organic Act of 1912 Congress made no attempt to provide proportional representation in the legislature but simply established four election districts, each coinciding in area with one of the judicial divisions.[28] The population of the four districts differed greatly. In the election of 1922 a combined total of 3,002 votes had been cast in the First Division for the two major candidates for the delegateship. The Second Division's vote for the two men together totaled 704; the Third Division's, 2,297; and the Fourth's 1,805.[29] While these numbers obviously represent only politically active adults, they also reflect the relative size of the population in each of the four divisions. Those differences in population accounted for some of the interdivisional rivalry that existed.

Disproportionate representation did not bother most politicians of the 1920s nearly as much as did the dominant position of the First Division in territorial affairs. In 1923, fifty-three (48.2 percent) of Alaska's 109 appointed and elected officials came from the First Division. George J. Love, United States Commissioner at Valdez, expressed an opinion typical of non-southeasterners when he wrote Dimond following the Senate dispute over selection of a secretary to congratulate him upon his victory over "those grafters in Juneau and southeastern Alaska."[30] Besides traditional distrust of a relatively remote government and resentment over the extent to which it was run by southeastern Alaskans, persons from other regions disliked the fact that the First Division could cast a larger vote than any other district in territory-wide elections. Since the Third Division (Dimond's) contained the second largest number of voters, elimination of one thousand First Division votes would have given to the Third the chief role as a makeweight in territorial politics.

In 1923 the only territory-wide elections consisted of those held to choose a delegate to Congress and a territorial attorney general, but in that year the Senate considered transferring most of Alaska's executive authority from the presidentially-appointed governor to a territorial Board of Control composed of officials elected at large throughout Alaska. The Wickersham/Sutherland faction strongly backed this "controller bill." Since the proposal raised the possibility that elected officials actually might possess power and exert increased control over patronage, some politicians from northern, central and western Alaska became even more eager than before to restrict the First Division's role in territorial affairs. Some also opposed the measure because they feared that, if it passed, Wickersham/Sutherland forces would dominate the Board of Control.[31]

Neither the literacy test nor the controller bill passed the Senate in 1923, both meeting defeat by four-to-four ties. Dimond voted against the controller bill and for the literacy test. Although the author of the literacy bill advanced frankly racist arguments in its favor, Dimond's support apparently did not stem from racial prejudice. On one occasion he expressed shock and disgust when informed of a rule barring persons of Indian descent from membership in the Elks, and his oldest daughter recalled that he had taught his children to be unprejudiced.[32] Probably his votes best can be explained as compatible with his own and his division's political interests.

In 1925 William Paul, a newly elected member of the Alaska House of Representatives, proposed expansion of Alaska's pension system to cover Natives as well as non-Natives. Many politicians and some newspapers opposed the suggestion, angrily decrying the expense involved in adding to territorial pension rolls persons who already received federal aid. Paul's presence in the legislature, the furor over his pension proposal, and the 1924 federal act declaring Indians to be citizens of the United States led to renewed controversy over the literacy bill. For example, the *Alaska Daily Empire* of Juneau, staunchly anti-Sutherland and therefore anti-Paul, editorialized:

> If anyone ever had any doubts about the need for a literacy test for voters in the election laws of Alaska, the attempt of Mr. Paul, leader of the organized Indian voting bloc in southeastern Alaska, to open...the Territorial pension list to Indians ought to clear away the doubt...
>
> Above all, the Legislature should pass the literacy test measure and alleviate the harm that is being done to both whites and Indians through political demagoguery that has created a race problem in Alaska and threatens to wreck our territorial government.[33]

The literacy bill proposed in 1925 included a clause exempting from its provisions all voters who had cast ballots legally in any prior election. Dimond twice tried to eliminate this exemption, but both attempts failed. He and three like-minded Senators then joined the other four to approve the measure unanimously.[34] As finally adopted, the Voter's Literacy Act of 1925 represented a hollow victory for those legislators who favored a literacy test, since it left Paul's political base intact.

The controller bill also resurfaced in 1925. It again failed when Dimond and the same three colleagues who had attempted unsuccessfully to amend the voters' literacy act voted against it.[35]

During 1925 Dimond again chaired the Committee on Judiciary and Federal Relations and also served on the Finance and Corporations Committee and the Committee on Education. He introduced thirteen bills, eleven of which passed the Senate unanimously and received the approval of the House of Representatives and the governor's signature. Most involved amendments to clarify or improve existing laws. One measure, for example, slightly modified the process of jury selection prescribed by the Dimond Jury Law of 1923. It provided that jurors had to be able to read, write, speak, and understand the English language; those who could not do so might be dismissed for cause. Another of his bills authorized diversion of some of the money originally appropriated for road construction in the Third Division into a fund for construction of airfields.[36]

Although for the most part the 1925 session proved unusually harmonious, Dimond once again tangled with the Sutherland faction. Amidst a patronage battle during which he attempted to discredit and dislodge several federal appointees in Alaska, most of whom happened to be Dimond's friends, Delegate Sutherland asserted in the United States House of Representatives that some regions of the territory suffered from a breakdown of law and order due to the incompetence of resident legal and judicial officials. His remarks apparently furnished the basis for statements made at a press conference by Supreme Court Justice Harlan Fiske Stone, who, according to the Associated Press, characterized Alaska as an uncivilized frontier where unruly citizens lacked respect for the law. Understanding that Sutherland had portrayed Alaska in strident, inaccurate tones to strengthen his hand in the patronage fight, Dimond and Representative Joseph H. Murray, Dimond's former prospecting partner, introduced identical memorials denouncing Stone's reported remarks as untrue and demanding the name of the person from whom Stone obtained such an impression so that the informant "might be branded from one end of Alaska to the other as the liar that he is." Sutherland's followers retaliated; Paul introduced a resolution condemning the Dimond/Murray memorial in highly emotional terms as an unjustified, politically-motivated attack upon Sutherland by the Democrats. His argument, although partially correct, ignored the fact that Murray belonged to the Republican party, albeit not the Sutherland wing. Both the resolution and the memorial failed to pass, but the dispute increased the enmity between Dimond and the Sutherland camp.[37]

Several Democrats urged Dimond to run for the delegateship in the 1924 and 1926 elections, but he declined. In August, 1923, he and T. J. Donohoe, his long-time mentor and Valdez law partner, had accepted a retainer from the Alaska Syndicate. The syndicate, a consortium formed by J. P. Morgan, the Guggenheim brothers, and other eastern investors, owned the Kennecott copper mines, the Copper River and Northwestern Railroad, a steamship line, and assorted salmon canneries and gold mines. His relationship with the syndicate, a favorite target of anti-monopolists, made Dimond vulnerable politically. It required no special astuteness to recognize that an attorney for the "Guggies" had little hope of winning a territorial election given existing anti-syndicate sentiment throughout much of Alaska. Following the 1925 Senate session, Dimond apparently intended to retire from politics, for he informed a friend, "I am glad that the session is over, and that I can do something else for awhile, being the last time that I shall ever appear in any legislative body. I thought it would be interesting, but it has been instead an awful bore."[38]

By 1926, however, Dimond had changed his mind, and he filed as a candidate for reelection to the Senate. Unopposed in the primary, he faced Republican nominee Arthur Frame in the general election. Frame, also a lawyer, had come to Alaska in 1905 and worked for several years in a Fairbanks law firm staffed by friends of James Wickersham before moving to Anchorage.[39] Frame did not campaign extensively. Instead Sutherland, a candidate for reelection to the delegate's seat, led the opposition to Dimond.

Wickersham's role in the 1926 campaign seems unclear, although in the past he had shown a pronounced tendency toward vindictiveness, neither forgetting nor forgiving anyone who disagreed with him on any issue. As Wickersham's protege, Sutherland may have acquired some of his patron's less endearing traits; certainly he adopted some of Wickersham's techniques. In the territorial Senate Dimond had opposed the controller bill, attacked the wording of the Sutherland faction's resolution protesting the fish reserves, and attempted to undercut the delegate's political base by supporting a literacy qualification for voters. Dimond had affronted Sutherland particularly by cosponsoring the memorial denouncing Justice Stone's allegations. In addition, several prominent Cordovans had retained Donohoe and Dimond to institute a libel suit against Sutherland, who had accused them of belonging to a bootleggers' ring during the 1925 patronage battle.[40] Although protected from the lawsuit by congressional immunity, Sutherland had ample reason to promote Dimond's defeat.

Even so, the delegate seems to have devoted a surprising amount of effort exclusively to attacking Dimond. Frame was not a dynamic speaker, so he doubtless needed help. Sutherland's opponent for the delegateship, Thomas Marquam of Fairbanks, had entered the race as an independent. Although the Democratic candidate had withdrawn to avoid splitting the anti-Sutherland vote, Marquam generated little enthusiasm outside the Fourth Division.[41] Sutherland remained popular throughout the territory and therefore could spare the time to concentrate upon Dimond, whom he seems to have regarded as a potentially dangerous rival as well as an effective opposition leader.

In a series of addresses given in the Third Division, Sutherland concentrated upon Dimond's connection with the Alaska Syndicate. Dimond's three children innocently attended a Republican rally in Valdez while their parents were out of town because they wanted to see the free movie which preceded the speeches. They then listened while Sutherland denounced their father as a tool of the "fish trust," a man who represented the salmon packers rather than the people both off and on the Senate floor. Dimond's oldest daughter later recalled, "And he banged and banged, and he said all those things, and here we were sitting there just kind of open-mouthed...I heard afterwards...he was terribly embarrassed."[42]

Sutherland wrongly charged Dimond with obstructing all proposals to authorize a test of the validity of the fish reserves. He attacked Dimond for opposing a bill to tax the fishing industry by means of a graduated tax on the number of salmon taken in fish traps rather than by a set fee per trap. He also charged that Donohoe and Dimond had engineered the selection of Marquam as the anti-Sutherland candidate and suggested that Dimond ran Marquam's campaign. The latter assertion may have hurt Dimond's chances with Native voters, since Marquam viewed the literacy test as a major issue and campaigned as an avowed racist, promising to save Alaska from "the menance of Indian controlled government."[43]

Sutherland's assertions contained just enough truth to put Dimond on the defensive. He would have been less vulnerable had voters been better informed about public affairs, but press coverage of legislative sessions ranged from the very spotty to the completely nonexistent. Only the Juneau *Empire* attempted complete coverage, and its editor's blatant anti-Sutherland bias made its accounts highly suspect. Hence, many voters accepted half-truths or plausible falsehoods because they had no factual basis for comparing the candidates' records. Dimond patiently tried to sort out Sutherland's allegations and to explain those charges he regarded as false or misleading. He acknowledged that he favored Marquam for delegate but denied organizing or administering Marquam's campaign. Indeed, prior to 1926 Dimond seems to have had no contact with Marquam, whom he apparently supported without great enthusiasm as the only alternative to Sutherland. Dimond explained in great detail his opposition to fish reserves and his votes on the legislative protests against them. He noted that Sutherland had described the existing fishery taxes erroneously, outlined his own attitude regarding the best system of taxation, and pointed out that both taxes on fisheries and appropriations for the relief of aged citizens and for the Alaska Agricultural College and School of Mines had more than doubled since 1919, the last year during which Sutherland had served in the territorial legislature. He affirmed that he had supported both the higher taxes and the larger appropriations, although he had voted against a proposal to tax fisheries solely by graduated fees on numbers of fish caught because he believed such a system impossible to enforce. He compared his own record in favor of territorial control over Alaskan resources to Sutherland's record, pointing out the delegate's undeniable ambiguity as to whether or not the territory should be allowed to regulate its own fisheries. He admitted acting as an attorney for the syndicate but stoutly denied representing any "fish trust." He asserted that in his capacity as a senator he always had sought to represent the people, not his corporate clients. Even Abraham Lincoln, he protested, once had performed legal work for corporations.[44]

Although his temper became frayed by election day, Dimond concluded his campaign on an ethical level unusually high by prevailing standards. Refusing to employ the opposition's tactics, he attempted to counter inaccurate, emotionally charged attacks calmly and logically. He received endorsements from the *Cordova Daily Times* and the *Anchorage Daily Times*. However, many voters clearly believed Sutherland, and Dimond lost to Frame.[45]

Still not satisfied, Sutherland Republicans struck at Dimond again in 1927 when Governor George A. Parks appointed him to the Board of Regents of the Alaska Agricultural College and School of Mines. Four Senators successfully blocked his confirmation because of his prominence in the Democratic party. They likewise rejected Dr. J. H. Romig of Fairbanks for membership on the Board, reportedly because he had played a major role in Marquam's campaign. As if to emphasize the point, the four voted to accept as regent a less politically active Fairbanks Democrat.[46]

Undaunted, Third Division Democrats nominated Dimond for a Senate seat again in 1928. Although unopposed in the primary, he once more found himself confronted by charges that he represented the "fish trust."[47] William Paul's monthly newsletter, *The Alaska Fisherman*, circulated distorted allegations similar to those made by Sutherland two years earlier:

> You have it in your power to elect men who will represent you and not the steamship company or the Kennecott Mine. You can put an end to the government of Alaska by carpet-baggers who look to Washington, D.C.
>
> But you cannot do so if you elect Tony Dimond, senator...

> Tony Dimond is the man who engineered the joker law that successfully tied the hands of our own attorney general and prevented this elected official from testing the infamous FISH RESERVATIONS.[48]

Voters responded less sympathetically to Paul than they had to Sutherland two years earlier. Dimond won.

During the ninth session of the Alaskan legislature (1929), Dimond introduced nineteen bills, fourteen of which passed. The governor vetoed one of these, the so-called "poor convict bill," which would have provided for the release of persons imprisoned solely because they could not pay a fine or a fine plus court costs. Dimond intended it, he said, to "put the poor man on the same footing with those who have money." The governor felt that the bill endangered effective law enforcement, and lawmakers failed to override the veto.[49]

The acts which Dimond sponsored successfully included one which authorized refunding the license fee required by law for each fish trap if the trap later could not be operated because of new government restrictions,[50] a second providing for creation of a public school teachers' pension fund,[51] and another, cosponsored by Senator John W. Dunn, designed to revise and codify all laws regarding Alaska's public schools. Dunn and Dimond proposed substituting a nonpartisan, appointed territorial Board of Education for the existing board, by law composed of the governor and the four senior senators and therefore necessarily politically-oriented. The Senate deleted this reform before passing the bill.[52]

The perennial controller bill became the chief issue facing the 1929 legislature, precipitating a dispute which remained unresolved until the clock had been stopped to keep the session from exceeding its sixty-day limit. Introduced by Senator Will Steel, now a senator from the First Division, the bill provided for creation of a Board of Control to assume all territorial executive duties, for the election of Alaska's Treasurer, and for the establishment of an elective office of Auditor. The bill passed the Senate over negative votes cast by Dimond, Dunn, and Luther C. Hess of the Fourth Division. Although supporters touted the measure as a method for increasing Alaskans' control over their territorial government, the Senate minority feared creation of a potentially powerful executive board at a time when political trends indicated that it would be staffed by Wickersham/Sutherland men.[53]

The territorial House amended the Senate version beyond recognition, eliminating the Board of Control entirely and passing only the sections relating to the positions of Auditor and Treasurer. The Senate majority refused to concur with the House amendments, while the House refused to rescind them. The conference committee deadlocked. The five pro-controller senators retaliated against House intransigence by holding a number of House bills in committee. Dimond led an unsuccessful effort to pry these bills loose. As part of a compromise settlement on the final day of the session, the Senate majority finally released a veritable flood of measures voluntarily.[54]

The version of the controller bill finally adopted contained no Board of Control. The act made the territory's Treasurer an elective rather than an appointive official. It created the new elective office of Auditor and gave that official many responsibilities, including most duties formerly performed by Alaska's Secretary, an appointed gubernatorial assistant.[55] Other acts originating in the House provided for election rather than appointment of the Commissioner of Education[56] and created the elective office of Highway Engineer.[57] Thus the legislature achieved the aim of the controller bill, increasing the power of elected officials and decreasing the influence of appointees, without enacting the entire measure. Both sides could express satisfaction.

Compared to 1929, the 1931 legislative session proved tranquil. Dimond introduced twenty-eight of the eighty-two Senate bills considered. More of his proposals than before involved local improvements to benefit Third Division constituents. These measures included requests for territorial funding of repair work upon the dike which protected Valdez from spring flooding and for money to build or repair schoolhouses at Longwood, Afognak, Oozinkie, and Matanuska. Of seven such bills, only the Valdez dike repair measure passed.[58]

The Territory of Alaska faced extraordinarily severe fiscal problems in 1931. The governor recommended strict austerity. In an effort to organize finances better, he asked the legislature to establish a Board of Budget. Dimond drafted the act which did so.[59] In another attempt to improve administration, Dimond successfully proposed creation of the office of Superintendent of Public Works. The Highway Engineer would also act as Superintendent, coordinating and supervising construction of all public buildings.[60] Dimond also convinced the legislature to remove the few remaining restrictions on married women's property rights.[61]

The 1931 legislature repealed Alaska's "Bone Dry Law," a stringent prohibition act which Wickersham had sponsored and vigorously defended through the years. Legislators also repealed the "Wickersham Mining Act" of 1912, which limited the size and number of placer claims that prospectors could stake. (Since both were federal laws, neither repeal could become effective without congressional assent. Both repeals simply constituted efforts to win sympathy in Washington, D.C.) Dimond introduced the act repealing the 1912 mining law as well as a companion measure which abrogated a similar territorial statute.[62]

By 1931 Dimond had begun to consider running for delegateship in 1932.[63] Wickersham/Sutherland influence had begun to wane, and 1932 promised to be a good year for Democrats. Dimond had proven his popularity with voters by returning from his 1926 defeat to weather a second attack by the Sutherland forces two years later. Fellow legislators had come to respect his ability and energy, and he had become something of a public figure throughout the territory. Despite allegations by political opponents, his legislative record indicated no favoritism for his corporate clients. Instead, he had consistently supported reforms of a progressive nature, measures designed to promote economic development in the territory, and proposals to insure equal rights and fair treatment to all citizens. From a present-day viewpoint, his support for a literacy qualification for voters may be interpreted as a smudge on his record; however, he seems to have been motivated by political considerations rather than by prejudice. In retrospect his record reveals almost none of the stains acquired by those involved in the grubby territorial political battles of the 1920s.

On March 16, 1931, Dimond gave a public lecture on the Declaration of Independence and the Constitution of the United States to Juneauites as part of a series of presentations sponsored by the local Order of Moose. He cautioned that "tyranny was to be feared not only through the accumulation of all power in one officer, but also through the operation of temporary majorities; that 'democracy has its own capacity for despotism'." These remarks doubtless reflected his own recent political experiences. However, the speech also may well have marked the opening of his campaign for the delegateship, which he was to win in 1932, for he also stressed a favorite Alaskan theme:

"When the speaker dwelt upon the necessity of self-rule in all local matters rather than a concentration of all power in the hands of the national government at Washington, he was enthusiastically applauded."[64]

ENDNOTES

[1]Alaska (Ter.), *Senate Journal of Alaska 1923*, pp. 9-13, 344.

[2]Ernest Gruening, *The State of Alaska*, rev. ed. (New York: Random House, 1968), p. 158.

[3]Jeannette Paddock Nichols, *Alaska: A History of Its Administration, Exploitation, and Industrial Development During the First Half Century under the Rule of the United States* (Cleveland: The Arthur H. Clark Company, 1924), pp. 358-62, 395-98; Gruening, *State of Alaska*, pp. 158, 186-187; William R. Hunt, *North of 53°--The Wild Days of the Alaska-Yukon Mining Frontier 1870-1914* (New York: Macmillan Publishing Co., Inc., 1974), pp. 281-285; William R. Cashen, *Farthest North College President: Charles E. Bunnell and the Early History of the University of Alaska* (Fairbanks: University of Alaska Press, 1972), pp. 39-60, 76.

[4]Gruening, *State of Alaska*, p. 158; Cashen, *Farthest North College President*, p. 76; Hunt, *North of 53°*, pp. 266-273.

[5]*An Act To Create a Legislative Assembly in the Territory of Alaska..., U.S. Statutes at Large* 37: 512-18 (1912); Gruening, *State of Alaska*, pp. 151-53; Melvin Crain, "Governance for Alaska; Some Aspects of Representation" (Ph.D. dissertation, University of Southern California, 1957), pp. 179-86; George Washington Spicer, *The Constitutional Status and Government of Alaska* (Baltimore: The Johns Hopkins Press, 1927), pp. 73-81.

[6]Anthony J. Dimond to A. F. Hoffman, 18 August 1914, T. J. Donohoe-John Y. Ostrander-Anthony J. Dimond Papers, Alaska and Polar Regions Collection (Archives), Elmer E. Rasmuson Library, University of Alaska Fairbanks (quotation). [Hereafter, this manuscript collection will be cited as "DOD."] Also see Gruening, *State of Alaska*, pp. 283, 285.

[7]For example, see Peter S. Erichsen to Dimond, 16 October 1912; telegram, R. F. Isaacson to Dimond, 19-21 [sic] October 1912; telegram, "Nizina, Kennecott Bunch" to Dimond, 22 October 1912; Isaacson to Dimond, 31 October 1912; Bill Salonka to Dimond, 5 November 1914, DOD.

[8]Dimond to Thomas C. Price, 20 January 1922; Dimond to L. Leo Wardell, 27 May 1922; Dimond to Joseph Murray, 2 November 1922 and 14 November 1922, DOD. *Valdez Miner*, 28 January 1922, p. 1; 25 February 1922, p. 4; 29 April 1922, pp. 1-2; 11 November 1922, p. 1; 17 February 1923, p. 3. *McCarthy Weekly News*, 21 October 1922, p. 1.

[9]*Senate Journal 1923*, pp. 8, 22-28, 36-37, 41-43, 84, 156, 242; *Alaska Daily Empire* (Juneau), 8 March 1923, p. 8.

[10]Dimond to E.S. Larson, 30 March 1923, DOD; *Senate Journal 1923*, pp. 103-104, 132, 181; Alaska (Ter.), *Session Laws of Alaska 1923*, Chapter 43, p. 53.

[11]*Senate Journal 1923*, pp. 35, 66, 85, 291; *Laws of Alaska 1923*,

Chapter 68, pp. 106-107.

[12]*Senate Journal 1923*, p. 138; *Alaska Empire*, 21 April 1923, p. 8; *Seward Weekly Gateway*, 10 October 1926, p. 11; *Laws of Alaska 1923*, Chapter 91, pp. 160-65.

[13]*Senate Journal 1923*, pp. 24, 50, 84, 101; *Laws of Alaska 1923*, Chapter 20, p. 28; Chapter 40, p. 51.

[14]*Senate Journal 1923*, pp. 23, 160-61; *Laws of Alaska 1923*, Chapter 53, pp. 70-79.

[15]*Seward Weekly Gateway*, 10, October 1926, p. 2; *Senate Journal 1923*, pp. 261, 268; *Laws of Alaska 1923*, Chapter 98, pp. 235-63.

[16]Dimond to W.C. Snook, 31 March 1923, DOD; *Alaska Empire*, 23 March 1923, p. 8; *Senate Journal 1923*, pp. 43, 94; *Laws of Alaska 1923*, Chapter 34, pp. 39-41.

[17]Gruening, *State of Alaska*, pp. 245-63; Henry W. Clark, *History of Alaska* (New York: The Macmillan Company, 1930), p. 182.

[18]Gruening, *State of Alaska*, pp. 263-64.

[19]Ibid.

[20]House Joint Memorial No. 1, *Laws of Alaska 1923*, pp. 319-20 (quotation, p. 319).

[21]*Anchorage Daily Times*, 29 October 1926, p. 3; Dimond to Larson, 30 March 1923; DOD; *Seward Weekly Gateway*, 10 October 1926, p. 11; *Senate Journal 1923*, pp. 129-30; *Laws of Alaska 1923*, pp. 320-21; *Alaska Empire*, 6 April 1923, p. 2.

[22]*Senate Journal 1923*, p. 138; Senate Joint Resolution No. 2 as quoted in *Anchorage Daily Times*, 29 October 1926, p. 3.

[23]*Alaska Empire*, 18 April 1923, pp. 1, 8.

[24]Ibid.

[25]*Alaska Empire*, 18 April 1923, p. 8; 2 May 1923, p. 4; *Anchorage Daily Times*, 29 October 1926, p. 3; *Senate Journal 1923*, pp. 137-38, 144, 148, 166, 170-71, 177, 184, 231.

[26]*Alaska Empire*, 3 April 1923, p. 3; 4 April 1923, p. 8; William L. Paul, Sr., "The Real Story of the Lincoln Totem," *Alaska Journal*, 1 (Summer 1971): 3, 5; Stephen Haycox, "William Paul, Sr., and the Alaska Voters' Literacy Act of 1925," *Alaska History* 2 (Winter 1986/87): 19-20.

[27]Dimond to Larson, 30 March 1923, DOD; *Alaska Empire*, 3 April 1923, p. 3 (quotation); 4 April 1923, p. 8.

[28]Spicer, *Status and Government of Alaska*, pp. 74-75; Crain, "Governance for Alaska," pp. 188-90.

[29]*Valdez Miner*, 17 February 1923, p. 3.

[30]Officeholders listed in *Laws of Alaska 1923*, pp. 5-8. The figures given above exclude the governor, usually someone from outside of Alaska, and the two senators and four representatives from each division. Quotation from George J. Love to Dimond, 15 March 1923, DOD.

[31]*Senate Journal 1923*, p. 41; *Alaska Empire*, 16 March 1923, p. 4.

[32]*Senate Journal 1923*, pp. 121, 176; *Alaska Empire*, 3 April 1923, p. 3; Dimond to I.D. Bogart, 22 July 1925, D-O-D; Sister Marie Therese, Notre Dame de Namur, interview with Claus-M. Naske, Washington, D.C., 20 April 1975 [transcript in author's possession].

[33]*Alaska Empire*, 6 March 1925, p. 4; 7 April 1925, p. 1; 8 April 1925, p. 4 (quotation); 21 April 1925, p. 4.

[34]*Senate Journal of Alaska 1925*, pp. 119, 143; Alaska (Ter.), *Session Laws of Alaska 1925*, Chapter 27, pp. 51-54.

[35]*Senate Journal 1925*, pp. 88-89, 164, 183, 190.

[36]*Alaska Empire*, 28 March 1925, p. 1; *Senate Journal 1925*, pp. 61-62, 73, 102, 104-106, 141-42, 171, 186, 192, 217, 231, 235, 272-84; *Laws of Alaska 1925*, Chapter 16, pp. 29-38 (jury selection); Chapter 62, pp. 106-107 (airfields).

[37]James Wickersham to J.W. Keith, 6 April 1925, Daniel Sutherland Papers, Alaska and Polar Regions Collection, Elmer E. Rasmuson Library, University of Alaska Fairbanks; *Alaska Empire*, 15 April 1925, pp. 1, 3 (quotation, p. 3); 17 April 1925, p. 1; 18 April 1925, pp. 1-2; 23 April 1925, pp. 1, 8; 1 May 1925, pp. 1-2; *Senate Journal 1925*, pp. 81, 172-73; *Valdez Miner*, 31 July 1926, p. 3; 2 October 1926, p. 2.

[38]Emmet Egan to Dimond, 10 November 1922; Dimond to Murray, 11 August 1923; Dimond to J. C. Murphy, 16 August 1923; John F. Coffey to Dimond, 28 June 1925, 7 August 1925; Dimond to Coffey, 18 July 1925; Dimond to Mrs. Agnes W.B. Shepard, 2 May 1925 (quotation), DOD; *Valdez Miner*, 1 September 1923, p. 2.

[39]*Valdez Miner*, 13 February 1926, p. 2; "Arthur Frame," *Alaska-Yukon Magazine*, January 1909, p. 317.

[40]*Cordova Daily Times*, 4 February 1926, p. 1.

[41]*New York Times*, 11 July 1926, p. 6.

[42]Sister Marie Therese, interview, 20 April 1975.

[43]*Valdez Miner*, 9 October 1926, p. 2; *Anchorage Daily Times*, 27 October 1926, p. 3; 28 October 1926, pp. 4-5; 29 October 1926, pp. 3, 6. For examples of Marquam's campaign: *Seward Weekly Gateway*, 10 October 1926, p. 9; *Anchorage Daily Times*, 27 October 1926, p. 1 (quotation); *Fairbanks Daily News-Miner*, 29 October 1926, p. 4.

[44]*Seward Weekly Gateway*, 10 October 1926, p. 2; *Anchorage Daily Times*, 28 October 1926, pp. 4-5; 29 October 1926, pp. 3, 6; *Fairbanks Daily News-Miner*, 29 October 1926, p. 4.

[45]*Valdez Miner*, 9 October 1926, p. 2; 6 November 1926, p. 1; *Anchorage Daily Times*, 28 October 1926, p. 4; *Cordova Daily Times*, 30 October 1926, p. 4; 1 November 1926, p. 4.

[46]*Alaska Empire*, 4 May 1927, p. 8; 5 May 1927, p. 4; *Valdez Miner*, 21 May 1927, p. 2.

[47]*Valdez Miner*, 10 December 1927, p. 2; 28 April 1928, p. 1; 13 October 1928, p. 2.

[48]*The Alaska Fisherman*, October 1928, p. 2.

[49]Alaska (Ter.), *Senate Journal of Alaska 1929*, pp. 45, 57-58, 62, 67, 70-71, 88, 93-94, 98-99, 106, 115, 122-23, 148, 152, 163, 168-69, 172, 174-76 (governor's veto message), 179, 223, 232, 262, 273, 306, 320, 350-76; *Alaska Empire*, 2 April 1929, p. 8 (quotation).

[50]*Senate Journal 1929*, pp. 70, 172, 273; Alaska (Ter.), *Session Laws of Alaska 1929*, Chapter 54, p. 123.

[51]*Senate Journal 1929*, pp. 163, 223, 306; *Laws of Alaska 1929*, Chapter 83, pp. 172-78.

[52]*Senate Journal 1929*, pp. 93, 186, 189, 194-95, 199, 202, 207, 218, 224, 228, 232, 249, 251, 274, 286, 291, 320; *Laws of Alaska 1929*, Chapter 97, pp. 194-233; *Alaska Empire*, 29 March 1929, pp. 1, 8; 22 April 1929, p. 8.

[53]*Senate Journal 1929*, pp. 49, 83; *Alaska Empire*, 25 March 1929, p. 2; 26 March 1929, p. 2.

[54]*Senate Journal 1929*, pp. 185-87, 203-204, 213-14, 225, 236-37; *Alaska Empire*, 20 April 1929, p. 8; 26 April 1929, p. 1; 27 April 1929, p. 1; 2 May 1929, p. 1.

[55]*Laws of Alaska 1929*, Chapter 118, pp. 279-94.

[56]*Laws of Alaska 1929*, Chapter 115, pp. 274-75.

[57]*Laws of Alaska 1929*, Chapter 114, pp. 272-73.

[58]Alaska (Ter.), *Senate Journal of Alaska 1931*, pp. 16, 49, 69, 83-84, 154, 161, 191-92, 203, 248, 272, 312, 317, 420-43; Alaska (Ter.), *Session Laws of Alaska 1931*, Chapter 10, pp. 55-57.

[59]*Alaska Empire*, 4 March 1931, p. 1; 5 March 1931, p. 1; *Senate Journal 1931*, p. 184; *Laws of Alaska 1931*, Chapter 72, pp. 128-30.

[60]*Senate Journal 1931*, pp. 184, 231, 363; *Laws of Alaska 1931*, Chapter 91, pp. 168-69.

[61]*Senate Journal 1931*, pp. 54, 90, 197; *Laws of Alaska 1931*, Chapter 16, p. 64.

[62]*Laws of Alaska 1931*, Chapter 95 (repeal of the "Bone Dry Law"), pp. 173-74; Chapter 65 (repeal of the Wickersham Mining Act), pp. 117-18; Chapter 64 (repeal of Alaska's mining act based upon the Wickersham law), p. 117; *Senate Journal 1931*, pp. 173.

[63]Sister Marie Therese, interview, 20 April 1975.

[64]*Alaska Empire*, 17 March 1931, p. 2.

PLANTING ALASKA*

James R. Shortridge

Alaska has long sought to capitalize upon its frontier image. Tourists have been asked to visit "the last frontier." Environmentalists, to the dismay of some Alaskan politicians, have accepted the notion that Alaska is a frontier, one which they wish to preserve. And non-resident writers such as John McPhee have depicted Alaska as the last refuge of the truly independent man, the prototypical pioneer.

In political terms, this frontier image has plagued Alaska from the time of its purchase by the United States. In the late 1860s and early 1870s Sitka, then the capital, experienced a minor boom as land speculators and other go-getters from western regions moved north, confidently anticipating that they would reap the rewards of rapid development similar to that occurring elsewhere in the American West. But, as Ted C. Hinckley has pointed out in *The Americanization of Alaska, 1867-1897* (Palo Alto, CA: Pacific Books, Publishers, 1972), the boom soon collapsed. Sitkans blamed the collapse on, among other things, lack of a homestead law. Yet, very little of the land near Sitka (and throughout southeastern Alaska) was suitable for homesteading, and a homestead act would have made no significant difference to the economy, which quickly fell into depression.

With hindsight, one can easily see that Sitka in 1870 lacked an economic base. The Russian American Company had sold its assets to a San Francisco firm, which transferred its operations from Sitka to Kodiak Island and the Pribilofs. Gold had not yet been found; the salmon industry, not yet developed; and tourism, not yet started. Military spending, the major economic component, proved insufficient to sustain the boom.

Yet American planners and politicians chose to ignore Sitka's example, if indeed they knew about it at all. They expected Alaska to follow the pattern set in the trans-Mississippi West, and part of that pattern consisted of yeoman farmers taming the land. In the early 1900s James Wickersham, then a federal district judge in Fairbanks, envisioned thousands of farms extending throughout the Tanana Valley. And in the 1930s, Franklin D. Roosevelt's New Deal revived the idea by sponsoring the Matanuska Colony. Today, state-funded farmers near Delta compete

---

*This article originally appeared in the *Pacific Northwest Quarterly* 69, no. 4 (October 1978): 145-158.

with rainy weather and hungry buffalo to try to raise enough barley to show a profit. The dream of the yeoman farmer dies hard.

James R. Shortridge, Professor of Geography at the University of Kansas, is one of the few scholars who have examined agriculture in Alaska in terms of both frontier mythology and profit and loss. Shortridge's interests include agriculture and the frontier, folk culture, and cultural regionalism.

In the following selection, Shortridge examines Alaskan agriculture between 1898 and 1929. He notes that Progressives, likening the concepts of frontier and agrarianism, sought agricultural self-sufficiency for Alaska. But he concludes that during the period in question no amount of experimentation and public relations could increase the market and lower production costs to the point that farmers could operate profitably.

* * *

Few people today doubt the basic marginality of Alaska for most farming activities. Climatic and soil conditions do not absolutely prohibit agriculture; the question is more one of economics. Production costs are high, and so few people are engaged in agriculture that marketing infrastructures are generally lacking. In 1973, only about 310 farmers remained in the state, and the number was declining.[1]

Today it is easy to scoff at the general optimism that pervaded Alaska following the discovery of gold in the Klondike. Contemporary publications that championed "the role of the cow and the plow in interior Alaska" or pronounced the region "a land of illimitable cereal and stock raising capabilities" now look very foolish to us. But the hopes for Alaska's agricultural future, when examined in the context of their time, seem not only rational but perhaps attainable. This paper is a sketch of the boom era, focusing on the potentially productive areas of the territory, the types of agriculture best suited to northern conditions, and the promotion of the Alaskan agricultural empire.[2]

Although by 1897 the United States had owned Alaska for 30 years, the agricultural potential of the vast area was largely unknown. A white population of only 4,300 in 1890 provided no market for commercial agriculture, and free land in Alaska generated little interest among American frontier farmers so long as closer homesteads were available in the Dakotas and Montana. Both of these conditions changed rather abruptly at the turn of the century.[3]

Some 34,000 people thronged to the Yukon Valley of Alaska and Canada during the Klondike rush. By late 1897 there were so many miners in the area that a major famine was predicted, a crisis that provided the first impetus for local agricultural development. The next year the U.S. Department of Agriculture began the establishment of experiment stations, and miners either too broke to buy imported food or too remote to obtain it sowed vegetable gardens from Dawson to the future site of Fairbanks. Success was general and soon full-time farmers emerged from the ranks of gold seekers.[4]

The natural isolation of interior Alaska created a protective tariff for the new farmers; even an inexperienced man could make a living. Foodstuffs were especially expensive: at Circle City in 1898, a breakfast of ham and eggs cost $2.50, and beef steak sold for $2.00 a pound. Prices reflected freight rates so high that the governor estimated that shipping one ton of goods from Seattle to mines in the Tanana Valley would cost $2,610. A serious food shortage at Fairbanks in the winter of 1903-1904, which sent the price of flour up to $35 per hundred weight was a clinching argument. Farmers were needed, and agriculture promised to be a lucrative venture.[5]

The internal changes in Alaska initiated by the mining boom generated considerable agricultural development by themselves. In addition, an external factor seemed almost to guarantee large-scale rural settlement in Alaska: the rapid exhaustion of the frontier in the American West during the 1890s. The agricultural frontier, which had been a part of American history from its beginnings, was believed to be nearly at an end. Many believed that its passing would have dour consequences: food prices would rise and wages would fall, destroying American prosperity. Alaska, with plentiful, free land, was the exception, and rapid settlement was predicted.[6]

Other Americans saw the frontier as essential for far more than the economic health of the nation. Agrarian idealism was strong, holding that farmers were the "chosen people of God," certainly the "core of the nation, 'the real genuine America.'" Following the lead of Frederick Jackson Turner, many Americans believed that nearly everything from Yankee ingenuity to democracy itself had roots in the frontier. Alaska, it seemed, simply had to prosper in the early 20th century.[7]

The perception that the Yukon country was a land of major agricultural potential can be observed as early as 1900 in the writings of C. C. Georgeson, head of the Alaska Agricultural Experiment Stations. That he did not hold this conviction in 1898 is shown by his location of the stations: headquarters was established at Sitka in that year, along with a branch at Kodiak, both at tidewater; the third station site was Kenai, still another coastal location. Thereafter, following his first tour through the Yukon Valley in 1900, Georgeson established all the new stations inland: Rampart in the Yukon Valley in 1900, Copper Center in the Copper River Basin in 1902, Fairbanks in the Tanana Valley in 1906, and Matanuska, inland from Cook Inlet, in 1915.[8]

Popular literature began to echo the new Georgeson theme shortly after 1900, and by the end of the decade, the virtues of the Yukon had wide acceptance. It became common knowledge, for example, that grain crops matured every summer at the Rampart station. The only question remaining was the quantity of land physically suited to agriculture. The immediate valley of the Yukon River itself, the only well-explored part of the huge drainage basin, offered only limited arable lands, but what about its tributary valleys and other lowlands and basins? Was the potential large enough to encourage bonanza farming, exporting products to the world? Though prospectors had begun exploration, the first generally accepted reports were from a series of organized government surveys undertaken by the army, the Geological Survey, and the Department of Agriculture.

One of the first places outside the Yukon Valley proper to attract attention was the so-called Fortymile country. It lay along a north-flowing river system by the same name which emptied into the Yukon between Dawson and Eagle. As one of its present town names, Bonanza Bar, suggests, the area was in the midst of early mining activities and thus had a sizable local market expectation. Probably because of this, C. C. Georgeson dispatched one of his assistants, Isaac Jones, to inspect the region in 1901. His report was glowing. In addition to finding an estimated 750,000 acres, "half of which could be brought under culture with ease," and a great deal more grassland, he learned of some cases of strayed livestock surviving the winters.[9]

The Fortymile area looked very good to reporters of the time, and as late as 1938 it was still mentioned as an area of considerable farming potential; but the popularity of the region was short-lived.

The mining boom moved westward to the Tanana Valley in 1903 and then on again to the Seward Peninsula. The resultant migration not only took the potential market of the older district, but was in large part responsible for the discovery of new agricultural regions both larger and less isolated than was the Fortymile. By 1910 the valley was noticeably absent from a map of potential agricultural lands.[10]

A second ephemeral agricultural region was the upper Koyukuk basin, just to the south of the Brooks Range. Although the gold rush never came to this area, the U.S. did maintain a commissioner there for awhile, at the village of Coldfoot. He reported gardening success as early as 1903, and in 1906 he specifically vouched for the growth of 8-pound cabbages and 16-pound turnips. The title of the commissioner gave authenticity to these reports, but a more important reason for their subsequent wide circulation was Coldfoot's location some 60 miles above the Arctic Circle; it was truly arctic farming.[11]

Nearly every Alaskan writer of the period repeated the story of the Coldfoot successes, but no one advocated rural settlement of the region, and it too was excluded from the 1910 map. Like the Fortymile, the upper Koyukuk lost favor largely because better farming lands were thought to exist farther south and closer to the mining market.

The principal competition for Coldfoot and the Fortymile country in the interior came from the Tanana Valley. This region, which had received a favorable agricultural report in 1885 from an army exploring party, was "rediscovered" for farming by Isaac Jones on the same journey in 1901 that had taken him to the Fortymile River. Jones found the valley to be about 25 miles wide where he crossed. It was fairly level, had "a dark, sandy loam" soil, and contained very few bothersome marshes. Even more significant for agriculture, the Tanana showed no evidence of having experienced its first autumn frost, although the date was September 18 and the Yukon Valley proper had already endured several killing frosts that fall. These findings were shortly corroborated by a report on the region requested by Georgeson from a Rampart lawyer, J. L. Green, who had made a recent extended tour of the Tanana. Green asserted that not only did the autumn frost date come late to the valley, but spring arrived there "almost a month earlier than anywhere on the Yukon River."[12]

Both Jones and Green predicted that hardy cereals and most vegetables would thrive in this valley, and they were especially impressed with the stock-raising possibilities. As Green described them:

> This soil was covered with a rank growth of grass...I have not been able to find anything in any other part of the country to equal it either in quantity or quality. The grass grows to the height of from 4 to 4 1/2 feet, and will produce from 2 to 3 tons of hay per acre. There are places where a mowing machine can be driven for 5 miles in one direction without lifting the sickle bar...As fine a quality of hay can be produced there as can be produced anywhere.[13]

During the next two years, nearly every wayfarer into the region voiced optimism. Enough favorable evidence had been accumulated by 1903 to allow Governor Brady to state confidently that "the Tanana Valley is looked upon as the real garden spot of Alaska."[14]

The Tanana Valley possessed a remarkable combination of physical traits favorable to agriculture, and just as people were becoming aware of them, gold was discovered. The first big strike came in 1902, not far from present-day Fairbanks, and the following year saw a stampede into the area. Here was a situation which had never before occurred in Alaska--a major mining bonanza in an area of major farming potential. Georgeson recommended an experiment station for the valley in 1905 and set it up the next year; homesteaders began to flow in; and soon nearly every report on Alaska had a large section devoted to the glories of the Tanana Valley. By the last years of the decade, entire articles were being devoted to Tanana agriculture.[15]

Just as the great potential of the Tanana region had cut short the development of the Fortymile and upper Koyukuk basins, it also curtailed the emergence of several other areas, most notably the upper valley of the Kuskokwim River. The first substantive agricultural information on the area came from the 1900 census agent, who related to Georgeson that Moravian missions at two locations in the valley raised "all the common vegetables." Grass was reported as abundant and the climate as not overly severe. Georgeson concluded from this that "there is no reason why agriculture should not succeed here, when grain ripens on the Yukon three or four degrees farther north."[16]

Having talked with numerous prospectors, in 1906 Georgeson reaffirmed his faith in the Kuskokwim district and termed it the probable equal of the Tanana. But the Kuskokwim never generated any sustained interest. A request in 1921 for an experiment station there was denied, and the press failed to pick up the cause. A later government report attributed the lack of development to "remoteness and inaccessibility," but this explanation only begs the issue. The attention enjoyed by Fairbanks worked to the detriment of the Kuskokwim. Transportation routes were developed to serve the Fairbanks-Tanana area because the population centered there, attracted initially by the gold rush of 1903 and kept on in part by acceptable local agricultural conditions.[17]

The upper Kuskokwim Basin could offer farming lands equal in quality to those of the Tanana, and major gold placers were discovered there in 1910, but the revelation of the agricultural potential of the area simply came too late to generate much enthusiasm or to allow the Kuskokwim to figure in the incipient overland transportation system. The Tanana already offered more good land than could be utilized in many years. Moreover, when gold first brought sizable numbers of people into the Kuskokwim Valley in 1910, a wagon road from the coast had already been constructed from Valdez through Big Delta on the upper Tanana River and down to Fairbanks. The permanent supremacy of the Tanana was assured shortly thereafter by the decision in 1915 to make Fairbanks the inland terminal of the government-owned Alaska Railroad.

Even as news of the farming viability of the Tanana Valley spread, preliminary agricultural investigations were underway in the Susitna and Copper River basins, the two major lowlands sandwiched between the Alaska Range and the coastal mountain system. Extensive gold placers existed in neither area, but the gold rush nevertheless was the indirect stimulus for exploration. These river valleys formed the two best overland approaches to the interior mining centers from the Alaskan coast. By developing one or both of them, the federal government hoped to provide an alternative to the largely Canadian-controlled trail from Skagway through Dawson and to the circuitous, highly seasonal route around the Alaska Peninsula and up the Yukon River.

Because the original plans for an "all-American" route predated 1900 when the Alaskan mining operations centered far to the east, around Circle City and Eagle, the Copper River Valley received most of the early attention. Captain W. R. Abercrombie of the U.S. Army inspected the area in 1898 and came back elated with the farming prospects. He personally observed "thousands and thousands of acres of the finest kind of bunch-grass," and found the soils to be from three to eight feet deep. A former Minnesota farmer living there assured him that "there were thousands of acres of land...that would certainly raise wheat, the conditions being about the same as those met with in northern Dakota and Minnesota."[18]

Words of praise soon found their way to the Department of Agriculture, and Georgeson asked the census enumerator in the Copper River area for his judgment. The report he gave was as enthusiastic as that of Abercrombie, and it prompted Georgeson to make one of his boldest pronouncements:

> In the judgment of the writer, the Copper River Valley has a great future. It will one day be a rich and flourishing country, and perhaps the most populous region in the future State of Alaska. Here are opportunities for thousands of families to make homes for themselves and gain independence.

To implement the vision, a new agricultural experiment station began work in 1902 at Copper Center, and the surveyor-general of Alaska elected to undertake his first rectilinear land surveys in this area.[19]

Agricultural enthusiasm reached its peak in the Copper basin in 1902. The future of the Copper River area seemed assured, but the bright predictions proved false. Frosts came to the experiment station on August 27 in 1903, and then on August 17 and August 14 in the following two years, killing all but the very earliest of the grains sown. In addition, local precipitation was found to be quite marginal and the soil an unproductive, slow-warming clay. The experiment station closed permanently in 1908, a year during which frost occurred every month.[20]

One might expect that the failures at the experiment station would have dictated the end of agricultural dreams in the Copper River country. They served instead as only a partial setback. Georgeson still claimed in 1909 that 15,000 square miles of farming lands existed there, and the government thought enough of the area in 1914 to send in a soil survey team. This persistence can be explained both by the importance of the valley as a transportation route to the deep interior, as already mentioned, and by the presence of a major copper ore body.

These factors produced a rash of local road and railroad building efforts, beginning with an abortive railroad attempt in 1897 and climaxing with the Copper River and Northwestern Railroad, constructed between 1905 and 1911.[21]

As the Copper River and Northwestern neared completion and mining operations began, farmers also arrived. Optimism in the face of decidedly negative experimental cropping results was contingent upon the continued operation of the copper mines and the heavy use of the Copper River route to the interior. When, in 1915, Woodrow Wilson announced that the federally financed railroad inland would ascend the Susitna rather than the Copper River, one of these supports collapsed. With it fell the already shaky farming community. The widely read *Handbook of Alaska* by A. W. Greely, for example, contained a favorable note on the area in its 1909 original edition, but the author deleted the reference from his 1925 revision.[22]

The final inland region to receive major agricultural attention was the Susitna-Matanuska lowland at the head of Cook Inlet. In several ways its early exploration resembled that of the Copper Valley. For both, the proposed all-American route to the interior served as the stimulus. Initial agricultural reports on the regions were also similar: the comments of Captain Edward F. Glenn on the Susitna echoed Abercrombie's on the Copper. "An abundance of good, nutritious grass" existed in the area, but Glenn found the cropping potential even more impressive. "There is no doubt that rye, oats, barley, and buckwheat can be profitably raised," he wrote in 1899, and there was even hope for hardy apples and "six-weeks corn." All in all, "from an agricultural standpoint, Cook Inlet and the country tributary thereto may be safely regarded as the garden spot of Alaska."[23]

Glenn's reports, and equally enthusiastic ones by the U.S. Geological Survey in 1898 and by Joseph Herron of the army in 1899, undoubtedly influenced Georgeson to locate one of his experiment station branches at Kenai in 1899, but they apparently generated little other interest. As late as 1904, for example, a traveler reported no farms and only a few gardens in the Susitna-Matanuska region. Virtually nothing about the area appeared in the popular literature before about 1913. The reasons for this omission are several. Foremost was the competition provided by the equally lush but also gold-rich and booming Tanana Valley. In addition, the lowland lacked an overland trail like the one that brought a measure of prosperity to the Copper Valley after 1898.[24]

The one suggestion of development for the Susitna Valley was the organization of the Alaska Central Railroad in 1902. Although a dozen homesteaders reportedly filed in the Matanuska Valley in anticipation of a boom, development was painfully slow in coming. The Alaska Central backers went broke in 1906 after laying only 52 miles of track, and the withdrawal of all Alaskan coal lands from public entry that same year discouraged new railroad promoters for several years. Further, the concurrent construction of the Copper River and Northwestern Railroad strongly suggested that the Yukon would shortly be tapped by that route.[25]

Potential reasons for development of the Susitna region were collapsing all around. In 1908 the Kenai experiment station closed, and the Susitna Valley seemed destined, like the Kuskokwim and Fortymile valleys, for obscurity. Only a miracle could remove the handicaps, but one came in 1915 when President Wilson selected the valley as the route for the government-owned Alaska Railroad. Immediately the Susitna's agricultural image reverted to that of the "garden spot of Alaska." By 1915, "several hundred" settlers were already reported in the area with some 500 acres in cultivation. Nearly 200 more homestead filings were made in 1916 and 1917, and, as a local historian has put it, "the picture for agriculture in the valley looked rosy indeed."[26]

Throughout the period of agricultural enthusiasm, the coastal region of Alaska was considered decidedly inferior to the Yukon country. In southeastern Alaska, an area of disconnected bits of flat land, high rainfall, and inadequate natural drainage, agriculture consisted only of occasional truck farms and dairies. Not even the most optimistic writers of the time ever portrayed it as a new commercial farming frontier.

Neglect of southwestern Alaska is more difficult to explain than that of the Panhandle, for the natural grasslands of Kodiak and the Alaska Peninsula received the highest praise accorded any portion of the territory throughout the 19th century. Expectations reached their peak during the Klondike period. At that time most people agreed that "cattle and sheep thrive well in the coast region" and assumed that the gold rush would precipitate the start of a sizable beef industry in the Southwest.[27]

But few ranchers came, and the region quietly disappeared from the agricultural spotlight. A great many Alaskan observers failed even to mention the area after about 1905, and many more accorded it only a few polite lines. The governor admitted the stagnation in 1920, saying that "the live-stock industry has hardly progressed beyond the demands for dairy products." He, like others before and after, quickly added that "eventually beef cattle will be grown in...the Territory," but hardly any ranches ever materialized.[28]

The failure of the stock industry in the Southwest gradually induced a change in the official estimates of potential agricultural lands. In 1909 Georgeson, who had earlier estimated that Alaska contained 100,000 square miles of land suitable for farming, broke down his assessment; on assigning a figure for the southern coast, however, he vacillated between 10,000 and 15,000 square miles. The reevaluation also can be seen by comparing a 1913 map of the potential agricultural lands with the 1910 one...The entire coastal area has suffered at the expense of the interior on the 1913 rendering, especially the Southwest from which most of the lands along the Alaska peninsula were stricken.[29]

The existence of large acreages of arable land in the Alaskan interior led to intensive speculation on the types of agriculture best suited to the country. Heretofore a local supply orientation had been the only one envisioned, but possible products for export quickly came to dominate discussions. Enthusiasts touted three possibilities: cattle and sheep ranching, wheat farming, and reindeer herding. The first two were traditional agricultural activities of the American frontier, and the third enterprise was ideally suited to the Alaskan environment. Together they seemed to hold a promise for a new agrarian empire.

Of livestock, wheat, and reindeer, the first to gain attention in Alaska was livestock. The lush grasslands around Kodiak had been heralded ever since 1867, and when the 20th century brought not only population to Alaska but a depletion of rangeland stateside, it was almost inevitable that some development would occur. Georgeson championed the cause in his early reports, and the overseer of some small herds kept by the Alaska Commercial Company in the Kodiak area had "little doubt but that with experienced men the business of stock raising might become a reasonably profitable industry on Kadiak and adjoining islands." In 1902 the governor reported that several stockmen were making inquiries.[30]

The Frye-Bruhn Company, a Seattle packing firm, placed some 9,000 sheep and 200 beef cattle (mostly Herefords) on Kodiak in 1902 and 1903. This move generated a new flurry of inquiries to the governor, and when a special Senate committee toured the area in 1903, it found the residents very optimistic, convinced that stock could be raised there "very profitably." The next season, the government dispatched an agrostologist to the southern Alaska grasslands in order to ascertain the ultimate scope of the apparent new empire.[31]

Early success promised a rapid development for the industry, but for a variety of reasons stagnation set in instead--a stagnation which was to last for some 20 years. During 1903 and 1904, the Frye-Bruhn holdings were decimated: over 70 percent of the cattle died, mostly by falling over cliffs, and sheep numbers plummeted from 9,000 to 80 as a result of an untreated scab outbreak, falls, and drowning. Although authorities emphasized that "all the mortality was due to causes entirely preventable," Frye-Bruhn did not restock its pastures, and no other companies rushed to fill the void.[32]

The rangelands were nearly empty after 1904, but both the government and general public remained excited about prospects for the industry. The Kodiak experiment station, for example, immersed itself completely in livestock research, bringing in Scottish Galloway cattle in 1906 and beginning work with sheep in 1910. The results, according to the secretary of agriculture, were "eminently successful." Most reputable observers agreed with Alfred Brooks, head of the U.S. Geological Survey in the region, that "the establishment of a cattle raising industry for export in this region will no doubt come," and they stubbornly refuted those who took the empty pastures to mean no potential.[33]

Sustaining enthusiasm naturally became more difficult as time passed, but in the middle 1920s sagging hopes were revived. First, in 1924, two companies each imported 1,000 sheep to Unalaska and Umnak islands. One of these brought in an additional 3,500 head by 1927 and reported "exceedingly promising results" from its project. A second impetus followed closely, as the Sixty-ninth Congress approved the creation of grazing districts on the public lands of the territory. Individuals could thus have assurance of their rangeland for extended periods, and would, therefore, be more likely to embark on capital ventures. On the eve of the Great Depression, the livestock future of Alaska seemed as bright as it had in 1902, before the Frye-

Bruhn debacle. The General Land Office reported having on file 80 applications for grazing leases in 1930, and an amazing 190 in 1931.[34]

The agricultural export hopes of Alaska resided almost exclusively in livestock for the first few years after the gold rush of 1897. Wheat, the other traditional American frontier standby, simply would not grow well on the coast, and its commercial potential in the interior was stymied by the inaccessibility of world markets. By around 1909, however, as a railroad to the sea seemed imminent, a few people began to extol the possibility of a new wheat bonanza country in the Tanana and other interior valleys.[35]

There was no great wave of boosterism, however, even after the Alaskan Railroad was announced. In fact, otherwise radiant articles sometimes included brief notes that "Alaska is not essentially a wheat country." Behind the cautious predictions for Alaska's wheat-growing future lay the indifferent experimental results obtained by the Department of Agriculture at Rampart and Fairbanks. By 1918, when barley, rye, and oats were all proven successes, Georgeson was still having trouble with his wheat. The spring varieties he described as "not very satisfactory" because of the short season, and the winter ones winter-killed when not protected by heavy snowfalls. Still, nearly everyone was confident that the wheat-breeding program would eventually be successful, and in the early 1920s their faith was borne out.[36]

Influential journals like *Science* and the *Rural New Yorker* claimed on the basis of Georgeson's confident report of 1920 that Alaska wheat fields were "destined to play an important part in the economic life of the nation." The optimistic outlook became general when the farmers' association at Fairbanks purchased a grain mill in 1921. Many waxed grandiloquent, and even though export dreams were not realized in the immediately ensuing years, most observers remained undaunted.[37]

Although both the wheat and cattle industries were enthusiastically promoted in the 1898-1929 period, their sporadic, very slow development rates were constant hindrances to public credibility. In contrast, the reindeer industry in this period was a model of rapid and smooth growth. It seemed to be an enterprise uniquely suited to the vast tundra lands, and it supplied a product for which abundant markets could be created in the coterminous U.S. and elsewhere.

The beginnings of Alaskan reindeer operations are curious in retrospect, for the government introduced the animals in 1891 not with export in mind, but to provide a means of subsistence for the destitute Alaskan Eskimo population. Nothing might have come of the experiment had the transplanted deer responded indifferently to their new environment, but the animals thrived. Given only minimal care, with no shelter or supplemental feeding, the herds doubled their numbers every three years. It seemed almost too good to be true, and Americans were quick to see the implications. The clarion call was sounded by Gilbert Grosvenor in 1903:

> There are 400,000 square miles of barren tundra in Alaska where no horse, cow, sheep, or goat can find pasture; but everywhere on this vast expanse of frozen land the reindeer can find the long, fibrous, white moss which is his food. There is plenty of room for 10,000,000 of these hardy animals. The time is coming when Alaska will have great reindeer ranches like the great cattle ranches of the southwest...[In 35 years] Alaska will be shipping each year to the United States anywhere from 500,000 to 1,000,000 reindeer carcasses and thousands of tons of delicious hams and tongues. At no distant day, it may be safely predicted, long reindeer trains from arctic and subarctic Alaska will roll into Seattle and our most western cities like the great cattle trains that now every hour thunder into the yards of Chicago.[38]

Grosvenor had made a most daring prophecy but one which the developments of the ensuing years seemed to substantiate. Law originally restricted ownership to Eskimos and missions, but the deer population grew so fast that officials soon realized that commercial exportation of surplus stock was necessary. The first herds passed into white ownership in 1914, and the literature exploded with enthusiastic predictions. Articles appeared bearing such titles as "Alaska, the World's Meat Shop," "The Reindeer Revolution," and "The T-Bone of Tomorrow," each espousing Grosvenor-like dreams.[39]

The new industry needed only a market, and no one doubted that one was waiting to be tapped. Reindeer meat could be delivered to the West Coast at a price one-fourth to one-half that of beef, with most cuts selling for 20 to 25 cents per pound. Coupled with this was the universal judgment that the meat was first class, both in quality and in taste.[40]

The first reindeer shipments stateside from the white-owned herds began in 1915, and success marked the next few years. It was claimed in 1919 that demand exceeded supply despite rapidly increasing exports. By the following year, the largest of the reindeer operators, Carl J. Lomen of Nome, had lined up distributors in eight major American cities, and had obtained contracts with several major hotels and passenger railroads.[41]

As the export business grew, so did the size of the herds. Total numbers rose steadily from 57,872 in 1914 through 98,582 in 1917 and 350,000 in 1924, to an estimated 700,000 in 1931, all concentrated along the Bering seacoast. With the coming of the Alaska Railroad to open up the interior of the country, it seemed only a matter of time before Alaska would contain the 4 to 10 million reindeer estimated to be the ultimate carrying capacity of the region. Figuring conservatively, this would have meant a net annual surplus of 1,200,000 deer--basis enough for a major export industry.[42]

Reindeer seemed ready to assume a permanent place on U.S. meat counters by the late 1920s. Exports continued to rise, and people in authority placed their approval on the endeavor. The eminent economic geographer, J. Russell Smith, for example, called the industry "thoroughly established" in 1924, and Governor Parks had stated that "at a date not far distant the United States may draw a considerable part of its meat supply from the reindeer herds..." Perhaps an even better indicator of general acceptance was the publication in 1929 of a Department of Agriculture leaflet entitled *Reindeer Recipes* and an article in the *Journal of Home Economics* praising this"new delicacy from the crisp, clean Northland" to America's homemakers.[43]

The reindeer, wheat, and cattle-sheep industries, together with the extensive interior valleys, the local mining economy, and the general land needs and beliefs existent in the U.S., comprised a tenable platform from which Alaskan agrarian dreams could be projected. These prospects, progressively supplemented by such things as more liberal land laws, the formal achievement of territorial status in 1912, and the announcement of the federally-financed Alaska Railroad, continually led people to predict an imminent settlement boom. The traditional mobility of war veterans prompted another round of anticipation around 1919, and during the 1920s similar sporadic outbursts of promotional fervor occurred. No one foresaw, or at least acknowledged, that changing economic and social conditions in America were taking away the traditional incentives for frontier farming.

Needless to say, no Alaskan settlement boom took place. The local white population remained virtually static at about 30,000 people, and the number of farms rose only from 12 in 1900 to 500 by 1929. A gain of 488 farmers in 30 years could hardly be termed a boom, and the trickling increase was only sufficient to perpetuate the boom talk, to keep alive hopes of a flood of settlement.[44]

The chief concern of Alaskans and other interested Americans was how to change the trickle into a flood. Some thought that time by itself would produce the desired result, but most authorities saw the need for advertising. The very successful promotional efforts for the plains provinces of Canada were familiar to many, as was the unpleasant fact that most of America still pictured Alaska as a snowy wasteland. As a perceptive commentator remarked in 1925: "Under the prevailing conception of Alaska as a polar region, the public is slow to believe that it contains any agricultural resources."[45]

Conventional American advertising methods had little potential since they depended on such private support as railroads and land speculators. In Alaska, where almost all the land was in government hands, where such abused laws as the Timber Culture and Desert Land acts did not apply, and where even the principal railroad was federally owned, private forces could not operate on any large scale. A massive, unabashed federal promotional program similar to the Canadian one might have been undertaken, but it had no precedent in American land tradition, and was never even discussed. With these two avenues closed, Alaskan agricultural promotion between 1900 and 1930 assumed a somewhat unique form, a hodgepodge of activities centered on ventures ostensibly private in nature but often subsidized in one way or another by the federal government.

Popular journalists provided a major source of propaganda for Alaska. Much of their material, though not intended solely as promotional literature, had a decidedly promotional flavor. After all, Alaskan agriculture was a topic that made good copy. The exotic nature and frontier status of the region were reasons enough for interest, but with agricultural promise in addition, the correspondents could contrast the popular image of snow and ice with the reality of mammoth vegetables. This contrast became a much-repeated theme and produced such attention-catching titles as "Wonders of Alaskan

Agriculture," "The Land of Tomorrow," and "Farming in a Bowl of Ice."[46]

Some journalistic efforts can be classified as pure advertising. Seattle, the stateside city that would have profited most from any Alaskan growth, had businessmen who commissioned several promotional books and articles. Government officials produced an even larger body of deliberately promotional literature; frustrated by the nondevelopment of Alaska, a surprising number of prominent men took up their pens. Georgeson, as might be expected, was one of the most prolific writers. He was joined by Governors John G. Brady, Walter E. Clark, and Scott C. Bone, and by other Alaskan officials such as Alfred Brooks. The movement even reached the national level: President Theodore Roosevelt, three secretaries of the interior, and several U.S. senators all wrote articles that appeared in major magazines.[47]

So enthusiastic was the federal government for Alaskan development that during the first third of the century it managed to undertake several direct promotional activities, in spite of past tradition. One was participation in the Alaska-Yukon-Pacific Exposition at Seattle in 1909. As official documents make clear, the government saw the exposition as a means of encouraging Alaskan settlement.[48]

Some 20 years after the Alaska-Yukon-Pacific Exposition, the federal government again directly involved itself in promoting Alaskan settlement. This time, the Department of the Interior, through the Alaska Railroad, published an information booklet, *The Newest Home Land*, and in January 1929 opened a branch information office in Chicago. Later that year, the railroad placed ads in newspapers and appointed a special agent to travel in the Midwest, distributing posters, showing pictures, and giving talks. It was an unprecedented program, but quite successful initially. By July 1929, 592 inquiries had been received, and by autumn the number had increased to 2,000. Many settlers were anticipated for the next year, but in late 1929 depression hit the country. Only 12 families made the long journey to settle in 1930, and although the railroad continued its program until 1934, a total of only 110 people responded.[49]

Whether private or federal, all Alaskan agricultural promotion undertaken in the first third of the 20th century emphasized similar attractions. Chief among these, as already discussed, were the vast acreages available in the interior and the exciting export possibilities offered by cattle and sheep raising, wheat growing, and reindeer herding. These, however, were by no means the only selling points. Prospective farmers learned that this northern land offered agricultural advantages not to be found in the States, and that Alaska possessed a variety of other assets to make living profitable and pleasurable. Promoters frequently employed analogies to Scandinavia and, in fact, gave special encouragement to settlers of Scandinavian extraction.[50]

Regarding practical agriculture, almost every promoter lauded the long summer days and their amazing effect on vegetable quality and size. One enthusiast called the tropical sun "too intense" for best plant growth whereas "the slanted light of the higher latitudes is always soft and delicate, stimulating growth and not retarding it." According to some, these magical conditions impart to Alaskan produce "such superior flavor that when a person has once eaten the vegetables grown in Alaska, other vegetables are insipid and tasteless."[51]

Other advantages of farming in high latitudes also received considerable publicity. Alaskan crops, because of the cold winters, were claimed to be free of damaging insect pests and fungus diseases. Moreover, farmers were sure to be interested in the natural subirrigation system accompanying every Yukon basin farm. The long, freezing winters there, according to writer after writer, made it possible for "every drop of water and every snowflake which falls" to be conserved as ground ice. This paid marvelous dividends during the growing season, "for as the moisture...is needed it comes up from below."[52]

Most promoters saw virtue in the undeveloped state of Alaskan agriculture. Demand created by the local mining and fishing population assured farmers a solid market for everything that could be grown. A favorite proof of the ready market consisted of the listing of annual farm imports to Alaska. Not the least of the economic attractions, the opportunity for a future beckoned to poor, rural Americans: they could cast their lot with that of the virgin country, and grow and prosper along with Alaska.[53]

Efforts to attract rural settlers to Alaska rarely stopped with strictly agricultural appeals. Other advantages of living in the North were also stressed. The scenery, of course, particularly the splendid beauty of the southeastern glacier and fjord country, always received emphasis, but so did matters of more direct concern to prospective immigrants. To dispel fears of the long winters, promoters published testimonies of Alaska residents who asserted that they actually preferred the local winters to the summers, and from all sides came assurances that the climate was extremely healthful.[54]

Like all promotional pictures, the Alaska of the 1900-1929 period looked extremely lucrative to homeseekers. The 1930 census, however, taken before the Great Depression had caused any turmoil, revealed that only minor agricultural development had taken place. No more than 500 farms could be counted, and although these occupied a fairly respectable 525,942 acres, only a minuscule 3,875 acres produced crops. On the average, less than eight acres of cultivated land existed per farm.[55]

An adequate explanation for the token rural settlement of Alaska seems obvious in retrospect. American life underwent tremendous change in the 1898-1929 period, and farming concepts were drastically altered. Growing urban amenities made life on a subsistence farm seem unattractive, and the virgin soil of a distant frontier held little allure as cheap fertilizers and improved plant varieties aided existing agricultural areas in the Middle West and elsewhere. Commercial production in Alaska was neither needed nor economically feasible, and although subsistence farming remained a theoretical possibility; it appealed only to a few.[56]

Americans in 1929 had not yet comprehended the new social and economic conditions, at least, as they affected Alaska. Apparently the pioneering idea was so deeply embedded in the culture that people could not admit that it no longer related to real conditions. Alaskan observers continued to focus on trends rather than absolute numbers, emphasizing, for example, the 37 percent increase in farms between 1920 and 1930 rather than the small total numbers. They still hoped that a little more time and a little more advertising would bring Alaska its long-awaited settlement boom.

ENDNOTES

[1]Burke G. Vanderhill, "Perspectives on Alaskan Agriculture", *Journal of Geography* 72 (February 1973): 38-52; Karl E. Francis, "Outpost Agriculture: The Case of Alaska," *Geographical Review* 57 (1967): 496-505.

[2]J. Paul Heritage, "Uncle Sam's Last Free Lands: The Role of the Cow and the Plow in Interior Alaska," *Scientific American Monthly* 4 (1921): 312-17;

Charles R. Tuttle, *The Golden North: A Vast Country of Inexhaustible Gold Fields, and a Land of Illimitable Cereal and Stock Raising Capabilities* (Chicago, 1897). The boom era is the only period of Alaskan agriculture lacking historical study: see James R. Gibson, *Imperial Russia in Frontier America: The Changing Geography of Supply of Russian America, 1784-1867* (New York, 1976); James R. Shortridge, "The Evaluation of the Agricultural Potential of Alaska, 1867-1897," *Pacific Northwest Quarterly* 68 (1977): 88-98; Orlando W. Miller, *The Frontier in Alaska and the Matanuska Colony* (New Haven, 1975); and James R. Shortridge, "The Collapse of Frontier Farming in Alaska," *Annals of the Association of American Geographers* 66 (1976): 583-604.

[3]*Report on Population of the United States at the Eleventh Census: 1890* (Washington, D.C., 1895), p. 967.

[4]Alfred H. Brooks, *Blazing Alaska's Trails*, ed. Burton L. Fryxell (College, Alaska, 1953), p. 349. *Relief of People in the Yukon River Country*, 55th Cong., 3rd Sess., 1899, House Document 244 (Serial 3812). C. C. Georgeson, *Fourth Report on the Agricultural Investigations in Alaska: 1900*, U.S. Department of Agriculture, Office of Experiment Stations Bulletin 94 (Washington, D.C., 1901), pp. 50-62 (hereafter cited OES Bulletin 94).

[5]Lt. W. P. Richardson to the adjutant-general, July 7, 1898, in *Relief of People*, p. 113; John G. Brady's annual report for 1900, in 56th Cong., 2nd Sess., 1900, House Document 5, p. 20 (Serial 4104). Cecil F. Robe, "The Penetration of an Alaskan Frontier: The Tanana Valley and Fairbanks," Ph.D. dissertation (Yale University, 1943), pp. 184-86.

[6]Josiah Strong, *Our Country: Its Possible Future and Its Present Crisis* (New York, 1885), p. 153; James Bryce, *The American Commonwealth*, Vol. 2, new ed. (New York, 1921), p. 913; William J. Trimble, "The Influence of the Passing of the Public Lands," *Atlantic Monthly* 113 (1914): 755-67.

[7]Thomas Jefferson, *Notes on the State of Virginia* (New York, 1964), p. 157; Henry N. Smith, *Virgin Land: The American West as Symbol and Myth* (Cambridge, Mass., 1950), p. 139. Frederick J. Turner, *The Frontier in American History* (New York, 1920). According to one modern historian, "The historic Turner essay seemed to rate only slightly lower in the popular estimation than the Bible, the Constitution, and the Declaration of Independence"; see Robert E. Riegel, "American Frontier Theory," *Journal of World History* 3 (1956): 367.

[8]Georgeson, OES Bulletin 94, p. 67.

[9]For Jones's findings, see Georgeson's annual report for 1901, in 57th Cong., 1st Sess., 1902, House Document 334, p. 300 (Serial 4301).

[10]One writer went so far as to call it "another Washington for fertility"; see Alice P. Henderson, "Alaska's Agricultural Possibilities," *Alaskan Magazine* 1 (1900): 60. Also see U.S. National Resources Committee, *Regional Planning.* Part VII: *Alaska--Its Resources and Development* (Washington, D.C., 1938), p. 122.

[11]Guy E. Mitchell, "Wonders of Alaskan Agriculture," *Illustrated World* 12 (1910): 526.

[12]Henry T. Allen, *Report of an Expedition to the Copper, Tanana, and*

Koyukuk Rivers, in the Territory of Alaska in the Year 1885, 49th Cong., 2nd Sess., 1887, Senate Executive Document 125, p. 164 (Serial 2449). Georgeson's annual report for 1901, pp. 302-303, 310.

[13]Georgeson's annual report for 1901, pp. 290, 309-10.

[14]Brady's annual report for 1903, in 58th Cong., 2nd Sess., 1903, House Document 5, p. 18 (Serial 4648).

[15]See, for example, Falcon Joslin, "Agriculture in the Tanana Valley, Alaska," *Alaska-Yukon Magazine* 9 (1909): 3-11; "Proof of Alaska's Agricultural Resources," *Alaska-Yukon Magazine* 9 (1910): 325-26; "Some Products of the Tanana Valley," *Alaska-Yukon Magazine* 11 (1911): 12-13; Gustav R. Stahl, "Farming in a Bowl of Ice," *Illustrated World* 20 (1913): 210-11.

[16]Georgeson, OES Bulletin 94, pp. 34-35.

[17]See Georgeson's essay on Alaska in Liberty H. Bailey, ed., *Cyclopedia of American Agriculture*, 3 vols. (New York, 1907), I, p. 96. *Alaska--Its Resources and Development*, p. 122.

[18]W. R. Abercrombie, "A Military Reconnaissance of the Copper River Valley," 1898, in *Compilation of Narratives of Exploration in Alaska*, 56th Cong., 1st Sess., 1900, Senate Report 1023, pp. 580-81 (Serial 3896). For more of Abercrombie's views see his "Copper River Country, Alaska," *Journal of the Franklin Institute* 158 (1904): 289-310, 353-66.

[19]Georgeson, OES Bulletin 94, p. 34. Idem, 1901 report, p. 306. See "Report of the Commissioner of the General Land Office" in *Annual Reports of the Department of the Interior for the Fiscal Year Ended June 30, 1901* (Washington, D.C., 1901), p. 471.

[20]C. C. Georgeson, *Report on Agricultural Investigations in Alaska, 1905*, U.S. Department of Agriculture, Office of Experiment Stations Bulletin 169 (Washington, D.C., 1906), p. 11; the shorter than expected growing season was a product of the high (2,000-3,000 ft.) elevation of the basin. Hugh H. Bennett and Thomas D. Rice, "Soil Reconnaissance in Alaska, with an Estimate of the Agricultural Possibilities," in U.S. Department of Agriculture, *Field Operations of the Bureau of Soils, 1914* (Washington, D.C., 1919), pp. 225-27.

[21]C. C. Georgeson, "Agricultural Capacity of Alaska," *National Geographic Magazine* 20 (1909): 678. Bennett and Rice, "Soil Reconnaissance in Alaska," p. 228. Franklin W. Burch, "Alaska's Railroad Frontier: Railroads and Federal Development Policy," Ph.D. dissertation (Catholic University of America, 1965), pp. 106-107.

[22]"Alaska's Farming Progress in 1910," *Alaska-Yukon Magazine* 10 (1910): 238; "A Real Farm in the Copper River Valley," *Alaska-Yukon Magazine* 11 (1911): 23-24. A. W. Greely, *Handbook of Alaska: Its Resources, Products, and Attractions* (New York, 1909), p. 46.

[23]Protected by the Kenai Mountains and the elongated nature of Cook Inlet, the Susitna, though technically located on the coast, has climatic conditions similar to those of the interior. Edward F. Glenn, "Explorations in and about Cooks Inlet," in *Compilation of Narratives*, pp. 721-22.

24George H. Eldridge, "A Reconnaissance in the Sushitna Basin and Adjacent Territory, Alaska, in 1898," in *Twentieth Annual Report of the United States Geological Survey*, 56th Cong., 1st Sess., 1900, House Document 5, part 7, pp. 24, 28-29 (Serial 3926); Joseph S. Herron, *Explorations in Alaska, 1899, for an All-American Overland Route from Cook Inlet, Pacific Ocean, to the Yukon*, 60th Cong., 2nd Sess., 1901, Senate Document 689, pp. 55-56 (Serial 5408). Norman F. Thomas, "Cook Inlet in 1904--H. P. Gallagher Journal," *Alaska Review* 3 (1969): 261-72.

25See, for example, Levi Chubbuck, "Alaska Agricultural Possibilities," *Bulletin of the American Geographical Society* 42 (1910): 896. "Alaska's Farming Progress," p. 328. Burch, "Alaska's Railroad Frontier," pp. 196-97.

26*Annual Reports of the Department of Agriculture for the Year Ended June 30, 1908* (Washington, D.C., 1909), p. 727. The "garden spot" term was used by Glenn, "Explorations in and about Cooks Inlet," p. 721. *Report of the Commissioner of the General Land Office to the Secretary of the Interior for the Fiscal Year Ended June 30, 1915* (Washington, D.C., 1915), p. 25; Bennett and Rice, "Soil Reconnaissance in Alaska," p. 112. Louise Potter, *A Study of a Frontier Town in Alaska: Wasilla to 1959* (Hanover, N.H., 1963), p. 57.

27C. C. Georgeson, *Report on Agricultural Investigations in Alaska in 1899*, U.S. Department of Agriculture, Office of Experiment Stations Bulletin 82 (Washington, D.C., 1900), pp. 39-40 (hereafter cited OES Bulletin 82). See also Shortridge, "The Evaluation of the Agricultural Potential."

28See, for example, Greely, *Handbook of Alaska* (1925 ed.), p. 143, and Agnes R. Burr, *Alaska, Our Beautiful Northland of Opportunity* (Boston, 1919), p. 331. Annual report of Thomas Riggs, Jr., for 1920, in *Reports of the Department of the Interior for the Fiscal Year Ended June 30, 1920*, Vol. 2 (Washington. D.C., 1920), p. 34 (also in Serial 7706).

29C. C. Georgeson, "Agriculture in Alaska," *Alaska-Yukon Magazine* 8 (1909): 300. Idem, "Agricultural Capacity," pp. 678-79.

30Georgeson, OES Bulletin 82, p. 40. Brady's annual report for 1902, in 57th Cong., 2nd Sess., 1903, House Document 5, p. 36 (Serial 4461).

31Brady's annual report for 1903, p. 20; testimony given to members of the subcommittee of the committee on territories in part 2 of *Conditions in Alaska*, 58th Cong., 2nd Sess., 1904, Senate Report 282, p. 216 (Serial 4570). C. V. Piper, *Grass Lands of the South Alaska Coast*, U.S. Department of Agriculture, Bureau of Plant Industry Bulletin 82 (Washington, D.C., 1905), p. 5.

32Piper, *Grass Lands of the South Alaska Coast*, pp. 22-24.

33 *Annual Reports of the Department of Agriculture for the Year Ended June 30, 1912* (Washington, D.C., 1913), p. 832. Brooks, *Blazing Alaska's Trails*, p. 457.

34[Scott C. Bone], *Report of the Governor of Alaska* (Washington, D.C., 1924), p. 33. U.S. Department of the Interior, *General Information Regarding the Territory of Alaska* (Washington, D.C., 1927), p. 76. Act of March 4, 1927 (*Statutes at Large*, 69th Cong., 2nd Sess., 1927, Vol. 44, part 2, p. 1452). The argument for assurance of rangeland appears in Committee on Public Lands and Surveys, *Grazing on Public Lands in Alaska*, 69th Cong., 1st Sess., 1926, Senate Report 681, p. 2 (Serial 8525). *Annual Report of the Commissioner of the General Land Office to the Secretary of the Interior, 1930* (Washington, D.C., 1930), p. 12; *Annual Report of the Commissioner of the General Land Office to the Secretary of the Interior, 1931* (Washington, D.C., 1931), p. 13.

[35]See, for example, Joslin, "Agriculture in the Tanana Valley," pp. 9-11; and E. S. Harrison, "Where Farmers May Find Homes," *Alaska-Yukon Magazine* 7 (1909): 279.

[36]J. J. Underwood, "What Alaska Offers to Agriculture," *Country Gentleman* 77 (March 1912): 5; another example is C. L. Andrews, "Agriculture in Alaska," *Alaska-Yukon Magazine* 12 (1911): 356. C. C. Georgeson, "The Selection and Hybridization of Cereals in Alaska, U.S.A.," *International Review of the Science and Practice of Agriculture* 9 (1918): 433-34.

[37]"Agriculture in Alaska," *Science* 52 (July 30, 1920): 101-102; A. H. Pulver, "Alaska as a Food Producer," *Rural New Yorker* 79 (1920): 1854; G. B. F., "Farming Possibilities in Alaska," *Rural New Yorker* 80 (1921): 1013. See, for example, Andrew J. Stone, "The Natural Resources of Alaska," *Century Magazine* 100 (1920): 842; [Scott C. Bone], *Report of the Governor of Alaska* (Washington, D.C., 1921), p. 41; Mary L. Davis, *Uncle Sam's Attic; The Intimate Story of Alaska* (Boston, 1930), pp. 285-86.

[38]Gilbert H. Grosvenor, "Reindeer in Alaska," *National Geographic Magazine* 14 (1903): 127, 147-48.

[39]The official herd estimates for 1902, 1907, and 1910, respectively, were 4,975, 13,839, and 26,000 (see Walter E. Clark's annual report for 1910 in *Reports of the Department of the Interior for the Fiscal Year Ended June 30, 1910*, Vol. 2 [Washington, D.C., 1911], p. 249 [Serial 5976]). By 1914 the herd population had reached 57,872 (see John F. A. Strong's annual report for 1915 in *Reports of the Department of the Interior for the Fiscal Year Ended June 30, 1915*, Vol. 2 [Washington, D.C., 1916], p. 472 [also in Serial 6992]). Emil E. Hurja, "Alaska, the World's Meat Shop," *Overland Monthly* 63 (1914): 120-25; "The Reindeer Revolution," *Independent* 77 (1914): 163; Francis J. Dickie, "The T-Bone of Tomorrow," *Sunset: The Pacific Monthly* 43 (December 1919): 41-42, 92.

[40]Clio Mamer, "Alaska's Prospective Contribution to Our Meat Supply," *Catholic World* 105 (1917): 647, 651. E. W. Nelson, "What Reindeer Mean to the United States," *U.S. Department of Agriculture Weekly News Letter* 8 (January 26, 1921): 9.

[41]Dickie, "The T-Bone of Tomorrow," p. 42. Shipments to the U.S. by the largest entrepreneur were as follows: in 1915, 74 carcasses (approx. 11,000 lbs.); in 1916, 10,650 lbs.; in 1917, 33,000 lbs.; in 1918, 99,000 lbs.; in 1919, 37,000 lbs.; and in 1920, 257,000 lbs. (see Carl J. Lomen, *Fifty Years in Alaska* [New York, 1954], p. 90).

[42]Strong's annual report for 1915, p, 472; annual report of Thomas Riggs, Jr., for 1918, in *Reports of the Department of the Interior for the Fiscal*

Year Ended June 30, 1918, Vol. 2 (Washington, D.C., 1919), p. 517 (also in Serial 7358); Bone's annual report for 1924, p. 43; and [George A. Parks], *Annual Report of the Governor of Alaska* (Washington, D.C., 1931), p. 111. Estimates of reindeer capacity varied widely. Alaska's governors, for example, placed the figure at 10,000,000 in 1912, 4,000,000 in 1923, and 10,000,00 again in 1926 (see Clark's annual report for 1912, in *Reports of the Department of the Interior for the Fiscal Year Ended June 30, 1912*, Vol. 2 [Washington, D.C., 1913], p. 538 [Serial 6409]; *Annual Report of the Secretary of the Interior for the Fiscal Year Ended June 30, 1923* [Washington, D.C. 1923], p. 110; and *Annual Report of the Secretary of the Interior for the Fiscal Year Ended June 30, 1926* [Washington, D.C., 1926], p. 38). The 1,200,000 figure is 30 percent of 4 million and represents the standard way of calculating the annual surplus of reindeer available for marketing.

[43]The export figures were as follows: in 1926, 968,000 lbs.; in 1927, 820,000 lbs.; in 1928, 1,319,000 lbs.; in 1929, 1,384,000 lbs.; and in 1930, 1,567,000 lbs.; see Albert L. Seeman, "Development of Reindeer Activities in Alaska," *Economic Geography* 9 (1933): 299; J. Russell Smith, "The Reindeer Industry in America: A Study of a New Industry and also of the Origins of Geographic Error," *Scottish Geographical Magazine* 40 (1924): 84; [George A. Parks], *Report of the Governor of Alaska* (Washington, D.C., 1925), p. 65. Louise Stanley and Fanny W. Yeatman, *Reindeer Recipes*, U.S. Department of Agriculture Leaflet 48 (Washington, D.C., 1929); Jean Bunnell, "The Alaska Reindeer Industry," *Journal of Home Economics* 21 (1929): 17-20.

[44]*Fifteenth Census of the United States: 1930. Outlying Territories and Possessions* (Washington, D.C., 1932), pp. 15, 29; and *Thirteenth Census of the United States Taken in the Year 1910: Vol. VII, Agriculture* (Washington, D.C., 1913), p. 971.

[45] Karel D. Bicha, "The Plains Farmer and the Prairie Province Frontier, 1897-1914," *Proceedings of the American Philosophical Society* 109 (1965): 398-440. Alfred H. Brooks, "The Future of Alaska," *Annals of the Association of American Geographers* 15 (1925): 172.

[46]Mitchell, "Wonders of Alaskan Agriculture," passim; William B. Stephenson, Jr., *The Land of Tomorrow* (New York, 1919); Stahl, "Farming in a Bowl of Ice," pp. 210-11.

[47]Wilds P. Richardson, "Alaska," *Atlantic Monthly* 141 (1928): 114. One of the most popular of the Seattle backed efforts was Charles R. Tuttle, *Alaska: Its Meaning to the World* (Seattle, 1914). On the relations between Alaska and Seattle, see William R. Siddall, "Seattle: Regional Capital of Alaska," *Annals of the Association of American Geographers* 47 (1957): 277-84. Beyond their annual reports, Alaska governors produced other writings both in and out of office: Brady wrote two articles for the *Independent* (52 [1900]: 165-68, and 66 [1909]: 1379-85); Clark wrote in *Sunset* (24 [1910]: 495-502, 29 [1912]: 27-36, and 32 [1914]: 299-309) and in *World's Work* (18 [1909]: 11941-44); and Bone contributed to *American Review of Reviews* (65 [1922]: 402-10). Brooks was another official

who added to the literature of Alaska: see his *Blazing Alaska's Trails*, "The Future of Alaska," and articles in *Geographical Review* (15 [1925]: 25-50) and *American Review of Reviews* (40 [1909]: 49-62). Roosevelt had two articles in *Outlook* (98 [1911]: 612-15 and 821-22); Walter L. Fisher wrote in the *Independent* (72 [1912]: 1094-96); Franklin K. Lane in *National Geographic Magazine* (25 [1914]: 183-95); and John Barton Payne in the *Independent* (103 [1920]: 330-31, 353-54). Two authors from the U.S. Senate were Simon Guggenheim (*Independent* 69 [1910]: 295-99) and George Chamberlain (*Independent* 77 [1914]: 372-73).

[48]Select Committee on Industrial Expositions, *Alaska-Yukon-Pacific Exposition at Seattle, Washington*, 59th Cong., 2nd Sess., 1909, Senate Report 6510, p. 6 (Serial 5060).

[49]U.S. Department of the Interior, Alaska Railroad, *The Newest Home Land* (Washington, D.C., 1928). Miller, *The Frontier in Alaska and the Matanuska Colony*, pp. 31-32. [George A. Parks], *Annual Report of the Governor of Alaska* (Washington, D.C., 1930), p. 9.

[50]A classic specimen of such an analogy appears in Floyd W. Parsons, "Our Last Undeveloped Empire," *Saturday Evening Post* 193 (Dec. 11, 1920): 34. Miller, *The Frontier in Alaska and the Matanuska Colony*, pp. 31-32.

[51]E. Davenport, "In Our Land of the Midnight Sun," *Country Gentleman* 93 (March 1928): 95. Joe King, "Farming in Alaska," *Alaska-Yukon Magazine* 8 (1909): 136.

[52]Stahl, "Farming in a Bowl of Ice," pp. 210-11. See also Henderson, "Alaska's Agricultural Possibilities," p. 60; T. A. Richard, *Through the Yukon and Alaska* (San Francisco, 1909), p. 282; and L. P. Bott, Jr., "Agricultural Opportunities in Alaska," *Market Growers Journal* 48 (1931): 160-62.

[53]See, for example, J. J. Underwood, "Alaska: Your Last Chance," *Illustrated World* 24 (1915): 365-70; Monroe Woolley, "Your Opportunities in Alaska," *Illustrated World* 27 (1917): 81.

[54]Mary L. Davis, "God's Pocket," *Scribner's Magazine* 75 (1924): 660-62. See, for example, C. C. Georgeson, "The Agricultural Capacity of Alaska," *See America First Magazine* 5 (1919): 25; Alfred Holman, "Alaska as a Territory of the United States," *Century Magazine* 85 (1913): 597-98; *Knik, Alaska, Its Resources* (n.p., 1911).

[55]*Fifteenth Census*, pp. 29-31. The only exception to the dismal agricultural picture was reindeer, but this industry underwent spectacular decline in the 1930s due to a combination of factors, including pressure from cattlemen's groups and overgrazing. For analysis see Shortridge, "Collapse," pp. 593-94.

[56]Shortridge, "Collapse," pp. 594-95, 602-604. *Fifteenth Census*, p. 29.

THE ALASKAN I.R.A.*

Kenneth R. Philp

The Indian Reorganization Act of 1934, passed in the early years of Franklin Roosevelt's New Deal, represented a dramatic change in American Indian policy. The I.R.A. recognized the legitimacy of Indian self-determination by permitting Indian businesses to be incorporated, establishing Indian credit agencies, protecting some forms of Indian land title, and granting limited power of self-government to Indian reservations. It was a reversal of the highly destructive Indian policies of the late 19th and early 20th centuries.

The I.R.A. was not immediately applicable to Alaska because there were no tribes in Alaska as that term was understood in the continental states. Delegate Tony Dimond and the Tlingit lawyer William Paul, Sr., worked with Interior department officials and congressional leaders to amend the I.R.A. for extension to Alaska, and a bill was passed in the U. S. Congress for that purpose in 1936.

In this article Professor Kenneth Philp at the University of Texas at Arlington discusses the Alaska Reorganization Act (as the amended I.R.A. was called) and some of the struggles of Alaska's Tlingit and Haida Indians which followed. Having earned his doctorate at Michigan State University, Philp published an important study on New Deal Indian Commissioner John Collier, *John Collier's Crusade for Indian Reform, 1920-1954* (Tucson: University of Arizona Press) in 1977. He has published a number of articles on 20th century Indian affairs, including "Dillion S. Meyer and the Advent of Termination, 1950-1953" *Western Historical Quarterly*, January 1988, and "Stride Toward Freedom: The Relocation of Indians to Cities, 1952-1960," *Western Historical Quarterly*, April 1985.

In the article printed here, Philp discusses the attempt of Secretary of the Interior Harold Ickes to persuade Alaska's Tlingit and Haida Indians to accept the establishment of reservations in Alaska to protect Native land title. Some Southeast villages did vote to create small reservations, but these were declared invalid by court action in the 1950s. Governor Gruening opposed the creation of Indian reservations as discriminatory toward the Native people and detrimental to the statehood movement.

* * *

On April 21, 1933, President Franklin D. Roosevelt appointed John Collier as commissioner of Indian affairs. During the previous

---

*This article originally appeared in *Pacific Historical Review* 50 (1981): 309-327.

decade Collier had been executive secretary of the American Indian Defense Association, an organization that opposed the Dawes General Allotment Act of 1887.[1] This legislation had destroyed much of the reservation system in the United States by abolishing tribal governments and providing the Indians with 160-acre, or smaller, homesteads. The Dawes Act was part of a broader effort by nineteenth-century Indian reformers to promote the objective of assimilation. Collier believed that the Dawes Act and similar efforts had led to poverty, landlessness, and the general social disorientation of native Americans. Shortly after taking office, he met with officials in the Department of the Interior and formulated a new federal Indian policy based on the concept of cultural pluralism. The centerpiece of this policy--the Indian New Deal--was the Indian Reorganization Act of 1934, which encouraged the use of reservations as homelands where tribes could engage in self-government and cooperative economic activity.[2]

Historians have recently provided new insights concerning the Indian New Deal, but they have neglected to analyze carefully how it effected the Eskimos, Aleuts, and Indians who resided in the territory of Alaska.[3] The Alaska Reorganization Act of 1936 allowed natives to establish village self-government and borrow money from a federal credit fund in order to combat the effects of the Great Depression.[4] The Interior Department used this legislation to create five reservations, and it held hearings to determine the extent of Haida and Tlingit claims to fishing rights and land in southeastern Alaska.

The Alaska Reorganization Act provided the natives with needed financial assistance, but it was poorly administered and inadequately funded by Congress. More importantly, the policy of setting aside reservations met opposition from white settlers and natives who had become assimilated after Alaska came under the jurisdiction of the United States in 1867.[5] Rather than listen to their critics, New Deal officials in the Interior Department pushed ahead with plans to establish reservations and determine the validity of native claims. They neglected, however, to consult with Congress or gain needed grass-roots support. The result was further delay in securing social justice for Alaska's native inhabitants.

After the purchase of Alaska, the United States did not sign treaties with the natives and provide them with reservations in return for ceded land rights. Instead, Congress passed the Alaska Organic Act of May 17, 1884, which allowed the natives to remain undisturbed on the land they occupied until their title was confirmed by future legislation. After 1890, some 126 reserves containing 1,338,700 acres for 2,063 natives were created by executive order. Most of these reserves were not bonafide reservations. Except for areas devoted to the grazing of reindeer, they consisted of forty-acre or smaller plots set aside for federal schools and hospitals. In 1898 and 1906, Congress permitted the natives to apply for homesteads, but the absence of surveyed land made it impossible to confirm land claims.[6]

The federal government had been concerned about the welfare of Alaska's natives long before the New Deal. Beginning in 1884, the Bureau of Education in the Interior Department provided the natives with schools, founded cooperative trading stores, and helped the Eskimos herd reindeer.[7] In 1905, President Theodore Roosevelt had requested an investigation of conditions among the Eskimos, Aleuts, and Indians of Alaska. This led to a report which recommended improved health and educational facilities, the development of native arts and crafts, the right of natives to own real estate and hold mineral claims, and increased federal supervision over the salmon industry.[8]

During the next four years, Congress passed legislation which implemented many of these recommendations. It regulated the fisheries of Alaska, established a school system for native children which included medical care, and in 1906 authorized the Secretary of the Interior to grant homesteads to Alaskan Indians and Eskimos. The natives were not given rights to mineral claims under this homestead law.[9]

The federal government in subsequent years demonstrated little concern for Alaska's natives until 1931, when the Bureau of Education was transferred to the Bureau of Indian Affairs in order better to coordinate federal programs. Before turning over his responsibilities, William Cooper, the U.S. Commissioner of Education, had obtained money from the Carnegie Foundation in order once again to survey the social status of Alaska's native inhabitants. This study rejected proposals to set aside large native reserves similar to those in Danish Greenland. It did, however, encourage the government to increase financial aid to native economic enterprises, use village councils for citizenship training, and take steps to end racial discrimination.[10]

Indian Commissioner John Collier hoped to implement many of these recommendations when he included the natives of Alaska under the Indian Reorganization Act (IRA) of 1934. The IRA abolished future land allotment, permitted tribal self-government, provided money for native educational loans, and authorized $2 million annually for the consolidation of checkerboarded reservations or the establishment of new homelands for propertyless Indians. It also set up a $10 million credit fund to encourage tribal economic development.[11] These steps were opposed by Anthony J. Dimond, an Alaskan politician, who believed that Collier had made a mistake by including Alaska's natives under the Indian Reorganization Act. Prior to his election in 1932 as a delegate to Congress, Dimond had been a member of the Alaskan Territorial Senate and served as mayor of Valdez.[12] Before the IRA passed, he convinced a congressional conference committee to exclude Alaska from several of its provisions. The committee omitted Alaska from sections of this legislation that ended the issuing of land allotments, allowed tribe to incorporate for business activity, and permitted the Secretary of the Interior to create new reservations.[13]

Dimond was convinced that the IRA did not meet the needs of the 4,462 Tlingit, 588 Haida, and 466 Tsimshean Indians located in southeastern Alaska, or the 4,028 Aleuts, 4,935 Athabascan, and 15,000 Eskimos who resided on the Aleutian Islands, in the interior, and along the coastal regions of the territory.[14] Except for the Metlakatla Tsimshean Indians, who had established a prosperous reservation on Annette Island in 1891, most of Alaska's aboriginal population consisted of small family groups which resided on town lots in villages. They lacked the tribal cohesiveness found in many parts of the United States.[15] Dimond's position on the IRA also reflected the hostile attitude of the Alaska Native Brotherhood toward the creation of reservations. The ANB had been founded at Sitka in 1912 by acculturated natives. They patterned the brotherhood after white fraternal lodges and local church societies. By the 1920s, almost every community in southeastern Alaska had established a local branch of this organization.[16]

Most of the founders of the Alaska Native Brotherhood had attended the Sitka Training School, where they were influenced by Sheldon Jackson, a Presbyterian missionary. An active participant in the Lake Mohonk Conference, Jackson was one of the humanitarian reformers who worked feverishly to Christianize and assimilate Native Americans in the decades after the Civil War. Jackson established church-state contract schools, secured reindeer to improve the Eskimos' economic status, and fought attempts to set aside reservations in Alaska. He feared that reservations would only promote segregation and lead to native dependence on government annuities.[17] Another influential person was Richard Henry Pratt. Several leaders of the ANB had also attended boarding schools in the United States where they learned the philosophy of Pratt, the director of the Carlisle Indian School. Pratt insisted that the reservation system and tribalism had to be eliminated before the natives could become first-class citizens. The leaders of the ANB promoted Pratt's and Jackson's assimilationist ideas by advocating equal citizenship rights, educational opportunities, and the abolition of what they considered to be outmoded aboriginal customs.[18]

William L. Paul, Sr., an officer in the ANB, had told Dimond about the natives' objections to the reorganization act. Paul, a mixed-blood Tlingit, had attended the Chemewa and Carlisle boarding schools. He had later studied law and in 1926 was elected to the territorial legislature as a Republican.[19] Although Paul favored loans from the IRA's credit fund to individual native fishermen, he argued that new reservations in Alaska administered by government bureaucrats would undermine principles of sound Americanism. Paul and many other natives were disappointed when the solicitor of the Interior Department ruled that tribal organization was a necessary prerequisite to securing federal money.[20]

Because the natives desperately needed financial help and secure title to their homesteads, Dimond agreed to support the passage of the Alaska Reorganization Act (ARA) in 1936. This measure enabled Alaska's natives to enjoy most of the benefits of the IRA. Groups of natives not previously recognized as bands or tribes, but having a bond of common occupation or association, could adopt constitutions for self-government and receive charters of incorporation required for federal loans. The ARA authorized the Secretary of the Interior to designate as reservations land previously set aside for the natives by executive order or congressional legislation, adjacent nearby public lands, and land actually occupied by Eskimos, Aleuts, and Indians. Congress required the Secretary of the Interior to secure native approval for any new reservations at special elections where thirty percent of the population would have to turn out.[21]

After the passage of the Alaska Reorganization Act, employees of the Indian Bureau persuaded 10,899 natives, out of a population of over 29,000, to draw up constitutions and charters of incorporation.[22] The constitutions drawn up by the forty-nine villages that organized under the ARA varied, but most allowed the formation of an elected municipal council. Many of these councils had been in existence since the passage of the Indian Village Act of 1915, which authorized settlements with more than forty members to establish self-government.[23] The councils had authority in all matters not prohibited by federal law, the right to employ legal counsel, and jurisdiction over any adjacent reservation set aside for native use.[24] But the refusal of Congress to appropriate the $200,000 needed to operate these village governments limited their effectiveness.[25]

Natives who adopted charters of incorporation could organize business corporations with the power to manage property of every description, make contracts, sue and be sued, and borrow money from the IRA's credit fund.[26] Members of chartered village credit associations and business cooperatives secured approval for 383 individual loans worth $604,158. Most of these loans were confined to southeastern Alaska where the Indians purchased new boats and fishing gear, repaired old equipment, and financed home payments at the village of Hoonah.[27] In 1939, the Haida Indians on the Prince of Wales Island established the Hydaburg Cooperative Association and borrowed $142,000 for the construction of a new salmon cannery building, dock, and related equipment. W. A. Pries, a white businessmen from Ketchikan, received a contract from the Interior Department to construct and operate this cannery. He received twenty-four percent of its profits until 1944, when an additional loan of $280,000 enabled the Haidas to assume complete financial control.[28] But they still had to pay a white manager to operate the cannery, because members of the village had little financial experience. A decline in the salmon run also made it difficult for the cooperative to repay the government.[29]

The natives received important benefits from the Alaska Reorganization Act but inept administration within the Interior Department caused numerous problems. The Indian Bureau had only three people to process loan applications. When Congress refused to provide money for field workers to supervise the loans, the bureau had to rely on thirty-three untrained school teachers for this important task. They often approved unsecured loans. Unfortunately, the educational loans authorized by the IRA were not used to train Alaska natives to become managers of their credit associations and business cooperatives. Seventy-seven students received over $34,500 for tuition and related expenses, but they used this money to become clerical workers or to enroll in liberal arts and teacher-training programs rather than to study business administration.[30]

There were other problems. The Eskimos, Aleuts, and Indians needed a secure land base in order to take full advantage of the Alaska Reorganization Act. For various reasons, plans for reservations failed to materialize until after the loans were made. Field studies of Alaska were virtually nonexistent and the Indian Bureau had to start from scratch in the compilation of the essential economic and human data necessary for the creation of reservations. When Indian Bureau officials finally submitted concrete proposals, they discovered that many natives and interested agencies in the Interior Department refused to cooperate.[31]

Commissioner Collier's own special efforts were often unsuccessful. During July 1937, he used section two of the ARA to withdraw extensive areas of land and water for the natives near Anchorage. His goal was to guarantee native fishing rights on water frontage adjacent to the Eklutna school site. He also requested a 1.6 million-acre reservation on the west side of Cook Inlet and an expanded 1,445,000-acre reservation for the 106 Athabascan villagers at Tyonek, with fishing rights three miles into the east side of the inlet and 100 miles along the shore.[32] Collier's proposals were never implemented because of legal objections raised by Nathan R. Margold, the solicitor of the Interior Department. In a ruling issued on September 14, 1937, Margold held that Congress never intended "to permit immense areas of land to be tacked upon existing reservations" when it passed the Alaska Reorganizition Act.[33] The two reservations under consideration, argued the solicitor, were illegal because the natives did not actually occupy all of that land as stipulated in the ARA. Margold also blocked the withdrawal of water frontage at Eklutna for nearby native fishermen because the adjacent land was a school site rather than a bonafide reservation.[34]

Officials in the General Land Office, who defended the interests of non-Indians, were pleased with Margold's decision. They had contributed to this impasse by raising difficult legal questions that caused endless debates among Interior Department lawyers. The General Land Office wanted to know how native claims would be affected by the creation of reservations, who would control subsurface mineral deposits, and whether proposed native fishing rights might interfere with federal authority to improve and regulate navigable waters.[35]

Margold's ruling forced Secretary of the Interior Harold L. Ickes to intervene in the reservation controversy. Before joining the Roosevelt administration, Ickes had supported liberal causes. As a lawyer in Chicago, he had accepted civil liberty cases without compensation, taught classes at Hull House, and fought against Samuel Insull's utility company. During the 1920s, Ickes had joined Collier's American Indian Defense Association and criticized the Republican-run Indian Bureau.[36] As head of the Interior Department, Ickes was determined to confirm native title to reservation land and to help the natives defend their hunting and fishing rights. But he had other motives as well. Native control over waters adjacent to reservations would enable him to gain more leverage over the powerful Alaska salmon industry. Ickes also favored reservations as a way of implementing conservation policies that would prevent the depletion of the country's natural resources. He was especially interested in preventing the Forestry Service from over-cutting timber on the mountain slopes in the Tongass National Forest in southeastern Alaska.[37]

In order to secure the necessary legal authority to carry out his plans, Ickes asked Solicitor Margold to consult with Felix S. Cohen, an associate solicitor in the Interior Department, on whether he had the power to close down the fish traps of non-Indians who were threatening the operation of native canneries and the livelihood of individual seiners. Cohen, who had a doctorate in philosophy from Harvard and a law degree from Columbia University, was one of the main architects of the IRA and a militant defender of native rights. His interest in applied anthropology and the philosophy of law eventually led to the publication of his *Handbook of Federal Indian Law*, which upheld both tribal sovereignty and the principle of federal jurisdiction in Indian affairs.[38]

Cohen made his influence felt on Margold, who used a legal brief compiled by the associate solicitor as the basis for a sweeping opinion issued on February 13, 1942. Margold upheld the natives' aboriginal claims to extensive areas of land and nearby fishing grounds. He based the reversal of his 1937 opinion on the U.S. Supreme Court decision of 1941 in the so-called Walpai case (*United States* v. *Sante Fe Pacific Railroad*) in which the court had recognized aboriginal possessory rights. According to Margold, the Supreme Court had held that aboriginal occupancy established rights of possession; that this possessory right extended to land under the prior sovereignty of European nations; that tribal right of occupancy need not be based upon a treaty or statute; and that extinguishment of occupancy rights could not be inferred from existing legislation or administrative action.[39] The use of waters or submerged lands by Alaska natives, concluded Margold, was similar to the Walpais's use of their lands for "agriculture, hunting, and seed-gathering."[40] Thus section two of the ARA could be invoked to set aside traditional lands and fishing areas of the Alaska natives.

Ickes used Margold's ruling to set aside four large reservations, in addition to the small one he had established in December 1941 at the Eskimo village of Unalakleet.[41] They were part of an overall plan to create twenty-five extensive reservations to protect the natives in central and northern Alaska who subsisted on a game and trapping economy.[42] During May and June 1943, Ickes reserved 72,000 acres for sixty-eight natives at Akutan; 32,200 acres and adjacent tidelands for the 185 villagers at Karluk on Kodiak Island; 1,408,000 acres for the 202 Athabascan inhabitants at Venetie, Arctic, and other Christian villages north of the Yukon River in the Brooks mountain range; and 7,200 acres of land and 14,000 acres of water for the 194 Eskimos at Wales on the Seward Peninsula.[43]

Two additional reservations that Ickes established in 1943 were rejected by the Eskimos at elections required by the ARA. These reserves included 3,000 acres for the residents at Shishmaref on the north side of the Seward Peninsula and 1,200 acres of land and water for White Mountain village on Norton Sound.[44] The Eskimos feared that fixed reservation boundaries might limit their hunting and fishing rights. They were also upset that the mineral rights to this land belonged to the United States pending future determination by the Interior Department. These Eskimos, who were converts to the Norwegian Lutheran and Catholic churches, agreed with the contention of the ANB that reservations would turn back the clock and promote racial segregation.[45] The Eskimos also remained suspicious of the government because it had mismanaged their reindeer herds. In September 1937, Congress had passed the Alaska Reindeer Act which placed the entire reindeer industry under native control.[46] While officials in the Interior Department carried on lengthy legal negotiations to compensate non-native owners for their reindeer and range equipment, thousands of reindeer were left to roam on an overgrazed, unsupervised range. The Eskimos became embittered as they watched thousands of their animals die from starvation and attacks from predators.[47]

The objections raised by the Eskimos did not prevent Ickes from imposing his reservation policy on the Haida and Tlingit Indians of southeastern Alaska. Ickes paid little attention to complaints by leaders of the Native American Brotherhood that reservations would result in the loss of their citizenship rights. Instead, he sought the support of elderly and less acculturated Indians who had concluded that reservations would offer them security. Many Haidas and Tlingits also believed that reservations were the best way to guarantee ownership of large areas of land and nearby fishing grounds.[48]

Ickes wanted to help the Haida and Tlingit Indians regain control over their fishing economy. The P.E. Harris Company, Pacific American Fisheries, Libby, McNeill and Libby, the Nakat Packing Company, the New England Fish Company, and several other absentee packing companies operated over fifty-six percent of the 434 fish traps granted by the War Department under legislation enacted in 1899. They harvested over $60 million worth of salmon and herring each year which made it difficult for many natives who fished in nearby streams to improve their economic condition.[49] Also a source of resentment was job discrimination. Under pressure from the Alaska Fisherman's Union, the canning companies had given preferential treatment to 17,398 whites, most of whom were nonresident unionized fishermen from Seattle and San Francisco. During the peak season harvest in 1937, the canneries employed 3,908 Filipinos, 967 Japanese, 634 Mexicans, and 556 Chinese aliens, who were viewed as a source of cheap labor.[50] The Alaska Native Brotherhood had bitterly complained to officials in the Interior Department about this type of employment discrimination, which resulted in only 6,600 natives being hired.[51]

One month after Margold's 1942 legal opinion upholding native occupancy rights, Ickes amended Alaskan fisheries regulations to prohibit fish traps on the Indians' property without their consent. Although he lacked authority from either Congress or the court system, Ickes invited the natives to request departmental hearings where they could present claims to land traditionally used for hunting and fishing and now used by non-Indians who had installed fish traps. If the Interior Department recognized these claims, the Indians could lease valuable fishing areas to the canneries, establish a native-run fishing industry, and request large reservations under the provisions of the ARA.[52]

The critical military situation in Alaska during the Second World War delayed hearings requested by the natives until 1944. During June of that year, Ickes sent associate solicitor Felix S. Cohen and other attorneys to Alaska to persuade the Tlingit and Haida Indians that reservations were necessary in order to protect their hunting and fishing rights. They succeeded in bringing many Indians around to their point of view and also helped the villagers at Hydaburg, Klawock, and Kake to prepare witnesses and legal cases for the hearings scheduled for September.[53]

Ickes tried to insure a fair hearing of the Indians' claims by persuading the Department of Justice to allow Richard Hanna, a special assistant to the Attorney General, to act as the presiding chairman at the hearings. Hanna had had a distinguished career on the New Mexico supreme court and during the 1920s had earned a reputation as a champion of Indian rights by helping the Pueblos to defend the title to their lands.[54] Though Hanna's temporary transfer was secured, some officials in the Department of Justice feared that it constituted a conflict of interest.[55] Hanna had been working on two cases pending in the court of claims that concerned the Haidas and Tlingits. After the passage of the Haida and Tlingit Claims Act of 1935, these Indians had sued the government for a cash settlement of all aboriginal rights destroyed with the tacit approval of the U.S. government. Hanna had prepared a legal brief for the Haida and Tlingit Indians at the Justice Department, and some government attorneys questioned whether he could impartially judge the validity of similar claims presented at Interior Department hearings.[56]

Hanna opened the hearings during the last two weeks of September 1944 in the federal school houses at the villages of Hydaburg, Klawock, and Kake.[57] The Indians' attorneys argued that neither Russia nor the United States had extinguished the aboriginal possessory rights to land and water used by the Haidas and Tlingits from time immemorial. The area that the Indians claimed included 3,339,000 acres in southeastern Alaska, including submerged land and water 3,000 feet from the shoreline, lakes and streams that emptied into the ocean, and nearby unpatented lands drained by these watersheds.[58]

Individuals, organizations, and corporations challenged the Indians' position. W. C. Arnold, an attorney from Ketchikan, represented the salmon packing industry and trap operators and argued that if the government recognized the Haida and Tlingit claims, it would have to confiscate a substantial portion of the salmon industry and turn over a third of the Alaska panhandle to less than a thousand natives. This would deprive the territory of needed tax revenues, threaten public navigation of waters, and overturn legislation that had opened the resources of Alaska to all citizens. Only Congress or "a court of competent jurisdiction," Arnold insisted, could determine possessory rights on the public domain.[59] This view received the endorsement of Stephen Carey, a lawyer representing the Pacific American Fisheries, and J. F. Jurich, a spokesman for the 22,000 International Fishermen and Allied Workers of America. The closing of the fish traps operated by the Pacific American Fisheries and Fidalgo Packing Company at Kasaan, claimed Carey, would jeopardize the $1.5 million investment of these canneries and lead to widespread unemployment.[60] Jurich feared that the Indians' claims would eliminate future job opportunities by ending the development of Alaska's mining, lumber, oil, and power resources.[61]

The Juneau and Ketchikan chambers of commerce also opposed the Haida and Tlingit claims. Juneau's representative stated that, contrary to Margold's ruling, native families had never established a right of occupancy except for small fishing villages.[62] The delegate from Ketchikan argued that the petitions presented by the residents of Hydaburg, Klawock, and Kake threatened the free enterprise system that had contributed to his community's steady growth. Furthermore, the government had not explained how the areas claimed by the Indians would be administered. If reservations were established, the Indians would lose their citizenship rights and face "Jim Crow" segregation.[63]

While Ickes waited for Hanna to rule on the conflicting testimony, he received criticism from Ernest Gruening, governor of Alaska. Gruening was considered a liberal; he had supported Robert La Follette, the Progressive party candidate in 1924; criticized U.S. military intervention in Latin America; and worked for *Nation* magazine. He had joined the Roosevelt administration in 1934 as director of the Division of Territories in the Interior Department. Five years later, when the president had appointed him governor of Alaska, Gruening had demonstrated his New Deal credentials by proposing a corporate income tax designed to retain wealth previously taken from the territory by absentee business corporations.[64]

Gruening believed that Ickes's attempt to create reservations in Alaska was a reactionary move that would promote racial disharmony.

In December 1944 he wrote Ickes a bitter letter, warning him that the policy of setting aside reservations "on a gigantic scale" not only threatened the economy of Alaska but would also "set the Natives back a full generation."[65] Gruening believed that Ickes had violated the spirit of the Alaska Reorganization Act which, he believed, only permitted the establishment of townsite reservations as a device for qualifying the natives to borrow money from the IRA's credit fund. The Indian Bureau, he complained, had pressured reluctant natives to accept large reservations in 1943, and this tactic savored "strongly of Hitlerism."[66]

Ickes was unmoved. He accused the governor of failing to distinguish between the attempt to determine native claims under the Supreme Court's doctrine of aboriginal occupancy rights and the Interior Department's authority to create reservations. The hearings, Ickes stressed, were merely a forum to give the natives an opportunity to present their claims so the government could determine their validity. The next step would be to decide what to do about these claims. Perhaps Congress would authorize negotiations with the natives that would determine "whether a given area should be set aside as a reservation or whether title to all or a portion of it should be extinguished."[67] In any event, the Secretary concluded, the native population was entitled to receive land on which it had lived for generations as well as adjacent areas necessary for "economic security."[68]

Ickes' problems multiplied when Richard Hanna submitted his report on March 7, 1945. Hanna rejected most of the Indians' claims because of deficiencies in the evidence provided by Interior Department lawyers. They had relied on the "diffuse and vague" oral testimony of natives over eighty years old.[69] Moreover, the claims to lands in the interior were contradicted by reports of anthropologists who testified that Haidas and Tlingits seldom ventured inland because of religious taboos and because virtually all their economic activity was confined to the coast. Conflicting statements by older and younger Indians also made it difficult to determine changing concepts of land use and those areas that had been held in common by villages.[70] Hanna also seriously undercut the Interior Department's plans to establish large reservations in southeastern Alaska. The inhabitants of Hydaburg, Klawock, and Kake, he concluded, had failed to present "substantial evidence" that they had exclusively used tidal ocean waters 3,000 feet from the shoreline except for "some small areas adjacent to the mouth of the salmon streams."[71] These

Indians had also abandoned fishing rights to most of the salmon trapsites by not objecting to the construction and operation of non-Indian canneries. Similarly, Hanna decided that the Haidas and Tlingits had, for the most part, abandoned their aboriginal rights to streams flowing into tidal waters, inland lakes, forests, and uplands used for hunting and trapping. The reduction in the native population in recent years, he concluded, had prevented use of much of this disputed area which white settlers had acquired in good faith under Alaska's homestead laws. Furthermore, the Indians had forfeited their claim to many towns and villages when they moved to different locations and accepted the "larger benefits of gainful employment in the new commercial fishing industry."[72] Hanna agreed that the claimants owned those lands that had been held for generations by Indian families, but the evidence presented at the hearings made it difficult to "measure or even approximate" the exact boundaries of these holdings.[73] Hanna recommended that Congress investigate the validity of Indian land titles and authorize cash compensation for property lost to white settlers through government neglect. If Congress failed to act, Ickes should set aside a reasonable portion of land where continuous Indian occupancy was apparent.[74]

Fowler Harper, the solicitor of the Interior Department, disagreed with Hanna's assertion that a congressional investigation was necessary.[75] Instead, he urged Ickes to use the factual data found in the 2,700 pages of testimony obtained at the hearings to establish administratively the precise boundaries of Indian possessions. Ickes's determinations could then be forwarded to Congress which could create reservations and provide compensation for the "cession of any areas in excess of those reserved for Indian occupancy.[76] The Secretary decided to follow Harper's advice because the Hanna report was "much less favorable to the Indians" than he had expected.[77]

On July 27, 1945, Ickes released a legal opinion (prepared by associate solicitor Felix S. Cohen) which held that the evidence presented at the hearings made it possible for the government to recognize as valid eight percent of the Indians' land claims.[78] He reserved 101,000 acres for Hydaburg; 95,000 acres for Klawock; and 77,000 acres for Kake. These lands, he ruled, could he set aside by "mutual consent" of the Indians and the federal government.[79] While the Indians had failed to prove exclusive possession to ninety-two percent of their claims, Ickes acknowledged, they had not abandoned the right to hunt, fish, and trap in those areas so long as the lands remained part of the public domain. Ickes promised to decide in the future whether the inhabitants of Kake and Klawock owned 2,008,000 acres, including all of Kuiu Island, after nearby Indian bands who were not represented at the departmental hearings presented their claims. Nor did these adjudications prevent the Indians from asking the Court of Claims for compensation due to "past invasions of their property rights."[80]

The Haidas and Tlingits of Hydaburg, Kake, and Klawock were not entirely satisfied with Ickes's decision, and in September 1945 they petitioned the Interior Department for a rehearing of their claims. At the new hearings they argued that the government had erred in not confirming their possessory rights to 1,120 acres of gardens, smokehouses, homes, cemeteries, and cannery facilities at Hunters Bay and Rose Inlet. In January 1946, Ickes agreed that most of their claims were justified and he awarded them an additional 800 acres.[81] He also concluded that the three villages owned nearby beaches down to the lowtide mark. This meant that those fish traps which were anchored on Indian land could be operated only "with the consent" of the natives.[82]

Ickes did not succeed in establishing reservations on the land he had awarded to the Indians of southeastern Alaska before he resigned from office in February 1946.[83] The effort had never gained widespread native support because government officials underestimated the extent of the Americanization of Alaska's aboriginal inhabitants. Christian missionaries and educators had successfully changed the lives and thought of many natives.[84] Moreover, the imbalance between white males and females on the Alaska frontier accelerated the process of acculturation. As early as the 1930s, every fourth individual in the native population had mixed-blood.[85]

Instead of carefully studying the social implications of contemporary native culture, New Deal reformers imposed their ideas of social justice on the Aleuts, Eskimos, and Indians. The Alaska Reorganization Act was drafted without native input, and when many natives resisted the creation of reservations, the Interior Department issued legal rulings that enabled the Secretary of the Interior to set aside extensive areas of land and water. This well-intentioned policy led to confusion within the Roosevelt administration, a premature dismissal of Haida and Tlingit claims, and increased tension between the territory's native and white residents.

In retrospect, it seems to have been a mistake to attempt a settlement of native hunting and fishing rights without the full cooperation of Congress and the Justice Department. Whites refused to accept the validity of the Interior Department's rulings which threatened the economic development of the territory and its progress toward statehood. They continued to oppose the creation of reservations through complicated litigation in the federal courts.[86] In 1946, Congress undercut the authority of the executive branch of the government to determine native claims when it authorized the establishment of the Indian Claims Commission.[87] The natives of Alaska would have to wait another twenty-five years before the Claims Commission and Congress resolved the questions that had surfaced during the New Deal debate over aboriginal rights.

ENDNOTES

[1]The activities of John Collier before he became commissioner are discussed in Kenneth R. Philp, *John Collier's Crusade for Indian Reform, 1920-1954* (Tucson, 1977), pp. 1-112.

[2]William Zimmerman, Jr., "The Role of the Bureau of Indian Affairs since 1933," *Annals of the American Academy of Political and Social Science* 311 (May 1957): 31-32.

[3]See Angie Debo, *A History of the Indians of the United States* (Norman, 1970), pp. 322-323; Lawrence C. Kelly, "The Indian Reorganization Act: The Dream and the Reality," *Pacific Historical Review* 44 (1975): 291-312; Philp, *John Collier's Crusade*, pp. 183-184; Graham D. Taylor, "The Tribal Alternative to Bureaucracy: The Indian New Deal," *Journal of the West* 13 (1974): 128-142; and Michael Smith, "The Indian New Deal," *Journal of the West* 10 (1971): 521-534.

[4]Throughout this essay the term native is used to include the Eskimos and Aleuts who are distinct from the Athabascan, Tlingit, Haida, and Tsimshian Indians. Felix S. Cohen, *Handbook of Federal Indian Law* (1942; reprint ed., Albuquerque, 1972), p. 401.

[5]June Helm, *The Indians of the Subarctic: A Critical Bibliography* (Bloomington, 1976), pp. 1-91; and Ted C. Hinckley, "Researching Alaska's Pioneer Years, 1867-1912," *Journal of the West* 16 (1977): 52-62, provide bibliographical information about the impact of white settlement in Alaska.

[6]U. S. Congress, Senate, Subcommittee of the Committee on Interior and Insular Affairs, *Hearings on S. 2037, Repeal Act Authorizing the Secretary of Interior to Create Indian Reservations in Alaska*, 80th Cong., 2d sess. (1948), pp. 44, 53-56; Ernest Gruening, *The State of Alaska* (New York, 1954), pp. 355-363; and Ted C. Hinckley, "Presbyterian Leadership in Pioneer Alaska," *Journal of American History* 52 (1966): 751.

[7]Glenn Smith, "Education for the Natives of Alaska: The Work of the United States Bureau of Education, 1884-1931," *Journal of the West* 6 (1967): 440.

[8]David E. Conrad, "Emmons of Alaska," *Pacific Northwest Quarterly* 69

(1978): 54, 57-58.

[9]Ibid., pp. 59-60.

[10]H. Dewey Anderson and Walter Crosby Eells, *Alaska Natives: A Survey of Their Sociological and Educational Status* (Stanford, 1935), pp. 5-6, 211-212.

[11]Philp, *John Collier's Crusade*, p. 159.

[12]*New York Times*, May 30, 1953, p. 15.

[13]William Zimmerman, memorandum for Secretary Harold L. Ickes, Nov. 16, 1944, Commissioner's Files, 1933-1953, National Archives, Record Group 48, Washington National Records Center, Suitland, Md (hereafter referred to as RG, NA).

[14]Merle Colby, *A Guide to Alaska: Last American Frontier* (New York, 1942), p. 44.

[15]Ibid., pp. 126-127; and Rita Singer, memorandum for Felix S. Cohen, Nov. 11, 1944, Records of the Solicitor's Office, Alaska Native Rights, RG 48, NA.

[16]Philip Drucker, *The Native Brotherhoods: Modern Intertribal Organizations on the Northwest Coast* (Washington, D. C., 1958), pp. 16-22.

[17]Useful accounts of Sheldon Jackson's work among the natives of Alaska are Ted C. Hinckley, "Sheldon Jackson as Preserver of Alaska's Native Culture," *Pacific Historical Review* 33 (1964): 411-424; Hinckley, "Presbyterian Leadership in Pioneer Alaska," pp. 742-756; Dorothy Jean Ray, "Sheldon Jackson and the Reindeer Industry of Alaska," *Journal of Presbyterian History* 43 (1965): 71-99; and Glenn Smith, "Education for the Natives of Alaska," pp. 440-445.

[18]Drucker, *The Native Brotherhoods*, pp. 41, 51-57.

[19]Ibid., pp. 34-39.

[20]William L. Paul to John Collier, April 1, 1935, Interior Department, Records of the Solicitor's Office, Alaska Native Rights, RG 48, NA.

[21]Theodore H. Haas, *Ten Years of Tribal Government under I.R.A.* (Washington, D. C., 1977), p. 42

[22]Ibid., pp. 29-30.

[23]Senate Subcommittee on Interior and Insular Affairs, *Hearings on S. 2037*, pp. 146-149.

[24]Ibid., pp. 75-79; *Constitution and By-Laws of the Native Village of Barrow, March 21, 1940* (Washington, D. C., 1941), pp. 1-3.

[25]U. S. Congress, House, Committee on Appropriations, *Hearings on the Interior Department Appropriation Bill for 1941*, 76th Cong., 3d sess. (1940), pt. II, p. 191.

[26]*Corporate Charter of the Village of Barrow, March 21, 1940* (Washington, D.C., 1941), pp. 1-2.

[27]Senate Subcommittee on Interior and Insular Affairs, *Hearings on S. 2037*, pp. 110, 190-191.

[28]Ibid., pp. 92-95.

[29]Gruening, *State of Alaska*, p. 400.

[30]Senate Subcommittee on Interior and Insular Affairs, *Hearings on S. 2037*, pp. 74, 110-111, 200-209.

[31]Nathan Margold, memorandum for Secretary Ickes, Sept. 14, 1937, Interior Department, Solicitor's Office, Administrative Correspondence Files, RG 48, NA.

[32]Harold L. Ickes, memorandum to the Commissioner of Indian Affairs, Sept. 16, 1937, ibid.

[33]Nathan Nargold, memorandum for Secretary Ickes, Sept. 14, 1937, ibid.

[34]Ibid.

[35]Warner W. Gardner, memorandum for the Assistant Secretary, Jan. 23, 1943, ibid.

[36]Maxine Block, ed., *Current Biography* (New York, 1941), pp. 426-428; and Ickes, "The Federal Senate and Indian Affairs," *Illinois Law Review* 24 (1930): 577.

[37]Paul H. Douglas, "A Sharp Tongue, a Hot Temper and a Tender Heart: A Recollection of Harold L. Ickes," *New Republic* 129 (Dec. 21, 1953): 14-15; Claude R. Wickard to the Secretary of the Interior, Feb. 5, 1945, office files of Oscar L. Chapman, 1933-1953, Alaska, RG 48, NA.

[38]*New York Times*, Oct. 20, 1953, p. 29; "Felix S. Cohen," *Nation* 177 (Dec. 19, 1953): 538; and Cohen, *Handbook of Federal Indian Law*, pp. vii-xi.

[39]Senate Subcommittee on Interior and Insular Affairs, *Hearings on S. 2037*, pp. 415-416.

[40]Ibid.

[41]Ibid., p. 13.

[42]Ibid., pp. 9-13; Oscar L. Chapman, memorandum for the Secretary, April 27, 1943, office files of Oscar L. Chapman, 1933-1953, Indians-Alaska, RG 48, NA.

[43]Senate Subcommittee on Interior and Insular Affairs, *Hearings on S. 2037*, p. 13.

[44]Ibid.

[45]Ibid., pp. 50, 371; and Anderson and Eells, *Alaska Natives*, pp. 206-207.

[46]For background material on the reindeer controversy, consult James and Catherine Brickey, "Reindeer: Cattle of the Arctic," *Alaska Journal* 5 (1975): 16-24; Hinckley, "Sheldon Jackson as Preserver of Alaska's Native Culture," pp. 411-424; Carl J. Lomen, *Fifty Years in Alaska* (New York, 1954), pp. 275-298; James R. Shortridge, "The Alaskan Agricultural Empire: An American Agrarian Vision, 1898-1929," *Pacific Northwest Quarterly* 69 (1978): 153-155; Ray, "Sheldon Jackson and the Reindeer Industry of Alaska," pp. 71-99; and Ray, *The Eskimos of the Bering Strait, 1650-1898* (Seattle, 1975), pp. 226-240.

[47]House Committee on Appropriations, *Hearings on the Department of Interior Appropriation Bill for 1941*, Pt. II, pp. 465-466.

[48]Drucker, *The Native Brotherhoods*, p. 52.

[49]Gruening, *State of Alaska*, pp. 395-396; and Jonathan M. Steere, ed., "Alaska Natives Seek Justice," *Indian Truth* 21 (1944): 1.

[50]Colby, *Guide to Alaska*, p. 49.

[51]Ibid.; Matthew K. Sniffen, ed., "From Alaska," *Indian Truth* 9 (1932): 3.

[52]Fowler Harper, memorandum for Assistant Secretary Oscar L. Chapman, April 27, 1944, office files of Oscar L. Chapman, 1933-1953, Indians-Alaska, RG 48, NA.

[53]Felix S. Cohen, "Report to the Commissioner of Indian Affairs," July 10, 1944, ibid.

[54]Press release (undated), Interior Department, Solicitor's Office, Alaska Native Rights, RG 48, NA.

[55]Fowler Harper to George W. Folta, Sept. 2, 1944, ibid.

[56]Ibid.; Senate Subcommittee on Interior and Insular Affairs, *Hearings on S. 2037*, pp. 459-460.

[57]Harper, memorandum for Secretary Ickes, March 10, 1945, Interior Department, Solicitor's Office, Alaska Native Rights, RG 48, NA; and Senate Subcommittee on Interior and Insular Affairs, *Hearings on S. 2037*, pp. 434-435.

[58]George W. Folta, Theodore H. Haas, and Kenneth R. L. Simmons, "Legal Brief, Proposed Findings of Fact, Conclusions of Law, and Recommendations of Petitioners," Sept. 1944, Interior Department, Solicitor's Office, Alaska Native Rights, RG 48, NA.

[59]W. C. Arnold "Supplemental Objection in the Matter of Hearings upon Claims of the Natives of Alaska Pursuant to the Provisions of Sections 201.21b," Sept. 15, 1944, ibid.

[60]Stephen Carey, "Protest on Behalf of the Pacific Fisheries," Sept. 16, 1944, ibid.

[61]J. F. Jurich, "Statement of the International Fishermen and Allied Workers of America," Sept. 16, 1944, ibid.

[62]Homer Garvin, "Protest of the Juneau Chamber of Commerce against the Establishment of Fishing Reservations Based on Aboriginal Claims," Aug. 31, 1944, ibid.

[63]A. M. Spaeth, "Protest by the Ketchikan Chamber of Commerce to the Granting of Exclusive Use and Occupancy of Lands and Waters to Certain Indian Tribes," Sept. 28, 1944, ibid.

[64]*New York Times*, June 27, 1974, p. 48; Charles Moritz, ed., *Current Biography* (New York, 1966), pp. 144-146; and Gruening, *The Battle for Alaska Statehood* (Seattle, 1967), pp. 1-2.

[65]Gruening, memorandum for the Secretary of the Interior, Dec. 11, 1944, Interior Department, Central Files, 1937-1953, RG 48, NA.

[66]Ibid.

[67]Ickes to Gruening, Dec. 14, 1944, ibid.

[68]Ibid.

[69]Harper to Folta, Nov. 6, 1944, Solicitor's Office, Interior Department, Alaska Native Rights Hearings, RG 48, NA.

[70]Haas to Zimmerman, Aug. 13, 1945, ibid.; Rita Singer, memorandum for Felix S. Cohen and Theodore H. Haas, Nov. 3, 1944; and Singer, interview with Father Cooper, Nov. 11, 1944, Solicitor's Office, Interior Department, General Correspondence Alaska, RG 48, NA.

[71]Senate Subcommittee on Interior and Insular Affairs, *Hearings on S. 2037*, pp. 426-429.

[72]Ibid.

[73]Ibid., p. 431.

[74]Ibid., pp. 432-433.

[75]Harper, memorandum for Secretary Ickes, March 10, 1945, Interior Department, Solicitor's Office, Alaska Native Rights Hearings, RG 48, NA.

[76]Ibid.

[77]Harold L. Ickes, Diary, July 28, 1945, p. 9907, Library of Congress.

[78]Senate Subcommittee on Interior and Insular Affairs, *Hearings on S. 2037*, p. 447; U. S. Dept. of the Interior press release, July 29, 1945, Interior Department, Solicitor's Office, Alaska Native Rights, RG 48, NA.

[79]Senate Subcommittee on Interior and Insular Affairs, *Hearings on S. 2037*, pp. 436, 439.

[80]Ibid., pp. 436, 440.

[81]Ibid., p. 451.

[82]Ibid., p. 452.

[83]Ickes resigned because of a dispute with President Harry S. Truman over the appointment of Edwin Pauley as Under-Secretary of the Navy. Harry S. Truman, *Memoirs, 1945: Year of Decisions* (New York, 1965), pp. 608-609.

[84]Hinckley, "The Presbyterian Leadership in Pioneer Alaska," pp. 749-750; Hinckley, *The Americanization of Alaska* (Palo Alto, 1972), pp. 113-117, 245-248; and Ray, *The Eskimos of the Bering Strait*, pp. 205-206, 241-253.

[85]Anderson and Eells, *Alaska Natives*, pp. 105-106.

[86]Haas to Assistant Secretary William Warne, June 28, 1949, Central Files, Interior Department, Alaska Native Rights, RG 48, NA.

[87]The operation of the Indian Claims Commission is discussed in Ralph A. Barney, "Some Legal Problems under the Indian Claims Commission Act," *Federal Bar Journal* 20 (1960): 235-239; Sandra C. Danforth "Repaying Historical Debts: The Indian Claims Commission," *North Dakota Law Review* 49 (1973): 359-403; Thomas Le Duc, "The Work of the Indian Claims Commission under the Act of 1946," *Pacific Historical Review* 26 (1961): 1-16; and Nancy Oestreich Lurie, "The Indian Claims Commission," *The Annals of the American Academy of Political and Social Science* 436 (1978): 97-110.

DR. ALASKA: ERNEST GRUENING*

Claus-M. Naske

Professor Claus-M. Naske, head of the history department at the University of Alaska in Fairbanks, has written a number of important studies furthering the understanding of Alaska history. His *An Interpretive History of Alaskan Statehood,* published in 1973, was republished in a revised edition in 1985 as *A History of Alaska Statehood* (Lanham, MD: University Press of America). His biography of Delegate Bob Bartlett, *Edward Lewis "Bob" Bartlett of Alaska: A Life in Politics,* was published in 1980 (Fairbanks: University of Alaska Press). His popular text, *Alaska: A History of the 49th State,* written with Herman Slotnick and originally published in 1979, was published in a revised edition in 1987 (Norman: University of Oklahoma Press). He has also published a number of articles on Alaska history.

In his article printed here on Ernest Gruening, Naske finds that the long-term governor of Alaska was very concerned about demonstrating his administrative abilities when he first came to the territory as governor in 1939. Gruening, who died in 1974, had been a journalist before he was appointed by Franklin Roosevelt as head of the new Division of Territories and Island Possessions in 1934. By 1939, it was clear to Roosevelt and other national leaders that the drive for Alaska statehood was not far off, and the president wanted a strong figure who could help lead Alaska toward full self-government. Gruening would serve with distinction as Alaska's wartime governor and through the turbulent period of unprecedented population growth following the war, stepping down in 1953. In 1958 he was elected one of the first U. S. Senators from Alaska, serving until 1968.

* * *

In May of 1934 President Franklin D. Roosevelt, by executive order created a new agency in the Department of the Interior, the Division of Territories and Island Possessions. This agency would supervise federal relations with outlying and dependent areas, and also assist them in every possible way to compensate for their lack of voting representation in Congress.

After the agency was created, the President appointed Ernest Gruening to be the director. Gruening brought an impressive background to his new job. Graduated from Harvard Medical School

---

*This article originally appeared in the *Journal of the West* 20, no. 1 (January 1981): 32-40.

in 1912, instead of practicing medicine, he pursued a career in journalism. After various newspaper jobs, he became editor and managing editor of *The Nation.* In his capacity as newspaperman, Gruening became acquainted with various New Deal personalities, including President Roosevelt. He caught the president's eye and in 1933 was appointed to serve as an advisor to the United States delegation at the Seventh Inter-American Conference at Montevideo. There he had a hand in fashioning the New Deal's policy toward Latin America.[1]

In his new position, Gruening quickly came into conflict, not only with his superior, Secretary of the Interior Harold L. Ickes, but also with Rexford Guy Tugwell who, in 1934, had gone to Puerto Rico on orders from the President and formed a committee of local leaders, which became known as the President's Policy Committee on Puerto Rico. Tugwell was involved in setting up Puerto Rico development programs. Gruening was doing the same thing in his agency.[2] At that point the President, disliking conflict, apparently decided to "kick" Gruening upstairs and make him governor of Alaska.

It was not surprising that Gruening, with his background and ambition, came to Alaska determined to make something out of the territory, to demonstrate to the President his capabilities.

Arriving in Alaska early in December of 1939, he took the oath of office in Juneau, the territory's capital, on 5 December. Almost immediately he discovered that the governor, "has really very little power: that he may be able, if he handles himself correctly, to exercise a good deal of influence and leadership which apparently has been lacking." Gruening then and there determined to supply that leadership. There was no question at all that a man of his talents, ability, determination, drive and ego would throw himself into his work--and lead Alaska superbly. It was equally clear that, in the process, he would disrupt established relationships, generating both intense dislike as well as admiration.[3]

Gruening also very soon discovered a number of Alaskan realities with which he had to deal. The first, and perhaps the most important, was the fact that Alaskans considered him an "Outsider." Although few whites had been born in the territory in those days, Alaskans carefully reminded each other of their length of residency in the North. The longer the stay, most believed, the more genuine was the honored term "pioneer" or "sourdough." Alaska's Indians, Eskimos, and Aleuts were collectively known as Natives, but apparently could not become pioneers or sourdoughs, on the assumption, perhaps, that you cannot be either on your native ground. More basically, most white Alaskans shared American racial attitudes of the day, considering Natives to be inferior to whites.

The governor also quickly discovered Alaska's intense regionalism, fostered by vast distances and different modes of making a living. Gruening determined to do his part of breaking down this regionalism. He found that until his arrival, most governors, either by choice or necessity, had been content to stay in Juneau. Gruening decided to make the governor's office a highly visible one throughout the territory. He traveled widely and incessantly, and interested himself in small as well as large problems, tackling all of them with singular gusto and enthusiasm. The governor, one acquaintance recalled, operated like a "trip hammer, he broke up everything that was in his way, he bored through, he had the determination of sixteen men, and a mind that was sharp and quick and ruthless." Once Gruening had made up his mind, he seldom changed it. He was a very athletic individual who, at times, exerted himself physically to the point of collapse, almost as if "to show his strength" to prospective opponents.[4] Gruening's swimming stunts in cold mountain lakes, his hiking expeditions with a string of panting and exhausted bureaucrats trying to keep up with him, and his fast tennis matches soon became legend in Alaska.

One of the first problems the governor tackled involved the discriminatory hiring practices of Navy defense contractors who engaged their labor through Seattle unions to the virtual exclusion of resident Alaskans. Gruening eventually carried his complaints to the Secretary of the Navy, Charles Edison, who ordered that contractor employment managers visit territorial towns at six week intervals and hire Alaskans on the same basis as men from Seattle. Gruening then successfully persuaded the Army to forego discriminatory practices in its defense construction program.[5]

Next the governor looked at Alaskan municipal government management and finances and found both to be lacking. He convinced the Juneau City Council to contribute $2,400 in matching funds for the construction of a swimming pool financed by the Works Progress Administration. Gruening counseled the Sitka municipal government to reassess all property adequately in order to stave off financial collapse and purchase the city light and water services, a private monopoly which, although charging exorbitant rates, did not meet expanding needs.[6]

One of the governor's chief concerns was the modernization of the outdated and inadequate Alaskan tax system. Gruening's predecessor, John W. Troy, had asked the territorial planning council to make a tax study in the late 1930s. The research was not completed until the fall of 1940. The authors of the report concluded that an annual revenue of $10,000,000 was entirely feasible. They recommended the adoption of a modern tax system, and urged that the revenue obtained be invested in a soundly planned and economically executed program of permanent improvements such as roads, schools, hospitals, and public buildings. Gruening enthusiastically endorsed these proposals, made them his own, and fully intended to push them through the legislature. The plan the governor presented to the 1941 legislature for adoption would abolish all obsolete mercantile taxes and license fees, imposing instead a very moderate income and profits tax, plus a nominal levy on property outside of incorporated towns.[7]

Governor Gruening, however, had waded into deep water with his proposal for a streamlined tax system. The scheme immediately mobilized the ever-alert economic interests, such as the canning and mining industries who were in no mood to relinquish their privileged status in Alaska. Many residents, depending for a livelihood on these industries, were unwilling to antagonize them. These feelings were reflected in the mood of the legislature which flatly rejected the governor's tax proposals in every legislative session between 1941 and 1947.

Although Gruening made many enemies in the territory rather quickly, he also won numerous friends. When renominated for another term in 1944, he was readily confirmed. When Harry S. Truman succeeded to the presidency after the death of Franklin D. Roosevelt, talk about a replacement for Gruening began to circulate in Washington. Two men were mentioned, both close Truman associates. Walter Walsh, who had received a Marine Corps commission at the beginning of the war with Truman's help, and Fred Canfil, a U. S. Marshal in Kansas City who had actively worked in one of the new president's senate campaigns.[8]

In the meantime, Gruening called a special session of the legislature to convene in March of 1946. The purpose was to have measures enacted designed to aid Alaska's veterans. Meeting for thirty days, the legislators passed most of Gruening's proposals. And although the governor was pleased, he was alarmed by a senate memorial which asked the President and the new Secretary of the Interior, Julius A. Krug, "to remove the present governor from office with all possible dispatch." It passed the senate by a vote of nine to six. Thereupon Steve McCutcheon, a Gruening supporter in the house, introduced a long memorial praising Gruening unqualifiedly. It passed by a vote of sixteen to seven. "The opposition," Gruening confided to E. L. "Bob" Bartlett, Alaska's Delegate to Congress, "are going to do everything to smear me in Washington." Bartlett, however, reassured the governor that he "should not attach any particular importance to any Senate memorial so far as its influence here [Washington, D.C.] is concerned."[9]

Complaints about the governor, however, trickled into Washington. Walter P. Sharpe, the territorial Commissioner of the Department of Labor told Robert E. Hennegan, the Chairman of the Democratic National Committee, that the governor had done everything to split the Democratic Party in Alaska. "Put in anyone, but get rid of this 'pinko' who has no ties in Alaska," Sharpe counseled. The commissioner essentially resented the fact that Gruening made appointments based on ability rather than party affiliation. But despite sniping from various quarters, the governor survived in office. When talk about his replacement once again revived late in 1947, Bartlett persuaded Robert S. Allen of the *Boston Daily Globe* to analyze Gruening's predicament. Such an article, Bartlett hoped, might help to force the president's hand. On 30 January 1948 the *Globe* carried the piece entitled "Next on List of New Dealers to be Dropped by Truman?" Allen stated that Gruening, one of the few Roosevelt appointees still holding high office, had only an outside chance of being reappointed for another term. "As of now," Allen claimed, "President Truman does not intend to rename Gruening." That could change, however, he continued, because the governor had strong Alaskan backing as well as powerful administration support both in and out of Congress, including "equally powerful Democratic opposition," most of it centered in Washington State, particularly in Seattle. For years the governor had been at loggerheads with Seattle business and transportation interests, accusing them of exploiting the territory like a colonial possession. Washington's Governor Mon Walgren and Seattle shipping and fishing magnate, Nick Bez, both Truman cronies, led the opposition to Gruening. The president faced a dilemma, Allen concluded, for he needed West Coast support in the upcoming election. Replacing Gruening, however, would upset the New Dealers whose support he needed as well.[10]

It may have been the piece in the *Globe* which prodded Secretary Krug to see the President and urge the reappointment. In any event, on 12 March, Truman sent Gruening's name to the Senate Interior and Insular Affairs Committee for confirmation. Bartlett was happy. "I won't forget ever," he told Krug, "that you went to the White House today and successfully urged President Truman to reappoint our friend, Ernest Gruening, as Governor of Alaska. It was a noble stroke of work." Unhappily, however, an informal poll of the committee revealed that the Republican majority favored "pigeonholing action until after the November election." One Republican member of the committee succinctly summed up majority opinion. "Why should we give a Democrat--and an ardent New Deal Democrat at that--a four-year term when after the Presidential election we could put in a good Republican?"[11]

Territorial Republicans were not satisfied with mere delays. The *Fairbanks Daily News-Miner*, owned by Alaska's foremost entrepreneur 'Cap' Austin E. Lathrop, long a Gruening opponent, urged that the governor be denied a third term. Lathrop argued that Gruening had enjoyed ample opportunities to prove himself as governor of Alaska, yet he had failed. Instead of fostering a sound legislative program for Alaska during the last five sessions of the legislature, he had "tried to promote tax legislation which was not acceptable" to the legislators. As a result, the territory's finances "are now as near complete disorganization as they have ever been." Even more disturbing, biennial territorial appropriations had increased from a modest $3,511,510 in the 1939-1940 period, the last before Gruening took office, to a record $8,476,309 appropriation passed by the last legislature. In short, Gruening had attempted "to use the power and prestige of his office and the resources of the federal government to transfer to himself the initiative and law-making powers of the citizens."[12] Lathrop left unclear how the governor had appropriated to himself all of these powers. In fact, Lathrop's editorial was transparently self-serving, for he was a chief beneficiary of Alaska's totally inadequate tax system. His many enterprises, ranging from banks to motion picture theaters, and from construction companies to a coal mine paid only negligible taxes to the territory.

In any event, the anti- and pro-Gruening forces quickly lined up for battle. While Lathrop urged his friends and associates to communicate their opposition to the Senate committee, the pro-Gruening forces similarly gathered support. Lathrop, for example, praised territorial senator Chas. D. Jones for the fine letter he had written to U.S. Senator Arthur H. Vandenberg, a member of the committee considering Gruening's confirmation. Lathrop was convinced that a sufficient number of protests had reached the Senators to convince them that "right or wrong, he [Gruening] has engendered so much bitterness and dissension in the Territory that very little of a constructive nature can be expected until there is a new governor." Foremost among Gruening's friends, Bartlett solicited support. Among many others, for example, he asked the Rt. Reverend John S. Bentley of the National Council of Protestant Churches to lend his help in the impending confirmation struggle.[13] Despite all the efforts, Senator Hugh Butler (R., Neb.) decided to allow Gruening's unconfirmed nomination to die.

In the meantime, however, territorial finances had run into trouble. On 31 December 1948 the general fund contained only $6,289.40 and the auditor held legitimate claims against the territory amounting to $758,209.59. It was only through individual and corporate pledges of $200,000 of interest-free loans, for example, that the doors of the University of Alaska had been kept open. Earlier on, the governor had rejected pleas for calling a special session, hoping that angry citizens would vote delinquent legislators out of office. Gruening's hopes were largely fulfilled when Alaskans trooped to the polls in October and "threw the rascals out." At that point, the governor summoned the newly-elected body not the lameduck legislature, into special session. Its only task was to consider the tax bills which territorial Attorney-General Ralph Rivers had prepared in his capacity as legislative counsel. From the extraordinary session which convened on 6 January 1949 and the regular one which followed on 24 January there emerged, at long last, a basic tax system.[14]

The first element of the new system consisted of a territorial income tax based on ten percent of the federal tax. A property tax of one percent was credited against the municipal and school district assessments, thus avoiding duplication. At the same time the territorial legislature took over and streamlined the old system of license fees from the federal government. For each separate business an initial application fee of $25 was charged. Beyond the initial fee, a sum equal to one-half percent above $100,000 received during the income year was to be remitted to the territory. This levy applied to those concerns which, so far, had paid no monies whatever to the Alaska territorial government. These included steamship companies, air and bus lines, lighterage companies, banks and motion picture theaters, oil and construction companies, garage and service stations, newspapers, radio stations, and logging operations. Professional registration, examination and insurance levies were to be collected by the various professional boards. The legislature changed the tax on the fishing industry from a case tax to one based on the wholesale value of the pack, amounting to four percent of the value of the raw fish processed for salmon cannieries to one percent of the value of raw fish for herring processing plants. Fishermen's license fees increased from $1 to $5 for residents, and from $25 to $50 for nonresidents. Fishing gear, such as traps, gill nets, and seines, was also taxed. Excise taxes on liquor were raised, and establishments serving alcohol were regulated by fees which varied from $75 to S5,000, according to the type of business, the size of the town, or the volume of the business. In addition, the usual motor fuel taxes, vehicle and drivers' licenses, and tobacco and various other miscellaneous taxes were modernized.[15]

Gruening was jubilant, and understandably so. It had been a long battle, finally crowned with victory. The special interests were furious. When word reached Alaska that Senator Joseph O'Mahoney (D., Wy.), the new chairman of the Committee on Interior and Insular Affairs, intended to hold hearings on Gruening's confirmation, a number of former legislators asked the committee to postpone any action until the territorial legislature had adjourned. Residents of Alaska, they telegraphed, should be given an opportunity "to present evidence and data supporting contention of many substantial citizens of territory that present governor's policies are not only definitely destructive to territorial development but will almost stop flow of badly needed investment capital from stateside sources." These disgruntled ex-legislators also asserted that the "present session being quarterbacked by governor is travesty of American tradition and legislative procedure."[16]

In the middle of March, the U.S. Senate appointed a subcommittee, headed by Clinton Anderson (D., N.M.) to investigate the various charges against the governor which had been accumulating in committee files. These charges ranged from bossism to the misuse of public funds, and from the refusal to permit an audit of territorial offices to furthering the spread of communism. Hearings on Gruening's confirmation were to be held on 1 April 1949. 'Cap' Lathrop decided to charter a plane and take a number of witnesses to Washington, D.C., to oppose the governor. When this mission became known, Stanley McCutcheon, legislator, Gruening friend and Anchorage attorney, gathered 44 individuals sympathetic to the governor and also chartered a plane so they could testify at the Washington hearings as well.[17]

Reactions to McCutcheon's flight were immediate. One Gruening foe advised the Senate Committee to "carefully screen the bunch of political dregs named as holding reservations," and not to "let this lot of grafters stay in Washington too long because it will be shameful to stink up the atmosphere by their presence." The critic had unkind words for most of the pro-Gruening witnesses, alleging that one, for example, supported the Governor only because he had a persecuted anti-Jewish feeling and was Jewish, while another was nothing more than a plain thief, another a tin-horn lawyer, a third a labor racketeer, while a fourth was a nice Eskimo who would vote for the Governor if he could be kept sober that long, and the like.[18]

According to the Washington *Evening Star*, Gruening's supporters "whooped" into D.C. "aboard a giant airliner, dubbed 'Ship of State, our Skipper Gov. Gruening' to break the glad tidings that everything's fine up their way, that the territory has launched a great development program and is preparing to realize its manifest destiny." Despite the hoopla, the delegation did not make a ripple, there were no pictures in the papers, no names, in part because the competition from the cherry blossoms and the eleven delegations from overseas in town to sign the Atlantic Pact.[19]

When the hearings opened, all the prior publicity had filled the large caucus room in the Old Senate Office Building to capacity, including eleven out of the thirteen committee members. The anti-Gruening witnesses were the first to be heard. Frank Angerman, Fairbanks machinist and member of the territorial house, accused the governor of buttonholing legislators and trying to convince them to support his program. Senator Eugene Milliken (R., Colo.) asked if Angerman charged Gruening with corruption. Angerman replied in the negative. Was there any charge that Gruening lacked intelligence for the job, Milliken persisted? Again, the witness replied no. Was there any charge that the governor attempted to influence legislators other than by talk, Milliken persisted? "No, not to my knowledge,"

Angerman stated. Milliken asked the same or similar questions of the next two witnesses and received the same answers.[20]

George Miscovich, house member and a Fairbanks placer gold miner, accused the governor of building the most powerful political machine ever seen in Alaska. Through his appointive powers, Gruening doled out territorial jobs and promised political favors "to selected individuals irrespective of party." This had practically destroyed the two-party system in Alaska. Perhaps worse, Gruening was attempting to establish a planned economy and was also encouraging radical elements. Milliken asked if Miscovich challenged Gruening's patriotism. Miscovich replied that he "certainly would like to, although I am not familiar with the routine procedure, and I do not know that it would be my duty to do it." Senator Bert Miller (D., Idaho) thereupon admonished witnesses to confine themselves to facts about Gruening's fitness for office.[21]

Charles D. Jones of Nome charged the chief executive with lobbying for his legislative program, and when that failed, "he plies the legislators with cocktails and cultured conversation in the Governor's Mansion amid surroundings more luxurious than most of these unpretentious Alaskans from mining and fishing communities and Eskimo villages have ever seen before." Jones then discarded his prepared statement and told the committee that this language was not his own, that the testimony had been prepared for him by Lathrop's secretary, and that he would "like to talk just as I talk." Encouraged by Senator Anderson, Jones stated that Gruening "takes them up and gives them plenty of booze and lots of conversation. Let me tell you, brother, the way he is throwing it out, you know, we have an expression, that what he peddles makes the grass grow green on the Kougarok. He's got it. Dairy farmers know what it is."[22]

Lathrop testified that Gruening had failed miserably as governor. "Never in my fifty-three years in Alaska have I seen the strife between parties and within parties, the friction between labor and capital, and the class and racial hatred that exists today--largely because of Gruening's leadership." Lathrop charged that the governor's policies, "almost without exception, have been motivated by personal or political considerations--certainly not by a constructive and sincere interest in Alaska." Lathrop stated that Gruening was a very intelligent and fine man, "I like Governor Gruening in many respects. I like him because I get ideas as well by talking with him." The rest of the opposition witnesses elaborated on various points, contending that the governor's opposition to absentee ownership and vested interests had prevented risk capital from coming into Alaska; that he used dictatorial methods; and that he campaigned with Alaska Native Service officials among the Natives, asking them to support his favored candidates for the territorial legislature. To a man, the seven witnesses asked the committee not to inflict Governor Gruening on Alaska for yet another term.[23]

Nine out of the forty-four Gruening supporters next testified. Their spokesman, Stanley McCutcheon, claimed that his group represented a good cross-section of Alaskan citizens. All asserted that Gruening had been a good, progressive governor who had the interests of the people at heart. They all approved of the tax program which just had become law. The added revenue was urgently needed for the rehabilitation of the school system, the public health program, and expansion of various other, vitally needed territorial activities. In short, the governor had transformed Alaska from a wilderness to a thriving and progressive community in the brief span of nine years.[24]

The opposition witnesses had been given the lion's share of the available time, but they had not used it to advantage. The seven were frequently put on the defensive chiefly by the Republican members of the committee. Impatient at times because of the piddling criticism offered, Senator Milliken repeatedly had asked if there had been any corruption in the Gruening administration? The answer had always been negative. Bartlett, although he did not speak, "spiritually rallied" to Gruening's side when the opposition testified, but then "became almost acutely ill to [my] stomach when the proponents had their turn," because they were so sickening in their lavish and uncritical praise of Gruening. Nothing the proponents could have done, however, could have been "so infantile as the opposition," Bartlett remarked, for "they were stupid, no less."[25]

After the witnesses had been heard, the committee asked the governor to take the stand. Gruening denied all charges. He stated that he had pressed for the enactment of his program for the development of Alaska, but had much less influence over the legislature than was generally assumed. In fact, Alaska's appointed governor had less power than even his Hawaiian counterpart. All important territorial officials were elected, not appointed, and therefore wholly independent of the governor. Finally, Gruening stated that it was his duty to tell Alaskans what he thought. The legislature had the responsibility to modify, adopt, or reject his views. With that the hearings concluded late in the evening.[26]

The following Monday, 4 April, territorial house representative Robert Hoopes, a Fairbanks filling station operator, filed a statement with the committee accusing Governor Gruening of having gone to England in the 1920s at the behest of the Mexican government to stir up British miners in the interest of world revolution. On his return from England, Hoopes asserted, Gruening again visited Mexico City and reported to President P. Elias Calles. Shortly thereafter, according to documents in Hoopes' possession, the Mexican government transmitted some $350,000 in two payments to England to aid the cause of communism. Hoopes also asserted that Gruening had received $10,000 from the Mexicans for his services.[27]

The committee thereupon decided to hold an executive session on 6 April to give Gruening an opportunity to respond to these new charges. The governor told the Senators that the document was a forgery and had been exposed as such. Gruening admitted that he had gone to Mexico in the fall of 1922 assigned to write articles for *Collier's* and other magazines. He had stayed in Mexico about six months and had become very interested in the country. Realizing that no book existed which answered all of his questions, he therefore decided to write such a volume and began the project after returning to the United States. Soon aware, however, that he had insufficient materials, he laid aside his notes, and did not start again until 1924 when President-elect Calles had returned from Europe to Mexico and made an official visit to Washington, D.C. Calles invited Gruening and others to attend his inauguration. The Governor went and his interest in the country was rekindled. During the next three years he spent approximately a year in Mexico working on his book. In 1927 Gruening had completed his research and went to Portland, Maine, where he started a daily newspaper and wrote the book in his spare time. In the late fall of 1928 a friend told Gruening that the New York Hearst papers had published on their front pages a photostatic reproduction of the letter Hoopes had given to the committee. Gruening immediately contacted Hearst and the editor of the New York *Evening Journal* and pointed out that the document was a forgery and grossly libelous and demanded a retraction. No retraction was forthcoming, however, and a few days later the paper published a series of photostatic letters purporting to show that four United States Senators had received $25,000 each for conducting propaganda in favor of the Calles government.[28]

Thereupon the United States Senate of the day ordered an investigation which showed the documents to be forgeries. The Hearst press, however, did not retract in Gruening's case, whereupon he sued. After some time, Hearst settled out of court and paid Gruening $75,000 and published retractions in his papers. Furthermore, Gruening told the Senators, he never went to England on an assignment for President Calles or anyone else--he merely went to Europe in 1926 to join his wife and three sons.[29]

It did not take the committee very long to recommend Gruening's reappointment by unanimous vote and the Senate confirmed it by a voice vote. As noted, the opposition to the governor had brought no substantial charges; in fact, they had made fools of themselves. But Gruening's supporters were far too lavish in their praise of his performance. The governor, however, acquitted himself superbly before the Senators. An eloquent speaker and a man of substantial achievements, his arguments totally demolished his opposition. Gruening had pointed out to the committee that many of the people who protested his confirmation had been retired from public life only because they had opposed his program--a decision made by the voters. Furthermore, the principal issue of the 1948 campaign in Alaska had involved the adoption of a tax program which the governor had urged since 1941. In 1948 Alaskans had decided the issue in favor of the governor by electing a legislature which had enacted the Gruening tax program.

Jack E. Eblen, a student of territorial government, has stated that the job of territorial governor was a difficult one in "which success might assure a bright future, and failure, oblivion." Territorial governors symbolized an often detested system of colonial government and had very limited powers. A governor's ability to adapt and succeed in the office, Eblen asserted, could be "measured roughly by the length of his tenure. It took an unusually capable man to be effective, either as a leader or as an administrator..." Gruening held office for more than thirteen years, from 1939 to 1953. Only Benjamin F. Pott, governor of Montana from 1870 to 1883, equaled that.[30] Gruening presided over a complex and difficult territory during a crucial period in its development. By any test, he was a very competent administrator and capable leader. Alaskans rewarded his service when they elected him one of their two United States Senators after the territory had become the 49th state in 1958.

In conclusion, Gruening's quest for territorial status was both political and personal. He certainly wanted to demonstrate his capabilities as an administrator to his superiors. At the same time, as the Alaska statehood movement gained momentum in the post-war period, the governor probably had his heart set on a U.S. Senate seat from Alaska.

ENDNOTES

[1]Sherwood Ross, *Gruening of Alaska* (New York: Best Books, Inc., 1968), pp. 77-89.

[2]Rexford Guy Tugwell, *The Stricken Land: The Story of Puerto Rico* (New York: Greenwood Press, Publishers, 1968), pp. 5, 71.

[3]Ernest Gruening Diary, December 5, 1939, Ernest Gruening Papers, University of Alaska Archives, Fairbanks, Alaska.

[4]Interview with Doris Steward, April 6, 1975, Sequim, Washington.

[5]Ernest Gruening, *Many Battles: The Autobiography of Ernest Gruening* (New York: Liveright, 1973), pp. 278-290.

[6]Ibid., pp. 288-294.

[7]Ernest Gruening to John F. Wiese, October 4, 1944, General Correspondence File, 1909-1953, Alaska Territorial Governor, Federal Records Center, Seattle, Washington.

[8]E. L. Bartlett to E. Gruening, May 26, 1945, ELB Papers, General Correspondence File, Ernest Gruening, 1944-45, box 11, UA Archives, Fairbanks, Alaska.

[9]Gruening, *Many Battles*, pp. 334-341; E. Gruening to E. L. Bartlett, March 29, 1946, E. L. Bartlett to E. Gruening, April 1, 1946, E. L. Bartlett Papers, General Correspondence File, E. Gruening, 1946, UA Archives, Fairbanks, Alaska.

[10]E. L. Bartlett to E. Gruening, February 5, 1948, E. L. Bartlett Papers, General Correspondence File, E. Gruening, 1948, Box 10, UA Archives, Fairbanks, Alaska; *Boston Daily Globe*, January 30, 1948.

[11]E. L. Bartlett to 'Cap' Krug, March 12, 1948, E. L. Bartlett Papers, General Correspondence File, Ernest Gruening, 1948, box 10, UA Archives, Fairbanks, Alaska; *The Daily Alaska Empire*, March 15, 1948.

[12]*Fairbanks Daily News-Miner*, March 15, 1948.

[13]A. E. Lathrop to Chas. D. Jones, March 29, 1948, Correspondence 1948, Jan.-June, File 8, box 1, Chas. D. Jones Collection, UA Archives, Fairbanks, Alaska; E. L. Bartlett to John S. Bentley, April 2, 1948, E. L. Bartlett Papers, General Correspondence File, Ernest Gruening, 1948, box 10, UA Archives, Fairbanks, Alaska.

[14]Alaska Legislature, House, *Journal*, 1949, p. 49: Gruening, *Many Battles*, p. 348; *The Daily Alaska Empire*, June 24, 1949; *Anchorage Daily Times*, December 18, 1948.

[15]63 Stat. 694; 62 Stat. 302: Alaska, *Session Laws*, 1949, Extraordinary

Session, pp. 54-56, Regular Session, pp. 136, 30-33, 205-206, 254.

[16]Joe Coble to Hugh Butler, March 7, 1949, E. Gruening Papers, File Pearson, Drew, 1949, box 11-A, UA Archives, Fairbanks, Alaska.

[17]Memorandum to Senators Anderson et. al. from S. French, counsel, Interior and Insular Affairs Committee, March 22, 1949, in author's files; E. L. Bartlett to E. Gruening March 21, 1949, Stanley McCutcheon to E L. Bartlett, March 28, 1949, E. L. Bartlett Papers, General Correspondence File, E. Gruening, 1949, box 10, UA Archives, Fairbanks, Alaska.

[18]Anonymous to Hugh Butler, March 24, 1949, E. Gruening Papers, Box 34-A, UA Archives, Fairbanks, Alaska.

[19]*Washington Evening Star*, April 5, 1949.

[20]*Nomination of Dr. Ernest Gruening to be Governor of Alaska, April 1, 1949, Hearings held before the U.S. Senate Committee on Interior and Insular Affairs* (Washington, D.C.: Ward & Paul, 1949), vol. 1, pp. 2-15. Hereafter referred to as *Hearings.*

[21]*Hearings*. pp. 16-28.

[22]Ibid., pp. 65-85.

[23]Ibid., pp. 98-140; *Ketchikan Daily News*, April 14, 1949.

[24]*Hearings*, pp. 141-199.

[25]E. L. Bartlett to Hugh Wade, April 7, 1949, E. L. Bartlett to Herb Hilscher, April 5, 1949, E. L. Bartlett Papers, General Correspondence File, Hugh Wade, 1945-51, Herb Hilscher, 1949, boxes 25 and 10, UA Archives, Fairbanks, Alaska.

[26]*The Daily Alaska Empire*, April 2, 1949.

[27]Ibid., April 5, 1949.

[28]*Hearings*, vol. II. pp. 277-311.

[29]Ibid.

[30]Jack Ericson Eblen, *The First and Second United States Empires* (Philadelphia, Pennsylvania: University of Pennsylvania Press, 1968), pp. 271-285.

KING SALMON*

James A. Crutchfield and Giulio Pontecorvo

From modest beginnings in 1878, the Alaska salmon canning industry became the most important economic enterprise in the territory in the first half of the 20th century, outdistancing gold and copper mining, timber and tourism in value of export, number of people employed, and the scope of the activity. The industry, headed by the Alaska Packers' Association, was the most significant absentee investment in Alaskan resources and one of the most powerful political forces both within Alaska and with Congress and the federal executive agencies which managed Alaska's resources. The industry's considerable lobbying effort often had a major effect on legislation and policy concerning Alaska. Many Alaskans found the effect to be detrimental to the interests of self-government and economic independence.

Overfishing during World War I, when the U. S. military purchased much of the annual salmon pack, and subsequent depletion of salmon stocks led to a debate over regulation of the fishery, within the territory and among federal bureaucrats. The result was major regulatory legislation, the 1924 White Act, which set the pattern for fisheries regulation virtually until statehood.

Professor Giulio Pontecorvo of the Graduate School of Business at Columbia University and Professor James Crutchfield, now retired from the School of Finance at the University of Washington, undertook a study of the regulation of the fishery while they were at the University of California in 1969. Their study was supported by Resources for the Future, a conservation research group funded by the Ford Foundation. Pontecorvo has since written several articles dealing with management of maritime resources, and in 1974, with John King Gamble, Jr., he edited the proceedings of the eighth annual Law of the Sea Conference, *Law of the Sea: The Emerging Regime of the Oceans* (Law of the Sea Institute).

In their study of the Alaska salmon industry, Pontecorvo and Crutchfield found that the new fisheries regulations of the 1920s did not adequately curtail overfishing. Nor did they save the resource from eventual severe depletion.

---

*This selection excerpted from *The Pacific Salmon Fisheries, A Study of Irrational Conservation* (Baltimore, MD: Published for Resources for the Future, Inc. by The John Hopkins Press, 1969), pp. 95-103.

* * *

The White Act

In the broadest sense, the White Act was the product of three forces: the biological state of the salmon resource; the economic condition of the Alaska fishing industry; and political attitudes in Washington, D.C.

In the summer of 1919, C. H. Gilbert and Henry O'Malley carried out an investigation of the fishery. Their report summarized and stated forcefully the feelings of some biologists concerned with the Alaska salmon stocks. They charged that the evidence pointing to overfishing was clear, and suggested that the necessity for economic regulation was self-evident in the rapid increase in inputs of men and equipment with no corresponding increase in the yield. This perceptive report indicated a partial understanding of the necessity of formulating a regulatory program consistent with both biological constraints on output and the price-profit motivated reactions of fishermen and processors. While biologists were by no means unanimous in their evaluation of the state of the salmon stocks or of the measures required to protect them, there was general concern for the future.

The industry had expanded rapidly during World War I. In 1915 there were some 86 canneries operating in Alaska, and by 1920 this number had jumped to 143. Almost 6.7 million cases were packed in 1918. After the war, in 1919, the government cancelled its contracts and returned its unused supplies to the packers. These heavy inventories presented difficult financial problems for the overexpanded industry, and prices broke sharply as dumping developed. In 1919 the opening price for red salmon (per dozen one-pound cans) was \$3.35, up \$1.00 from 1918. In 1920 the market opened at \$3.25, down 10 cents, and by 1921 it had fallen to \$2.35.[1] The general economic depression which began in January 1920 complicated the problems of the industry, and a number of failures occurred among the canning firms. These economic pressures altered industry attitudes sharply, and conservation suddenly became good business as well as good biology.[2] This position relaxed somewhat as prices stabilized in 1922 and 1923, but at least part of the impetus for legislation reflected the weak economic position of the industry.

Finally, Secretary of Commerce [Herbert] Hoover was favorably disposed toward the conservation issue and was prepared to accept the increase in the regulatory powers of his [Commerce] Department required to mount a more effective program.

The legislation that emerged in 1924 was a compromise between economic interests and biological necessity. With two major exceptions the Act represented an extension of the existing pattern of regulation. The first change, in Section 6, involved the scope of federal authority and penalties for the violation of regulations. As had been suggested by Gilbert and O'Malley, this change put the regulatory process more on a par with that in continental United States by giving the Bureau [of Fisheries] the legal power to arrest and also to seize gear. The latter was a more serious threat to fishermen and canners than the usual small fines, and its implementation caused widespread resentment against the Bureau.

The most striking innovation, however, was in Section 2 of the Act, which required not less than 50 percent escapement in most streams. This meant that the commercial fishery had to be regulated in such a manner as to allow 50 percent of the fish in any given stream to escape the fishery. Unfortunately, the application of a rigid percentage escapement rule, like almost all other inflexible regulations, is not well adapted to the peculiar characteristics of the Pacific salmon. Depending on the size of the returning run, a 50 percent harvest could easily be either too large or too small for optimal escapement.

More interesting are the implications of the rule for the regulatory agency. A policy aimed at maintenance of maximum sustained yield through assurance of adequate escapement requires the regulatory agency to mount a research and enforcement effort sufficient for the task. At the time the White Act was passed only a few persons had any real grasp of the complexity of the regulatory problem. The development of an organization capable of carrying out the requirements of the Act would have taken many years in the best of circumstances. In the face of subsequent congressional neglect, partisan sniping, and conflicting pressures from vested interests, only very modest results could have been expected. The lack of general recognition of the difficulties became a source of disappointment and disillusionment with the results achieved under the Act.

At first, however, the industry thought highly of the Act, and this opinion was reflected in the trade journals. Some 15 years later,

Gregory and Barnes, without adequate knowledge of the biological situation, could regard the Act as

> ...making possible greater production of salmon than previously, yet this has taken place despite the restrictions imposed to insure proper escapement, and therefore presumably without jeopardizing the future.[3]

Writing in the late 1930's, they could not foresee the catastrophic decline in the fishery that was to come, nor could they appreciate the inadequacy of both the research and enforcement capabilities of the regulatory agency.

Other authors were critical of the Act for other reasons. Writing in the 1950's, Ernest Gruening emphasized what eventually was recognized as a key omission in the Act from the standpoint of the emerging regional consciousness of the Territorial residents:

> By the White Act of 1924, Congress had foreclosed Alaskans' principal aspiration--control of their fisheries.[4]

By any reasonable standards the program developed under the Act of 1924 must, in retrospect, be judged a failure. Certainly it did not prevent depletion of the fishery. Yet, once the self-delusion about the status of the resource had been dispelled in the 1950's, the Act became the basis of a greatly expanded federal program of research and enforcement. In spite of the provision about escapement and the penalties provided for enforcement, however, the Act really did not change *de facto* conditions in the fishery. The status quo was maintained after 1924 largely as before.

Boom and Bust: 1924 to Statehood

After the contraction in the fishery in the early 1920's, the industry began to expand again in the latter part of the decade. New firms entered and some mergers occurred. The most important entrant was Nakat Packing (A&P) and the key merger, the creation of the Alaskan Pacific Salmon Company in 1928. After 1924, prices rose sharply, fluctuated around those higher levels until 1928, then began to decline again. The entries and mergers that took place, in part as a result of financial speculation, did not change the basic structure of the industry.

There were other changes, perhaps the most significant being the introduction of high-speed canning lines in 1926 and extension of the market by vigorous national advertising. The level of industry activity continued to respond to market conditions, with heavy pressure to pack as much as possible as long as price expectations were firm, and to curtail operations (as in Bristol Bay in 1935) when they were not. Prices showed severe cyclical variations. The opening price for reds (per dozen one-pound cans) dropped from $3.10 in 1930 to $1.45 in 1932. Thereafter it recovered, and the industry began another period of expansion.

During the initial stages of the depression, economy measures in the federal government curtailed the already slender enforcement capability in Alaska. The aerial survey program was cut back and the number of stream guards reduced. There was some increase in enforcement later in the decade but expenditures for research were minimal, averaging less than $25,000 per year until 1939.

With the outbreak of war in 1939, price increases put more and more pressure on the resource. The price of salmon rose 63 percent from 1940 to 1942--an increase of 25 percent even after adjustment for changes in the general price level. At this point, the catch began to decline, a development that simply intensified the industry's efforts to obtain relaxation of regulations.

During the 1930's a more cohesive and vocal Alaskan position toward regulation was developing.[5] This position gradually polarized around two central issues: opposition to outside interests and dissatisfaction with federal control. Public concern with both matters increased in the later 1930's and came to a head in 1939. Early in that year the Commissioner of Fisheries resigned. In May the Bureau of Fisheries was transferred to the Department of the Interior and became part of the Fish and Wildlife Service, and in July the House of Representatives passed a resolution calling for a congressional investigation of the administration of the Alaska fishery. The principal result of the investigation was to break down some of the isolation surrounding the industry. For the first time Congressmen were exposed to a full airing of the divergent interests in the Alaska fisheries: the complaints of Alaskans, mostly directed against traps and absentee administration; the attitudes of the canners; and the actual operating conditions in Alaska. Despite evidence of congressional dissatisfaction (and confusion) over the situation, the advent of war in 1941 prevented any major overhauling of administrative programs.

There was a strong tendency to rationalize the economic structure of the fishery during World War II. Regulations were relaxed, the fishery moved further inshore, fishing was permitted in areas previously restricted, and canners were required to consolidate operations in a limited number of joint units. For example, in 1942 the Bristol Bay season was allowed to open two weeks earlier than usual and the midweek closing was suspended, and in 1943 only 83 canneries operated in all of Alaska. Military security requirements and the drain on manpower in the fishery reduced the number and range of operating units to a point where relatively full and efficient utilization of gear became possible.

The trend of output continued downward, however. Landings of salmon averaged 560 million pounds during the 1935-39 period. During the war (1940-44), despite curtailment of the number of operating units, the catch had dropped to 453 million pounds, and in the immediate postwar period (1945-49) it was only 381 million pounds--a 32 percent decline over the decade. In the 1950's, the catch declined further to a 259 million pound yearly average for the next five years, and only moderate recovery in the 1960's seems indicated. These aggregate figures conceal much greater variation in the catch by species and in the finer detail of yield by species, by area, or by particular race of fish.

This was the pattern predicted in 1919, when Gilbert and O'Malley had written (in reference to the Kvichak-Naknek area in Bristol Bay):

> The sequence of events is always the same. Decreased production is accomplished by increase of gear. Fluctuations in the seasons become more pronounced. Good seasons still appear in which nearly maximum packs are made. But the poor seasons become more numerous. When poor seasons appear no attempt is made to compensate by fishing less closely. On the contrary, efforts are redoubled to put up the full pack. The poorer years strike constantly lower levels, until it is apparent to all that serious depletion has occurred.[6]

This behavior hypothesis was supported by the investigations of Rich and Ball and was consistent with the general decline in the fishery.[7]

In addition to the decline in abundance, the postwar period produced a shift in the political situation in Alaska. In 1940 Ernest

Gruening was elected Governor [*sic*]. One of his proposals involved a basic tax reform program that was bitterly opposed by the Alaska fishing and mining industries. The ultimate passage of this program in 1949 marked, in the opinion of one observer, the end of effective opposition by the salmon lobby in the Territory.[8] In 1949 the Territorial legislature also established a Department of Fisheries. This was a shadow department, assisting and supplementing by means of Territorial appropriations the work of the U.S. Bureau of Commercial Fisheries. It also provided the training ground necessary for eventual assumption of control by the state.

As indicated above, production fell sharply in the 1950's to the level of output prevailing before World War I. Specific areas were very hard hit and political pressures increased further. In a statewide referendum in 1952 Alaskans voted 20,500 to 5,500 to request Congress to turn control of the fisheries over to the Territory on the grounds that local management would be better management.[9] The publication of Gruening's book in 1954 restated the Territorial version of the history of congressional neglect, the power of the lobbies, and the case for statehood. From that time, given the level of economic development reached in Alaska and the hardening of political attitudes, it seems probable that a shift to state control was inevitable, especially since no rehabilitation program for the fishery, no matter how well conceived, could be effective in the short run.

There were two other structural changes of great importance in the overall salmon management program. The decline in landings forced the government and the industry to turn to a greatly expanded program of biological research. Expenditures on research by the Bureau of Commercial Fisheries were less than $100,000 per year until 1948. By 1956 they had reached almost a quarter of a million, and in 1959, the last year before statehood, they exceeded $900,000. In addition, the industry supported the formation, in 1947, of the Fisheries Research Institute at the University of Washington, largely because of dissatisfaction with the level and orientation of the federal program. Today the Institute, in cooperation with the federal and state programs, provides for a broad-based attack on the complex biological problems of the fishery. The Institute has been supported financially by both the industry and the Bureau of Commercial Fisheries, and the latter is currently the major contributor.

Fully as important as the biological factors, and largely misunderstood or ignored in the political debate, were the massive economic problems of the fishery. In addition to the core problems of inefficiency and the stifling effect of regulation on innovation and technical progressiveness, the spectre of unemployment in the precarious Alaskan economy and the special role of the immobile native fishermen have exerted constant pressure on the fishery administrators.

The problems posed by the economics of the fishery have been as ubiquitous as the problem of depletion. Pre-World War I proposals for economic controls included suggestions that both fishing units and the number of canneries in an area be limited. After the war Gilbert and O'Malley emphatically stated the need for economic control, and during World War II, in a proposed revision of the White Act, detailed legislation was presented that included direct measures for economic regulation.[10] Finally, the problem of the amount of fishing effort and its regulation weighed heavily on the minds of those who formulated the revised federal regulatory program in the 1950's. All these efforts suffered from the same deficiency that had plagued those charged with formulation of meaningful biological regulations: the lack of detailed empirical and theoretical economic knowledge of the fishery, which made it impossible to specify the implications and costs of unrestricted entry.

In spite of the long history of bad feelings, the transfer of regulatory authority over the fisheries to the state was accomplished smoothly. The Alaskan department already in existence had established its competence. Its much greater public acceptance made its task easier, and thus far it has retained this respect. Operating details of the conservation problem are obviously easier to administer from Juneau than from Washington, although today there are many issues, primarily international, that are basically beyond the capacity of any state to handle in a satisfactory manner, and some critical potential conflicts between state and national interest are yet to be faced.

Within the existing framework, the question of economic performance of the industry under regulation remains the overriding issue. The furor over the Japanese high-seas fishery and the recent mild upturn in the catch have tended to obscure this question, but the state can ill afford, either in terms of its own needs or as an instrument in international bargaining, to let the fishery dissipate millions each year in manifestly inefficient operations.

ENDNOTES

[1]*Pacific Fisherman Yearbook*, 1918-22.

[2]For a detailed account of these attitudes see Richard A. Cooley, *Politics and Conservation: The Decline of the Alaska Salmon* (New York: Harper & Row, 1963), pp. 109 ff.

[3]Homer E. Gregory and Kathleen Barnes, *North Pacific Fisheries*, Studies of the Pacific, No. 3 (San Francisco: American Institute of Pacific Relations, 1939)

[4]Ernest Gruening, *The State of Alaska* (New York: Random House, 1954), p. 282.

[5]George W. Rogers, *The Future of Alaska* (Baltimore: The Johns Hopkins Press, 1962), chapter 5.

[6]C. H. Gilbert and Henry O'Malley, "Special Investigations of the Salmon Fishery in Central and Western Alaska," *Alaska Fishery and Fur-Seal Industries in 1919*, Bureau of Fisheries (Washington: U.S. Government Printing Office, 1920), p. 151

[7]Willis H. Rich and Edward M. Ball, *Statistical Review of Alaska Salmon Fisheries*. Bureau of Fisheries Document No. 1041 (Washington: U.S. Government Printing Office, 1928), p. 65.

[8]Rogers, *The Future of Alaska*, pp. 255 ff.

[9]Gruening, *The State of Alaska*, p. 406.

[10]Hearings on S.930, Committee on Commerce, January 20, 1944. See the report of the Secretary of the Interior and amendments, pp. 97-98.

THE ROLE OF THE ALASKA HIGHWAY*

M. V. Bezeau

M. V. Bezeau is Director of Ceremonial for National Defence Headquarters in Ottawa. In 1982, while serving as head of the Directorate of History for the agency, he participated in a 40th Anniversary Symposium on the Alaska Highway at Northern Lights College in Fort St. John, British Columbia, near the beginning of the highway. The symposium, organized by Curtis Nordman, presented papers by a number of scholars on all aspects of the history of the road that connects the north with the Outside.

Bezeau challenged a particularly tenacious northern nostrum in his article dealing with the decision to construct the road--that it was a supply road needed by the military to support the defense of the north. Prewar British Columbian Premier T. D. Patullo had for many years pushed for a northern road as a way to encourage development in the northern tier of his province. But he had met with a cool reception both in Ottawa and in Washington, D. C., where he also went to attempt to enlist support. The Ottawa government was not eager to spend the money which such a venture would cost and not happy about the implications for Canadian sovereignty of a road across Canada to connect two U. S. areas. On the other hand, while some officials in Washington were enthusiastic, the American military saw the project as unnecessary and too far outside its defense mission to be justifiable.

The onset of World War II changed some minds. But as Bezeau points out, the road was not intended as a supply route; it was too primitive, problematical and unreliable for such use. Moreover, the American military only grudgingly gave approval to the project, and then only on the condition that its construction would divert no military resources needed for the war effort.

* * *

At first glance, the strategic reasons for building the Alaska Highway appear obvious. On 7 December 1941, the Japanese attacked Pearl Harbor, Hawaii and destroyed a large part of the U.S. Navy Pacific Fleet. American territorial vulnerability immediately increased, especially in the north. Although the Great Circle route, the shortest distance linking Tokyo with the west coast of the United States, passed through the Aleutian Islands, American military

---

*This article originally appeared in Kenneth Coates, ed., *The Alaska Highway: Papers of the 40th Anniversary Symposium* (Vancouver: University of British Columbia Press, 1985), pp. 25-35.

planners earlier had concluded that a road to Alaska had little military value. Now, facing a greatly increased threat, they declared that a land link was imperative. Both American and Canadian authorities approved the construction of a highway as a defensive measure. These facts seem to indicate that the military recommendation to build the road stemmed from a careful strategic reassessment of changing defense requirements under wartime conditions. In reality, it did not.

For many years prior to the outbreak of the Second World War, various Canadians and Americans advocated construction of a road to Alaska. They stressed economic and developmental advantages but also noted the possible value of such a road for defense.[1] In response, the United States War Department repeatedly examined these suggestions and rejected them. From a military point of view, the strategic areas of Alaska were the Panhandle, the south coast, the Alaska Peninsula, and the Aleutian Islands. These all lay near ocean transport and probable air routes. Other areas had low temperatures and poor communications which made year-round operations difficult. The sea lanes connecting all the valued areas were shorter in both time and distance than any highway route. Moreover, the proposed roads did not provide links to such areas as the Alaska Peninsula, and could not do so to Kodiak, Unalaska, and other islands where important installations were located. Thus, sea transport would be required in any case. The navy saw little likelihood of any permanent interruption to sea communications in the event of war with Japan. Shipping could be in short supply in an emergency, but this was more quickly corrected by new marine construction than by building a road. Hence, the defensive value of a highway to Alaska was "negligible," and construction on the basis of military necessity alone was unjustified and unsupportable.[2] The Canadian-American Permanent Joint Board on Defense (P.J.B.D.) reached similar conclusions on 15 November 1940.[3]

Of course, military communications to Alaska could not be, and were not, ignored. Primary reliance was placed on the sea, but air routes were developed along the coast and from the prairie interior. The prairie link, the Northwest Staging Route, was especially important since it avoided the poorer coastal weather, was removed from potential enemy interruption, and was connected to the continental heartland. The staging route originated in 1935 with a Canadian Department of Transport survey for a Great Circle air route to the Orient. The line from Edmonton to Alaska was chosen and airfield sites selected at Grande Prairie, Fort St. John, and Fort

Nelson, B.C., and Watson Lake and Whitehorse, Yukon. Survey parties were in the field when the European war broke out in September 1939. With the British Commonwealth Air Training Plan and other expanded air force construction about to begin, consideration was given to ending the program. It was decided, however, that if the U.S. were to enter the war, the strategic value of the airfields would increase, so work continued. By September 1941, the route was considered usable in daylight, and radio range stations were operational along its Canadian length by the end of the year.[4]

During this construction, but unrelated to it, a new move was launched in the U.S. House of Representatives to build a highway north. On 5 February 1941, Delegate Anthony J. Dimond of Alaska introduced Bill HR 3095 to construct a road along a route to be selected by the president.[5] The army's War Plans Division was asked to examine the issue once more, and it concluded that there still appeared to be little military justification for constructing a land route to the north. The division recommended, as it had before, that the bill not be considered favorably in the interests of national defense.[6] This staff work took time, however, and was not finished until early June. By then the strategic balance was about to undergo a dramatic change.

On 22 June 1941, Hitler launched a massive invasion of the U.S.S.R., slicing easily and deeply into Soviet territory, and the great Russian empire trembled. In the Far East, Japan was an Axis power, allied with Germany and Italy for mutual aid and assistance since the previous September. Although Japan had also signed a neutrality treaty with the Soviet Union in April 1941, the United States had no guarantee that the German attack would not ultimately lead to a Japanese presence in Siberia if the Soviet armies collapsed. Prudence seemed necessary, at least until the situation became clearer.[7]

Two days after the German invasion, the American chief of staff, Gen. Marshall, returned the War Plans Division's report. "In view of recent developments in the international situation," he advised, a highway was "desirable as a long range defense measure, providing this construction is controlled so as not to delay or interfere with other more pressing military construction requirements." Marshall directed that the report "be rewritten to interpose no objection to the passage of the authorization bill."[8] This new War Department position was subsequently passed to the House Committee on Roads. A recommendation which mentioned "certain military limitations" which justified only "a low priority" and merely interposed "no further objection" was scarcely a ringing endorsement of quick construction.[9] Nonetheless, it was a significant shift from clear opposition to gentle support and helped ensure that the issue did not die.

A few short months later, the Japanese attacked Pearl Harbor, and the United States was at war. Delegate Dimond and others now pressed William Cartwright, the chairman of the House Committee on Roads, to give active consideration to the bill. In turn, Cartwright solicited departmental views and on 6 January asked the War Department if the changing international situation now increased the military importance of the road.[10] The War Plans Division referred the request to the G-4 staff, responsible for logistics, noting in passing that the division now felt that conditions justified more active support than before.[11]

Meanwhile, other departments were also concerned with the highway proposal. On 16 January, Secretary Ickes of the Department of the Interior raised the issue at a cabinet meeting. President Roosevelt, who had previously gone on record as favoring an early route survey, was interested, and cabinet sentiment was generally favorable. Roosevelt appointed Secretaries Stimson (war), Knox (navy), and Ickes as a committee to "agree on the necessity for a road and the proper route."[12] Since the matter was then being studied by the War Department, a meeting of the committee was delayed until the army's in-house assessment was complete and its expert opinion obtained.[13]

The critical moment for a professional military contribution had arrived. Soldiers are carefully trained to make staff estimates--"appreciations of the situation" in Canadian terminology--and to weigh all factors, such as the enemy threat and considerations of time and distance, before giving their balanced conclusions. The G-4 staff's procedure was less dispassionate but perhaps more interesting.

The House Roads Committee's request, with the War Plans Division's note, went to the Transportation Branch, which would be responsible for the effective use of the highway if built. The branch disagreed with giving more active support to the bill. To do so without also giving funds, manpower, and other resources, it argued, would be ineffectual, while allocating these would only divert scarce assets. The branch strongly suggested that the immediate needs of higher priority projects meant that more support was unjustified.[14]

This advice led to some soul-searching within the G-4's staff. The War Department, it felt, was now forced to take a definite stand on the issue. The Transportation Branch's opinion, if accepted, would reverse the chief of staff's 1941 position, repeated by the secretary of war, that highway construction should no longer be opposed, and this in spite of the fact that the international situation had since deteriorated. On the other hand, it was argued, a road would eventually have to be built to Alaska anyway, and "it could be started now in the interests of the national defense," even if this meant "diverting materials and machinery from other necessary important road projects." Under the current wartime circumstances, Canada could be expected to look favorably on the project but might not do so later. Accordingly, it was recommended that the War Department "take advantage of the present war to secure the necessary agreements from Canada to start work now and finish perhaps many years to come."[15]

Col. A. R. Wilson, the author of this recommendation, drafted a carefully-worded reply, which was repeated to the War Plans Division.[16] He wrote:

> It is believed that hearings should be scheduled on this Bill as early a date as practicable...construction of a highway to Alaska...is a desirable undertaking to initiate. However, the amount of work to be undertaken at the present time or in the immediate future depends upon a careful evaluation of the amount of machinery, material, engineering talent, labor and funds which can be diverted from other national defense projects which may be more important.
>
> The Bill should provide that no unit of work should be started or no funds appropriated...until approval has been obtained from the War and Navy Departments and the necessary priorities board.[17]

This reply seemed "generally favorable" to the division, which had a predisposition toward more active support. To the chief of staff, the division noted that increased Alaskan garrisons and the possibility of enemy interference with water routes indicated a greater need for an alternate land route for supplies and reinforcements. The road should follow the line of the Northwest Staging Route airfields in order to supply them and to support additional airfield construction.[18] The proposal now had a life of its own.

A subsequent War Plans Division draft paper clearly spelled out the army's position. It acknowledged that the cost of the highway in man hours, equipment, and supplies would be greater than the same expenditure for an equivalent amount of transport ship-building; that the estimated construction time of two years made the road "unavailable in the present emergency"; and that the road would not reach vital installations such as Kodiak, Dutch Harbor, and Sitka-all of which would still need sea transport. Nevertheless, the division concluded, somewhat unconvincingly, that the security of a supply line to the central portion of Alaska outweighed all disadvantages. It recommended that the highway be authorized.[19] The gist of this paper was passed orally to the secretary of war on 2 February.[20]

By then, both Stimson and Knox had also received the State Department's opinion. They were told that the highway would have to be negotiated with Canada, but "if the United States Government really wanted it, Canada would accede." Route selection was left to the expert opinion of the army engineers, but since a road would be needed to ease northwest airfield supply difficulties, that route seemed logical: a choice, it was noted, which would "break the hearts of the politicians in our Pacific Northwest." The State Department deliberately refused to advise on whether or not the highway was important enough to justify immediate construction.[21] The army, of course, had already recommended that it was.

Armed with this information, the American cabinet committee decided to obtain engineer surveys of the highway route and the availability of road-building equipment and to commence the survey work before the spring thaw in the north.[22] Brig.-Gen. C. L. Sturdevant, assistant chief of engineers, was immediately given this task. He was told that the decision was to build the highway via the airfield line and was ordered to submit a survey and construction plan within a few days.[23] Sturdevant's report was ready two days later, on 4 February 1942.[24]

Although Knox, the secretary of the navy, was a member of the special cabinet committee, the chief of naval operations had not yet been formally asked for his opinion, in spite of recommendations to consult him and the persistent concern over the security of sea links. On the day that Sturdevant returned his outline plan, Gen. Marshall finally signed a letter to Adm. King. He asked for "a brief statement as to the ability of the Navy, considering all its commitments and probable future requirements, to maintain, under all circumstances, uninterrupted communications" to Alaska. King replied immediately. Guarantees of uninterrupted communications were impossible, but he assured Marshall that the Navy would provide adequate protection for the garrisons and civilian population. King believed it improbable that the enemy could gain any foothold in Alaska which would make the communication links dangerous. Specifically, he rejected the thesis that a road to Alaska was necessary because the navy could not afford adequate shipping defense.[25] By now, however, this opinion was irrelevant.[26] Plans were already being made. On the 11th of February, President Roosevelt approved the project and authorized the army to proceed immediately.[27]

Canadian permission to build was still necessary, but the State Department's confidence that American approval would gain Canadian concurrence was firmly based. Such support had been all but guaranteed previously when American officials visited the Canadian Department of External Affairs in mid-1941. Canada, then already at war, made it clear that the primary consideration in such matters was national defense, but the Permanent Joint Board on Defense had downplayed the highway's importance in 1940. If the board now recommended construction, however, Canada would do its share. It was strongly implied that if the United States put up the bulk of the money, it could probably choose the route. After the meeting, Norman Robertson, the Canadian under-secretary of state for external affairs, conferred further with J. Pierrepont Moffat, the U.S. representative in Ottawa. Robertson said that he was personally sympathetic to the project, but that the government would only agree to it if it were really needed for the war effort. He assured Moffat that if the United States Army "really went to the mat for it in the Permanent Joint Defense Board...then...any opposition at this end would automatically disappear."[28] The U.S. Army was now quite prepared to take such action. Shortly after the initial plans were ready, the army's senior member on the joint board, Lieut.-Gen. S. D. Embick, took steps to ensure that the American Army and Navy representatives would speak with one voice favoring the project. Presidential approval assured that this would be so.[29]

There was still some reason to expect opposition from Canada. After all, the Canadian members of the board had joined in the 1940 judgment that the military value of such a road was "negligible." There was no reason for them to have reversed their opinions. As late as 4 February 1942, the Canadian chiefs of staff considered the question and decided that, from their point of view, a highway to

Alaska would only indirectly affect the defense of the west coast, even if it could be completed during the war. Canadian construction of the road, therefore, was unwarranted.[30] American construction for American purposes, however, was another question.

On 10 February, the secretary to the Canadian Cabinet War Committee noted that Canada was about to receive a request to allow American army engineers to survey a highway route via the Peace River to Whitehorse. The matter was discussed at a meeting two days later. The committee agreed to allow the survey. Such permission, noted C. D. Howe, the minister of munitions and supply, would in any event not commit Canada to actual construction.[31]

The American request was formally presented by Moffat the next day. It asked for permission both to make a survey and to construct a pioneer road, noting that four regiments of engineers were scheduled for employment on the project and that the United States would defray all associated costs. In reply, Norman Robertson passed on the Cabinet War Committee's approval of the survey but queried the definition of a "pioneer road." Specifically, he wished to know if, by approving it, the Canadian government would be automatically committing itself to the construction of the entire road. This, he said, would require further cabinet consideration, since only the survey had been approved so far. Moffat sought clarification from Washington and reported back the same day that a commitment for the final road would be sought later through the joint board. As for the pioneer road, he defined it as "a rough working road...considered part of the survey...[which] would be in part the site of an eventual road." Robertson was satisfied with this explanation and was pleased that Canada and the United States had come to a mutual understanding about limiting Canadian liability.[32]

The United States War Department now directed its chief of engineers to proceed with the project. Robertson may have visualized the pioneer road as a rough trail for survey parties, but the American army engineers were under no such delusions. Orders were given for a corridor thirty-two feet wide, subsequently much enlarged, with log bridges and culverts, to provide complete access for the whole distance for civilian contractors who would build the permanent road.[33] The United States Army's official historical chronology rightly regards 13 February, the day Robertson and Moffat met, as the date that Canada approved construction.[34]

In Canada, discussion continued. It was decided that the Canadian members of the board would agree to a proposal to build the highway if the Americans asked for it for defense reasons and accepted all construction and maintenance costs. Subsequently, the board formally advocated this proposal on 25-26 february 1942. The Canadian chiefs of staff still did not think the road warranted by Canadian defense standards but were willing to accept American reasons for justifying construction at their own expense.[35]

Others were more frank. H. L. Keenleyside, the Canadian assistant under secretary of state for external affairs and the secretary of the joint board's Canadian section, noted before final Cabinet approval that the board's recommendation should be accepted, but not for defense reasons. The military arguments advanced were questionable, especially since the road was not expected to be finished until 1944, and adequate ship construction and other plans would obviate its requirement by then. Nonetheless, he concluded, "the United States Government is now so insistent...that the Canadian Government cannot possibly allow itself to be put into the position of barring...land access to Alaska." Canada "should agree," he declared:

> but this agreement should be recognized, in our own minds at least, as being based on political and not on strategic grounds. The political argument, given the attitude of Washington, is inescapable; the strategic argument, in my opinion, is a most dubious egg.[36]

To this Norman Robertson could only add: "I agree that on political grounds we cannot be put into the position of blocking its construction."[37]

Whatever the value of the arguments, the board had supported the proposal, and now the Canadian government prepared to do its part. On 5 March 1942, the Cabinet War Committee approved the recommendation.[38] The last legal obstacle to construction had been passed.

We now know that the Japanese never intended to invade mainland Alaska. Planners in 1942 did not, and they had to be prepared to respond to any reasonable enemy capability. Still, it is fair to assess both the actual and perceived strategic requirements for building the highway during the war. Two issues stand out: the ability of the U.S. Navy to protect the sea lanes of communication north, and the availability of sufficient sea transport to handle all the foreseeable supply and reinforcement requirements of Alaska.

Prior to Pearl Harbor, the U.S. Navy's ability was virtually unquestioned. With the destruction of a large part of the American Pacific fleet, however, it was reasonable for the issue to be reexamined. The U.S. Army certainly voiced some doubts about the navy's capability to maintain sea communications to Alaska but carried out no detailed assessments to see if they were valid. The Navy was not asked for its opinion until after all vital decisions had been made. Its rejection of the idea that it could not provide adequate protection was then no longer relevant. Beyond this general point, there are two additional significant facts. There always was a reasonably secure route along the Inside Passage as far north as Skagway--and the Americans took steps to increase the Passage's defenses--with only the few hundred additional miles of open sea to Seward remaining.[39] From there, sea transport was required, highway or no highway, to the important forward installations on Kodiak Island and points west. Navy protection had to be relied upon at these advanced locations in any case.

Sea transport required ships, and these were the Allies' most critical logistical resource. Losses were then far exceeding new construction, and the highway could have been justified on the basis of freeing a depleting resource for other uses. Plans were already underway for massive new ship-building programs, however, and from the summer of 1942, the Allies experienced a net gain, not loss, in available cargo space. Military shipping requirements to destinations other than Alaska had a much higher priority, but there was no reason to suspect such a severe shortage of ships in 1944--the planned highway completion date--that the essential maintenance of the Alaskan garrison and population would be prevented. Indeed, the road at first contributed to existing shortages, since a great deal of construction material in the critical summer of 1942 was transported by water to Skagway and mainland Alaska.[40]

There were other opportunity costs as well. Despite assurances that sufficient men and material were available, resources sent to Canada reduced those available elsewhere.[41] In early 1942, it was already clear that the U.S. Army did not have enough engineers to handle all its tasks. To provide them for the highway required breaking an existing policy not to send black troops to extreme northern climates.[42] Demands for heavy transport trucks led to shortages and shipping difficulties as far away as the Persian Gulf, while later reallocations of road-building machinery designated for British use led to controversy and compromise in the Allied Munitions Assignments Board.[43] All this would have been justified, of course, if it had been needed to meet real or perceived strategic requirements. But it was not.

With hindsight, one can see that the highway never really contributed much to Alaskan supply even after its completion. Although the first trucks from Dawson Creek rolled into Fairbanks on 21 November 1942, in essence the territory remained an "island" for military transportation purposes throughout the war.[44] When Gen. DeWitt, the commanding general of the U.S. Western Defense Command, was informed at the end of October 1942 that the opening of the highway would lead to a curtailment of available shipping, he took immediate steps to stop such action. Completion of the highway, he pointed out, did not alleviate the need for shipping during the westward movement to the Aleutians.[45] As a strategic measure for the direct support of Alaska, therefore, the highway's impact was, as previously assessed, virtually "negligible."

But as a construction project, it was a great success. It captured the public imagination as few things did in those dark and forbidding midwar years. Work on it had a frontier spirit on a scale which seemed to typify the best in American pioneering tradition: men and machines against the wilderness in a race against time.[46] It was a magnificent achievement carried out as a military project in time of war. But it was not needed for defense. The highway was actually planned and built for other reasons.

ENDNOTES

1Karl C. Dod, *The Corps of Engineers: the War Against Japan*, United States Army in World War II (Washington: United States Army, 1966), p. 299; C. P. Stacey, *The Military Problems of Canada* (Toronto: Ryerson, 1940) pp. 36-37.

2Stimson to Cartwright, 2 August 1940, McNarney to Cofs, 24 April 1941. NARS, RG 165, WPD 4327.

3Army Service Forces, "The Alaska Highway," May 1945, exhibit B (Gen. Somervell's desk file), NARS, RG 160.

4Stanley W. Dziuban, *Military Relations Between the United States and Canada 1939-1945*, United States Army in World War II (Washington: Department of the Army, 1959), pp. 201-2; C. P. Stacey, *Arms, Men and Governments: The War Policies of Canada 1939-1945* (Ottawa: Queen's Printer, 1970) pp. 379-80.

[5]Army Service Forces, "The Alaska Highway," exhibits B and E.

[6]Gerow to Cofs, 9 June 1941, NARS, RG 165, WPD 4327-11.

[7]See, for example, warnings to Western and Alaska Defense Commands in early July 1941, in U.S. Army, Western Defense Command, "History of the Western Defense Command," MS (1945), I: ch. 1, p. 6, ch. 2, pp. 5-6, copy in U.S. Army Military History Institute, Carlisle Barracks, Carlisle, Pa.

[8]Ward to Cofs, 24 June 1941, NARS, RG 407, WPD, AG 611.

[9]Gerow to Cofs, 30 June 1941, NARS, RG 165, WPD 4327; Stimson to Cartwright, 6 October 1941, in Army Service Force, "The Alaska Highway," exhibit E.

[10]Cartwright to Stimson, 6 January 1942, NARS, RG 407, AG 611.

[11]Gerow to Cofs, 19 January 1942, NARS, RG 165, WPD 4327-25.

[12]"Notes on Cabinet Meeting of January 16, 1942," in Army Service Force, "The Alaska Highway," exhibits B and F.

[13]Smith to Cofs, 19 January 1942, Stimson to Ickes, 21 January 1942, NARS, RG 165, WPD 4327-25, 26.

[14]Hamblen to Construction and Real Estate Branch, 17 January 1942, NARS, RG 407, AG 611.

[15]Wilson to chief, Construction and Real Estate Branch, 18 January 1942, Ibid.

[16]Ibid.

[17]Somervell to WPD, 20 January 1942, Ibid.

[18]Gerow to Cofs, 23 January 1942, Ibid.

[19]Draft Gerow to Cofs, n.d., NARS, RG 165, WPD 4327-27.

[20]Tully minute, n.d., Ibid.

[21]Hickerson to Berle, Berle to Knox, 31 January 1942, Knox to Berle, 3 February 1942 (Knox Office File 4-1-2), NARS, RG 80.

[22]Gerow to Cofs, 6 February 1942, NARS, RG 165, WPD 4327-27.

[23]Excerpt from Sturdevant's notes, in Army Services Force, "The Alaska Highway," exhibit F.

[24]Gerow to Cofs, 6 February 1942, NARS, RG 165, WPD 4327-27.

[25]Marshall to King, 4 February 1942, memo for record, 21 February 1942, Ibid.

[26]The navy did not seem to really care and in the future treated the highway with some indifference. See Knox to Cartwright, 9 March 1942 (Knox office file 4-1-2), NARS, RG 80; and lack of correspondence on CNO Confidential 1942 file on highways, Ibid, NS--N2 = 8/ND3.

[27]Crawford minute, 11 February 1942, on Gerow to Cofs, 6 February 1942, NARS, RG 165, WPD 4327-27.

[28]"Memorandum of Conversation," 6 August 1941, enclosed with Hickerson to Embick, 11 August 1941, Ibid.

[29]Senior army representative to A. Cofs, 8 February 1942, memo for record, 21 February 1942, Ibid.

[30]Stacey, *Arms, Men and Governments*, p. 382.

[31]Cabinet War Committee minutes, 12 February 1942, in Canada, External Affairs, *Documents on Canadian External Relations, 9: 1941-1943*, ed. J. F. Hilliker (Ottawa: Minister of Supply and Services, 1980), p. 1175 (hereafter cited as *DCER 9*).

[32]Minister of United States memorandum on conversation with Robertson and Hickerson, 13 February 1942, Ibid., pp. 1176-78.

[33]Dod, *Engineers: The War Against Japan*, pp. 300, 307.

[34]Mary H. Williams, *Chronology, 1941-1945*, United States Army in World War II (Washington: Department of the Army, 1960).

[35]Memorandum on Alaska Highway, n.d., journal extracts, 26th P.J.B.D. Meeting, 25-26 February 1942, extracts from Cabinet War Committee minutes, 5 March 1942, *DCER 9*, pp. 1178-82, 1185-87.

[36]Keenleyside memorandum: assistant under secretary of state for external affairs to under secretary of state for external affairs, 3 March 1942, Ibid., pp. 1182-85.

[37]Robertson note on Keenleyside memorandum, Ibid., p. 1183n.

[38]Extracts from Cabinet War Committee minutes, 5 March 1942, Ibid., pp. 1185-87.

[39]AG to CG Field Forces, 10 February 1942, Ulio to CG WDC, 4 June 1942, WDC to AG, 25 August 1942, NARS, RG 407, AG 611.

[40]R. M. Leighton and R. W. Coakley, *Global Logistics and Strategy, 1940-1943*, United States Army in World War II (Washington: Department of the Army, 1955), p. 583, appendix E; R. W. Coakley and R. M. Leighton, *Global Logistics and Strategy, 1943-1945*, United States Army in World War II (Washington: United States Army, 1968), appendix F-1.

[41]Gerow to Cofs, 6 February 1942, NARS, RG 165; WPD 4327-27; extracts from minutes of 26th Meeting of P.J.B.D., 25-26 February 1942, *DCER 9*, pp. 1180-82.

[42]B. D. Coll, et al., *The Corps of Engineers: Troops and Equipment*, United States Army in World War II (Washington: Department of the Army, 1958), p. 143; Ulysses Lee, *The Employment of Negro Troops*, United States Army in World War II (Washington: United States Army, 1966), p. 439. Ultimately, more than a third of the engineers working on the road were black, Ibid., p. 609.

[43]Leighton and Coakley, *Global Logistics and Strategy, 1940-1943*, pp. 294, 576, 582.

[44]Dod, *Engineers: The War Against Japan*, p. 315; Stetson Conn, Rose C. Engelman, Byron Fairchild, *Guarding the United States and its Outposts*, United States Army in World War II (Washington: Department of the Army, 1964), p. 225.

[45]Western Defense Command, "History of the Western Defense Command," I: ch. 2, p. 17.

[46]Lee, *The Employment of Negro Troops*, p. 609; Harold W. Richardson, "Alcan--America's Glory Road," Part I: "Strategy and Location," *Engineering Newsrecord* (17 December 1942): 859, copy in U.S. CMH, HRC 228.03, Geog., E., Alaska 611, "Alcan Highway."

STATEHOOD FOR ALASKA AND HAWAII*

John S. Whitehead

Professor John Simms Whitehead earned his doctoral degree at Yale University in 1971. He has taught at the University of Alaska in Fairbanks since 1978. He has written *Hydroelectric Power in Twentieth Century Alaska: Anchorage, Juneau, Ketchikan and Sitka* (Fairbanks: University of Alaska, Institute of Water Resources, 1983) and *The Separation of College and State: Columbia, Dartmouth, Harvard and Yale, 1776-1876* (New Haven, CT: Yale University Press, 1973). His journal articles include "Hydroelectric Power in Juneau: Technology as a Guide to the Development of an Alaskan Community," *Pacific Northwest Quarterly*, April 1984.

A comparative analyst, Professor Whitehead has devoted much of his recent research effort to a comparison of the Alaska and Hawaii statehood movements and their aftermath. He also has become schooled in the techniques of oral history as a research tool.

In this article, Whitehead brings his oral history training to bear on the question of how Alaskans and Hawaiians have understood their states' respective histories since statehood. Residents of each state feel differently, Whitehead found: even though their options are limited by federal policy and jurisdiction, Alaskans generally seem to view statehood as more beneficial than do the Hawaiians. Whitehead shows in this piece that when used carefully, oral history can yield great dividends in the interpretation of the past.

* * *

The first constitutional conventions held in the statehood movements of Alaska and Hawaii were strikingly similar in their organization and planned purpose. Both conventions were called by the legislatures of the respective territories in the first decade after World War II (Hawaii in the spring of 1950; Alaska in the winter of 1955-56) for the conscious purpose of prodding the U.S. Congress to pass statehood legislation after years of delay. The conventions would be living proof that the territories were ready and able to be states. Both territories were quite aware of the historical significance

---

*This selection is excerpted from John S. Whitehead and William S. Schneider, "The Singular Event and The Everyday Routine: The Interplay of History and Culture in the Shaping of Memory," *Oral History Review* 15 (Fall 1987): 43-79.

of calling such constitutional conventions. Fifteen American territories had done so in advance of Congressional enabling legislation; in all previous cases statehood followed in a reasonable period of time.[1]

The delegates to both conventions, 63 in Hawaii and 55 in Alaska, were elected on a non-partisan basis using a geographic apportionment much broader than that in the existing territorial legislatures. Each convention was hailed at the time of its election as the most representative political assembly ever held in either territory, both because of the new apportionment and because of the election of people who had not previously participated in politics. Each convention sought to produce a model constitution, using guidelines prepared by the National Municipal League. Both bodies produced such constitutions in roughly the same number of days (79 in Hawaii and 75 in Alaska), and their delegates achieved near unanimity in approving the documents. In both Alaska and Hawaii only one delegate refused to sign the completed constitution. To finish the list of similarities, both territories were admitted as states to the union in 1959 and began their political existence with the constitutions those conventions produced.

Despite these similarities in original organization and purpose, the memories of people who participated in the two respective conventions as recorded in oral history interviews twenty-five to thirty-five years after the events could not be more different. The Alaskans remember their convention in the mystical, almost religious tones of a transcendent experience. In the quarter century since statehood they have turned the convention into a political legend that is revered and perpetuated even by people who did not participate in the event. In January 1986 Alaska governor William Sheffield, who had not been involved in the 1955-56 convention, announced in his State of the State message to the Alaska legislature:

> Thirty years ago this winter, on a hill outside of Fairbanks, a group of Alaskans sat down in a university gymnasium and wrote a constitution for a state that didn't exist. That took patience, courage, pride, and confidence. Patience--because governments must be carefully constructed. Courage--because there were no guarantees for statehood. Pride--because Alaskans had dreams to fulfill. And confidence, confidence above all else--because they knew Alaskans had the will to turn potential into success. The 30th anniversary of our constitution is a time for reflection and celebration. It's also a

time to reaffirm our pride in Alaska, and our confidence in the future.[2]

For both the governor and his audience the 1955-56 Alaska Constitutional Convention had become a time in history never to be forgotten, a touchstone of political achievement and devotion against which all past and future governmental actions were to be measured. The convention symbolized the genesis of the political entity known as the State of Alaska. To Alaskans the Fairbanks convention was every inch the legend or miracle that the Philadelphia Convention of 1787 had been to America's founders and the generations that followed them. When Alaskans celebrated their twenty-fifth anniversary of statehood in 1984, they revered the convention delegates at a gala dinner in Fairbanks with a ceremony of "investitute" for the Founders of Alaska Statehood thus creating a new order of "northern nobility." One by one the living delegates walked across the stage to the applause of several hundred people and were presented with a specially struck silver medallion. Earlier in the day they had been feted at a public reception to the cheers of thousands.[3]

In Hawaii the 1950 convention commands no similar legendary status. Participants remember it as an important occurrence, but no more so than many other public displays made in support of statehood after World War II. The constitution the convention wrote is more often noted than the experience of participating in the convention itself. For the people of Hawaii, the 1950 convention in no way symbolizes, as it does in Alaska, the genesis of the state they love and serve. When they celebrated their Silver Jubilee a few months after Alaska in August 1984, they made no mention of the convention or its delegates. Instead, they staged a three hour musical extravanganza replete with flowers, hulas, and tributes in song and dance to the spirit and history of the islands.[4]

By the mid-1980s the evidence of public celebrations and political speeches suggested that Alaska's convention had become legend while Hawaii's had virtually fallen into oblivion. This surprising contrast becomes even more evident when examining the quality of memory in the oral history interviews of participants in these two events.

My first interviews with the Alaskans came in 1981 when the Alaska Statehood Commission, an agency created by the state legislature to investigate the relationship of the state of Alaska to the

United States, commissioned an oral history of the statehood movement. Two other historians and I were charged with interviewing the principal actors in the statehood movement. There was little question in Alaska as to who the principal actors were; they were the delegates to the convention along with a handful of other people. Our specific mission was to ask them if the development of Alaska since statehood--particularly its relation to the federal government--met the expectations they had held in the late 1950s. Beyond this specific social science objective our broader goal was to uncover the depth of feeling, mission or conviction that surrounded the birth of the state of Alaska.[5]

The answer to the specific question was an overwhelming affirmative. The reasons were not difficult to discern. When Alaska became a state in 1959 there was some doubt over the state's ability to raise sufficient revenues to pay the cost of a functioning government. By 1981 the state's share of Alaska's oil wealth was not only paying the cost of state government, without the need for a personal income or sales tax, but was also building a permanent fund to defray the cost of government in the future. This was a level of prosperity undreamed of in 1959 by those I interviewed. One of the principal goals of statehood had been the creation of a stable economy; the participants in the movement could not have been more pleased. Anchorage businessman Barrie White, a delegate to the convention, said his only disappointment was that "Alaska has become normal so quickly."[6]

As the interviews with the Alaskans progressed, I quickly became struck not so much with the answers to the specific question on state development as with the emotional intensity, the precision of detail, the almost reverential tone with which people described their participation in the statehood movement, particularly in the 1955-56 convention. Barrie White noted, "It was an extraordinary experience, one of those rare experiences in life. I think everyone got caught up in it." New Orleans businessman George Lehleitner, who visited the convention as a public spirited outsider, noted that the delegates conducted their work with a "sense of mission"; he went as far as saying the delegates were moved by a "divine injunction." Ernest Bartley, a political consultant to the convention from the University of Florida, thoughtfully called the convention "a peaceful rebellion" by a people who had been "kicked from pillar to post by a less than beneficent government." Possibly the most moving memory of the convention came from Les Nerland, a delegate from Fairbanks. On the day the convention adjourned, February 6, 1956, Nerland took a signed copy of the constitution to his family's furniture store and showed it to his father Andrew Nerland, a long time statehood supporter who was too old to serve as a delegate. Andrew Nerland looked over the document with pride, seeing it as a giant step toward statehood; fifteen minutes later he collapsed and died. It seemed as if even heaven waited for the delegates to complete their work! Comments such as these were the rule rather than the exception in the 54 interviews.[7]

The 1981 interviews and my observation of the January 1984 Alaska Statehood celebration suggested to me that participation in a singular or once-in-a-lifetime event such as a constitutional convention created the heightened, precise quality of memory I had discovered in Alaska. The upcoming Silver Jubilee in Hawaii in August 1984 attracted my interest. I assumed it would be similar to the silver celebration in Alaska and that people in Hawaii would recall their constitutional convention in much the same way. I decided to go to Hawaii and wrote various people in advance whom I thought could give me expert advice.

My first indication that Hawaii would be different came in an answer to a letter I wrote Robert Kamins, a member of Hawaii's Legislative Reference Bureau at the time of the 1950 convention. Kamins responded, "My memories of Hawaii's statehood movement and tactic are no longer any shade of green and many years ago I cleared out my files on the period."[8] Kamins' response was certainly different from anything I had encountered in Alaska. My subsequent attendance at the Silver Jubilee, which has already been described, only confirmed Kamins' reaction to my request for a recollection of the 1950 convention. This led me to search deeper to understand Hawaii's reaction to a convention that seemed so similar to the one in Alaska. What might have caused the difference in these reactions and celebrations? Possibly the people of Hawaii were simply less boastful than their northern neighbors. In a land where the climate and hours of daylight remain relatively constant every day, so may the emotional peaks and valleys of political intensity. If the islands' silver Jubilee differed from Alaska's, this may simply have been an indication of the style rather than the factual basis of Hawaii's political culture.

I decided to approach Hawaii as I had done in Alaska with oral history supplemented by documentary evidence of the convention. My oral history research in Hawaii was two-pronged. I used transcripts of existing oral histories and conducted new interviews.

The transcripts in the massive John A. Burns Oral History Project at the University of Hawaii remove any doubt that the people of Hawaii *can* reach emotional peaks over politics. Interview after interview with associates and adversaries of Hawaii's governor from 1962 to 1974 describe in intense detail and passion the building and operation of the Burns political machine from the early 1950s to the present day. These interviews did not center on statehood or the 1950 convention, but the interviewees were usually asked to give an account of their political lives in Hawaii as an introduction. Those who had been delegates to the convention or who had been in Hawaii when the convention took place made only the most passing reference to it. In some cases, they did not mention it at all.[9]

Nelson Doi, a delegate to the 1950 convention and later lieutenant governor of Hawaii, merely noted that he was elected to the convention and was "the youngest guy there." Delegate Chuck Mau, the first judge in Hawaii of full-blooded Chinese ancestry, went into vivid detail about his trip to the 1948 Democratic National Convention where he convinced the platform committee to endorse immediate statehood for Hawaii. Mau recounted how he sat through three days of committee meetings without leaving the room for fear he would be absent when called to speak. He made no mention at all of his participation in the constitutional convention two years later. William Quinn, who was not a delegate to the convention but who became Hawaii's last territorial governor in 1957 and its first elected governor in 1959, made no mention of the convention. In only one interview in the Burns project did anything like the response of the Alaskan delegates appear. Toshio Serizawa, a delegate from Kauai, recalled, "It was a very emotional experience to sign the document. Not knowing when or ever in my lifetime will I see statehood...I swore at the time of the signing of the constitution...that the day we get statehood, even if I'm 90 years old, I would run for the state legislature."[10]

In my interviews with the delegates, I asked specifically for a recollection of the convention. I also described the Alaska experience as a point of comparison. The direct questioning only reinforced the indirect impression I had received in the Burns' transcripts. Judge Mau reaffirmed the importance of the 1948 Democratic convention over the later constitutional event: "Not only was it more important to me," he said, "but perhaps more important to the people of the then territory of Hawaii." He emphasized that the Democratic convention was the first occasion at which either of the two national parties had endorsed *immediate* rather than eventual, statehood. Mau recounted in vivid detail how Delegate Bob Bartlett of Alaska had taken him to dinner at 3:00 a.m. after the platform committee approved the statehood plank. The New York *Times* had interviewed him and the Honolulu *Star-Bulletin* ran a banner headline "Mau Wins Statehood Plank." Mau clearly expressed emotion, but not for the 1950 convention. He merely noted that he had run as a delegate to ensure that Hawaii had a *fair* constitution.[11]

The memories of other participants were similar to Mau's. Delegate Richard Lyman, Jr., a native Hawaiian and now trustee of the Bishop Estate (Hawaii's principal charitable land trust), compared the convention to the sowing of a seed which later grew into a plant, but a plant which needed to be pruned this way or bent that way. Adam "Bud" Smyser, who covered the 1950 convention for the Honolulu *Star-Bulletin* and later became its editor, emphasized the idealism of the convention. But as a memorable event in the statehood movement Smyser categorized it as a "milestone" rather than a watershed. Hiram Fong, vice-president of the convention and later one of Hawaii's original U. S. Senators, noted, "It was not such a big event, although we felt it was important. In the hearts of the people it wasn't big." Honolulu lawyer Hebden Porteus, secretary of the 1950 convention, put it this way:

> I don't want to take anything away from the idea of the 1950 convention, but if you say where did it loom in my life, I'd say it loomed as the absolute No. 1 thing *at that time*...But then there were other problems. You had to deal with those. You couldn't live on "I was a member of that and wasn't it a wonderful thing."

Porteus emphasized the value of the constitution the convention produced. Having successfully drafted a governing document, people turned their attention to other things. "Problems once encountered and met are forgotten," said Porteus. "The problems that aren't solved are the nagging ones."[12]

Whether I talked with a Democrat such as Chuck Mau or Republicans such as Fong and Porteus in the 1980s, it was clear that the 1950 Hawaii convention, unlike the 1955-56 Alaska event, simply did not hold a place in the minds of its participants as a once-in-a-lifetime event that could never be duplicated. The memory of this singular event had somehow faded over the years. A check of

Honolulu newspapers that carried extensive coverage of the convention in 1950 revealed that this fading memory had begun even before statehood was achieved. As late as 1956 the newspapers still gave broad coverage to the convention. In that year territorial governor Samuel Wilder King, who had been president of the convention, proclaimed a Constitution Day to celebrate the six-year old event. The Honolulu *Advertiser* gave the day extensive coverage and published pictures of all the delegates. Only three years later in 1959, the year Hawaii entered the union, the convention was almost forgotten by the newspapers. The *Advertiser* published a 300 page Statehood Edition on June 23 which carried extensive stories on almost every aspect of Hawaii's history and life. The constitution itself was printed on a two-page spread, but the convention which produced it received only the scantest mention. The paper merely noted in two short paragraphs that the convention had been held and that voters later ratified the document. No pictures of the delegates or the signing of the document which had filled the paper 9 years earlier were in evidence.[13]

All the sources I obtained, written and oral, led me to the same conclusion. While the achievement of statehood was as important in Hawaii as in Alaska, the experience of participating in the 1950 constitutional convention did not engender the sense of destiny, mission and history that Alaskans vividly. Why? How could the memory of, and the reaction to, these seemingly identical events have been so different? In searching for an answer to this question I returned to the oral history interviews and to newspapers and other documentary records of the conventions. The combination of the written and oral sources revealed an answer which illuminates not only the shaping of memory, but also much about the political culture of the two states. I believe the difference in the quality of the two sets of memories stems from differences in the conventions themselves and in the linkage of the conventions to past traditions, concurrent events, and future developments in the history of the two states. Four such differences particularly stand out.

1) The Uniqueness of Each Convention as a Constitution Writing Experience

While both conventions were unique in being the only constitutional convention held in territorial days to achieve statehood, the Hawaii convention was only one of several in the islands' overall history. Honolulu newspapers noted in 1950 that the delegates would be writing Hawaii's sixth constitution. Four constitutions had been written under the monarchy between 1840 and 1887, and a fifth in 1894 for the Republic of Hawaii. Five delegates to the 1950 convention were related to members of the 1894 event, including Charles Rice of Kauai who remembered being there with his father![14]

While it is unlikely that memories from 1894 had a direct influence on the delegates, other constitution writing activities in the preceding decade were on their minds. The Hawaii Statehood Commission, the territory's principal information service and lobby for statehood, had worked since 1947 on a draft constitution for the consideration by the convention. Many of the men who prepared this draft, including Samuel Wilder King and Hebden Porteus, were also delegates to the convention. Though Porteus assured me that the 1950 constitution was not based solely on this draft, it is nonetheless clear that many of the delegates were not approaching constitution writing for the first time. By 1950 constitution writing in Hawaii had both historic and immediate precedents.[15]

In contrast, the 1955-56 Alaska convention was the first such event ever held in the territory. The Alaska Statehood Committee, an organization similar in function to the Hawaii Statehood Commission, did gather background information for the convention, but it did not write a draft constitution. There were also popular pro-statehood groups in Alaska that examined other state constitutions such as Operation Statehood in Anchorage and the All-Alaska Constitutional Study Group in Fairbanks. Members from both organizations were delegates to the convention. But they did not have a draft constitution to present to the convention for consideration. Political scientist John Bebout noted shortly after the 1956 convention, "The constitution was literally written by the delegates in convention assembled. It was more truly a 'do-it-yourself' convention on the part of the delegates than any other in modern times--certainly in this century."[16]

2) The Emotional Tone of the Alaska and Hawaii Conventions

Emotion is often a strong factor in securing the memory of an event in the minds of its participants. Here again the tone of the conventions differed. Though Toshio Serizawa remembered the Hawaii convention in strong emotional tones, his description was not echoed by others. Newspaper accounts reported more an air of festivity and informality. The Hawaii convention opened in Honolulu at Iolani Palace, the territorial capital, with pageantry, music, flowers, and pledges of Americanism which included a mandatory anti-communist loyalty oath from each delegate. The Honolulu *Star-Bulletin* proudly reported, "Hawaii stressed Americanism but didn't forget its beloved flowers and dancing as the state constitutional convention began...Flowers were banked high on the delegates' desks--anthuriums, tulips, orchids, gladiolas, carnations and roses vying in the splash of color."[17]

Three months later when the delegates signed the constitution, the newspapers again emphasized the floral and musical aspects of the ceremony. The delegates chose to sign the document in the Throne Room of Iolani Palace which admitted only a small public audience. As each stepped forward to sign, local musicians performed a special song. Said the Honolulu *Advertiser* of the signing:

> The Convention's 79th and perhaps most moving day was easily its most colorful and significant. The solemn seriousness of the occasion was lightened by the traditional presence of Hawaiian informality.
>
> Delegates and the austere throne room were bedecked with flowers and an all-star troupe of nine brightly dressed Hawaiian ladies and their ukuleles brought old Hawaii into the ceremony with their frequent incidential music.[18]

Once the constitution was endorsed, President King handed it for safe-keeping to Territorial Secretary Oren Long. Long accepted, noted the excellent qualities of the constitution, and reminded the delegates that they had been involved in an historic mission. Upon the conclusion of Long's speech, the delegates presented King with a fountain pen set. According to the official proceedings, "In a few well-chosen words, the President thanked the members for this tribute of aloha." He then turned to the musicians and expressed appreciation for their efforts which "had contributed so much to the typically Hawaiian atmosphere which had pervaded the ceremonies." The 1950 Hawaii constitutional convention then adjourned, subject to the call of the chair.[19]

Reports of Alaska's convention could not have been more different. The Northerners seemed unworried about their "Americanness." Though the delegates took a loyalty oath similar to that in Hawaii, they began their convention on the campus of the University of Alaska in Fairbanks with speeches soundly criticizing federal territorial rule. On the second day former territorial governor Ernest Gruening lambasted the government's continual neglect of the territory and implored the delegates to throw off the shackles of American colonialism. He told them that even the president of the United States showed a pathetic lack of understanding for Alaska's plight. He described the convention as a "mobilization" for the battle to win Alaska statehood.

At the end of the convention, the Alaska constitution was signed in the university's gymnasium before a crowd of nearly a thousand people. Each delegate came forward to sign the parchment document at a table brightened by the glow of a small jade lamp commissioned specifically for the occasion by delegate Marvin "Muktuk" Marston.

Tears stained the faces of many people that day, but the emotional finale came the next morning when the delegates met to adjourn and presented convention president William Egan with a portrait of himself. Fairbanks *Daily News-Miner* reporter Florence Douthit recorded the event in these terms:

> The convention ended in a state of highly charged emotion. The closing ceremonies and the attendant private and public function had been reinforcing the delegate's feelings for one another and their appreciation of the historic significance of the work they had now completed. The moment that destroyed the last vestige of defense against emotionalism came when delegates presented Egan with a painting of himself.[20]

Egan was so overwhelmed by this gesture that he broke into tears. "At that point," reported Douthit, "Egan had fifty-three other delegates for company."

The delegates composed themselves and gave the last word to their oldest colleague, E. B. Collins of Fairbanks, who had been a member of the first territorial legislature in 1913. In a short speech which capsulized the beginning and hoped for ending of territorial rule, Collins recalled that first legislature and told his friends:

> We wound up our duties with the same emotional scene as I have experienced here today. In that legislature, we formed a friendship that was enduring...I can see here today that the association and the friendship and the existence that are here

> within this convention are going to bind the personalities of each and every one of you that will endure for time to come when we enjoy the statehood of Alaska.[21]

The Alaska convention then adjourned *sine die*, the legend forming even as the delegates filed from the hall.

The bond of personal emotion at the Alaska convention clearly differed from that in Hawaii. It played a decisive role in forging the legendary character of the Alaska event. But some reflection on the emotional qualities of politics in Hawaii is necessary for a proper perspective. Clearly the 1950 convention was not bland. The music, the flowers, and the dancing infused a sensual emotion throughout all the ceremonies. But in Hawaii, emotion formed the backdrop of the convention, the "typically Hawaiian atmosphere;" it was not created in the interaction of the delegates. The Alaskans made a legend of their politics. The people of Hawaii tended to blend their politics into the existing emotion and traditions of the islands. Symbolically the Alaska convention adjourned *sine die*--a moment closed and captured in time. The Hawaii convention adjourned subject to the call of the chair--an open-ended event blending into the flow of time.

3) The Connection of the Conventions to Statehood Legislation in Congress

The 1950 Hawaii convention took place at the same time that the Hawaii Statehood Bill (H.R. 49) came to a vote in the 81st Congress (1949-51). Hawaii's statehood advocates were quite conscious of a direct connection between the convention and action in the Congress. Hawaii Statehood Commission chairman and convention president Samuel Wilder King noted repeatedly in the newspapers that a successful convention was likely to bring a favorable vote on statehood. Enthusiasm mounted in Hawaii when the House passed the Hawaii Statehood Bill in March 1950. By the time the convention opened in April, the Senate was ready to consider the bill in committee. Sixteen delegates including convention president King and all four convention vice-presidents left the convention for several days to go to Washington in May to testify for the statehood hearings. After signing the constitution in July, statehood leaders made elaborate efforts to convene a special session of the legislature to approve the constitution so that voters could ratify it in the November general elections. Thus a constitution approved by the people could be presented to the Senate after the election recess when a floor vote was anticipated. When the Senate vote was permanently stalled by a threatened filibuster, hopes for statehood in the 81st Congress came to an end. The constitutional convention had not brought about the main hope of its organizers. The excellent constitution it produced almost served as a consolation prize.

Had the U. S. Senate passed the statehood bill in 1950, the convention might well have figured more prominently in the memories of its delegates. Had Hawaii then entered the union in 1951, Samuel Wilder King would very likely have been the first elected governor, thus tieing leadership in the convention to leadership in the new state. Hawaii's congressional contingent would likely have included delegates from the convention. Hebden Porteus told me that the names most mentioned in 1950 for Hawaii's senators were Joseph Farrington and convention delegate William Heen. Porteus said that less attention was given to the seat in the House of Representatives, but he indicated that he was considered a likely possibility.[22]

Statehood did not come until 1959. By that time King, who had been appointed territorial governor by Eisenhower in 1953, had been removed from office by his own party. He died in March 1959, a few weeks after Congress passed the Hawaii statehood bill. His long tradition of political leadership would not continue into the new state. Heen was defeated in the 1959 Democratic primary for the Senate, and Porteus did not run for the House seat. Hiram Fong, a vice-president of the convention, was elected as one of Hawaii's first U.S. senators. But he told me in 1986 that his election was not linked directly to his previous leadership in the convention and territorial politics. Fong was defeated for the legislature in 1954 and turned his attention to managing his personal business affairs for the next five years. His 1959 senate victory, which he said came as a surprise, marked the beginning of a new episode in his career, not the direct continuation of an earlier political role.[23]

In contrast, the 1955-56 Alaska convention did not coincide with activities in the Congress. No statehood legislation reached the floor of either house in the 84th Congress (1955-57). Nor would a statehood vote in the 85th Congress (1957-59) take place until late in the second session. Thus Alaska's delegates were totally absorbed in the experience of writing a constitution, and building a bond among themselves without the distraction of Congress. Several convention delegates noted in their interviews with me that they were not sure in

1955-56 when statehood would come. Some thought there might be a ten year wait.

In 1958 Congress passed the Alaska Statehood Bill in the first house and senate votes since the convention was held. William Egan, president of the convention, became Alaska's first governor and led the state from 1959 to 1966, and again from 1970 to 1974. Another convention delegate Ralph Rivers became Alaska's first U. S. Representative. The Alaska convention became more historically linked to the achievement of statehood and leadership in the new state than did Hawaii's.

4) The Convention as a Break from Past Tradition

The Alaska convention and the constitution it produced constituted a major break from the territory's previous tradition of government and politics. That tradition was characterized by outside economic control, weak executive rule, and constant governmental interference by the U. S. Department of Interior. The territory's legislative tradition was not positive; it had been too blatantly influenced by lobbyists, particularly the canned salmon industry. Convention delegates Steve McCutcheon and Herb Hilscher told me that this excessive influence was evident even inside the legislative chambers. McCutcheon remembered one instance in which a legislator changed his vote on a tax bill for a case of whisky, an overcoat, and a ticket to Seattle. Hilscher claimed he had even taken a photograph of a prominent lobbyist instructing legislators how to vote from the balcony.[24]

The convention was consciously planned as a break from this legislative tradition. Holding the convention on the campus of the University of Alaska in Fairbanks rather than in the territorial capital of Juneau was a major part of the break. Convention Secretary Tom Stewart explained that the university setting allowed the delegates to escape the capital's atmosphere of bars and poolrooms in which lobbyists peddled their influence. In the 1981 interviews delegate after delegate mentioned the positive, even ennobling, atmosphere of the university campus. Stewart, who was from Juneau, told me that he paid a price for this nobility. He remembered that a local friend gave him a hard kick in the shins when he said he favored holding the convention in Fairbanks![25]

Delegates to the Alaska Constitutional Convention stated repeatedly in the 1981 interviews that the convention was unique in the absence of lobbyists and representatives of the outside interests (fishing, canning, mining) that had long controlled Alaska's economy. Even delegates who noted the presence of representatives of these interests emphasized their ineffectiveness in influencing the constitution. The absence of special interests at the convention requires some explanation. The delegates themselves did have interests and opinions. But by an absence of interests, the delegates meant an absence of the blatant lobbying and influence that had characterized legislatures in the past. As delegate Victor Fischer wrote in his analysis of the convention, "The usual type of lobbyist who frequents legislative halls attempting to influence bills on insurance, banking, labor, or other legislative issues was completely missing from the convention, except insofar as individual delegates represented special interests." What was significant about the convention was not the absence of any interest or opinion, but the break with the tradition of influence that had so poisoned the past. The Alaska convention with its university setting, and relative absence of lobbying pressure, was indeed a "peaceful rebellion" in which Alaskans began to create a new state they could control.[26]

Hawaii's territorial tradition was different from Alaska's. Its economy had long been controlled by local corporations, and the kind of Interior Department influence which characterized Alaska's territorial government did not inhibit Hawaii. Only in the federal appointment of judges from the mainland was there widespread irritation. The "interests" in Hawaii, both economic and political, were primarily local. Hawaii's 1950 convention reflected the prevailing state of these interests. Management and labor, the dominant Republicans and the old guard Democrats, outer island and Oahu politicians were all there. The "newcomers" to the convention were as likely to be Henry A. White, president of the Hawaiian Pineapple Co., as John R. Phillips, 33 year old World War II veteran and University of Hawaii student.

The Hawaii convention was in no way a break from the legislative tradition of the territory, nor was it planned to be so. The convention was held in Honolulu; the opening and closing sessions at Iolani Palace were in the House of Representatives--though the main sessions were held across the street in the Honolulu Armory which had more space. Every known distraction of the capital competed for the attention of the delegates and the public. Leadership in the convention also paralleled leadership in the legislature and the Hawaii Statehood Commission.

The delegates to the Hawaii convention were not so much creating a new political community as trying to get an existing community which had long functioned like many mainland states into the union. Statehood, not a new Hawaii, was their goal. The leaders of the convention had never pretended that they were making a break with past traditions. Possibly this makes it easier to understand why the delegates remembered the convention as simply one of many episodes in the struggle for statehood. It did not stand out as a particularly memorable event because it had been planned to blend with existing island traditions rather than to break from them.

The people of Hawaii were capable of breaking the political traditions of the territory. The break or "peaceful revolution" in Hawaii's political life came four years later in 1954 when a rejuvenated Democratic party controlled by John A. Burns secured a majority in the territorial legislature. Burns, a former Honolulu police captain, built a major faction within the Democratic party in the early 1950s. His power was based largely on the support of young World War II veterans of Japanese ancestry. Burns went on to become Hawaii's delegate to Congress in 1956 and later its governor from 1962 to 1974. His lieutenant governor George Ariyoshi succeeded him, and held the governorship through 1986.[27]

Burns and a number of his supporters ran for the constitutional convention. Most, including Burns, were not elected. Only a few delegates such as Chuck Mau even represented the ideas for Hawaii's future on which Burns would build his career. Had this new group of Democrats assembled at the convention, the writing of a state constitution might have signalled the start of a new wave in Hawaii politics. It might have been the first major act of a new group in Hawaii's political history. But this was not the case. To present day Burns Democrats, the "1950 convention" does not mean the Hawaii Constitutional Convention or Con-Con as it is called. For them the important event was the 1950 Democratic Party convention at which the Burns faction dramatically split from the Old Guard (who had represented the party at the constitutional convention) and began to vie for control of the party.

Statehood came when Burns was Hawaii's delegate to Congress. His supporters have credited him with its achievement.

These people have been the dominant political figures in Hawaii since statehood and have truly created a Burns legend. To them John Burns is the father of modern Hawaii politics. At the 1984 Silver Jubilee, statehood and Burns were carefully linked. There was no mention of the constitutional convention, though there was acknowledgement of the contributions of Samuel Wilder King and Joseph Farrington as delegates to Congress. There was also no mention of Republican William Quinn, the state's first elected governor who defeated Burns in the 1959 election. But amidst the dancing and the singing there was a repeated message from the master of ceremonies that John Burns was the "architect of statehood."[28]

Many people with whom I have talked in Hawaii consider the Revolution of 1954 the most important event in post-World War II Hawaii. It brought a new group of people into full participation in the islands' political life. There is no doubt that the Revolution of 1954 is remembered today as far more important than the constitutional convention. The John A. Burns Oral History Project bears ample testimony to this.

The people of Hawaii, like their counterparts in Alaska, have been capable of making dramatic breaks in their political life and creating legends to go with them. In the story of statehood and the development of new political traditions, the watershed occurred in Alaska at its constitutional convention. In Hawaii, it did not. It came with the rise of a new group of people to political power who had not been prominent at the convention. The quality of memories as evidenced in the oral history interviews serves as an invaluable litmus test to show when such watersheds did--or did not--occur. The intensity of memory of the Hawaii convention was weak not only in the interviews with Burns' followers who later came to power but also in the interviews with prominent convention participants.

For the reader concerned with the nature of oral history and the quality of memory this foray into Alaska and Hawaii's political history may seem a strange diversion. I hope it has been done with some effect. By placing the intensity of the memories in the context of the broader historical and political cultures from which they emerged, it becomes possible to understand their differences. Equally important, the quality of the memories provides a crucial guide for what to look for in the documentary record. Had it not been for the difference in the intensity of the memories, I would have been drawn to the similarities in the two constitutional conventions that I mentioned in the beginning of the paper. The oral history turned my attention to items in the documentary record such as flowers and music in Hawaii or tears and oil portraits in Alaska. These items might have initially appeared of secondary importance compared to apportionment systems or concise constitutions. With the guide of the participants' memories they took on a new significance. I was also alerted to the need of tracing the subsequent careers of convention participants and their political allies to understand the significance they later placed on an event, albeit of singular importance, that took place at only one point in their lives.

What makes the singular or once-in-a-lifetime event memorable? Or for that matter why can such an event be rather easily forgotten? By now I think it should be clear, at least in the context of twentieth century Alaska and Hawaii, that no event stands isolated in time, regardless of the attention it attracted at the moment it occurred. It is connected in some fashion to what came before and what came after. It may have been carefully planned at the time it occurred to reflect prevailing traditions as in Hawaii or to be a break from those traditions as in Alaska. Those initial plans may succeed or fail in the future. What was being remembered or forgotten in Hawaii and Alaska was not simply the constitutional conventions but a quarter century of tradition and emotion before them and a quarter century of development afterward. For a political historian such as myself who uses the technique of oral history, the memories of these two unique events, particularly their intensity and vividness, provided not only colorful vignettes of a point in time, but a first answer to the vexing question of what to look for next. In the story of Alaska and Hawaii statehood movements oral history thus became the indispensable key for understanding political history. In the same vein the political history was the necessary clue for understanding the differences in the oral histories.

ENDNOTES

[1]For a general description of the Alaska convention see Victor Fischer, *Alaska's Constitutional Convention*, National Municipal League, State Constitutional Convention Studies, Number Nine (Fairbanks: University of Alaska Press, 1975). For Hawaii see Norman Meller, *With An Understanding Heart, Constitution Making in Hawaii*, National Municipal League, State Constitutional Convention Studies, Number Five (New York: National Municipal League, 1971); and Richard H. Kosaki, "Constitutions and Constitutional Conventions of Hawaii," *The Hawaiian Journal of History* 12 (1978): 120-138.

[2]Governor Bill Sheffield, *The State of the State and Budget Addresses Before a Joint Session of the Second Session of the 14th Alaska State Legislature January 14 and January 16, 1986*. Pamphlet printed by the State of Alaska.

[3]For details of the Alaska silver anniversary celebration see Fairbanks *Daily News-Miner*, January 3 & 4, 1984. The author was present at the dinner and "investiture."

[4]For details on Hawaii's silver anniversary celebration, see Honolulu *Star-Bulletin*, August 21, 1984; Honolulu *Advertiser*, August 22, 1984. The author was present at the musical celebration "A Lifetime of Aloha." Statements in this paper about the celebration are confirmed on a videotaped produced by KITV (Honolulu) which is in the author's possession.

[5]The results of these interviews appear in: John S. Whitehead, Claus-M. Naske, William Schneider, *Alaska Statehood: The Memory of the Battle and the Evaluation of the Present by Those Who Lived it, An Oral History of the Remaining Actors in the Alaska Statehood Movement*, (Fairbanks: Alaska Statehood Commission, 1981). The tapes of the interviews with summaries and logs are on file at Oral History Program, Rasmuson Library, University of Alaska Fairbanks.

[6]Interview with Barrie White in Whitehead, *Alaska Statehood.*

[7]Interview with Barrie White, George Lehleitner, Ernest Bartley and Les Nerland in Whitehead, *Alaska Statehood.* (The interview with Les Nerland was conducted by Bill Schneider.)

[8]Robert Kamins to John Whitehead, March 15, 1984. Letter in author's possession.

[9]Transcripts of the interviews in John A. Burns Oral History Project are located in the Hamilton Library, University of Hawaii. Most of the interviews took place in 1975, 1976, and 1977. Additional interviews have been added after those dates. I have also utilized transcripts of interviews on Hawaii statehood prepared in 1985-86 by Warren Nishimoto and Chris Conybeare for the Oral History Project, University of Hawaii.

[10]Interviews with Nelson Doi, 1977; Chuck Mau, 1977; William Quinn, 1984; Toshio Serizawa, 1977 in Burns Oral History Project.

[11]Interview with Chuck Mau January 8, 1986. All of the interviews conducted by Whitehead in Hawaii in 1985-86 are on tape in the author's possession. (Funds have not yet become available to produce transcripts.)

[12]Interviews with Richard Lyman, Jr., August 4, 1985; Adam Smyser, August 6, 1985; Hiram Fong, January 7, 1986; Hebden Porteus, August 1, 1985. (In author's possession.)

[13]Honolulu *Advertiser*, July 22, 1956; June 23, 1959.

[14]For the link of the 1950 convention to previous conventions see Honolulu *Star-Bulletin*, February 25, 1950, March 10, 1950, March 25, 1950 and April 8, 1950. Three men were sons of 1894 delegates; one was a grandson and another a nephew.

[15]Interview with Hebden Porteus, August 1, 1985. (In author's possession.)

[16]John E. Bebout, as quoted in Fischer, *Alaska's Constiutional Convention*, p. iv.

[17]Honolulu *Star-Bulletin*, April 5, 1950.

[18]Honolulu *Advertiser*, July 23, 1950.

[19]*Proceedings of the Constitutional Convention of Hawaii 1950* (Honolulu: State of Hawaii, 1961), vol. 1, p. 143.

[20]Fairbanks *Daily News-Miner*, February 6, 1956.

[21]*Alaska Constitutional Convention Proceedings* (Juneau: Alaska Legislative Council, March 1965), p. 3982.

[22]Interview with Hebden Porteus, August 1, 1985. (In author's possession.)

[23]Interview with Hiram Fong, January 7, 1986. (In author's possession.)

[24]Interview with Steve McCutcheon and Herb Hilscher in Whitehead, *Alaska Statehood.*

[25]Interview with Tom Stewart, January 24, 1986. (In author's possession.)

[26]Whitehead, *Alaska Statehood*, p. 14; Fischer, *Alaska's Constitutional Convention*, p. 171.

[27]For the rise of the Burns led Democratic party see Paul C. Phillips, *Hawaii's Democrats Chasing the American Dream* (Lanham, MD: University Press of America, 1982).

[28]Videotape, "A Lifetime of Aloha," KITV-Honolulu, August 21, 1984. There was no mention or recognition of Quinn at the official ceremony. However, KITV interviewed Quinn during intermission. Thus the television audience saw Quinn prominently featured, while the live audience did not.

THE WILDERNESS AND ALASKA*

Morgan Sherwood

Morgan Sherwood is the dean of Alaska historians. His many careful books and articles and his encouragement of new students in the field have advanced the understanding of the subject as has the work of few other scholars.

Sherwood grew up in Anchorage, Alaska, before leaving to complete his college and advanced studies at the University of California, Berkeley. He has taught at the University of California, Davis, since receiving his doctoral degree for a study which was published in 1965, *Exploration of Alaska, 1865-1900* (New Haven, CT: Yale University Press), a pioneering work which is perhaps the single most important book in Alaska studies. He has published numerous journal articles, including "Ardent Spirits: Hooch and the Osprey Affair at Sitka," *Journal of the West*, July 1965, and "Science in Russian America," *Pacific Northwest Quarterly*, January 1967. His *Big Game in Alaska: A History of Wildlife and People* (New Haven, CT: Yale University Press, 1981) traces the history of game regulation in Alaska from 1925 to 1945 and argues that Alaskans were slow to recognize the necessity for regulation of the resource. In 1967 Sherwood published the first anthology of scholarly articles on Alaska history, *Alaska and Its History* (Seattle: University of Washington Press).

Sherwood's article here offers the challenging thesis that the Alaska wilderness may be a thing of the past. With easy access to the wilderness now a routine affair, man has become a part of the landscape everywhere. Hikers and pilots lost in the wilds now have their positions located by reconnaissance satellites. It may be that if "wilderness" means "wild," the taming reach of man may have gone so far as to render the term "wilderness" meaningless any longer.

* * *

Environmental historians should face the problem of wilderness, which is a problem of definition, or of the failure to frame our analysis of wilderness precisely. If historians continue to treat wilderness only as an idea, the meaning of which has changed over time, they will have little to contribute to the preservation of natural environments and, *reductio ad absurdum*, "wilderness" will become a

---

*This article originally appeared in *Environmental Review* 9, no. 3 (Fall 1985): 197-209.

city park or perhaps a suburban lawn.[1] Historiographically, wilderness will cease to be a place or even an idea and become only a word. Maybe it already has.

My thesis may be stated simply: We are in the wilderness about wilderness. The central reason for the confusion is our inability or reluctance to treat technology as a crucial factor. To argue the case, I will assay a number of definitions of wilderness, and indicate the failure of these definitions to define what is called wilderness in Alaska (not always officially designated wilderness units), given the availability of certain technologies. In the conclusion, I will deal briefly with policy for existing natural environments.

But first, if you do not think that the meaning of wilderness has become too vague, your attention is called to the title of a recent television documentary about Alaska, narrated by Lorne Green and entitled "New Wilderness," as though our lawmakers can declare an area "wilderness" and make it so, as though wilderness can be "new." The Kachemak Bay Wilderness Lodge, a few miles across the bay from the town of Homer, has been listed as America's best wilderness lodge in Sterling Publications' "America's Best 100";[2] apparently, the trail to wilderness lodges is brightly blazed by their own version of the Michelin guidebook. Still another example of confusion over the meaning of wilderness comes from a summer issue of the *Homer News*.[3]

An Alaska Wilderness Marathon was planned for the Kenai Peninsula last summer. It would cross fifty miles of the Kenai National Moose Range, through which motorized access was requested to set up a check point. Runners could carry portable rafts, tents and other modern accoutrements needed to "rough it" outdoors. Michael Hedrick, manager of the refuge, denied a permit, saying, "There have to be places where some species of wildlife have top billing." The organizer of the race was a biologist with the Alaska State Fish and Game Department; he responded: "I deal with environmental issues every day and this just isn't an environmental issue." He said that a dog sled race was held in the Gates of the Arctic National Wildlife Refuge last year, and argued: Why not a marathon through the Kenai Moose Range? Ted Stevens, one of Alaska's U.S. senators, persuaded the federal agency to reverse Hedrick' s decision. Stevens told a newspaper reporter: "The agency implied that the traffic, 50 to 75 pairs of feet, running over the Resurrection Trail is too much. I couldn't buy that. If people can't walk or run in the Alaska wilderness, what can be in it?"

Evidence from the wilderness marathon controversy supports the notion that citizens who wish to protect the natural environment may sometimes have reason to fear public employees charged with its protection as much as exploitative entrepreneurs. Another example of this problem, and also of the strange ways in which the word "wilderness" is used, appears in a questionnaire distributed by the Alaska Division of Parks. Respondents were asked whether they favored development of recreational facilities in Kachemak Bay State Wilderness Park. The developments included boat-launch facilities, lodges, shelter cabins, and landing strips for airplanes.[4] (The response for both the Wilderness Park and neighboring State Park was overwhelmingly for low or no development.)

If you still do not think that "wilderness" is a vague concept, so vague that it may not really be a place anymore, read the third part of John McPhee's *Coming Into the Country*, in which the Yukon River people are forever proclaiming themselves to be genuine frontiersmen and frontier women while they criticize their neighbors for the lack of ennobling frontier virtues. One of them characterizes another as more frontiersman-like because he hand-loads his ammunition.[5] The hand-loader thinks that *how much* technology is the issue. He is correct but the insight dissolves when he says: "people who have tried to get away from technology completely have always failed. Meanwhile, what this place has to offer is wilderness that is nowhere else." One may read that part of McPhee's book as an attempt to determine how much technology is permissible in a wilderness, and to measure it by the amount of technology available where civilization ends, which supports my thesis that technology is the crucial variable.

Sadly, however, McPhee concludes that he must carry a gun out of fear of the bears, which brings us to solitude, one quality invoked to identify wilderness. According to this definition, wilderness provides solitude that inspires a kind of subtle unease and quiet wonder. The definition is one of a large category that dwells on the literary and psychological effects of wilderness on the individual. Wilderness (or a natural environment where one is alone) inspires poetry, impresses one philosophically with, for example, man's insignificance, tempering his destructive impulses, or inspires a kind of delicious fear. McPhee's fear of bears brings home to him a deep philosophical contradiction. He writes: "If bears were no longer in the country, I would not have come. I am here...because they survive. So I am sorry--truly rueful and perplexed--that without a means of killing them I cannot feel at ease."[6] McPhee thought he needed a gun to travel alone in a natural environment relatively unpopulated by other humans. He might have carried a toy cap pistol to frighten the animal, or more mundanely, a couple of saucepans to rattle the bears. Better still, using no technology whatever, he might have done what a Swedish-American pioneer in Alaska once recommended: "Sing loudly on the trail." (I know of no case of an experienced outdoorsman being attacked without provocation by a bear, although I admit the point hangs on the definition of provocation.)[7]

In his firearm, McPhee had the power of industrial technology to help him appreciate the wilderness. There was more than a gun in his wilderness. He was carried there in airplanes and in boats propelled by outboard motors. There is a road to Eagle; it is gravel, narrow, tortuous and not maintained from October to April, but for half of the year it will take you 160 miles to the Alaska Highway, which will in turn get you by auto to Chicago (if the urban wilderness happens to be your cup of tea). All-terrain vehicles and snowmobiles penetrate McPhee's country, along with airplanes equipped with "tundra tires" and skis to reduce the need for cleared landing strips. Bulldozers tear up the country looking for gold, chainsaws reduce the spare forests for fuel, just as axes and saws--even power saws at an early date--did to feed steamboats from the late nineteenth century to quite recent times. Voices fill the radio waves to reduce still further the isolation from urban environments. Probably, like many rural Alaskans, some of McPhee's people have erected satellite antennae for television reception of the same adolescent inanities that are inflicted on the remainder of American society.

There is no solitude (read "wilderness") if an aircraft may thunder overhead at any time and land, if a skiff with a noisy outboard motor may splash by your "wilderness" beach at any time, if jet boats ignore low water to crunch over sandbars on their way up a remote stream, if a snowmobile marathon can scatter wildlife, if a bear's misunderstood ferocity can be silenced by a bullet before the animal's intentions are determined. So much for solitude as a sign of wilderness, given the widespread use of modern technology in Alaska.

In one sense, solitude is only a variation of Frederick Jackson Turner's famous criterion. According to him, the frontier disappears, and by implication wilderness too, when a certain man-land ratio changes. Turner and the Superintendent of the Census of 1890 "regarded as unsettled" any area with less than two inhabitants in a square mile.[8] (Table 1.) The number of square miles per person in Alaska dropped, between 1880 and 1980, from a high of 18.3 square miles.

Table 1

Date		Population	Square Miles Per Person
	1880	33,400	17.5
	1890	32,000	18.3
	1900	63,600	9.2
	1910	64,400	9.1
Jan. 1	1920	55,000	10.65
Oct. 1	1929	59,300	9.9
Oct. 1	1939	72,500	8.1
Apr. 1	1950	128,600	4.6
Apr. 1	1960	226,200	2.6
	1970	300,400	1.95
	1980	401,800	1.45

The figures are rounded, and 586,000 square miles is divided by the population. Source: A.M. Rollins, comp. *Census of Alaska: Numbers of Inhabitants, 1791-1970* (Anchorage: University of Alaska Anchorage Library, 1978). U.S. Bureau of the Census, *General Social and Economic Characteristics: United States Summary, 1980.*

miles in 1890 to 1.45 in 1980. By this measure, Alaska, as a whole, is still a frontier region. But that conclusion is unsatisfactory for a couple reasons. First, the method is arbitrary, and fails to account for the distribution of population. As recently as 1950, the population of

Alaska was only 27% urban; now the population is about 50-50, urban-rural. Most of the urbanites and suburbanites live in an area embracing Anchorage, part of the Kenai Peninsula, and the lower Matanuska and Susitna river valleys near the big city. The concentration of population means that large areas of Alaska are sparsely settled; with a low man-land ratio, they may qualify as wilderness. However, such areas are *accessible* with modern transportation technologies, and *vulnerable* if other technologies employed in the war against nature are introduced. One person (it does not require two) could make a mess of his one square mile even in 1890. Imagine what a bulldozer operator can do to a square mile quickly, nowadays. Instead of counting people in rural areas, machines should be counted in the entire area which they may affect.

Scrappy data on airplanes will illustrate the importance of counting machines that permit access to what people call wilderness. As early as 1944, sixty-two airplanes were used by hunting parties flying out of Anchorage, a city of perhaps six or seven thousand people then.[9] In one month of the following year, Merrill Field, the town's airstrip, had 10,000 landings and take-offs, more than LaGuardia Field in New York City.[10] There were twenty-nine "air carriers" operating out of Anchorage in 1947, or about one air service for every 325 people in town.[11] These were mainly bush pilots, taking people to and from natural environments. In 1956, 77% of the hunters who traveled by air were successful in attempting to kill caribou from the Nelchina herd; only 20% of the hunters traveling on foot were successful, although they came a long part of the way by auto. Later regulations prohibited aircraft from driving animals to exhaust them and make them easier to kill, and also prohibited herding animals to landing places, shooting from the air, and spotting (locating) animals from the air.[12] Spotting is still common. In 1960 there was one aircraft for every 194 Alaskans, including children, and in 1967 there was one for every 100 persons. That year, one in fifty residents had a pilot's license, and Lake Hood in Anchorage was the largest seaplane base in the United States. A Federal Aviation Administration pamphlet describing all of this is entitled *The Alaskan Region: A Family Affair*.[13]

Counting machines is not the most dramatic way to argue that accessibility made possible by modern technology is the important determinant of wilderness status. Instead, consider a place which would, at first thought, be chosen by many people as the least accessible spot in Alaska: the slopes of Mount McKinley, the tallest mountain in North America. Surely, "Denali" (as romantics prefer to call the mountain) can be "regarded as unsettled" and offers the psychological rewards of solitude. Not necessarily true, during the summer months. In 1970, 124 people were on the mountain, in 1976 nearly 600, a number topped in each of the next four years.[14] During early May of 1983, perhaps 200 people were already on the mountain or waiting for an air taxi to fly them from Talkeetna to Kahiltna Glacier, elevation 7,000-8,000 feet. This year one pilot told a reporter: "Packing the plane is like loading a sports car for a two-week vacation."[15] Size and distance is difficult to estimate from Kahiltna Glacier except during climbing season, when perspective is provided by other mountaineers; in the words of the pilot, "you can see people coming into view...and you can see them all day long." From Kahiltna Glacier, climbing parties may be guided as high as 14,000 feet.[16] The mountain is 20,300 feet in elevation. One guide climbed it twenty-five times.[17] If you do not have the physical stamina, the sense of adventure, or the suicidal drive it takes to ascend Mount McKinley, you can sightsee around the mountain by airplane, or fly to a camp on Ruth Glacier that offers sled dog tours.

A third definition of wilderness refers to the biological integrity of an area and the absence of man and his works. In the Wilderness Act of 1964 that means an area "where the earth and its community of life are untrammeled by man...," an area which "generally appears to have been affected primarily by the forces of nature, with the imprint of man's work substantially unnoticeable."[18] How noticeable are the works of man, his technology, in remote areas of Alaska? In answer to that question, this paper should, but will not, discuss the greenhouse effect on the earth's climate, or "Arctic haze," or the sight and the sound of airliners flying the Great Circle Route between Europe and Asia. Instead, a single example will suffice here to demonstrate that man's work is ubiquitous.

The example is Anaktuvuk Pass, in the Brooks Range, and its residents in 1963, including a five-year-old Eskimo girl named Dorothy Ahgook. In that year the *Tundra Times* reported unhappily that Dorothy had "the highest, or one of the highest radiation counts of any person in the United States."[19] Her sister Vera, one year older, had a high count too. The village council was told by a representative of the Atomic Energy Commission that "whole body counts" of radiation--strontium 90 and cesium 137--had increased substantially in Anaktuvuk. A reporter for the *Tundra Times* claimed that residents had "about forty times the amount of radiation absorbed by the average U.S. citizen," another record for Anaktuvuk.

The problem was ecological. Radioactive debris from the atmospheric testing of nuclear bombs had been carried by air currents over the Arctic. Common plants of the tundra, lichens and sedges, got their nutrients from dust in the air as it fell with rain and snow, not from the soil, and stored what they absorbed. Migrating caribou had several times as much strontium 90 as the flesh of cattle elsewhere in the U.S. The Eskimos of Anaktuvuk relied heavily on caribou for food. Among some Alaskan Natives, the marrow of caribou bone is especially favored.

What the long-range effects are of overdosing radiation by the people of Anaktuvuk is not clear. Events there did help to cancel the Atomic Energy Commission's Project Chariot, to blow a hole on the Arctic coast west of Anaktuvuk. Opposition to Project Chariot united northern Alaskan Eskimos politically for the first time and led to publication of the *Tundra Times*, which became an influential voice for Eskimo causes. (Physicist Edward Teller, in promoting Chariot, told an Anchorage audience jokingly: "If your mountain is not in the right place, just drop us a card.")[20] Anaktuvuk Pass is now the principal village in Gates of the Arctic National Park and Preserve, though not in an area designated wilderness. The village is just north of Mt. Doonerak, made famous by Robert Marshall, founder of the Wilderness Society.[21] Residents still hunt, fish and gather in the region. The *Alaska Geographic* reported in 1981: "A desire to maintain cultural integrity for Native communities and rural life style within the newly created national parks generated provisions [in the Alaska National Interest Lands Conservation Act of 1980] to continue subsistence activities including hunting, fishing and trapping using motorized vehicles such as snow machines and motorboats *where traditionally practiced.*"[22] And so much for the natural biological integrity of wilderness areas, where man's technology is unnoticeable.

The fourth and final characteristic of wilderness considered here is the oldest, in many ways the most attractive and, at first glance, the easiest way to identify wilderness. In this scheme, wilderness is measured by the presence of wildlife, especially the large animals, living more or less as they did before the appearance of mechanized man. The abundance and variety of wild creatures in a natural environment defines the wilderness condition.

Most of the wild species that were in Alaska when the Russians came in 1741 are still there, though certain species have been threatened over time, for example, the whales, fur seals and otter at sea, and large mammals on land during the gold rushes. One may still see the giant Kenai moose going its own way, and the formidable Kodiak brown bear still ranges the island after which it was named. But "things are not what they seem." The presence of wildlife in Alaska is due to the rise of conservation as a potent political movement, and a social institution--wildlife management--created to achieve the goals of conservationists has itself become heavily dependent on technology. Not even the brown bear, once called by DeWitt Clinton, "the ferocious tyrant of the American Woods,"[23] can count on roaming freely in his territory without being shot with a tranquilizer, tagged and equipped with a radio transmitter.

Management of Alaska's wild animals began long before such high technology was available, and predates wildlife management as a profession. In the 1830s, the Russians introduced conservation practices to the Pribilof Island fur seal rookeries.[24] The United States, after 1870, also regulated the killing of fur seals on land. The decisions of both governments followed periods of indiscriminate slaughter. Alaska's first game laws were a response to wholesale destruction of edible wildlife during the gold rushes northward in the late nineteenth century and early in the twentieth. A decision made late in the nineteenth century to import reindeer from Siberia for the relief of Eskimos suffering from the commercial depletion of marine mammals contributed to a little-publicized ecological disaster. The reindeer competed with the native caribou for browse, overgrazing the range. Both populations crashed dramatically in the 1930s and 1940s. Meantime, the federal Alaska Game Commission policed the health of other wildlife, a job made easier by the low human population.[25]

Major demographic, economic, political and technological changes occurred during and after World War II. "Traditional" uses of aircraft, snowmobiles and motorboats became common *after* the war. The population tripled, federal spending for defense boomed the economy, and the new state of Alaska assumed management of its resources in 1959, when public support of science was more generous than it had been before the war. High-tech wildlife biology came to Alaska with these changes. The Eskimos were not uniformly delighted.

The *Tundra Times*, in 1966, reported that two investigators from eastern universities had killed several polar bears while conducting a scientific experiment. The *Times* did not have all of its facts straight, but using other sources as well, a rough picture of what happened can be sketched. The two biologists came to Alaska to develop methods of immobilizing the bears in order to tag them and, eventually, attach radio transmitters which would be monitored by satellite and thus track the animal around its frigid habitat. Two airplanes were used, one to spot the bear; when spotted, another airplane would deposit the scientists someplace ahead and return to help the first aircraft herd the bear toward the waiting savants, who were armed with a rifle and tranquilizing dart, or syringe. The syringe was loaded with succinylcholine chloride; the size of the dose was determined by an estimate of the bear's size, made by the pilot of the spotter airplane. When the bear was chased, perhaps exhausted, within range, it was shot with the dart, then marked with a long-lasting red dye. Splattered would be a better word than marked; the dye could not be sprayed on because of low temperatures so it was dumped on the animal's backside.

The first polar bear to be anesthetized stirred during the handling and was given another dose of succinylcholine chloride; it died. The second bear was "marked recovered," the scientists reported; it may be the bear that was shot soon thereafter by a hunter who easily could have spotted its red posterior on the white landscape. (The hunter was distressed because the fur was spoiled.) A third bear was not immobilized. The fourth bear that was hit died in five minutes; the fifth in ten minutes; the sixth in twenty-five minutes. Succinylcholine chloride had no effect on the next two bears coming within range, according to the two investigators. They also anesthetized two other polar bears, but their data about these animals are incomplete. The score: four bears killed and three immobilized and marked, one of which was shot by a hunter shortly thereafter. The experiment was reported at a national conference and in *Scientific American*. Newspaper reports emphasized the derring-do. Whether any science needed to protect the polar bear emerged from the carnage (as both biologists firmly believe) is moot because the effect of the drug on large animals apparently was known before the episode.[26]

More than 3,000 polar bears have been immobilized, marked and studied worldwide since then, out of a total population estimated at 20,000-25,000, or 12% to 15%. Alaska's polar bears number either 6,000 to 9,000 animals, or 3,000 to 5,000, depending upon the expert you consult. The discrepancies suggest that all of the capturing and tracking can only have been partially successful. The presence of scientists in the polar bears' Alaskan wilderness has not even resulted in wildlife management program for the animal. The Marine Mammal Protection Act of 1972 gave supervision of polar bears to the federal government. Sport hunting was prohibited but Congress allowed Natives the right to hunt the animal using "traditional" methods at any time, without bag limits and with no protection for females and cubs. Products made from the bear's skin may be sold, reviving the specter of market hunting which wildlife protectionists thought they had banished decades ago. Clearly, the polar bear is not "master of the northern ice," as a federal biologist titled his article about Nanook.[27] Man and his technology are.

Biologists continue to drug and tag Alaska's wild animals and to equip them with radios. An article in *Alaska* magazine by a state biologist entitled, "Wildlife That Goes Beep-beep," describes how transmitters have been attached to brown bears, black bears, polar bears, caribou, moose, wolves, walruses, and geese.[28] Another article in the same magazine reports how the Forest Service and the State Department of Fish and Game moved mountain goats by helicopter to a place where they could be seen by tourists from a highway. The reclusive animals were tranquilized with a dart shot from a helicopter, examined, tagged and then carried in a net by helicopter to a place where motorists could better appreciate the Kenai "wilderness."

"Darting wildlife from the air is tricky," said one biologist. "A goat can travel some distance in the seven to eight minutes it takes the drug to work...If a goat reaches a steep slope before going down, chances of retrieving it are slim."[29]

The state undertook a large investigation during the 1970s to explain the disappearance of moose from an area in the interior that is not officially a wilderness unit. Moose is a favorite game meat of Alaskans. The wolves were blamed by the hunters, and when the state decided to shoot some wolves, the national news media triggered a popular uproar. In the experiment, more than 100 adult moose were tranquilized and fitted with radio collars or other identification devices. One hundred twenty calves were also equipped with radios; this was accomplished by chasing the cow away with a helicopter. One hundred wolves were killed, sixty wolves were removed from the area, and another 150 wolves were given radio collars. Twenty-three adult brown bears were also equipped with radios, and forty-seven were drugged and taken miles away by helicopter, airplane and truck; 70% returned in sixty days. The main culprit was the brown bear, who feasted on baby moose and cut the calf survival rate which eventually reduced the population of moose.[30]

Did this massive intrusion of technology into a natural environment end the wolf control controversy? No. It and other studies have led to specific population goals for moose, caribou and wolves in several areas. Statistics on the effects of these management practices on the individual animals are not readily available. One hopes that mortality rates are lower than they were in the polar bear experiment, or in the record of management in Yellowstone Park, where eighty-six grizzlies have been killed by wildlife professionals since 1970, most by drug overdoses.[31]

The public is apparently not alarmed by the adventures of its wildlife managers. Perhaps people have become accustomed to such activities by watching Marlin Perkins, Jacques Cousteau and William Conrad tinker with wild animals weekly on television. In outdoor magazines, thrilling stories by biologists confronting dangerous wild beasts often replace the bear stories of hunters. Frequently the articles feature cute pictures of, for example, a tranquilized brown bear embracing a biologist, or a giant sedated polar bear resting on the lap of a scientist, or a wildlife expert with his arm around the neck of a cow moose. Such photographs are becoming as common in outdoor magazines as pictures of big game hunters posing with rifle and kill were in former times.

So, if you spot a mountain goat while visiting Alaska, remember that it may have been placed there for you to see, and to provide "photo opportunities" (a term that wildlife managers have borrowed from the public relations industry). If you agree with Aldo Leopold that knowledge alone of the presence of wildlife certifies an area's classification as wilderness, remember that the biggest game animal out there may have tatooed gums, a tag on its ear, and go beep-beep. Even the fish in your Alaskan wilderness may have been put there by humans. In Kachemak Bay, state biologists have planted thousands of young salmon where they cannot reproduce. The fish return at the end of their cycle to mill around, vainly searching for a fresh-water stream with gravel in which to spawn, turning red and black and decaying. Fishermen are invited to catch them by net or snag in an orgy of unsportsmanlike "taking" that would chill the spirit of Izaak Walton. The other rotting salmon are left for the eagles, ravens, and bears.

Is all of this wildlife management--or farming, or ranching, or zookeeping? Sam White was a veteran warden who pioneered the use of airplanes when he worked for the Alaska Game Commission. In the late 1970s I asked him what he considered the gravest threat to Alaskan big game. He answered in one word: "Biology." His judgment was too severe. Some reductionist science and high-tech game management maybe necessary to the animals' survival. But modern technology has made "wildlife" management a contradiction in terms, and these days, the presence of indigenous animals does not necessarily identify wilderness.

In 1967 Robert Heilbronner published his controversial article which asked: "Do Machines Make History?" The answer sounded too much like technological determinism.[32] But if machines do not always make history, machines do unmake wilderness. The lesson for policy makers is fairly clear. Just as early conservationists leaned heavily on technological obsolescence and outright prohibition of certain technologies to protect wildlife, the fisheries and national parklands, society should now move with deliberate speed to restrict the use of destructive technologies in relatively untouched natural environments. Congress should legislate off-road vehicles, all-terrain vehicles, airplanes, helicopters, snowmobiles and motor boats out of such areas, except when the machines are on rescue missions. Purchase anywhere of an off-road vehicle for recreational purposes should be considered *prima facie* evidence of intention to engage in destructive trespass, and the sale of these vehicles should be prohibited except for occupational purposes. This action would be a major step forward to environmental sanity, in town as well as in the woods (and, incidentally, improve America's balance of payments with Japan).

What about policy for high-tech wildlife management? The wolf-moose-bear study concluded with the statement: "Unfortunately, the answers we have found, although they provide valuable clues and good basic information for other parts of Alaska, apply only to the Nelchina Basin and our study area, and for the years 1975 through 1981."[33] In other words, the study was inconclusive for Alaska as a whole and will have to be repeated again and again in the Nelchina basin and all other places where the moose population declines. The scientific caution is admirable in principle, consistent with ecological theory, and promotes full employment of wildlife technicians. It also raises an economic question: Has the cost of management been translated into dollars-per-pound of moosemeat? Political and ethical questions arise too. The Alaska State Department of Fish and Game defers to wildlife advisory boards for policy based on such experiments, and these advisors encourage the management of animals for use by people, either to kill and eat, for "photo opportunities", or to protect people from wild creatures. In addition to these concerns, which will not disappear from Alaska in the foreseeable future, the beasts should be managed and studied with the welfare of the animals themselves a consideration. The ethical issues associated with animal science are almost never addressed in print by the biologists involved. Meanwhile, in response to pressure from animal rights organizations, the federal government and universities in the contiguous United States have created institutions to oversee the ethical use of animals in research. University committees, consisting of scientists mainly but also with public representatives and representatives from the humanities, now appraise an experiment with the animal's welfare in mind. Does it suffer unalleviated pain or distress and if so, is the distress justified, given the significance of the experiment? Perhaps similar institutions are needed to evaluate wildlife studies.

To conclude: existing definitions of wilderness as a place where there is solitude, a low man-land ratio, biological integrity, and wildlife, do not work because disruptive modern technologies are not taken into account. Technologies that provide easy access have threatened Alaskan natural environments increasingly since the end of World War II. Between then and the 1960s, Alaska lost its frontier innocence and wilderness became only a word, not a place. Ironically, wilderness in America may have ended at the same time that society, by passage of the Wilderness Act of 1964, decided it was worth saving. There are still ways, however, to reverse or at least to ameliorate the damage.

ENDNOTES

[1]The tendency to view the history of wilderness as the history of an idea comes, of course, from the well-deserved success of Roderick Nash's *Wilderness and the American Mind* (New Haven: Yale University Press, 1967).

[2]Reported in a brochure for the Lodge, 1984.

[3]July 12, 1984.

published 1977), p. 195.

[6]Page 339.

[7]The issue is discussed in M. Sherwood, *Big Game in Alaska: A History of Wildlife and People* (New Haven: Yale University Press, 1981), p. 36-38.

[8]Frederick Jackson Turner, "The Significance of the Frontier in American History," in Turner, *The Frontier in American History* (New York: Henry Holt, 1950; originally published 1920. The paper was read in 1893), p. 3. U.S. Census Office, *Compendium of the Eleventh Census, 1890, Part I* (Washington: GPO, 1892) p.xlv.

[9]Annual Report, Alaska Game Commission, 1944, A.G.C. Records, Alaska State Library, Juneau.

[10]Jean Potter, *The Flying North* (New York: Macmillan, 1965; originally published 1945), p. 7.

[11]Tewkesbury's *Who's Who in Alaska and Alaska Business Index* (Juneau: Tewkesbury Publishers, 1947).

[12]*Annual Report*, Alaska Game Commission, 1956, A.G.C. Records. Alaska State Library, Juneau.

[13](Washington: GPO, 1967). U.S. Federal Aviation Agency, General Aviation in Alaska (Washington: GPO, 1960).

[14]*Alaska* 49 (May 1983): 27.

[15]C. Swaney, "Air Taxi Owner Picks High Life in Talkeetna," *Anchorage Times*, July 1, 1983, Business section, p. 1.

[16]National Public Radio, "Alaska," cassette ME-82-08-23.

[17]*The Milepost, 1983* (Anchorage: Alaska Northwest,1983), p. 231.

[18]The law is reprinted in C. W. Allin, *The Politics of Wilderness Preservation* (Westport, Connecticut: Greenwood Press, 1982), Appendix A.

[19]*Tundra Times*, Sept. 3, 1963. Information about Anaktuvuk, and background, is drawn from this issue and from: *Tundra Times*, Dec. 23, 1966; P. Brooks and J. Foote, "The Disturbing Story of Project Chariot," *Harper's* 224 (Apr. 1962): 60-67; R. D. Arnold, et al, *Alaska Native Land Claims* (Anchorage: Alaska Native Foundation, 1976), pp. 94, 95.

[20]Quoted in Brooks and Foote, "Disturbing Story," p. 67.

[21]Marshall, *Alaska Wilderness* (Berkeley: University of California Press, 1970; originally published 1956).

[22]*Alaska National Interest Lands* (Anchorage: Alaska Geographic Society, 1981), p. 12. Italics added. See U.S. Statutes at Large, 94 State. 2371 passim, especially 2423, 2428, 2430.

[23]Quoted in J. M. Holzworth, *The Wild Grizzlies of Alaska* (New York: G. P. Putnam's Sons, 1930), p. 232.

[24]C. L. Andrews, *The Story of Alaska* (Caldwell, Idaho: Caxton Printers, 1947), p. 147.

[25]Sherwood, *Big Game in Alaska*, pp. 27, 84, 85, passim.

[26]The incident can be documented from periodicals, a paper by the biologists, and correspondence with one of them and with Alaska officials, but names are not important. The episode is included here to demonstrate further that high-tech science can be dangerous to wildlife. Specific documentation will be provided upon request, if needed for scholarly purposes.

[27]F. Bruemmer, "Nanook Bears Watching," *National Wildlife* 21 (Dec.-

provided upon request, if needed for scholarly purposes.

[27]F. Bruemmer, "Nanook Bears Watching," *National Wildlife* 21 (Dec.-Jan. 1983): 38-42. S. C. Amstrup, "Masters of the Northern Ice," *Alaska* 50 (Nov. 1984): 35, 36. J. Rearden, "Alaska's Unmanaged Polar Bears," *Alaska* 50 (Nov. 1984): 36.

[28]By Sterling Miller. *Alaska* 50 (June 1984).

[29]D. Allen, "Movin' Goats," *Alaska* 50 (Oct, 1983): 71.

[30]W. G. Ballard, "The Case of the Disappearing Moose," *Alaska* 49 (Jan. 1983): 22-25, (Feb. 1983): 36-39, (March 1983): 38-41.

[31]Bil Gilbert, "Can We Live in Peace with the Grizzly?" *Sports Illustrated* 61 (July 1983): 72.

[32]*Technology and Culture* 8 (July 1967): 335-345.

[33]Ballard, "Disappearing Moose," p. 42.

HISTORY AS HISTORY*

Terrence Cole

In 1924 Jeannette Paddock Nichols published one the the few political histories of Alaska. It was Nichols' argument that Alaska had suffered as a result of federal neglect, which, had it been forthcoming, would have facilitated Alaska's growth and development. In this she was consistent with Alfred Swineford and James Wickersham before her and Ernest Gruening afterward. Well researched and organized, Nichols' book became a mainstay of the traditionalist school, those historians whom William H. Wilson criticized in 1970 for their use of the federal government as a scapegoat for the history of Alaska.

Dr. Terrence Cole is a prolific young historian who earned his doctorate at the University of Washington in 1983 for a dissertation on the Nome gold rush of 1898. He worked for several years as editor of *Alaska Journal* and for Alaska Northwest Publishing Company. In 1988 he joined the faculty of the University of Alaska at Fairbanks. He has published *E. T. Barnette: The Strange Career of the Man Who Founded Fairbanks* (Anchorage: Alaska Northwest Publishing Co., 1981), *Nome: City of the Golden Beaches* (Anchorage: Alaska Geographic Society, 1984), *Ghosts of the Gold Rush: A Walking Tour of Fairbanks* (Fairbanks: Tanana-Yukon Historical Society, 1977), and a number of scholarly articles, including "Raymond Robins in Alaska: the Conversion of a Progressive," *Pacific Northwest Quarterly*, April 1981.

In his history and assessment of Nichols' work, printed here, Cole finds that while Nichols' presumption of federal neglect of Alaska had many faults, her work is nonetheless an indispensable source for Alaskan political development.

* * *

When Alaska became the 49th state in 1959, Ernest Gruening credited Edna Ferber's novel *Ice Palace* with convincing many people of the need for Alaska statehood. Ferber's romantic novel described how Alaska residents were ruthlessly exploited by absentee cannery owners and corporate giants in Seattle and San Francisco. It was a classic American battle: a neglected colony subject to taxation without representation.

---

*This article originally appeared in the *Pacific Northwest Quarterly* 77, no. 4 (October 1986): 130-138.

"Don't you know that Alaska has no Congressman or Senator in Washington!" one of the heroes of Ferber's novel explains. "Everything we do, and everything the Territory yields, goes out. Outside. Everything goes out and nothing stays in. Gold, Copper, Timber, Fish. Millions and millions and millions a year. Outside, We're slaves."[1]

Ferber's Alaskan novel may have been one of her less distinguished artistic efforts, but it carried a strong political message. That message was first delivered nearly 40 years earlier by another woman writer named Jeannette Paddock Nichols, who wrote the first political history of Alaska.

Jeannette Paddock Nichols's *Alaska: A History of Its Administration, Exploitation, and Industrial Development during Its first Half Century under the Rule of the United States* is one of the classics in Alaskan literature. When it first appeared in 1924, a reviewer in the New York *Evening Post* predicted that her study would relegate "all other histories of Alaska to unimportance, and may fairly be expected to hold its place for a long time as the only comprehensive account of Alaska's political history that it is worth any one's time to consult." Even today, more than 60 years later, Nichols's book is still the most detailed study ever written about Alaska's early political development. More important, her thesis, that Alaska was a neglected stepchild of the federal government, has been the major issue in Alaskan historical and political debate during the 20th century.[2]

After a long career at the University of Pennsylvania, where she taught with her husband, Roy F. Nichols, Jeannette Paddock Nichols died in the summer of 1982 in a nursing home outside Philadelphia. She was 91. Recently, some of her papers in the archives at the University of Pennsylvania have been opened to the public. Among other items, her collection includes most of her correspondence from the 1920s with her publisher, the Arthur H. Clark Company of Cleveland, as well as scattered correspondence with some prominent Alaskans and government officials. Altogether, her papers reveal a great deal about her methods of research and writing and her interpretations of Alaska's past. They may also provide the answers to several puzzling questions about her landmark book on Alaskan political history.[3]

Jeannette Paddock was born at Rochelle, Illinois, on August 17, 1890. She graduated from Knox College at Galesburg, Illinois, in 1913 and taught high school history in Oregon for several years. She traveled widely during the summer months and took courses in history and philosophy at the University of Oregon. But what changed her professional life was a month-long trip she made to Alaska with her aunt in 1916.[4]

The young high school teacher was overwhelmed by the spectacular scenery along the Inside Passage. "This is the *greatest* country I have ever witnessed," she wrote to her father from Wrangell on July 5, 1916. The people she met in the territory were as interesting as the sights. A chance shipboard conversation introduced the future historian to the topic of Alaskan history. As she told the story later, her interest in the subject really began with a box of candy.[5]

Among the passengers on board the steamship as it sailed between Skagway and Juneau were the Alaska governor J. F. A. Strong, and his wife, Anna. Governor and Mrs. Strong had boarded the steamship at Skagway, where the residents of the city had presented them with a box of candy as a going-away gift. While relaxing in a deck chair, Mrs Strong offered a piece to a young woman nearby named Jeannette Paddock. "The governor began to tell the girl and her aunt about the struggles of Alaska to get proper recognition from the national government, etc.," an account of their chance meeting explained after Nichols's history of Alaska was published. "The conversation continued until a late hour. The girl was intensely interested."[6]

John Franklin Alexander Strong could tell a good story of federal indifference to the needs of Alaskans, and he had been doing so for many years as a newspaper editor and a politician. The people of every western territory and state believed that they were discriminated against in Washington, D.C., either because of greed or lack of knowledge, and of course, many westerners still feel that way. But Alaskans have always felt uniquely burdened by the ignorance of those who controlled the region from afar. "Judging by the indifference and neglect [with] which we in Alaska are treated by congress and the federal government," Strong had written in 1901 when he was the editor of the Nome *Nugget*, "we might reasonably suppose that if we were to 'secede' and set up a little republic of our own Uncle Sam would think it no serious matter."[7]

Though the issues have changed, this basic complaint of Alaskan pioneer politicians about federal neglect is still heard today on the editorial page and the campaign trail, even if it is no longer quite as popular as it once was. The most eloquent exponent of the idea was probably Ernest Gruening, the dynamic politician and scholar who served as Alaska's territorial governor from 1939 to 1953, and as its U.S. senator from 1959 to 1968. Gruening was one of the main advocates in the Alaska statehood movement, and he argued that Alaska needed statehood or it would forever remain an exploited colony run by outside interests. His 1954 history of territorial Alaska, purposely titled *The State of Alaska*, divides Alaska's history into periods of varyingly inept rule by Washington, including "The Era of Total Neglect, 1867-1884," "The Era of Flagrant Neglect, 1884-1898," "The Era of Mild but Unenlightened Interest, 1898-1912," etc.[8]

Gruening's theory of Alaska history grew out of his own experiences as territorial governor and from the dissatisfaction and suspicion long felt in the territory for the federal government and powerful outside economic interests. But the first person to formulate a scholarly thesis in those terms to explain Alaskan development was the young woman who heard Governor Strong's "neglect lecture" on a southbound steamer in 1916.

Two years after her Alaskan vacation, Jeannette Paddock gave up teaching history at Jefferson High School in Portland. In the closing months of World War I, at age 28, she moved to New York and began work on a Master's degree in history at Columbia University. She studied at first with James Harvey Robinson, and as always, she was a hard worker and kept a well-disciplined schedule, even during Christmas vacation. "School begins again tomorrow," Jeannette wrote her mother on January 4, 1919, "and I go back with the knowledge that I've read 5 books, & had an exceptionally pleasant amount of exercise, fresh air and sleep. I face the next five months with the desire to *keep* my five jobs and *yet* pass the oral exam in history with *credit*."[9]

She passed her Master's examination in 1919 and continued on in the Ph.D. program at Columbia under Professor William A. Dunning, the noted scholar of the Civil War and Reconstruction, who was also the author of a famous article on the Alaska Purchase. Many students had left the university during the war, and there was still a high proportion of women graduate students. Jeannette was one of 10 students in Dunning's seminar in the fall of 1919, 7 of whom were women. Among the three men was Roy Franklin Nichols, who was six years her junior and who said that he and Jeannette "attracted each other almost from the moment of meeting."[10]

Early in 1920 they were engaged to be married. Amid all the preparations for their wedding, both still had to study for their oral preliminary examinations. "What is happening to my studying--I don't know," Jeannette wrote her mother in late February, "but I get in what I can and will pull through somehow." Yet, she was certain about her future career, "I plan to stay in the college or university professional field with my husband," she wrote. "And we hope to collaborate on our books."[11]

Despite a bout of "nervous indigestion" that laid Jeannette low for a few days in April, the two graduate students passed their comprehensive exams in the spring of 1920, and they were married on May 27. "We have been working together ever since," Roy Nichols wrote nearly 50 years later, "completely sharing our professional as well as our personal interests." Roy won the Pulitzer Prize for history in 1949 for a political history of the 1850s, and he and Jeannette earlier wrote several books together, including *The Growth of American Democracy* and *The Republic of the United States*. But her major book was her study of the Alaska home rule movement from 1867 to 1912, for which she earned her Ph.D. in 1923.[12]

At first Nichols's professors at Columbia warned her against the topic. For one thing, some faculty members apparently did not consider the subject of "sufficient importance" for a doctoral dissertation. In addition they thought that adequate records on Alaskan history would be unavailable and that, since some of what she hoped to cover was so controversial and had occurred so recently--less than a decade earlier--maintaining impartiality would be difficult. Such faculty opposition was hard to resist. When Roy, seeking a dissertation topic, had specified his interest in early American politics, and especially in Hamilton and Jefferson, Dunning replied that his students had mostly been interested in either Reconstruction or the Republican party but that "he had always hoped for some Democratic studies." As Roy recounted the episode years later in his autobiography, "Though I was about as rock-ribbed a Republican as there was I did not blink, and agreed." The dissertation was published in 1923 as *The Democratic Machine, 1850-1854*.[13]

Unlike her husband and many other graduate students both then and now, however, Jeannette Paddock Nichols knew her own mind and could not be easily dissuaded when she believed she was right. She had no interest in following in anyone's footsteps, and the fact that no one had ever tried to write a political history of Alaska made the subject irresistible. Ever since visiting the territory and meeting Governor Strong, she had been determined to investigate the controversies surrounding Alaskan development since 1867. It was the progressive era, and she sensed an opportunity to expose the sorry record of the first 45 years of American rule in Alaska. She judiciously stated that her goal was to "write an accurate, interesting account of the affairs of that Territory as affected by the peculair [sic] economic conditions in the north and the special political situations in Washington, D.C."[14]

Jeannette and Roy Nichols returned from a four-month-long European honeymoon in the summer of 1920, and they soon moved to Washington, D.C., to begin work on their dissertations in the Library of Congress. While he examined the story of the Democratic party before the Civil War, she delved into a field that had not been explored in depth since Hubert Howe Bancroft's literary factory had assembled an Alaskan history 35 years earlier.

"The history of Alaska has not as yet commanded the interest of many students," Nichols wrote when her book was published. "One who sets to work upon it therefore becomes a pioneer and must blaze his own trail." It was the chance to be a trailblazer that so strongly appealed to her, and Nichols took great delight in uncovering new sources. As her husband later wrote (about another research project in which she was involved), "Her most exciting and gratifying work was the ferreting out of hitherto undiscovered manuscript collections, to which she was the first person to gain access."[15]

Alaskan sources are difficult enough to track down today, but research was far more arduous in the early 1920s, before any significant archival collections of Alaskan materials had been gathered, before newspapers and periodicals were readily available on microfilm, before any comprehensive bibliographies on the literature of Alaska had yet been published, and before the holdings of the territorial museum and library had been adequately cataloged. Nichols could find few collections of personal correspondence or other private records to help her trace the history of Alaska's recent political development. She believed that much of Alaska's history was the "crude product of Wall Street Exploitation," as she once put it, but finding documents to prove that was difficult. She explained the problem in a letter to Professor Edmond S. Meany at the University of Washington in September 1921, asking for assistance in locating other sources:

> Here at the Library of Congress the file of newspapers and U.S. Documents is fairly satisfactory, or at least as good as one could expect for a field that has never been worked up since Bancroft. But there is sad dearth of personal correspondence available, and I am particularly in need of proof of the part played in Alaskan administration and politics by the vested interests in the District.[16]

Writing a political history without having access to any significant collections of letters, memoirs, or other private papers posed a tremendous challenge, and to compensate for the lack of such materials, Nichols had to make imaginative use of what was available. She relied heavily on three major sources: newspapers, government documents, and interviews with prominent persons or officials associated with Alaska. Some of her research techniques, such as using newspapers and oral history, are today considered modern innovations.

Nichols read the back files of dozens of newspapers published inside and outside Alaska. She said she "examined all of the newspaper files of Alaskan papers on the Atlantic seaboard, as well as some of those which could be obtained only by special loans from the Pacific Coast." Because during the first 30 years of American rule Alaska had few newspapers of its own, and during later years, the American press gave generous coverage to Alaskan events, she also combed the papers of Seattle, Boston, Chicago, New York, Philadelphia, San Francisco, and many other cities.[17]

Even more significant than her newspaper research was her reading of the government documents related to Alaska. "The pioneer student of Alaska's political history," she explained, "is largely dependent upon the official documents." She studied all references to Alaska that appeared in the *Congressional Globe* and the *Congressional Record* over a period of more than 50 years, as well as the voluminous files of Senate and House reports and hearings on Alaska housed in the Library of Congress.[18]

Finally, Nichols relied on interviews and correspondence with people she called her "living sources." Though her study opens with the transfer ceremony at Sitka in 1867, her main emphasis is on later events, especially those that led the federal government to grant Alaskans a small measure of home rule by authorizing the creation of a territorial legislature in 1912. About two-thirds of her text is devoted to the 15 years between the 1897 Klondike stampede and the passage of the Second Organic Act in 1912.[19]

Many of the key figures from those years were still alive in the early 1920s. Among them were some of the most knowledgeable people in the world on Alaska, including: William H. Dall, Henry W. Elliott, the Reverend S. Hall Young, Captain G. T. Emmons, W. T. Lopp, James Wickersham, William Sulzer, General Wilds P. Richardson, Alfred H. Brooks, C. L. Andrews, John Underwood, David Starr Jordan, Frank A. Golder, Charles Sheldon, Gifford Pinchot, Walter L. Fisher, and the former governors Walter E. Clark, J. F. A. Strong, and Thomas Riggs, and others.[20]

Nichols found Dan Sutherland, who was serving his first term as Alaska's delegate to Congress in 1921, especially helpful. "The Delegate from Alaska and his wife are very nice to me," she wrote her mother in September 1921. "They try to assist in the getting of material as much as they can. Congressmen are not often so helpful."[21]

Out of her eminent cast of advisers, James Wickersham was the figure many readers naturally thought had the greatest influence on Nichols while she was preparing her history. He was the most prominent Alaskan politician of the early 20th century and, like Gruening a generation later, a scholar and a man of many talents, in addition to being a fierce political battler for the rights of Alaskans. Wickersham wrote the introduction for Nichols's book; his long political career, his interest in Alaskan history, and his unmatched collection of Alaskana supported the belief that she worked closely with him--a belief that persists to the present day. According to one often-repeated legend, Nichols was actually Wickersham's secretary while he was the Alaskan delegate in Washington, D.C.[22]

In fact, Nichols was not in Washington at the same time that Wickersham was, nor was she intimately associated with him. She never had access to his extensive library on Alaska. A reviewer who thought otherwise reported after interviewing Nichols that "she is only slightly acquainted with Judge Wickersham and that his views on Alaskan problems affected her not in the least." Wickersham, however, was one of many experts who did read and comment on her manuscript, and for the most part he heartily endorsed her interpretation of federal mistreatment of Alaska. "He went over my book by chapters, as I finished them," Nichols later wrote her publisher, "making occasional contributions as to fact and others as to interpretation. The former I verified and used where applicable; the latter I considered carefully before rejecting or embodying them."[23]

Nichols was frankly puzzled about why Wickersham liked her book. Perhaps he had a different attitude toward history "than one might expect from a political controversialist." She speculated that the old judge may have approved of her study because she had sifted through the many lies his enemies were fond of telling about him and had left them out. She had also omitted the story of his celebrated conviction for the seduction of Sadie Brantner in Tacoma in 1889. Wickersham's "love intrigue" had no bearing on Alaskan history, Nichols argued, and was therefore not worth mentioning. Despite her muckraking inclinations and her desire to demonstrate how the government's wanton neglect had greatly hindered Alaska's development and allowed monopolistic corporations to take control, Nichols had no interest in dredging up scandals. "I do not consider that the dregs or the scum of politics belong in serious research," she wrote, "unless they actually affect issues. Every Alaskan knows that Wickersham made a serious mistake at one time; but, like frontiersmen the world over, that kind of a mistake had absolutely no effect upon their votes."[24]

It was not Nichols's idea to have Wickersham write the introduction to her book. She had actually opposed his involvement and agreed only because her publisher insisted that his name would help sales. Nichols feared that readers would think hers a partisan account if Wickersham introduced it. Though she respected Wickersham for his unsurpassed knowledge of Alaskan politics his magnificent library of Alaskana, and his "strength of character," she warned Clark confidentially that "the heat of controversy has, naturally, warped his understanding on some points and his remarks and conduct while prominent in Washington did not always show a strict regard for the truth, as far as I am capable of judging it."[25]

Continuing her private assessment of Wickersham's character, Nichols was far more candid than she dared to be in print.

> He is brilliant, resourceful; has sometimes chosen strange means for the confounding of his enemise [sic]...In Alaska, his endorsement of the book would certainly be accepted by a majority of the people. In the United States--in the Northwest, the enemies whom the man has made would be inclined to doubt the value of his endorsement. In the United States--in the East, such men as Justice [William Howard] Taft, ex-Attorney General [George] Wickersham, and [Gifford] Pinchot might be likely to consider the book biased if it carried a Wickersham introduction; but on the other hand the fact that it had one would arouse their interest, too, because Wickersham is always interesting.[26]

The publisher thought that Nichols's reservations about Wickersham's objectivity were the very reasons the former judge and delegate to Congress should write the introduction. "Wickersham may be on one side of the controversy," Clark wrote. "At the same time, the fellows on the other side...are going to want to know what their enemy is up to and what he is saying--perhaps more so than if a member of their own side of the controversy were writing. If it starts an argument, so much better for the sale and the place which the volume will take in historical source work."[27]

The man whom Nichols would have preferred to write an introduction to her political history was not a politician at all, but a professional geologist, Alfred H. Brooks of the U.S. Geological Survey, the man for whom the Brooks Range is named. More than any of her "living sources," Brooks was her guide and inspiration during the course of her work. "Throughout my study of Alaskan affairs," Nichols wrote in one letter, "the only person who has impressed me with a strict attempt at impartiality has been Dr. Alfred H. Brooks." She said that "his absolute aloofness from controversy, his complete dissociation from politics, and his scientific impartiality are an inspiration to the student who has the privilege of his criticism." Without his help,she believed, the book could not have been written.[28]

In November 1920 Brooks had recommended the history of Alaska's fight for a territorial legislature as a topic for her dissertation, and he edited and critiqued her manuscript as she wrote it. Providing Nichols with the historical account he was writing (which was published in 1953, long after his death, as *Blazing Alaska's Trails*), he shared with her his own extensive knowledge of conditions in Alaska. The geologist admitted that "as a historian I am but an amateur," but he said he nevertheless liked to think of himself as a "silent partner" in her book.[29]

In late June 1922, after nearly two years of work, Jeannette Nichols put the finishing touches on the manuscript she had tentatively called: "Alaska: A Struggle for Home Rule." Immediately, she began looking for a publisher, and she early approached the Arthur H. Clark Company of Cleveland, a firm well known for its distinguished list of Western Americana, including Frank A. Golder's 1914 work *Russian Expansion in the Pacific, 1641-1850.* "My own ideal in writing this book," Nichols wrote Clark,

> the ideal which I have had before me constantly in the two years and more I have been at work, is to produce a strictly reliable, authoritative work, based on the sources, of a quality to give me recognition in the historical field, as a fair, dispassionate writer of recent history.[30]

Nichols wanted to place her book with a commercial publisher if at all possible (her second choice was Columbia University), so she sent her manuscript to Clark in September 1922 and began waiting impatiently for the verdict. Meanwhile, Nichols's advisers at Columbia had determined that her manuscript would be acceptable for consideration as a Ph.D. dissertation if the university's requirements could be met. These included the acceptance of the work for publication, an examination or defense of the dissertation once it was in galley proof, and the deposit of 30 copies of the book in the university library. She admitted that her main concern was "to have those letters Ph.D. after my name on the author page of my book."[31]

Finally, after much hesitation, Clark offered her a contract in March 1923, stipulating that Nichols pay in advance $1,200, or about one-third the total publication costs of the book. Clark told her he was interested only in putting out a high-quality edition, and it was going to be expensive.

"Most of the paper used at the present time on publications will have disintegrated within ten or twelve years," Clark wrote Nichols, "consequently I cannot use such paper in my publications if they are to remain for permanent historical research." He intended that Nichols's history of Alaska would be around for a long time to come. "So far, I have not issued a publication that will not stand the ravages of time for at least four hundred or five hundred years; in other words, none of our publications are made on anything but paper of at least a certain percentage of linen rag--the same can be said of the ink."[32]

Nichols received the first bound copies of her book in mid-December 1923. Though it may have been printed to last 500 years, its sales seemed depressingly slow. The press run was 1,200; more than five years passed before Clark sold enough copies to start paying the author back for her share of the publication costs. Nichols thought that at $6 a copy her book may have been too expensive for most Alaskans to buy. Clark thought otherwise.

> Frankly I look for very little sale in Alaska, not because there are not many people there who can well afford to own the volume, but because there is at present little or no culture there of the kind which would lead to the formation of libraries or of the more serious reading. There is little sold at present in Alaska outside of the most ephemeral of literature...I am almost inclined to the belief that there will be a larger sale for the work in Japan than there will be in Alaska.[33]

Always thinking of ways to promote her book, Nichols suggested placing copies in the libraries on the ships that served Alaska, so that on rainy days tourists might find her volume more interesting than the scenery. But she warned Clark that the Alaska Steamship Company and, in her opinion, the Pacific Steamship Company were part of the monopolistic Alaska Syndicate, and therefore it was possible that "they would not wish the book on their steamers if they knew what was in it."[34]

Unfortunately, Nichols was correct: officials of the Alaska Steamship Company refused to buy any copies whatsoever. John H. Bunch, the firm's traffic manager in Seattle, pointed to an error in the introduction--that the 1909 Alaska-Yukon-Pacific Exposition had occurred in 1902--and insinuated that such a mistake proved that the whole book was worthless. Nichols thought the real reason lay in Wickersham's involvement. "The evident distaste of the officials of the Alaska Steamship Company for the thought of purchasing volumes for their ships' library," she wrote, "is readily accounted for by the relations between that company and the author of the introduction to the book. If the proof-reading slip mentioned in Mr. Bunch's letter is the worst error he can discover in the history, he has indeed endorsed the book highly."[35]

A reviewer in the New York *Times* praised Nichols's book, but he thought that Wickersham's forceful introduction, which claimed that the Alaska struggle for home rule "defeated President Taft for reelection in 1912; elected Woodrow Wilson President of the United States; and changed the course of the history of our country," was perhaps a bit overstated. The *Times* reviewer also remarked that "a note of indignation" at the shabby treatment Alaska had received at the hands of the federal government "sounds plainly all through the book."[36]

Most reviewers were kinder to Nichols's work than the officials of the Alaska Steamship Company, including a young Samuel Eliot Morison, who reviewed the book for the *English Historical Review*, and Frederic L. Paxson in the *American Historical Review*. Morison thought that Nichols's study would be of interest to all students of imperialism. He concluded, however, that Nichols had demonstrated that Alaskans traditionally had a habit of "violently quarreling among themselves over the pettiest matters, and only uniting to attack their federal officials." Modern observers of the Alaskan political scene often have a similar reaction, as did Paxson. "Her book is a history of petty politics," he commented, "but it is a good history, founded upon real sources and intelligently put together."[37]

Petty or otherwise, Alaska's post-1867 political development has undergone no major investigation since Nichols's. Her book does, however, have obvious gaps. Hers is primarily a study of politics in southeastern Alaska, the most populous region of Alaska, as seen from Washington, D.C., through newspapers and government documents; this narrow topical and geographical focus, which the work of Morgan Sherwood and others makes clear, led Nichols to overlook the active role of the federal government in Alaskan exploration and development. She also hardly scratched Alaska's social or economic history in the period between the purchase and the turn of the century, as Ted Hinckley demonstrates in *The Americanization of Alaska, 1867-1897*.[38]

Probably the most puzzling gap in the book is that it virtually ignores the biggest political scandal in Alaska's history, the reign of the "Spoilers" in turn-of-the-century Nome. Without even mentioning Judge Arthur H. Noyes or the receiver Alexander McKenzie by name, Nichols says only that they engineered "one of the most audacious

grafts in mining history" but that "it is not necessary for our purposes to describe the scandal."[39]

Even in the 1920s Alexander McKenzie's big swindle in Nome was not a subject of polite conversation among members of the Republican party. Though Nichols had no desire to dig up the "dregs or the scum of politics" as she said when she omitted from her book the skeletons in Wickersham's closet, it seems impossible to justify her decision to leave out the scandal that, reaching from Nome to the White House, was in some ways Alaska's worst case of federal mistreatment. Ignoring the Spoilers in an Alaskan political history devoted primarily to the years 1897-1912 is almost like writing a history of the Nixon presidency without mentioning Watergate.

It may simply have been that the Spoilers controversy did not easily fit into Nichols's main theme of Alaska's fight for home rule. In her view, Alaska's political history featured a struggle for supremacy between the pioneer residents of the north and the "vested interests," the greedy monopolistic corporations head-quartered in Seattle, San Francisco, or New York, like the Alaska Syndicate, which controlled the resources of the district. Congress was Alaska's legislature before 1913, and Nichols maintained that the federal government had neglected the needs of the residents and instead had catered to the wishes of the Morgans and the Guggenheims. Only with the passage of the Second Organic Act in 1912, which provided for a locally elected legislature, did the residents gain the political voice that would enable them to develop the territory's resources in a just and democratic fashion.[40]

Nichols predicted in 1923 that someday the struggle for home rule would begin again, with statehood the eventual result. Advocates of statehood a generation later embraced her thesis that the U.S. government had neglected Alaskans in favor of outside economic interests, such as the salmon-canning industry. The battle for a legislature, as Nichols had depicted it, neatly paralleled the struggle for statehood during the 1940s and 1950s. But after Alaska became a state, some historians began to challenge the Nichols-Gruening thesis: had Alaska in fact suffered from federal misadministration and neglect, or were there other factors that retarded its economic and political development?[41]

In a thoughtful article in 1970, the historian William H. Wilson argued that traditionalists like Nichols and Gruening had seriously

overemphasized the federal neglect of Alaska and that, compared with other western territories and states, Alaska had not been abused or neglected at all. Partisan political battles of Alaskans with Washington, D.C., had forged the neglect thesis, and in the heat of the campaigns for home rule or statehood, it was natural that reformers like James Wickersham, Jeannette Nichols, and Ernest Gruening would see federal misadministration and neglect wherever they looked.[42]

Yet, for all of its faults, Jeannette Nichols's *Alaska* has withstood the test of time. As Hinckley has concluded, it "remains an excellent, indeed, the indispensable source for Alaska's territorial political development." Reprinted by Russell and Russell of New York in 1963 but once again out of print, it is nonetheless extraordinarily influential among modern-day Alaskans. No sooner do new residents arrive than they start to complain that "outsiders" who don't understand the country are determining its fate. Alaskans still fear that powerful outside interests--whether the Sierra Club or Standard Oil--will come before their own. "Resident hire" has been a hotly debated political issue in Alaska during the 1980s. Even though the 49th state, with a population of about half a million people, has two members in the Senate, just like New York and California, many of its citizens continue to believe that their voice has never been heard in Washington, D.C., that they do not receive treatment equal to that accorded residents of other states.[43]

In the early 1970s, Joe Vogler, a Fairbanks miner with a law degree who has battled with the federal government on many issues, founded the Alaskan Independence party. Since that time, he has been a perennial candidate for governor, running on a platform of peaceful secession from the Union. Though many consider his candidacy a joke, in the 1986 election, Vogler garnered a respectable 5 percent of the vote.[44]

Vogler and those who support him may be extremists, but they come out of a long-established political tradition in Alaska, one first defined by Jeannette Nichols and later by Ernest Gruening. In 1974, about six months before Gruening died, Vogler wrote to him, saying, "If I did not feel that it would be a gross imposition upon your energies, I would ask you to seriously consider stepping up to lead our Independence Movement. We are seeking the same thing that you were--the right to determine our destiny." The former governor and U.S. senator, a leader of the Alaska statehood movement, gave an encouraging reply. Gruening noted on the bottom of Vogler's letter that he had told him he "was not ready to join YET--not until we had exhausted every means" of settling the issue, then under dispute, of excessive federal land withdrawals in Alaska and had proved "that total secession was the only answer." James Wickersham or J. F. A. Strong, the man who first introduced Jeannette Paddock Nichols to the subject of federal neglect of Alaska, might have answered Vogler in exactly the same way.[45]

ENDNOTES

[1]Edna Ferber, *Ice Palace* (New York, 1958), p. 15; for his views on the effect of the novel, see Ernest Gruening, *The Battle for Alaska Statehood* (College, Alaska, 1967), p. 102-103.

[2]*Literary Review of the New York Evening Post*, March 22, 1924, p. 610; Ted C. Hinckley, "Researching Alaska's Pioneer Years, 1867-1912," *Journal of the West* 16 (October 1977): 54. For the history of the statehood movement, see Claus-M. Naske, *An Interpretative History of Alaskan Statehood* (Anchorage, 1973).

[3]Philadelphia *Inquirer*, June 24, 1982. Unless otherwise noted, all Nichols's correspondence is from the University of Pennsylvania Archives in Philadelphia. Unfortunately, the records of the Arthur H. Clark Company during the years in which Nichols was corresponding with the company were destroyed by fire before the firm moved from Cleveland to California in 1930 (Robert A. Clark to Terrence Cole, July 8, 1983).

[4]Vita of Jeannette Paddock Nichols (hereafter JP or JPN), 1923, Nichols Papers, University of Pennsylvania.

[5]JP to Charles Paddock, July 5, 1916; *Alaska Weekly* (Seattle), Sept. 5, 1924.

[6]*Alaska Weekly*, Sept. 5, 1924 (quotation); JPN to Arthur H. Clark, July 24, 1922.

[7]Nome *Nugget* July 30, 1901.

[8]Earnest Gruening, *The State of Alaska* (New York, 1954).

[9]JP to "Mother and All," Jan. 4, 1919.

[10]William A. Dunning, "Paying for Alaska," *Political Science Quarterly* 27 (1912): 385-98; Roy F. Nichols (hereafter RFN), *A Historian's Progress* (New York, 1968), p. 33.

[11]JP to mother, Feb. 29, 1920.

[12]Ibid., April 4, 1920; RFN, *A Historian's Progress*, p. 33. The books that the Nicholses wrote together include *The Growth of American Democracy* (New York, 1939); *The Republic of the United States* (New York, 1942); *A Short History of American Democracy* (New York, 1943). Roy Nichols's Pulitzer Prize was for *The Disruption of American Democracy* (New York, 1948).

[13]*Alaska Weekly*, Sept. 5, 1924 (first quotation); RFN, *A Historian's Progress*, p. 33.

[14]JPN to Clark, July 24, 1922.

[15]Jeannette Paddock Nichols, *Alaska: A History of Its Administration, Exploitation, and Industrial Development during Its first Half Century under the Rule of the United States* (Cleveland, 1924), p. 419; RFN, *A Historian's Progress*, p. 45.

[16]JPN, *Alaska*, p. 423; a partial manuscript copy of James Wickersham's *Bibliography of Alaskan Literature, 1724-1924*, Miscellaneous Publications of the Alaska Agricultural College and School of Mines, Vol. 1 (Cordova, 1927), was available to Nichols. The phrase "crude product of Wall Street Exploitation" was originally Clark's--see Clark to JPN, April 27, 1923; JPN to E. S. Meany, Sept. 28, 1921, Box 37, Edmond S. Meany Papers, University of Washington Libraries, Seattle.

[17]JPN to Clark, July 24, 1922 (draft) (quotation); JPN, *Alaska*, p. 429

[18]JPN, *Alaska*, p. 427.

[19]JPN to Clark, July 24, 1923.

[20]Ibid., April 10, 1923; JPN, *Alaska*, pp. 12-15.

[21]JPN to mother, Sept. 7, 1921.

[22]Stephen W. Haycox and Betty J. Haycox, eds., *Melvin Ricks' Alaska Bibliography: An Introductory Guide to Alaskan Historical Literature* (Portland, Oreg., 1977), s.v. "Nichols, Jeannette"; Hinckley,"Researching Alaska's Pioneer Years," p. 54.

[23]JPN to editor, *Alaska Weekly*, April 23, 1924; undated, unidentified clipping, "Population of Alaska Greatly Reduced Lately," Nichols Papers (slightly); JPN to Clark, April 10, 1923.

[24]JPN to Clark, April 18, 1923 (quotations); Evangeline Atwood, *Frontier Politics: Alaska's James Wickersham* (Portland, 1979), pp. 31-34.

[25]JPN to Clark, April 18, 1923.

[26]Ibid.

[27]Clark to JPN, April 26 1923.

[28]JPN to Clark, April 10, 1923 (first quotation); JPN, *Alaska*, p. 15 (second quotation).

[29]Alfred H. Brooks to JPN, Dec. 26, 1923.

[30]Theodore Grivas, "The Arthur H. Clark Company, Publisher of the West," *Arizona and the West* 5 (1963): 63-78; JPN to Clark, July 24, 1924 (draft).

[31]JPN to Clark, Oct. 31, 1922, April 18, 1923 (quotation).

[32]Clark to JPN, Feb. 20, 1923 (first quotation), March 6, 1923 (second quotation). The book was very well made, but at least one copy, discarded by the New Jersey State Library and purchased by the author of this article some years ago at a used book store, has not survived the "ravages of time" as well as Clark might have hoped. Although the paper is obviously superior to that used in most modern books, the binding has nearly disintegrated.

[33]Statement, July 1, 1929, "Nichols Alaska Publication Account," Nichols Papers; RFN to JPN (telegram), Feb. 27, 1923; Clark to JPN, March 6, 1923, Aug. 13, Sept. 4, 1929, and April 18, 1924 (quotation); JPN to Clark, Aug. 10, 1929; Brooks to JPN, Dec. 26, 1923.

[34]JPN to Clark, April 3, 1924.

[35]Ibid., May 16, 1924.

[36]*New York Times Book Review* 29 (May 18, 1924): 21; JPN, *Alaska*,

p. 17 (first quotation).

[37]*English Historical Review* 39 (1924): 452; *American Historical Review* 29 (1924): 579-80.

[38]Morgan R. Sherwood, in *Exploration of Alaska, 1865-1900* (New York, 1965), p. 8, explains that a "fundamental thesis" of his book is that "exploratory activities by the federal government in Alaska were extensive in light of contemporary social altitudes in the United States.... This does not mean exploration was as rapid as it should have been, but only that it proceeded as rapidly as it could in the context of the time." Ted C. Hinckley, *The Americanization of Alaska, 1867-1897*, (Palo Alto, Calif., 1972).

[39]JPN, *Alaska*, p. 192.

[40]Ibid., pp. 405-409.

[41]Ibid., p. 409.

[42]William H. Wilson, "Alaska's Past, Alaska's Future," *Alaska Review* 4 (1970): 1-11.

[43]Hinckley, "Researching Alaska's Pioneer Years," p. 54.

[44]Anchorage *Daily News*, Nov. 5, 1986.

[45]Joe Vogler to Gruening, Jan. 15, 1974, Gruening Collection, University of Alaska Archives, Correspondence file 1916-1972.